DEPARTMENT OF COMMERCE
R. P. LAMONT, Secretary
BUREAU OF THE CENSUS
W. M. Steuart, *Director*

WOMEN IN GAINFUL OCCUPATIONS
1870 TO 1920

A STUDY OF THE TREND OF RECENT CHANGES IN
THE NUMBERS, OCCUPATIONAL DISTRIBUTION,
AND FAMILY RELATIONSHIP OF WOMEN
REPORTED IN THE CENSUS AS
FOLLOWING A GAINFUL
OCCUPATION

BY

JOSEPH A. HILL

CENSUS MONOGRAPHS
IX

GREENWOOD PRESS, PUBLISHERS
WESTPORT, CONNECTICUT

Library of Congress Cataloging in Publication Data

Hill, Joseph Adna, 1860-1938.
    Women in gainful occupations, 1870 to 1920.

    At head of title: Department of Commerce, Bureau of
the Census.
    Reprint of the 1929 ed. published by U.S. Govt.
Print. Off., Washington, which was issued as no. 9 of
Census monographs.
    1. Women--Employment--United States--History.
I. Title. II. Series: United States. Bureau of the
Census. Census monographs ; 9.
[HD6095.H54 1979]   331.4'0973   78-12048
ISBN 0-313-20679-1

Originally published in 1929 by the United States Government
Printing Office, Washington

Reprinted in 1978 by Greenwood Press, Inc.,
51 Riverside Avenue, Westport, CT 06880

Printed in the United States of America

10 9 8 7 6 5 4 3 2 1

CONTENTS

TEXT TABLES

CHAPTER I

CHAPTER II

CHAPTER III

DIAGRAMS

FOREWORD

In the Foreword of the census monograph on "The Integration of Industrial Operation" Dr. Wesley C. Mitchell points out that while the Industrial Revolution began in eighteenth-century England, it is still in progress in twentieth-century America. Beginning with the later years of the nineteenth century, industrial evolution in this country has perhaps been particularly characterized by the high degree of attention which has been directed to the reorganization and improvement of the human processes of production as well as the mechanical processes. The greater consideration accorded to the human element in industry has given rise, at least in part, to an increasing need for—and opportunity for—the participation of women in economic activities. Whatever opinions may be held as to the proper sphere of woman, the fact is that, to a considerable extent, woman's place to-day is no longer in the home. In addition to her social contributions to the preservation and welfare of mankind, the contributions of her sex to economic production in its commercial aspects are of such substantial proportions that not only is it impossible to ignore them as a factor in industrial progress, but they are worthy of serious study as an important element in this progress.

Happily, the schedule of inquiries used in connection with the decennial censuses of population has included an inquiry as to the occupation of each person enumerated. In the present monograph Doctor Hill presents a comprehensive statistical analysis of the occupational data obtained at these censuses as to that portion of the total adult female population of the United States recorded as gainfully employed. At the latest census 24 per cent of all women were engaged in gainful occupations; and women comprised 20 per cent of the total working population.

It is to be noted that, since this census was taken nearly 14 months after the conclusion of the World War, its results are not appreciably affected by the temporary employment needs and opportunities incident to that conflict; in general, the figures may properly be regarded as representative of conditions after the readjustment to peace-time habits. In view of the seasonal and cyclical fluctuations which characterize many lines of economic activity, however, even in periods of undisturbed economic life, census results relative to employment are inevitably more or less affected by the date of the enumeration. The date of the latest census was January 1, 1920.

Unfortunately for occupational statistics, the first of any year marks a season when employment in agriculture, taken as a whole, is relatively slack; and the consequent effect of an enumeration at such a time is an understatement of the number of women engaged in agriculture, as is pointed out in Chapter III. In the case of nonagricultural pursuits as a whole, the date of January 1 can not be said to distort employment figures from a seasonal standpoint; but it might be well to bear in mind the fact that the beginning of the year 1920 happens to have been a time of high production in relation to the normal trend of industrial growth. While this fact is not of sufficient moment to prejudice comparisons of statistics as to employment in industrial occupations in 1920 with similar data obtained at earlier censuses, yet it presumably should have some significance in any independent consideration of industrial employment as a whole in 1920 and its distribution by occupations.

One of the many commendable features of the monograph as a census publication lies in the fact that the textual comments are confined to explanations, interpretations, and conclusions directly associated with the data presented. Doctor Hill carefully refrains from excursions into realms of speculation and theory beyond the purview of the facts available. The volume contains no moralizations as to the presumed effect upon home life of the participation of women in gainful occupations. It does not pretend to determine whether such participation is indicative of lower or of higher "standards of living." Answers to broad sociological and economic questions such as these are undoubtedly desirable if they can be accurately given; but it is doubtful if it is within the province of a governmental statistical organization, such as the Bureau of the Census, to venture beyond the presentation and direct analysis of the recorded facts at its disposal. Accordingly, it is appropriate that this monograph should present, in an organized manner and in suitable detail, the underlying facts as to an important phase of our economic and social life, leaving to others the tasks of relating these facts to other facts outside the scope of the census inquiry and of reaching conclusions of a qualitative nature as to the broader significance of these facts.

SEYMOUR L. ANDREW.

I
INTRODUCTION

This monograph is based on the data obtained through the census in regard to women engaged in gainful occupations. The census gives their numbers, the occupations in which they are engaged, their ages, marital condition, race, nativity, and other personal data. From the census one can learn also something about their home connections, as indicated by the size of the family in which they live, their relationship to the head of the family, and the number of other members of the family also having gainful occupations. Data of this general character, though varying somewhat in detail, have been obtained by each decennial census since, and including, that of 1860.

This is the second time that the Bureau of the Census has published a special study of women in gainful occupations. The first time was shortly after the census of 1900, when the bureau issued a special report on this subject in a separate volume entitled "Women at Work." [1]

The term "women" as here used includes all persons of the female sex 16 years of age and over. Persons under that age are classified in the occupation census as children; and the statistics regarding their employment belong in a discussion of children in occupations, a subject which is covered in detail in a chapter of the occupation report of the Fourteenth Census. In some connections, however, the figures in this monograph include all females 10 years of age—in cases, for instance, where data are not separately available for those 16 and over, and it is safe to assume that the number under 16 in the particular class under consideration is relatively inconsiderable.

Except so far as may be indicated by the generally known facts regarding the various occupations in which women are engaged, the data obtained through the population census furnish no information as to the wages or compensation which women receive, or their hours of labor, or the conditions under which they work. Information of this kind is obviously important, but it can not be obtained through the instrumentality of a general population census, and while data covering these subjects are to some extent available from other sources this monograph, as just stated, is restricted to the data derived from the census.

---

[1] Statistics of Women at Work, 1900, Bureau of the Census.

The following statement is introduced here to show the relative numerical importance of women and of children in the total number of gainful workers of all ages:

TABLE 1.—PERSONS 10 YEARS OF AGE AND OVER ENGAGED IN GAINFUL OCCU-
PATIONS, BY AGE AND SEX: 1920

AGE AND SEX	Total number	PERSONS ENGAGED IN GAINFUL OCCUPATIONS: 1920		
		Number	Per cent distribution	Per cent of total
Total 10 years of age and over	82,739,315	41,614,248	100.0	50.3
Children 10 to 16	12,502,582	1,060,858	2.5	8.5
Male	6,294,985	714,248	1.7	11.3
Female	6,207,597	346,610	0.8	5.6
Men 16 and over [1]	35,994,984	32,350,489	77.7	89.9
Women 16 and over [1]	34,241,749	8,202,901	19.7	24.0

[1] Includes age not reported.

The occupations reported in the census include only those which are termed gainful. While the term is not formally defined, its scope is indicated by the instructions issued to the enumerators, in which they are told to report as an occupation the particular kind of work done, by which the person enumerated earns money or a money equivalent. Thus the gainful occupation is a money earning occupation. It is made clear that this is not to include home housework, for it is explicitly stated that in the case of a woman doing housework in her own home and having no other employment the entry should be "none"; that is, no gainful occupation.

The fact that the occupations listed in the census do not include the home housekeeper should not, however, be taken to indicate that those who have been responsible for determining the scope of the census inquiries have failed to appreciate the economic as well as the social value of the work done by women in the home. On the contrary, it has been explicitly recognized in the census reports that "the wife, sister, or adult daughter who keeps house for her family, though she receives nominally no pecuniary return for her services and does not regard herself as having a gainful occupation, is helping to sustain the productive capacity of the community quite as truly as her male relatives who are earning money wages." [2]

But while home housekeeping is technically a productive occupation, it is not a money earning occupation. The home housekeeper ordinarily receives no wages for her services and presumably is not engaged in that occupation primarily for the sake of getting a living. Her occupation lies outside the field of economic competition. It does

[2] Supplementary Analysis, 1900, p. 439.

not affect and is not affected by the labor supply and market demand. Moreover, the service which the home housekeeper renders to society in her capacity as wife or mother is not solely economic or even mainly so. It is much more than that, and can not be adequately evaluated in terms of a wage equivalent. So, while there is some analogy between the woman who is a wage earner and the home housekeeper, it does not extend very far. The two belong in quite different classes, and a total which included them both without differentiation would have little significance.

The history of the census occupation inquiry is of interest in this connection. While an attempt was made in 1820 and again in 1840 to classify the population by main divisions of industry, distinguishing agriculture, manufactures, and commerce, the first complete census of occupations was taken in 1850, when for the first time the name of each person enumerated was recorded on the census schedule, together with sex, age, and other personal data including occupation. The earlier censuses had been taken by families, the schedules recording opposite the name of the head of the family simply the number of persons in the family, classified by color, sex, and age groups.

The 1850 occupation inquiry was restricted to adult males, the instructions being to report "the profession, occupation, or trade of each male person over 15 years of age." In 1860 the scope of the question was expanded to cover "each male and female over 15 years of age," and in 1870 it applied to "each person, male or female," without limitation as to age.

As regards the home housekeeper, in 1870 and again in 1880 the enumerators were instructed that "women keeping house for their own families or for themselves without any other gainful occupation" were to be entered on the schedules as "keeping house," and grown daughters assisting them were to be reported as without occupation, the term "housekeeper" being reserved for such persons as received wages or salaries for their services.

In 1890 the enumerators were instructed to distinguish between "housekeepers," or women who receive a stated wage or salary for their services, and "housewives" who keep house for their own families or themselves without pay. The occupation of grown daughters assisting in the household duties without fixed remuneration was to be recorded as "housework—without pay."

Thus, if the enumerators followed instructions the occupation of the home housekeeper was recorded on the census schedules as that of "keeping house" in 1870 and 1880 and as that of "housewife" in 1890. But no tabulation of the returns as to home housekeepers was made at any of these censuses.

At the census of 1900, in view of the fact that the occupation tabulation of previous censuses had included only those persons who were gainfully employed, it is not surprising that the enumerators were instructed to make no entry in the occupation column for the "wife or daughter living at home and assisting only in the household duties without pay," or for a person who had retired or was too old to work, or for a child under 10 years of age not at school. There was some economy in thus relieving the enumerators from the labor of recording facts which were not to be tabulated. But when the plans for the next census, that of 1910, were under consideration, in order to guard against the danger that the occupation question as applying to women and children might be overlooked or not asked, it was thought best to require the enumerator to make an entry in the occupation column for every person enumerated. Accordingly, he was instructed to write "none" for persons not having any gainful occupation. This included the home housekeepers. The same rule was followed in 1920.

While the home housework performed by women has an unquestioned economic value, its importance can not be measured by a mere enumeration of the number of women engaged in that work. For the amount of housekeeping done by the individual home housekeeper and hence the economic value of the service she renders is a very elastic and indefinite unit. One woman's home housekeeping may be limited to dusting off the furniture once a day, while another works from early morn until late at night cooking, washing, ironing, sweeping, mending. Should each alike be enumerated as a home housekeeper or a home maker, or should a minimum amount of home housekeeping be prescribed as a qualification for inclusion in this class? Then there is the woman whose housework is done through the employment of servants, but who supervises and directs the affairs of her household, and in that way performs an economic service which bears some analogy to that of the management of a business concern. These conditions make it impossible to obtain through a census any satisfactory statistical record of the work done by women not gainfully employed. Moreover, not all the unremunerated work performed by women is housework. Women form the bulk of the church workers and of welfare workers in other largely unremunerated fields of work. So that without any census enumeration it may be taken for granted that all but a very small and insignificant minority of the women outside the gainful occupations are engaged in some form of work, at least to some extent.

The interest in women's occupations lies not so much in the number occupied or in the amount of work that they are doing as in the change that is taking place in the character of their occupations and the extent to which their work takes them away from the home which was once the sole field of occupational activity for most women.

When the spinning wheel and the loom were part of the home equipment, the number of women engaged in their use was of small concern; but when the manufacture of cloth and clothing was transferred to the factory, and women went from home to the factory to work, and from one kind of factory to another, their occupations took on the character of those in which men were engaged, and the social problems which always accompany economic changes arose and have continued to exist and to keep alive the interest in the occupations of women gainfully employed.

It may be noted furthermore, in this connection, that, although the census in its present scope does not directly enumerate or specifically distinguish the home housekeepers, it does obtain a very considerable amount of data, which has never yet been exploited, regarding women in the home. Thus, it is possible on the basis of the present census schedule to distinguish the number of women who, as wives and mothers, are maintaining homes without following a gainful occupation; also the number of other women living in the family but having no gainful occupation and therefore probably participating in the housework and care of the family; also the number of women who are both maintaining homes and following a gainful occupation. These and other data regarding homes and home makers are obtainable in the census with its present scope, as has well been shown by a special tabulation relating to women home makers which was recently made from the census sheets for the city of Rochester, N. Y.[3] This gave, in addition to other facts, the number of women in Rochester who were or had been married and were maintaining homes; the number of other women equally responsible as custodians of family life who were boarding or lodging or living with relatives; the number of women who were maintaining homes and also mothering children; also the number who were mothering children without maintaining homes; the number of women who were custodians and caretakers of the home and at the same time were contributing to the family income by working for money either in or outside the home.

Without making any actual enumeration of housekeepers or any elaborate tabulation of the census data it is possible to estimate approximately, on the basis mainly of the published figures of the census, the number of women working in their own homes without salary or wages and having no other employment; and such an estimate has been made in connection with this study. It indicates that the number of women home housekeepers without other occupation is between 22,000,000 and 23,000,000. Suppose that we call it 22,500,000. Adding this figure to the 8,202,901 women reported

[3] Nienburg, Bertha M.: "The Woman Home Maker in the City—A study of statistics relating to married women in the city of Rochester, N. Y., at the census of 1920."—U. S. Bureau of the Census.

as employed in money earning pursuits gives a total of 30,702,901 women occupied in the home or out, representing 89.7 per cent of the 34,241,749 women 16 years of age and over.   This is practically the same as the proportion of men 16 years of age and over reported as engaged in gainful occupations—89.9 per cent; and it should not be forgotten in this connection that very many of the women who are wage earners are likewise maintaining homes and mothering children. How the work done by women compares in quantity or in social value with that done by men is another question and one which can not be answered by statistics.   No aggregate of the amount of work done by women measured in hours or in any other unit can be obtained through the instrumentality of a population census either for the gainful workers or for the unremunerated home housekeepers. Still less can any one estimate or measure on the basis of any obtainable statistical data the value of the social service rendered by women as home makers and as wives and mothers.

TABLE 2.—WOMEN 16 YEARS OF AGE AND OVER: 1920

CLASS	Number	Per cent distribution
Total	34, 241, 749	100. 0
Engaged in gainful occupations	8, 202, 901	24. 0
Home housekeepers without gainful occupations (estimated)	22, 500, 000	65. 7
Attending school, college, or other educational institution	1, 436, 840	4. 2
All other	2, 102, 008	6. 1

II

THE EXTENT TO WHICH WOMEN HAVE TAKEN UP GAINFUL OCCUPATIONS

The gainfully employed women as reported in the census of 1920 constituted 24 per cent, or almost one-fourth, of the total number of women 16 years of age and over.

GEOGRAPHIC DIVISIONS

As is shown by the following table, the percentage was in general higher in the Eastern States than in the Western. In fact, going from East to West, the percentage shows a steady decline by geographic divisions until the Pacific coast is reached, where it shows some increase or recovery. Thus, the percentage of women gainfully employed was 32.3 in New England, 27.2 in the Middle Atlantic division, 21.5 in the East North Central, 18.8 in the West North Central, 17.9 in the Mountain division, and 23.0 in the Pacific division. There is a similar decrease going westward in the southern half of the country, from 26.9 in the South Atlantic division to 23.4 in the East South Central and 20.1 in the West South Central. The main explanation of these differences is found in the fact that in the East, as compared with the West, there is more manufacturing and less agriculture, and likewise a larger urban and a smaller rural population, the result being that there are greater demands and greater opportunities for the employment of women in gainful occupations.

In general, it can be said that the percentage of women gainfully employed in any State or section of the country is determined largely by the number of cities or by the percentage of urban population in the total population. But in the Southern States another factor which has considerable influence is the large Negro element in the total population, since, as noted elsewhere, a large proportion of the Negro women are gainfully employed, most of them as servants or laundresses or as farm laborers.

7

TABLE 3.—NUMBER AND PERCENTAGE OF WOMEN ENGAGED IN GAINFUL OCCU-
PATIONS, BY GEOGRAPHIC SECTIONS AND DIVISIONS: 1920

GEOGRAPHIC SECTION AND DIVISION	WOMEN 16 YEARS OF AGE AND OVER: 1920		
	Total number	Engaged in gainful occupations	
		Number	Per cent
United States	34, 241, 749	8, 202, 901	24. 0
The North	21, 395, 384	5, 205, 146	24. 3
New England	2, 621, 950	846, 244	32. 3
Middle Atlantic	7, 579, 969	2, 063, 007	27. 2
East North Central	7, 147, 542	1, 535, 641	21. 5
West North Central	4, 045, 923	760, 254	18. 8
The South	10, 003, 943	2, 392, 609	23. 9
South Atlantic	4, 280, 480	1, 151, 407	26. 9
East South Central	2, 701, 751	632, 866	23. 4
West South Central	3, 021, 712	608, 336	20. 1
The West	2, 842, 422	605, 146	21. 3
Mountain	971, 112	174, 123	17. 9
Pacific	1, 871, 310	431, 023	23. 0

IN CITIES

While the difference between city and country as regards the extent
to which women engage in gainful occupations can not be precisely
determined on the basis of the census statistics, since the occupation
data were not tabulated separately either for rural districts or for
individual cities of less than 25,000 inhabitants, an indication of how
great the difference is may be obtained from the following table, in
which the percentages are given for three classes of cities of over 25,000
and for cities having a population less than 25,000 combined with
rural districts.

In the United States as a whole 31.9 per cent of the women living in
the larger cities (those having more than 25,000 inhabitants) were
engaged in gainful occupations, as compared with 18.8 per cent of
those living in smaller cities or country districts. Doubtless the contrast would be still more striking if percentages could be shown for
rural areas apart from the smaller cities.

The differences between the three classes of cities are not as great
as the difference between the total for cities of over 25,000 and the
rest of the country. As a rule, however, the percentage is highest in
the class of largest cities—those of over 100,000 inhabitants. This
is the case for every division distinguished in the table, except New
England, where the percentage is highest for cities of 50,000 to 100,000.

Table 4.—Number and Percentage of Women Engaged in Gainful Occupations for Cities of 25,000 Inhabitants or More, Classified by Size,
and for Smaller Cities and Rural Areas, by Geographic Divisions:
1920

AREA	Total number	WOMEN 16 YEARS OF AGE AND OVER: 1920	
		Engaged in gainful occupations	
		Number	Per cent
United States	34, 241, 749	8, 202, 901	24. 0
Cities of 25,000 inhabitants or more	13, 478, 835	4, 301, 788	31. 9
Cities of 100,000 inhabitants or more	9, 803, 818	3, 191, 006	32. 5
Cities of 50,000 to 100,000 inhabitants	1, 871, 747	581, 357	31. 1
Cities of 25,000 to 50,000 inhabitants	1, 803, 270	529, 425	29. 4
Smaller cities and rural areas	20, 762, 914	3, 901, 113	18. 8
New England division	2, 621, 950	846, 244	32. 3
Cities of 25,000 inhabitants or more	1, 407, 543	514, 424	36. 5
Cities of 100,000 inhabitants or more	795, 166	294, 859	37. 1
Cities of 50,000 to 100,000 inhabitants	298, 003	115, 116	38. 6
Cities of 25,000 to 50,000 inhabitants	314, 374	104, 449	33. 2
Smaller cities and rural areas	1, 214, 407	331, 820	27. 3
Middle Atlantic division	7, 579, 969	2, 063, 007	27. 2
Cities of 25,000 inhabitants or more	4, 547, 188	1, 451, 130	31. 9
Cities of 100,000 inhabitants or more	3, 721, 840	1, 209, 534	32. 5
Cities of 50,000 to 100,000 inhabitants	480, 599	139, 589	29. 0
Cities of 25,000 to 50,000 inhabitants	344, 749	102, 007	29. 6
Smaller cities and rural areas	3, 032, 781	611, 877	20. 2
North Central divisions	11, 193, 465	2, 295, 895	20. 5
Cities of 25,000 inhabitants or more	4, 322, 083	1, 272, 019	29. 4
Cities of 100,000 inhabitants or more	3, 128, 422	953, 234	30. 5
Cities of 50,000 to 100,000 inhabitants	535, 059	148, 387	27. 7
Cities of 25,000 to 50,000 inhabitants	658, 602	170, 398	25. 9
Smaller cities and rural areas	6, 871, 382	1, 023, 876	14. 9
The South	10, 003, 943	2, 392, 609	23. 9
Cities of 25,000 inhabitants or more	2, 041, 476	733, 691	35. 9
Cities of 100,000 inhabitants or more	1, 286, 763	473, 853	36. 8
Cities of 50,000 to 100,000 inhabitants	425, 185	145, 898	34. 3
Cities of 25,000 to 50,000 inhabitants	329, 528	113, 940	34. 6
Smaller cities and rural areas	7, 962, 467	1, 658, 918	20. 8
The West	2, 842, 422	605, 146	21. 3
Cities of 25,000 inhabitants or more	1, 160, 545	330, 524	28. 5
Cities of 100,000 inhabitants or more	871, 627	259, 526	29. 8
Cities of 50,000 to 100,000 inhabitants	132, 901	32, 367	24. 4
Cities of 25,000 to 50,000 inhabitants	156, 017	38, 631	24. 8
Smaller cities and rural areas	1, 681, 877	274, 622	16. 3

In the following diagram, which is based on the above table, the
relative number of women gainfully employed in each class of cities
is indicated by the extent of the heavily shaded areas in comparison
with the areas of lighter shading representing the women not gainfully
employed.

DIAGRAM 1.—WOMEN ENGAGED IN GAINFUL OCCUPATIONS, IN SPECIFIED
CLASSES OF CITIES: 1920

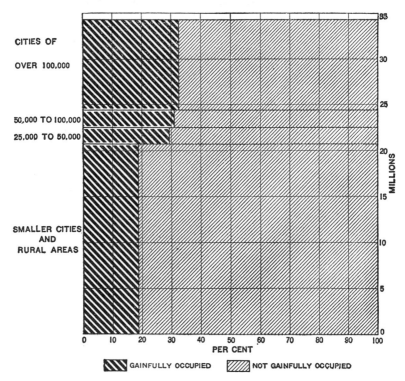

CITIES OF

OVER 100,000

50,000 TO 100,000
25,000 TO 50,000

SMALLER CITIES
AND
RURAL AREAS

PER CENT

GAINFULLY OCCUPIED   NOT GAINFULLY OCCUPIED

In most cities of over 100,000 population not far from one-third
of the total number of women 16 years of age and over are engaged
in gainful occupations. (See table on p. 11.) There is, in fact, a
remarkably close approach to uniformity in the percentages for many
of the larger cities. Thus, in New York the percentage of women in
gainful occupations is 34.2; in Chicago, 32.3; in Philadelphia, 32.2;
in St. Louis, 33.0; in Baltimore, 33.5; and in San Francisco, 33.2.
Boston has a percentage of 37.2, which is somewhat above the general
range for cities of this class. Washington, however, stands out as
having by far the highest percentage, namely 49.6, or almost one-half
of the total number of women in that city. This represents an advance
from a percentage of 39.8 in 1910. Large numbers of women came
to Washington as war workers in 1917 and 1918 and a considerable
proportion of them were still there when the census of 1920 was taken.
Some of the mill cities of New England show exceptionally high percentages, notably Fall River, 45.7; Lowell, 43.1; and New Bedford,
46.1. Comparatively low percentages are shown for Detroit, 26.4;

Cleveland, 28.0; Pittsburgh, 28.1; and Buffalo, 27.4. The lowest percentage of all is that for Youngstown, Ohio, 21.3, this, and the percentage of 24.8 in Salt Lake City, being the only instances in which the percentage falls below 25, or represents less than one-fourth of the total number of women in the city. Doubtless the character of the leading industries in the various cities goes far toward accounting for the variations in the percentage, some industries, textiles for instance, affording a much better opportunity for the employment of women than others, such as iron and steel.

TABLE 5.—PERCENTAGE OF WOMEN ENGAGED IN GAINFUL OCCUPATIONS, FOR CITIES OF 100,000 INHABITANTS OR MORE: 1920

CITY	Percentage of women 16 years of age and over gainfully occupied: 1920	CITY	Percentage of women 16 years of age and over gainfully occupied: 1920
Total, cities of 100,000 or more____	32. 5	North Central divisions—Continued.	
New England division:		Dayton, Ohio_____	27. 0
Boston, Mass._____	37. 2	Des Moines, Iowa_____	32. 1
Bridgeport, Conn_____	31. 6	Detroit, Mich_____	26. 4
Cambridge, Mass_____	37. 6	Grand Rapids, Mich._____	30. 0
Fall River, Mass._____	45. 7	Indianapolis, Ind _____	29. 7
Hartford, Conn_____	34. 9	Kansas City, Kans_____	26. 5
Lowell, Mass._____	43. 1	Kansas City, Mo._____	31. 9
New Bedford, Mass._____	46. 1	Milwaukee, Wis._____	30. 7
New Haven, Conn._____	32. 3	Minneapolis, Minn._____	32. 7
Providence, R. I._____	36. 7	Omaha, Nebr _____	31. 0
Springfield, Mass._____	35. 2	St. Louis, Mo._____	33. 0
Worcester, Mass._____	32. 2	St. Paul, Minn_____	32. 5
Middle Atlantic division:		Toledo, Ohio_____	27. 2
Albany, N. Y._____	31. 7	Youngstown, Ohio_____	21. 3
Buffalo, N. Y_____	27. 4	The South:	
Camden, N. J._____	26. 8	Atlanta, Ga._____	41. 2
Jersey City, N. J_____	28. 7	Baltimore, Md_____	33. 5
New York, N. Y_____	34. 2	Birmingham, Ala._____	31. 5
Bronx Borough_____	29. 9	Dallas, Tex._____	36. 2
Brooklyn Borough_____	30. 3	Fort Worth, Tex._____	28. 9
Manhattan Borough_____	40. 2	Houston, Tex._____	33. 3
Queens Borough_____	27. 9	Louisville, Ky._____	36. 3
Richmond Borough_____	25. 6	Memphis, Tenn_____	37. 7
Newark, N. J._____	29. 0	Nashville, Tenn_____	38. 4
Paterson, N. J_____	37. 2	New Orleans, La._____	33. 8
Philadelphia, Pa_____	32. 2	Norfolk, Va._____	35. 3
Pittsburgh, Pa._____	28. 1	Richmond, Va._____	39. 1
Reading, Pa._____	33. 1	San Antonio, Tex._____	29. 0
Rochester, N. Y_____	33. 9	Washington, D. C._____	49. 6
Scranton, Pa._____	27. 8	Wilmington, Del._____	30. 1
Syracuse, N. Y_____	29. 3	The West:	
Trenton, N. J._____	28. 0	Denver, Colo._____	30. 0
Yonkers, N. Y_____	31. 6	Los Angeles, Calif._____	29. 5
North Central divisions:		Oakland, Calif._____	25. 5
Akron, Ohio._____	25. 9	Portland, Oreg._____	29. 9
Chicago, Ill._____	32. 3	Salt Lake City, Utah_____	24. 8
Cincinnati, Ohio._____	31. 8	San Francisco, Calif._____	33. 2
Cleveland, Ohio._____	28. 0	Seattle, Wash._____	29. 5
Columbus, Ohio._____	28. 5	Spokane, Wash._____	28. 3

RACE AND NATIVITY

The proportion of women gainfully employed differs considerably in the different race and nativity classes. Of the native white women whose parents were also native, 20 per cent were gainfully employed;

for those whose parents, one or both, were immigrants, the percentage is 29.2; for the white women who were themselves immigrants it is 18.8; and for the Negro women it is 43.7.

TABLE 6.—NUMBER AND PERCENTAGE OF WOMEN ENGAGED IN GAINFUL OCCU- PATIONS, BY RACE AND NATIVITY: 1920

RACE AND NATIVITY	WOMEN 16 YEARS OF AGE AND OVER: 1920		
	Total number	Engaged in gainful occupations	
		Number	Per cent
All classes	34, 241, 749	8, 202, 901	24. 0
Native white—Native parentage	17, 969, 950	3, 596, 397	20. 0
Native white—Foreign or mixed parentage	6, 990, 685	2, 042, 804	29. 2
Foreign-born white	5, 872, 366	1, 102, 697	18. 8
Negro	3, 312, 081	1, 445, 935	43. 7
All other [1]	96, 667	15, 068	15. 6

[1] Includes Indians, Chinese, Japanese, and other races.

To a large extent these differences in the percentages are accounted for by differences in age composition and in the geographic distribution of the several classes. Thus, the marked difference between the two classes of native white women—20 per cent for one, as against 29.2 per cent for the other—is partly explained by the fact that, as compared with those whose parents were native Americans, the white women who were born in this country of immigrant parents are concentrated to a greater degree in cities and industrial centers, and comprise a somewhat larger proportion of young women and a considerably larger proportion of single women. At the same time, it is probable that, as compared with the daughters of native Americans, the daughters of immigrants begin working at a younger age and are more frequently under the necessity of earning their living or of contributing to the family income.

The relatively high percentage of Negro women gainfully employed is probably attributable mainly to their low economic status as compared with the other classes. In other words, they are under a greater necessity of working for a living.

The comparatively small percentage gainfully employed among foreign born white women is largely explained by the fact that as a class they are older than the native women and consequently comprise a relatively small percentage of young unmarried women. Thus, only 13.5 per cent of the foreign-born white women are single, as compared with 35.0 per cent of the native white of foreign or mixed parentage and 26.3 per cent of the native white of native parentage.

TABLE 7.—PERCENTAGE OF SINGLE WOMEN 16 YEARS OF AGE AND OVER, BY RACE AND NATIVITY: 1920

RACE AND NATIVITY	WOMEN 16 YEARS OF AGE AND OVER: 1920		
	Total number	Single	
		Number	Per cent
All classes	34, 241, 749	8, 694, 469	25. 4
Native white—Native parentage	17, 969, 950	4, 717, 463	26. 3
Native white—Foreign or mixed parentage	6, 990, 685	2, 448, 946	35. 0
Foreign-born white	5, 872, 366	794, 781	13. 5
Negro	3, 312, 081	717, 168	21. 7
All other [1]	96, 667	16, 111	16. 7

[1] Includes Indians, Chinese, Japanese, and other races.

If the difference noted between the women of foreign or mixed parentage and those of native parentage as regards the extent to which they have taken up gainful occupations is, as suggested, partly due to the fact that the one class is concentrated in cities to a greater degree than the other, then the difference should be less striking when the comparison is confined to the representatives of the two classes living in cities. The following table shows that to be the case:

TABLE 8.—NUMBER AND PERCENTAGE OF WOMEN ENGAGED IN GAINFUL OCCUPATIONS, BY RACE AND NATIVITY, FOR CITIES OF 100,000 INHABITANTS OR MORE AND FOR SMALLER CITIES AND RURAL AREAS: 1920

RACE AND NATIVITY	WOMEN 16 YEARS OF AGE AND OVER ENGAGED IN GAINFUL OCCUPATIONS: 1920			
	In cities of 100,000 inhabitants or more		In smaller cities and rural areas	
	Number	Per cent	Number	Per cent
All classes	3, 191, 006	32. 5	5, 011, 895	20. 5
Native white—Native parentage	1, 110, 218	33. 2	2, 486, 179	17. 0
Native white—Foreign or mixed parentage	1, 068, 872	37. 4	973, 932	23. 6
Foreign-born white	655, 349	22. 4	447, 348	15. 2
Negro	353, 619	53. 7	1, 092, 316	41. 2
All other [1]	2, 948	25. 9	12, 120	14. 2

[1] Includes Indians, Chinese, Japanese, and other races.

Table 9, which carries the analysis a step further by introducing the age classification, brings out the interesting fact that in cities of more than 100,000 population the difference as regards the percentage gainfully employed between the native white women of native parentage and those of foreign or mixed parentage, although quite marked in the age group 16 to 24, largely disappears in the next older age group, 25 to 44. Thus in the younger age group 51.5 per cent of the native white women of native parentage were gainfully employed as compared with 61.9 per cent of the native white women of foreign or mixed parentage, while in the age group 25 to 44, the percentage is 30.6 for the former class and 31.3 for the latter. As already remarked it is quite probable that, as compared with the daughters of native Americans, the daughters of immigrants begin working at an earlier age, which would explain the high percentage shown for them in the younger age group. For each of these two classes the percentage is smaller in the older age group than in the younger mainly because of the large numbers of women who give up their occupations when they marry. But the reduction in the percentage is not so great for the women of native parentage as it is for those of foreign or mixed parentage. This might suggest that the latter marry and give up their occupations at a younger age. That may be true to some extent. It is more probable, however, that the main reason for the approach to equality as regards the percentages employed in the older age group is to be found in the undoubted fact that large numbers of single women of native parentage migrate to the cities from rural districts in order to obtain employment, thus recruiting the ranks of the breadwinners in the city population and taking the places of those who marry. It is safe to say that there is no correspondingly large cityward migration on the part of the native women of foreign or mixed parentage because there is no equally large representation of this class in the rural districts.[1] In other words, most of the daughters of immigrants are born in cities and therefore do not need to migrate in order to obtain employment. Consequently, this class of breadwinners in cities is not being recruited by any very large influx from the country.

TABLE 9.—PERCENTAGE OF WOMEN ENGAGED IN GAINFUL OCCUPATIONS, CLASSIFIED BY AGE, RACE, AND NATIVITY, FOR CITIES OF 100,000 INHABITANTS OR MORE: 1920

RACE AND NATIVITY	PERCENTAGE OF WOMEN IN CITIES OF 100,000 INHABITANTS OR MORE ENGAGED IN GAINFUL OCCUPATIONS: 1920			
	16 years of age and over	16 to 24 years of age	25 to 44 years of age [a]	45 years of age and over
All classes	32.5	55.3	29.8	18.3
Native white—Native parentage	33.2	51.5	30.6	18.6
Native white—Foreign or mixed parentage	37.4	61.9	31.3	19.0
Foreign-born white	22.4	50.7	21.4	13.6
Negro	53.7	53.2	55.0	50.9
All other [b]	25.9	25.7	25.1	31.1

[a] Includes age not reported.   [b] Includes Indians, Chinese, Japanese, and other races.

[1] In the rural districts of the United States the native white population of native parentage outnumbers the native white population of foreign or mixed parentage by almost 5 to 1, while in the cities the ratio is only about 3 to 2. In the North, which, as defined in the census, comprises New England and the Middle Atlantic and North Central States, the ratio is about 3 to 1 in the rural districts, as contrasted with 6 to 5 in the cities.

The following table presents this comparison between the two classes for each of the 12 cities of more than 500,000 inhabitants. In all these cities the same general relationship obtains, the percentage gainfully employed in the younger age group being invariably considerably higher for the women of foreign parentage than for those of native parentage, while in the older age group the difference is less pronounced, and in several instances the higher percentage is that shown for the women of native parentage.

TABLE 10.—PERCENTAGE OF NATIVE WHITE WOMEN OF NATIVE PARENTAGE AND OF NATIVE WHITE WOMEN OF FOREIGN OR MIXED PARENTAGE ENGAGED IN GAINFUL OCCUPATIONS, CLASSIFIED BY AGE AND PARENT NATIVITY, FOR CITIES OF 500,000 INHABITANTS OR MORE: 1920

CITY	PERCENTAGE ENGAGED IN GAINFUL OCCUPATIONS: 1920			
	16 years of age and over	16 to 24 years of age	25 to 44 years of age [1]	45 years of age and over
BALTIMORE:				
Native parentage	29.6	50.3	25.8	16.2
Foreign or mixed parentage	30.4	57.2	25.8	16.9
BOSTON:				
Native parentage	39.7	57.4	42.7	24.3
Foreign or mixed parentage	46.9	66.5	41.5	27.7
BUFFALO:				
Native parentage	32.0	53.3	26.4	16.7
Foreign or mixed parentage	32.4	58.1	26.5	14.8
CHICAGO:				
Native parentage	37.1	56.4	33.2	21.8
Foreign or mixed parentage	40.2	65.3	31.2	19.0
CLEVELAND:				
Native parentage	33.3	50.9	30.3	17.8
Foreign or mixed parentage	34.9	57.3	27.1	15.4
DETROIT:				
Native parentage	30.4	47.0	25.6	16.2
Foreign or mixed parentage	31.9	54.1	24.2	15.1
LOS ANGELES:				
Native parentage	29.9	41.0	33.5	19.4
Foreign or mixed parentage	31.4	44.6	33.1	20.0
NEW YORK:				
Native parentage	37.8	59.2	33.6	19.9
Foreign or mixed parentage	41.9	66.3	32.6	19.9
PHILADELPHIA:				
Native parentage	32.9	55.6	29.9	18.6
Foreign or mixed parentage	37.3	61.7	31.7	20.7
PITTSBURGH:				
Native parentage	30.6	47.8	27.2	17.2
Foreign or mixed parentage	32.8	55.3	27.3	15.7
ST. LOUIS:				
Native parentage	36.6	55.7	30.2	20.8
Foreign or mixed parentage	30.6	60.8	28.7	17.7
SAN FRANCISCO:				
Native parentage	37.7	51.3	36.8	24.1
Foreign or mixed parentage	35.3	55.4	33.7	21.2

[1] Includes age not reported.

III

WHY THE PERCENTAGE OF WOMEN REPORTED AS GAINFULLY OCCUPIED WAS SMALLER IN 1920 THAN IN 1910

From 1870 to 1910 the percentage of women reported in the successive censuses as gainfully employed regularly increased. It was 14.7 in 1870, 16.0 in 1880, 19.0 in 1890, 20.6 in 1900, and 25.5 in 1910, indicating that within this period of 40 years the proportion of women engaged in gainful occupations increased from about one in seven to one in four. Then the percentage declined to 24.0 in 1920. There are some reasons for doubting whether this decrease in the percentage for the decade 1910 to 1920 represents an actual decrease in the extent to which women are engaging in gainful occupations. In this connection one must take account of certain disturbing factors that impair the comparability of the occupation figures of the last three censuses. One of these factors is the change in the date of the census.

The census of 1910 was taken as of April 15, while that of 1920 was taken as of January 1; and though this change probably did not have much effect upon the number of women reported in clerical, or industrial, or professional pursuits, it probably had considerable effect upon the number reported as engaged in agriculture, the census of 1920 being taken at a time of the year (January) when farm work is mostly at a standstill, while the census of 1910 was taken at the season (April and May) when the crops are being planted and the farmer's wife and children as well as the hired help may be actively employed in farm work.

The census question, to be sure, calls for the occupation usually followed, without regard to whether the person enumerated is actually engaged in that occupation at the time when the census is taken. Nevertheless, it is very probable that many women who might think of themselves, or be thought of, as agricultural laborers when actually employed in farm work would not be reported as such at a season when they were not so employed.

CHANGES IN INSTRUCTIONS TO ENUMERATORS

Another disturbing factor was a change in instructions to census enumerators regarding the recording of women as farm laborers. In 1910 the enumerators were instructed to return as a farm laborer—

16

"a women working regularly at outdoor farm work, even though she works on the home farm for her husband, son, or other relative and does not receive money wages * * *."

In 1920 the corresponding paragraph of the instructions read as follows:

"For a woman who works *only occasionally*, or *only a short time each day* at outdoor farm or garden work, or in the dairy, or in caring for livestock or poultry, the return should be '*none*'; but for a woman who works *regularly* and *most of the time* at such work, the return should be *farm laborer—home farm; farm laborer—working out; laborer—garden; laborer—dairy farm; laborer—stock farm;* or *laborer—poultry yard,* as the case may be."

It is evident that there are some rather essential differences in these two definitions of a woman farm laborer. It is partly, however, a matter of emphasis. In 1910 the emphasis was upon *returning* as a farm laborer every woman working regularly at outdoor farm work; in 1920 the emphasis was upon *not returning* as a farm laborer any woman who worked at outdoor work only occasionally or only a short time each day, thus indicating in the one case an apprehension that the enumerator might fail to return as a farm laborer some woman who ought to be so returned and in the other case that he might return as a farm laborer some woman who ought not to be so returned. This change of emphasis came about because a study of the occupation returns convinced those who had charge of the tabulation in 1910 that many women had been returned as farm laborers who could not be properly regarded as such—that there was, in short, an overenumeration of women farm laborers. But it is not only a difference of emphasis. There is obviously a change in the substance of the definition of farm laborer. In 1910 a woman was a farm laborer if she worked regularly at outdoor farm work; but according to the instructions in 1920 she must work not only regularly but most of the time. This narrowed the denotation of the term farm laborer very materially. Either definition, however, leaves a good deal of latitude to the discretion of the enumerator who must decide what constitutes regularity and how large a proportion of the time is "most of the time."

There is, however, still another important difference between the two censuses as regards this matter of defining a farm laborer. In 1910 the enumerators were told that a woman working regularly on the farm was to be returned as a farm laborer even though she worked on the home farm for her husband, son, or other relative and did not receive any money wages; but in 1920 nothing was said about working on the home farm without money wages. At both censuses, however,

6436°—29——3

the enumerator was instructed to distinguish "farm laborer—home farm" from " farm laborer—working out," thus recognizing, at least by implication, the possibility that a woman might work as a laborer on the home farm.

In the 1900 instructions for enumerators there were no specific directions regarding the return of women working as laborers on farms; nor was there, indeed any mention of them as farm laborers. A farm laborer, in general, was defined as a person "who works on a farm for a stated wage (in money or its equivalent) even though he may be a son or other relative of the person who conducts the farm." "Other relative" would include wife and daughter unless the use of the masculine pronoun ("he") was understood as excluding female relatives.

FLUCTUATIONS IN THE REPORTED NUMBER OF FARM LABORERS

In view of these changes in the instructions to the enumerators in the three censuses 1900, 1910, and 1920, and the change of date already noted between 1910 and 1920, it is not altogether surprising that, as shown by the following table, the number of women returned as agricultural laborers increased from 456,405 in 1900 to 1,112,490 in 1910 and then fell off to 611,972 in 1920:

TABLE 11.—NUMBER OF WOMEN IN ALL OCCUPATIONS, IN THE PRINCIPAL AGRICULTURAL PURSUITS, AND IN NONAGRICULTURAL PURSUITS, AS REPORTED IN THE CENSUSES OF 1920, 1910, AND 1900, WITH NUMBER AND PER CENT OF INCREASE

	WOMEN 16 YEARS OF AGE AND OVER ENGAGED IN GAINFUL OCCUPATIONS						
CLASS OF OCCUPATION	Number			Increase [1]			
				1910-1920		1900-1910	
	1920	1910	1900	Number	Per cent	Number	Per cent
All occupations	8, 202, 901	7, 438, 686	4, 833, 630	764, 215	10. 3	2, 605, 056	53. 9
Agricultural pursuits	896, 057	1, 397, 324	[2] 770, 483	−501, 267	−35. 9	626, 841	81. 4
Agricultural laborers	611, 972	1, 112, 490	456, 405	−500, 518	−45. 0	656, 085	143. 8
Farm laborers (home farm)	403, 009	826, 523	[3]	−423, 514	−51. 2	[3]	[3]
Farm laborers (working out)	198, 979	278, 637	[3]	−79, 658	−28. 6	[3]	[3]
Other agricultural laborers	9, 984	7, 330	[3]	2, 654	36. 2	[3]	[3]
Farmers, dairy farmers, and stock raisers	256, 160	265, 200	307, 204	−9, 040	−3. 4	−42, 004	−13. 7
All other agricultural pursuits	27, 925	19, 634	6, 874	8, 291	42. 2	12, 760	185. 6
Nonagricultural pursuits	7, 306, 844	6, 041, 362	4, 063, 147	1, 265, 482	20. 9	1, 978, 215	48. 7

[1] A minus sign (−) denotes decrease.
[2] Number determined by adding fisherwomen and oysterwomen to number reported in agriculture.
[3] Figures not available.

The table brings out the contrast between the decrease of 35.9 per cent from 1910 to 1920 in the number of women reported as engaged in agricultural pursuits and the increase of 20.9 in the number engaged in nonagricultural pursuits. The decrease in the number of women farmers, it may be noted, is a continuation of the decrease between 1900 and 1910; but the large decrease in the number of agricultural laborers between 1910 and 1920 is a reversal of the large increase that took place in the earlier decade. There is little, if any, reason to suppose that the changes in the instructions or in the date of the censuses made any material difference as regards the number of women reported as farmers, and therefore the figures may be accepted as indicating that there was an actual though small decrease in this occupation between 1910 and 1920 following a more marked decrease in the preceding decade. But as regards the number of women reported as farm laborers the great increase between 1900 and 1910, and the great decrease between 1910 and 1920 can not, for reasons already given, be accepted as measuring actual changes in the extent to which women were employed as laborers on farms.

PERCENTAGE IN NONAGRICULTURAL PURSUITS

It is evident that these fluctuations in the reported number of farm laborers, which appear to be due largely to changes in the instructions and in the date of the census, seriously impair the significance of any comparisons of the total number and proportion of women reported as engaged in all gainful occupations at the censuses of 1900, 1910, and 1920; and may largely explain the very marked increase between 1900 and 1910 in the percentage of women so reported and the slight decrease in that percentage between 1910 and 1920. The changes in the instructions here considered should, however, have no effect—and the change of date very little, if any, effect—upon the number of women returned as engaged in nonagricultural pursuits; and the table which follows presents, by way of comparison, separate figures for the women employed in gainful occupations outside of agriculture. These proportions are also shown graphically in the diagram on page 20.

TABLE 12.—NUMBER AND PERCENTAGE OF WOMEN ENGAGED IN ALL OCCUPATIONS, IN AGRICULTURAL PURSUITS, AND IN NONAGRICULTURAL PURSUITS: 1870–1920

CENSUS YEAR	WOMEN 16 YEARS OF AGE AND OVER					
	Total number	Engaged in gainful occupations				
		All occupations		Agricultural pursuits		Nonagricultural pursuits
		Number	Per cent	Number	Per cent	Number	Per cent
1920	34, 241, 749	8, 202, 901	24.0	896, 057	2.6	7, 306, 844	21.3
1910	29, 188, 575	7, 438, 686	25.5	1, 397, 324	4.8	6, 041, 362	20.7
1900	23, 485, 559	4, 833, 630	20.6	770, 483	3.3	4, 063, 147	17.3
1890	18, 957, 672	3, 596, 615	19.0	[1] 595, 711	3.1	[1] 3, 000, 904	15.8
1880	14, 752, 258	2, 353, 988	16.0	458, 709	3.1	1, 895, 279	12.8
1870	11, 205, 910	1, 645, 188	14.7	323, 824	2.9	1, 321, 364	11.8

[1] Estimated in part.

DIAGRAM 2.—WOMEN ENGAGED IN AGRICULTURAL PURSUITS AND IN
NONAGRICULTURAL PURSUITS: 1870–1920

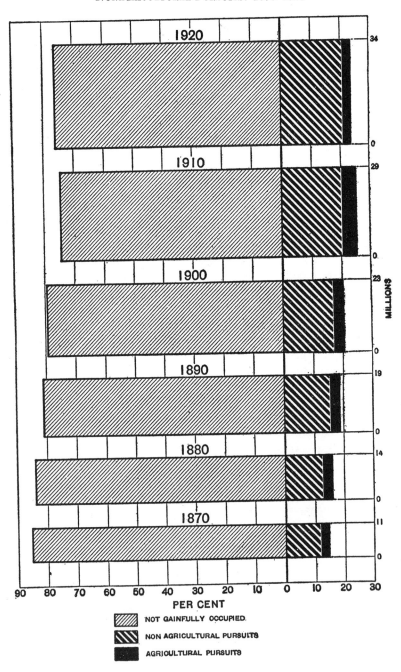

Eliminating agricultural pursuits, the percentage of women gainfully employed as given in the last column of the preceding table shows an increase between 1910 and 1920, but the increase is so small compared with that shown for earlier decades that it seems to call for explanation almost as loudly as does the decrease in the percentage reported as engaged in all occupations. Is this small increase in turn to be explained by some factitious circumstance affecting the comparability of the figures or does it represent an actual check in the tendency of women to take up gainful occupations, or is there possibly some other explanation?

While it is obvious that the changes in the definition of farm laborer would not have any effect on the number of women reported as employed in occupations outside of agriculture, there was one other change in the instructions to enumerators which may have had some effect upon the number of women reported, not only in agriculture, but in other classes of occupations as well. The change here referred to was the omission in 1920 of the paragraph inserted in the instructions in 1910 emphasizing the importance of returning the occupations of women and children. The paragraph read as follows:

"Column 18, Trade or profession.—An entry should be made in this column for *every* person enumerated. The occupation, if any, followed by a child, of any age, or by a woman is just as important, for census purposes, as the occupation followed by a man. Therefore it must never be taken for granted, without inquiry, that a woman, or child, has no occupation."

How much effect the insertion of this paragraph in 1910 and its omission in 1920 may have had upon the returns it is of course not possible to determine. It expressed a more or less obvious truth and the writer doubts whether its omission in 1920 made very much difference. At both censuses the enumerator was required to make an entry in the occupation column of the schedule for every woman enumerated, writing the word "none" in case she had no gainful occupation. Hence, if he were a conscientious enumerator he could not overlook the question at either census.

It seems probable, therefore, that as regards the employment of women in nonagricultural pursuits the returns of the 1910 and 1920 censuses may be accepted as indicating changes which actually took place, and that there was, in fact, only a small increase in the proportion of women following wage-earning occupations. But that seems rather surprising and opposed to the popular impression as to what is taking place; and the question naturally arises as to what it signifies or how it may be explained. To obtain light upon that question it is desirable to ascertain whether this check to the increase in the extent to which women are engaging in industrial, commercial, clerical, professional, or other nonagricultural occupations was general, or whether, on the contrary, the percentage of increase for the total is a result of diverging tendencies among the different classes composing the total. It might almost be enunciated as an axiom in statistics that what is true of the whole is seldom true of all the parts composing the whole; and in any statistical analysis one of the first questions to be considered is whether the particular phenomenon which attracts attention can be localized. The analysis of the statistics by race, nativity, and age, as given in the following section, brings out some facts of significance in this connection.

ANALYSIS BY AGE, RACE, AND NATIVITY

On the basis of nativity and race, the occupation statistics distinguish four main classes of women, and the following table gives for each of these classes the percentage engaged in nonagricultural pursuits at the censuses of 1890, 1900, 1910, and 1920:

TABLE 13.—PERCENTAGE OF WOMEN ENGAGED IN NONAGRICULTURAL PURSUITS, BY RACE AND NATIVITY: 1890–1920

| CENSUS YEAR | PERCENTAGE OF WOMEN 16 YEARS OF AGE AND OVER ENGAGED IN NONAGRICULTURAL PURSUITS | | | | |
	All classes [1]	Native white— Native parentage	Native white— Foreign or mixed parentage	Foreign-born white	Negro
1920	21.3	18.3	28.6	18.1	28.4
1910	20.7	15.9	27.8	21.1	30.9
1900	17.3	12.4	24.8	18.1	26.5
1890	15.8	10.6	25.4	18.6	23.1

[1] Includes Indians, Chinese, Japanese, and other races.

The above table brings out some rather remarkable features of difference between the last two decades, 1900 to 1910 and 1910 to 1920. In the earlier decade the three classes of white women, so far as the percentage employed in nonagricultural pursuits is concerned, kept even pace, one with the other, the percentage of each class increasing by exactly or approximately three units. But for the following decade the figures for the three classes show a decided divergence. For the native white of native parentage the percentage increased considerably, or by 2.4, although not as much as in the preceding decade, when the increase was 3.5. For the native white of foreign or mixed parentage there was only a slight increase in the percentage (0.8). For the foreign-born white there was a decided decrease (3.0).

In the case of the Negro women the fluctuation in the percentage seems rather erratic—an increase from 26.5 in 1900 to 30.9 in 1910 being followed by a decrease to 28.4 in 1920.

These differences and variations, it will be found, are in part the result of a rather pronounced change that took place during the last decade in the age composition of the adult female population, the change consisting of a decrease in the percentage of women under the age of 25, and a nearly corresponding increase in the percentage over 45. Thus, in 1920, of the total number of women 16 years of age and over, 25 per cent were under 25 years of age, as compared with 27.9 per cent in 1910; and 30.3 per cent were over 45 as compared with 28.1 per cent in 1910. This change in the proportionate numbers under 25 and over 45 is not a new development, but is, in fact, the continuation of a tendency that has been revealed by each successive census for the last 50 years, or more; the change, however, was more pronounced between 1910 and 1920 than in the earlier decades, as is shown by the following table.

TABLE 14.—PER CENT DISTRIBUTION, BY AGE, OF WOMEN 16 YEARS OF AGE AND OVER: 1870–1920

AGE PERIOD	PER CENT DISTRIBUTION OF WOMEN 16 YEARS OF AGE AND OVER					
	1920	1910	1900	1890	1880	1870
Total	100.0	100.0	100.0	100.0	100.0	100.0
16 to 24 years	25.0	27.9	28.8	30.4	31.2	31.7
25 to 44 years	44.5	43.7	43.4	42.3	42.7	44.0
45 to 64 years	23.1	21.4	21.0	20.7	20.3	19.1
65 years and over	7.2	6.7	6.5	6.2	5.8	5.1
Age not reported	0.2	0.2	0.3	0.3	----------	(1)

1 Less than one-tenth of 1 per cent.

In 1870, 31.7 per cent of the women 16 years of age and over were under 25 years of age; in 1920 the corresponding percentage was only 25. Meantime, the percentage 45 years and over increased from 24.2 in 1870 to 30.3 in 1920. Changes in age distribution such as these are bound to have some rather important sociological results.

The above-noted change in the age composition of the adult female population may have come about through what might be termed the growing up or aging of a young population, representing a change which may normally take place in the early history of new country recently peopled largely by immigration.[1] But it is a change which may also result from an improvement in sanitation, hygiene, and medical knowledge, influences tending to reduce the death rate and prolong human life. A declining birth rate may be another factor contributing to produce an increase in the proportion of older people

[1] This might not be so confidently asserted if we were considering the age distribution of the total—as distinguished from the adult—population, since the settlement of a new country is often followed by a high birth rate and a consequent increase in the proportion of children.

in the total adult population. In the decade 1910 to 1920, however, still another cause was operating, and that was the very decided check to immigration.

Any designated age class (except the youngest) is recruited in two ways, first, by the persons of younger years who enter the given age group simply by growing older, and secondly, by the arrival of immigrants who are already within the given age class. Now, with the outbreak of the World War, immigration to this country was greatly curtailed. The effect as regards the immigration of females is shown by the following figures:

FEMALE IMMIGRANTS ARRIVING IN THE UNITED STATES

Fiscal year ending June 30—	Number
1911	308, 493
1912	308, 241
1913	389, 748
1914	419, 733
1915	139, 679
1916	116, 597
1917	120, 926
1918	48, 738
1919	57, 860
1919 (July 1 to Dec. 31)	76, 844

The total immigration of females from July 1, 1914 to December 31, 1919, a period of five and one-half years, was only 560,644, as compared with a total of 1,426,215 in the preceding four years. Since a large proportion of arriving immigrant women are young, the immediate effect of this check to immigration, as shown by the table which follows, was a decrease of over 20 per cent in the number of foreign-born white women in the United States 16 to 24 years of age; and as a further consequence, the percentage of women under 25 years of age in the total number of white women of foreign birth decreased from 16.5 in 1910 to 11.9 in 1920, while the percentage over 45 increased from 38.4 in 1910 to 41.6 in 1920.

There was a similar but less marked change in the age composition of the native white women 16 years of age and over, the percentage under 25 years of age in the case of the native white of native parentage decreasing from 29.2 in 1910 to 27.1 in 1920, and in the case of the native white of foreign or mixed parentage from 32.7 in 1910 to 27.9 in 1920. In neither of these two classes, however, did the actual number of younger women decrease, as was the case among the foreign-born whites.

TABLE 15.—NUMBER OF FOREIGN-BORN WHITE WOMEN, WITH NUMBER AND PER CENT OF INCREASE, AND WITH PER CENT DISTRIBUTION, BY AGE PERIODS: 1920 AND 1910

| AGE PERIOD | FOREIGN-BORN WHITE WOMEN 16 YEARS OF AGE AND OVER | | | | | |
| | Number | | Increase (+) or decrease (−) | | Per cent distribution | |
	1920	1910	Number	Per cent	1920	1910
Total	5,872,366	5,408,190	+464,176	+8.6	100.0	100.0
16 to 24 years	696,909	890,352	−193,443	−21.7	11.9	16.5
16 to 19 years	227,053	283,891	−56,838	−20.0	3.9	5.2
20 to 24 years	469,856	606,461	−136,605	−22.5	8.0	11.2
25 to 29 years	662,275	672,120	−9,845	−1.5	11.3	12.4
30 to 34 years	704,657	617,047	+87,610	+14.2	12.0	11.4
35 to 44 years	1,354,032	1,148,042	+205,990	+17.9	23.1	21.2
45 to 64 years	1,799,118	1,497,783	+301,335	+20.1	30.6	27.7
65 years and over	648,843	576,341	+72,502	+12.6	11.0	10.7
Age not reported	6,532	6,505	+27	+0.4	0.1	0.1

TABLE 16.—PER CENT DISTRIBUTION, BY AGE, OF WOMEN CLASSIFIED BY RACE AND NATIVITY: 1920 AND 1910

| AGE PERIOD | WOMEN 16 YEARS OF AGE AND OVER | | | | | | | |
| | Native white— Native parentage | | Native white— Foreign or mixed parentage | | Foreign-born white | | Negro | |
	1920	1910	1920	1910	1920	1910	1920	1910
Total	100.0	100.0	100.0	100.0	100.0	100.0	100.0	100.0
16 to 24 years	27.1	29.2	27.9	32.7	11.9	16.5	31.0	33.2
25 to 44 years	43.4	41.9	45.1	46.6	46.3	45.1	46.1	44.5
45 to 64 years	21.6	21.2	23.2	18.4	30.6	27.7	17.8	17.1
65 years and over	7.6	7.4	3.8	2.2	11.0	10.7	4.8	4.7
Age not reported	0.2	0.2	0.1	0.1	0.1	0.1	0.3	0.5

Since the women engaging in gainful occupations are predominantly young women, it follows that decreases—such as those just noted—in the relative numerical importance of the younger age groups, or in the proportion of young women, would, apart from any other influences, tend to reduce the total percentage of women gainfully employed. It is possible to measure statistically and to eliminate the effect of this change in age composition by ascertaining how many women would have been gainfully employed in 1920 if, without any change in the percentage employed in each separate age group, the proportion of the total number of women in the several age groups had remained the same as it was in 1910. Working out this computation for each of the principal race and nativity classes we get the results shown in Table 17.

TABLE 17.—NUMBER AND PERCENTAGE OF WOMEN ENGAGED IN NONAGRICUL-
TURAL PURSUITS IN 1920, CLASSIFIED BY RACE AND NATIVITY, COMPARED
WITH THE NUMBER AND PERCENTAGE THAT WOULD HAVE BEEN SO OCCUPIED
HAD THE AGE DISTRIBUTION OF THE TOTAL NUMBER OF WOMEN REMAINED
AS IT WAS IN 1910

	WOMEN 16 YEARS OF AGE AND OVER: 1920			
		Engaged in nonagricultural pursuits		
RACE AND NATIVITY	Total number	As actually enumerated		On the assumption that the age distribution had remained as it was in 1910	
		Number	Per cent	Number	Per cent
All classes_____	34, 241, 749	7, 306, 844	21. 3	7, 564, 270	22. 1
Native white—Native parentage_____	17, 969, 950	3, 293, 327	18. 3	3, 344, 605	18. 6
Native white—Foreign or mixed parentage_____	6, 990, 685	1, 996, 811	28. 6	2, 128, 908	30. 5
Foreign-born white_____	5, 872, 366	1, 064, 724	18. 1	1, 143, 713	19. 5
Negro_____	3, 312, 081	941, 172	28. 4	936, 395	28. 3.
All other [1]_____	96, 667	10, 810	11. 2	10, 649	11. 0

[1] Includes Indians, Chinese, Japanese, and other races.

On the supposition that the age composition for each of the several
race and nativity classes had remained the same as it was in 1910,
the percentage of women employed in nonagricultural pursuits, as
shown by the above table, would have been 22.1, which is higher,
though not very much higher, than the percentage actually reported,
21.3. The computation, however, affects the percentage for the several
classes in varying degrees. The percentage for the native white of
native parentage is increased slightly, or from 18.3 to 18.6; that for
the native white of foreign or mixed parentage, considerably, or
from 28.6 to 30.5; that for the foreign-born white, appreciably, or
from 18.1 to 19.5; while that for the Negro remains practically
unchanged.

TABLE 18.—PERCENTAGE OF WOMEN ENGAGED IN NONAGRICULTURAL PURSUITS
IN 1920 AND IN 1910, CLASSIFIED BY RACE AND NATIVITY, WITH THE INCREASE
OR DECREASE ON THE 1910 AGE BASIS

BASIS	PERCENTAGE OF WOMEN 16 YEARS OF AGE AND OVER ENGAGED IN NONAGRICULTURAL PURSUITS				
	All classes	Native white—Native parentage	Native white—Foreign or mixed parentage	Foreign-born white	Negro
1920 as enumerated_____	21. 3	18. 3	28. 6	18. 1	28. 4
1920 as adjusted to 1910 age basis_____	22. 1	18. 6	30. 5	19. 5	28. 3
1910 as enumerated_____	20. 7	15. 9	27. 8	21. 1	30. 9
Increase (+) or decrease (−) from 1910 to 1920, on 1910 age basis_____	+1. 4	+2. 7	+2. 7	−1. 6	−2. 6

When the adjusted percentages for 1920—using that term to designate the figures obtained by the computation shown in Table 17—are compared with the actual percentages for 1910 (see Table 18) they show an identical and normal increase for the two native white classes, not as great, it is true, as the increase from 1900 to 1910, but greater than that from 1890 to 1900. Therefore, as regards native white women, the above analysis of the census figures seems to justify the conclusion that the tendency to engage in gainful occupations to an increasing extent did not come to an end or undergo in fact any material check or retardation in the last decade. But the figures above presented do not justify the same conclusion as regards the foreign-born white and the Negro women, since for each of these classes the percentage employed in nonagricultural pursuits as adjusted for 1920 is still smaller than the actual percentage in 1910, the 1920 percentage for Negroes being hardly affected by the adjustment and that for the foreign born being increased somewhat but not enough to make it equal the 1910 figure. The situation as regards these two classes will be given further consideration in another section. (See Chs. XII and XIII.)

CONCLUSIONS

The general conclusions reached by the preceding study of figures may be briefly restated as follows: The decrease in the percentage of women reported in the census as gainfully employed—from 25.5 in 1910 to 24.0 in 1920—cannot be accepted as indicating an actual decline in the tendency of women to engage in gainful occupations. It is accounted for in part by the change in the date of the census and in the instructions to enumerators in regard to returning women as farm laborers and in part by a decrease in the proportion of young women in the total adult female population. When agricultural pursuits are excluded and an adjustment is made to eliminate the effect of the change in age composition, the percentage of women engaged in nonagricultural pursuits shows an increase from 20.7 in 1910 to 22.1 (as adjusted) in 1920, or, confining the comparison to native white women, an increase from 19.1 in 1910 to 21.9 in 1920.

A further study of the statistics in relation to this question of the change that is taking place in the extent to which women are following gainful occupations reveals the fact that there are five important occupations for their sex in which not only the percentage but the actual number of women employed has materially decreased, a fact which of course would check the increase in the total percentage of women gainfully employed to the extent that it was not offset by increases in the numbers employed in other occupations. The five occupations here referred to are those of servant, dressmaker or seamstress (not in factory), laundress (not in laundry), milliner, and boarding or lodging house keeper. The total number of women employed in these five occupations decreased from 2,458,737 in 1910 to 1,785,036 in 1920, and the percentage of women employed in these occupations decreased from 8.4 to 5.2.

TABLE 19.—NUMBER AND PER CENT DISTRIBUTION OF WOMEN EMPLOYED IN ALL NONAGRICULTURAL PURSUITS AND IN 5 DECREASING OCCUPATIONS: 1920 AND 1910

OCCUPATION	WOMEN 16 YEARS OF AGE AND OVER GAINFULLY EMPLOYED			
	Number		Per cent distribution	
	1920	1910	1920	1910
All occupations	34, 241, 749	29, 188, 575	100. 0	100. 0
All nonagricultural pursuits	7, 306, 844	6, 041, 362	21. 3	20. 7
Five decreasing occupations	1, 785, 036	2, 458, 737	5. 2	8. 4
Servants	981, 557	1, 234, 758	2. 9	4. 2
Dressmakers and seamstresses (not in factory)	235, 519	446, 555	0. 7	1. 5
Laundresses (not in laundry)	383, 622	513, 586	1. 1	1. 8
Milliners and millinery dealers	69, 598	121, 446	0. 2	0. 4
Boarding and lodging house keepers	114, 740	142, 392	0. 3	0. 5
Nonagricultural pursuits (exclusive of five decreasing occupations)	5, 521, 808	3, 582, 625	16. 1	12. 3

The percentage of women employed in nonagricultural pursuits exclusive of the five occupations above mentioned increased from 12.3 in 1910 to 16.1 in 1920, an increase of 3.8. On account of changes in the occupational classification it is not possible to show how this compares with the increase in the corresponding percentage for the preceding decade 1900 to 1910. But the conclusion seems to be justified that, if agricultural pursuits (for which the census figures are misleading) and the five occupations above mentioned (from which women are apparently turning away) are left out of account, the movement of women into other gainful occupations—commercial, clerical, industrial, and professional—underwent no check or retardation in the last decade. On the contrary, when due allowance is made for the changes noted in age composition, it seems probable that the increase in the tendency for women to engage in gainful occupations, outside of those above excluded, was greater between 1910 and 1920 than in the preceding decade.

IV

COMPARISON BY STATES AND CITIES AS REGARDS CHANGES IN THE PERCENTAGE GAINFULLY OCCUPIED

In considering the figures presented in the following table, showing by States, from 1880 to 1920, the percentage of women reported as engaged in all gainful occupations, one should bear in mind the preceding discussion regarding the comparability of the figures for the last three censuses. In most of the Northern States the percentage of women reported as gainfully employed showed little change in 1920 as compared with 1910, but a very considerable increase as compared with 1900. In most of the Southern States the percentage in 1920 was much lower than it was in 1910 and not much, if any, higher than it was in 1900. Since a large proportion of the gainfully employed women in the Southern States are engaged in agriculture, it is probable that the changes noted in the date of the census and in the instructions relating to agricultural laborers had more effect upon the figures for that section than was the case in the Northern States.

In fact, if agricultural pursuits are eliminated from the comparison and a percentage is given based upon the number of women engaged in nonagricultural pursuits, as in the last three columns of the following table, it will be found that, while this exclusion reduces the percentages for the northern divisions but slightly, it makes a material reduction in the percentages for the southern divisions; and in many States it does away with the decrease from 1910 to 1920, which is so marked when agricultural pursuits are included.

In cities the enumeration of women engaged in gainful occupations would obviously not be affected by the changes previously noted in the instructions regarding the return of agricultural laborers, so that no allowance or qualification need be made for that factor. In nearly all cities of 100,000 population or more for which statistics are available, the percentage of women gainfully employed was higher, and in most cases considerably higher, in 1920 than it was in 1900, 20 years earlier. There are in fact only three cities, Lowell, Atlanta, and Memphis, which show a lower percentage for 1920 than for 1900. As compared with 1910, however, the percentages for 1920 do not show any very striking changes or any uniform tendency. In 30 of the 48 cities, the percentage in 1920 was higher but usually not very much higher than it was in 1910, while in 17 cities, it was lower, but usually not very much lower, and in New York City the percentages were the same in the two years. (See Table 21.)

TABLE 20.—PERCENTAGE OF WOMEN ENGAGED IN GAINFUL OCCUPATIONS, BY DIVISIONS AND STATES: 1880–1920

DIVISION AND STATE	ALL OCCUPATIONS					NONAGRICULTURAL PURSUITS		
	1920	1910	1900	1890	1880	1920	1910	1900
UNITED STATES	24.0	25.5	20.6	19.0	16.0	21.3	20.7	17.3
GEOGRAPHIC DIVISIONS:								
New England	32.3	31.9	27.8	26.4	21.7	32.0	31.5	27.3
Middle Atlantic	27.2	26.8	22.6	20.7	17.4	26.9	26.4	22.1
East North Central	21.5	20.6	16.8	14.6	10.6	20.8	19.6	15.8
West North Central	18.8	18.6	15.3	14.0	9.5	17.7	17.0	13.9
South Atlantic	26.9	32.5	25.0	23.3	21.4	19.7	19.2	16.8
East South Central	23.4	31.8	23.1	20.4	18.7	14.2	14.6	12.4
West South Central	20.1	25.2	17.9	18.3	17.2	13.8	13.0	10.1
Mountain	17.9	18.7	15.5	14.2	8.6	16.6	17.0	14.0
Pacific	23.0	21.5	17.6	16.1	11.7	22.2	20.4	16.4
NEW ENGLAND:								
Maine	24.2	23.9	20.5	18.6	14.3	23.4	22.9	19.2
New Hampshire	30.9	30.3	26.6	24.9	22.2	30.3	29.4	25.6
Vermont	21.9	22.7	18.4	16.3	13.4	21.0	21.6	17.2
Massachusetts	35.1	35.0	30.8	30.2	25.2	34.9	34.7	30.6
Rhode Island	35.7	34.9	31.4	30.0	27.0	35.6	34.7	31.2
Connecticut	30.1	29.7	26.2	24.9	20.3	29.8	29.2	25.8
MIDDLE ATLANTIC:								
New York	30.2	29.8	25.0	22.9	19.5	30.0	29.4	24.5
New Jersey	26.6	26.5	22.4	21.0	16.9	26.4	26.2	22.1
Pennsylvania	23.5	23.1	19.5	18.0	14.9	23.2	22.6	19.0
EAST NORTH CENTRAL:								
Ohio	20.9	20.6	16.9	14.7	10.8	20.4	19.9	15.8
Indiana	18.1	16.6	13.8	11.9	8.3	17.4	15.7	12.6
Illinois	24.1	22.5	18.2	16.1	11.2	23.7	21.9	17.4
Michigan	20.7	19.7	16.5	14.1	10.8	20.0	18.6	15.4
Wisconsin	21.0	21.3	17.4	15.4	11.5	19.8	19.3	16.1
WEST NORTH CENTRAL:								
Minnesota	21.6	22.9	18.7	17.4	11.1	20.3	21.0	17.4
Iowa	17.5	17.9	15.1	13.8	9.5	16.6	16.6	13.9
Missouri	20.7	19.0	15.4	13.8	9.9	19.5	17.6	13.8
North Dakota	15.8	18.4	17.0	16.3 }	9.2 {	14.1	15.7	14.9
South Dakota	15.8	16.9	13.7	13.2 }		14.3	14.1	11.9
Nebraska	17.4	17.2	14.8	14.6	8.9	16.4	15.8	13.4
Kansas	16.0	15.1	12.3	11.1	7.3	15.1	13.9	10.9
SOUTH ATLANTIC:								
Delaware	23.4	24.5	19.8	17.5	15.6	22.8	23.2	19.1
Maryland	26.9	27.8	23.3	23.1	18.6	26.3	26.8	22.5
District of Columbia	49.6	39.8	37.0	36.1	30.5	49.6	39.7	37.0
Virginia	21.3	24.6	20.6	19.6	16.3	18.9	19.9	17.0
West Virginia	13.4	14.7	10.6	9.5	6.2	12.1	12.5	8.7
North Carolina	24.5	34.3	23.3	21.3	17.0	15.8	15.5	13.5
South Carolina	37.0	49.9	37.9	33.9	36.5	15.7	16.0	15.2
Georgia	29.8	38.5	28.8	26.4	28.2	17.9	17.7	17.0
Florida	27.1	29.9	22.8	22.4	19.9	22.8	20.9	15.8
EAST SOUTH CENTRAL:								
Kentucky	17.0	19.5	15.5	14.4	10.7	14.7	16.0	12.9
Tennessee	19.7	23.2	17.5	14.5	10.8	15.6	15.8	13.0
Alabama	27.8	40.8	30.4	26.1	28.1	14.2	14.0	12.3
Mississippi	31.7	48.6	33.4	31.4	31.1	11.4	12.0	10.8
WEST SOUTH CENTRAL:								
Arkansas	19.7	29.5	17.7	14.6	11.6	9.6	10.5	8.0
Louisiana	25.8	32.2	27.8	29.6	28.5	17.6	17.9	14.7
Oklahoma	15.5	15.3	9.9	6.8		12.5	10.4	6.4
Texas	20.0	24.5	15.1	14.2	12.4	14.4	12.8	9.6
MOUNTAIN:								
Montana	17.9	19.3	16.9	16.4	7.8	16.5	17.6	15.9
Idaho	14.5	15.2	11.5	10.1	5.0	13.4	13.4	9.7
Wyoming	17.6	17.3	14.5	13.6	11.4	16.1	15.7	13.4
Colorado	20.6	21.1	17.2	17.4	11.6	19.6	19.6	16.5
New Mexico	14.5	15.9	11.1	8.7	6.3	12.8	12.5	9.6
Arizona	18.8	19.5	20.3	11.7	6.3	16.0	18.1	14.1
Utah	16.7	17.3	13.6	12.3	7.1	16.0	16.5	12.3
Nevada	20.3	21.0	17.6	17.1	12.1	19.4	20.0	16.4
PACIFIC:								
Washington	21.5	20.0	15.3	13.5	6.5	20.7	18.9	13.9
Oregon	21.2	20.2	15.6	13.1	6.9	20.3	18.9	14.3
California	24.0	22.4	18.7	17.5	13.0	23.2	21.5	17.6

The general trend or movement as regards the extent to which women in cities are engaged in gainful occupations is shown by Table 22.

TABLE 21.—PERCENTAGE OF WOMEN ENGAGED IN GAINFUL OCCUPATIONS, FOR SPECIFIED CITIES OF 100,000 INHABITANTS OR MORE: 1920, 1910, AND 1900

CITY	PERCENTAGE OF WOMEN 16 YEARS OF AGE AND OVER ENGAGED IN GAINFUL OCCUPATIONS			CITY	PERCENTAGE OF WOMEN 16 YEARS OF AGE AND OVER ENGAGED IN GAINFUL OCCUPATIONS		
	1920	1910	1900		1920	1910	1900
NEW ENGLAND DIVISION				NORTH CENTRAL DIVISIONS— continued			
Boston, Mass	37.2	38.0	33.1				
Bridgeport, Conn	31.6	32.6	29.2	Grand Rapids, Mich	30.0	26.8	24.5
Cambridge, Mass	37.6	36.1	32.1	Indianapolis, Ind	29.7	28.1	24.8
Fall River, Mass	45.7	45.8	44.7	Kansas City, Mo	31.9	30.0	26.8
Lowell, Mass	43.1	45.4	45.1	Milwaukee, Wis	30.7	29.2	25.6
New Haven, Conn	32.3	31.6	28.0	Minneapolis, Minn	32.7	32.3	28.1
Providence, R. I	36.7	36.4	33.5	Omaha, Nebr	31.0	30.0	28.4
Worcester, Mass	32.2	32.1	28.8	St. Louis, Mo	33.0	29.8	25.5
				St. Paul, Minn	32.5	34.3	29.6
MIDDLE ATLANTIC DIVISION				Toledo, Ohio	27.2	27.3	22.3
Albany, N. Y	31.7	31.4	27.5	SOUTHERN DIVISIONS			
Buffalo, N. Y	27.4	27.6	23.1				
Jersey City, N. J	28.7	26.9	22.8	Atlanta, Ga	41.2	42.8	42.1
New York, N, Y	34.2	34.2	29.3	Baltimore, Md	33.5	35.3	30.6
Newark, N. J	29.0	29.2	26.2	Louisville, Ky	36.3	35.7	29.2
Paterson, N. J	37.2	35.2	30.6	Memphis, Tenn	37.7	40.4	40.8
Philadelphia, Pa	32.2	33.7	29.3	Nashville, Tenn	38.4	38.6	36.7
Pittsburgh, Pa	28.1	27.6	¹22.2	New Orleans, La	33.8	33.5	26.2
Rochester, N. Y	33.9	33.8	31.5	Richmond, Va	39.1	41.6	36.9
Scranton, Pa	27.8	25.8	24.1	Washington, D. C	49.6	39.8	37.0
Syracuse, N. Y	29.3	30.1	26.2				
				WESTERN DIVISIONS			
NORTH CENTRAL DIVISIONS				Denver, Colo	30.0	28.4	24.8
Chicago, Ill	32.3	30.8	25.1	Los Angeles, Calif	29.5	26.2	21.8
Cincinnati, Ohio	31.8	33.0	29.4	Oakland, Calif	25.5	23.0	20.9
Cleveland, Ohio	28.0	27.9	23.4	Portland, Oreg	29.9	28.7	24.8
Columbus, Ohio	28.5	28.0	24.5	San Francisco, Calif	33.2	29.3	25.2
Dayton, Ohio	27.0	26.2	24.1	Seattle, Wash	29.5	25.8	22.8
Detroit, Mich	26.4	29.1	25.4				

¹ Figures include Allegheny in 1900.

TABLE 22.—NUMBER AND PERCENTAGE OF WOMEN GAINFULLY OCCUPIED IN 1920, WITH PERCENTAGE FOR 1910 AND 1900, FOR THE COMBINED CITIES OF 100,000 INHABITANTS OR MORE IN EACH GEOGRAPHIC DIVISION

GEOGRAPHIC SECTION AND DIVISION	WOMEN 16 YEARS OF AGE AND OVER IN CITIES OF 100,000 INHABITANTS OR MORE				
	Total number, 1920	Engaged in gainful occupations			
		Number, 1920	Per cent		
			1920	1910	1900
United States	9,803,818	3,191,006	32.5	32.3	28.0
The North:					
New England division	795,166	294,859	37.1	37.3	33.3
Middle Atlantic division	3,721,840	1,209,534	32.5	32.8	28.1
East North Central division	2,332,883	697,089	29.9	29.7	25.3
West North Central division	795,539	256,145	32.2	30.9	27.2
The South:					
South Atlantic division	676,203	265,360	39.2	38.3	33.0
East South Central division	264,412	94,797	35.9	36.9	32.9
West South Central division	346,148	113,696	32.8	33.5	26.2
The West:					
Mountain division	135,610	38,558	28.4	28.4	24.8
Pacific division	736,017	220,968	30.0	26.9	24.4

V

THE OCCUPATIONS WHICH WOMEN ARE ENTERING

Every year large numbers of women join the ranks of the wage earners by taking up some gainful occupation. Their choice of an occupation, while in some degree a matter of preference or liking, is restricted of course to those occupations for which they are individually qualified by education, experience, or natural abilities, and in which at the same time there is a demand or opportunity for their employment. Every year, likewise, large numbers of women give up their occupations on account of marriage or for other reasons. Probably there is at the same time considerable shifting from one occupation to another.

Under these conditions the occupational classification of women gainfully employed may change materially in a comparatively short time. Such changes may, of course, be temporary, as was the case to a large extent during the World War; or they may be indicative of a permanent tendency, or of an adjustment to conditions that are likely to continue. It is by no means certain that women have as yet filled the place they will ultimately come to occupy in the industrial world. The general employment of women in wage-earning pursuits is still a comparatively recent development, and the census statistics indicate that they may be going through a period of adjustment to changing conditions in industry and in society.

In Table 23 the principal nonagricultural occupations or occupational groups in which women are employed have been arranged in the order of the increase between 1910 and 1920 in the number of women in the occupation, so as to give prominence to those occupations which attract the largest numbers of women or offer the largest opportunities for their employment. Diagram 3 (p. 34) is a graphic presentation of these changes.

OCCUPATIONS SHOWING INCREASES

The occupation of clerk (outside of stores) stands at the head of the list, the increase in the number of women employed in this occupation being 344,185. This occupation showed also the largest percentage of increase, 288.3 per cent, so that the number of women employed as clerks in 1920 was almost four times what it was in 1910.

The next largest absolute increase was that shown for semiskilled operatives in manufacturing and mechanical industries, whose numbers increased from 955,423 in 1910 to 1,274,719 in 1920, an increase of 319,296, or 33.4 per cent. There was an increase of 298,546, or 114.3 per cent, in the number of stenographers and typists; of 171,304, or 92.4 per cent, in the number of bookkeepers, cashiers, and accountants; and of 163,333, or 46.6 per cent, in the number of clerks and saleswomen in stores. Women school-teachers increased from 476,661 in 1910 to 635,207 in 1920, an increase of 158,546, or 33.3 per cent.

TABLE 23.—NUMBER OF WOMEN EMPLOYED IN THE PRINCIPAL NONAGRICUL-
TURAL PURSUITS IN 1920 AND 1910, WITH INCREASE

| OCCUPATION | WOMEN 16 YEARS OF AGE AND OVER GAIN-FULLY EMPLOYED | | | |
| | 1920 | 1910 | Increase [1] | |
			Number	Per cent
All nonagricultural pursuits	7, 306, 844	6, 041, 362	1, 265, 482	20. 9
Clerks (except clerks in stores)	463, 570	119, 385	344, 185	288. 3
Semiskilled operatives (manufacturing) (n. o. s.[2])	1, 274, 719	955, 423	319, 296	33. 4
Stenographers and typists	559, 748	261, 202	298, 546	114. 3
Bookkeepers, cashiers, and accountants	356, 603	185, 299	171, 304	92. 4
Saleswomen and clerks in stores	514, 056	350, 723	163, 333	46. 6
Teachers (school)	635, 207	476, 661	158, 546	33. 3
Telephone operators	175, 469	86, 081	89, 388	103. 8
Laborers (manufacturing) (n. o. s.[2])	160, 133	80, 048	80, 085	100. 0
Trained nurses	143, 664	76, 481	67, 183	87. 8
Waitresses	114, 718	83, 597	31, 121	37. 2
Housekeepers and stewardesses	204, 350	173, 280	31, 070	17. 9
Midwives and nurses (not trained)	137, 431	116, 746	20, 685	17. 7
Religious, charity, and welfare workers	26, 927	8, 877	18, 050	203. 3
Retail dealers	78, 957	67, 010	11, 947	17. 8
Barbers, hairdressers, and manicurists	33, 091	22, 011	11, 080	50. 3
Forewomen and overseers (manufacturing)	30, 171	19, 740	10, 431	52. 8
Telegraph operators	16, 860	8, 199	8, 661	105. 6
Librarians	13, 502	5, 828	7, 674	131. 7
Janitors and sextons	28, 929	21, 357	7, 572	35. 5
College presidents and professors	10, 075	2, 958	7, 117	240. 6
Manufacturers, officials, and managers (manufacturing)	13, 276	6, 161	7, 115	115. 5
Agents, canvassers, and collectors	15, 741	8, 754	6, 987	79. 8
Laundry operatives	78, 548	73, 393	5, 155	7. 0
Restaurant, café, and lunch room keepers	15, 644	10, 515	5, 129	48. 8
Postmasters	11, 208	8, 718	2, 490	28. 6
Actresses and showwomen	14, 220	12, 817	1, 403	10. 9
Hotel keepers and managers	14, 134	14, 235	−101	−0. 7
Artists, sculptors, and teachers of art	14, 566	15, 354	−788	−5. 1
Charwomen and cleaners	24, 744	26, 443	−1, 699	−6. 4
Compositors, linotypers, and typesetters	11, 306	14, 025	−2, 719	−19. 4
Tailoresses	31, 828	40, 370	−8, 542	−21. 2
Musicians and teachers of music	72, 431	83, 851	−11, 420	−13. 6
Boarding and lodging house keepers	114, 740	142, 392	−27, 652	−19. 4
Milliners and millinery dealers	69, 598	121, 446	−51, 848	−42. 7
Laundresses (not in laundry)	383, 622	513, 586	−129, 964	−25. 3
Dressmakers and seamstresses (not in factory)	235, 519	446, 555	−211, 036	−47. 3
Servants	981, 557	1, 234, 758	−253, 201	−20. 5
All other nonagricultural pursuits	225, 982	147, 083	78, 899	53. 6

[1] A minus sign − denotes decrease.   [2] Not otherwise specified.

In the aggregate the number of women employed in the six occupations above mentioned, which include clerks, factory operatives, stenographers, typists, cashiers, bookkeepers, accountants, saleswomen, clerks in stores, and school-teachers, increased 1,455,210, or 62 per cent. Of course, the number of women entering these occupations in the interval between 1910 and 1920 must have been considerably greater than the recorded net increase, because before there can be any increase in an occupation the new recruits must be sufficient in number to take the places of those who die or give up the occupation for any reason.

The number of telephone operators more than doubled, increasing by 89,388, or 103.8 per cent. The increase in the number of women employed as laborers in manufacturing industries was almost as great, being 80,085, or 100 per cent.

The number of religious, charity, and welfare workers, and of college presidents and professors, increased by more than 200 per cent. But in point of numbers these are occupations of minor importance, and the absolute numerical increase is therefore relatively small as compared with the increase in the number of clerks, factory operatives, and stenographers.

DIAGRAM 3.—INCREASE AND DECREASE IN NUMBER OF WOMEN EMPLOYED IN THE PRINCIPAL NONAGRICULTURAL PURSUITS: 1910–1920

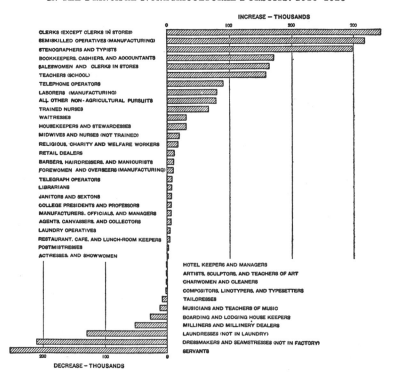

OCCUPATIONS SHOWING DECREASES

At the foot of the list in Table 23 are the principal occupations in which the number of women decreased. Most noteworthy of all is the decrease of 253,201, or 20.5 per cent, in the number employed as servants. There were decreases, likewise, in the number of dressmakers, laundresses, milliners, tailoresses, and boarding and lodging house keepers. The occupation of musician and music teacher seems hardly to belong in this class. Nevertheless it shows a decrease.

Table 23 seems to indicate, in general, that women are turning away from the occupation of servant, dressmaker, laundress (not in laundry), milliner, and boarding house keeper to accept employment in stores, factories, and offices as clerks, operatives, laborers, saleswomen, cashiers, stenographers, etc. The inducements may be better pay in many cases, regular and shorter hours, more congenial companionship, and pleasanter surroundings, also probably a better social standing, since the occupation of domestic servant and that of laundress or washerwoman, in particular, are very commonly looked upon as being menial pursuits.

This explanation, however, probably does not fully account for the change. The decrease shown by some of these occupations is probably due, in part at least, to a decreasing demand or opportunity for the employment of women in that occupation rather than to their preference for other pursuits; and to that extent it might be said that women are not leaving the occupation, so much as the occupation is leaving them. This is probably the case as regards the occupations of home dressmakers and seamstresses and home laundresses. They seem to be occupations of declining importance, because to an increasing extent housekeepers send work to the steam laundry rather than to the washerwoman; and women in general are more and more inclined to purchase ready-made dresses in preference to employing a dressmaker.

The keeping of a boarding house is another occupation of declining importance. The total number of boarding and lodging house keepers of both sexes decreased from 165,452 in 1910 to 133,392 in 1920. Probably no one will be surprised at the fact of a decrease. But it may create some surprise to learn that the reported number of hotel keepers and managers also decreased—from 64,504 in 1910 to 55,583 in 1920. The hotel business, if one may judge by appearances, is not languishing; and the explanation of the decrease probably is to be found in a reduction in the number of small hotels—many of which were little more than boarding houses with ambitious names— and the multiplication of the large hotels which in the extent of the accommodation provided take the place of many small ones. It is quite probable that in the hotel and boarding-house business, as in many other industries, the big establishments are absorbing or displacing the smaller ones.

THE DECREASING SERVANT CLASS

While the census of 1920 was the first to report a decrease in the number of servants, the statistics of earlier censuses show that the occupation was not keeping up with the growth of other employments. That is to say, it was steadily losing ground in its relative importance as an occupation for women. This is shown by Table 24, in which, however, in order to obtain comparable figures going back to the earlier censuses, certain other occupations of a similar nature have been included with that of servant. For the same reason (i. e., to secure comparable figures) the table includes all females 10 years of age and over and not only those 16 and over.

TABLE 24.—NUMBER AND PERCENTAGE OF WOMEN AND GIRLS EMPLOYED AS SERVANTS, ETC.: 1870–1920

CENSUS YEAR	FEMALES 10 YEARS OF AGE AND OVER ENGAGED IN NONAGRICULTURAL PURSUITS		
	Total number	Employed as servants and in kindred occupations [1]	
		Number	Per cent of total
1920	7,465,383	1,358,665	18.2
1910	6,268,271	1,595,572	25.5
1900	4,341,599	1,430,692	33.0
1890	3,235,424	1,302,728	40.3
1880	2,052,582	970,273	47.3
1870	1,439,285	873,738	60.7

[1] Includes servants, waitresses, charwomen, cleaners, porters, housekeepers, and stewardesses, based on 1900 classification.

In 1870, as shown by the above table, 60.7 per cent of the women and girls engaged in nonagricultural pursuits were servants or had taken up similar employments. This percentage declined at each successive census, and in 1920 reached 18.2, marking the change of half a century, from the time when the occupation of servant constituted the principal opportunity for women seeking to earn a living, to the present time, when less than one-fifth of the wage-earning women outside of agriculture are servants.

The decrease between 1910 and 1920 in the number of women employed as servants (using this term in the more limited classification of the past two censuses), while it was general throughout the United States, was much more marked in the Northern States than in the Southern and Western, as shown by the following table:

TABLE 25.—DECREASE IN THE NUMBER OF WOMEN EMPLOYED AS SERVANTS: 1910-1920

GEOGRAPHIC SECTION AND DIVISION	WOMEN 16 YEARS OF AGE AND OVER EMPLOYED AS SERVANTS		Decrease, 1910 to 1920	
	1920	1910	Number	Per cent
United States	981, 557	1, 234, 758	253, 201	20. 5
The North	585, 179	799, 580	214, 401	26. 8
New England	76, 478	111, 125	34, 647	31. 2
Middle Atlantic	249, 636	340, 996	91, 360	26. 8
East North Central	166, 674	222, 050	55, 376	24. 9
West North Central	92, 391	125, 409	33, 018	26. 3
The South	333, 611	368, 534	34, 923	9. 5
South Atlantic	168, 512	185, 921	17, 409	9. 4
East South Central	83, 734	101, 134	17, 400	17. 2
West South Central	81, 365	81, 479	114	0. 1
The West	62, 767	66, 644	3, 877	5. 8
Mountain	19, 913	22, 564	2, 651	11. 7
Pacific	42, 854	44, 080	1, 226	2. 8

While the number of men employed as servants did not decrease, it underwent only a very small increase, as shown by the following table:

TABLE 26.—TOTAL PERSONS 10 YEARS OF AGE AND OVER EMPLOYED AS SERVANTS, 1920 AND 1910, BY SEX AND AGE, WITH NUMBER AND PER CENT OF INCREASE OR DECREASE

SEX AND AGE	SERVANTS 10 YEARS OF AGE AND OVER		Increase (+) or decrease (−)	
	1920	1910	Number	Per cent
Total	1, 270, 946	1, 572, 225	−301, 279	−19. 2
Men 16 years of age and over	251, 209	247, 959	+3, 250	+1. 3
Women 16 years of age and over	981, 557	1, 234, 758	−253, 201	−20. 5
Children 10 to 15 years of age	38, 180	89, 508	−51, 328	−57. 3

The check to immigration during the latter half of the decade 1910 to 1920, of course, reduced the supply of women of foreign birth available for employment as servants. But if this had been the only— or indeed the principal—factor influencing the situation, it would seem that there would have been no decrease in the other nativity groups, but rather an increase, to make good the deficiency in the supply of foreign-born servants. But, as a matter of fact, the number of native white servants likewise decreased, although the percentage of decrease was not as great as it was for foreign born. The number of Negro women servants, it is true, showed no decrease, but it did not appreciably increase. It remained practically stationary. There was, however, as noted elsewhere (p. 114), a very considerable increase of Negro servants in the Northern States, where to some extent the Negro woman seems to have taken the place of the immigrant in the field of domestic service.

TABLE 27.—NUMBER OF WOMEN EMPLOYED AS SERVANTS, BY RACE AND NATIVITY, WITH INCREASE OR DECREASE AND PER CENT DISTRIBUTION: 1920 AND 1910

RACE AND NATIVITY	WOMEN 16 YEARS OF AGE AND OVER EMPLOYED AS SERVANTS					
	Number		Increase (+) or decrease (−): 1910–1920		Per cent distribution	
	1920	1910	Number	Per cent	1920	1910
All classes _ _ _ _ _ _ _ _ _ _ _ _ _ _ _ _ _ _ _	981, 557	1, 234, 758	−253, 201	−20. 5	100. 0	100. 0
Native white—Native parentage _ _ _ _ _ _ _ _ _ _	238, 357	310, 474	−72, 117	−23. 2	24. 3	25. 1
Native white—Foreign or mixed parentage _ _	143, 208	200, 042	−56, 834	−28. 4	14. 6	16. 2
Foreign-born white _ _ _ _ _ _ _ _ _ _ _ _ _ _ _ _ _	207, 811	333, 011	−125, 200	−37. 6	21. 2	27. 0
Negro _	389, 276	388, 659	+617	+0. 2	39. 7	31. 5
All other [1] _	2, 905	2, 572	+333	+12. 9	0. 3	0. 2

[1] Includes Indians, Chinese, Japanese, and other races.

The increase in servants' wages, accompanying a general increase in the cost of living, makes the keeping of a servant more and more in the nature of a luxury which only people with liberal incomes can afford. On the other hand, it might seem that this increase in wages, by making the position of servants more attractive, should have induced more women to seek that employment; but it has apparently not had that effect, partly, perhaps, because wages have increased also in other competing employments for women. Housekeepers very generally complain of the increasing difficulty experienced in obtaining and retaining good servants even at high wages.

Another factor which may be both a cause and a result of the decrease in the number of servants is to be found in the simplification of housekeeping resulting from the use of apartments, the resort to cafés and restaurants for meals, the invention of mechanical improvements in housekeeping equipment—such as electrical ranges, vacuum cleaners, and washing machines—and the opportunities for having laundry work, cooking (to some extent), and many other tasks, which were formerly included in housework, done outside the home.

Servants are not so indispensable in housekeeping as they once were; and people are finding or inventing ways of doing without them. Of course, only a small minority of the housekeepers have ever had servants. But that minority is becoming still smaller. Just how many private families keep servants it is not possible to determine from the census figures, because the total number of servants includes without distinction many that are employed in hotels, boarding houses, and restaurants; and on the other hand there are some families that have more than one servant.

It is fairly evident, however, that the number of families having servants must have been considerably smaller in 1920 than it was in 1910, and somewhat smaller in 1910 than it was at earlier censuses. This is indicated by the following table giving the number of servants, waiters, etc., per 1,000 of the population at each census from 1870 to 1920.

TABLE 28.—NUMBER OF SERVANTS, WAITERS, AND HOUSEKEEPERS AND STEWARDS PER 1,000 OF POPULATION: 1870–1920

CENSUS YEAR	NUMBER OF SERVANTS, WAITERS, AND HOUSEKEEPERS AND STEWARDS, OF BOTH SEXES AND ALL AGES, PER 1,000 OF POPULATION				
	Total number	Servants and waiters			Housekeepers and stewards
		Total	Servants	Waiters	
1920	17.3	15.2	13.0	2.2	2.1
1910	22.4	20.3	18.3	2.1	2.1
1900	22.6	20.5	19.1	1.4	2.0
1890	24.7	23.2	(¹)	(¹)	1.5
1880	23.0	(¹)	(¹)	(¹)	(¹)
1870	25.9	(¹)	(¹)	(¹)	(¹)

¹ Figures not available.

THE INCREASING STORE AND OFFICE CLASS

The decline in the relative importance of the servant class involves, of course, a corresponding increase in the relative importance of other occupational groups. Most remarkable is the increase in the clerical group, which we will here define to include clerks, saleswomen,[1] stenographers, typists, bookkeepers, cashiers, and accountants. In 1870 the total number of women or girls reported as employed in these occupations was only 10,798, representing less than 1 per cent of the women employed in nonagricultural occupations. In 1920, 50 years later, the number reported in these occupations was 1,910,695, representing 25.6 per cent of the employed women and girls outside of agriculture.

[1] In the recent censuses the saleswomen and the clerks in stores are classified under trade, instead of under clerical occupations; but in the earlier censuses clerks in stores are not distinguishable from clerks not in stores.

TABLE 29.—NUMBER AND PERCENTAGE OF WOMEN AND GIRLS EMPLOYED IN CLERICAL AND SIMILAR OCCUPATIONS: 1870–1920

CENSUS YEAR	FEMALES 10 YEARS OF AGE AND OVER ENGAGED IN NONAGRICULTURAL PURSUITS		
	Total number	Employed as clerks, saleswomen, stenographers, typists, bookkeepers, cashiers, and accountants [1]	
		Number	Per cent of total
1920	7,465,383	1,910,695	25.6
1910	6,268,271	930,763	14.8
1900	4,341,599	394,747	9.1
1890	3,235,424	171,712	5.3
1880	2,052,582	38,088	1.9
1870	1,439,285	10,798	0.8

[1] Based on 1900 classification.

FACTORY WORKERS

About one-fifth of the women reported as gainfully employed in 1920 were semiskilled operatives or laborers in manufacturing industries. The numbers in these occupations were not separately reported in the earlier censuses. But it is possible to obtain a figure which will represent approximately the total number of factory workers, including under that designation all women employed in factories either as machine operatives or in some other kind of semiskilled or unskilled manual labor, or in supervisory positions. This figure is derived from the census statistics by deducting from the total for "manufacturing and mechanical pursuits" at each census the dressmakers and seamstresses, not employed in factories, and then including laundry operatives and managers, classified under "domestic and personal service."

TABLE 30.—NUMBER AND PERCENTAGE OF WOMEN AND GIRLS EMPLOYED IN MANUFACTURING AND MECHANICAL PURSUITS: 1870–1920

CENSUS YEAR	FEMALES 10 YEARS OF AGE AND OVER ENGAGED IN NONAGRICULTURAL PURSUITS		
	Total number	Employed in mills and factories [1]	
		Number	Per cent of total
1920	7,465,383	1,777,022	23.8
1910	6,268,271	1,450,151	23.1
1900	4,341,599	966,167	22.3
1890	3,235,424	657,661	20.3
1880	2,052,582	429,132	20.9
1870	1,439,285	252,702	17.6

[1] Found by deducting from the total for manufacturing and mechanical pursuits the figures for dressmakers and seamstresses (not in factory) and then adding laundry operatives and laundry officials and managers.

The total number of factory workers as thus determined increased from 252,702 in 1870 to 1,777,022 in 1920. The percentage which they constituted of the total number of females employed in all nonagricultural pursuits increased from 17.6 in 1870 to 20.9 in 1880. It reached 22.3 in 1900 and 23.8 in 1920. So it shows no such increase in recent years as is shown for clerical occupations.

WOMEN IN THE PROFESSIONS

There has been a marked gain in the relative importance of the professions as occupations for women. Teaching has always been the leading profession for that sex, and the percentage of teachers in the total number of women and girls employed in nonagricultural pursuits increased from 5.8 in 1870 to 8.7 in 1920, equivalent to approximately 1 in 19 at the earlier census and 1 in 12 at the later. These figures do not include women music teachers, the number of whom, as already noted, showed a decrease at the last census. The occupation of trained nurse is the professional pursuit ranking next to that of teacher as regards the number of women following it. It was not distinguished as a professional pursuit 50 years ago, but was covered under the general designation of "nurses and midwives" in the domestic and personal service group.

TABLE **31.**—NUMBER OF WOMEN AND GIRLS IN THE PRINCIPAL PROFESSIONAL PURSUITS FOR WOMEN: 1870–1920

| CENSUS YEAR] | FEMALES 10 YEARS OF AGE AND OVER ENGAGED IN NONAGRICULTURAL PURSUITS | | |
| | Total number | Engaged in the principal professional pursuits [1] | |
		Number	Per cent of total
1920	7,465,383	992,638	13.3
1910	6,268,271	724,176	11.6
1900	4,341,599	433,862	10.0
1890	3,235,424	307,774	9.5
1880	2,052,582	175,351	8.5
1870	1,439,285	91,963	6.4

[1] For detail by occupations, see Table 32.

On account of the special interest attaching to the subject, the following table is introduced to show the number of females 10 years of age and over reported in each of the principal professional pursuits at each census from 1870 to 1920, inclusive. It should be noted that while the table does not include quite all the occupations now classified as professional in the census reports, it includes all those in which any considerable numbers of women were reported. Some of the minor occupations had to be omitted because the changes in the census classification made it impossible to give figures for all six censuses.

TABLE 32.—NUMBER OF FEMALES 10 YEARS OF AGE AND OVER ENGAGED IN THE PRINCIPAL PROFESSIONAL PURSUITS FOR WOMEN: 1870–1920

OCCUPATION	FEMALES 10 YEARS OF AGE AND OVER IN THE PROFESSIONS					
	1920	1910	1900	1890	1880	1870
Total (specified occupations)	992,638	724,176	433,862	307,774	175,351	91,963
Actresses	13,237	11,992	6,374	3,949	1,820	692
Architects, designers, draftsmen, and inventors	[1] 7,340	3,130	1,041	327	73	14
Artists, sculptors, and teachers of art	14,617	15,429	11,021	10,815	2,061	412
Clergymen, etc	28,714	9,574	3,373	1,143	165	67
Clergymen	1,787	685	(2)	(2)	(2)	(2)
Religious, charity, and welfare workers	26,927	8,889	(2)	(2)	(2)	(2)
Dentists	1,829	1,254	807	337	61	24
Editors and reporters	5,730	4,181	2,193	888	288	35
Lawyers, judges, justices, etc	3,221	1,343	1,010	208	75	5
Lawyers, judges, and justices	1,738	558	(2)	(2)	(2)	(2)
Abstracters, notaries, and justices of peace	1,483	785	(2)	(2)	(2)	(2)
Literary and scientific persons	25,205	13,521	5,984	2,764	[3] 368	159
Authors	3,006	2,058	(2)	(2)	(2)	(2)
Chemists, assayers, and metallurgists	1,714	579	*248	39	48	
Librarians	13,502	5,829	} 3,122 {	(2)	(2)	43
Librarians' assistants and attendants	1,212	2,792		(2)	(2)	(2)
Other literary, etc., persons	5,771	2,263	(2)	(2)	(2)	(2)
Musicians and teachers of music	72,678	84,478	52,359	34,519	13,182	5,753
Photographers	7,119	4,964	3,580	2,201	451	228
Physicians, surgeons, etc	16,784	13,687	7,387	4,557	2,432	527
Osteopaths	1,663 } 9,015 {		(2)	(2)	(2)	(2)
Physicians and surgeons	7,219		(2)	(2)	(2)	(2)
Other healers	7,902	4,672	(2)	(2)	(2)	(2)
Teachers and professors in college, etc	652,500	484,115	327,614	246,066	[3] 154,375	84,047
College presidents and professors [4]	10,075	2,958	463	695	(2)	(2)
Teachers [3]	639,241	478,027	}327,151	245,371 {	(2)	(2)
Demonstrators	3,184	3,130			(2)	(2)
Trained nurses	143,664	76,508	11,119	(2)	(2)	(2)

[1] Includes an estimate involving about 6.4 per cent of the total women in the occupation in 1920.
[2] Figures not available.
[3] Scientific persons combined in 1880 with teachers.
[4] Probably includes some teachers in schools below collegiate rank.

The table shows a steady and rapid increase in the number of women engaged in teaching, an increase from 84,047 in 1870 to 652,500 in 1920. This reflects mainly the growth of the teachers' occupation. Within this period of 50 years the total number of teachers, male and female, increased more than sixfold, or from 126,822 to 799,996, while the total population multiplied only threefold. So in 1920 there was one teacher to every 132 persons, as compared with one to 304 in 1870. But the increase in the number of female teachers is accounted for only in part by the growth of the profession. It reflects also an increase in the proportion of women teachers, or a replacement of men by women. In 1870, 66.3 per cent of the teachers of all ages were women; in 1920 the percentage was 81.7.

Fifty years ago the only three generally recognized professions of any considerable importance outside of teaching were law, medicine, and the ministry.[2]   In those days women were practically debarred from the practice of these professions by legal barriers as well as by public sentiment.   The former have mostly been removed;[3] and people no longer think it strange or unnatural for a woman to take up one of these professions.   But the number who have taken up law (1,738) or the ministry (1,787) is still comparatively small, although on a percentage basis it shows a marked increase.   The number of women physicians, including osteopaths and "other healers," is, however, fairly large, being 16,784.

The musician's or music teacher's profession is one which has given employment to a large—and up to 1910 an increasing—number of women (72,678 in 1920); and the various employments grouped as literary or scientific are also represented by a fairly large number of women (25,205 in 1920).

The only important profession in which women are not represented to any appreciable extent is that of engineering, only 41 women being reported in this profession in 1920.   In 1910 the number was 11. Not insignificant, but still very small, is the number of women reported as architects—137 in 1920.

WOMEN IN AGRICULTURE

In this chapter no reference has been made as yet to the women employed in agricultural pursuits, nor have they been included in the totals for which figures have been presented.   The main reason for leaving them out of consideration, as explained in Chapter III, is that the figures relating to them for the last three censuses are not comparable, owing to changes in the date of the census and in the definition of the term farm laborer as applied to women.

It is probable, however, that the figures for 1900 are so far comparable with those for 1920 that the comparison has some significance in indicating a decline in the relative importance of agriculture in the list of occupations pursued by women.   The number of women reported as employed in agricultural pursuits, it is true, increased from 770,483 in 1900 to 896,057 in 1920, an increase of 16.3 per cent. The increase, however, was confined to the number of women reported as agricultural laborers, the number so reported increasing from 456,405 to 611,972, an increase of 34.1 per cent, which is probably attributable in part to the fact that while at the census of 1900 the enumerators' instructions made no mention of women as agricultural laborers, the corresponding instructions in 1920 gave a careful definition of farm laborer with special reference to women.

---

[2] Although the census reports in those days included in the professional class Government officials, who in point of numbers outranked clergymen and lawyers.

[3] At the present time, according to figures obtained from the Bureau of Education, 62 theological schools out of 1,880, 105 law schools out of 135, 61 medical schools out of 77, and 31 engineering schools out of 139 have women students; and of the various schools which do not have any women students on their rolls, there are many which admit them.

The number of women reported as farmers, which was probably not affected by any changes in the enumerator's instructions, showed a decrease of 16.6 per cent—from 307,204 in 1900 to 256,160 in 1920. The percentage which the women reported as engaged in agricultural pursuits form of the total number of women gainfully employed decreased from 15.9 in 1900 to 10.9 in 1920. This is a result of the fact that while the total number of women reported in the census as employed in agricultural pursuits had, as just noted, increased 16.3 per cent since 1900, the number of women in nonagricultrual pursuits increased by nearly 80 per cent in the same period. This difference, in turn, doubtless reflects mainly the change that is taking place in the relative importance of agriculture and manufactures in the national economy.

Table 33 brings together for ready comparison figures which have been presented and discussed in the preceding pages of this chapter. It is an attempt to give a summary occupational classification which will show the general character of the development that has taken place as regards women's occupations within the last 50 years. In order to obtain a classification which would be significant in that connection and at the same time would present comparable figures going as far back as 1870, it was necessary to make some readjustments in the established census classification and to resort to estimates to some extent. This was partly because the census classification has undergone some changes within that interval and partly because of new developments in the industrial world.

Many occupations have come into existence or acquired importance only within the last 50 years. In 1870, for instance, there were no telephone operators and very few stenographers and trained nurses. But in 1920 these three occupations gave employment to nearly 900,000 women and girls. The distinction between trained nurses (classified under professional pursuits) and other nurses (classified under domestic and personal service) was first introduced in the census of 1900. That was also the first census in which laundry operatives were distinguished from home laundresses.

For the purpose of Table 33, therefore, it was necessary either to estimate or to ignore the number of trained nurses and of laundry operatives prior to 1900.

TABLE 33.—SUMMARY OCCUPATIONAL CLASSIFICATION OF WOMEN AND GIRLS EMPLOYED IN NONAGRICULTURAL PURSUITS: 1870–1920

CENSUS YEAR	FEMALES 10 YEARS OF AGE AND OVER GAINFULLY EMPLOYED					
	Total, in all nonagricultural occupations	Servants, waitresses, and kindred occupations	Clerks, saleswomen, stenographers, etc.	In the principal professions	Mill and factory workers	In all other nonagricultural occupations
	NUMBER					
1920	7,465,383	1,358,665	1,910,695	992,638	1,777,022	1,426,363
1910	6,268,271	1,595,572	930,763	724,176	1,450,151	1,567,609
1900	4,341,599	1,430,692	394,747	433,862	966,167	1,116,131
1890	3,235,424	1,302,728	171,712	307,774	657,661	795,549
1880	2,052,582	970,273	38,088	175,351	429,132	439,738
1870	1,439,285	873,738	10,798	91,963	252,702	210,084
	PER CENT OF TOTAL					
1920	100.0	18.2	25.6	13.3	23.8	19.1
1910	100.0	25.5	14.8	11.6	23.1	25.0
1900	100.0	33.0	9.1	10.0	22.3	25.7
1890	100.0	40.3	5.3	9.5	20.3	24.6
1880	100.0	47.3	1.9	8.5	20.9	21.4
1870	100.0	60.7	0.8	6.4	17.6	14.6

The residual or "all other" group in the above table is large, but the occupations included in it are so diverse that it did not seem to the writer that an attempt at further subdivision was worth while. It included in 1920, 385,874 home laundresses, 235,519 dressmakers and seamstresses not in factories, 178,379 telephone operators, 114,740 boarding and lodging house keepers, and 78,980 retail dealers. These five occupations account for almost seven-tenths of the total in this group. The decline in relative importance of the group between 1910 and 1920 as indicated by the percentages in the table is probably largely due to the decrease already noted (see Table 19, Ch. III) in the numbers of dressmakers, laundresses, and boarding house keepers.

VI
RANGE OF WOMEN'S OCCUPATIONS

The 1920 census classification of the gainfully employed distinguished 572 occupations or occupational titles; and of this number there are only 35 in which women are not represented. This fact is given an undue significance when, as has sometimes been the case, it is accepted as indicating that women are engaging in practically all the occupations that are followed by men. It is true that there is hardly any important branch of industry in which women are not employed in some capacity; but that does not mean that they are doing all or even nearly all the various kinds of work that men are doing. The variety of occupations in the field of modern industry is very great; and the census classification of occupations is necessarily a very summary one, in which many of the designations cover composite occupational or industrial groups, rather than single specific occupations. This is especially true in the field of manufacturing industries, in which a great diversity of employments is comprehended under the terms "laborer" and "semiskilled operative." For example, 2,198 women are classified as laborers in blast furnaces and steel rolling mills. But the term "laborer" as applied to this industry covers a great number of distinct employments, possibly more than a hundred. Just what these women laborers were doing in the rolling mills no one without an intimate knowledge of the industry could venture to say. It is quite probable that many of them were employed in some such occupation as that of "scrubber" or "sweeper." Without doubt their field of employment—as is indicated by the relatively small numbers reported—was rather limited and definitely marked off from that of the 255,330 men classed as laborers in that industry.

No serious significance should be attached to the fact that in successive censuses, a certain small number of women have been reported as carpenters, masons, blacksmiths, plumbers, and even as locomotive engineers. These are sporadic cases, and many of them probably represent errors occurring in the original schedules or in the tabulation of the returns. The small numbers reported in such occupations fluctuate from census to census, and there is no reason to suppose that they indicate even the small beginning of a general movement of women into occupations of this class. The newspaper space writer or cartoonist may delight in featuring the woman blacksmith of the census as a village smithy in skirts or knickers working with hammer and anvil under the wide-spreading chestnut tree. But it is safe to say that it is a purely fanciful picture. The woman

46

may have been called a blacksmith because she had charge of the blacksmith shop of her recently deceased husband, or the enumerator may have made an entry on the wrong line. Some errors of this kind may and inevitably do occur, without impairing the statistical value and substantial accuracy of the census totals.

In addition to the 35 occupations in which no women were reported, there were 58 other occupations in each of which the number of women was less than 0.1 per cent of the total number of workers, and 107 in which it was 0.1 per cent or over but less than 1 per cent. In the aggregate these occupations, in which none or less than 1 per cent of the workers were women, gave employment to 10,097,505 men, which represents 31.2 per cent of the 32,350,489 men reported in all occupations; while the total number of women employed in these occupations was but 17,356, which represents but 0.2 per cent of the 8,202,901 women reported in the census as gainfully employed.

It is evident, then, that a large proportion of the male workers are engaged in occupations in which there are either very few women or none at all. On the other hand, a large proportion of the gainfully employed women, about 60 per cent of them, are concentrated in occupations in which men are a minority.

There are 131 occupations in which 20 per cent or more of the adult workers are women; and the total number of women employed in these occupations is 7,091,492, which is 86.4 per cent of the total number of women in all occupations. The total number of men in these occupations is 5,424,611, which is only 16.7 per cent of the total number in all occupations.

The contrast between men and women workers as regards their occupational distribution is brought out by the following table and by the diagram on page 48, which graphically depicts these figures.

TABLE 34.—MEN AND WOMEN ENGAGED IN GAINFUL OCCUPATIONS, DISTRIBUTED BY OCCUPATIONAL GROUPS AS DETERMINED BY THE PERCENTAGE OF WOMEN IN THE TOTAL NUMBER OF ADULT WORKERS: 1920

OCCUPATIONAL GROUP ACCORDING TO PERCENTAGE OF WOMEN	Number of occupations	GAINFUL WORKERS 16 YEARS OF AGE AND OVER: 1920						
		Number			Per cent of total		Per cent distribution	
		Both sexes	Men	Women	Men	Women	Men	Women
All occupations	572	40,553,390	32,350,489	8,202,901	79.8	20.2	100.0	100.0
Occupation in which, in 1920—								
No women were reported	35	952,047	952,047		100.0		2.9	
Less than 0.1 per cent women	58	4,591,065	4,590,243	822	100.0	(1)	14.2	(1)
From 0.1 to 1 per cent women	107	4,571,749	4,555,215	16,534	99.6	0.4	14.1	0.2
From 1 to 5 per cent women	108	11,162,555	10,778,579	383,976	96.6	3.4	33.3	4.7
From 5 to 10 per cent women	70	4,526,226	4,137,843	388,383	91.4	8.6	12.8	4.7
From 10 to 20 per cent women	63	2,233,645	1,911,951	321,694	85.6	14.4	5.9	3.9
From 20 to 50 per cent women	81	6,411,332	4,185,234	2,226,098	65.3	34.7	12.9	27.1
50 per cent and over women	50	6,104,771	1,239,377	4,865,394	20.3	79.7	3.8	59.3

1 Less than one-tenth of 1 per cent.

DIAGRAM 4.—MEN AND WOMEN ENGAGED IN GAINFUL OCCUPATIONS, CLASSIFIED ACCORDING TO THE PROPORTION OF WOMEN IN THE TOTAL NUMBER OF ADULT WORKERS: 1920

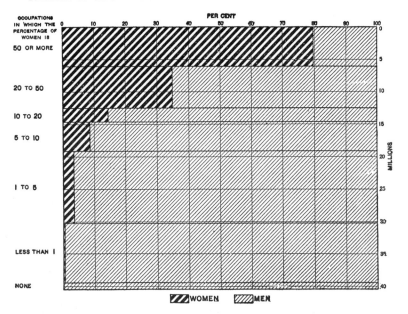

It is of interest to inquire whether this concentration of women in certain classes of occupations is becoming less pronounced or more so. Is the present tendency toward greater concentration or toward greater dispersion? Without doubt there is less concentration in a few occupations than there was 50 years ago. The figures presented in Chapter V indicate that. Women are engaged in a much greater variety of occupations now than they were then. They are more widely dispersed over the occupational field. But whether that tendency is still in progress is not quite so certain. It is not altogether improbable that women are taking more and more complete possession of those occupations for which experience has shown that they are best fitted and are replacing men in these occupations, with the result that the present movement may be in the direction of a more pronounced differentiation between the sexes in the industrial world rather than in the opposite direction.

With the hope of obtaining some light on this question, we may ask whether the concentration of women in those occupations in which they represent a large percentage of the total number of workers was greater or less in 1920 than it was in 1910. Since, for reasons already set forth, the inclusion of the figures for agricultural pursuits impairs the comparability of the results of the two censuses, it seems best to base the distribution on the total for nonagricultural employments, as in the table which follows:

TABLE 35.—MEN AND WOMEN ENGAGED IN NONAGRICULTURAL PURSUITS, 1920 AND 1910, DISTRIBUTED BY OCCUPATIONAL GROUPS AS DETERMINED BY THE PERCENTAGE OF WOMEN IN THE TOTAL NUMBER OF ADULT WORKERS IN 1920

OCCUPATIONAL GROUP ACCORDING TO PERCENTAGE OF WOMEN	MEN				WOMEN			
	1920		1910		1920		1910	
	Number	Per cent distribution	Number	Per cent distribution	Number	Per cent distribution	Number	Per cent distribution
All nonagricultural pursuits	22,940,697	100.0	18,909,095	100.0	7,306,844	100.0	6,041,362	100.0
Nonagricultural pursuits in which, in 1920—								
No women were employed	920,270	4.0	648,748	3.4			9	(¹)
Less than 0.1 per cent women	4,576,989	20.0	3,732,285	19.7	816	(¹)	2,120	(¹)
From 0.1 to 1 per cent women	4,310,215	18.8	3,542,849	18.7	15,866	0.2	11,278	0.2
From 1 to 5 per cent women	4,654,439	20.3	4,487,900	23.7	124,205	1.7	98,464	1.6
From 5 to 10 per cent women	2,108,556	9.2	1,567,293	8.3	173,933	2.4	106,788	1.8
From 10 to 20 per cent women	1,826,366	8.0	1,331,613	7.0	304,487	4.2	192,682	3.2
From 20 to 50 per cent women	3,304,485	14.4	2,394,047	12.7	1,822,143	24.9	1,164,394	19.3
50 per cent or more women	1,239,377	5.4	1,204,360	6.4	4,865,394	66.6	4,465,627	73.9

¹ Less than one-tenth of 1 per cent.

The above table brings out the fact that, of the total number of women engaged in nonagricultural pursuits, 73.9 per cent in 1910 and 66.6 per cent in 1920 were in occupations in which a majority of the workers were women. The concentration in this class of occupations was therefore much less marked in 1920 than it was in 1910. But the explanation is to be found mainly in the decrease, elsewhere noted, in the number of women employed as servants, laundresses, dressmakers, etc. Outside of these occupations, the distribution of gainfully employed women with respect to occupations, grouped on the basis of the percentage of women in the total number of workers, underwent little change between 1910 and 1920, as is shown by Table 36.

6436°—29——5

TABLE 36.—MEN AND WOMEN ENGAGED IN NONAGRICULTURAL PURSUITS, 1920 AND 1910, DISTRIBUTED BY OCCUPATIONAL GROUPS AS DETERMINED BY THE PERCENTAGE OF WOMEN IN THE TOTAL NUMBER OF ADULT WORKERS IN 1920, EXCLUDING SERVANTS, DRESSMAKERS, LAUNDRESSES, MILLINERS, AND BOARDING HOUSE KEEPERS

OCCUPATIONAL GROUP ACCORDING TO PERCENTAGE OF WOMEN	MEN				WOMEN			
	1920		1910		1920		1910	
	Number	Per cent distribution	Number	Per cent distribution	Number	Per cent distribution	Number	Per cent distribution
Total	22,656,157	100.0	18,617,510	100.0	5,521,808	100.0	3,582,625	100.0
Nonagricultural pursuits in which, in 1920—								
No women were engaged	920,270	4.1	648,748	3.5			9	(1)
Less than 0.1 per cent women	4,576,989	20.2	3,732,285	20.0	816	(1)	2,120	0.1
From 0.1 to 1 per cent women	4,310,215	19.0	3,542,849	19.0	15,866	0.3	11,278	0.3
From 1 to 5 per cent women	4,654,439	20.5	4,487,900	24.1	124,205	2.2	98,464	2.7
From 5 to 10 per cent women	2,108,556	9.3	1,567,293	8.4	173,933	3.1	106,788	3.0
From 10 to 20 per cent women	1,826,366	8.1	1,331,613	7.2	304,487	5.5	192,682	5.4
From 20 to 50 per cent women	3,304,485	14.6	2,394,047	12.9	1,822,143	33.0	1,164,394	32.5
50 per cent or more women	954,837	4.2	912,775	4.9	3,080,358	55.8	2,006,890	56.0

1 Less than one-tenth of 1 per cent.

The results of this test, then, appear to be negative, showing no marked change in the per cent distribution of women workers by occupational groups in 1920 as compared with 1910. The next table carries this analysis a step farther, showing what the percentage of women was to the total number of workers—men and women—in each group of occupations in 1910 and 1920. In every group the percentage of women increased in 1920, as it did likewise in the total. There are some variations as regards the extent of the increase as between the different groups, but on the whole these do not indicate that the distribution of women by occupations is tending to parallel that of men. If there were such a tendency, and if it continued until in some distant future the parallelism became complete, the percentage of women would then, of course, be the same in all occupational groups. It would be as great among manual laborers as among clerks. No one, it may be presumed, anticipates any such consummation as that or desires it. It is safe to say that in economic as well as in other relationships of life, there will always be functional distinctions based on sex.

TABLE 37.—PERCENTAGE OF WOMEN IN THE TOTAL NUMBER OF ADULT WORKERS IN EACH SPECIFIED GROUP OF OCCUPATIONS, 1920 AND 1910, NOT INCLUDING AGRICULTURAL PURSUITS, OR THE OCCUPATIONS OF SERVANTS, DRESSMAKERS, LAUNDRESSES, MILLINERS, AND BOARDING HOUSE KEEPERS

OCCUPATIONAL GROUP ACCORDING TO PERCENTAGE OF WOMEN	PERCENTAGE OF WOMEN IN TOTAL NUMBER OF ADULT WORKERS	
	1920	1910
Total	19. 6	16. 1
Occupations in which, in 1920—		
No women were engaged	(¹)	(¹)
Less than 0.1 per cent women		0. 1
From 0.1 to 1 per cent women	(¹)	0. 3
From 1 to 5 per cent women	0. 4	2. 1
From 5 to 10 per cent women	2. 6	6. 4
From 10 to 20 per cent women	7. 6	12. 6
From 20 to 50 per cent women	14. 3	32. 7
50 per cent or more women	35. 5	68. 7
	76. 3	

¹ Less than one-tenth of 1 per cent.

Certain occupations, in which women predominate and in which they are employed in large numbers, are declining in importance and consequently the number of women finding employment in these occupations is decreasing. There are other occupations in which the number of women, already large, is increasing with the growth of the occupation and with the replacement of men by women. But there is no evidence in the census that women are entering new occupations in large numbers, or gaining ground to any marked degree in occupations in which they have been heretofore represented by small numbers.

VII

PROPORTION OF WOMEN AMONG THE GAINFULLY OCCUPIED

At the last census women formed about one-fifth of the total number of gainful workers 16 years of age and over. The proportion showed no increase as compared with the preceding census, being 20.6 per cent in 1910 and 20.2 in 1920. Prior to 1910, however, the percentage of women in the total number of workers had been steadily increasing census by census. It advanced from 14 per cent in 1870 to 20.6 in 1910. In other words, in 1870 one gainful worker in seven was a woman, and in 1910 and in 1920, one in five.

TABLE **38.**—NUMBER AND PERCENTAGE OF WOMEN IN THE TOTAL NUMBER OF ADULT WORKERS: 1870–1920

CENSUS YEAR	GAINFUL WORKERS 16 YEARS OF AGE AND OVER		
	Total, both sexes	Women	
		Number	Per cent
1920	40, 553, 390	8, 202, 901	20. 2
1910	36, 177, 111	7, 438, 686	20. 6
1900	27, 323, 055	4, 833, 630	17. 7
1890 [1]	21, 814, 412	3, 596, 615	16. 5
1880	16, 273, 743	2, 353, 988	14. 5
1870	11, 766, 759	1, 645, 188	14. 0

[1] Figures partly estimated.

The numbers and percentages of women workers as given in the above table are represented graphically by Diagram 5, in which the width of the bars is proportioned to the total number of workers of both sexes as enumerated in the successive censuses.

Since the comparability of the last two censuses, as already explained, is to a considerable degree impaired by the changes in the definition of agricultural laborers, it seems desirable to supplement the preceding table with the table on page 54, which shows the percentage of women among the gainful workers in occupations exclusive of agricultural pursuits. The percentage shows an increase from 1870 to 1910, but was exactly the same in 1920 as it was in 1910, being 24.2 at each of these censuses. So, in either case, whether agricultural pursuits are included or excluded, the percentage of women in the total number of workers was no larger in 1920 than it was in 1910.

52

DIAGRAM 5.—PROPORTION OF WOMEN IN TOTAL NUMBER OF ADULT
WORKERS: 1870–1920

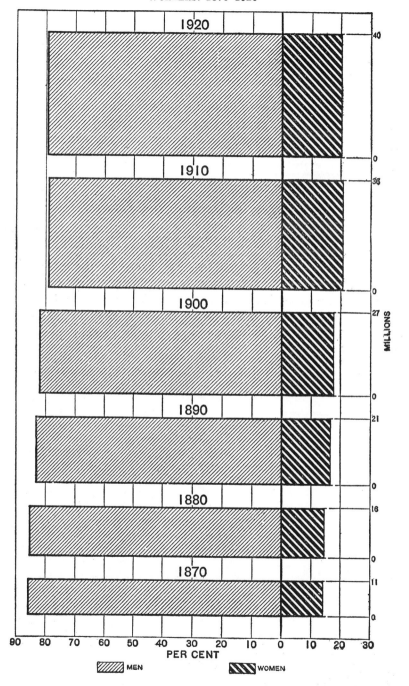

TABLE 39.—NUMBER AND PERCENTAGE OF WOMEN IN THE TOTAL NUMBER OF ADULT WORKERS IN NONAGRICULTURAL PURSUITS: 1870–1920

CENSUS YEAR	GAINFUL WORKERS 16 YEARS OF AGE AND OVER ENGAGED IN NONAGRICULTURAL PURSUITS		
	Total, both sexes	Women	
		Number	Per cent
1920	30, 247, 541	7, 306, 844	24. 2
1910	24, 950, 457	6, 041, 362	24. 2
1900	17, 936, 315	4, 063, 147	22. 7
1890 [1]	13, 518, 005	3, 000, 904	22. 2
1880	9, 240, 368	1, 895, 279	20. 5
1870	6, 291, 477	1, 321, 364	21. 0

[1] Figures for 1890 partly estimated.

CLASSIFICATION BY RACE AND NATIVITY

While the percentage of women in the total number of adult gainful workers showed no increase in the last decade, the percentage of native white women in that total, as shown by the table below, increased from 12.4 to 13.9, this increase being offset by a decline in the percentage of foreign-born white women, from 3.3 to 2.7, and of Negro women, from 4.8 to 3.6. Thus it may be said that the ground gained by the native whites was lost by the foreign whites and Negroes.

TABLE 40.—NUMBER AND PERCENTAGE OF WOMEN, CLASSIFIED BY RACE AND NATIVITY, IN THE TOTAL NUMBER OF ADULT WORKERS IN ALL OCCUPATIONS AND IN NONAGRICULTURAL PURSUITS: 1920 AND 1910

SEX, RACE, AND NATIVITY	PERSONS 16 YEARS OF AGE AND OVER GAINFULLY EMPLOYED							
	All occupations				Nonagricultural pursuits			
	1920		1910		1920		1910	
	Number	Per cent distribution	Number	Per cent distribution	Number	Per cent distribution	Number	Per cent distribution
All classes	40, 553, 390	100. 0	36, 177, 111	100. 0	30, 247, 541	100. 0	24, 950, 457	100. 0
Men	32, 350, 489	79. 8	28, 738, 425	79. 4	22, 940, 697	75. 8	18, 909, 095	75. 8
Women	8, 202, 901	20. 2	7, 438, 686	20. 6	7, 306, 844	24. 2	6, 041, 362	24. 2
Native white	5, 639, 201	13. 9	4, 481, 058	12. 4	5, 290, 138	17. 5	3, 962, 257	15. 9
Native parentage	3, 596, 397	8. 9	2, 847, 982	7. 9	3, 293, 327	10. 9	2, 388, 095	9. 6
Foreign or mixed parentage	2, 042, 804	5. 0	1, 633, 076	4. 5	1, 996, 811	6. 6	1, 574, 162	6. 3
Foreign-born white	1, 102, 697	2. 7	1, 195, 953	3. 3	1, 064, 724	3. 5	1, 140, 078	4. 6
Negro	1, 445, 935	3. 6	1, 744, 752	4. 8	941, 172	3. 1	926, 559	3. 7
All other [1]	15, 068	(2)	16, 923	(2)	10, 810	(2)	12, 468	(2)

[1] Includes Indians, Chinese, Japanese, and other races.
[2] Less than one-tenth of 1 per cent.

IN INDIVIDUAL OCCUPATIONS

Although, in the total number of adult gainful workers the percentage of women does not appear to be increasing at the present time,
this is not true in all divisions of the occupational field. On the
contrary, there are many important individual occupations or classes
of occupations in which the percentage showed a very decided increase
in 1920 as compared with 1910; and, in fact, this was the case in most
of the occupations in which considerable numbers of women are
employed. But the gains they made in these occupations were offset
partly by the decrease in the percentage of women in some other
occupations, partly by the growth of occupations in which women are
not represented in any considerable numbers, and partly by the
decline of some occupations (servants, dressmakers, etc.) which are
largely women's occupations. Any one of these three factors, so far
as it is not offset by other counteracting tendencies, would produce a
decrease in the proportion of women in the total number of gainful
workers.

The table on the next page presents a list of the occupations in
which as many as 5,000 women were employed in 1920, the occupations being arranged in the order of their importance as measured by
the percentage of women employed of the total number of adult
workers.

Of the important occupations for women—using that term here to
distinguish those occupations which gave employment to not less
than 5,000 women in 1920—the one which shows the greatest
increase in the percentage of women employed is that of clerk.
Among clerks, not including those in stores, the percentage increased
from 16.9 in 1910 to 31.6 in 1920, an increase of 14.7. Almost as
great was the increase among clerks in stores—from 28.8 per cent
in 1910 to 41.2 per cent in 1920, an increase of 12.4. The percentage
of women among bookkeepers, cashiers, and accountants increased
from 38.3 to 48.8, an advance of 10.5; and among stenographers
and typists from 83.2 to 91.8, an advance of 8.6. Especially noteworthy, though not exceptionally large, is the increase of women
among school teachers, the percentage advancing from 80.1 to 84.5,
and thus continuing the increase which, as noted elsewhere (see p.
42), has been in progress for at least a half century. There was a
still greater increase in the percentage of women teachers in the field
of higher education, or among college or university professors, the
percentage being 30.2 in 1920 as compared with 18.9 in 1910. Thus
the occupation of teaching appears to be more and more passing into
the hands of women, a movement which has sometimes been deplored,
and is probably partly due to the fact that the low level of salaries
paid in that profession fails to attract men having the requisite degree
of education. As regards teaching in colleges, however, it is probable

that the great development of higher education for women has increased the demand for women teachers of that grade and at the same time has increased the number of those who are qualified for that occupation.

TABLE 41.—NUMBER AND PERCENTAGE OF WOMEN IN THE TOTAL NUMBER OF ADULT WORKERS IN EACH OCCUPATION IN WHICH, IN 1920, 5,000 OR MORE WOMEN WERE EMPLOYED, WITH PERCENTAGE FOR 1910

	GAINFUL WORKERS 16 YEARS OF AGE AND OVER: 1920				
		Women			
			Per cent		
OCCUPATION	Total, both sexes, 1920	Number, 1920	1920	1910	Increase (+) or decrease (−)
All occupations	40,553,390	8,202,901	20.2	20.6	−0.4
Dressmakers and seamstresses (not in factory)	235,855	235,519	99.9	99.6	+0.3
Launderers and laundresses (not in laundry)	394,308	383,622	97.3	97.4	−0.1
Trained nurses	149,128	143,664	96.3	92.9	+3.4
Milliners and millinery dealers	73,255	69,598	95.0	95.7	−0.7
Telephone operators	186,972	175,469	93.8	90.3	+3.5
Housekeepers and stewards	221,612	204,350	92.2	91.6	+0.6
Stenographers and typists	609,480	559,748	91.8	83.2	+8.6
Librarians	15,297	13,502	88.3	78.6	+9.7
Midwives and nurses (not trained)	156,769	137,431	87.7	88.0	−0.3
Boarding and lodging house keepers	133,392	114,740	86.0	86.1	−0.1
Teachers (school)	752,055	635,207	84.5	80.1	+4.4
Servants	1,232,766	981,557	79.6	83.3	−3.7
Charwomen and cleaners	36,401	24,744	68.0	78.8	−10.8
Laundry operatives	117,887	78,548	66.6	67.6	−1.0
Religious, charity, and welfare workers	41,078	26,927	65.6	55.7	+9.9
Musicians and teachers of music	129,752	72,431	55.8	60.7	−4.9
Attendants and helpers (professional service)	29,602	16,046	54.2	45.9	+8.3
Healers (except osteopaths, physicians, and surgeons)	14,774	7,902	53.5	68.4	−14.9
Waiters and waitresses	225,579	114,718	50.9	45.3	+5.6
Bookkeepers, cashiers, and accountants	731,350	356,603	48.8	38.3	+10.5
Actors and actresses	28,161	13,114	46.6	42.1	+4.5
Artists, sculptors, and teachers of art	35,289	14,566	41.3	45.2	−3.9
Clerks in stores	398,869	164,487	41.2	28.8	+12.4
Designers	15,410	5,652	36.7	21.8	+14.9
Semiskilled operatives (manufacturing) (n. o. s.[1])	3,519,707	1,274,719	36.2	36.8	−0.6
Postmasters	31,935	11,208	35.1	31.3	+3.8
Clerks (except clerks in stores)	1,465,384	463,570	31.6	16.9	+14.7
Farm laborers (home farm)	1,280,295	403,009	31.5	38.4	−6.9
Salesmen and saleswomen (stores)	1,110,461	349,569	31.5	28.3	+3.2
College presidents and professors	33,407	10,075	30.2	18.9	+11.3
Packers, wholesale and retail trade	18,963	5,582	29.4	20.4	+9.0
Hotel keepers and managers	55,583	14,134	25.4	22.1	+3.3
Telegraph operators	79,434	16,860	21.2	11.7	+9.5
Photographers	33,992	7,048	20.7	15.6	+5.1
Elevator tenders	40,150	7,233	18.0	0.1	+17.9
Restaurant, café, and lunch room keepers	87,987	15,644	17.8	17.3	+0.5
Farm foremen, general farms	79,018	13,767	17.4	18.1	−0.7
Editors and reporters	34,197	5,730	16.8	12.2	+4.6
Tailors and tailoresses	192,232	31,828	16.6	19.8	−3.2
Janitors and sextons	177,216	28,929	16.3	19.0	−2.7
Barbers, hairdressers, and manicurists	215,285	33,091	15.4	11.4	+4.0
Messenger, bundle, and office boys and girls	64,994	9,947	15.3	10.8	+4.5
Farm laborers (working out)	1,991,286	198,979	10.0	11.7	−1.7
Foremen and overseers (manufacturing)	307,413	30,171	9.8	11.3	−1.5
Agents, canvassers, and collectors	175,193	15,741	9.0	8.4	+0.6
Compositors, linotypers, and typesetters	140,165	11,306	8.1	11.0	−2.9
Garden laborers	78,214	5,773	7.4	5.7	+1.7
Laborers, porters, and helpers in stores	120,024	7,987	6.7	4.0	+2.7
Real estate agents and officials	149,135	9,208	6.2	2.3	+3.9

[1] Not otherwise specified.

TABLE 41.—NUMBER AND PERCENTAGE OF WOMEN IN THE TOTAL NUMBER OF ADULT WORKERS IN EACH OCCUPATION IN WHICH, IN 1920, 5,000 OR MORE WOMEN WERE EMPLOYED, WITH PERCENTAGE FOR 1910—Continued

OCCUPATION	GAINFUL WORKERS 16 YEARS OF AGE AND OVER: 1920				
	Total, both sexes, 1920	Women			
		Number, 1920	Per cent		
			1920	1910	Increase (+) or decrease (−)
Retail dealers	1,327,916	78,957	5.9	5.6	+0.3
Physicians, surgeons, and osteopaths	150,007	8,882	5.9	6.0	−0.1
Laborers (manufacturing) (n. o. s.[1])	2,892,800	160,133	5.5	3.3	+2.2
Gardeners	98,591	5,068	5.1	5.5	−0.4
Insurance agents	119,918	5,083	4.2	2.9	+1.3
Farmers, general farms	6,004,580	247,253	4.1	4.4	−0.3
Manufacturers and officials (manufacturing)	231,615	8,326	3.6	1.8	+1.8
Laborers, steam-railroad	467,644	6,488	1.4	0.6	+0.8
All other occupations	11,813,608	151,458	1.3	1.2	+0.1

[1] Not otherwise specified.

The percentage of women among factory operatives (semiskilled operatives in manufacturing, not otherwise specified) underwent a small decrease from 36.8 to 36.2; among laborers in manufacturing pursuits, there was a small increase, from 3.3 to 5.5. Both of these occupational groups cover many different industries, in some of which the percentage of women shows a decrease, as shown by Table 43, at the end of this chapter. Thus, there was a marked decrease in the percentage of women among the semiskilled operatives in carpet mills, from 52.7 to 44.2; in bakeries, from 67.5 to 59.3; in paper and pulp mills, from 28.3 to 23.9; in rubber factories, from 32.0 to 21.3, and in a number of other industries. But in a majority of the manufacturing industries distinguished in the census classification the percentage shows an increase, some of the more noteworthy instances being the increases from 46.1 to 57.2 in percentage of women among the semiskilled operatives in cigar and tobacco factories, from 53.3 to 58.6 in the percentage for candy factories, and from 32.2 to 35.3 for shoe factories. Thus, women as factory operatives lost ground in some industries and gained in others, the net results being, however, a small decrease in the percentage of women among semiskilled operatives for all industries combined.

The situation is the same as regards the occupation of factory laborers. In some industries, as shown by Table 43, the percentage of women in this occupation has increased, in others it has decreased, but the net result is a slight gain.

While in retail trade taken as a whole the percentage of women in the total number of dealers is not very large and shows only a small increase—from 5.6 in 1910 to 5.9 in 1920—there are, as indicated by

Table 115, some lines of retail trade in which the percentage is large and is increasing, the percentage for the total in this occupational group being the net result of widely varying conditions in the several subdivisions of the group. The percentage of women among retail dealers increased from 17.5 to 24.8 in art stores, from 10.3 to 14.3 in book stores, and from 13.1 to 22.7 in stores dealing in curios, antiques, and novelties. There was some increase, also, in the percentage of women among florists—from 13.8 to 16.7. There are other lines of retail trade in which women form a considerable, but apparently a decreasing, percentage of the total number of dealers. Thus the percentage of women among dealers in candy and confectionery decreased from 26.8 to 19.3; among proprietors of delicatessen stores from 23.7 to 17.7; and among proprietors of 5 and 10 cent and variety stores from 23.9 to 17.9. There was a slight decrease, also, in the percentage of women among dealers in dry goods, fancy goods, and notions (from 12.2 in 1910 to 12.1 in 1920), and among stationery dealers (from 11.8 in 1910 to 11.6 in 1920).

Among the minor occupations shown in Table 41 the most conspicuous as regards the increase in the percentage of women is that of elevator tender. This is virtually a new occupation for that sex, being one in which women were first employed in considerable numbers during the war. In 1910 only 25 women were reported as tending elevators, but by 1920 the number had increased to 7,233, while the percentage of women in that occupation increased from practically nothing—0.1—to 18.0.

Another occupation in which women were employed for the first time in considerable numbers during the war is that of street car conductor. In 1910 no women were reported in this occupation. But after this country entered the war and men were called away for military service women took their places to some extent in this as well as in many other occupations. For a time a large proportion of the conductors on surface cars in the city of New York were women. Most of the women street car conductors, however, were replaced by men soon after the war was over; so that in the census of 1920 the number of women reported in this occupation was only 253, which was about four-tenths of 1 per cent of the total number of street car conductors in the United States.

The next largest increase of the percentage was that for the occupation rather vaguely defined by the term "designer," 36.7 per cent of the total number of designers in 1920 being women as compared with 21.8 per cent in 1910—an increase of 14.9. Probably many of these women were clothing or dress designers.

The percentage of women showed an increase of 9.9 (from 55.7 to 65.6) among religious, charity, and welfare workers (representing, of course, only those who were paid salaries); of 9.7 (from 78.6 to 88.3) among librarians;[1] of 9.5 (from 11.7 to 21.2) among telegraph operators; of 9.0 (from 20.4 to 29.4) among packers, wholesale and retail trade; of 8.3 (from 45.9 to 54.2) among attendants and helpers in professional service; and of 5.1 (from 15.6 to 20.7) among photographers.

The occupations in which the percentage of women is increasing are sometimes referred to as those in which women are displacing or crowding out men. But, looking at the matter from another point of view, it might be said with equal validity that they are the occupations in which women are releasing men for employment in other pursuits, just as in the period of the war women, by engaging in factory and farm work, released men for military service. Where the percentage of women is increasing it does not necessarily mean that men are leaving that occupation or that they are being forced out of it in order to give place to women, although that process may go on to some extent. But it is more probable that the change comes about mainly through the fact that, among the new recruits who enter that occupation, either contributing to its growth or taking the place of those who have died or withdrawn from it, there is an increasing percentage of women and a diminishing percentage of men.

In periods of industrial depression when there is a large amount of unemployment, it is quite probable that, to some extent, the women who engage in gainful occupations stand in the way of men who are seeking to find work. But in normal times, and especially in periods of industrial expansion, it is doubtful whether their employment keeps any able-bodied or able-minded man out of a job.

The present indications seem to point toward greater industrial development, bringing an increasing demand for workers in the factory, the store, and the office. With immigration restricted and with the proportion of men gainfully employed close to the maximum proportion employable,[2] it would seem that any great increase in the aggregate demand for workers, in so far as it is not met by the growth of population, must be met mainly by an increase in the employment of women. The proportion of women gainfully occupied is much lower in the United States than in most of the leading countries of Europe, and it is quite probable that the near future will show a considerable increase in the proportion gainfully occupied in the United States.[3]

---

[1] This increase in the percentage of women among librarians doubtless resulted in part from the fact that cataloguers in libraries were classified with librarians' assistants in 1910 and with librarians in 1920. Probably the great majority of these cataloguers were women.

[2] In 1920, 68 per cent of the males 16 to 19, 91 per cent of those 20 to 24, 97.2 per cent of those 25 to 44, and 93.8 per cent of those 45 to 64 years of age were gainfully occupied.

[3] Because of the difference between countries in reporting the occupations of women especially as regards the extent to which they report all farm women as gainfully employed, accurate comparison can not be made. However, the statistics appear fully to warrant the statement that the proportion of women gainfully employed is considerably lower in the United States than in most of the leading countries of Europe.

The percentage of women in the total number of servants showed an appreciable decrease, from 83.3 in 1910 to 79.6 in 1920. This accompanied a falling off, already noted in Chapter V, in the total number of servants of both sexes. The census classification does not distinguish domestic servants from hotel servants, but it seems rather improbable that the latter class decreased appreciably, if at all; and in that case the decrease in the total must have been the result of a falling off in the number of domestic servants, of whom no doubt women form a far larger percentage than they do of hotel servants. So it seems probable that it was a change in the relative importance of the two classes of servants—in one class, that in which women predominated, decreasing and the other probably increasing—rather than any substitution of men for women in domestic service, which brought about the decrease in the percentage of women in the total number of servants of all classes.

While in the occupation of servant the percentage of women decreased, in the allied occupation of waiter it increased, from 45.3 in 1910 to 50.9 in 1920. This change accompanied an increase of 22.1 per cent in the total number of waiters of both sexes, and of 44.7 per cent in the number of restaurant keepers, which suggests that the decrease in the number of domestic servants may in some degree have either resulted from, or resulted in, an increase in the practice of eating at the public restaurant and cafeteria rather than in a boarding house or at home.

Outside the occupation of servant there are but few of the important occupations for women in which the percentage of women decreased appreciably. One of these few is the occupation of musician and music teacher, in which for some reason the percentage of women decreased from 60.7 in 1910 to 55.8 in 1920. The percentage among artists, sculptors, and teachers of art decreased from 45.2 to 41.3. There was a very marked decrease—from 68.4 to 53.5—in the percentage of women among "healers," a term which as used in the census includes chiropractors, Christian Science healers, divine healers, faith healers, magnetic healers, mental healers—in fact, all persons professing to heal or cure the ailments of the human body or mind, except osteopaths and physicians and surgeons. There was a decrease also in the percentage for janitors and sextons, from 19.0 to 16.3; and in that for compositors, linotypers, and typesetters, from 11.0 to 8.1. Other instances may be found in the table at the end of this chapter.

Although in all but 20 of the 57 occupations distinguished in Table 41 the percentage of women was larger in 1920 than in 1910, in the total number of workers the percentage, as already noted, remained nearly stationary. In this connection it may not be superfluous to remind the reader that changes in the total percentages do not always reflect the changes in the percentages for the individual occupations, but are determined largely by differences in the rate of growth of different occupations, the growth of an occupation in which the percentage of women is above the average tending, of course, to increase the percentage for the total, and the decline of such an occupation having the opposite effect.   Conversely, the growth or decline of an occupation in which the percentage of women is below the average tends, respectively, to decrease or to increase the total percentage.   In fact, the percentage of women in every single occupation in which they are employed might decrease while the total percentage increased, and vice versa, an increase in the percentage in every occupation might accompany a decrease in the total.   These relationships are perhaps too elementary and too obvious to mention, but they must be taken into account because, as already noted, some of the leading occupations for women underwent a pronounced decline between 1920 and 1910.   The occupations here referred to are those of servant, home laundress, dressmaker or seamstress, milliner, and boarding-house keeper.   The number of adult persons of both sexes reported in these five occupations decreased from 2,750,322 in 1910 to 2,069,576, and the number of women employed in them decreased from 2,458,737 to 1,785,036.   It is evident, therefore, that these occupations had a greatly diminished weight in 1920 in determining the percentage of women in the total number of nonagricultural pursuits.

Leaving out the five occupations just mentioned, the percentage of women in the total for all other nonagricultural occupations, as shown by the next table, increased from 16.1 to 19.6, and in the total for those other nonagricultural occupations which employed at least 5,000 women each it increased from 32.7 to 38.2.   If the number of women employed as servants, laundresses, etc., had been as large in 1920 as it was in 1910—the number of men so employed remaining unchanged—the percentage of women in the total number of gainful workers outside of agriculture would have been 25.8, instead of 24.2, the reported percentage.

It seems fairly evident, then, that one reason why the percentage of women in the total number of nonagricultural workers showed no increase between 1910 and 1920 is found in the fact that five of the leading occupations for that sex are nevertheless occupations of diminishing importance, as indicated by the decrease in the total number of persons employed in them.   Within these occupations the number of women decreased greatly in the last decade—by more than 27 per cent—and at the same time the percentage of women in the total number of workers in these occupations decreased somewhat—or from 89.4 in 1910 to 86.3 in 1920. In nonagricultural pursuits outside these occupations the number of women increased by about 54 per cent, while the number of men increased but 21.7 per cent, with the result that the percentage of women in the total number of workers in these pursuits increased appreciably, or, as just noted, from 16.1 in 1910 to 19.6 in 1920.

TABLE 42.—PROPORTION OF WOMEN IN THE TOTAL NUMBER OF GAINFUL WORKERS 16 YEARS OF AGE AND OVER IN EACH SPECIFIED GROUP OF NON-AGRICULTURAL OCCUPATIONS: 1920 AND 1910

CLASS OF OCCUPATION	GAINFUL WORKERS 16 YEARS OF AGE AND OVER					
	1920	1910	Increase,[1] 1910-1920		Per cent distribution by sex	
			Number	Per cent	1920	1910
All nonagricultural occupations:						
Total	30, 247, 541	24, 950, 457	5, 297, 084	21. 2	100. 0	100. 0
Men	22, 940, 697	18, 909, 095	4, 031, 602	21. 3	75. 8	75. 8
Women	7, 306, 844	6, 041, 362	1, 265, 482	20. 9	24. 2	24. 2
Servants, laundresses, dressmakers, milliners, and boarding and lodging house keepers:						
Total	2, 069, 576	2, 750, 322	−680, 746	−24. 7	100. 0	100. 0
Men	284, 540	291, 585	−7, 045	−2. 4	13. 7	10. 6
Women	1, 785, 036	2, 458, 737	−673, 701	−27. 4	86. 3	89. 4
All other nonagricultural occupations:						
Total	28, 177, 965	22, 200, 135	5, 977, 830	27. 0	100. 0	100. 0
Men	22, 656, 157	18, 617, 510	4, 038, 647	21. 7	80. 4	83. 9
Women	5, 521, 808	3, 582, 625	1, 939, 183	54. 1	19. 6	16. 1
Other nonagricultural occupations each employing at least 5,000 women in 1920:						
Total	14, 124, 024	10, 699, 023	3, 425, 001	32. 0	100. 0	100. 0
Men	8, 729, 136	7, 205, 619	1, 523, 517	21. 1	61. 8	67. 3
Women	5, 394, 888	3, 493, 404	1, 901, 484	54. 1	38. 2	32. 7
Nonagricultural occupations each employing less than 5,000 women in 1920:						
Total	14, 053, 941	11, 501, 112	2, 552, 829	22. 2	100. 0	100. 0
Men	13, 927, 021	11, 411, 891	2, 515, 130	21. 9	99. 1	99. 2
Women	126, 920	89, 221	37, 699	42. 4	0. 9	0. 8

[1] A minus sign (−) denotes decrease.

If it be asked why the decrease in the number of women employed in the five declining occupations is not fully offset by an increase in the number employed in other occupations, or why, in other words, the women who fail to obtain, or are unwilling to accept, employment as servants, dressmakers, etc., do not go into other occupations, it may be said that it seems probable that the native white women who would have entered domestic service or would have taken up similar occupations if conditions had remained as they were in 1910, did in fact turn to other occupations, since, as previously noted, the percentage of native white women in the total number of gainful workers increased between 1910 and 1920, as did also the percentage of native white women gainfully employed. But as regards Negro women the decrease in the numbers employed in domestic pursuits was not fully offset by the increase in other occupations; and the same is true of the foreign born or immigrant women. What probably took place as regards these two classes is discussed in Chapters XII and XIII.

TABLE 43.—SPECIFIED OCCUPATIONS IN WHICH WOMEN IN 1920 FORMED 5 PER CENT OR MORE OF TOTAL NUMBER OF WORKERS 16 YEARS OF AGE AND OVER, 1920 AND 1910, WITH INCREASE OR DECREASE

OCCUPATION	GAINFUL WORKERS 16 YEARS OF AGE AND OVER						Increase (+) or decrease (−) in percentage of women
	1920			1910			
	Total number	Women		Total number	Women		
		Number	Per cent		Number	Per cent	
All occupations	40,553,390	8,202,901	20.2	36,177,111	7,438,686	20.6	−0.4
Agriculture, forestry, and animal husbandry:							
Farm laborers (home farm)	1,280,295	403,009	31.5	2,153,211	826,523	38.4	−6.9
Farm laborers (working out)	1,991,286	198,979	10.0	2,377,153	278,637	11.7	−1.7
Farm foremen, general farms	79,018	13,767	17.4	41,521	7,505	18.1	−0.7
Florists	8,345	938	11.2	9,028	1,051	11.6	−0.4
Fruit growers	55,402	3,194	5.8	43,531	2,276	5.2	+0.6
Gardeners	98,591	5,068	5.1	79,894	4,413	5.5	−0.4
Garden laborers	78,214	5,773	7.4	78,654	4,493	5.7	+1.7
Greenhouse laborers	15,891	1,120	7.0	17,153	903	5.3	+1.7
Poultry raisers	14,116	2,324	16.5	12,119	3,226	26.6	−10.1
Manufacturing and mechanical industries:							
Apprentices to dressmakers and milliners	2,337	2,330	99.7	5,814	5,785	99.5	+0.2
Compositors, linotypers, and typesetters	140,165	11,306	8.1	127,511	14,025	11.0	−2.9
Dressmakers and seamstresses (not in factory)	235,855	235,519	99.9	448,127	446,555	99.6	+0.3
Buffers and polishers (metal)	30,295	1,970	6.5	30,046	2,184	7.3	−0.8
Foremen and overseers (manufacturing)	307,413	30,171	9.8	175,098	19,740	11.3	−1.5
Jewelers and lapidaries (factory)	8,757	1,056	12.1	10,575	1,798	17.0	−4.9
Laborers (n. o. s.[1])—							
Cigar and tobacco factories	34,198	13,396	39.2	15,035	4,493	29.9	+9.3
Glass factories	27,789	2,295	8.3	22,604	827	3.7	+4.6
Potteries	11,514	1,078	9.4	8,994	556	6.2	+3.2
Shirt, collar, and cuff factories	2,517	1,283	51.0	1,939	1,215	62.7	−11.7
Suit, coat, cloak, and overall factories	3,737	1,667	44.6	2,650	1,133	42.8	+1.8
Other clothing factories	5,663	2,945	52.0	4,700	1,959	41.7	+10.3
Bakeries	7,861	1,347	17.1	4,141	635	15.3	+1.8
Butter, cheese, and condensed milk factories	15,018	995	6.6	4,744	127	2.7	+3.9
Candy factories	6,199	1,983	32.0	2,606	916	35.1	−3.1
Fish curing and packing	6,140	975	15.9	4,819	218	4.5	+11.4
Fruit and vegetable canning, etc.	12,816	3,200	25.0	4,497	908	20.2	+4.8
Slaughter and packing houses	59,143	4,055	6.9	33,370	1,345	4.0	+2.9
Other food factories	50,033	2,931	5.8	25,745	1,500	5.8	+0.1
Clock and watch factories	2,990	1,143	38.2	1,778	582	32.7	+5.5
Tinware, enamelware, etc., factories	17,153	2,067	12.1	7,017	779	11.1	+1.0
Furniture, piano, and organ factories	39,421	3,232	8.2	26,301	816	3.1	+5.1
Other woodworking factories [2]	33,131	2,835	8.6	27,001	1,168	4.3	+4.3
Printing and publishing	10,821	2,379	22.0	6,566	1,698	25.9	−3.9
Shoe factories	18,183	4,740	26.1	9,330	2,068	22.2	+3.9
Cotton mills	71,770	15,440	21.5	33,113	4,744	14.3	+7.2
Knitting mills	11,061	4,868	44.0	6,569	2,865	43.6	+0.4
Silk mills	9,237	2,381	25.8	3,233	913	28.2	−2.4
Woolen and worsted mills	21,427	3,713	17.3	11,467	1,780	15.5	+1.8
Other textile mills	31,683	3,918	12.4	24,077	3,163	13.1	−0.7
Electrical supply factories	26,353	3,111	11.8	11,189	1,308	11.7	+0.1
Rubber factories	50,903	3,824	7.5	13,124	1,203	9.2	−1.7
Officials (manufacturing)	48,229	3,381	7.0	21,484	401	1.9	+5.1
Milliners and millinery dealers	73,255	69,598	95.0	126,900	121,446	95.7	−0.7

[1] Not otherwise specified.   [2] Exclusive of saw and planing mills.

TABLE **43.**—SPECIFIED OCCUPATIONS IN WHICH WOMEN IN 1920 FORMED 5 PER CENT OR MORE OF TOTAL NUMBER OF WORKERS 16 YEARS OF AGE AND OVER, 1920 AND 1910, WITH INCREASE OR DECREASE—Continued

OCCUPATION	GAINFUL WORKERS 16 YEARS OF AGE AND OVER						Increase (+) or decrease (−) in percentage of women
	1920			1910			
	Total number	Women		Total number	Women		
		Number	Per cent		Number	Per cent	
Manufacturing and mechanical industries—Continued.							
Semiskilled operatives (n. o. s.[1])—							
Powder, cartridge, dynamite, fuse, and fireworks factories____	7,280	2,503	34.4	5,000	2,208	44.2	−9.8
Soap factories_____	6,057	2,900	47.9	4,122	1,731	42.0	+5.9
Other chemical factories_____	35,629	11,988	33.6	19,924	8,451	42.4	−8.8
Cigar and tobacco factories_____	141,243	80,757	57.2	143,346	66,087	46.1	+11.1
Glass factories_____	43,206	6,709	15.5	38,999	3,445	8.8	+6.7
Potteries_____	16,968	4,842	28.5	15,668	4,140	26.4	+2.1
Corset factories_____	12,077	11,035	91.4	12,289	10,960	89.2	+2.2
Glove factories_____	22,625	16,212	71.7	18,525	13,299	71.8	−0.1
Hat factories (felt)_____	20,689	6,162	29.8	32,220	9,768	30.3	−0.5
Shirt, collar, and cuff factories____	49,933	39,892	79.9	56,443	43,570	77.2	+2.7
Suit, coat, cloak, and overall factories____	141,082	62,415	44.2	131,649	57,723	43.8	+0.4
Other clothing factories_____	152,057	120,925	79.5	117,446	87,159	74.2	+5.3
Bakeries_____	18,282	10,836	59.3	7,706	5,200	67.5	−8.2
Butter, cheese, and condensed milk factories_____	18,648	2,666	14.3	11,484	513	4.5	+9.8
Candy factories_____	48,778	28,564	58.6	28,048	14,950	53.3	+5.3
Fish curing and packing_____	7,313	3,077	42.1	2,642	918	34.7	+7.4
Fruit and vegetable canning, etc_	9,874	6,059	61.4	4,923	2,872	58.3	+3.1
Slaughter and packing houses____	49,609	7,936	16.0	25,605	2,282	8.9	+7.1
Other food factories_____	28,782	8,615	29.9	18,894	5,706	30.2	−0.3
Automobile factories_____	120,436	12,582	10.4	20,789	820	3.9	+6.5
Other iron and steel factories [3]___	274,491	38,036	13.9	209,422	18,485	8.8	+5.1
Brass mills_____	17,186	3,799	22.1	16,310	2,372	14.5	+7.6
Clock and watch factories_____	17,825	7,953	44.6	15,334	6,235	40.7	+3.9
Gold and silver factories_____	6,071	1,724	28.4	5,638	1,585	28.1	+0.3
Jewelry factories_____	14,149	5,662	40.0	10,289	4,139	40.2	−0.2
Tinware, enamelware, etc., factories_____	18,707	6,882	36.8	9,707	3,542	36.5	+0.3
Other metal factories (except iron and steel)_____	14,592	3,066	21.0	9,716	1,691	17.4	+3.6
Furniture factories_____	54,725	6,588	12.0	43,092	3,408	7.9	+4.1
Piano and organ factories_____	19,401	2,740	14.1	18,442	1,440	7.8	+6.3
Saw and planing mills_____	56,350	3,085	5.5	64,138	2,119	3.3	+2.2
Other woodworking factories____	34,884	5,333	15.3	36,851	5,757	15.6	−0.3
Paper and pulp mills_____	53,867	12,901	23.9	35,484	10,046	28.3	−4.4
Blank book, envelope, tag, paper bag, etc., factories_____	13,101	8,153	62.2	9,359	6,107	65.3	−3.1
Printing, publishing, and engraving_____	63,894	31,165	48.8	55,945	27,809	49.7	−0.9
Shoe factories_____	199,707	70,517	35.3	173,564	55,824	32.2	+3.1
Tanneries_____	31,774	3,465	10.9	33,224	1,759	5.3	+5.6
Carpet mills_____	22,769	10,055	44.2	36,111	19,043	52.7	−8.5
Cotton mills_____	285,124	139,037	48.8	244,268	121,491	49.7	−0.9
Knitting mills_____	100,495	75,250	74.9	78,035	57,924	74.2	+0.7
Lace and embroidery mills_____	17,759	11,980	67.5	14,679	10,579	72.1	−4.6
Silk mills_____	106,541	66,314	62.2	71,093	44,227	62.2	-------
Textile dyeing, finishing, and printing mills_____	17,021	5,303	31.2	15,590	4,858	31.2	-------
Woolen and worsted mills_____	120,141	57,923	48.2	98,209	47,851	48.7	−0.5
Hemp and jute mills_____	3,924	2,080	53.0	4,359	2,467	56.6	−3.6
Linen mills_____	2,347	1,566	66.7	1,810	1,170	64.6	+2.1
Rope and cordage factories_____	8,167	3,578	43.8	5,971	3,123	52.3	−8.5
Other textile mills_____	61,592	35,194	57.1	50,170	30,687	61.2	−4.1
Broom and brush factories_____	12,262	2,294	18.7	10,735	1,947	18.1	+0.6
Button factories_____	12,494	4,911	39.3	10,617	4,271	40.2	−0.9
Electrical supply factories_____	63,385	26,626	42.0	23,708	10,467	44.1	−2.1
Leather belt, leather case, etc., factories_____	16,610	4,115	24.8	11,009	2,768	25.1	−0.3
Paper box factories_____	18,883	12,171	64.5	15,830	11,291	71.3	−6.8
Rubber factories_____	84,662	18,023	21.3	30,468	9,747	32.0	−10.7
Straw factories_____	13,745	6,091	44.3	5,710	3,804	66.6	−22.3
Tailors and tailoresses_____	192,232	31,843	16.6	203,966	40,370	19.8	−3.2
Upholsterers_____	29,605	2,267	7.7	20,100	1,280	6.4	+1.3

[1] Not otherwise specified.
[3] Exclusive of blast furnaces and steel rolling mills, car and railroad shops, and ship and boat building.

TABLE 43.—SPECIFIED OCCUPATIONS IN WHICH WOMEN IN 1920 FORMED 5 PER CENT OR MORE OF TOTAL NUMBER OF WORKERS 16 YEARS OF AGE AND OVER, 1920 AND 1910, WITH INCREASE OR DECREASE—Continued

OCCUPATION	GAINFUL WORKERS 16 YEARS OF AGE AND OVER						Increase (+) or decrease (−) in percentage of women
	1920			1910			
	Total number	Women		Total number	Women		
		Number	Per cent		Number	Per cent	
Transportation:							
Ticket and station agents	26,585	2,261	8.5	24,115	1,206	5.0	+3.5
Telegraph operators	79,434	16,860	21.2	69,888	8,199	11.7	+9.5
Telephone operators	186,972	175,469	93.8	95,285	86,081	90.3	+3.5
Trade:							
Bankers and bank officials	82,375	4,226	5.1	56,059	1,672	3.0	+2.1
Clerks in stores	398,869	164,487	41.2	371,491	106,961	28.8	+12.4
Decorators, drapers, and window dressers	8,779	1,142	13.0	5,310	438	8.2	+4.8
Floorwalkers and foremen in stores	20,604	4,039	19.6	17,946	3,046	17.0	+2.6
Inspectors, gaugers, and samplers	13,714	1,031	7.5	13,187	1,521	11.5	−4.0
Laborers, porters, and helpers in stores	120,024	7,987	6.7	96,592	3,865	4.0	+2.7
Real estate agents and officials	149,135	9,208	6.2	125,853	2,925	2.3	+3.9
Retail dealers	1,327,916	78,957	5.9	1,193,649	67,010	5.6	+0.3
Demonstrators (stores)	4,823	3,184	66.0	4,370	3,121	71.4	−5.4
Salesmen and saleswomen (stores)	1,110,461	349,569	31.5	860,909	243,762	28.3	+3.2
Fruit graders and packers	7,947	3,020	38.0	4,470	1,889	42.3	−4.3
Packers, wholesale and retail trade	18,963	5,582	29.4	12,767	2,605	20.4	+9.0
Public service (not elsewhere classified):							
Officials and inspectors (county)	22,092	3,262	14.8	19,044	1,575	8.3	+6.5
Postmasters	31,935	11,208	35.1	27,841	8,718	31.3	+3.8
Professional service:							
Actors	28,161	13,114	46.6	27,905	11,750	42.1	+4.5
Showmen	19,611	1,106	5.6	19,860	1,067	5.4	+0.2
Artists, sculptors, and teachers of art	35,289	14,566	41.3	33,954	15,354	45.2	−3.9
Authors	6,665	3,005	45.1	4,368	2,058	47.1	−2.0
Editors and reporters	34,197	5,730	16.8	34,363	4,181	12.2	+4.6
Chemists, assayers, and metallurgists	32,941	1,714	5.2	16,268	579	3.6	+1.6
College presidents and professors	33,407	10,075	30.2	15,668	2,958	18.9	+11.3
Designers	15,410	5,652	36.7	11,776	2,572	21.8	+14.9
Musicians and teachers of music	129,752	72,431	55.8	138,243	83,851	60.7	−4.9
Osteopaths	5,030	1,663	33.1	(4)	(4)	(4)	(4)
Photographers	33,992	7,048	20.7	31,572	4,917	15.6	+5.1
Teachers (athletics, dancing, etc.)	9,711	4,034	41.5	3,931	1,163	29.6	+11.9
Teachers (school)	752,055	635,207	84.5	595,080	476,661	80.1	+4.4
Trained nurses	149,128	143,664	96.3	82,300	76,481	92.9	+3.4
Librarians	15,297	13,502	88.3	7,412	5,828	78.6	+9.7
Abstracters, notaries, and justices of peace	10,071	1,483	14.7	7,445	785	10.5	+4.2
Healers (except osteopaths, physicians, and surgeons)	14,774	7,902	53.5	6,831	4,669	68.4	−14.9
Keepers of charitable and penal institutions	12,884	4,931	38.3	7,491	2,245	30.0	+8.3
Officials of lodges, societies, etc	11,736	2,162	18.4	8,215	1,970	24.0	−5.6
Religious, charity, and welfare workers	41,078	26,927	65.6	15,948	8,877	55.7	+9.9
Theatrical owners, managers, and officials	18,395	1,257	6.8	11,316	295	2.6	+4.2
Attendants and helpers (professional service)	29,602	16,046	54.2	17,576	8,074	45.9	+8.3
Domestic and personal service:							
Barbers, hairdressers, and manicurists	215,285	33,091	15.4	193,680	22,011	11.4	+4.0
Boarding and lodging house keepers	133,392	114,740	86.0	165,444	142,392	86.1	−0.1
Charwomen and cleaners	36,401	24,744	68.0	33,552	26,443	78.8	−10.8
Elevator tenders	40,150	7,233	18.0	24,438	25	0.1	+17.9
Hotel keepers and managers	55,583	14,134	25.4	64,504	14,235	22.1	+3.3
Housekeepers and stewards	221,612	204,350	92.2	189,210	173,280	91.6	+0.6
Janitors and sextons	177,216	28,929	16.3	112,180	21,357	19.0	−2.7
Laborers (domestic and professional)	32,399	1,631	5.0	52,229	3,113	6.0	−1.0
Launderers and laundresses (not in laundry)	394,308	383,622	97.3	527,134	513,586	97.4	−0.1
Laundry operatives	117,887	78,548	66.6	108,624	73,393	67.6	−1.0
Midwives and nurses (not trained)	156,769	137,431	87.7	132,672	116,746	88.0	−0.3

4 No comparable figures available for 1910.

6436°—29——6

TABLE 43.—SPECIFIED OCCUPATIONS IN WHICH WOMEN IN 1920 FORMED 5 PER CENT OR MORE OF TOTAL NUMBER OF WORKERS 16 YEARS OF AGE AND OVER, 1920 AND 1910, WITH INCREASE OR DECREASE—Continued

OCCUPATION	GAINFUL WORKERS 16 YEARS OF AGE AND OVER						Increase (+) or decrease (−) in percentage of women
	1920			1910			
	Total number	Women		Total number	Women		
		Number	Per cent		Number	Per cent	
Domestic and personal service—Con.							
Restaurant, café, and lunch room keepers	87,987	15,644	17.8	60,822	10,515	17.3	+0.5
Servants	1,232,766	981,557	79.6	1,482,717	1,234,758	83.3	−3.7
Waiters	225,579	114,718	50.9	184,712	83,597	45.3	+5.6
Cleaners and renovators (clothing, etc.)	21,518	4,533	21.1	14,592	2,567	17.6	+3.5
Clerical occupations:							
Agents	130,338	8,910	6.8	50,598	2,285	4.5	+2.3
Canvassers	14,349	4,124	28.7	18,506	4,589	24.8	+3.9
Collectors	30,506	2,707	8.9	35,463	1,880	5.3	+3.6
Bookkeepers, cashiers, and accountants	731,350	356,603	48.8	483,845	185,299	38.3	+10.5
Clerks (except clerks in stores)	1,465,384	463,570	31.6	707,807	119,385	16.9	+14.7
Messenger, bundle, and office boys and girls [5]	64,994	9,947	15.3	55,847	6,005	10.8	+4.5
Stenographers and typists	609,480	559,748	91.8	313,986	261,202	83.2	+8.6

[5] Except telegraph messengers.

VIII

AGE AND MARITAL CONDITION IN RELATION TO OCCUPATION

A large proportion of the 8,202,901 women 16 years of age and over who were engaged in gainful occupations in 1920 were young women, nearly 40 per cent of them being not over 25 years of age. The corresponding figure for men gainfully employed is 20.6 per cent. The main reason for the difference is, of course, to be found in the fact that a large proportion of the older women, 78.2 per cent of those between the ages of 25 and 45, are married women; for notwithstanding the recent increase in the number of married women gainfully employed, the great majority—over 90 per cent—of all the women who are married do not follow a gainful occupation, and are therefore presumably free to devote themselves wholly to the care of their homes and families.

The extent to which the percentage of women gainfully employed declines in each of the older ages after the age of 20 is shown by the following table:

TABLE 44.—PROPORTION OF WOMEN AND OF MEN IN EACH SPECIFIED AGE PERIOD GAINFULLY OCCUPIED IN 1920, WITH A PER CENT DISTRIBUTION OF THOSE GAINFULLY OCCUPIED, BY AGE PERIODS

AGE PERIOD	WOMEN 16 YEARS OF AGE AND OVER: 1920				MEN 16 YEARS OF AGE AND OVER: 1920	
	Total number	Gainfully occupied			Per cent gainfully occupied	Per cent distribution of those gainfully occupied
		Number	Per cent of total	Per cent distribution		
All ages	34,241,749	8,202,901	24.0	100.0	89.9	100.0
16 and 17 years	1,925,264	609,192	31.6	7.4	58.0	3.4
18 and 19 years	1,895,734	802,235	42.3	9.8	78.3	4.5
20 to 24 years	4,749,976	1,809,075	38.1	22.1	91.0	12.7
25 to 44 years	15,249,602	3,417,373	22.4	41.7	97.2	48.2
45 to 64 years	7,915,205	1,352,479	17.1	16.5	93.8	26.4
65 years and over	2,450,144	196,900	8.0	2.4	60.1	4.6
Age not reported	55,824	15,647	28.0	0.2	61.5	0.2

Diagram 6, based upon the above table, shows by shaded areas the total number of women in each age period, as well as the number and percentage gainfully employed.

67

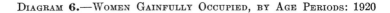

DIAGRAM 6.—WOMEN GAINFULLY OCCUPIED, BY AGE PERIODS: 1920

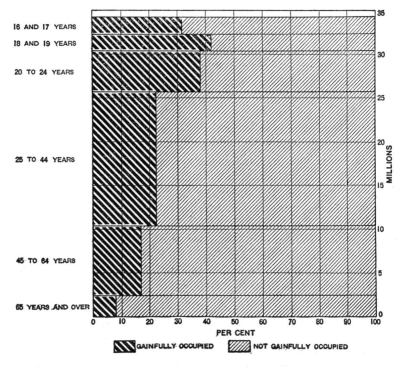

Of the young women 18 and 19 years of age 42.3 per cent, or more than two-fifths, are employed in gainful occupations. This is the maximum percentage for any age group shown in the table. In the next older age group, 20 to 24, the percentage is 38.1. It declines further to 22.4 for the age group 25 to 44 and to 17.1 and 8.0, respectively, for the next two older groups. While these figures clearly establish the fact that in each generation the percentage of women gainfully employed diminishes very materially as they grow older, the age groups are too comprehensive to show how rapidly or how gradually the change takes place in the successive years of life. It is probable, however, that if we had figures for each year of age, we should find that the percentage of women in gainful occupations decreases rapidly in the period between 20 and 30 years of age, this being the decade of life in which there is a rapid increase in the percentage of married women and a corresponding decrease in the percentage remaining single. Thus, in this interval of 10 years the percentage married increases from 38.4 for women who are 20 years of age to 78.4 for those 29 years of age, while the percentage single declines from 60.0 to 17.5, as shown by the following table:

TABLE 45.—PER CENT DISTRIBUTION, BY MARITAL CONDITION, OF THE TOTAL NUMBER OF WOMEN IN EACH YEAR OF AGE FROM 20 TO 29, INCLUSIVE: 1920

AGE	PER CENT OF WOMEN 20 TO 29 YEARS OF AGE: 1920		
	Single	Married	Widowed or divorced
20 years	60.0	38.4	1.3
21 years	52.5	45.8	1.6
22 years	44.9	52.9	2.0
23 years	38.3	59.2	2.3
24 years	33.0	64.2	2.6
25 years	29.0	67.8	3.0
26 years	25.3	71.4	3.2
27 years	22.0	74.4	3.5
28 years	20.2	75.9	3.9
29 years	17.5	78.4	4.0

In the census report on Women at Work, published in 1907, there is an attempt to obtain through an analysis of the age statistics some indication of the extent to which young women on account of marriage or for other reasons give up their occupations as they grow older. On the basis of figures there presented it seems, in the language of the report, to be "a very conservative conclusion that not less than one-half of the native white women 15 to 24 years of age who were breadwinners in 1890 and were still living in 1900 (being then 25 to 34 years of age) had given up their gainful occupation in the interval." No similar computation can be made for a later decade, either 1900 to 1910 or 1910 to 1920, since the requisite age detail for women gainfully employed was not tabulated in the census of 1910.

That the decrease in the percentage of women gainfully employed in older years is mainly accounted for by marriage is further indicated by Table 46, in which separate figures are presented for the married and the "not married." The latter, it may be noted, include the widowed and divorced as well as the single women, separate figures for these classes not being available. But, since the great majority of the unmarried women in the age groups under 45 are single, the fact that the percentage gainfully employed in the case of those not married shows no decrease up to that age may be accepted as indicating that most of the single women who take up a gainful occupation in early life continue to follow it, if they remain single, until well past middle age.

In Diagram 7 (pp. 70 and 71) are two figures showing the proportionate number of married women gainfully occupied at each age period, in comparison with corresponding proportions for unmarried women. It should be noted that the scale for the total numbers of women for the married groups is not the same as that for the not married groups, but the scale for percentage occupied is the same in the two diagrams.

DIAGRAM 7.—MARRIED WOMEN AND WOMEN NOT MARRIED,

FIGURE 1.—Married women

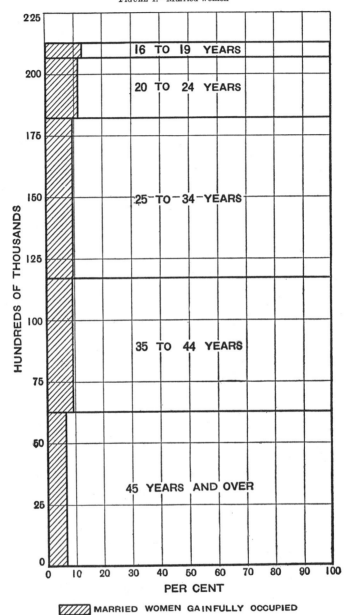

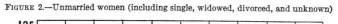

ENGAGED IN GAINFUL OCCUPATIONS, BY AGE PERIODS: 1920

FIGURE 2.—Unmarried women (including single, widowed, divorced, and unknown)

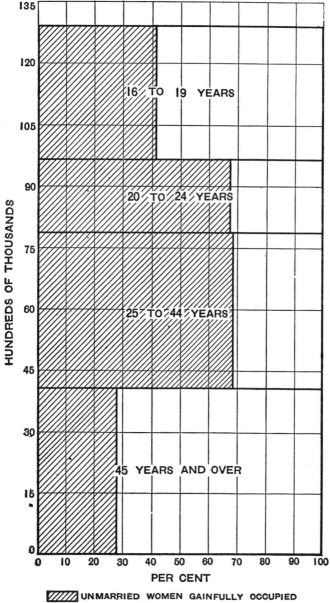

Table 46.—Number and Percentage of Married Women and of Women Not Married, Engaged in Gainful Occupations, by Age Periods: 1920

AGE PERIOD	WOMEN 16 YEARS OF AGE AND OVER AND MARRIED: 1920			WOMEN 16 YEARS OF AGE AND OVER AND NOT MARRIED: 1920		
	Total number	Gainfully occupied		Total number	Gainfully occupied	
		Number	Per cent		Number	Per cent
Total	21, 306, 099	1, 920, 281	9. 0	12, 935, 650	6, 282, 620	48. 6
16 to 19 years	583, 708	74, 305	12. 7	3, 237, 290	1, 337, 122	41. 3
20 to 24 years	2, 483, 697	283, 870	11. 4	2, 266, 279	1, 525, 205	67. 3
25 to 34 years	6, 492, 355	627, 580	9. 7	3, 330, 813	2, 273, 667	68. 3
35 to 44 years	5, 426, 434	516, 126	9. 5			
45 years and over	6, 296, 432	414, 436	6. 6	4, 068, 917	1, 134, 943	27. 9
Age not reported	23, 473	3, 964	16. 9	32, 351	11, 683	36. 1

As shown by the above table, over two-thirds of the unmarried (single, widowed, or divorced) women from 20 to 44 years of age are following gainful occupations. But among the older unmarried women (45 years of age and over) the proportion gainfully employed is very much smaller, being only 27.9 per cent. While this difference is doubtless due in part to the fact that many single women as they approach old age give up their occupation either voluntarily or because of disability, it must be borne in mind that in the older years of life the ranks of the "not married" are recruited by large numbers of widows. In fact, in the total population, the "not married" women in the age period 45 and over are 77.6 per cent widows or divorced women. There are no recent census figures showing to what extent widows are engaged in gainful occupations. But in 1890, at a time when the percentage of single women (15 years of age and over) gainfully employed was 40.5, the corresponding percentage for widows was 29.3; and in the age period 45 and over the percentage gainfully employed was 33.8 for single women compared with 22.2 for widows.[1] It is probable, therefore, that the decrease after the age of 45 in the percentage gainfully employed among women not married results mainly from the fact that large numbers of women become widows at this period of life without taking up any gainful occupation.

Of the total number of women 16 years of age and over in 1920, 19.4 per cent, or nearly one-fifth, were neither married nor gainfully employed. The number of women in this class was 6,653,030. Of these, 1,900,168, or 28.6 per cent, were young women between 16 and 20 years of age; and 2,933,974, or 44.1 per cent, were women past 45 years of age. Of the latter about 75 per cent probably were widows or divorced women. These statistics indicate that a large proportion of the women who are neither married nor engaged in a gainful

[1] Statistics of Women at Work, 1907, p. 14—Bureau of the Census.

occupation are either very young women hardly past the school age, or else they are women past middle life, many of whom are widows, and were therefore married women at one time, while others may have followed a gainful occupation in earlier life.

Of women between the ages of 25 and 44, 70.7 per cent were married and not engaged in any gainful occupation; 14.9 per cent were gainfully employed and not married; 7.5 were both married and gainfully employed; and 6.9 per cent were neither married nor gainfully employed. The last-named class, numbering 1,057,146, doubtless includes a limited number of women of whom it might be said that they are not contributing to the work of the world, or to the maintenance of a home or family. Probably, however, the number to whom that description applies is not large, for the fact that a woman is neither married nor engaged in a gainful occupation does not by any means indicate that she is idle. Large numbers of unmarried women are engaged in home housework, and not a few of them have the responsibility of caring for the family or the home; others are occupied in church or charity work, or in the nonprofessional pursuits of music, art, or literature, or in some other unremunerated and, therefore, unenumerated, occupation. Moreover, the range of ages here considered, from 25 to 44 years inclusive, makes it certain that a considerable number of the unmarried and not gainfully employed within these ages will sometime marry or take up an occupation. It might be interesting to inquire how many women reach the age of 45 without either marrying or taking up a gainful occupation or engaging in home housework. The number is unascertainable from the census or other statistics, but one may safely assume that it is rather small, and would be made up in part of those who, through the misfortune of ill health, deformity, or some mental or physical defect, are cut off from participation in the activities of life.

It still remains true, although less true now than it once was, that to a woman marriage normally supersedes or precludes the pursuit of a gainful occupation, in that it involves the establishment and care of a home, with the housework or household duties incident thereto, and at the same time provides her with a livelihood; so that, as a rule, the woman who marries is not as free to follow a wage-earning occupation as she was before marriage, nor under the same necessity for doing so. But there are, of course, plenty of exceptions which will occur to any reader. There are cases in which the woman is under no necessity of earning a living either before marriage or after; and there are cases in which it is necessary after marriage for the woman to become or to continue to be a wage earner, in order to contribute to the support of herself and her family. But more commonly, marriage relieves her of that necessity. With some women, particularly those having a superior education, ambition for a career or the desire for a wider sphere of activity than the domestic hearth affords is a motive which leads them to follow a profession or gainful occupation after marriage.   This class, it is safe to say, is not very numerous. More frequent, probably, are the cases in which the married woman is a wage earner not strictly from necessity but rather from choice, for the sake of securing a better living for herself and husband than his income alone would provide.   The fact remains, that in 1920, 91 per cent of the married women were not engaged in any gainful occupation.   But it is also a fact that the percentage of married women following a gainful occupation appears to be increasing, as will be shown in the next chapter.

IX

MARRIED WOMEN IN GAINFUL OCCUPATIONS

NUMBER AND PERCENTAGE

The 1,920,281 married women 16 years of age and over reported in the census of 1920 as engaged in gainful occupations constituted 23.4 per cent of the total number of gainfully employed women, and 9 per cent of the total number of married women. That is to say, in 1920, 1 married woman in 11 was following a gainful occupation; and 2 out of 9 women at work in gainful occupations were married women. It may be noted by way of contrast that of the unmarried women 48.6 per cent, or almost one-half, were following gainful occupations.

TABLE 47.—NUMBER AND PERCENTAGE OF MARRIED WOMEN AND OF WOMEN NOT MARRIED ENGAGED IN GAINFUL OCCUPATIONS: 1920

| | WOMEN 16 YEARS OF AGE AND OVER: 1920 | | | |
| MARITAL CLASS | Total number | Gainfully occupied | | |
		Number	Per cent of total	Per cent distribution
All classes	34,241,749	8,202,901	24.0	100.0
Married	21,306,099	1,920,281	9.0	23.4
Not married [1]	12,935,650	6,282,620	48.6	76.6

[1] Includes single, widowed, divorced, and unknown.

INCREASE, 1890–1920

The percentage of married women reported in the census as engaged in a gainful occupation was slightly smaller in 1920 than it was in 1910. But the decrease in the last decade is in all probability attributable to the changes previously mentioned in the date of the census and in the instructions to the enumerators regarding the reporting of women working on farms, since one effect of these changes was to reduce very materially the number of married women (most of them, doubtless, farmers' wives) reported as agricultural laborers on the home farm, this number falling off from 495,423 in 1910 to 225,503 in 1920. (See p. 83.) If agricultural pursuits are omitted, it will be found that the percentage of the married women employed in other occupations consistently increased from 3.3 in 1890, to 3.9 in 1900,

75

6.8 in 1910, and 7.3 in 1920.   Thus, the proportion of married women employed in nonagricultural occupations increased from approximately 1 in 30 in 1890, to 1 in 14 in 1920.

TABLE 48.—NUMBER AND PERCENTAGE OF MARRIED WOMEN ENGAGED IN ALL OCCUPATIONS AND IN NONAGRICULTURAL PURSUITS: 1890–1920

CENSUS YEAR	MARRIED WOMEN 16 YEARS OF AGE AND OVER				
			Engaged in gainful occupations		
	Total number	All occupations		Nonagricultural pursuits	
		Number	Per cent	Number	Per cent
1920	21,306,099	1,920,281	9.0	1,548,744	7.3
1910	17,674,396	1,890,626	10.7	1,197,901	6.8
1900	13,810,057	769,477	5.6	1 542,358	3.9
1890	1 11,117,051	1 515,124	4.6	1 362,268	3.3

1 Figures partly estimated.

The following table gives the percentage of increase in the number of married and of unmarried women, respectively, engaged in nonagricultural pursuits in each decade from 1890 to 1920:

TABLE 49.—PERCENTAGE OF INCREASE IN NUMBER OF WOMEN ENGAGED IN NONAGRICULTURAL PURSUITS: 1890–1920

DECADE	PERCENTAGE OF INCREASE	
	Married	Not married 1
1910 to 1920	29.3	18.9
1900 to 1910	120.9	37.6
1890 to 1900	49.7	33.4

1 Includes single, widowed, divorced, and unknown.

The percentages in the above table would indicate that the advent of the twentieth century was followed by a great increase in the number of married women who took up wage-earning occupations, but that after this first inrush, the tide subsided somewhat, the next decade showing a less pronounced increase.   One naturally wonders why that was so or whether there really was such an exceptional increase between 1900 and 1910.   There is the lurking possibility that the changes and inconsistencies previously noted in the instructions to the enumerators in the last three censuses may account in part for these fluctuations in the figures.   Yet it is not apparent why that should be so, since women employed in agricultural pursuits are not included in the above comparison.

PROPORTION MARRIED IN THE TOTAL NUMBER OF WOMEN EMPLOYED

As a result of the fact that in nonagricultural pursuits the number of married women has increased faster than the number not married, an increasing proportion of the total number of women engaged in nonagricultural pursuits are married women. The extent of this change is indicated by the table which follows, showing that in 1890 12.1 per cent, or approximately one in eight, of the women engaged in gainful occupations outside of agriculture were married women, while 30 years later, in 1920, the proportion was 21.2 per cent, or more than one in five. The most marked change took place between 1900 and 1910, in which interval the percentage married in the total number of women in nonagricultural pursuits increased from 13.3 to 19.8.

TABLE 50.—NUMBER AND PERCENTAGE OF MARRIED WOMEN IN THE TOTAL NUMBER OF WOMEN ENGAGED IN NONAGRICULTURAL PURSUITS: 1890–1920

CENSUS YEAR	WOMEN 16 YEARS OF AGE AND OVER ENGAGED IN NONAGRICULTURAL PURSUITS		
	Total number	Married women	
		Number	Per cent of total
1920	7, 306, 844	1, 548, 744	21. 2
1910	6, 041, 362	1, 197, 901	19. 8
1900	4, 063, 147	1 542, 358	13. 3
1890	1 3, 000, 904	1 362, 268	12. 1

1 Figures partly estimated.

RACE AND NATIVITY

Slightly more than one-third, or 34.5 per cent, of the married women reported as engaged in gainful occupations in 1920 were Negro women. This represents a disproportionately large number for a race which comprises only 9.9 per cent of the total population of the United States and only 9.6 per cent of the total number of married women. So it is evident that in proportion to their numbers the married women of the Negro race are engaged in gainful occupations to a much greater extent than the married white women. In fact, 32.5 per cent, or nearly one-third, of the married Negro women are gainfully employed, as compared with 6.5 per cent of the married white women. Most of the gainfully occupied Negro married women—80.1 per cent of them—are employed as servants, farm laborers, or laundresses; and the 531,094 Negro women so employed account for 27.7 per cent, or more than one-fourth, of the total number of married women engaged in gainful occupations.

TABLE 51.—NUMBER AND PERCENTAGE OF MARRIED WOMEN ENGAGED IN GAINFUL OCCUPATIONS, BY RACE AND NATIVITY: 1920

RACE AND NATIVITY	MARRIED WOMEN 16 YEARS OF AGE AND OVER: 1920			
	Total number	Engaged in gainful occupations		
		Number	Per cent of total	Per cent distribution
All classes	21,306,099	1,920,281	9.0	100.0
Native white	15,077,337	952,814	6.3	49.6
Native parentage	11,187,355	707,503	6.3	36.8
Foreign or mixed parentage	3,889,982	245,311	6.3	12.8
Foreign-born white	4,122,932	296,126	7.2	15.4
Negro	2,036,419	662,684	32.5	34.5
All other [1]	69,411	8,657	12.5	0.5

[1] Includes Indians, Chinese, Japanese, and other races.

AGE

Attention has already been called to the fact that the percentage of married women who have taken up gainful occupations decreases in each older age group. (See p. 67.) In other words, a larger proportion of the younger married women are breadwinners than of the older. This would indicate that married women as they grow older give up their gainful occupations in many cases. The coming of children may make it more difficult to carry on a breadwinning pursuit, or an improvement in the husband's income may make it less necessary. Another explanation, however, may be that the younger generation of married women are engaging in gainful occupations to a greater extent than their predecessors—the older generation—ever did. Figures already presented show that married women in general are engaging in gainful occupations to an increasing extent, and it seems probable that this change, like any other change of habits or customs, would be more marked in the younger and less conservative generation than in the older. Either of these causes or both of them may be operative in producing the decrease shown in the percentage gainfully occupied in each successive older age group of married women.

But there is still another possible contributory cause or explanation that may be suggested, namely, the possibility that those women who are willing and competent to continue in or to take up a gainful occupation after marriage may marry at a younger age than other women. There are many cases in which a young couple can live quite comfortably on their combined earnings but would have to defer marriage if they had to depend entirely on the husband's wages for their support. Thus, one serious barrier to early marriages, namely, the man's inability to support a wife, is removed when the wife is competent and ready to support herself, or to contribute to the family income. And this, as just suggested, may be another reason why the percentage gainfully employed is considerably larger for young married women than for those of older years. It should be noted, however, that the decrease of the percentage in the older years is much less marked when the comparison is restricted to non-agricultural pursuits, as shown by the last two columns of Table 52.

TABLE 52.—NUMBER AND PERCENTAGE OF MARRIED WOMEN ENGAGED IN GAINFUL OCCUPATIONS, BY AGE PERIODS: 1920

AGE PERIOD	MARRIED WOMEN 16 YEARS OF AGE AND OVER				
	Total number	Engaged in all gainful occupations		Engaged in nonagricultural pursuits	
		Number	Per cent	Number	Per cent
Total	21,306,099	1,920,281	9.0	1,548,744	7.3
16 to 19 years	583,708	74,305	12.7	50,611	8.7
20 to 24 years	2,483,697	283,870	11.4	222,049	8.9
25 to 34 years	6,492,355	627,580	9.7	517,596	8.0
35 to 44 years	5,426,434	516,126	9.5	422,855	7.8
45 years and over	6,296,432	414,436	6.6	332,059	5.3
Age not reported	23,473	3,964	16.9	3,574	15.2

The table which follows brings out the fact that this decrease in the percentage of married women gainfully employed in the older age periods is considerably more marked for the foreign-born white and the native white of foreign or mixed parentage than it is for the native white of native parentage, while in the case of Negro married women there is up to the age of 45 no decrease whatever in the percentage gainfully employed, but, on the contrary, an increase.

TABLE 53.—NUMBER AND PERCENTAGE OF MARRIED WOMEN ENGAGED IN GAINFUL OCCUPATIONS, BY AGE, RACE, AND NATIVITY: 1920

AGE PERIOD	MARRIED WOMEN 16 YEARS OF AGE AND OVER ENGAGED IN GAINFUL OCCUPATIONS: 1920							
	Native white—Native parentage		Native white—Foreign or mixed parentage		Foreign-born white		Negro	
	Number	Per cent	Number	Per cent	Number	Per cent	Number	Per cent
Total	707,503	6.3	245,311	6.3	296,126	7.2	662,684	32.5
16 to 19 years	29,980	8.0	7,677	11.3	4,382	11.4	31,911	28.0
20 to 24 years	106,191	7.6	37,284	8.8	27,876	9.6	111,095	31.1
25 to 34 years	225,760	6.6	83,255	6.7	95,802	8.3	219,432	33.7
35 to 44 years	182,009	6.6	63,130	6.3	93,336	8.1	175,484	34.5
45 years and over	162,154	5.0	53,669	4.7	74,331	5.0	122,925	30.4
Age not reported	1,409	10.5	296	14.7	399	11.9	1,837	41.0

OCCUPATIONS

The employment of married women in gainful occupations is frequently deplored as an evil on the ground that it takes them away from their homes, necessitating the neglect of their children, or perhaps deters them from having any children. Since the objections that may be urged against their employment are considerably lessened if not entirely removed when the occupation is one that is carried on in the home, it is of interest to inquire regarding the extent to which the occupations followed by married women are, in fact, of a kind that would presumably take them away from their homes during working hours. While the question is one that can not be definitely answered by reference to census statistics, the following classification of gainfully employed married women by occupations throws some light upon it.

TABLE 54.—PRINCIPAL OCCUPATIONS OF MARRIED WOMEN, WITH PER CENT DISTRIBUTION: 1920

OCCUPATION	MARRIED WOMEN 16 YEARS OF AGE AND OVER GAINFULLY EMPLOYED: 1920	
	Number	Per cent distribu- tion
All occupations	1, 920, 281	100. 0
Semiskilled operatives (manufacturing) (n. o. s. [1])	312, 478	16. 3
Servants	228, 270	11. 9
Farm laborers (home farm)	225, 503	11. 7
Laundresses (not in laundry)	187, 510	9. 8
Clerical occupations	129, 038	6. 7
Saleswomen and clerks in stores	103, 340	5. 4
Farm laborers (working out)	93, 078	4. 8
Dressmakers and seamstresses (not in factory)	66, 094	3. 4
Teachers (school)	61, 483	3. 2
Laborers (manufacturing) (n. o. s. [1])	48, 863	2. 5
Boarding and lodging house keepers	42, 431	2. 2
Farmers, general farms	39, 093	2. 0
Housekeepers and stewardesses	36, 688	1. 9
Retail dealers	34, 801	1. 8
Waitresses	31, 037	1. 6
Midwives and nurses (not trained)	27, 444	1. 4
Laundry operatives	26, 237	1. 4
Musicians and teachers of music	17, 830	0. 9
Telephone operators	17, 225	0. 9
Janitors and sextons	15, 394	0. 8
Milliners and millinery dealers	12, 735	0. 7
Barbers, hairdressers, and manicurists	12, 728	0. 7
Trained nurses	10, 706	0. 6
Charwomen and cleaners	10, 398	0. 5
All other occupations	129, 877	6. 8

[1] Not otherwise specified.

In the above list of principal occupations for married women there are some which do not ordinarily separate the worker from her home. That is obviously true as regards farmers and laborers on the home farm, and as regards boarding and lodging house keepers. It is probably true to a large extent as regards laundresses not working in a laundry, dressmakers not employed in factories, and retail dealers. On the other hand, it is fairly certain that such occupations as those of clerk, semiskilled operative in a manufacturing industry, servant, school teacher, and saleswoman or clerk in a store, would in most cases necessitate absence from home during working hours plus the time required for going from the home to the place of employment and returning. Therefore, while it is evident that not all the married women reported in the census as following a gainful occupation are separated from their homes while at work, that is undoubtedly the case as regards a large proportion of them—a proportion which probably is somewhere between two-thirds and three-fourths of the total.

TABLE 55.—NUMBER OF MARRIED WOMEN ENGAGED IN NONAGRICULTURAL PURSUITS, BY SPECIFIED OCCUPATION, WITH NUMBER AND PER CENT INCREASE, AND PER CENT DISTRIBUTION: 1920 AND 1910

OCCUPATION	MARRIED WOMEN 16 YEARS OF AGE AND OVER GAINFULLY EMPLOYED					
	Number		Increase: 1910 to 1920 [1]		Per cent distribution	
	1920	1910	Number	Per cent	1920	1910
All nonagricultural pursuits	1,548,744	1,197,901	350,843	29.3	100.0	100.0
Semiskilled operatives (manufacturing) (n. o. s.[2])	312,478	[3] 154,278	158,200	102.5	20.2	12.9
Clerical occupations	129,038	33,074	95,964	290.1	8.3	2.8
Saleswomen and clerks in stores	103,340	43,534	59,806	137.4	6.7	3.6
Laborers (manufacturing) (n. o. s.[2])	48,863	17,384	31,479	181.1	3.2	1.5
Teachers (school)	61,483	30,319	31,164	102.8	4.0	2.5
Servants	228,270	209,988	18,282	8.7	14.7	17.5
Waitresses	31,037	13,350	17,687	132.5	2.0	1.1
Telephone operators	17,225	[4] 4,354	12,871	295.6	1.1	0.4
Laundry operatives	26,237	16,489	9,748	59.1	1.7	1.4
Barbers, hairdressers, and manicurists	12,728	5,452	7,276	133.5	0.8	0.5
Trained nurses	10,706	5,412	5,294	97.8	0.7	0.5
Retail dealers	34,801	29,755	5,046	17.0	2.2	2.5
Housekeepers and stewardesses	36,688	31,874	4,814	15.1	2.4	2.7
Midwives and nurses (not trained)	27,444	23,386	4,058	17.4	1.8	2.0
Janitors and sextons	15,394	11,854	3,540	29.9	1.0	1.0
Musicians and teachers of music	17,830	17,092	738	4.3	1.2	1.4
Charwomen and cleaners	10,398	10,298	100	1.0	0.7	0.9
Milliners and millinery dealers	12,735	18,776	−6,041	−32.2	0.8	1.6
Boarding and lodging house keepers	42,431	59,062	−16,631	−28.2	2.7	4.9
Dressmakers and seamstresses (not in factory)	66,094	122,609	−56,515	−46.1	4.3	10.2
Laundresses (not in laundry)	187,510	263,772	−76,262	−28.9	12.1	22.0
All other nonagricultural occupations	116,014	75,789	40,225	53.1	7.5	6.3

[1] A minus sign (−) denotes decrease.
[2] Not otherwise specified.
[3] Partly estimated; persons reported as sewers in the various industries in 1910 were presented as a separate occupation, but were classified in 1920 with the semiskilled operatives of the respective industries. The number of sewers in each industry in 1910 is available and has been included with the semiskilled for comparative purposes, but marital condition was tabulated for the whole number of sewers only. The number of married sewers in each industry in 1910 has been estimated on the basis of the total number of married sewers.
[4] Estimated to a slight degree.

A comparison of the occupational classification in 1920 with that in 1910 as applied to married women indicates that for them as well as for the unmarried the present drift is in the direction of employment in factory, office, and store, and away from domestic pursuits and home occupations. Within that period of 10 years the number of married women employed as semiskilled operatives in manufacturing pursuits more than doubled, increasing from 154,278 in 1910 to 312,478 in 1920, an absolute increase of 158,200. The largest relative, or percentage, increases are those shown for clerical occupations and telephone operators, the number of married women in these occupations being nearly three times as large in 1920 as it was in 1910. In absolute numbers, however, the increase in these occupations—95,964 for clerical occupations and 12,871 for telephone operators—was considerably less than that in the number of married factory operatives as just noted.

It may be noted as a matter of some interest that while, as pointed out in another connection (p. 36), the total number of women servants showed a decided decrease (20.5 per cent) between 1910 and 1920, the number of married women employed as servants showed an appreciable, though not large, increase, from 209,988 in 1910 to 228,270 in 1920, or 8.7 per cent. This probably means that the check to immigration and the inclination to prefer other occupations affected mainly the supply of young women available for domestic service, the older women continuing in that employment and in some degree replacing the younger women.

TABLE 56.—NUMBER OF MARRIED WOMEN AND WOMEN NOT MARRIED EMPLOYED AS SERVANTS: 1920 AND 1910

MARITAL CLASS	WOMEN 16 YEARS OF AGE AND OVER EMPLOYED AS SERVANTS			
	1920	1910	Increase (+) or decrease (−): 1910 to 1920	
			Number	Per cent
Total_____	981,557	1,234,758	−253,201	−20.5
Married_____ _____	228,270	209,988	+18,282	+8.7
Not married [1]_____	753,287	1,024,770	−271,483	−26.5

[1] Includes single, widowed, divorced, and unknown.

In the following table the occupations which gave employment to not less than 10,000 women in 1920 have been arranged in the order of the percentage of married women in the total number of women employed. The six occupations at the head of the list are of a kind that may be followed without necessarily separating the worker from her home. The janitress or caretaker very commonly lives in the building in which she works. Of the 320,348 married women reported as farm laborers, 225,503 were employed on the home farm. Most of the 187,510 married women reported as laundresses (not in laundries) were, in all probability, doing the work in their own homes, "taking in washing," as the phrase runs. Nearly four-fifths of them—79 per cent—were Negro women. The woman who engages in retail trade very frequently lives in or near the building in which she has her shop or store. In each of these occupations, however, the percentage married in the total number of women employed was smaller in 1920 than it was in 1910, although in the case of retail dealers the decrease was very slight. There was a decided decrease in the percentage of married in the total number of women reported as boarding-house keepers and as farmers. These also are home occupations.

TABLE 57.—NUMBER AND PERCENTAGE OF MARRIED WOMEN GAINFULLY EMPLOYED, IN SPECIFIED OCCUPATIONS: 1920 AND 1910

OCCUPATION	WOMEN 16 YEARS OF AGE AND OVER ENGAGED IN GAINFUL OCCUPATIONS					
	Total number		Married			
			Number		Per cent of total	
	1920	1910	1920	1910	1920	1910
All occupations	8,202,901	7,438,686	1,920,281	1,890,626	23.4	25.4
Janitors and sextons	28,929	21,357	15,394	11,854	53.2	55.5
Farm laborers	605,668	1,108,613	320,348	634,896	52.9	57.3
Home farm	*403,009*	*826,523*	*225,503*	*495,423*	*56.0*	*59.9*
Working out	*198,979*	*278,637*	*93,078*	*137,543*	*46.8*	*49.4*
Laundresses (not in laundry)	383,622	513,586	187,510	263,772	48.9	51.4
Hotel keepers and managers	14,134	14,235	6,544	6,946	46.3	48.8
Restaurant, café, and lunch room keepers	15,644	10,515	7,244	5,143	46.3	48.9
Retail dealers	78,957	67,010	34,801	29,755	44.1	44.4
Charwomen and cleaners	24,744	26,443	10,398	10,298	42.0	38.9
Postmasters	11,208	8,718	4,609	(1)	41.1	(1)
Actresses and showwomen	14,220	12,817	5,817	5,514	40.9	43.0
Barbers, hairdressers, and manicurists	33,091	22,011	12,728	5,452	38.5	24.8
Boarding and lodging house keepers	114,740	142,392	42,431	59,062	37.0	41.5
Laundry operatives	78,548	73,393	26,237	[2] 16,489	33.4	22.5
Manufacturers, officials, and managers (manufacturing)	13,276	6,161	4,181	1,910	31.5	31.0
Laborers (manufacturing) (n. o. s.[3])	160,133	80,048	48,863	17,384	30.5	21.7
Tailoresses	31,828	40,370	9,176	7,464	28.8	18.5
Dressmakers and seamstresses (not in factory)	235,519	446,555	66,094	122,609	28.1	27.5
Waitresses	114,718	83,597	31,037	13,350	27.1	16.0
Agents, canvassers, and collectors	15,741	8,754	3,905	2,366	24.8	27.0
Musicians and teachers of music	72,431	83,851	17,830	17,092	24.6	20.4
Semiskilled operatives (manufacturing) (n. o. s.[3])	1,274,719	955,423	312,478	[2] 154,278	24.5	16.1
Servants	981,557	1,234,758	228,270	209,988	23.3	17.0
Saleswomen and clerks in stores	514,056	350,723	103,340	43,534	20.1	12.4
Compositors, linotypers, and typesetters	11,306	14,025	2,273	1,546	20.1	11.0
Midwives and nurses (not trained)	137,431	116,746	27,444	23,386	20.0	20.0
Artists, sculptors, and teachers of art	14,566	15,354	2,880	3,677	19.8	24.0
Forewomen and overseers (manufacturing)	30,171	19,740	5,807	2,162	19.2	11.0
Milliners and millinery dealers	69,598	121,446	12,735	18,776	18.3	15.5
Housekeepers and stewardesses	204,350	173,280	36,688	31,874	18.0	18.4
Farmers	253,836	261,956	40,466	48,534	15.9	18.5
Telegraph operators	16,860	8,199	2,463	1,044	14.6	12.7
Farm foremen, general farms	13,767	7,505	1,878	1,365	13.6	18.2
Bookkeepers, cashiers, and accountants	356,603	185,299	41,061	13,142	11.5	7.1
College presidents and professors	10,075	2,958	1,140	295	11.3	10.0
Religious, charity, and welfare workers	26,927	8,877	2,995	1,452	11.1	16.4
Clerks (except clerks in stores)	463,570	119,385	46,265	8,548	10.0	7.2
Telephone operators	175,469	86,081	17,225	4,354	9.8	5.1
Teachers (school)	635,207	476,661	61,483	30,319	9.7	6.4
Trained nurses	143,664	76,481	10,706	5,412	7.5	7.1
Librarians	13,502	5,828	1,000	(1)	7.4	(1)
Stenographers and typists	559,748	261,202	37,095	8,835	6.6	3.4
All other occupations	248,768	166,333	69,442	46,749	27.9	28.1

[1] Figures not available.   [2] Includes a slight estimate.   [3] Not otherwise specified.

In most of the other occupations listed in this table the percentage of married women either remained nearly stationary or showed a considerable increase in 1920. Especially notable is the increase in the percentage married among the large number of women employed as semiskilled operatives in manufacturing industries, an increase from 16.1 in 1910 to 24.5 in 1920. There is a similar increase in the percentage married among women employed as laborers in manufacturing industries (from 21:7 to 30.5) and as laundry operatives (from 22.5 to 33.4). These are mostly factory occupations, usually necessitating absence from home during hours of employment.

There was a marked increase also in the proportion of married women among servants and among waitresses.

In the occupations of clerk (not in store), telephone operator, and stenographer the percentage of married women is relatively small, but increased considerably between 1910 and 1920. That is also true in the occupation of teaching school, the percentage increasing from 6.4 to 9.7.

Some other facts of interest in regard to married women employed in gainful occupations are revealed by a special tabulation made for a number of selected cities, classifying gainfully employed women with respect to the relationship to the head of the family in which the employed woman lives, also with respect to the number of other breadwinners in the family. The results of this tabulation are presented and discussed in Chapters XIV and XV. But it may be noted here that in these 11 cities, 37.6 per cent of the married women engaged in gainful occupations were apparently not living with their husbands in homes of their own, but were either boarders or lodgers or living in the home of the father or the mother, or some other relative of the wife or the husband, or were living apart from their husbands. If, therefore, the normal home life for a married woman be defined as living with her husband in a home of her own, then somewhat more than one-third of these married women gainfully employed did not have a normal home life.

The tabulation referred to indicates also that of the employed married women having a home life (i. e., not boarding or lodging), 91.5 per cent represented families in which there were one or more other breadwinners, including as a rule, presumably, the husband of the married woman; and 45 per cent represented families in which there were no unemployed members, and therefore presumably no young children or other dependents. For a more detailed discussion of this line of inquiry the reader is referred to the chapters cited above.

X

NATIVE WHITE WOMEN OF NATIVE PARENTAGE IN GAINFUL OCCUPATIONS

Of the 8,202,901 women reported in the census of 1920 as following gainful occupations, 3,596,397 were native white women who were the children of native white parents and therefore represented at least two generations of native Americans. Farther back than that in indicating ancestry the census records do not go. Accordingly in the census statistics the native grandchildren of immigrants are not distinguishable from the native Americans whose ancestors came to this country prior to the American Revolution. Both classes are included under the designation, "native white of native parentage," and doubtless both are represented in the number of women gainfully employed.

TABLE 58.—NUMBER AND PERCENTAGE OF NATIVE WHITE WOMEN OF NATIVE PARENTAGE IN THE TOTAL NUMBER OF WOMEN ENGAGED IN GAINFUL OCCUPATIONS: 1890–1920

CENSUS YEAR	WOMEN 16 YEARS OF AGE AND OVER ENGAGED IN GAINFUL OCCUPATIONS		
	Total number	Native white—Native parentage	
		Number	Per cent of total
1920	8, 202, 901	3, 596, 397	43. 8
1910	7, 438, 686	2, 847, 982	38. 3
1900	4, 833, 630	1, 771, 966	36. 7
1890	3, 596, 615	[1] 1, 268, 462	35. 3

[1] Partly estimated.

The native white women of native parentage comprised 43.8 per cent of the total number of women gainfully employed in 1920. In 1910 the percentage was 38.3. The increase is a natural result of the fact that with the decrease in foreign immigration and the retardation in the growth of the Negro population the proportion of native white of native parentage in the total population increased appreciably between 1910 and 1920—from 53.8 per cent of the total in 1910 to 55.3 per cent in 1920—and at the same time the percentage of women reported as gainfully employed increased in this class of the population, while it decreased among the Negroes and the foreign-born white. (See p. 54.)

TABLE 59.—NUMBER AND PERCENTAGE OF NATIVE WHITE WOMEN OF NATIVE PARENTAGE ENGAGED IN GAINFUL OCCUPATIONS, AS COMPARED WITH THEIR PROPORTION IN THE TOTAL POPULATION, BY GEOGRAPHIC SECTIONS AND DIVISIONS: 1920

GEOGRAPHIC SECTION AND DIVISION	NATIVE WHITE WOMEN OF NATIVE PARENTAGE 16 YEARS OF AGE AND OVER: 1920				
	Total number	Engaged in gainful occupations			Per cent of total women in the population
		Number	Per cent of total	Per cent of total women gainfully occupied	
United States	17,969,950	3,596,397	20.0	43.8	52.5
The North	10,040,427	2,246,230	22.5	43.2	46.9
New England	983,854	276,850	28.1	32.7	37.5
Middle Atlantic	3,207,246	819,665	25.6	39.7	42.3
East North Central	3,660,289	746,036	20.4	48.6	51.2
West North Central	2,189,038	403,679	18.4	53.1	54.1
The South	6,434,847	1,035,079	16.1	43.3	64.3
South Atlantic	2,659,052	493,943	18.6	42.9	62.1
East South Central	1,795,743	252,161	14.0	39.8	66.5
West South Central	1,980,052	288,975	14.6	47.5	65.5
The West	1,494,676	315,088	21.1	52.1	52.6
Mountain	545,622	96,579	17.7	55.5	56.2
Pacific	949,054	218,509	23.0	50.7	50.7

The percentage which the native white of native parentage form of the total number of women gainfully employed varies considerably in different parts of the United States, being determined largely by the composition of the total population. It is lowest in New England, where the foreign element in the total population is larger than in any other section. As compared with the percentage of native white of native parentage in the total population it is relatively low in the South, which means, of course, that in that section women of this class have not taken up gainful occupations to the same extent that they have in the North. The difference is shown by column 3 of the above table. Thus, in the North the percentage of native white women of native parentage gainfully employed is 22.5, while the corresponding percentage in the South is 16.1. This difference might be interpreted as indicating that in the South, as compared with the North, the native white women are less ready to take up wage-earning pursuits. It may be due in some degree to the survival in the South of a sentiment or tradition averse to the idea of native white women becoming wage earners. It may be noted, furthermore, that there are some occupations, notably that of domestic servant, which in the North are followed by large numbers of white women but in the South are largely preempted by Negro women. Doubtless these are factors which have considerable influence. But to a greater degree, probably, the difference between the North and South as regards the employment of native white women in wage-earning pursuits is attributable to the fact that the South is so largely rural and agricultural, and thus in comparison with the urban and industrial North affords fewer opportunities for the employment of women in wage-earning pursuits. This conclusion is borne out by the fact that when the comparison is made by cities the difference between the North and South is not so striking, although taking the larger southern cities in the aggregate the percentage gainfully employed—31.6—is lower than in the total for the same class of northern cities—34.0.

TABLE 60.—NUMBER AND PERCENTAGE OF NATIVE WHITE WOMEN OF NATIVE PARENTAGE ENGAGED IN GAINFUL OCCUPATIONS IN CITIES OF 100,000 INHABITANTS OR MORE, BY GEOGRAPHIC SECTIONS AND DIVISIONS: 1920

GEOGRAPHIC SECTION AND DIVISION	NATIVE WHITE WOMEN OF NATIVE PARENTAGE 16 YEARS OF AGE AND OVER, IN CITIES OF 100,000 OR MORE INHABITANTS		
	Total number	Engaged in gainful occupations	
		Number	Per cent
United States	3,345,797	1,110,218	33.2
The North	2,278,385	775,057	34.0
New England	196,482	71,954	36.6
Middle Atlantic	992,406	344,756	34.7
East North Central	747,592	243,012	32.5
West North Central	341,905	115,335	33.7
The South	677,512	214,125	31.6
South Atlantic	358,697	123,557	34.4
East South Central	137,786	38,861	28.2
West South Central	181,029	51,707	28.6
The West	389,900	121,036	31.0
Mountain	66,145	19,769	29.9
Pacific	323,755	101,267	31.3

But there are individual southern cities which have just as high a percentage as some of the northern cities. Thus, the percentage of native white women of native parentage engaged in gainful occupations in 1920 was practically as high in Atlanta (30.4) and in Richmond (30.2) as it was in Detroit (30.4) and Pittsburgh (30.6), and as high in Dallas (32.4) as it was in Grand Rapids (32.4). (See Table 157, p. 270.)

As shown by Table 61, the total number of native white women of native parentage reported at the census of 1920 as engaged in gainful occupations included 486,407—nearly half a million—who were classified as semiskilled operatives in manufacturing pursuits. To any one not familiar with occupation statistics it may be a matter of some surprise that the number of women of native white stock in this class of occupations should be so large. It is a well-known fact that in the history of the New England textile mill industry the native American female labor originally employed and composed largely of the farmers' daughters was early displaced by the influx of immigrants. But that development has not by any means been paralleled in the history of other factory industries; and at the present time 38.2 per cent of the women employed as semiskilled operatives in manufacturing pursuits are native white women of native parentage. Their relative numerical importance varies widely in different sections of the country and in different industries. In the South, where there are comparatively few foreign immigrants in the population, nearly all (97.5 per cent) of the semiskilled women operatives in the cotton mills are of native white stock; while in New England the proportion is only 12.9 per cent. But in the shoe industry of New England the proportion of native white of native parentage among the adult female semiskilled operatives is over one-third (34.2 per cent), which, in view of the fact that only 32.7 per cent of the total number of the women gainfully employed in New England are of native white parentage, would seem to be a due proportion.

TABLE **61.**—PRINCIPAL OCCUPATIONS OF NATIVE WHITE WOMEN OF NATIVE PARENTAGE, WITH PER CENT DISTRIBUTION AND RANK: 1920

OCCUPATION	NATIVE WHITE WOMEN OF NATIVE PARENTAGE 16 YEARS OF AGE AND OVER GAINFULLY EMPLOYED		
	Number	Per cent distribution	Rank
All occupations	3,596,397	100.0	
Semiskilled operatives (manufacturing) (n. o. s.[1])	486,407	13.5	1
Teachers (school)	425,983	11.8	2
Stenographers and typists	302,180	8.4	3
Saleswomen and clerks in stores	284,863	7.9	4
Clerks (except clerks in stores)	262,600	7.3	5
Servants	238,357	6.6	6
Bookkeepers, cashiers, and accountants	194,001	5.4	7
Farm laborers, general farms	151,065	4.2	8
Farmers, general farms	125,872	3.5	9
Dressmakers and seamstresses (not in factory)	110,245	3.1	10
Telephone operators	106,403	3.0	11
Housekeepers and stewardesses	99,910	2.8	12
Trained nurses	80,673	2.2	13
Midwives and nurses (not trained)	67,105	1.9	14
Laborers (manufacturing) (n. o. s.[1])	66,787	1.9	15
Boarding and lodging house keepers	59,862	1.7	16
Waitresses	51,180	1.4	17
Laundresses (not in laundry)	50,279	1.4	18
Musicians and teachers of music	47,382	1.3	19
Milliners and millinery dealers	34,764	1.0	20
Retail dealers	29,220	0.8	21
Laundry operatives	28,103	0.8	22
Religious, charity, and welfare workers	14,770	0.4	23
Forewomen and overseers (manufacturing)	12,479	0.3	24
Telegraph operators	10,696	0.3	25
Barbers, hairdressers, and manicurists	10,579	0.3	26
Agents, canvassers, and collectors	10,022	0.3	27
All other occupations	234,610	6.5	

[1] Not otherwise specified.

The occupation which gives employment to the next largest number of native white women of native parentage is that of teaching school, the number of school teachers, 425,983, being not far below the number of semiskilled factory operatives, 486,407. One-fourth of the total number of native white women of native parentage gainfully employed are included in one or the other of these two leading occupational groups. The occupation next in numerical importance for this class of the population is that of stenographer or typist (302,180), then that of saleswoman or clerk in a store (284,863), followed by that of clerk not in a store (262,600). The five leading occupations here named give employment to nearly one-half of the total number of native white women of native parentage employed in gainful occupations. The occupation which ranks next as regards the number of representatives of this class of the population is that of servant. Here again it may be a matter of surprise to many people that nearly one-fourth (24.3 per cent) of the women servants reported in the census were the daughters of native white parents. The proportion varies widely in different sections of the country as shown by the following table, which, for purposes of comparison, gives percentages for other race and nativity classes:

TABLE **62.**—NUMBER AND PERCENTAGE OF NATIVE WHITE WOMEN OF NATIVE PARENTAGE, AS COMPARED WITH OTHER RACE AND NATIVITY CLASSES, IN THE TOTAL NUMBER OF WOMEN EMPLOYED AS SERVANTS, FOR GEOGRAPHIC SECTIONS AND DIVISIONS: 1920

GEOGRAPHIC SECTION AND DIVISION	WOMEN 16 YEARS OF AGE AND OVER EMPLOYED AS SERVANTS: 1920			PER CENT OF TOTAL		
	Total number [1]	Native white—Native parentage		Native white—Foreign or mixed parentage	Foreign-born white	Negro
		Number	Per cent of total			
United States	981,557	238,357	24.3	14.6	21.2	39.7
The North	585,179	171,346	29.3	21.2	30.9	18.5
New England	76,478	18,190	23.8	17.6	50.7	7.9
Middle Atlantic	249,636	57,852	23.2	15.5	37.4	23.9
East North Central	166,674	61,694	36.6	25.3	21.2	16.4
West North Central	92,391	33,610	36.4	32.6	14.3	16.6
The South	333,611	44,309	13.3	1.7	2.5	82.5
South Atlantic	168,512	20,357	12.1	1.1	2.0	84.8
East South Central	83,734	11,183	13.4	1.0	0.4	85.1
West South Central	81,365	12,769	15.7	3.4	5.7	75.0
The West	62,767	22,702	36.2	21.3	30.1	9.1
Mountain	19,913	8,822	44.3	22.4	22.2	8.7
Pacific	42,854	13,880	32.4	20.8	33.7	9.3

[1] Includes Indians, Chinese, Japanese, and other races.

Doubtless the percentage of women of native white stock among servants is larger in the rural districts than in the cities. The difference can not, however, be determined on the basis of the census, the occupation data not being tabulated separately either for rural districts or for individual cities of less than 25,000 population; but it may be noted, as bearing out the above statement, that in the city of New York only 7.2 per cent of the women servants are native white women of native parentage while in the rest of the State the percentage is 36.5. In Illinois there is a similar contrast between a percentage of 9.5 for Chicago and one of 47.1 for the rest of the State. In Massachusetts the percentage is 7.9 for Boston and 18.2 outside of Boston.

Another occupation in which it might not be supposed that there would be any very large representation of white women of native parentage is that of farm laborer. The number of women of this population class reported in the census of 1920 as farm laborers was, however, 152,768. But of that number 118,119, or about 77 per cent, were reported as employed on the home farm, which means that they were mostly farmers' wives or daughters assisting in the home farm work.

The principal changes between 1910 and 1920 in the relative importance of the nonagricultural occupations in which native white women of native parentage engage are shown by Table 63.

TABLE **63.**—NONAGRICULTURAL PURSUITS SHOWING A LARGE INCREASE OR DECREASE, FROM 1910 TO 1920, IN THE NUMBER OF NATIVE WHITE WOMEN OF NATIVE PARENTAGE GAINFULLY EMPLOYED

OCCUPATION	NATIVE WHITE WOMEN OF NATIVE PARENTAGE 16 YEARS OF AGE AND OVER GAINFULLY EMPLOYED					
	Number		Increase: 1910–1920 [1]		Per cent distribution	
	1920	1910	Number	Per cent	1920	1910
All nonagricultural pursuits	3,293,327	2,388,095	905,232	37.9	100.0	100.0
Clerks (except clerks in stores)	262,600	62,746	199,854	318.5	8.0	2.6
Semiskilled operatives (manufacturing) (n. o. s.[2])	486,407	318,134	168,273	52.9	14.8	13.3
Stenographers and typists	302,180	136,970	165,210	120.6	9.2	5.7
Teachers (school)	425,983	306,920	119,063	38.8	12.9	12.9
Saleswomen and clerks in stores	284,863	171,528	113,335	66.1	8.6	7.2
Bookkeepers, cashiers, and accountants	194,001	93,889	100,112	257.4	5.9	3.9
Telephone operators	106,403	51,783	54,620	105.5	3.2	2.2
Trained nurses	80,673	38,644	42,029	108.8	2.4	1.6
Laborers (manufacturing) (n. o. s.[2])	66,787	28,072	38,715	137.9	2.0	1.2
Midwives and nurses (not trained)	67,105	46,989	20,116	42.8	2.0	2.0
Waitresses	51,180	32,314	18,866	58.4	1.6	1.4
Housekeepers and stewardesses	99,910	87,460	12,450	14.2	3.0	3.7
Religious, charity, and welfare workers	14,770	4,745	10,025	211.3	0.4	0.2
Retail dealers	29,220	20,992	8,228	39.2	0.9	0.9
Telegraph operators	10,696	4,811	5,885	122.3	0.3	0.2
Forewomen and overseers (manufacturing)	12,479	7,380	5,099	69.1	0.4	0.3
Agents, canvassers, and collectors	10,022	5,807	4,215	72.6	0.3	0.2
Laundry operatives	28,103	24,202	3,901	16.1	0.9	1.0
Barbers, hairdressers, and manicurists	10,579	8,242	2,337	28.4	0.3	0.3
Musicians and teachers of music	47,382	55,304	−7,922	−14.3	1.4	2.3
Boarding and lodging house keepers	59,862	70,830	−10,968	−15.5	1.8	3.0
Laundresses (not in laundry)	50,279	74,728	−24,449	−32.7	1.5	3.1
Milliners and millinery dealers	34,766	66,086	−31,322	−47.4	1.1	2.8
Servants	238,357	310,474	−72,117	−23.2	7.2	13.0
Dressmakers and seamstresses (not in factory)	110,245	212,745	−102,500	−48.2	3.3	8.9
All other occupations	208,477	146,300	62,177	42.5	6.3	6.1

[1] A minus (−) sign denotes decrease.   [2] Not otherwise specified.

There were large increases in the number of women of this class employed as clerks (not in stores), as semiskilled operatives in factories, as stenographers, as teachers, as saleswomen and clerks in stores, and as bookkeepers, cashiers, and accountants; and large decreases in the numbers reported as dressmakers (not in factories), servants, milliners, and laundresses (not in laundries). The table thus indicates that the women of native stock shared in and largely determined the general movement of women away from domestic pursuits into office, store, and factory occupations. In 1910 the number of native white women of native parentage employed as clerks (not in stores) or as stenographers or typists or as bookkeepers, cashiers, or accountants—all of which may be termed office employments—was 293,605, which was 12.3 per cent of the total number employed in all occupations outside of agriculture. In 1920—10 years later—the number in these occupations had increased to 758,781 and the percentage of the total to 23.0. In the same interval the corresponding percentage employed as servants, dressmakers, laundresses, and milliners decreased from 27.8 to 13.2.

In the following table all those occupations in which more than 10,000 women were reported at the census of 1920 have been ranked in the order of the percentage of native women of native parentage in the total number of women engaged in the occupation.

The percentage of women of native stock is exceptionally large among postmistresses, teachers, college presidents and professors, and librarians; it is relatively small among farm laborers, servants, charwomen, and janitors, and least among laundresses not in laundries. In general and as would be expected, the women of native white parentage attain their greatest numerical prominence in intellectual pursuits or in occupations requiring more than an ordinary degree of education, and they are less prominent in manual occupations which require little skill and more especially those which are looked upon as menial.

In most occupations the percentage of women of native white parentage was larger in 1920 than in 1910. There are in fact only three occupations in the following list in which the percentage showed a pronounced decrease—namely, the occupation of milliner, that of barber, hairdresser, or manicurist, and that of charwoman.

The percentage of women of native white parentage increased materially in the total number reported in the census as college presidents and professors; nurses, either trained or untrained; saleswomen and clerks in stores; manufacturers and officials or managers in manufacturing enterprises; waitresses; restaurant, café, and lunch room keepers; laborers in manufacturing industries; and retail dealers.

TABLE **64.**—NUMBER AND PERCENTAGE OF NATIVE WHITE WOMEN OF NATIVE PARENTAGE IN THE TOTAL NUMBER OF WOMEN EMPLOYED IN EACH OF THE PRINCIPAL OCCUPATIONS PURSUED BY WOMEN IN 1920, WITH INCREASE OR DECREASE IN THE PERCENTAGE: 1910–1920

OCCUPATION	WOMEN 16 YEARS OF AGE AND OVER ENGAGED IN GAINFUL OCCUPATIONS				
		Native white of native parentage			
	Total number, 1920	Number, 1920	Per cent of total		
			1920	1910	Increase (+) or decrease (−)
All occupations	8, 202, 901	3, 596, 397	43.8	38.3	+5.5
Postmasters	11, 208	8, 791	78.4	78.3	+0.1
College presidents and professors	10, 075	7, 428	73.7	65.0	+8.7
Librarians	13, 502	9, 890	73.2	75.8	−2.6
Farm foremen, general farms	13, 767	9, 917	72.3	70.0	+2.3
Teachers (school)	635, 207	425, 983	67.1	64.4	+2.7
Musicians and teachers of music	72, 431	47, 382	65.4	66.0	−0.6
Agents, canvassers, and collectors	15, 741	10, 022	63.7	66.3	−2.6
Artists, sculptors, and teachers of art	14, 566	9, 275	63.7	67.6	−3.9
Telegraph operators	16, 860	10, 696	63.4	58.7	+4.7
Hotel keepers and managers	14, 134	8, 775	62.1	60.1	+2.0
Compositors, linotypers, and typesetters	11, 306	6, 861	60.7	61.9	−1.2
Telephone operators	175, 469	106, 403	60.6	60.2	+0.4
Clerks (except clerks in stores)	463, 570	262, 600	56.6	52.6	+4.0
Trained nurses	143, 664	80, 673	56.2	50.5	+5.7
Actresses and showwomen	14, 220	7, 920	55.7	53.6	+2.1
Saleswomen and clerks in stores	514, 056	284, 863	55.4	48.9	+6.5
Religious, charity, and welfare workers	26, 927	14, 770	54.9	53.5	+1.4
Bookkeepers, cashiers, and accountants	356, 603	194, 001	54.4	50.7	+3.7
Stenographers and typists	559, 748	302, 180	54.0	52.4	+1.6
Boarding and lodging house keepers	114, 740	59, 862	52.2	49.7	+2.5
Manufacturers, officials, and managers (manufacturing)	13, 276	6, 863	51.7	44.1	+7.6
Farmers	253, 836	129, 451	51.0	51.6	−0.6
Milliners and millinery dealers	69, 598	34, 764	49.9	54.4	−4.5
Housekeepers and stewardesses	204, 350	99, 910	48.9	50.5	−1.6
Midwives and nurses (not trained)	137, 431	67, 105	48.8	40.2	+8.6
Dressmakers and seamstresses (not in factory)	235, 519	110, 245	46.8	47.6	−0.8
Waitresses	114, 718	51, 180	44.6	38.7	+5.9
Restaurant, café, and lunch room keepers	15, 644	6, 550	41.9	34.5	+7.4
Laborers (manufacturing) (n. o. s.[1])	160, 133	66, 787	41.7	35.1	+6.6
Forewomen and overseers (manufacturing)	30, 171	12, 479	41.4	37.4	+4.0
Semiskilled operatives (manufacturing) (n. o. s.[1])	1, 274, 719	486, 407	38.2	33.3	+4.9
Retail dealers	78, 957	29, 220	37.0	31.3	+5.7
Laundry operatives	78, 548	28, 103	35.8	33.0	+2.8
Barbers, hairdressers, and manicurists	33, 091	10, 579	32.0	37.4	−5.4
Farm laborers	605, 668	152, 768	25.2	28.0	−2.8
Tailoresses	31, 828	7, 858	24.7	22.4	+2.3
Servants	981, 557	238, 357	24.3	25.1	−0.8
Janitors and sextons	28, 929	6, 235	21.6	18.0	+3.6
Charwomen and cleaners	24, 744	4, 250	17.2	22.8	−5.6
Laundresses (not in laundry)	383, 622	50, 279	13.1	14.6	−1.5
All other occupations	248, 768	128, 715	51.7	49.9	+1.8

[1] Not otherwise specified.

XI

NATIVE WHITE WOMEN OF FOREIGN OR MIXED PARENTAGE IN GAINFUL OCCUPATIONS

The native white women of foreign or mixed parentage are the grown-up children of immigrants. Born and reared in this country but having parents one or both of whom were aliens by birth, they may be said to constitute the present-day first generation of native Americans. Compared with the native white of native parentage they are concentrated to a much greater extent in the eastern industrial districts and in cities. In fact, of the total native white population of foreign or mixed parentage, 54.3 per cent in 1920 were resident in northern and eastern cities—using that term to designate all cities of over 2,500 population in New England and the Middle Atlantic and East North Central divisions—while the corresponding percentage for the native white of native parentage was only 23.6. As a class, the native white women of foreign or mixed parentage are somewhat younger than those of native parentage and include a considerably larger percentage of single women.

These differences in age composition, marital status, and geographic distribution—and particularly the last named—go far toward accounting for the fact that the percentage gainfully employed is so much larger for native white women of foreign or mixed parentage (29.2 per cent) than it is for those of native parentage (20 per cent). At the same time, it is probable that as compared with the women of native stock, the women whose parents were immigrants are, as a class, not so well to do and are therefore more frequently under the necessity of earning money, either to support themselves or to contribute to the support of their families.

The difference as regards the percentage gainfully employed is no less striking when the two classes are compared by geographic divisions. In New England, for instance, 44 per cent of the daughters of immigrants are wage earners, as compared with 28.1 per cent of the women of native parentage. In the Middle Atlantic division the percentages are, respectively, 34.8 and 25.6; in the South, 22.7 and 16.1. But when the comparison is restricted to the large cities the difference becomes less pronounced. (See Ch. II.) In cities of more than 100,000 population the percentage of the native white women of foreign or mixed parentage gainfully employed, 37.4, is not greatly in excess of the corresponding percentage for the women of native parentage, 33.2.

The native white women of foreign or mixed parentage comprise 24.9 per cent, or nearly one-fourth, of the total number of women gainfully employed in 1920, as shown by the figures in Table 65.

TABLE 65.—NUMBER AND PERCENTAGE OF NATIVE WHITE WOMEN OF FOREIGN OR MIXED PARENTAGE IN THE TOTAL NUMBER OF WOMEN ENGAGED IN GAINFUL OCCUPATIONS: 1890–1920

CENSUS YEAR	WOMEN 16 YEARS OF AGE AND OVER ENGAGED IN GAINFUL OCCUPATIONS		
	Total number	Native white—Foreign or mixed parentage	
		Number	Per cent of total
1920	8,202,901	2,042,804	24.9
1910	7,438,686	1,633,076	22.0
1900	4,833,630	1,090,744	22.6
1890	3,596,615	751,016	20.9

In the North, in the total number of women gainfully employed, the percentage of native white women of foreign or mixed parentage is 33.8, and in the West, 28.7; but in the South it is only 4.5, these differences, of course, reflecting differences in the composition of the total population.

TABLE 66.—NUMBER AND PERCENTAGE OF NATIVE WHITE WOMEN OF FOREIGN OR MIXED PARENTAGE ENGAGED IN GAINFUL OCCUPATIONS, AS COMPARED WITH THEIR PROPORTION IN THE TOTAL POPULATION, BY GEOGRAPHIC SECTIONS AND DIVISIONS: 1920

GEOGRAPHIC SECTION AND DIVISION	NATIVE WHITE WOMEN OF FOREIGN OR MIXED PARENTAGE 16 YEARS OF AGE AND OVER: 1920				
	Total number	Engaged in gainful occupations			Per cent of total women in the population
		Number	Per cent of total number	Per cent of total women gainfully occupied	
United States	6,990,685	2,042,804	29.2	24.9	20.4
The North	5,800,131	1,760,286	30.3	33.8	27.1
New England	725,971	319,283	44.0	37.7	27.7
Middle Atlantic	1,951,208	679,431	34.8	32.9	25.7
East North Central	1,949,781	513,449	26.3	33.4	27.2
West North Central	1,173,171	248,123	21.1	32.6	29.0
The South	479,802	108,847	22.7	4.5	4.8
South Atlantic	181,354	50,405	27.8	4.4	4.2
East South Central	83,794	19,034	22.7	3.0	3.1
West South Central	214,654	39,408	18.4	6.5	7.1
The West	710,752	173,671	24.4	28.7	25.0
Mountain	229,847	46,675	20.3	26.8	23.7
Pacific	480,905	126,996	26.4	29.5	25.7

Of the 2,042,804 native white women of foreign or mixed parentage reported in the census of 1920 as engaged in gainful occupations, 436,889, or more than one-fifth, of the total were semiskilled operatives in manufacturing industries. About half as many, 223,735, were stenographers and typists, 171,600 were saleswomen and clerks in stores, 169,747 were clerks not in stores, and 153,716 were schoolteachers. These five occupational groups comprise 56.6 per cent of the total number of native white women of foreign or mixed parentage reported in all occupations. The five leading occupations here designated are the same as those for the native white women of native parentage. (See p. 88.) The occupation of semiskilled operatives heads the list in both cases but includes 13.5 per cent, or less than one-eighth, of the gainfully employed white women of native parentage as compared with 21.4 per cent, or more than one-fifth, of those of foreign or mixed parentage. Teaching school, which ranks second among the occupations followed by the women of native parentage, ranks fifth for those of foreign or mixed parentage, or 11.8 per cent of the total number gainfully occupied in the one case as compared with 7.5 per cent in the other.

TABLE 67.—PRINCIPAL OCCUPATIONS OF NATIVE WHITE WOMEN OF FOREIGN OR MIXED PARENTAGE, WITH PER CENT DISTRIBUTION AND RANK: 1920

OCCUPATION	NATIVE WHITE WOMEN OF FOREIGN OR MIXED PARENTAGE 16 YEARS OF AGE AND OVER GAINFULLY EMPLOYED		
	Number.	Per cent distribution	Rank
All occupations	2,042,804	100.0	
Semiskilled operatives (manufacturing) (n. o. s.[1])	436,889	21.4	1
Stenographers and typists	223,735	11.0	2
Saleswomen and clerks in stores	171,600	8.4	3
Clerks (except clerks in stores)	169,747	8.3	4
Teachers (school)	153,716	7.5	5
Servants	143,208	7.0	6
Bookkeepers, cashiers, and accountants	132,898	6.5	7
Telephone operators	61,654	3.0	8
Dressmakers and seamstresses (not in factory)	60,526	3.0	9
Housekeepers and stewardesses	50,462	2.5	10
Trained nurses	38,138	1.9	11
Laborers (manufacturing) (n. o. s.[1])	33,930	1.7	12
Midwives and nurses (not trained)	29,976	1.5	13
Waitresses	26,387	1.3	14
Milliners and millinery dealers	24,234	1.2	15
Boarding and lodging house keepers	21,266	1.0	16
Farmers, general farms	20,762	1.0	17
Retail dealers	19,535	1.0	18
Musicians and teachers of music	18,528	0.9	19
Laundresses (not in laundry)	18,204	0.9	20
Laundry operatives	17,366	0.9	21
Farm laborers, general farms	17,363	0.8	22
Forewomen and overseers (manufacturing)	13,199	0.6	23
Tailoresses	10,752	0.5	24
All other occupations	128,729	6.3	

[1] Not otherwise specified.

Comparatively few, only 2.3 per cent, of the native white women of foreign or mixed parentage engaged in gainful occupations have taken up agricultural pursuits. The corresponding percentage for the native white of native parentage is 8.4. The occupation of farm laborer, which ranks eighth in the list of principal occupations for white women of native parentage, is the twenty-second occupation in the corresponding list for those of foreign or mixed parentage; and the occupation of farmer (general farm), ranking ninth in the former list, is seventeenth in the latter.

As shown by Table 68 the number of women of foreign or mixed parentage employed as clerks (not including clerks in stores) increased from 46,783 in 1910 to 169,747 in 1920, which is the largest numerical increase (122,964) as well as the largest percentage of increase (262.8 per cent) shown for this class of women in any of the occupations listed in the preceding table. The number employed as stenographers or typists increased by 115,018, or 105.8 per cent. The next largest numerical increase was that of 98,431 in the number employed as semiskilled operatives in manufacturing industries, which, however, represented a percentage increase of only 29.1. There was a decrease of 65,345, or 51.9 per cent, in the number of dressmakers or seamstresses (not in factories) in this population class, a decrease of 56,834, or 28.4 per cent, in the number of servants; of 16,631, or 40.7 per cent, in the number of milliners, and of 9,488, or 34.3 per cent, in the number of laundresses not in laundries.

TABLE 68.—NONAGRICULTURAL PURSUITS SHOWING A LARGE INCREASE OR DECREASE, FROM 1910 TO 1920, IN THE NUMBER OF NATIVE WHITE WOMEN OF FOREIGN OR MIXED PARENTAGE GAINFULLY EMPLOYED

OCCUPATION	NATIVE WHITE WOMEN OF FOREIGN OR MIXED PARENTAGE 16 YEARS OF AGE AND OVER GAINFULLY EMPLOYED					
	Number		Increase: 1910–1920 [1]		Per cent distribution	
	1920	1910	Number	Per cent	1920	1910
All nonagricultural pursuits	1,996,811	1,574,162	422,649	26.8	100.0	100.0
Clerks (except clerks in stores)	169,747	46,783	122,964	262.8	8.5	3.0
Stenographers and typists	223,735	108,717	115,018	105.8	11.2	6.9
Semiskilled operatives (manufacturing) (n. o. s.[2])	436,889	338,458	98,431	29.1	21.9	21.5
Bookkeepers, cashiers, and accountants	132,898	75,331	57,567	76.4	6.7	4.8
Saleswomen and clerks in stores	171,600	138,555	33,045	23.8	8.6	8.8
Teachers (school)	153,716	122,612	31,104	25.4	7.7	7.8
Telephone operators	61,654	30,933	30,721	99.3	3.1	2.0
Trained nurses	38,138	18,881	19,257	101.9	1.9	1.2
Laborers (manufacturing) (n. o. s.[2])	33,930	20,624	13,306	64.5	1.7	1.3
Housekeepers and stewardesses	50,462	40,380	10,082	25.0	2.5	2.6
Midwives and nurses (not trained)	29,976	22,806	7,170	31.4	1.5	1.4
Waitresses	26,387	21,018	5,369	25.5	1.3	1.3
Forewomen and overseers (manufacturing)	13,199	9,073	4,126	45.5	0.7	0.6
Retail dealers	19,535	15,841	3,694	23.3	1.0	1.0
Musicians and teachers of music	18,528	21,210	−2,682	−12.6	0.9	1.3
Tailoresses	10,752	14,689	−3,937	−26.8	0.5	0.9
Boarding and lodging house keepers	21,266	24,427	−3,161	−12.9	1.1	1.6
Laundry operatives	17,366	22,410	−5,044	−22.5	0.9	1.4
Laundresses (not in laundry)	18,204	27,692	−9,488	−34.3	0.9	1.8
Milliners and millinery dealers	24,234	40,865	−16,631	−40.7	1.2	2.6
Servants	143,208	200,042	−56,834	−28.4	7.2	12.7
Dressmakers and seamstresses (not in factory)	60,526	125,871	−65,345	−51.9	3.0	8.0
All other occupations	120,861	86,944	33,917	39.0	6.1	5.5

[1] A minus sign (−) denotes decrease.   [2] Not otherwise specified.

Thus, it is evident that the women who were the daughters of immigrants, like the women of native parentage, are taking up clerical pursuits and similar occupations in preference to domestic service.

As shown by the following table, which lists all occupations in which more than 10,000 women were engaged, native white women of foreign or mixed parentage, while including 24.9 per cent, or very nearly one-fourth, of the total number of women engaged in gainful occupations, included 34.3 per cent, or more than one-third, of the semiskilled women operatives in manufacturing industries and a still larger percentage of the women employed as stenographers and typists; bookkeepers, cashiers, and accountants; clerks (not in stores); telephone operators; and milliners and millinery dealers. The percentage reaches its maximum—43.7—in the occupation of forewomen and overseers in manufacturing industries. The women of foreign or mixed parentage comprise a due proportion of the women school-teachers, the percentage, 24.2, being not far below the percentage which this class forms of the total number of women gainfully employed. But in the field of higher education, as represented by college presidents and professors, their percentage falls off to 16.9. They come far short of contributing their due proportion of servants, their percentage of the total number of servants being only 14.6, or about one in seven.

Although the percentage of white women of foreign or mixed parentage in the total number of gainfully employed women increased between 1910 and 1920, in about one-half of the occupations listed in Table 69 the percentage shows a decrease. The decrease was rather marked among laundry operatives, barbers, hairdressers, and manicurists, saleswomen and clerks in stores, and laborers in manufacturing industries. In most of the occupations, however, there was not much change in the relative numerical importance of this class of workers.

6436°—29——8

TABLE 69.—NUMBER AND PERCENTAGE OF NATIVE WHITE WOMEN OF FOREIGN OR MIXED PARENTAGE IN THE TOTAL NUMBER OF WOMEN EMPLOYED, IN EACH OF THE PRINCIPAL OCCUPATIONS PURSUED BY WOMEN IN 1920, WITH INCREASE OR DECREASE IN THE PERCENTAGE: 1910–1920

	WOMEN 16 YEARS OF AGE AND OVER ENGAGED IN GAINFUL OCCUPATIONS				
OCCUPATION	Total number, 1920	Native white of foreign or mixed parentage			Increase (+) or decrease (−)
		Number, 1920	Per cent of total		
			1920	1910	
All occupations	8, 202, 901	2, 042, 804	24. 9	22. 0	+2. 9
Forewomen and overseers (manufacturing)	30, 171	13, 199	43. 7	46. 0	−2. 3
Stenographers and typists	559, 748	223, 735	40. 0	41. 6	−1. 6
Bookkeepers, cashiers, and accountants	356, 603	132, 898	37. 3	40. 7	−3. 4
Clerks (except clerks in stores)	463, 570	169, 747	36. 6	39. 2	−2. 6
Telephone operators	175, 469	61, 654	35. 1	35. 9	−0. 8
Milliners and millinery dealers	69, 598	24, 234	34. 8	33. 6	+1. 2
Semiskilled operatives (manufacturing) (n. o. s.[1])	1, 274, 719	436, 889	34. 3	35. 4	−1. 1
Tailoresses	31, 828	10, 752	33. 8	36. 4	−2. 6
Saleswomen and clerks in stores	514, 056	171, 600	33. 4	39. 5	−6. 1
Telegraph operators	16, 860	5, 275	31. 3	35. 1	−3. 8
Manufacturers, officials, and managers (manufacturing)	13, 276	4, 111	31. 0	27. 7	+3. 3
Compositors, linotypers, and typesetters	11, 306	3, 488	30. 9	31. 7	−0. 8
Actresses and showwomen	14, 220	3, 800	26. 7	26. 7	--------
Trained nurses	143, 664	38, 138	26. 5	24. 7	+1. 8
Artists, sculptors, and teachers of art	14, 566	3, 767	25. 9	23. 2	+2. 7
Dressmakers and seamstresses (not in factory)	235, 519	60, 526	25. 7	28. 2	−2. 5
Musicians and teachers of music	72, 431	18, 528	25. 6	25. 3	+0. 3
Agents, canvassers, and collectors	15, 741	3, 966	25. 2	21. 9	+3. 3
Housekeepers and stewardesses	204, 350	50, 462	24. 7	23. 3	+1. 4
Retail dealers	78, 957	19, 535	24. 7	23. 6	+1. 1
Religious, charity, and welfare workers	26, 927	6, 513	24. 2	21. 2	+3. 0
Teachers (school)	635, 207	153, 716	24. 2	25. 7	−1. 5
Waitresses	114, 718	26, 387	23. 0	25. 1	−2. 1
Librarians	13, 502	3, 006	22. 3	19. 9	+2. 4
Laundry operatives	78, 548	17, 366	22. 1	30. 5	−8. 4
Midwives and nurses (not trained)	137, 431	29, 976	21. 8	19. 5	+2. 3
Laborers (manufacturing) (n. o. s.[1])	160, 133	33, 930	21. 2	25. 8	−4. 6
Hotel keepers and managers	14, 134	2, 932	20. 7	20. 8	−0. 1
Janitors and sextons	28, 929	5, 913	20. 4	24. 0	−3. 6
Barbers, hairdressers, and manicurists	33, 091	6, 224	18. 8	27. 6	−8. 8
Restaurant, café, and lunch room keepers	15, 644	2, 889	18. 5	18. 4	+0. 1
Boarding and lodging house keepers	114, 740	21, 266	18. 5	17. 2	+1. 3
Postmasters	11, 208	2, 063	18. 4	16. 9	+1. 5
Charwomen and cleaners	24, 744	4, 397	17. 8	17. 7	+0. 1
College presidents and professors	10, 075	1, 700	16. 9	19. 5	−2. 6
Servants	981, 557	143, 208	14. 6	16. 2	−1. 6
Farm foremen, general farms	13, 767	1, 911	13. 9	12. 6	+1. 3
Farmers	253, 836	22, 252	8. 8	7. 6	+1. 2
Laundresses (not in laundry)	383, 622	18, 204	4. 7	5. 4	−0. 7
Farm laborers	605, 668	18, 130	3. 0	3. 2	−0. 2
All other occupations	248, 768	64, 517	25. 9	28. 2	−2. 3

[1] Not otherwise specified.

XII
FOREIGN-BORN WHITE WOMEN IN GAINFUL OCCUPATIONS

It is necessary, occasionally, to remind oneself and others that the foreign-born population of the United States is a composite group of widely differing races and nationalities. To such an extent is this the case that generalizations based on total figures for all foreign born combined do not, as a rule, hold good even approximately for any of the constituent classes of which the total is composed. However, as regards the occupations of the foreign born, the only up-to-date statements that can be made relate to the foreign born as a whole, as there has been no tabulation of the census occupation data by country of birth since the census of 1900.

Of the foreign-born white females (of all ages) in the United States, 15 per cent are presumably of English or Scotch stock, having been born either in England or Scotland or Canada (excluding French-Canadians), 9.4 per cent are natives of Ireland, 7.1 per cent came from Norway or Sweden, and 12.9 per cent from Germany.

The total number coming from the countries above mentioned and from other countries of northwestern Europe represents 49.6 per cent—practically one-half—of the total number of white women of foreign birth in the United States in 1920.

The immigration from central, southern, and eastern Europe prior to 1920 came largely from three countries—Italy, Russia, and Poland—these countries contributing, respectively, 10.5, 10.1, and 8.0 per cent of the total number of white females of foreign birth in the United States in 1920.

The other European countries from which there is a considerable number of immigrants include Austria, Czechoslovakia, Hungary, and Finland. The total number of female immigrants from these four countries constituted 10.7 per cent of the total foreign-born white female population. No other European country contributed as much as 1 per cent of the total.

The French-Canadian female immigrants constitute 2.4 per cent of the total foreign-born white female population, and the Mexican 3.3 per cent.

TABLE 70.—COUNTRY OF BIRTH OF FOREIGN-BORN WHITE FEMALES, IN THE
UNITED STATES: 1920

COUNTRY OF BIRTH	Number	Per cent distri- bution	COUNTRY OF BIRTH	Number	Per cent distri- bution
All countries	6,184,432	100.0	Europe—Continued.		
			Eastern Europe	790,498	12.8
Europe	5,310,397	85.9	Russia	626,476	10.1
			Finland	64,537	1.0
Northwestern Europe	2,644,856	42.8	Other countries	99,485	1.6
England	387,790	6.3			
Scotland	120,612	2.0	Southern Europe	725,802	11.7
Ireland	581,662	9.4	Italy	651,835	10.5
Norway	161,105	2.6	Other countries	73,967	1.2
Sweden	280,647	4.5			
Denmark	75,091	1.2	Other Europe	2,236	(¹)
France	73,539	1.2			
Germany	794,813	12.9	Asia	38,677	0.6
Other countries	169,597	2.7			
			America	804,969	13.0
Central Europe	1,147,005	18.5			
Poland	493,591	8.0	Canada—French	150,038	2.4
Czechoslovakia	166,185	2.7	Canada—Other	420,483	6.8
Austria	252,174	4.1	Mexico	206,819	3.3
Hungary	180,368	2.9	Other countries	27,629	0.4
Yugoslavia	54,687	0.9			
			All other countries	30,389	0.5

¹ Less than one-tenth of 1 per cent.

The number of foreign-born white women of all nationalities
reported in the census of 1920 as having a gainful occupation was
1,102,697, which represents 13.4 per cent, or rather more than one-
eighth, of the total number of gainfully employed women.

TABLE 71.—NUMBER AND PERCENTAGE OF FOREIGN-BORN WHITE WOMEN
ENGAGED IN GAINFUL OCCUPATIONS, AS COMPARED WITH THEIR PROPORTION
IN THE TOTAL POPULATION, BY GEOGRAPHIC SECTIONS AND DIVISIONS: 1920

GEOGRAPHIC SECTION AND DIVISION	FOREIGN-BORN WHITE WOMEN 16 YEARS OF AGE AND OVER: 1920				
	Total number	Engaged in gainful occupations			Per cent of total women in the popula- tion
		Number	Per cent of total num- ber	Per cent of total women gainfully occupied	
United States	5,872,366	1,102,697	18.8	13.4	17.1
The North	4,999,000	953,351	19.1	18.3	23.4
New England	883,012	235,944	26.7	27.9	33.7
Middle Atlantic	2,192,814	447,418	20.4	21.7	28.9
East North Central	1,350,733	203,396	15.1	13.2	18.9
West North Central	572,441	66,593	11.6	8.8	14.1
The South	319,984	55,149	17.2	2.3	3.2
South Atlantic	123,858	28,477	19.0	2.0	2.9
East South Central	28,671	4,426	15.4	0.7	1.1
West South Central	167,455	27,246	16.3	4.5	5.5
The West	553,382	94,197	17.0	15.6	19.5
Mountain	163,640	22,920	14.0	13.2	16.9
Pacific	389,742	71,277	18.3	16.5	20.8

Over three-fifths (62 per cent) of the foreign-born white women reported as gainfully employed were in the New England and Middle Atlantic divisions, and in these divisions the percentage which they formed of the total number of women gainfully employed is exceptionally high, 27.9 in New England and 21.7 in the Middle Atlantic division, or more than one woman in four in the one case and more than one in five in the other.

The percentage of foreign-born whites among women workers decreased somewhat gradually from approximately 20.4 in 1890 to 13.4 in 1920. In the main, this was the result of a corresponding decrease in the percentage which foreign-born whites constituted of the total female population 16 years of age and over—from 19.9 per cent in 1890 to 17.1 per cent in 1920. But during the decade 1910 to 1920 there was a decrease also in the proportion of foreign-born white women gainfully occupied—a decrease from 22.1 per cent in 1910 to 18.8 per cent in 1920. (See p. 102.) That is to say, in 1920 as compared with 1910 there was a smaller proportion of foreign born in the total female population and at the same time a smaller proportion of the foreign born were gainfully employed.

TABLE 72.—NUMBER AND PERCENTAGE OF FOREIGN-BORN WHITE WOMEN IN THE TOTAL NUMBER OF WOMEN ENGAGED IN GAINFUL OCCUPATIONS, AS COMPARED WITH THEIR PROPORTION IN THE TOTAL POPULATION: 1890–1920

CENSUS YEAR	WOMEN 16 YEARS OF AGE AND OVER			
	Engaged in gainful occupations			Per cent of foreign-born white women in the population
	Total number	Foreign-born white		
		Number	Per cent of total	
1920	8,202,901	1,102,697	13.4	17.1
1910	7,438,686	1,195,953	16.1	18.5
1900	4,833,630	840,011	17.4	18.7
1890	[1] 3,712,144	[1] 756,006	[1] 20.4	19.9

[1] The figures for 1890 cover the number 15 years of age and over instead of 16 years of age and over.

As shown by the following summary, the percentage of foreign-born white women engaged in gainful occupations declined slightly between 1890 and 1900, increased considerably between 1900 and 1910, and then declined quite markedly between 1910 and 1920. The percentage in 1920, it may be noted, was slightly lower than in 1890—30 years before.

TABLE 73.—NUMBER AND PERCENTAGE OF FOREIGN-BORN WHITE WOMEN
ENGAGED IN GAINFUL OCCUPATIONS: 1890–1920

| CENSUS YEAR | FOREIGN-BORN WHITE WOMEN 16 YEARS OF AGE AND OVER | | |
| | Total number | Engaged in gainful occupations | |
		Number	Per cent of total
1920	5,872,366	1,102,697	18.8
1910	5,408,190	1,195,953	22.1
1900	4,403,494	840,011	19.1
1890	1 3,809,919	1 756,006	1 19.8

1 The figures for 1890 cover the number 15 years of age and over, instead of 16 years and over.

The increase from 1900 to 1910 in the percentage of foreign-born white women reported as engaged in gainful occupations corresponds with a similar increase for every other population class, indicating that foreign-born white women contributed to the general increase that took place during this decade in the extent to which women were engaging in gainful occupations. (See p. 22.) Since comparatively few foreign-born women take up agricultural pursuits, it is hardly probable that the percentage reported as gainfully employed was affected appreciably by the changes in the census definitions of farmer and farm laborer as applied to women. (See p. 17.)

The marked decline between 1910 and 1920 in the percentage of foreign-born white women engaged in gainful occupations was largely the result of the change in the age distribution of foreign-born white women, brought about by the practical cessation of immigration to the United States during the World War. Since the arriving women immigrants are mostly young women, and since the women who engage in gainful occupations are likewise mostly young women, it was to be expected that with the cessation of immigration the number of young women in the foreign-born population of the United States would decrease and that there would consequently be a decrease in the percentage of foreign-born women gainfully employed.

The change in the age composition of the foreign-born white here referred to is shown in Table 15, Chapter III. The number of women 16 to 24 years of age in the foreign-born white population fell off from 890,352 to 696,909, a decrease of 21.7 per cent; and the proportion under the age of 25 in the total number of foreign-born white women 16 years of age and over decreased from 16.5 per cent in 1910 to 11.9 per cent in 1920. Such a striking change as this in the age composition of any class of women would almost inevitably produce a decrease in the proportion employed in gainful occupations. The check to immigration, however, had a still further effect upon employment in that it reduced the number and proportion of single women among the foreign born—a natural result of the fact that among the foreign born the single are recruited only through immigration, while the married are recruited partly through the immigration of married women and partly through the marriage of single immigrant women already in this country; and the latter source of increase in the number married may continue to be operative for a considerable period after immigration ceases. Thus, while the number of foreign-born white women who were single decreased by 16.9 per cent between 1910 and 1920, the number who were married increased by 13.8 per cent in the same period, as shown by the following table:

TABLE 74.—TOTAL FOREIGN-BORN WHITE WOMEN CLASSIFIED BY MARITAL CONDITION FOR 1920 AND 1910, WITH INCREASE OR DECREASE, AND WITH PER CENT DISTRIBUTION

MARITAL CLASS	FOREIGN-BORN WHITE WOMEN 16 YEARS OF AGE AND OVER					
	Number		Increase (+) or decrease (−)		Per cent distribution	
	1920	1910	Number	Per cent	1920	1910
All classes	5,872,366	5,408,190	+464,176	+8.6	100.0	100.0
Single	794,781	956,649	−161,868	−16.9	13.5	17.7
Married	4,122,932	3,623,544	+499,388	+13.8	70.2	67.0
Widowed or divorced	946,881	820,632	+126,249	+15.4	16.1	15.2
Unknown	7,772	7,365	+407	+5.5	0.1	0.1

In view of these decreases in the proportion of young women and of single women in this class of the population, it is not surprising that the proportion gainfully employed, as already noted, decreased from 22.1 per cent in 1910 to 18.8 per cent in 1920. A computation which is given in the Appendix (p. 161) shows that if the distribution of foreign-born white females by age and marital condition had been the same in 1920 as it was in 1910, then without any change in the proportion gainfully occupied in each age period and marital class, the proportion of foreign-born white women 16 years of age and over gainfully occupied in 1920 would have been 21.7 per cent instead of 18.8 per cent as actually reported. The percentage thus arrived at, it may be noted, is only slightly below the percentage for 1910 (22.1), and so substantiates the conclusion that the decrease in the percentage of foreign-born white women gainfully employed was largely the result of the decrease noted in the proportion of young and of single women in this class of the population.

PRINCIPAL OCCUPATIONS OF FOREIGN-BORN WHITE WOMEN

While the activities of the 1,102,697 foreign-born white women gainfully employed extended over a wide range of occupations and into practically all divisions of the occupational field, more than 9 out of 10 of these breadwinners (1,017,927, or 92.3 per cent) were employed in one or another of the 22 occupations or occupation groups listed in the following table:

TABLE 75.—PRINCIPAL OCCUPATIONS OF FOREIGN-BORN WHITE WOMEN, WITH PER CENT DISTRIBUTION AND RANK, FOR THE UNITED STATES: 1920

| OCCUPATION | FOREIGN-BORN WHITE WOMEN 16 YEARS OF AGE AND OVER GAINFULLY EMPLOYED | | |
	Number	Per cent distribution	Rank
All occupations	1,102,697	100.0	
Semiskilled operatives (manufacturing) (n. o. s.[1])	307,339	27.9	1
Servants	207,811	18.8	2
Saleswomen and clerks in stores	52,720	4.8	3
Housekeepers and stewardesses	40,232	3.6	4
Dressmakers and seamstresses (not in factory)	37,479	3.4	5
Laundresses (not in laundry)	32,763	3.0	6
Stenographers and typists	31,768	2.9	7
Bookkeepers, cashiers, and accountants	27,979	2.5	8
Clerks (except clerks in stores)	27,752	2.5	9
Retail dealers	26,939	2.4	10
Laborers (manufacturing) (n. o. s.[1])	26,605	2.4	11
Midwives and nurses (not trained)	26,327	2.4	12
Teachers (school)	26,032	2.4	13
Boarding and lodging house keepers	23,950	2.2	14
Waitresses	23,039	2.1	15
Trained nurses	21,556	2.0	16
Farmers, general farms	19,876	1.8	17
Tailoresses	12,505	1.1	18
Laundry operatives	12,267	1.1	19
Farm laborers, general farms	11,653	1.1	20
Janitors and sextons	11,329	1.0	21
Milliners and millinery dealers	10,006	0.9	22
All other occupations	84,770	7.7	

[1] Not otherwise specified.

Considerably over one-fourth (27.9 per cent) of the gainfully occupied foreign-born white women are semiskilled factory operatives, who are employed in a variety of specific occupations, pursued in many different industries. Taken together, however, they form a group which, broadly considered, is occupationally homogeneous. If to these semiskilled operatives be added the laborers in manufacturing industries, the total represents 30.3 per cent of the gainfully occupied foreign-born white women. In other words more than 3 out of 10 of the immigrant white women at work in gainful occupations are either semiskilled operatives or laborers in mills and factories.

The occupation second in importance for this class is that of servant, 18.8 per cent of the total number of gainfully occupied foreign-born white women being employed in that occupation. Thus, almost one-half (49.1 per cent) of the total number of occupied immigrant women are either factory employees or servants.

The third occupation in point of numbers—that of saleswomen and clerks in stores—falls far below the first two, giving employment to only 4.8 per cent of the foreign-born white women workers, while none of the remaining occupations represented as large a proportion as 4 per cent, or 1 in 25. No clerical or professional pursuit, it will be noted, included as many as 3 per cent of the total.

The following table shows by occupation the increase or decrease from 1910 to 1920 in the number of foreign-born white women employed in nonagricultural pursuits:

TABLE 76.—NONAGRICULTURAL PURSUITS SHOWING A LARGE INCREASE OR DECREASE FROM 1910 TO 1920 IN THE NUMBER OF FOREIGN-BORN WHITE WOMEN EMPLOYED

	FOREIGN-BORN WHITE WOMEN 16 YEARS OF AGE AND OVER GAINFULLY EMPLOYED					
OCCUPATION	Number		Increase: 1910–1920 [1]		Per cent distribution	
	1920	1910	Number	Per cent	1920	1910
All nonagricultural pursuits	1,064,724	1,140,078	−75,354	−6.6	100.0	100.0
Semiskilled operatives (manufacturing) (n. o. s.[2])	307,339	279,958	27,381	9.8	28.9	24.6
Clerks (except clerks in stores)	27,752	8,886	18,866	212.3	2.6	0.8
Stenographers and typists	31,768	14,698	17,070	116.1	3.0	1.3
Saleswomen and clerks in stores	52,720	38,367	14,353	37.4	4.9	3.4
Bookkeepers, cashiers, and accountants	27,979	15,135	12,844	84.9	2.6	1.3
Laborers (manufacturing) (n. o. s.[2])	26,605	19,320	7,285	37.7	2.5	1.7
Housekeepers and stewardesses	40,232	35,087	5,145	14.7	3.8	3.1
Trained nurses	21,556	16,770	4,786	28.5	2.0	1.5
Teachers (school)	26,032	24,439	1,593	6.5	2.4	2.1
Janitors and sextons	11,329	9,943	1,386	13.9	1.1	0.9
Waitresses	23,039	22,920	119	0.5	2.2	2.0
Retail dealers	26,939	27,121	−182	−0.7	2.5	2.4
Midwives and nurses (not trained)	26,327	27,687	−1,360	−4.9	2.5	2.4
Laundry operatives	12,267	14,720	−2,453	−16.7	1.2	1.3
Milliners and millinery dealers	10,006	13,513	−3,507	−26.0	0.9	1.2
Tailoresses	12,505	16,213	−3,708	−22.9	1.2	1.4
Boarding and lodging house keepers	23,950	37,790	−13,840	−36.5	2.2	3.3
Laundresses (not in laundry)	32,763	53,523	−20,760	−38.8	3.1	4.7
Dressmakers and seamstresses (not in factory)	37,479	69,293	−31,814	−45.9	3.5	6.1
Servants	207,811	333,011	−125,200	−37.6	19.5	29.1
All other occupations	78,326	61,684	16,642	27.0	7.4	5.4

[1] A minus sign (−) denotes decrease.   [2] Not otherwise specified.

The figures here presented indicate that the foreign-born white women participated to some extent in the general movement away from domestic service and allied occupations into industrial and clerical pursuits. But the fact that the decrease in the numbers employed as servants, dressmakers, laundresses, etc., was not, as was the case with both classes of native white women, more than offset by an increase in the numbers employed in other occupations, indicates that it was caused in part by a decrease in the total number of foreign-born women available for employment of any kind.

TABLE 77.—NUMBER AND PERCENTAGE OF FOREIGN-BORN WHITE WOMEN IN THE TOTAL NUMBER OF WOMEN EMPLOYED IN EACH OF THE PRINCIPAL OCCUPATIONS PURSUED BY WOMEN IN 1920, WITH INCREASE OR DECREASE IN THE PERCENTAGE: 1910–1920

OCCUPATION	WOMEN 16 YEARS OF AGE AND OVER ENGAGED IN GAINFUL OCCUPATIONS			
	Total number, 1920	Foreign-born white women		
		Number, 1920	Per cent of total	
			1920	1910	Increase (+) or decrease (−)
All occupations	8, 202, 901	1, 102, 697	13. 4	16. 1	−2. 7
Tailoresses	31, 828	12, 505	39. 3	40. 2	−0. 9
Janitors and sextons	28, 929	11, 329	39. 2	46. 6	−7. 4
Charwomen and cleaners	24, 744	8, 991	36. 3	33. 4	+2. 9
Retail dealers	78, 957	26, 939	34. 1	40. 5	−6. 4
Semiskilled operatives (manufacturing) (n.o.s.[1])	1, 274, 719	307, 339	24. 1	29. 3	−5. 2
Servants	981, 557	207, 811	21. 2	27. 0	−5. 8
Boarding and lodging house keepers	114, 740	23, 950	20. 9	26. 5	−5. 6
Waitresses	114, 718	23, 039	20. 1	27. 4	−7. 3
Housekeepers and stewardesses	204, 350	40, 232	19. 7	20. 2	−0. 5
Midwives and nurses (not trained)	137, 431	26, 327	19. 2	23. 7	−4. 5
Religious, charity, and welfare workers	26, 927	4, 866	18. 1	21. 6	−3. 5
Manufacturers, officials, and managers (manufacturing)	13, 276	2, 289	17. 2	27. 1	−9. 9
Restaurant, café, and lunch room keepers	15, 644	2, 680	17. 1	20. 8	−3. 7
Laborers (manufacturing) (n.o.s.[1])	160, 133	26, 605	16. 6	24. 1	−7. 5
Dressmakers and seamstresses (not in factory)	235, 519	37, 479	15. 9	15. 5	+0. 4
Laundry operatives	78, 548	12, 267	15. 6	20. 1	−4. 5
Trained nurses	143, 664	21, 556	15. 0	21. 9	−6. 9
Hotel keepers and managers	14, 134	2, 076	14. 7	16. 4	−1. 7
Milliners and millinery dealers	69, 598	10, 006	14. 4	11. 1	+3. 3
Forewomen and overseers (manufacturing)	30, 171	4, 295	14. 2	16. 4	−2. 2
Actresses and showwomen	14, 220	1, 887	13. 3	14. 8	−1. 5
Barbers, hairdressers, and manicurists	33, 091	3, 531	10. 7	17. 5	−6. 8
Saleswomen and clerks in stores	514, 056	52, 720	10. 3	8. 5	+1. 8
Farm foremen, general farms	13, 767	1, 349	9. 8	13. 5	−3. 7
Artists, sculptors, and teachers of art	14, 566	1, 407	9. 7	8. 3	+1. 4
Laundresses (not in laundry)	383, 622	32, 763	8. 5	10. 4	−1. 9
Farmers	253, 836	21, 148	8. 3	10. 1	−1. 8
Agents, canvassers, and collectors	15, 741	1, 213	7. 8	9. 3	−1. 5
Bookkeepers, cashiers, and accountants	356, 603	27, 979	7. 8	8. 2	−0. 4
Compositors, linotypers, and typesetters	11, 306	747	6. 6	5. 3	+1. 3
Musicians and teachers of music	72, 431	4, 348	6. 0	5. 9	+0. 1
Clerks (except clerks in stores)	463, 570	27, 752	6. 0	7. 4	−1. 4
Stenographers and typists	559, 748	31, 768	5. 7	5. 6	+0. 1
Telegraph operators	16, 860	867	5. 1	6. 0	−0. 9
College presidents and professors	10, 075	448	4. 4	13. 0	−8. 6
Librarians	13, 502	559	4. 1	4. 0	+0. 1
Teachers (school)	635, 207	26, 032	4. 1	5. 1	−1. 0
Telephone operators	175, 469	6, 892	3. 9	3. 8	+0. 1
Postmasters	11, 208	305	2. 7	4. 0	−1. 3
Farm laborers	605, 668	12, 112	2. 0	2. 3	−0. 3
All other occupations	248, 768	34, 289	13. 8	15. 9	−2. 1

[1] Not otherwise specified.

Large numbers of foreign-born white women on arriving in this country seek employment as servants, partly because they have no special aversion to such work, and not being qualified by education or training for other employments, find it is easier to secure work in domestic service than in other fields. Many of them give up this occupation when they marry; while others, once they have become familiar with our language and customs, and perhaps acquired some of the native white women's aversion to domestic service, may shift to other occupations. And, of course, in this, as in every occupation, there are also losses through deaths. It is obvious, therefore, that the number of foreign-born white women in domestic service can be kept up only by the constant arrival of new recruits from abroad; and it is probable that the striking decrease from 1910 to 1920 in the number of foreign-born white women engaged in domestic service was due to the cessation of immigration during the War rather than to any increase in the number of foreign-born white women leaving domestic service. We have, it is true, no statistical measure of the actual tendency of foreign-born white women to leave domestic service for other pursuits; but, whatever the extent of this tendency may be, if the present restrictions on immigration are maintained, the number of foreign-born white women engaged in domestic service will in all probability continue to decrease.

There is a wide variation between different occupations as regards the proportion of foreign-born white women in the total number of women employed. In the occupations included in the preceding table, this proportion ranges from 39.3 per cent for tailoresses to 2.0 per cent for farm laborers. It will be noted that the occupations in which foreign-born white women were especially prominent were mostly factory occupations, needle trades, and domestic service. But the proportion of foreign-born women was also high among retail dealers (34.1 per cent); and it was fairly high among religious, charity, and welfare workers (18.1 per cent), manufacturers, officials and managers (17.2 per cent), trained nurses (15.0 per cent), and forewomen and overseers in manufacturing pursuits (14.2 per cent).

The clerical and most of the professional occupations, as shown by the above table, are near the bottom of the list as regards the percentage of foreign-born white women. The exceptions in professional occupations, as noted above, include religious, charity, and welfare workers and trained nurses.

In view of the fact that there was a very considerable decrease in the percentage of foreign born in the total number of women gainfully employed, it is not surprising that there were decreases in this percentage in most of the individual occupations. In the above list there are, in fact, only two occupations, that of milliner and that of charwoman, in which the percentage increased appreciably—from 11.1 in 1910 to 14.4 in 1920 in the occupation of milliner and from 33.4 to 36.3 in that of charwoman. There are some occupations in which the percentage showed little change. They include the occupations of housekeeper or stewardess, dressmaker or seamstress, stenographer or typist, and bookkeeper, cashier, or accountant. As regards these and some other occupations it may be said that the foreign-born women held their own. · But in most occupations they lost ground relatively. Notwithstanding the great increase previously noted in the number of foreign-born women employed as semiskilled operatives and as laborers in manufacturing industries, the percentage of foreign born among the total number of women in these pursuits decreased materially—from 29.3 to 24.1 among semiskilled operatives and from 24.1 to 16.6 among laborers. Among women servants the percentage foreign born declined from 27.0 to 21.2.   So, in general, it looks as if the immigrant woman is a factor of diminishing importance in the labor supply of this country for mills and factories as well as in domestic service.

XIII

NEGRO WOMEN IN GAINFUL OCCUPATIONS

The total number of Negro women reported in the census of 1920 as employed in gainful occupations was 1,445,935. Of this total 420,148 were reported as farm laborers, 389,276 as servants, and 281,761 as laundresses (not in laundries), these three occupational groups comprising 75.5 per cent, or almost exactly three-fourths, of the total number of Negro women gainfully employed.

TABLE 78.—PRINCIPAL OCCUPATIONS OF NEGRO WOMEN, WITH PER CENT DISTRIBUTION AND RANK: 1920

OCCUPATION	NEGRO WOMEN 16 YEARS OF AGE AND OVER GAINFULLY EMPLOYED: 1920		
	Number	Per cent distribution	Rank
All occupations	1,445,935	100.0	
Farm laborers, general farms	420,148	29.1	1
Servants	389,276	26.9	2
Laundresses (not in laundry)	281,761	19.5	3
Farmers, general farms	79,773	5.5	4
Semiskilled operatives (manufacturing) (n. o. s.[1])	40,779	2.8	5
Laborers (manufacturing) (n. o. s.[1])	32,582	2.2	6
Teachers (school)	29,189	2.0	7
Dressmakers and seamstresses (not in factory)	26,961	1.9	8
Laundry operatives	20,463	1.4	9
Midwives and nurses (not trained)	13,888	1.0	10
Waitresses	13,836	1.0	11
Housekeepers and stewardesses	13,250	0.9	12
Barbers, hairdressers, and manicurists	12,631	0.9	13
Boarding and lodging house keepers	9,536	0.7	14
All other occupations	61,862	4.3	

[1] Not otherwise specified.

The Negro women gainfully employed comprise 17.6 per cent, or rather more than one-sixth, of the total number of women engaged in gainful occupations. In the South the percentage is 49.8, or practically one-half. The percentage in the Northern States is naturally much smaller because of the smaller proportion of Negroes in the total population.

109

TABLE 79.—NUMBER AND PERCENTAGE OF NEGRO WOMEN ENGAGED IN GAINFUL OCCUPATIONS, AS COMPARED WITH THEIR PROPORTION IN THE TOTAL POPULATION, BY GEOGRAPHIC SECTIONS AND DIVISIONS: 1920

GEOGRAPHIC SECTION AND DIVISION	NEGRO WOMEN 16 YEARS OF AGE AND OVER: 1920				
		Engaged in gainful occupations			Per cent of total women in the population
	Total number	Number	Per cent of total number	Per cent of total women gainfully occupied	
United States	3,312,081	1,445,935	43.7	17.6	9.7
The North	536,490	243,160	45.3	4.7	2.5
New England	28,311	13,915	49.2	1.6	1.1
Middle Atlantic	226,075	115,867	51.3	5.6	3.0
East North Central	181,947	72,066	39.6	4.7	2.5
West North Central	100,157	41,312	41.2	5.4	2.5
The South	2,749,360	1,191,354	43.3	49.8	27.5
South Atlantic	1,312,669	582,824	44.4	50.6	30.7
East South Central	793,083	357,106	45.0	56.4	29.4
West South Central	643,608	251,424	39.1	41.3	21.3
The West	26,231	11,421	43.5	1.9	0.9
Mountain	8,650	3,602	41.6	2.1	0.9
Pacific	17,581	7,819	44.5	1.8	0.9

For two decades—or from 1890 to 1910, inclusive—the number of Negro women reported in the census as having a gainful occupation increased, and the percentage which they constituted of all gainfully employed women remained nearly constant—not far from 24 per cent. But between 1910 and 1920 the number decreased and the percentage fell off to 17.6. (See Table 80.) The percentage of Negro women gainfully employed likewise increased from 1890 to 1910 and then decreased in 1920. (See Table 81.)

TABLE 80.—NUMBER AND PERCENTAGE OF NEGRO WOMEN IN THE TOTAL NUMBER OF WOMEN ENGAGED IN GAINFUL OCCUPATIONS: 1890–1920

CENSUS YEAR	WOMEN 16 YEARS OF AGE AND OVER ENGAGED IN GAINFUL OCCUPATIONS		
	Total number	Negro	
		Number	Per cent of total
1920	8,202,901	1,445,935	17.6
1910	7,438,686	1,744,752	23.9
1900	4,833,630	1,119,621	23.2
1890 [1]	3,712,144	867,717	23.4

[1] Figures for 1890 cover the number 15 years of age and over instead of 16 years and over.

This decrease in the number and percentage of Negro women gainfully employed was doubtless due in large part to the changes already noted in the date of the census and in the instructions to the enumerators regarding the return of women working on farms (see pp. 16 to 18); and in so far as that was the case it did not represent a change in actual conditions. If, however, the comparison is restricted to occupations outside of agriculture, there is still a decrease in the percentage, although it is not so pronounced as it is when all occupations are included. Thus, while the percentage of Negro women employed in all occupations decreased from 58.2 to 43.7 and the percentage employed in agricultural pursuits decreased from 27.3 to 15.2, the percentage employed in nonagricultural pursuits decreased only from 30.9 to 28.4. Accepting the decrease in the percentage employed in agricultural pursuits as being mainly due to the changes referred to in the instructions and in the date of the census, we must seek some other explanation of the decrease in the percentage employed in nonagricultural pursuits.

TABLE 81.—NUMBER AND PERCENTAGE OF NEGRO WOMEN ENGAGED IN ALL GAINFUL OCCUPATIONS AND IN AGRICULTURAL AND NONAGRICULTURAL PURSUITS: 1890–1920

CENSUS YEAR	NEGRO WOMEN 16 YEARS OF AGE AND OVER						
	Total number	In all occupations		In agricultural pursuits		In nonagricultural pursuits	
		Number	Per cent of total	Number	Per cent of total	Number	Per cent of total
1920	3,312,081	1,445,935	43.7	504,763	15.2	941,172	28.4
1910	2,997,710	1,744,752	58.2	818,193	27.3	926,559	30.9
1900	2,589,988	1,119,621	43.2	434,065	16.8	685,556	26.5
1890 [1]	2,175,550	867,717	39.9	357,883	16.5	509,834	23.4

[1] Figures for 1890 cover the number 15 years of age and over instead of 16 years and over.

That the decrease between 1910 and 1920 in the percentage of Negro women employed in nonagricultural pursuits was general throughout the United States is indicated by the following table:

TABLE 82.—NUMBER AND PERCENTAGE OF NEGRO WOMEN ENGAGED IN NON-AGRICULTURAL PURSUITS, BY GEOGRAPHIC SECTIONS AND DIVISIONS: 1920 AND 1910

GEOGRAPHIC SECTION AND DIVISION	NEGRO WOMEN 16 YEARS OF AGE AND OVER					
	Total number		Engaged in nonagricultural pursuits			
			Number		Per cent of total	
	1920	1910	1920	1910	1920	1910
United States	3,312,081	2,997,710	941,172	926,559	28.4	30.9
The North	536,490	378,168	241,871	189,854	45.1	50.2
New England	28,311	24,779	13,863	13,676	49.0	55.2
Middle Atlantic	226,075	162,109	115,720	92,713	51.2	57.2
East North Central	181,947	106,712	71,766	45,526	39.4	42.7
West North Central	100,157	84,568	40,522	37,939	40.5	44.9
The South	2,749,360	2,601,745	688,063	728,309	25.0	28.0
South Atlantic	1,312,669	1,214,491	365,173	375,363	27.8	30.9
East South Central	793,083	801,972	180,974	206,283	22.8	25.7
West South Central	643,608	585,282	-141,916	146,663	22.1	25.1
The West	26,231	17,797	11,238	8,396	42.8	47.2
Mountain	8,650	7,514	3,545	3,669	41.0	48.8
Pacific	17,581	10,283	7,693	4,727	43.8	46.0

To understand the significance of this decrease in the percentage of Negro women engaged in nonagricultural pursuits a study of the statistics by occupations is necessary.

As shown by figures already presented the range of occupations in which Negro women are employed is a comparatively narrow one. Of the 941,172 Negro women in nonagricultural pursuits 671,037, or 71.3 per cent, are either servants or laundresses. Between 1910 and 1920 the number of Negro women reported as servants increased but slightly, and the number of Negro women reported as laundresses decreased 20.9 per cent, or from 356,275 in 1910 to 281,761 in 1920. It is fairly evident that this large decrease in the number of laundresses must have gone far toward bringing about the decrease just noted in the total percentage of Negro women employed in all nonagricultural pursuits. In fact, if the number of laundresses had merely remained as large as it was in 1910, without undergoing any increase, there would have been hardly any decrease—only from 30.9 to 30.7—in that percentage.

DECREASE IN THE NUMBER OF LAUNDRESSES

The term "laundress," synonym of "washerwoman," is rather elastic in its application. It includes the woman who regularly takes in washing, doing the work at home, as well as the one who goes out to wash or gives her entire time to that work, since according to the instructions to the census enumerators both in 1910 and 1920 a woman "who regularly takes in washing" in addition to doing housework in her own home was to be considered as a laundress or washerwoman. If these instructions were followed to the letter, the amount of washing which the woman regularly took in would not matter. However small it might be, if it was taken in regularly she would be returned as a washerwoman or laundress under the census definition strictly construed. But it is hardly probable that the enumerators were such strict constructionists. In the actual enumeration they were probably guided largely by their own judgment as to what constitutes a laundress or washerwoman, or by the answer which the woman herself gave to the occupation question. Therefore, as regards the great decrease in the number of laundresses reported in the census of 1920, when compared with that of 1910, it is quite possible that at the earlier census, when the instructions contained the clause emphasizing the importance of returning occupations followed by women (see p. 21), the enumerators may have been more zealous in discovering representatives of this occupation than they were in 1920, when there was no corresponding clause in the instructions. But on the other hand, it seems very probable that the occupation is one which is in fact declining in importance, the woman who does washing being supplanted to some extent by the operative working in the steam laundry. On that theory, the decrease in the total number of laundresses—a decrease of 25.3 per cent for all classes, white and colored—should be accompanied by an increase in the total number of laundry operatives. And there was such an increase, although it was not very great, being in fact only 7 per cent. That it was not larger is, however, not surprising, since a single laundry operative continuously employed represents in amount of work done the equivalent of several women taking in varying amounts of washing at home and devoting only a part of their time to that work.

There is another factor that may have had some effect in reducing the number of women gainfully employed as washerwomen, and that is the invention and use of electrically operated home washing machines and ironing appliances, making it easier for the thrifty housewife to do her own laundry work. Changes in styles, particularly as regards women's dress, and in kind of materials which they wear, have also had considerable effect in reducing the amount of necessary laundry work. It seems quite probable, therefore, that there is a diminishing demand for the services of the washerwoman, and that she is gradually being deprived of her occupation. This may go far toward accounting for the decrease noted in the number of women, white and colored, reported in the census as laundresses (not in steam laundries), a decrease from 513,586 in 1910 to 383,622 in 1920.

SLIGHT INCREASE IN THE NUMBER OF SERVANTS

The decrease in the number of Negro laundresses, in so far as it was not offset by an increase in the number of Negro women engaged in other occupations, would of course produce a decrease in the total number and percentage of Negro women gainfully employed. It might be supposed, however, that the Negro woman who lacked the opportunity of earning money by washing would seek some other employment. How persistent or how successful she may have been in doing that is a question of some interest to which, however, only a partial answer may be found or suggested in the census statistics. Outside of agriculture the principal alternative occupation to which she might turn is that of household servant. But, as already noted, the census statistics indicate that this is also a declining occupation, the total number of female servants of all ages and all classes as reported in the census having fallen off from 1,309,549 in 1910 to 1,012,133 in 1920, a decrease of 22.7 per cent. In so far as this decrease resulted from a diminution in the supply of potential servants consequent upon the check to immigration, it would seem that it should have brought about an increased demand for the services of Negroes to fill the places formerly occupied by the foreign-born servant; and to some extent it appears to have done that, particularly in the North, where the percentage of Negroes in the total number of female servants increased from 11.5 in 1910 to 18.5 in 1920 and the actual number of Negro women servants increased from 92,318 to 108,342, an increase of about 17 per cent. But, notwithstanding the very considerable northward migration of Negroes in the latter part of the decade 1910-1920, the great mass of the Negro population remains in the South, where the servant situation, outside of one or two cities, could not have been much affected by the check to immigration, because in that section of the country there are relatively few immigrants and the Negro woman has always had nearly complete possession of the field of employment in domestic service.   So the check to immigration created hardly any new demand or opportunity for her services in that field.

TABLE 83.—NUMBER AND PERCENTAGE OF NEGRO WOMEN IN THE TOTAL NUMBER OF WOMEN EMPLOYED AS SERVANTS, BY GEOGRAPHIC SECTIONS AND DIVISIONS: 1920 AND 1910

GEOGRAPHIC SECTION AND DIVISION	WOMEN 16 YEARS OF AGE AND OVER EMPLOYED AS SERVANTS								
	Total number		Negro						
			Number		Increase (+) or decrease (−)		Per cent of total number		
	1920	1910	1920	1910	Number	Per cent	1920	1910
United States	981,557	1,234,758	389,276	388,659	+617	+0.2	39.7	31.5
The North	585,179	799,580	108,342	92,318	+16,024	+17.4	18.5	11.5
New England	76,478	111,125	6,012	6,214	−202	−3.3	7.9	5.6
Middle Atlantic	249,636	340,996	59,688	52,757	+6,931	+13.1	23.9	15.5
East North Central	166,674	222,050	27,306	19,139	+8,167	+42.7	16.4	8.6
West North Central	92,391	125,409	15,336	14,208	+1,128	+7.9	16.6	11.3
The South	333,611	368,534	275,223	292,453	−17,230	−5.9	82.5	79.4
South Atlantic	168,512	185,921	142,886	149,655	−6,769	−4.5	84.8	80.5
East South Central	83,734	101,134	71,293	82,509	−11,216	−13.6	85.1	81.6
West South Central	81,365	81,479	61,044	60,289	+755	+1.3	75.0	74.0
The West	62,767	66,644	5,711	3,888	+1,823	+46.9	9.1	5.8
Mountain	19,913	22,564	1,736	1,765	−29	−1.6	8.7	7.8
Pacific	42,854	44,080	3,975	2,123	+1,852	+87.2	9.3	4.8

In the North the Negro population is largely concentrated in a few large cities, so that outside these cities there are few Negro women available for employment as servants.   But in those northern cities where there is a considerable Negro population the increase in the number and percentage of Negro women among female servants is quite striking.

TABLE 84.—INCREASE IN ⁻NUMBER OF NEGRO FEMALE SERVANTS IN 10
NORTHERN CITIES: 1910–1920

CITY	FEMALE SERVANTS 16 YEARS OF AGE AND OVER								
	Total number		Negro						
			Number		Increase: 1910–1920		Per cent of total number	
	1920	1910	1920	1910	Number	Per cent	1920	1910
Total	187,894	238,022	57,807	43,778	14,029	32.0	30.8	18.4
New York	84,272	111,590	18,932	13,951	4,981	35.7	22.5	12.5
Chicago	25,834	33,631	6,206	3,473	2,733	78.7	24.0	10.3
Philadelphia	28,076	36,320	15,120	14,037	1,083	7.7	53.9	38.6
Detroit	7,502	6,523	1,744	404	1,340	331.7	23.2	6.2
Cleveland	6,426	7,338	1,961	668	1,293	193.6	30.5	9.1
Pittsburgh	8,611	12,518	2,538	2,156	382	17.7	29.5	17.2
Cincinnati	6,750	8,559	2,158	1,819	339	18.6	32.0	21.3
Indianapolis	3,941	3,733	2,413	1,814	599	33.0	61.2	48.6
St. Louis	11,814	12,944	3,909	3,114	795	25.5	33.1	24.1
Kansas City, Mo	4,668	4,866	2,826	2,342	484	20.7	60.5	48.1

The list of 10 cities in the above table includes all northern cities in which the total Negro population in 1920 was more than 30,000. The total number of Negro female servants 16 years of age and over in these cities increased from 43,778 in 1910 to 57,807 in 1920, an increase of 32 per cent; and the percentage of Negroes in the total number of female servants increased from 18.4 to 30.8.

In brief, then, the situation as regards the entry of Negro women into domestic service in the decade 1910 to 1920 appears to have been as follows: In the South there are relatively few immigrants and consequently no increased demand for native servants resulted from the check to immigration. There the number of Negro women servants decreased. In most portions of the North, on the other hand, there was no supply of Negro women to meet any increased demand which might result from the shortage in the supply of foreign-born servants. But as regards those large cities of the North in which there was a considerable Negro population it might be said that demand and supply overlapped, and there the number of Negro female servants increased materially between 1910 and 1920.

INCREASE IN OTHER NONAGRICULTURAL PURSUITS

In contrast with the very slight increase in the number of Negro servants in the United States as a whole and the large decrease in the number of Negro laundresses, there was a very striking increase—48.7 per cent, or from 181,625 in 1910 to 270,135 in 1920—in the number of Negro women reported in "All other nonagricultural pursuits," which is all the more noteworthy because the preceding decade, 1900 to 1910, showed practically no increase of Negro women in this group of occupations. These occupations, it is true, furnish employment to only a small percentage of the total number of Negro women 16 years of age and over. But the noteworthy fact is that this percentage has appreciably increased, from 6.1 in 1910 to 8.2 in 1920. Of the total number of Negro women engaged in all nonagricultural occupations 28.7 were in this "all other" group in 1920, as compared with 19.6 per cent in 1910.

TABLE 85.—NUMBER OF NEGRO WOMEN EMPLOYED AS SERVANTS, AS LAUNDRESSES, AND IN ALL OTHER NONAGRICULTURAL PURSUITS, 1920, 1910, AND 1900, WITH INCREASE

OCCUPATION	NEGRO WOMEN 16 YEARS OF AGE AND OVER ENGAGED IN NONAGRICULTURAL PURSUITS						
				Increase [1]			
	1920	1910	1900	1910 to 1920		1900 to 1910	
				Number	Per cent	Number	Per cent
All nonagricultural pursuits_	941,172	926,559	685,556	14,613	1.6	241,003	35.2
Servants_____	389,276	388,659	[2] 296,984	617	0.2	91,675	30.9
Laundresses (not in laundry)_____	281,761	356,275	[3] 208,591	−74,514	−20.9	147,684	70.6
All other nonagricultural pursuits_	270,135	181,625	179,981	88,510	48.7	1,644	0.9

[1] A minus sign (−) denotes decrease.
[2] Estimated number according to the classification of 1910 and 1920.
[3] Estimated that of the total 215,042 Negro women 16+ reported as laundresses in 1900 the same proportion were employed in steam laundries as was true of all women 16+ reported as laundresses—3 per cent. (See Women at Work, pp. 56 and 57.)

Considering these facts it seems safe to infer that to some extent those Negro women who failed to find or did not choose to seek employment as servants and laundresses found opportunities in other pursuits, and that in some directions there has been in consequence, at least temporarily, a rather marked extension of the field of employment for the women of that race, and some letting down of the bars.

This residuary group of "other nonagricultural pursuits" comprises a number of diverse employments, as is shown by Table 86. This table also shows a very considerable increase in the number of Negro women employed as semiskilled operatives and laborers in manufacturing industries, the number being 73,361 in 1920 as compared with 25,220 in 1910. This results from an increased employment of Negro women in cigar and tobacco factories (increase of 11,681), clothing industries (5,322), textile mills (5,044), etc. It may be noted that the considerable number of Negro women who have found employment in manufacturing industries comprises only a small proportion—3.2 per cent—of all the women classed as semiskilled operatives in those industries but a fairly large proportion— 20.3 per cent—of those classed as laborers. (See Table 88, on p. 120.)

TABLE 86.—Increase or Decrease from 1910 to 1920 in the Number of Negro Women Employed in Specified Nonagricultural Pursuits

OCCUPATION	NEGRO WOMEN 16 YEARS OF AGE AND OVER ENGAGED IN NONAGRICULTURAL PURSUITS					
	Number		Increase: 1910–1920 [1]		Per cent distribution	
	1920	1910	Number	Per cent	1920	1910
All nonagricultural pursuits_____	941,172	926,559	14,613	1.6	100.0	100.0
Servants_____	389,276	388,659	617	0.2	41.4	41.9
Laundresses (not in laundry)_____	281,761	356,275	−74,514	−20.9	29.9	38.5
All other nonagricultural pursuits_____	270,135	181,625	88,510	48.7	28.7	19.6
Semiskilled operatives (manufacturing) (n. o. s.[2])_	40,779	13,331	27,448	205.9	4.3	1.4
Laborers (manufacturing) (n. o. s.[2])_____	32,582	11,889	20,693	174.1	3.5	1.3
Teachers (school)_____	29,189	22,410	6,779	30.2	3.1	2.4
Dressmakers and seamstresses (not in factory)_	26,961	38,053	−11,092	−29.1	2.9	4.1
Laundry operatives_____	20,463	11,889	8,574	72.1	2.2	1.3
Midwives and nurses (not trained)_____	13,888	19,190	−5,302	−27.6	1.5	2.1
Waitresses_____	13,836	7,100	6,736	94.9	1.5	0.8
Housekeepers and stewardesses_____	13,250	10,010	3,240	32.4	1.4	1.1
Barbers, hairdressers, and manicurists____	12,631	3,765	8,866	235.5	1.3	0.4
Boarding and lodging house keepers_____	9,536	9,182	354	3.9	1.0	1.0
Charwomen and cleaners_____	7,075	6,841	234	3.4	0.8	0.7
Janitors and sextons_____	5,413	2,444	2,969	121.5	0.6	0.3
Saleswomen and clerks in stores_____	4,488	2,140	2,348	109.7	0.5	0.2
Clerks (except clerks in stores)_____	3,388	941	2,447	260.0	0.4	0.1
Elevator tenders_____	3,036	2	3,034	([3])	0.3	([4])
All other occupations_____	33,620	22,438	11,182	49.8	3.6	2.4

[1] A minus sign (−) denotes decrease.
[2] Not otherwise specified.
[3] Per cent not shown where base is less than 100.
[4] Less than one-tenth of 1 per cent.

This striking increase from 1910 to 1920 in the number of Negro women employed as laborers and as semiskilled operatives in factories arouses our interest, in view of the fact that until recently Negro women have not been employed in factories to any appreciable extent, partly, it may be, because of racial antipathy on the part of white employers and workers, reinforced probably by a general conviction, whether wellfounded or not, that Negro women are not well qualified for factory work. We shall need the statistics of at least one more census to determine whether the large increase from 1910 to 1920 marks the beginning of a more general employment of Negro women in factories, or whether, being an increase due to the great temporary demand for factory workers which came with the World War, it will not outlast the exceptional conditions which caused it. Much depends, perhaps, upon whether—with continued restricted immigration—there will be a sufficient supply of white workers.

Outside the manufacturing industries there were increases in the number of Negro women employed as teachers, laundry operatives, waitresses, housekeepers, barbers, hairdressers and manicurists, janitors, saleswomen or clerks in stores, clerks not in stores, stenographers, bookkeepers, accountants, etc. Most of these increases were not very large in absolute numbers, but many of them represent large percentage increases. The number of Negro women employed as tenders of elevators increased from practically none—or 2 only—to 3,036. For women this is a new occupation which came into existence during the war.

The great increase during the decade 1910 to 1920 in the number and proportion of the gainfully occupied Negro women employed as barbers, hairdressers, and manicurists doubtless is indicative of a great increase during this period in the number of "beauty parlors" and hair dressing parlors for women. These establishments give employment to large numbers of Negro women. In fact, many of them are operated by and for Negro women.

Two occupations listed under "all other nonagricultural pursuits" show a decrease, namely, the occupation of dressmaker or seamstress and that of midwife or untrained nurse. Dressmaking, as has been noted, is an occupation of diminishing importance for white women as well as for Negroes.

TABLE 87.—INCREASE OR DECREASE, 1910–1920, IN THE NUMBER OF NEGRO WOMEN EMPLOYED AS SERVANTS, AS LAUNDRESSES, AND IN ALL OTHER NONAGRICULTURAL PURSUITS, BY GEOGRAPHIC SECTIONS

GEOGRAPHIC SECTION AND CLASS OF OCCUPATION	NEGRO WOMEN 16 YEARS OF AGE AND OVER ENGAGED IN NONAGRICULTURAL PURSUITS		Increase: 1910–1920 [1]	
	1920	1910	Number	Per cent
United States	941,172	926,559	14,613	1.6
Servants	389,276	388,659	617	0.2
Laundresses	281,761	356,275	−74,514	−20.9
All other nonagricultural pursuits	270,135	181,625	88,510	48.7
The North	241,871	189,854	52,017	27.4
Servants	108,342	92,318	16,024	17.4
Laundresses	46,914	53,747	−6,833	−12.7
All other nonagricultural pursuits	86,615	43,789	42,826	97.8
The South	688,063	728,309	−40,246	−5.5
Servants	275,223	292,453	−17,230	−5.9
Laundresses	233,205	300,734	−67,529	−22.5
All other nonagricultural pursuits	179,635	135,122	44,513	32.9
The West	11,238	8,396	2,842	33.8
Servants	5,711	3,888	1,823	46.9
Laundresses	1,642	1,794	−152	−8.5
All other nonagricultural pursuits	3,885	2,714	1,171	43.1

[1] A minus sign (−) denotes decrease.

The changes between 1910 and 1920 as regards the employment of Negro women in gainful occupations may be summarized as follows: The number of Negro women reported in the census as employed in agricultural pursuits underwent a marked decrease between 1910 and 1920, which, however, was largely due to changes in the definition of farm laborers as applied to women. The number of Negro women employed in nonagricultural pursuits showed only a very slight increase from 1910 to 1920, with the result that the percentage so employed showed a pronounced decrease. This was caused mainly by the decrease in the number of Negro women employed as laundresses or washerwomen. The number employed as servants underwent hardly any change, a considerable increase in the North and West being offset by a decrease in the South. But the number of Negro women employed in other nonagricultural pursuits increased very materially, both in the North and in the South, the absolute increase being nearly the same in the two sections, although the percentage increase was much greater in the North.

The increase noted in the number of Negro women employed in "other nonagricultural pursuits" was, however, not much more than large enough to offset the decrease in the numbers reported as laundresses, so that there was only a slight increase in the total number employed in all nonagricultural pursuits, and the percentage of Negro women so employed, as already noted, fell off from 30.9 in 1910 to 28.4 in 1920. In other words, Negro women, according to the census, were not so generally employed in 1920 as they were in 1910. To some extent—but the writer believes to a small extent—this falling off in the percentage may have been due to the changes already noted in the instructions to the enumerators as regards the emphasis placed upon the importance of returning the occupations of women. Beyond that it may have resulted from difficulty in finding employment outside of domestic service and laundry work in the cities to which Negroes migrated in large numbers in the period immediately preceding the census of 1920. It is probable, also, that many of the Negro women who would be ready to take in washing if they had the opportunity, or if their services were solicited, are not qualified for regular employment in other occupations, or are not in a position to accept employment outside their homes. At the same time, in a period of high wages, and despite high costs of living, it is not improbable that the Negroes may have experienced some improvement in their economic position, making it less imperative for the women to contribute to the support of the family. All things considered, it does not seem remarkable that a decrease in the number of Negro washerwomen took place and was not offset by a corresponding increase in numbers reported in other occupations, and that there should have been in consequence a decrease in the proportionate number of Negro women reported in the census as gainfully employed in all pursuits outside of agriculture.

PROPORTION OF NEGROES IN THE TOTAL NUMBER OF WOMEN WORKERS

Table 88 shows the changes between 1910 and 1920 in the percentage which Negro women form of the total number of women engaged in the specified occupations.

TABLE 88.—NUMBER AND PERCENTAGE OF NEGRO WOMEN IN THE TOTAL NUMBER OF WOMEN EMPLOYED IN THE PRINCIPAL NONAGRICULTURAL OCCUPATIONS PURSUED BY NEGRO WOMEN IN 1920, WITH INCREASE OR DECREASE IN THE PERCENTAGE: 1910–1920

OCCUPATION	WOMEN 16 YEARS OF AGE AND OVER ENGAGED IN NONAGRICULTURAL OCCUPATIONS				
	Total number, 1920	Negro women			Increase (+) or decrease (−) in per cent of Negro women
		Number, 1920	Per cent of total		
			1920	1910	
All nonagricultural occupations	7, 306, 844	941, 172	12. 9	15. 3	−2. 4
Servants	981, 557	389, 276	39. 7	31. 5	+8. 2
Laundresses (not in laundry)	383, 622	281, 761	73, 4	69. 4	+4. 0
Semiskilled operatives (manufacturing) (n. o. s.[1])	1, 274, 719	40, 779	3. 2	1. 4	+1. 8
Laborers (manufacturing) (n.o. s.[1])	160, 133	32, 582	20. 3	14. 9	+5. 4
Teachers (school)	635, 207	29, 189	4. 6	4. 7	−0. 1
Dressmakers and seamstresses	235, 519	26, 961	11. 4	8. 5	+2. 9
Laundry operatives	78, 548	20, 463	26. 1	16. 2	+9. 9
Midwives and nurses (not trained)	137, 431	13, 888	10. 1	16. 4	−6. 3
Waitresses	114, 718	13, 836	12. 1	8. 5	+3. 6
Housekeepers and stewardesses	204, 350	13, 250	6. 5	5. 8	+0. 7
Barbers, hairdressers, and manicurists	33, 091	12, 631	38. 2	17. 1	+21. 1
Boarding and lodging house keepers	114, 740	9, 536	8. 3	6. 4	+1. 9
Charwomen and cleaners	24, 744	7, 075	28. 6	25. 9	+2. 7
Janitors	28, 929	5, 413	18. 7	11. 4	+7. 3
All other	2, 899, 536	44, 532	1. 5	1. 5	

[1] Not otherwise specified.

In all but two of the occupational groups listed in the above table, the percentage of Negroes in the total number of women employed increased. The list includes all nonagricultural occupational groups in which more than 5,000 Negro women were reported. In the servant's occupation the percentage of Negro women increased from 31.5 in 1910 to 39.7 in 1920. This resulted from the fact that while the number of white women employed as servants materially decreased, the number of Negro women in that occupation remained nearly stationary. In the total number of laundresses the percentage of Negro women also increased—from 69.4 to 73.4—indicating that while, as already noted, the number of Negro women reported as laundresses decreased, it did not decrease as much, proportionately, as the number of white women in that occupation. There were notable increases in the percentage of Negroes among women reported as laborers in manufacturing industries, as dressmakers and seamstresses, as laundry operatives, as waitresses, as barbers, hairdressers, and manicurists, and as janitors and sextons. In all these occupations and in a number of others Negro women gained ground; and of all the occupations designated in the above table the only one in which the percentage of Negroes materially decreased was that of untrained nurse.

It may seem like an anomaly that the percentage of Negro women decreased in the total for all nonagricultural pursuits combined and at the same time increased in nearly all those nonagricultural pursuits in which Negro women are employed in considerable numbers. The explanation is found mainly in the fact that the two leading occupations for Negro women, namely, those of servant and laundress, declined in importance very materially between 1910 and 1920, so that they had much less weight in determining the percentage for the total at the later census than they had at the earlier; and in the further fact that many of the occupations in which few or no Negro women were employed increased very greatly. The contrast is brought out by the following table:

TABLE 89.—TOTAL NUMBER OF WOMEN EMPLOYED AS SERVANTS, AS LAUNDRESSES, AND IN OTHER IMPORTANT OCCUPATIONS FOR NEGRO WOMEN, AND IN ALL OTHER NONAGRICULTURAL PURSUITS, WITH INCREASE: 1910–1920

CLASS OF OCCUPATION	NUMBER OF WOMEN 16 YEARS OF AGE AND OVER GAINFULLY EMPLOYED					
	Number		Increase: 1910 to 1920 [1]		Percentage of Negro women	
	1920	1910	Number	Per cent	1920	1910
Nonagricultural pursuits	7,306,844	6,041,362	1,265,482	20.9	12.9	15.3
Servants and laundresses	1,365,179	1,748,344	−383,165	−21.9	49.2	42.6
Other important occupations for Negro women [2]	3,042,129	2,617,906	424,223	16.2	7.4	6.0
All other nonagricultural pursuits	2,899,536	1,675,112	1,224,424	73.1	1.5	1.5

[1] A minus sign (−) denotes decrease.
[2] Includes all nonagricultural occupations (other than those of servant and laundress) in which at least 5,000 Negro women were employed.

In the occupations of servant and laundress, in which there are large numbers of Negro women, the total number of women, white and colored, decreased 21.9 per cent; the group of other occupations in which considerable numbers of Negro women are engaged increased only 16.2 per cent; but the group of occupations in which there were very few Negro women increased 73.1 per cent. It is the great increase of this last group which explains the decrease in the percentage of Negro women in the total for all nonagricultural pursuits.

XIV

FAMILY RELATIONSHIP

From the population census schedules some information may be obtained as to the home relationship or environment of the women who are wage earners, or are otherwise gainfully employed. It is possible to distinguish those women who live in the family relationship, or with relatives, and therefore have presumably a home life, from those who are boarding or lodging; and it is further possible to classify the former with respect to their relationship to the head of the family, whether it is that of wife or of daughter or some other relationship. These distinctions were believed to be so important and fundamental that the Bureau of the Census made a special tabulation for a few cities, classifying the women reported as gainfully employed in the census of 1920 with respect to their relationship to the heads of families in which they were living.

On account of the expense involved, a tabulation covering the entire United States, or even all the larger cities, was considered out of the question. But the results obtained for the following 11 selected cities can doubtless be accepted as fairly typical of conditions prevailing generally in individual cities.

Fall River, Mass.	St. Paul, Minn.
Providence, R. I.	Kansas City, Mo.
Rochester, N. Y.	Atlanta, Ga.
Paterson, N. J.	Louisville Ky.
Cincinnati, Ohio	New Orleans, La.
Indianapolis, Ind.	

This group of cities is composed of two from each of the northern geographic divisions—New England, Middle Atlantic, East North Central, and West North Central—and one from each of the southern geographic divisions—South Atlantic, East South Central, and West South Central.

Following the census of 1900 a similar tabulation was made for 27 selected cities, and the results were presented in the report on Women at Work, published in 1907. The 11 cities selected for the census of 1920 were all included in the earlier tabulation, so that for these cities comparisons of the results of the two tabulations are possible.

The total number of gainfully employed women in the 11 selected cities in 1920 was 373,204, which is 4.5 per cent of the total number gainfully employed in the entire country, and 11.7 per cent of the gainfully employed women in all cities of 100,000 population and over.

Each of the cities, except Fall River and Paterson, had a population in excess of 200,000 in 1920. Paterson was selected as having the highest proportion of gainfully occupied women of any city with a population of 100,000 or more in the Middle Atlantic division of States. Fall River had the highest proportion among the New England cities, with the exception of New Bedford, which was not selected because it was not included in the 27 cities for which similar statistics are available for 1900.

The basis of this special tabulation is the relationship of the woman breadwinner to the head of the family or household in which she lives. This relationship is reported for each individual enumerated in the census. The woman who was either herself the head of the family, or was related (as wife, daughter, etc.) to the head of the family in which she lived, was considered to be "living at home," and was further classified with respect to this relationship as living with father (i. e., in a family the head of which was the woman's father), with mother, with husband, or with other relatives, as the case might be. The woman not living at home was classified as boarding or lodging whenever her relationship to the head of the family as reported on the census schedule was that of boarder or lodger. Finally, a considerable number of women, mostly servants and housekeepers, were reported and classified as living in the family of their employer.

The result of this basic classification was as follows:

TABLE 90.—NUMBER AND PER CENT DISTRIBUTION, BY FAMILY RELATIONSHIP, OF GAINFULLY OCCUPIED WOMEN, FOR THE 11 SELECTED CITIES COMBINED: 1920

FAMILY RELATIONSHIP	WOMEN 16 YEARS OF AGE AND OVER ENGAGED IN GAINFUL OCCUPATIONS: 1920	
	Number	Per cent
Total	373, 204	100. 0
Living at home	293, 213	78. 6
Head of family	56, 659	15. 2
Living with father	96, 281	25. 8
Living with mother	44, 360	11. 9
Living with husband	53, 411	14. 3
Living with other relative	42, 502	11. 4
Boarding or lodging	50, 297	13. 5
Living with employer	29, 694	8. 0

Of the women reported as having gainful occupations in these 11 cities, 78.6 per cent, or almost 4 out of 5, were living at home, 13.5 per cent were boarding or lodging, and 8 per cent were living with the employer's family.

As regards the considerable number of women designated as heads of families in the above classification, it should be noted that some of them are not heads of families in the usual sense of the term, but only in the somewhat technical sense in which the term is defined by the census. The woman who keeps house by herself, in an apartment for instance, is classified as constituting a family and as being the head of a family; and the single woman or widow who keeps a boarding house is considered by the census as the head of a family of boarders.[1]

COMPARISON BY OCCUPATIONS

The distribution of women by family relationship varies greatly in different occupation groups, as is shown by the following table:

TABLE 91.—PER CENT DISTRIBUTION, BY FAMILY RELATIONSHIP, OF WOMEN EMPLOYED IN EACH SPECIFIED OCCUPATION COMMON TO THE 11 SELECTED CITIES: 1920

	WOMEN 16 YEARS OF AGE AND OVER GAINFULLY EMPLOYED: 1920								
		Living at home							
OCCUPATION	Total	Total	Head of family	Living with—				Boarding or lodging	Living with employer
				Father	Mother	Husband	Other relative		
All occupations	100.0	78.6	15.2	25.8	11.9	14.3	11.4	13.5	8.0
Boarding and lodging house keepers	100.0	98.8	73.1	0.4	0.7	23.4	1.3	1.0	0.3
Bookkeepers, cashiers, and accountants	100.0	85.7	5.6	43.1	19.4	5.6	12.0	14.1	0.3
Clerks (except clerks in stores)	100.0	85.8	5.5	44.2	18.5	5.4	12.2	13.9	0.3
Dressmakers and seamstresses (not in factory)	100.0	83.3	31.0	10.5	8.8	17.5	15.4	12.8	4.0
Housekeepers and stewardesses	100.0	46.0	18.8	4.0	2.4	7.4	13.5	12.6	41.7
Laborers (manufacturing) (n. o. s.)	100.0	82.6	16.4	25.0	9.8	19.1	12.3	17.2	0.2
Laundresses (not in laundry)	100.0	89.2	37.7	2.9	3.7	37.1	7.9	9.3	1.5
Laundry operatives	100.0	81.3	22.3	14.2	9.8	22.2	12.8	16.4	2.2
Midwives and nurses (not trained)	100.0	56.4	17.7	7.3	5.4	9.9	16.1	22.0	21.6
Milliners and millinery dealers	100.0	80.5	11.1	27.3	15.8	10.7	15.4	19.5	0.1
Musicians and teachers of music	100.0	87.0	13.8	33.7	13.6	15.1	10.8	11.5	1.5
Retail dealers	100.0	94.2	38.1	8.5	5.7	33.4	8.5	5.2	0.6
Saleswomen and clerks in stores	100.0	84.7	9.1	34.7	14.5	13.0	13.5	15.2	0.1
Semiskilled operatives (manufacturing) (n. o. s.)	100.0	89.5	11.8	34.0	13.9	17.1	12.6	10.5	(2)
Servants	100.0	49.3	16.5	5.0	4.9	14.3	8.6	14.6	36.1
Stenographers and typists	100.0	84.6	3.4	47.7	18.8	3.5	11.1	15.3	0.1
Teachers (school)	100.0	69.6	9.5	28.3	14.7	4.3	12.7	13.3	17.1
Telephone operators	100.0	83.5	3.6	44.7	19.3	3.5	12.4	16.0	0.5
Trained nurses	100.0	29.9	6.8	8.5	4.5	3.2	6.8	18.9	51.3
Waitresses	100.0	52.7	14.1	8.9	6.8	15.1	7.9	37.7	9.6
All other occupations	100.0	83.1	19.8	22.0	11.5	17.9	11.8	14.0	2.9

1 Not otherwise specified.   2 Less than one-tenth of 1 per cent.

It is evident that to some extent the distribution by family relationship is determined by the nature of the occupation. That is the case as regards servants, housekeepers, and nurses, a large proportion of whom live in the families of their employers. Of the boarding

[1] The term "family," as used in the census, signifies a group of persons, whether related by blood or not, who live together, as one household, usually sharing the same table. One person living alone is counted as a family, and, on the other hand, all the occupants and employees of a hotel, boarding house, or lodging house—if that is their usual place of abode—and all the inmates of an institution, however numerous, are treated as constituting a single family.

house keepers, dressmakers, laundresses, and retail dealers, a large proportion are reported as heads of families, probably because these are occupations which, to a large extent, are carried on in the homes of the workers and by women who, as a class, are older than the women in most other occupations. • Keeping a boarding house, in particular, is an occupation which is very commonly resorted to by women in the later years of life, when, through the death of a husband or for other reasons, they are thrown upon their own resources and compelled to find some means of supporting themselves and those dependent upon them.

Of the women employed as bookkeepers, cashiers, accountants, clerks (other than clerks in stores), stenographers, and telephone operators, a large proportion are reported as living at home with father and mother. This is mainly because these are occupations in which most of the workers are young unmarried women.

The proportion of women living with husband is naturally high in those occupations in which the proportion of married women is high, which is the case as regards boarding and lodging house keepers, laundresses, and retail dealers. On the other hand, in the occupations of stenographer, telephone operator, and trained nurse, the percentage living with husband is small, because as already noted, the women in these occupations are mostly young and unmarried. (See Ch. IX.)

COMPARISON BY CITIES

The table which follows shows that as regards the family relationship of the gainfully employed women there are rather wide differences in different cities. Thus 90 per cent of the women wage earners in Fall River are living at home, as compared with 68.2 per cent of those in Kansas City, Mo. The percentage reported as heads of families ranges from 9.8 in Fall River to 21.2 in Atlanta, while the percentage living with father ranges from 13.9 in Atlanta to 38.8 in Paterson. The percentage living with husband is large in Atlanta (22.6) and small in St. Paul (8.3), and, naturally, the percentage boarding or lodging varies inversely with the percentage living at home.

Some reasons for these differences may readily be suggested. There will naturally be a large percentage of boarders and lodgers among women gainfully employed in any city to which single women from the surrounding territory or from more distant regions migrate in large numbers, leaving their homes in the smaller towns or rural communities under the attraction of an opportunity to live and earn their living in a large city. This may explain the relatively large percentage of boarders and lodgers in Kansas City, St. Paul, and Atlanta. On the other hand, in a city in which the employed women

TABLE 92.—NUMBER AND PER CENT DISTRIBUTION, BY FAMILY RELATIONSHIP, OF GAINFULLY OCCUPIED WOMEN, FOR EACH OF 11 SELECTED CITIES: 1920

CITY	Total number	Living at home						Boarding or lodging	Living with employer
		Total	Head of family	Father	Mother	Husband	Other relative		
				Living with—					
NUMBER									
Total	373,204	293,213	56,659	96,281	44,360	53,411	42,502	50,297	29,694
Fall River	19,111	17,192	1,881	7,063	2,298	4,022	1,928	921	998
Providence	32,099	25,339	3,732	10,187	4,272	3,254	3,894	3,366	3,394
Rochester	36,956	28,657	3,897	11,349	4,409	4,683	4,319	5,289	3,010
Paterson	17,999	15,964	1,856	6,976	2,298	2,973	1,861	1,223	812
Cincinnati	50,231	40,709	8,852	14,074	7,206	5,077	5,500	4,121	5,401
Indianapolis	35,454	27,624	5,557	9,009	3,511	5,526	4,021	5,442	2,388
St. Paul	27,863	20,151	2,765	8,908	3,418	2,310	2,750	4,625	3,087
Kansas City, Mo	39,925	27,244	5,824	7,704	3,671	6,279	3,766	9,442	3,239
Atlanta	31,553	24,492	6,677	4,380	3,064	7,130	3,241	5,324	1,737
Louisville	33,655	27,185	6,469	7,505	4,185	5,144	3,882	4,118	2,352
New Orleans	48,358	38,656	9,149	9,126	6,028	7,013	7,340	6,426	3,276
PER CENT DISTRIBUTION									
Total	100.0	78.6	15.2	25.8	11.9	14.3	11.4	13.5	8.0
Fall River	100.0	90.0	9.8	37.0	12.0	21.0	10.1	4.8	5.2
Providence	100.0	78.9	11.6	31.7	13.3	10.1	12.1	10.5	10.6
Rochester	100.0	77.5	10.5	30.7	11.9	12.7	11.7	14.3	8.1
Paterson	100.0	88.7	10.3	38.8	12.8	16.5	10.3	6.8	4.5
Cincinnati	100.0	81.0	17.6	28.0	14.3	10.1	10.9	8.2	10.8
Indianapolis	100.0	77.9	15.7	25.4	9.9	15.6	11.3	15.3	6.7
St. Paul	100.0	72.3	9.9	32.0	12.3	8.3	9.9	16.6	11.1
Kansas City, Mo	100.0	68.2	14.6	19.3	9.2	15.7	9.4	23.6	8.1
Atlanta	100.0	77.6	21.2	13.9	9.7	22.6	10.3	16.9	5.5
Louisville	100.0	80.8	19.2	22.3	12.4	15.3	11.5	12.4	7.0
New Orleans	100.0	79.9	18.9	18.9	12.5	14.5	15.2	13.3	6.8

are recruited mostly from resident families the percentage boarding or lodging will be comparatively small. This is probably the case in such cities as Fall River and Paterson. These are mill cities in which the textile industries predominate, and the population is largely of foreign origin, consisting mostly of immigrants and their children; and while the textile mills afford employment for large numbers of persons of both sexes, the country woman of native American stock who may be looking for an opportunity to earn her living in the city is not apt to be attracted by cities of this type. This may account for the fact that an exceptionally small percentage of the working women in these cities are boarders or lodgers and an exceptionally large percentage are living at home. The large proportion of working women reported as living with father in both these cities probably reflects the fact that a large proportion of the women employed in the mills are young unmarried women. At the same time, in Fall River, though not in Paterson, the proportion living with husband is large as compared with other cities, indicating a considerable employment of married women in that city. Atlanta is another city in which the percentage living with husband is large, representing probably the many cases in which married colored women are following some gainful occupation, usually that of laundress or that of servant.

The following table gives the percentage living at home for each city by principal occupations. For most occupations this percentage is highest in either Fall River or Paterson and lowest in either Atlanta, Kansas City, or St. Paul. And within the same city the percentage living at home is almost always relatively high among boarding house keepers and retail dealers; and relatively low among teachers, nurses, servants, waitresses, and housekeepers. It is evident, therefore, that the percentage is determined to some extent by conditions peculiar to the occupation in which the workers are engaged and to some extent by conditions peculiar to the city in which the occupation is carried on.

TABLE 93.—PERCENTAGE LIVING AT HOME OF THE TOTAL NUMBER OF WOMEN EMPLOYED IN EACH SPECIFIED OCCUPATION, FOR EACH OF 11 SELECTED CITIES: 1920

OCCUPATION	WOMEN 16 YEARS OF AGE AND OVER GAINFULLY EMPLOYED—PER CENT LIVING AT HOME: 1920 [1]										
	Total, 11 cities	Fall River	Paterson	Cincinnati	Louisville	New Orleans	Providence	Indianapolis	Atlanta	Rochester	St. Paul	Kansas City, Mo.
All occupations	78.6	90.0	88.7	81.0	80.8	79.9	78.9	77.9	77.6	77.5	72.3	68.2
Boarding and lodging house keepers	98.8			97.8	100.0	98.4	98.5	99.6	100.0	100.0	99.3	97.4
Retail dealers	94.2	99.0	98.7	95.4	96.9	97.5	96.1	96.4	83.8	92.6	88.2	84.4
Semiskilled operatives (manufacturing) (n. o. s.[2])	89.5	94.7	93.2	93.4	84.8	89.4	90.3	85.1	83.0	85.5	83.9	79.3
Laundresses (not in laundry)	89.2		89.9	89.3	92.5	86.1	82.6	87.6	95.2	82.8	82.1	81.9
Musicians and teachers of music	87.0			88.9	88.0	82.2	91.3	91.4	88.0	88.3	86.1	81.2
Clerks (except clerks in stores)	85.8	97.5	94.5	92.6	87.8	89.9	89.2	85.4	75.3	86.9	86.7	75.8
Bookkeepers, cashiers, and accountants	85.7	97.1	96.4	93.2	90.1	90.0	89.5	82.0	73.9	86.8	84.6	75.0
Saleswomen and clerks in stores	84.7	96.6	92.2	91.0	89.2	91.2	84.7	84.2	74.8	83.4	80.5	73.9
Stenographers and typists	84.6	98.9	97.7	93.5	88.6	90.4	91.1	83.9	72.5	87.4	84.6	71.0
Telephone operators	83.5	95.6	97.2	92.1	87.9	91.0	93.2	83.8	60.3	82.4	81.9	75.2
Dressmakers and seamstresses (not in factory)	83.3	88.2	88.9	85.1	82.6	85.6	84.1	82.0	89.4	79.4	71.6	80.2
Laborers (manufacturing) (n. o. s.[2])	82.6		87.7	85.5	81.2	81.9	93.2	81.0	86.8	76.6	81.6	77.0
Laundry operatives	81.3			90.6	81.9	80.5	82.0	80.8	82.8	82.1	75.7	75.6
Milliners and millinery dealers	80.5			87.3	88.1	88.8	85.0	81.7	72.0	83.8	72.5	70.2
Teachers (school)	69.6	72.8	82.7	61.6	68.2	73.5	74.1	77.5	76.9	63.2	62.1	64.9
Midwives and nurses (not trained)	56.4	71.2	76.4	51.8	64.0	58.5	54.9	52.9	62.4	49.2	61.1	46.4
Waitresses	52.5			63.5	65.3	56.7	44.8	57.7	60.7	46.6	40.3	48.0
Servants	49.3	32.3	28.6	41.7	59.0	62.6	23.5	54.3	68.9	25.7	23.7	40.1
Housekeepers and stewardesses	46.0	49.7	51.4	52.3	46.1	52.2	42.5	43.9	43.1	42.0	41.4	43.8
Trained nurses	29.9	35.3	49.5	32.9	27.7	42.9	23.6	28.1	29.5	33.0	27.2	18.7

[1] Per cent not shown where base is less than 100. [2] Not otherwise specified.

MARITAL CONDITION

In the following table family relationship is shown by marital status:

TABLE 94.—NUMBER AND PER CENT DISTRIBUTION, BY FAMILY RELATIONSHIP, OF GAINFULLY OCCUPIED WOMEN OF EACH SPECIFIED MARITAL CLASS, FOR THE 11 SELECTED CITIES COMBINED: 1920

| | | WOMEN 16 YEARS OF AGE AND OVER ENGAGED IN GAINFUL OCCUPATIONS: 1920 | | | | | |
| | | Number | | | Per cent distribution | | |
FAMILY RELATIONSHIP	Total number	Single [1]	Married	Widowed or divorced	Single [1]	Married	Widowed or divorced
Total	373,204	224,428	85,642	63,134	100.0	100.0	100.0
Living at home	293,213	170,170	74,099	48,944	75.8	86.5	77.5
Head of family	56,659	13,883	8,129	34,647	6.2	9.5	54.9
Living with father	96,281	87,571	5,568	3,142	39.0	6.5	5.0
Living with mother	44,360	37,968	3,269	3,123	16.9	3.8	4.9
Living with husband	53,411		53,411			62.4	
Living with other relative	42,502	30,748	3,722	8,082	13.7	4.3	12.7
Boarding or lodging	50,297	31,826	9,033	9,438	14.2	10.5	14.9
Living with employer	29,694	22,432	2,510	4,752	10.0	2.9	7.5

[1] Includes those whose marital condition was not reported.

Since single women are as a class younger than the married or the widowed, and are more likely to be foot free, so that they can seek employment where the opportunities are most favorable or most attractive, it is not surprising that the percentage living at home, as shown by the above table, is considerably smaller for them than it is for the married and somewhat smaller than it is for the widowed and divorced.

Of the 170,170 single women living at home slightly more than one-half (87,571) were living with father and rather more than one-fifth (37,968) were living with mother, who in most cases, it may be assumed is a widow. A somewhat smaller number (30,748) were living with some other relative, and a considerable number (13,883) were reported as heads of families. Regarding these last it is probable that some of them were living alone, i. e., were not living with any relatives and were not boarders or lodgers. Others may have been "heads of families" in the ordinary sense of the term, being charged with the responsibility of maintaining, or helping to maintain, a home in which there were dependent children, or younger brothers or sisters. Some indication of the relative numbers in each class may be found in figures presented in the next chapter (p. 148). As would be expected, a large proportion of the single women living at home are living either with father or with mother.

Of the married women gainfully employed, 62.4 per cent were reported as living with husband (i. e., in a family the head of which is the husband of the employed woman). The fact that the others were not "living with husband" in the sense in which the phrase is here used, does not necessarily imply separation, or that the husband and wife are living apart, because they may both be living with the father or with the mother of the husband or of the wife or boarding in the same family or boarding house. When, however, the married woman is returned as the head of the family, as was the case with 9.5 per cent of the married women gainfully employed, there is a presumption that she is living apart from her husband.

The 62.4 per cent living with husband, represents, therefore, the proportion or percentage living with their husbands in homes of their own. The others were either living in the home of some other relative or were boarding or were living apart from their husbands. There has never been any tabulation made of the census data to show the home connections of the married women who are not gainfully employed. But it seems rather improbable that the proportion living with their husbands in homes of their own is as small as the 62.4 per cent shown for working women, which is equivalent to about 3 married women out of 5; and it seems reasonable to expect that the proportion of married couples who avoid the burden and responsibility of housekeeping by boarding or by living with relatives would be much larger in those cases in which the wife has taken up a money earning occupation, than in those cases where she is free to give her entire attention to housekeeping and the care of the home.

Of the widowed and divorced women gainfully employed more than one-half, 54.9 per cent, were reported as heads of families and about one-seventh, 14.9 per cent, as boarding.

RACE AND NATIVITY

In the next table the family relationship is shown for gainfully employed women as classified by race and nativity.

The preceding discussion brought out the fact that the family relationship of any group or class of gainfully employed women is to some extent determined by their occupations and also to some extent by age and marital status; and these factors partially explain the difference between the different population classes as shown in Table 95.

6436°—29——10

TABLE 95.—NUMBER AND PER CENT DISTRIBUTION, BY FAMILY RELATIONSHIP, OF GAINFULLY OCCUPIED WOMEN CLASSIFIED BY RACE AND NATIVITY, FOR THE 11 SELECTED CITIES COMBINED: 1920

FAMILY RELATIONSHIP	WOMEN 16 YEARS OF AGE AND OVER ENGAGED IN GAINFUL OCCUPATIONS, IN 11 SELECTED CITIES: 1920				
	Total number [1]	Native white		Foreign-born white	Negro
		Native parentage	Foreign or mixed parentage		
	NUMBER				
All classes	373, 204	156, 686	102, 064	44, 572	69, 808
Living at home	293, 213	120, 168	85, 516	32, 910	54, 575
Head of family	56, 659	18, 997	11, 770	7, 467	18, 417
Living with father	96, 281	46, 183	37, 008	8, 264	4, 822
Living with mother	44, 360	20, 939	16, 215	2, 495	4, 698
Living with husband	53, 411	16, 202	7, 275	10, 210	19, 707
Living with other relative	42, 502	17, 847	13, 248	4, 474	6, 931
Boarding or lodging	50, 297	26, 588	8, 906	4, 329	10, 462
Living with employer	29, 694	9, 930	7, 642	7, 333	4, 771
	PER CENT DISTRIBUTION				
All classes	100. 0	100. 0	100. 0	100. 0	100. 0
Living at home	78. 6	76. 7	83. 8	73. 8	78. 2
Head of family	15. 2	12. 1	11. 5	16. 8	26. 4
Living with father	25. 8	29. 5	36. 3	18. 5	6. 9
Living with mother	11. 9	13. 4	15. 9	5. 6	6. 7
Living with husband	14. 3	10. 3	7. 1	22. 9	28. 2
Living with other relative	11. 4	11. 4	13. 0	10. 0	9. 9
Boarding or lodging	13. 5	17. 0	8. 7	9. 7	15. 0
Living with employer	8. 0	6. 3	7. 5	16. 5	6. 8

[1] Includes Indians, Chinese, Japanese, and other races.

Thus, among the employed foreign-born white women the percentage living with employers is exceptionally large simply because a large proportion of them are following the occupation of servant. Again, because a large proportion of both the Negro and the foreign-born working women are married women, the proportion living with husbands is relatively large for both these classes. The fact that a large proportion also of the Negro women gainfully employed are widows partially accounts for the relatively large percentage reported as heads of families, since the widow is much more frequently the head of a family than either the married or the single woman. The differences here noted as regards the marital status of the several classes are shown in the following table:

TABLE 96.—GAINFULLY OCCUPIED WOMEN CLASSIFIED BY RACE AND NATIVITY AND BY MARITAL CONDITION, FOR THE 11 SELECTED CITIES COMBINED: 1920

MARITAL CONDITION	GAINFULLY OCCUPIED WOMEN				
	Total number [1]	Native white		Foreign-born white	Negro
		Native parentage	Foreign or mixed parentage		
	NUMBER				
Total	373,204	156,686	102,064	44,572	69,808
Single [2]	224,428	104,182	78,234	23,104	18,869
Married	85,642	28,606	12,457	13,713	30,844
Widowed or divorced	63,134	23,898	11,373	7,755	20,095
	PER CENT DISTRIBUTION				
Total	100.0	100.0	100.0	100.0	100.0
Single [2]	60.1	66.5	76.7	51.8	27.0
Married	22.9	18.3	12.2	30.8	44.2
Widowed or divorced	16.9	15.3	11.1	17.4	28.8

[1] Includes Indians, Chinese, Japanese, and other races.
[2] Includes those whose marital condition was not reported.

As compared with Negro and immigrant women, the native white women engaged in gainful occupations comprise a smaller percentage of servants; they also include a larger percentage of young women and therefore a smaller percentage of married women and of widows. This explains, at least in part, why the percentage living with parents—either father or mother—is larger for each class of native white women gainfully employed than it is for either the foreign born or the Negro.

As compared with those whose parents were immigrants, the native white women of American parentage engaged in gainful occupations include a larger percentage of boarders and lodgers and a smaller percentage living at home with their parents. The main reason, probably, for the difference is found in the fact that, as the immigrants have mostly located in large cities or industrial centers, their children—the native white of foreign or mixed parentage—find opportunities for employment without leaving home or separating from their families, whereas a large proportion of the daughters of native American parents were born in rural districts or small towns, and, therefore, if they are to find employment in a city, must give up their home connections and become boarders or lodgers. So it comes about that in the 11 selected cities 17 per cent of the native white women of native parentage employed in gainful occupations are boarding or lodging, as compared with 8.7 per cent of the native white women of foreign or mixed parentage, and that only 42.9 per cent of the former are living at home with their parents as compared with 52.2 per cent of the latter.

The following summary presents for 1920 and for 1900 the distribution by family relationship of the gainfully employed women in the 11 selected cities:

TABLE 97.—NUMBER AND PER CENT DISTRIBUTION, BY FAMILY RELATIONSHIP, OF GAINFULLY OCCUPIED WOMEN, FOR THE 11 SELECTED CITIES COMBINED: 1920 AND 1900

FAMILY RELATIONSHIP	WOMEN 16 YEARS OF AGE AND OVER ENGAGED IN GAINFUL OCCUPATIONS			
	1920		1900	
	Number	Per cent distribution	Number	Per cent distribution
Total	373,204	100.0	212,761	100.0
Living at home	293,213	78.6	151,549	71.2
Head of family	56,659	15.2	34,245	16.1
Living with father	96,281	25.8	53,040	24.9
Living with mother	44,360	11.9	28,700	13.5
Living with husband	53,411	14.3	35,564	16.7
Living with other relative	42,502	11.4		
Boarding or lodging	50,297	13.5	61,212	28.8
Living with employer	29,694	8.0		

The table shows a marked increase in the percentage of gainfully employed women reported as living at home—an increase from 71.2 per cent in 1900 to 78.6 per cent in 1920, with a corresponding decrease in the percentage living away from home, i. e., either boarding or lodging or living with employer—a decrease from 28.8 per cent in 1900 to 21.5 per cent in 1920. It appears further that the increase in the percentage living at home represents mainly an increase in the percentage reported as living with husband or "other relative"— an increase from 16.7 in 1900 to 25.7 per cent in 1920. The other classes in the living at home group show no very great change in their relative importance. There is a slight decrease—from 16.1 to 15.2— in the percentage reported as heads of families; some decrease—from 13.5 to 11.9—in the percentage living with mother; and a slight increase—from 24.9 to 25.8—in the percentage living with father.

The increase noted in the percentage reported as living with husband or some relative other than father or mother is due mainly to the increase in the extent to which married women are taking up gainful occupations. In these 11 cities the number of married women gainfully employed increased by nearly 200 per cent, while for single women and for widows and divorced women the corresponding increase was only 52.5 per cent and 70.6 per cent, respectively; and the percentage which married women formed of the total number of women wage earners increased from 13.4 in 1900 to 22.9 in 1920.

Under these conditions there would naturally be a very considerable increase in the proportion of female bread-winners reported as living with husband. But just how great that increase was can not be determined, because in the 1900 classification, as just noted, the women living with husbands were included, without being separately distinguished, in the total number living with some relative other than father or mother.

TABLE 98.—NUMBER AND PER CENT OF GAINFULLY OCCUPIED WOMEN IN EACH MARITAL CLASS, 1920 AND 1910, WITH INCREASE, FOR THE 11 SELECTED CITIES COMBINED

MARITAL CLASS	WOMEN 16 YEARS OF AGE AND OVER ENGAGED IN GAINFUL OCCUPATIONS, IN 11 SELECTED CITIES					
	1920	1900	Increase: 1900 to 1920		Per cent distribution	
			Number	Per cent	1920	1900
All classes	373,204	212,761	160,443	75.4	100.0	100.0
Single [1]	224,428	147,181	77,247	52.5	60.1	69.2
Married	85,642	28,577	57,065	199.7	22.9	13.4
Widowed or divorced	63,134	37,003	26,131	70.6	16.9	17.4

[1] Includes those whose marital condition was not reported.

This phenomenon of an exceptionally large increase in the number of married women gainfully employed is common to all the 11 cities included in this tabulation, as is shown by the following table:

TABLE 99.—NUMBER OF GAINFULLY OCCUPIED WOMEN IN EACH MARITAL CLASS, 1920 AND 1910, WITH INCREASE, FOR EACH OF 11 SELECTED CITIES

CITY AND MARITAL CLASS	WOMEN 16 YEARS OF AGE AND OVER ENGAGED IN GAINFUL OCCUPATIONS			
	1920	1900	Increase: 1900 to 1920	
			Number	Per cent
TOTAL, 11 SELECTED CITIES				
All classes	373,204	212,761	160,443	75.4
Single [1]	224,428	147,181	77,247	52.5
Married	85,642	28,577	57,065	199.7
Widowed or divorced	63,134	37,003	26,131	70.6
FALL RIVER, MASS.				
All classes	19,111	16,170	2,941	18.2
Single [1]	12,142	11,303	839	7.4
Married	5,489	3,688	1,801	48.8
Widowed or divorced	1,480	1,179	301	25.5
PROVIDENCE, R. I.				
All classes	32,099	22,068	10,031	45.5
Single [1]	22,813	17,501	5,312	30.4
Married	5,433	2,118	3,315	156.5
Widowed or divorced	3,853	2,449	1,404	57.3

[1] Includes those whose marital condition was not reported.

TABLE 99.—NUMBER OF GAINFULLY OCCUPIED WOMEN IN EACH MARITAL
CLASS, 1920 AND 1910, WITH INCREASE, FOR EACH OF 11 SELECTED
CITIES—Continued

CITY AND MARITAL CLASS	WOMEN 16 YEARS OF AGE AND OVER ENGAGED IN GAINFUL OCCUPATIONS			
	1920	1900	Increase: 1900 to 1920	
			Number	Per cent
ROCHESTER, N. Y.				
All classes	36,956	18,910	18,046	95.4
Single [1]	25,255	15,574	9,681	62.2
Married	7,587	1,511	6,076	402.1
Widowed or divorced	4,114	1,825	2,289	125.4
PATERSON, N. J.				
All classes	17,999	10,958	7,041	64.3
Single [1]	11,990	8,771	3,219	36.7
Married	4,243	1,132	3,111	274.8
Widowed or divorced	1,766	1,055	711	67.4
CINCINNATI, OHIO				
All classes	50,231	35,150	15,081	42.9
Single [1]	33,735	27,518	6,217	22.6
Married	8,403	2,557	5,846	228.6
Widowed or divorced	8,093	5,075	3,018	59.5
INDIANAPOLIS, IND.				
All classes	35,454	15,444	20,010	129.6
Single [1]	19,511	10,481	9,030	86.2
Married	8,876	1,811	7,065	390.1
Widowed or divorced	7,067	3,152	3,915	124.2
ST. PAUL, MINN.				
All classes	27,863	15,444	12,419	80.4
Single [1]	21,223	13,268	7,955	60.0
Married	3,699	944	2,755	291.8
Widowed or divorced	2,941	1,232	1,709	138.7
KANSAS CITY, MO.				
All classes	39,925	15,684	24,241	154.6
Single [1]	21,389	9,857	11,532	117.0
Married	10,347	2,394	7,953	332.2
Widowed or divorced	8,189	3,433	4,756	138.5
ATLANTA, GA.				
All classes	31,553	14,257	17,296	121.3
Single [1]	12,659	6,092	6,567	107.8
Married	11,112	3,659	7,453	203.7
Widowed or divorced	7,782	4,506	3,276	72.7
LOUISVILLE, KY.				
All classes	33,655	21,831	11,824	54.2
Single [1]	18,429	13,949	4,480	32.1
Married	8,078	3,216	4,862	151.2
Widowed or divorced	7,148	4,666	2,482	53.2
NEW ORLEANS, LA.				
All classes	48,358	26,845	21,513	80.1
Single [1]	25,282	12,867	12,415	96.5
Married	12,375	5,547	6,828	123.1
Widowed or divorced	10,701	8,431	2,270	26.9

[1] Includes those whose marital condition was not reported.

The changes noted in the family relationship of women gainfully employed do not, however, appear to be entirely due to the increased employment of married women, for when the classification is shown for each marital class separately, as in the following table, it appears that there is a marked increase in the percentage of single women living at home—from 67.6 per cent in 1900 to 75.8 per cent in 1920—and also some increase in the corresponding percentage for married women.

TABLE 100.—PER CENT DISTRIBUTION, BY FAMILY RELATIONSHIP, OF GAINFULLY OCCUPIED WOMEN OF EACH MARITAL CLASS, FOR THE 11 SELECTED CITIES COMBINED: 1920 AND 1900

FAMILY RELATIONSHIP	WOMEN 16 YEARS OF AGE AND OVER ENGAGED IN GAINFUL OCCUPATIONS					
	Single		Married		Widowed or divorced	
	1920	1900	1920	1900	1920	1900
Total	100.0	100.0	100.0	100.0	100.0	100.0
Living at home	75.8	67.6	86.5	82.3	77.5	77.3
Head of family	6.2	5.3	9.5	14.4	54.9	60.2
Living with father	39.0	34.1	6.5	5.9	5.0	3.3
Living with mother	16.9	17.6	3.8	3.8	4.9	4.5
Living with husband			62.4	} 58.2		} 12.7
Living with other relative	13.7	10.6	4.3		12.7	9.2
Boarding or lodging	14.2	} 32.4	10.5	} 17.7	14.9	} 22.7
Living with employer	10.0		2.9		7.5	

As already shown (see p. 124) the percentage of gainfully employed women living at home depends to some extent upon the occupations in which they are engaged, and therefore a decrease in the percentage living at home for all women gainfully employed may be accounted for in part by occupational shifts. The most important change of this kind in recent years has been the decrease in the relative numbers of women employed in domestic service and the increase in the numbers employed in clerical and kindred pursuits. In the 11 cities here considered the percentage of servants and waitresses in the total number of women following gainful occupations decreased from 23.9 in 1900 to 13.6 in 1920. Since the proportion living at home is much smaller among servants and waitresses than in most other occupational groups (see Table 91), a reduction in the relative importance of this group would tend to increase the percentage living at home in the total number of women gainfully employed.

To eliminate the effect which the decline of the servants occupation may have had on the total, the following table has been prepared, showing the distribution by family relationship of the women gainfully employed in 1920 and 1900, exclusive of servants and waitresses.

TABLE 101.—PER CENT DISTRIBUTION, BY FAMILY RELATIONSHIP, OF GAIN-FULLY OCCUPIED WOMEN, EXCLUSIVE OF SERVANTS AND WAITRESSES, OF EACH MARITAL CLASS, FOR THE 11 SELECTED CITIES COMBINED: 1920 AND 1900

| FAMILY RELATIONSHIP | WOMEN 16 YEARS OF AGE AND OVER ENGAGED IN GAINFUL OCCUPATIONS, EXCLUSIVE OF SERVANTS AND WAITRESSES [1] | | | | | | | |
| | All classes | | Single | | Married | | Widowed or divorced | |
	1920	1900	1920	1900	1920	1900	1920	1900
All classes	100.0	100.0	100.0	100.0	100.0	100.0	100.0	100.0
Living at home	83.1	83.2	81.1	81.6	89.6	88.9	81.9	85.0
Head of family	15.0	17.9	6.1	5.8	9.4	15.5	58.0	67.3
Living with father	29.0	30.5	42.6	42.1	7.2	6.6	5.7	3.7
Living with mother	13.0	16.1	18.1	21.4	3.9	3.9	5.3	4.9
Living with husband	14.3 } 18.7		} 14.3 { 12.2		64.9 } 63.0		} 12.9 { 9.1	
Living with other relative	11.8				4.2			
Boarding or lodging	12.9 } 16.8		13.9 } 18.4		9.4 } 11.1		14.2 } 15.0	
Living with employer	4.0		5.0		1.0		3.9	

[1] Servants and waitresses, in the occupation classification of 1900, included charwomen, cleaners, and porters—occupations which were not included with servants and waitresses in 1920.

When servants and waitresses are eliminated from the com-parison, and the figures are shown for each marital class separately, the changes between 1900 and 1920 which were shown in Table 100 largely disappear, the percentage of working women living at home remaining practically unchanged as regards both single and married women. But in the case of married women there is still a rather marked decrease in the percentage reported as heads of families (from 15.5 to 9.4), and an increase (from 63.0 to 69.1) in the percentage reported as living with husband or with some relative other than father or mother. This change reflects a difference in the rate of increase of the two classes, for while in the 11 cities the number of gainfully employed married women reported as heads of families increased 97.2 per cent between 1900 and 1920, the number of those reported as living with husband, including the relatively small but indistinguishable number living with "other relative," increased 243.7 per cent. The gainfully employed married woman reported as the head of a family represents in most cases probably the deserted or deserting wife who finds it necessary to earn a living for herself and those dependent on her; and the decline in the relative importance of this class among the married women gainfully employed means that an increasing proportion are married women who either from necessity or choice take up a gainful occupation in order to supplement the wages earned by their husbands or other members of the family.

As regards the single women gainfully employed it is noteworthy that, leaving servants and waitresses out of account, there was little change in this interval of 20 years in the distribution by family relationship. The percentage living at home remained practically the same, and so, of course, did its complement, the percentage boarding, lodging, or living with employer. There was some decrease in the percentage living with mother, some increase in the percentage living with some relative other than father or mother, and a slight increase in percentage reported as heads of families, which, it may be well to note in this connection, would include the single woman who is living by herself in an apartment, and the one who is operating a boarding house.

The decrease in the percentage of single women living with mother may not improbably reflect a decrease in the relative importance of that class of single women—widows' daughters and others—who take up an occupation largely from necessity, or in order to support themselves and those dependent upon them. For while that class may not have decreased, it probably has not increased to the same extent as the other class consisting of women who are following a gainful occupation more or less as a matter of choice or preference without being absolutely compelled to do so in order to make a living. Of course, the two classes here mentioned are not sharply differentiated. But the statistics indicate, or at any rate suggest, that an increasing proportion of the women who follow gainful occupations do so from choice or preference and not solely from necessity. The economic motive for following a gainful occupation is doubtless almost always present with women as it is with men. But while the number of gainfully employed women with whom it is mainly a question of getting a living may not have decreased, the number of those with whom it is mainly a question of getting a better living and more independence has probably greatly increased.

For widowed and divorced women gainfully employed the change between 1900 and 1920 in the distribution by family relationship, as shown by Table 101, was more marked than for either of the other two marital classes, the change consisting mainly of a rather striking decrease in the percentage reported as heads of families. The explanation may be that a diminishing proportion of the gainfully employed widows are engaged in the widow's traditional occupation of keeping boarders or lodgers. It is quite probable that to an increasing extent they are seeking and finding employment in other occupations, and for that reason are less likely to be heads of families and more likely to live with some relative or become boarders or roomers.

SERVANTS AND WAITRESSES "LIVING OUT"

It is of interest to note in this connection that, as shown by Table 102, the percentage of servants and waitresses living at home increased very materially between 1900 and 1920, the percentage being 49.6 for 1920 as compared with 33.2 for 1900. This indicates, of course, that the practice of living in the family of the employer is becoming less usual for servants, and that an increasing proportion of them are "living out." We do not, it is true, know just how many of those not living at home in 1900 were in fact living in their employer's family and how many were boarders or lodgers in other families. But probably in 1900, as in 1920, the majority of those not living at home were living with employer; and the proportion would doubtless be still larger if the figures were shown for servants separately, not including waitresses. But unfortunately it is not possible to make this segregation in the 1900 figures.

TABLE 102.—NUMBER AND PER CENT DISTRIBUTION, BY FAMILY RELATIONSHIP, OF WOMEN EMPLOYED AS SERVANTS AND WAITRESSES, 1920 AND 1910, WITH INCREASE OR DECREASE, FOR THE 11 SELECTED CITIES COMBINED

FAMILY RELATIONSHIP	WOMEN 16 YEARS OF AGE AND OVER EMPLOYED AS SERVANTS AND WAITRESSES					
	Number		Increase (+) or decrease (−): 1900 to 1920		Per cent distribution	
	1920	1900	Number	Per cent	1920	1900
Total	50,709	50,871	−162	−0.3	100.0	100.0
Living at home	25,161	16,873	+8,288	+49.1	49.6	33.2
Head of family	8,251	5,309	+2,942	+55.4	16.3	10.4
Living with father	2,747	3,605	−858	−23.8	5.4	7.1
Living with mother	2,559	2,643	−84	−3.2	5.0	5.2
Living with husband or other relative	11,604	5,316	+6,288	+118.3	22.9	10.4
Living with husband	7,289	(1)	(1)	(1)	14.4	(1)
Living with other relative	4.315	(1)	(1)	(1)	8.5	(1)
Boarding or lodging or living with employer	25,548	33,998	−8,450	−24.9	50.4	66.8
Boarding or lodging	8,593	(1)	(1)	(1)	16.9	(1)
Living with employer	16,955	(1)	(1)	(1)	33.4	(1)

1 Figures not available.

Table 102 shows also that while the number of servants living with employer or boarding or lodging decreased very materially, the number living with husband or with some relative other than father or mother more than doubled. This reflects the increased employment of married women as servants. The number reported as heads of families also increased, though not to so marked a degree, but the relatively small number living with father or with mother decreased.

The increase in the number of married servants and waitresses in these 11 cities is shown by the following table:

TABLE 103.—NUMBER OF WOMEN IN EACH MARITAL CLASS EMPLOYED AS SERVANTS AND WAITRESSES, 1920 AND 1910, WITH INCREASE, FOR THE 11 SELECTED CITIES COMBINED

MARITAL CLASS	WOMEN 16 YEARS OF AGE AND OVER EMPLOYED AS SERVANTS AND WAITRESSES			
	1920	1900	Increase [1]	
			Number	Per cent
Total	50,709	50,871	−162	−0.3
Single [2]	23,755	35,779	−12,024	−33.6
Married	14,568	6,307	8,261	131.0
Widowed or divorced	12,386	8,785	3,601	41.0

[1] A minus sign (−) denotes decrease.　　　[2] Includes those whose marital condition was not reported.

An increase in the percentage of servants and waitresses living at home took place not only, as just indicated, in the total for all cities combined, but also in each of the 11 cities covered by this tabulation as is shown by the table below. At each census, 1900 and 1920, the percentage living at home is noticeably larger in each of the three southern cities than in any of the northern cities; but in 1920 the percentage in the northern cities, though remaining smaller, showed a greater increase than in the southern cities. In 1920 the percentage was largest in Atlanta (68.5) and smallest in Providence (25.8).

TABLE 104.—NUMBER AND PERCENTAGE LIVING AT HOME IN THE TOTAL NUMBER OF WOMEN EMPLOYED AS SERVANTS AND WAITRESSES, FOR EACH OF 11 SELECTED CITIES: 1920 AND 1910

CITY AND CENSUS YEAR	WOMEN 16 YEARS OF AGE AND OVER EMPLOYED AS SERVANTS AND WAITRESSES [1]		
	Total number	Living at home	
		Number	Per cent
Total:			
1920	50,709	25,161	49.6
1900	50,871	16,873	33.2
Fall River:			
1920	701	250	35.7
1900	988	154	15.6
Providence:			
1920	3,371	869	25.8
1900	4,322	656	15.2
Rochester:			
1920	2,856	826	28.9
1900	3,293	466	14.2
Paterson:			
1920	817	248	30.4
1900	1,186	173	14.6
Cincinnati:			
1920	7,445	3,257	43.7
1900	8,499	2,331	27.4
Indianapolis:			
1920	4,459	2,440	54.7
1900	3,966	1,198	30.2
St. Paul:			
1920	3,387	930	27.5
1900	4,694	682	14.5

[1] Charwomen, cleaners, and porters were included with servants and waitresses in 1900 but not in 1920.

TABLE **104.**—Number and Percentage Living at Home in the Total Number of Women Employed as Servants and Waitresses, for Each of 11 Selected Cities: 1920 and 1910—Continued

CITY AND CENSUS YEAR	WOMEN 16 YEARS OF AGE AND OVER EMPLOYED AS SERVANTS AND WAITRESSES [1]		
	Total number	Living at home	
		Number	Per cent
Kansas City, Mo.:			
1920	5,730	2,380	41.5
1900	4,228	940	22.2
Atlanta:			
1920	6,847	4,689	68.5
1900	4,139	2,613	63.1
Louisville:			
1920	4,635	2,755	59.4
1900	6,657	2,770	41.6
New Orleans:			
1920	10,461	6,517	62.3
1900	8,899	4,890	54.9

[1] Charwomen, cleaners, and porters were included with servants and waitresses in 1900 but not in 1920.

In general, and in way of summary, it may be said that as regards the proportion of working women living in the family relationship in these 11 cities there were no marked changes between 1900 and 1920 apart from those caused by the large increase in the number of married women gainfully employed, and by the decrease in number of women employed as servants. The reduction in the number of servants, coupled with the increasing practice of having servants live out, had the effect of lowering the percentage of working women living with employer; and the increase in the number of married women engaged in gainful occupations had the effect of lowering the percentage of working women who were boarders or lodgers. A lower percentage boarding or lodging or living with employer involves, of course, a correspondingly higher percentage living at home, or with relatives. But as regards the working women who were not married and were not servants there appears to have been no marked change between 1900 and 1920 in the proportion living in the family relationship, or with relatives.

The above conclusion applies to the totals for the 11 cities combined. In some of the individual cities included in this total there have been changes other than those here noted, as is shown in the section which follows.

COMPARISON WITH 1900 BY INDIVIDUAL CITIES

In the following table the changes between 1900 and 1920 in the distribution by family relationship of women gainfully employed are shown for the individual cities:

TABLE 105.—NUMBER AND PER CENT DISTRIBUTION, BY FAMILY RELATIONSHIP, OF GAINFULLY OCCUPIED WOMEN, FOR EACH OF 11 SELECTED CITIES: 1920 AND 1900

CITY AND CENSUS YEAR	WOMEN 16 YEARS OF AGE AND OVER ENGAGED IN GAINFUL OCCUPATIONS						
	Total number	Living at home					Boarding or lodging or living with employer
		Total	Head of family	Living with—			
				Father	Mother	Husband or other relative	
NUMBER							
Total:							
1920	373,204	293,213	56,659	96,281	44,360	95,913	79,991
1900	212,761	151,549	34,245	53,040	28,700	35,564	61,212
Fall River:							
1920	19,111	17,192	1,881	7,063	2,298	5,950	1,919
1900	16,170	13,220	1,245	5,847	2,116	4,012	2,950
Providence:							
1920	32,099	25,339	3,732	10,187	4,272	7,148	6,760
1900	22,068	15,056	2,294	6,650	3,057	3,055	7,012
Rochester:							
1920	36,956	28,657	3,897	11,349	4,409	9,002	8,299
1900	18,910	12,955	1,738	6,078	2,808	2,331	5,955
Paterson:							
1920	17,999	15,964	1,856	6,976	2,298	4,834	2,035
1900	10,958	8,709	1,068	4,268	1,758	1,615	2,249
Cincinnati:							
1920	50,231	40,709	8,852	14,074	7,206	10,577	9,522
1900	35,150	25,868.	5,530	10,069	6,079	4,190	9,282
Indianapolis:							
1920	35,454	27,624	5,557	9,009	3,511	9,547	7,830
1900	15,444	10,487	2,434	3,807	1,887	2,359	4,957
St. Paul:							
1920	27,863	20,151	2,765	8,908	3,418	5,060	7,712
1900	15,444	7,819	1,355	3,679	1,341	1,444	7,625
Kansas City, Mo.:							
1920	39,925	27,244	5,824	7,704	3,671	10,045	12,681
1900	15,684	9,540	2,732	2,871	1,590	2,347	6,144
Atlanta:							
1920	31,553	24,492	6,677	4,380	3,064	10,371	7,061
1900	14,257	11,424	4,347	1,709	1,598	3,770	2,833
Louisville:							
1920	33,655	27,185	6,469	7,505	4,185	9,026	6,470
1900	21,831	15,893	4,207	4,665	3,030	3,991	5,938
New Orleans:							
1920	48,358	38,656	9,149	9,126	6,028	14,353	9,702
1900	26,845	20,578	7,295	3,397	3,436	6,450	6,267
PER CENT OF TOTAL							
Total:							
1920	100.0	78.6	15.2	25.8	11.9	25.7	21.4
1900	100.0	71.2	16.1	24.9	13.5	16.7	28.8
Fall River:							
1920	100.0	90.0	9.8	37.0	12.0	31.1	10.0
1900	100.0	81.8	7.7	36.2	13.1	24.8	18.2
Providence:							
1920	100.0	78.9	11.6	31.7	13.3	22.3	21.1
1900	100.0	68.2	10.4	30.1	13.9	13.8	31.8
Rochester:							
1920	100.0	77.5	10.5	30.7	11.9	24.4	22.5
1900	100.0	68.5	9.2	32.1	14.8	12.3	31.5
Paterson:							
1920	100.0	88.7	10.3	38.8	12.8	26.9	11.3
1900	100.0	79.5	9.7	38.9	16.0	14.7	20.5
Cincinnati:							
1920	100.0	81.0	17.6	28.0	14.3	21.1	19.0
1900	100.0	73.6	15.7	28.6	17.3	11.9	26.4
Indianapolis:							
1920	100.0	77.9	15.7	25.4	9.9	26.9	22.1
1900	100.0	67.9	15.8	24.7	12.2	15.3	23.1

TABLE 105.—NUMBER AND PER CENT DISTRIBUTION, BY FAMILY RELATION-
SHIP, OF GAINFULLY OCCUPIED WOMEN, FOR EACH OF 11 SELECTED CITIES:
1920 AND 1900—Continued

CITY AND CENSUS YEAR	WOMEN 16 YEARS OF AGE AND OVER ENGAGED IN GAINFUL OCCUPATIONS						
	Total number	Living at home					Board-ing or lodg-ing or living with em-ployer
		Total	Head of family	Living with—		Hus-band or other relative	
				Father	Mother		
	PER CENT OF TOTAL—continued						
St. Paul:							
1920	100. 0	72. 3	9. 9	32. 0	12. 3	18. 2	27. 7
1900	100. 0	50. 6	8. 8	23. 8	8. 7	9. 3	49. 4
Kansas City, Mo.:							
1920	100. 0	68. 2	14. 6	19. 3	9. 2	25. 2	31. 8
1900	100. 0	60. 8	17. 4	18. 3	10. 1	15. 0	39. 2
Atlanta:							
1920	100. 0	77. 6	21. 2	13. 9	9. 7	32. 9	22. 4
1900	100. 0	80. 1	30. 5	12. 0	11. 2	26. 4	19. 9
Louisville:							
1920	100. 0	80. 8	19. 2	22. 3	12. 4	26. 8	19. 2
1900	100. 0	72. 8	19. 3	21. 4	13. 9	18. 3	27. 2
New Orleans:							
1920	100. 0	79. 9	18. 9	18. 9	12. 5	29. 7	20. 1
1900	100. 0	76. 7	27. 2	12. 7	12. 8	24. 0	23. 3

As a rule the changes in each city are the same in character as those
shown in the totals for the 11 cities combined. Thus, in every city
except Atlanta there was a pronounced increase in the percentage
of gainfully employed women living at home and a corresponding
decrease in the percentage boarding or lodging or living with employer; and in every city the increase in the percentage living at home
reflects an increase in the percentage living with husband or some
relative other than father or mother. The percentage reported as
heads of families decreased to a marked degree in Kansas City,
Atlanta, and New Orleans, but increased or remained practically
stationary in the other cities; the percentage living with father underwent little change, as a rule, but shows a striking increase in St. Paul
and New Orleans; while the percentage living with mother decreased
in the total and in every city except St. Paul.

The analysis of the totals for the 11 cities combined brought out
the fact that the increase in the percentage of gainfully employed
women living at home was largely the result of a decrease in the
relative number of servants and waitresses, a large proportion of
whom (50.4 per cent in 1920) do not live at home, but are living with
their employers or boarding or lodging. To determine how far this
same factor may have affected the figures for the individual cities
the following table has been prepared in which the distribution by
family relationship is shown for women gainfully employed, exclusive
of servants and waitresses.

TABLE **106.**—NUMBER AND PER CENT DISTRIBUTION, BY FAMILY RELATIONSHIP,
OF GAINFULLY OCCUPIED WOMEN, EXCLUSIVE OF SERVANTS AND WAITRESSES,
FOR EACH OF 11 SELECTED CITIES: 1920 AND 1900

CITY AND CENSUS YEAR	WOMEN 16 YEARS OF AGE AND OVER ENGAGED IN GAINFUL OCCUPATIONS, EXCLUSIVE OF SERVANTS AND WAITRESSES						
	Total number	Living at home					Boarding or lodging or living with employer
		Total	Head of family	Living with—			
				Father	Mother	Husband or other relative	
					NUMBER		
Total:							
1920	322,495	268,052	48,408	93,534	41,801	84,309	54,443
1900	161,890	134,676	28,936	49,435	26,057	30,248	27,214
Fall River:							
1920	18,410	16,942	1,783	7,027	2,262	5,870	1,468
1900	15,182	13,066	1,213	5,817	2,094	3,942	2,116
Providence:							
1920	28,728	24,470	3,366	10,108	4,205	6,791	4,258
1900	17,746	14,400	2,103	6,483	2,956	2,858	3,346
Rochester:							
1920	34,100	27,831	3,578	11,278	4,357	8,618	6,269
1900	15,617	12,489	1,618	5,938	2,735	2,198	3,128
Paterson:							
1920	17,182	15,716	1,770	6,940	2,275	4,731	1,466
1900	9,772	8,536	1,019	4,209	1,735	1,573	1,236
Cincinnati:							
1920	42,786	37,452	7,582	13,663	6,923	9,284	5,334
1900	26,651	23,537	4,836	9,328	5,670	3,703	3,114
Indianapolis:							
1920	30,995	25,184	4,805	8,699	3,294	8,386	5,811
1900	11,478	9,289	2,117	3,480	1,675	2,017	2,189
St. Paul:							
1920	24,476	19,221	2,488	8,789	3,345	4,599	5,255
1900	10,750	7,137	1,229	3,362	1,268	1,278	3,613
Kansas City, Mo.:							
1920	34,195	24,864	5,078	7,507	3,452	8,827	9,331
1900	11,456	8,600	2,461	2,674	1,399	2,066	2,856
Atlanta:							
1920	24,706	19,803	5,152	3,998	2,504	8,149	4,903
1900	10,118	8,811	3,256	1,454	1,243	2,858	1,307
Louisville:							
1920	29,020	24,430	5,557	7,174	3,892	7,807	4,590
1900	15,174	13,123	3,295	4,191	2,592	3,045	2,051
New Orleans:							
1920	37,897	32,139	7,249	8,351	5,292	11,247	5,758
1900	17,946	15,688	5,789	2,499	2,690	4,710	2,258
					PER CENT DISTRIBUTION		
Total:							
1920	100.0	83.1	15.0	29.0	13.0	26.1	16.9
1900	100.0	83.2	17.9	30.5	16.1	18.7	16.8
Fall River:							
1920	100.0	92.0	9.7	38.2	12.3	31.9	8.0
1900	100.0	86.1	8.0	38.3	13.8	26.0	13.9
Providence:							
1920	100.0	85.2	11.7	35.2	14.6	23.6	14.8
1900	100.0	81.1	11.9	36.5	16.7	16.1	18.9
Rochester:							
1920	100.0	81.6	10.5	33.1	12.8	25.3	18.4
1900	100.0	80.0	10.4	38.0	17.5	14.1	20.0
Paterson:							
1920	100.0	91.5	10.3	40.4	13.2	27.5	8.5
1900	100.0	87.4	10.4	43.1	17.8	16.1	12.6
Cincinnati:							
1920	100.0	87.5	17.7	31.9	16.2	21.7	12.5
1900	100.0	88.3	18.1	35.0	21.3	13.9	11.7

TABLE 106.—NUMBER AND PER CENT DISTRIBUTION, BY FAMILY RELATIONSHIP, OF GAINFULLY OCCUPIED WOMEN, EXCLUSIVE OF SERVANTS AND WAITRESSES, FOR EACH OF 11 SELECTED CITIES: 1920 AND 1900—Continued

CITY AND CENSUS YEAR	WOMEN 16 YEARS OF AGE AND OVER ENGAGED IN GAINFUL OCCUPATIONS, EXCLUSIVE OF SERVANTS AND WAITRESSES						
	Total number	Living at home					Boarding or lodging or living with employer
		Total	Head of family	Living with—			
				Father	Mother	Husband or other relative	
	PER CENT DISTRIBUTION—continued						
Indianapolis:							
1920	100.0	81.3	15.5	28.1	10.6	27.1	18.7
1900	100.0	80.9	18.4	30.3	14.6	17.6	19.1
St. Paul:							
1920	100.0	78.5	10.2	35.9	13.7	18.8	21.5
1900	100.0	66.4	11.4	31.3	11.8	11.9	33.6
Kansas City, Mo.:							
1920	100.0	72.7	14.9	22.0	10.1	25.8	27.3
1900	100.0	75.1	21.5	23.3	12.2	18.0	24.9
Atlanta:							
1920	100.0	80.2	20.9	16.2	10.1	33.0	19.8
1900	100.0	87.1	32.2	14.4	12.3	28.2	12.9
Louisville:							
1920	100.0	84.2	19.1	24.7	13.4	26.9	15.8
1900	100.0	86.5	21.7	27.6	17.1	20.1	13.5
New Orleans:							
1920	100.0	84.8	19.1	22.0	14.0	29.7	15.2
1900	100.0	87.4	32.3	13.9	15.0	26.2	12.6

When the percentages are based upon the total number of women gainfully employed, Atlanta, as shown by Table 105, is the only one of the 11 cities in which the percentage living at home decreased between 1900 and 1920. But when servants and waitresses are eliminated from the total, as in Table 106, there are four cities besides Atlanta which show a decrease in this percentage, namely, Cincinnati, Kansas City, Louisville, and New Orleans; and as regards each of the remaining cities the increase in this percentage, though not entirely eliminated, becomes much less marked.

To a large extent, therefore, the increase in the percentage of gainfully employed women living at home was simply the result of the fact that in every city there was a smaller proportion—and in 7 of the 11 cities a smaller actual number—of servants and waitresses in 1920 than in 1900, as shown by Table 107.

Atlanta, as just noted, is exceptional in showing a rather marked decrease in the percentage of working women living at home; St. Paul, on the other hand, shows a marked increase in that percentage. The statistics are not, however, to be accepted as proving or even indicating that the working women of St. Paul show an increasing inclination for home life and those of Atlanta an increasing aversion to it. While it is not easy to explain fully the reasons for the changes noted in these percentages, it is safe to say that they are not to any great extent, if at all, a reflection of changing preferences or of differing habits on the part of working women, but are determined mainly by other factors.

TABLE 107.—NUMBER AND PER CENT OF SERVANTS AND WAITRESSES IN THE TOTAL NUMBER OF GAINFULLY OCCUPIED WOMEN, FOR EACH OF 11 SELECTED CITIES: 1920 AND 1900

CITY AND CENSUS YEAR	WOMEN 16 YEARS OF AGE AND OVER ENGAGED IN GAINFUL OCCUPATIONS		
	Total number	Employed as servants and waitresses [1]	
		Number	Per cent of total
Total:			
1920	373, 204	50, 709	13. 6
1900	212, 761	50, 871	23. 9
Fall River:			
1920	19, 111	701	3. 7
1900	16, 170	988	6. 1
Providence:			
1920	32, 099	3, 371	10. 5
1900	22, 068	4, 322	19. 6
Rochester:			
1920	36, 956	2, 856	7. 7
1900	18, 910	3, 293	17. 4
Paterson:			
1920	17, 999	817	4. 5
1900	10, 958	1, 186	10. 8
Cincinnati:			
1920	50, 231	7, 445	14. 8
1900	35, 150	8, 499	24. 2
Indianapolis:			
1920	35, 454	4, 459	12. 6
1900	15, 444	3, 966	25. 7
St. Paul:			
1920	27, 863	3, 387	12. 2
1900	15, 444	4, 694	30. 4
Kansas City, Mo.:			
1920	39, 925	5, 730	14. 4
1900	15, 684	4, 228	27. 0
Atlanta:			
1920	31, 553	6, 847	21. 7
1900	14, 257	4, 139	29. 0
Louisville:			
1920	33, 655	4, 635	13. 8
1900	21, 831	6, 657	30. 5
New Orleans:			
1920	48, 358	10, 461	21. 6
1900	26, 845	8, 899	33. 1

[1] Charwomen, cleaners, and porters were included with servants and waitresses in 1900 but not in 1920.

As regards the exceptional decrease between 1900 and 1920 in the percentage of working women living at home in the city of Atlanta—a decrease from 80.1 in 1900 to 77.6 in 1920, or when servants and waitresses are left out of account, from 87.1 to 80.2—it may be noted that within that interval of 20 years a marked change took place in the proportions white and colored among women gainfully employed in that city. Thus in 1900 only 28.3 per cent of the total were white; but by 1920 this percentage had advanced to 48.1, the number of white women at work having increased by 276 per cent while the number of Negro women at work increased by only 60 per cent.

It may be noted further that Atlanta is a city which had a very exceptional growth, the population having increased 123 per cent, or from 89,872 in 1900 to 200,616 in 1920. Since very little immigration of foreign origin goes to this city, this population growth must in large part have resulted from the immigration of native population from the surrounding region or from more distant parts of the United States; and it is probable that this domestic immigration included many single white women, who left their homes to find employment in this city, and thus recruited the number of working women living away from home.

This inference is borne out by the figures in the following table, which shows that the decrease in the percentage living at home was confined mainly to the white women gainfully employed and was most marked for single white women. Since comparatively few of the white women were servants living with employer, the decrease in the percentage living at home means mainly an increase in the percentage boarding or lodging.

TABLE **108.**—NUMBER AND PERCENTAGE LIVING AT HOME OF THE TOTAL NUMBER OF GAINFULLY OCCUPIED WOMEN, CLASSIFIED BY RACE AND MARITAL CONDITION, FOR ATLANTA, GA.: 1920 AND 1900

| | WOMEN 16 YEARS OF AGE AND OVER GAINFULLY EMPLOYED IN ATLANTA | | |
| RACE AND MARITAL CLASS | Total number | Living at home | |
		Number	Per cent of total
All classes:			
1920	[1] 31, 553	24, 492	77. 6
1900	14, 257	11, 424	80. 1
White—			
1920	15, 173	10, 894	71. 8
1900	4, 037	3, 149	78. 0
Single:			
1920	9, 070	6, 221	68. 6
1900	2, 585	1, 972	76. 3
Married:			
1920	3, 479	2, 767	79. 5
1900	561	470	83. 8
Widowed or divorced:			
1920	2, 624	1, 906	72. 6
1900	891	707	79. 3
Negro—			
1920	16, 377	13, 598	83. 0
1900	10, 220	8, 275	81. 0
Single:			
1920	3, 588	2, 488	68. 5
1900	3, 507	2, 400	68. 4
Married:			
1920	7, 633	6, 740	88. 3
1900	3, 098	2, 775	89. 6
Widowed or divorced:			
1920	5, 156	4, 370	84. 8
1900	3, 615	3, 100	85. 8

[1] Includes 3 other than whites and Negroes.

In contrast with Atlanta, St. Paul is a city in which there was a very marked increase in the percentage of working women living at home—an increase from 50.6 per cent in 1900 to 72.3 in 1920. If servants and waitresses are excluded from the totals the increase in this percentage—from 66.4 to 78.5 (see Table 106)—is not as great but is still quite striking, especially as compared with a decrease from 87.1 to 80.2 in Atlanta.

In further contrast with Atlanta, St. Paul in 1920 was a city which had not been growing rapidly. Its population, it is true, increased 31.7 per cent from 1900 to 1910, but only 9.3 per cent from 1910 to 1920, while the corresponding percentages of growth for Atlanta were 72.3 and 29.6, respectively. This contrast in the rate of growth of the two cities probably goes far toward explaining the fact that in the one city—the city of rapid growth—the percentage of working women living away from home increased while in the other city it decreased.

Considering the figures of growth for St. Paul it seems reasonable to suppose that by 1920 the numbers of young women coming to that city to take up gainful occupations had fallen off, and that many of the earlier arrivals had joined the home making, or home sharing, class, while the new recruits in the local army of gainful workers came mostly from resident families with the result that the census of 1920 showed a great increase in the percentage of gainfully employed women living at home.

In 1900 the percentage of working women living at home was exceptionally small in St. Paul. In 1920 it was more in line with the percentages for other cities. So it looks as if in that city conditions were becoming more settled and home or family life for working women was becoming more common or general, as a natural result of a retardation in the growth of that city.

XV

OTHER WAGE EARNERS; BOARDERS AND LODGERS

When the woman following a gainful occupation is living at home the census records show what other members of her family, if any, are also following gainful occupations, thus making it possible to classify the woman who is a breadwinner with respect to the number of other breadwinners in the family to which she belongs, and also with respect to the number of "dependents," using that term to designate those members of the family who are not gainfully employed. Such a classification has been made for the 293,213 women, in 11 selected cities, reported as gainfully employed and living at home, the cities being the same as those covered in the tabulation by family relationship, as presented in the preceding chapter. (See p. 122.)

(See p. 122.)

NUMBER OF OTHER WAGE EARNERS IN THE FAMILY

The classification here described distinguishes those cases in which the woman following the gainful occupation appears to be the only wage earner from those cases in which her earnings supplement those of one or more other members of the family, and thus affords some indication of the extent to which women at work are supporting families. Of course, these statistics, like statistics in general, do not tell the whole story. We have no information as to what the woman earns, or as to the relative importance of her contribution to the family income. There may be absent members who are contributing to the support of the family or, on the other hand, are drawing upon the family income instead of contributing to it. Again, where there are other wage earners in the family, the woman at work may spend all her earnings on herself, making no contribution to the family budget nor any payments even for her board or lodging. She may be working for pin money. Nevertheless, a classification with respect to the number of breadwinners and of dependents in the family does throw some light upon the question of the extent to which women in gainful occupations are supporting families by their own unaided efforts and the extent to which they share the burden with other members of the family; for where the woman is the only wage earner in the family the presumption is that the burden of supporting the family rests upon her alone, and where the employed woman is one of two or more breadwinners it is evident that the family is not entire-

148

ly dependent upon her earnings.   Moreover, the ratio of breadwinners to dependents in the family affords some indication of the burden or responsibility resting upon the individual wage-earning woman.[1]

It should be explained at the outset that the term family as used in this chapter has a more restricted scope than it has in the established census terminology, in that it does not as here used include persons boarding or lodging with the family.   It includes only those persons living together in the same household who are related by kinship or marriage.   It seems hardly necessary to point out the reason for this limiting of the definition for the purposes of this tabulation, since it is obvious that a classification of women gainfully employed with respect to the number of other breadwinners and number of dependents in the family would largely lose its significance if boarders and lodgers were included and counted in the family, either as breadwinners or dependents.

The results of this classification of the gainfully employed women living at home in these 11 selected cities are presented in the following table:

TABLE **109.**—GAINFULLY EMPLOYED WOMEN LIVING AT HOME, CLASSIFIED ACCORDING TO THE NUMBER OF OTHER EMPLOYED MEMBERS, AND NUMBER OF UNEMPLOYED MEMBERS IN THE FAMILY, FOR THE 11 SELECTED CITIES COMBINED: 1920

CLASS	GAINFULLY EMPLOYED WOMEN LIVING AT HOME					
	Total	Unemployed members in family				
		None	1	2	3	4 or more
All classes	293, 213	79, 768	88, 505	56, 247	32, 069	36, 624
Number in family having—						
No other employed member	44, 153	22, 191	12, 863	5, 580	2, 100	1, 419
1 other	111, 112	38, 638	32, 813	19, 131	10, 247	10, 283
2 others	69, 825	12, 375	22, 891	15, 221	8, 979	10, 359
3 or more others	68, 123	6, 564	19, 938	16, 315	10, 743	14, 563
Per cent of total	100. 0	27. 2	30. 2	19. 2	10. 9	12. 5
In family having—						
No other employed member	15. 1	7. 6	4. 4	1. 9	0. 7	0. 5
1 other	37. 9	13. 2	11. 2	6. 5	3. 5	3. 5
2 others	23. 8	4. 2	7. 8	5. 2	3. 1	3. 5
3 or more others	23. 2	2. 2	6. 8	5. 6	3. 7	5. 0

While the great majority of the gainfully employed women included in the above tabulation—in fact, 84.9 per cent of them—belong to families in which there were one or more other gainfully employed persons or wage earners, there were 44,153 women—15.1 per cent of the total number—who were the only breadwinners in the family.

[1] It should perhaps be noted that in this classification the same family may be represented more than once, or two or more times in case there are two or more women in the family who are gainfully employed. It is a classification not of families but of individual working women with respect to conditions in the families in which they live.

Regarding these it should be immediately noted that about one-half of them—22,191—were classified as living in a family having no unemployed persons or dependents. That means that the woman was living alone, in the sense at least of not living with any relatives. She may, however, have had boarders or lodgers or other persons not related to her living with her; or she may have been keeping house quite by herself, living perhaps in an apartment, and either doing her own cooking or taking her meals out. The remaining number of women who were the only breadwinners in the family—constituting 7.5 per cent of the gainfully employed women living at home in the 11 cities—represented families in which there were one or more dependents or members not gainfully employed. So far as the evidence of this tabulation goes for this group of cities, comparatively few of these single breadwinners are supporting large families. Of 293,213 women included in this table, only 3,519, or 1. 2 per cent, represented cases in which one employed woman is apparently supporting unaided a family comprising three or more dependents, and only 9,099, or 3. 1 per cent, represented cases in which one woman was apparently supporting two or more dependents.

The above classification with respect to breadwinners and dependents, it may be noted (Table 109), distinguishes 20 primary classes, of which the largest consists of women living in families in which there is one other person gainfully employed and none unemployed. In other words, the family in these cases consists of the woman herself and one other wage earner and it is of interest to note that of the 38,638 women tabulated in this class 24,239 (as shown by Table 110) were married women, who, assuming that the other member of the family is the husband, represent cases in which husband and wife are both working and have apparently no children or other persons dependent upon them. It is of further interest to note that the married women in this class comprise nearly one-third (32.7 per cent) of the total number of married women reported as living at home and following a gainful occupation in these 11 cities.

The next most numerous class in the above classification is that in which the gainfully employed woman is one of two wage earners in a family having one unemployed person—a family of three. This class would include families in which the father and the only daughter are working and the mother is the home carer; also families in which the widowed mother is supported by two children, one of them a daughter. Although it has never been done it would be quite possible on the basis of available census data to classify families in any area not only with respect to the number of breadwinners and number of dependents, as has been done here, but with respect to the particular members of family—father, mother, sons, daughters, etc.—who are, respectively, breadwinners and dependents.

The third largest class distinguished in Table 109 is composed of gainfully employed women living in families of four, comprising three breadwinners and one dependent.

The three classes here mentioned comprise in the aggregate 32.2 per cent of the total number of women included in this tabulation, which means that nearly one-third of the women living at home and gainfully employed in these 11 cities belonged to families in which there were either one or two other breadwinners and either only one dependent or none.

The cases in which the woman gainfully employed was either the sole breadwinner or was one of two breadwinners in a family comprising not less than three dependents, numbered 24,049, representing 8.2 per cent, or nearly one-twelfth, of the total number.

The cases in which the gainfully employed women belonged to a large, or fairly large, family comprising three or more breadwinners and three or more dependents numbered 44,644, representing 15.2 per cent of the total number of women included in this tabulation.

In Table 110 the classification with respect to number of other breadwinners and number of dependents is shown for the gainfully employed women classified by marital condition.

Of the single women included in the above classification 7,858, or 4.6 per cent of the total number, are classified as being in families in which there were "no other employed members" and "no unemployed members," which means that the woman, though classified as living at home, was either living alone or else living with people to whom she was not related by kinship. Some of these lone single women, however, may have kept boarders or taken lodgers. The woman who is herself a boarder or lodger, it may be noted, would not be included in this tabulation, as she is not living at home.

There were 10,079 single women—5.9 per cent of the total—who were the only breadwinners, or gainfully employed persons, in families comprising one or more dependents, or persons not gainfully employed. These represent cases in which the woman at work is apparently supporting the family unaided. On the other hand, 16,636 single women—9.8 per cent of the total number—were reported as belonging to families in which there were one or more other wage earners and no dependents. The remaining number of single women, representing 79.7 per cent, or about four-fifths of the total number, belonged to families in which there were one or more other wage earners and one or more dependents. As shown in the preceding chapter, 87,571, or about one-half of the 170,170 single women gainfully employed and living at home were reported as "living with father," in which cases it may be presumed that the father was one of the other wage earners.

TABLE 110.—GAINFULLY EMPLOYED WOMEN LIVING AT HOME, CLASSIFIED BY MARITAL CONDITION AND BY NUMBER OF OTHER EMPLOYED MEMBERS, AND OF UNEMPLOYED MEMBERS IN THE FAMILY, FOR THE 11 SELECTED CITIES COMBINED: 1920

NUMBER OF OTHER GAINFULLY EMPLOYED MEMBERS OF FAMILY	GAINFULLY EMPLOYED WOMEN LIVING AT HOME					
	Total	Unemployed members in family				
		None	1	2	3	4 or more
SINGLE WOMEN						
Total	170, 170	24, 494	59, 563	37, 678	21, 902	26, 533
In family having—						
No other employed member	17, 937	7, 858	6, 691	2, 334	672	382
1 other	49, 729	7, 860	19, 248	10, 676	5, 737	6, 208
2 others	48, 059	5, 196	17, 082	11, 220	6, 660	7, 901
3 or more others	54, 445	3, 580	16, 542	13, 448	8, 833	12, 042
Per cent of total	100. 0	14. 4	35. 0	22. 1	12. 9	15. 6
In family having—						
No other employed member	10. 5	4. 6	3. 9	1. 4	0. 4	0. 2
1 other	29. 2	4. 6	11. 3	6. 3	3. 4	3. 6
2 others	28. 2	3. 1	10. 0	6. 6	3. 9	4. 6
3 or more others	32. 0	2. 1	9. 7	7. 9	5. 2	7. 1
MARRIED WOMEN						
Total	74, 099	33, 374	17, 235	11, 031	6, 148	6, 311
In family having—						
No other employed member	6, 310	2, 731	1, 819	976	445	339
1 other	44, 971	24, 239	9, 424	5, 607	2, 988	2, 713
2 others	13, 686	4, 468	3, 686	2, 531	1, 433	1, 568
3 or more others	9, 132	1, 936	2, 306	1, 917	1, 282	1, 691
Per cent of total	100. 0	45. 0	23. 3	14. 9	8. 3	8. 5
In family having—						
No other employed member	8. 5	3. 7	2. 5	1. 3	0. 6	0. 5
1 other	60. 7	32. 7	12. 7	7. 6	4. 0	3. 7
2 others	18. 5	6. 0	5. 0	3. 4	1. 9	2. 1
3 or more others	12. 3	2. 6	3. 1	2. 6	1. 7	2. 3
WIDOWED OR DIVORCED WOMEN						
Total	48, 944	21, 900	11, 707	7, 538	4, 019	3, 780
In family having—						
No other employed member	19, 906	11, 602	4, 353	2, 270	983	698
1 other	16, 412	6, 539	4, 141	2, 848	1, 522	1, 362
2 others	8. 080	2, 711	2, 123	1, 470	886	890
3 or more others	4, 546	1, 048	1, 090	950	628	830
Per cent of total	100. 0	44. 7	23. 9	15. 4	8. 2	7. 7
In family having—						
No other employed member	40. 7	23. 7	8. 9	4. 6	2. 0	1. 4
1 other	33. 5	13, 4	8. 5	5. 8	3. 1	2. 8
2 others	16. 5	5. 5	4. 3	3. 0	1. 8	1. 8
3 or more others	9. 3	2. 1	2. 2	1. 9	1. 3	1. 7

Slightly more than one-half—51.8 per cent—of the single women represented families which included one or more other breadwinners and either one or two dependents; and more than one-fourth—27. 8 per cent—represented families in which, in addition to one or more other bread winners, there were three or more dependents.

Of the 74,099 married women gainfully employed and living at home 44,971, or 60.7 per cent, as shown by Table 110, were living in families in which there was only one other employed member, presumably the husband of the employed woman; and in 24,239, or more than half of these cases, there was no unemployed, or dependent, person in the family.

In all, 45 per cent of the married women gainfully employed represented families in which there were no dependents.   The cases in which the married woman is the sole breadwinner in a family comprising one or more dependent members constitute only about 4.9 per cent of the total.   In about one-half, or 50.1 per cent, of the cases tabulated the married woman shared with one or more other breadwinners the burden of supporting one or more dependents, who in most cases, probably, were her children.

Of the widowed and divorced women included in this tabulation 23.7 per cent were living alone, in the sense in which that term is here used, 21 per cent were living in families with one or more other breadwinners and no dependents, and 16.9 per cent were the only breadwinners in families comprising one or more dependents.   That leaves 38.4 per cent representing families having one or more other breadwinners and one or more dependents.

To go back to the married group, if we may assume that the husband is always the other breadwinner wherever one other is reported, or is one of the other breadwinners if more than one are reported, we can make the following classification of the employed wives living at home:

TABLE 111.—MARRIED WOMEN GAINFULLY EMPLOYED AND LIVING AT HOME, CLASSIFIED ACCORDING TO NUMBER OF OTHER WAGE EARNERS AND NUMBER OF DEPENDENTS IN FAMILY: 1920

CLASS	Number	Per cent distribution
Wives gainfully employed and living at home	74, 099	100. 0
Wife alone working, no dependents	2, 731	3. 7
Wife alone working, one dependent	1, 819	2. 5
Wife alone working, two or more dependents	1, 760	2. 4
Husband and wife both working, no dependents	24, 239	32. 7
Husband and wife both working, one dependent	9, 424	12. 7
Husband and wife both working, two or more dependents	11, 308	15. 3
Husband, wife, and one or more other members of the family working	22, 818	30. 8
No dependents	6, 404	8. 6
One dependent	5, 992	8. 1
Two or more dependents	10, 422	14. 1

It is of interest to note again in this connection that a large proportion—about 45 per cent—of the married women in the above tabulation represent families in which there were no dependents and therefore, presumably, no young children.

It may be well to remind the reader that in the 11 cities covered by the above tabulation, there were, as shown in Chapter XIV, 11,543 employed married women who were not living at home but were either boarders or were living in the family of their employer. They are not included in the above total, because in such cases the facts as to number of dependents and other breadwinners are not available.

In the table which follows, the scope of the classification has been expanded to include in the total the women boarding or lodging or living with the family of their employer. The percentage living with one or more relatives, i. e., in a family of two or more, is largest for married women and smallest for widowed and divorced women. Of the latter a relatively large proportion—18.4 per cent—were reported as living alone, in the sense of not living with any relative. The proportion boarding or lodging is about the same for single women as it is for the widows and divorced women, representing in each case about 1 in 7; for married women the proportion is somewhat smaller, about 1 in 10.

TABLE 112.—WOMEN GAINFULLY EMPLOYED CLASSIFIED ACCORDING TO MARITAL CONDITION, FAMILY RELATIONSHIP, AND NUMBER OF OTHER WAGE EARNERS IN THE FAMILY, FOR THE 11 SELECTED CITIES COMBINED: 1920

FAMILY RELATIONSHIP	GAINFULLY EMPLOYED WOMEN 16 YEARS OF AGE AND OVER: 1920							
	All classes		Single [1]		Married		Widowed or divorced	
	Number	Per cent distribution	Number	Per cent distribution	Number	Per cent distribution	Number	Per cent distribution
Total	373, 204	100. 0	224, 428	100. 0	85, 642	100. 0	63, 134	100. 0
Living in family of 2 or more members	271, 022	72. 6	162, 312	72. 3	71, 368	83. 3	37, 342	59. 1
No other employed member	21, 962	5. 9	10, 079	4. 5	3, 579	4. 2	8, 304	13. 1
1 other	111, 112	29. 8	49, 729	22. 2	44, 971	52. 6	16, 412	26. 0
2 or more others	137, 948	37. 0	102, 504	45. 7	22, 818	26. 6	12, 626	20. 0
Living alone	22, 191	5. 9	7, 858	3. 5	2, 731	3. 2	11, 602	18. 4
Boarding or lodging	50, 297	13. 5	31, 826	14. 2	9, 033	10. 5	9, 438	14. 9
Living in employer's family	29, 694	8. 0	22, 432	10. 0	2, 510	2. 9	4, 752	7. 5

[1] Includes those whose marital condition was not reported.

BOARDERS OR LODGERS

When the woman who is gainfully employed lives at home, it is possible to ascertain whether the family to which she belongs is taking boarders or lodgers by noting whether there are persons whose relationship to the head of the family as reported on the census schedules is that of boarder or lodger. Using that source of information we find that 40,733, or 13.9 per cent, of the 293,213 employed women living at home in the 11 selected cities were classified as belonging to families which took boarders or lodgers. The number so classified includes presumably the 5,870 women living at home whose occupation was that of boarding or lodging house keeper. But in the remaining cases the woman was pursuing some other occupation, and the taking of boarders or lodgers must have been a supplementary source of family income. Whether, however, she herself had the burden of taking care of the boarders or lodgers in addition to her other employment, or whether that duty devolved upon some other member of the family—her mother for instance—is not revealed by the census.

The percentage of employed women representing families in which there were boarders or lodgers was largest in those cases in which the woman was the only breadwinner, as shown by the table below; and probably in a large proportion of such cases the keeping of boarders or lodgers was the woman's occupation. The percentage decreases with the increase in the number of other breadwinners in the family, possibly because the need of obtaining an income from this source likewise decreases with the increase in the number of other wage earners.

TABLE 113.—GAINFULLY EMPLOYED WOMEN LIVING AT HOME, CLASSIFIED ACCORDING TO THE NUMBER OF OTHER EMPLOYED MEMBERS IN THE FAMILY, WITH THE NUMBER AND PER CENT IN EACH CLASS LIVING IN FAMILIES HAVING BOARDERS OR LODGERS, FOR THE 11 SELECTED CITIES COMBINED: 1920

CLASS	GAINFULLY EMPLOYED WOMEN LIVING AT HOME: 1920		
	Total number	In families having boarders or lodgers	
		Number	Per cent of total
All classes	293, 213	40, 733	13. 9
In family having—			
No other employed member	44, 153	11, 620	26. 3
One other	111, 112	15, 597	14. 0
Two others	69, 825	7, 778	11. 1
Three or more others	68, 123	5, 738	8. 4

In the table which follows the percentage of gainfully employed women whose families have boarders or lodgers is shown for each marital class. That it is largest for widowed and divorced women is doubtless indicative of the fact that a large proportion of them are keeping boarders as an occupation, this being a means of earning a livelihood very commonly resorted to by the woman who, through the death of her husband, is left dependent upon her own resources. The percentage is especially large (30.2) for those widows who are the sole breadwinners in the family, having either no relatives living with them or none that are earning money.

The percentage is also large (27.6) for those married women who are either living alone or, if not, are the sole breadwinners in their families, the latter doubtless including cases in which wife and children are living apart from the husband as well as cases in which the husband is incapacitated for work through illness, accident, or old age, so that it devolves upon the wife to support him and the other members of the family if there are any.

TABLE **114.**—GAINFULLY EMPLOYED WOMEN LIVING AT HOME, CLASSIFIED BY MARITAL CONDITION AND WITH RESPECT TO THE NUMBER OF OTHER EMPLOYED MEMBERS IN THE FAMILY, WITH THE NUMBER AND PER CENT IN EACH CLASS LIVING IN FAMILIES HAVING BOARDERS OR LODGERS, FOR THE 11 SELECTED CITIES COMBINED: 1920

CLASS	GAINFULLY EMPLOYED WOMEN LIVING AT HOME: 1920		
	Total number	In families having boarders or lodgers	
		Number	Per cent
All classes	293, 213	40, 733	13. 9
In family having—			
No other employed member	44, 153	11, 620	26. 3
1 other	111, 112	15, 597	14. 0
2 others	69, 825	7, 778	11. 1
3 or more others	68, 123	5, 738	8. 4
Single women	170, 170	17, 759	10. 4
In family having—			
No other employed member	17, 937	3, 856	21. 5
1 other	49, 729	5, 689	11. 4
2 others	48, 059	4, 370	9. 1
3 or more others	54, 445	3, 844	7. 1
Married women	74, 099	11, 657	15. 7
In family having—			
No other employed member	6, 310	1, 744	27. 6
1 other	44, 971	6, 638	14. 8
2 others	13, 686	2, 034	14. 9
3 or more others	9, 132	1, 241	13. 6
Widowed or divorced women	48, 944	11, 317	23. 1
In family having—			
No other employed member	19, 906	6, 020	30. 2
1 other	16, 412	3, 270	19. 9
2 others	8, 080	1, 374	17. 0
3 or more others	4, 546	653	14. 4

APPENDIX

EFFECT OF CHANGES IN DISTRIBUTION BY AGE AND BY MARITAL CON-
DITION UPON NUMBER OF WOMEN GAINFULLY EMPLOYED

From 1910 to 1920 the number of foreign-born white women engaged in gainful occupations fell off from 1,195,953 to 1,102,697, and the proportion of such women gainfully occupied declined from 22.1 to 18.8 per cent.

To what extent was this decline from 1910 to 1920 in the number and proportion of foreign-born white women engaged in gainful occupations the result of the changes in age distribution and in distribution by marital condition, which in turn were the result of the practical cessation of immigration to the United States during the World War?

EFFECT OF THE CHANGE IN AGE DISTRIBUTION

The following statement shows that between 1910 and 1920 there was a marked change in the age distribution of foreign-born white females, the proportion in each of the lower age periods or years having declined and the proportion in each of the higher periods having increased:

AGE	FOREIGN-BORN WHITE FEMALES			
	1920		1910	
	Number	Per cent distri- bution	Number	Per cent distri- bution
All ages	6,184,432	100.0	5,821,757	100.0
Under 16 years	312,066	5.0	413,567	7.1
16 years	51,145	0.8	50,574	0.9
17 years	52,539	0.8	58,782	1.0
18 and 19 years	123,369	2.0	174,535	3.0
20 to 24 years	469,856	7.6	606,461	10.4
25 to 44 years	2,720,964	44.0	2,437,209	41.9
45 to 64 years	1,799,118	29.1	1,497,783	25.7
65 years and over	648,843	10.5	576,341	9.9
Age unknown	6,532	0.1	6,505	0.1

Had the 6,184,432 foreign-born white females of all ages in the United States in 1920 been distributed by age as were the foreign-born white females in 1910, then the number and distribution of those 16 years of age and over would have been as shown in the first column

157

in the statement below; and had the proportion gainfully occupied been the same for each age period or year as actually prevailed in 1920, then the number and distribution of the gainfully occupied 16 years of age and over in 1920 would have been as shown in the last column of the statement:

AGE	FOREIGN-BORN WHITE WOMEN: 1920		
	Number there would have been had the age distribution of foreign-born white females been as it was in 1910	Per cent occupied in 1920 by age periods	Number that would have been occupied in 1920 had the age distribution been as it was in 1910
16 years and over	5,741,175	20.1	1,155,807
16 years	55,616	49.4	27,474
17 years	61,795	60.3	37,262
18 and 19 years	185,387	58.6	108,637
20 to 24 years	642,676	37.7	242,289
25 to 44 years	2,589,241	18.6	481,599
45 to 64 years	1,588,150	13.9	220,753
65 years and over	611,778	5.9	36,095
Age unknown	6,532	26.0	1,698

Thus, had the age composition of foreign-born white females been the same in 1920 as in 1910, and had the proportion in each age gainfully occupied been as it was in 1920, then there would have been 1,155,807 foreign-born white women gainfully occupied in 1920 as against 1,195,953 in 1910, and the proportion of such women gainfully occupied would have been 20.1 per cent in 1920 as against 22.1 per cent in 1910. It appears, therefore, that while the decline from 1910 to 1920 in the number and proportion of foreign-born white women gainfully occupied resulted in considerable measure from the difference in the age composition of the foreign-born white female population some other contributing cause or causes existed.

EFFECT OF THE CHANGE IN DISTRIBUTION BY MARITAL CONDITION

It is evident that a check to immigration, such as prevailed during the World War, would have a direct effect upon the distribution of foreign-born women among the marital classes, and in this way an indirect effect upon the proportion of foreign-born women gainfully occupied.

A check on immigration at once checks the immigrant recruits in each respective marital class. But since the single class is recruited entirely from immigrants while each of the other classes is recruited partly from immigrants and partly from entrants from one or more of the other marital classes, it follows that when immigration largely ceases the single class will decline in numbers through the marriage and death of many of its members, while the married class will continue to increase so long as new marriages exceed the decrease from death, divorce, and widowhood. And it is possible, also, for the number of foreign-born widows and divorced women to increase for a time even though immigration cease entirely.

The following statement shows that while from 1910 to 1920 there was a considerable increase in the number of foreign-born white married women, and in the number of widowed and divorced, there was a large decrease in the number of single—a decrease of 161,868, or 16.9 per cent—and a decrease, also, in the per cent the single constituted of the total.

MARITAL CONDITION	1920		1910	
	Number	Per cent distribution	Number	Per cent distribution
Aggregate	5,872,366	100.0	5,408,190	100.0
Married	4,122,932	70.2	3,623,544	67.0
Single, widowed, divorced, and unknown	1,749,434	29.8	1,784,646	33.0
Single	794,781	13.5	956,649	17.7
Widowed and divorced	946,881	16.1	820,632	15.2
Unknown	7,772	0.1	7,365	0.1

The decrease from 1910 to 1920 in the number of single women produced a net decrease in the total number of single, widowed, divorced, and unknown; and, since the proportion gainfully occupied in 1920 was 46.1 per cent for the total of these classes, as against only 7.2 per cent for the married, this decrease in the number of single, widowed, divorced, and unknown, accompanied, as it was, by an increase in the number married would naturally result in a reduction in the proportion of all foreign-born white women gainfully occupied.

Had the proportion of foreign-born white women who were married been the same in 1920 as in 1910, and had the proportion of gainfully occupied for each of the two classes been the same as reported for 1920, then the proportion of foreign-born white women gainfully occupied in 1920 would have been 20 per cent instead of the 18.8 per cent reported. It would, however, still have been considerably below the 22.1 per cent reported for 1910. The figures are summarized in the next statement. Of course, a somewhat different result would be obtained if we could distinguish in the analyses the single from the widowed and divorced.

MARITAL CONDITION	FOREIGN-BORN WHITE WOMEN: 1920			
	Distributed by marital condition as in 1910		Engaged in gainful occupations	
	Number	Per cent	Number	Per cent
Aggregate --	5, 872, 366	100. 0	1, 176, 546	20. 0
Married --	3, 934, 485	67. 0	283, 283	7. 2
Single, widowed, divorced, and unknown ----------	1, 937, 881	33. 0	893, 263	46. 1

COMBINED EFFECT OF CHANGES IN AGE DISTRIBUTION AND MARITAL CONDITION

Had the distribution of foreign-born white females of all ages, by age and also by marital condition, been the same in 1920 as in 1910, then in 1920 the total number of foreign-born white women 16 years of age and over would have been 5,741,175, and the distribution of these women by age and marital condition would have been as shown in the following statement:

AGE	Total	MARRIED		SINGLE, WIDOWED, DIVORCED, AND UNKNOWN	
		Number	Per cent	Number	Per cent
16 years and over ---------------------	5, 741, 175	3, 847, 913	67. 0	1, 893, 262	33. 0
16 to 19 years ---------------------------------	302, 798	44, 209	14. 6	258, 589	85. 4
20 to 24 years ---------------------------------	642, 676	348, 973	54. 3	293, 703	45. 7
25 to 44 years ---------------------------------	2, 589, 241	2, 115, 410	81. 7	473, 831	18. 3
45 years and over and unknown ---------------	2, 206, 460	1, 339, 321	60. 7	867, 139	39. 3

Had the proportion gainfully occupied in each age and marital condition class been as reported in 1910, then in 1920 the number gainfully occupied would have been as follows:

AGE	MARRIED			SINGLE, WIDOWED, DIVORCED, AND UNKNOWN		
	Total number	Engaged in gainful occupations		Total number	Engaged in gainful occupations	
		Number	Per cent		Number	Per cent
16 years and over ---------------	3, 847, 913	279, 059	7. 3	1, 893, 262	964, 695	50. 6
16 to 19 years -------------------------	44, 209	5, 128	11. 6	258, 589	170, 669	66. 0
20 to 24 years -------------------------	348, 973	33, 501	9. 6	293, 703	242, 599	82. 6
25 to 44 years -------------------------	2, 115, 410	173, 464	8. 2	473, 831	356, 321	75. 2
45 years and over and unknown --------	1, 339, 321	66, 966	5. 0	867, 139	195, 106	22. 5

Summarizing the figures of the above statement, we have the following:

FOREIGN-BORN WHITE WOMEN: 1920

Aggregate_____ 5, 741, 175
Engaged in gainful occupations_____ 1, 243, 754
Per cent engaged in gainful occupations_____ 21. 7

Thus, according to the figures presented, had the age and marital condition distribution of foreign-born white females of all ages been the same in 1920 as in 1910, then in 1920 the proportion of the foreign-born white women 16 years and over gainfully occupied would have been 21.7 per cent as compared with the 18.8 per cent reported for 1920 and with the 22.1 per cent reported for 1910.

With the age and marital condition distribution the same in 1920 as in 1910, the percentage gainfully occupied would have been only 0.4 below what it was in 1910—a slight difference that might easily be due to the change in the date of enumeration or to the changes made in the instructions to enumerators as explained in the text (Ch. III).

6436°—29——12

DETAILED TABLES

163

TABLE 115.—WOMEN EMPLOYED IN EACH SPECIFIED OCCUPATION, WITH

	OCCUPATION	ALL CLASSES		RACE AND NATIVITY:		
				Native white		Foreign-born white
		1920	1910	Native parentage	Foreign or mixed parentage	
1	All occupations	8,202,901	7,438,686	3,596,397	2,042,804	1,102,697
2	Agriculture, forestry, and animal husbandry	896,057	1,397,324	303,070	45,993	37,973
3	Dairy farmers, farmers, and stock raisers	253,836	261,956	129,451	22,252	21,148
4	Dairy farmers	3,946	2,576	1,888	1,017	944
5	Farmers, general farms	247,253	257,706	125,872	20,762	19,876
6	Stock raisers	2,637	1,674	1,691	473	328
7	Dairy farm, farm, and stock farm laborers	605,668	1,108,613	152,768	18,130	12,112
8	Dairy farm laborers	2,412	2,566	1,180	599	370
9	Farm laborers (home farm)	403,009	826,523	118,119	12,733	4,927
10	Farm laborers (working out)	198,979	278,637	32,946	4,630	6,726
11	Farm laborers (turpentine farm)	268	292	19	1	
12	Stock herders, drovers, and feeders	1,000	595	504	167	89
13	Dairy farm, farm, garden, orchard, etc., foremen	14,340	7,776	10,250	2,041	1,444
14	Dairy farm foremen	140	85	72	36	32
15	Farm foremen, general farms	13,767	7,505	9,917	1,911	1,349
16	Farm foremen, stock farms	94	11	62	18	13
17	Garden and greenhouse foremen	176	88	101	35	27
18	Orchard, nursery, etc., foremen	163	87	98	41	23
19	Fishermen and oystermen	365	468	170	26	48
20	Foresters, forest rangers, and timber cruisers	2		2		
21	Gardeners, florists, fruit growers, and nurserymen	9,283	7,834	5,499	1,626	1,544
22	Florists	938	1,051	537	230	158
23	Fruit growers	3,194	2,276	1,820	653	666
24	Gardeners	5,068	4,413	3,085	726	713
25	Landscape gardeners	25	15	17	8	
26	Nurserymen	58	79	40	9	7
27	Garden, greenhouse, orchard, and nursery laborers	8,699	6,798	2,455	1,276	1,174
28	Cranberry bog laborers	5	61	3		1
29	Garden laborers	5,773	4,493	1,384	661	743
30	Greenhouse laborers	1,120	903	536	308	192
31	Orchard and nursery laborers	1,801	1,341	532	307	238
32	Lumbermen, raftsmen, and woodchoppers	262	74	90	33	49
33	Owners and managers of log and timber camps	13	4	4	5	4
34	Managers and officials	5			4	1
35	Owners and proprietors	8	4	4	1	3
36	Other agricultural and animal husbandry pursuits	3,589	3,801	2,381	604	450
37	Apiarists	134	124	97	30	7
38	Corn shellers, hay balers, grain threshers, etc.	4		3		1
39	Irrigators and ditch tenders	3	9		1	2
40	Poultry raisers	2,324	3,226	1,571	396	321
41	Poultry yard laborers	946	357	622	150	96
42	Other and not specified pursuits	178	85	88	27	23
43	Extraction of minerals	2,718	1,023	1,104	497	778
44	Foremen, overseers, and inspectors	8	10	6	2	
45	Foremen and overseers	6	9	5	1	
46	Inspectors	2	1	1	1	
47	Operators, officials, and managers	182	107	120	45	16
48	Managers	23	12	11	6	6
49	Officials	41	9	31	8	1
50	Operators	118	86	78	31	9
51	Coal mine operatives	1,388	368	475	238	508
52	Copper mine operatives	136	19	23	27	84
53	Gold and silver mine operatives	34	39	14	12	6
54	Iron mine operatives	97	36	1	17	48

DISTRIBUTION BY RACE AND NATIVITY, MARITAL CONDITION, AND AGE: 1920

1920		MARITAL CONDITION: 1920		AGE: 1920							
Negro	All other	Married	Single, widowed, divorced, or unknown	16 and 17 years	18 and 19 years	20 to 24 years	25 to 44 years	45 to 64 years	65 years and over	Not reported	
1,445,935	15,068	1,920,281	6,282,620	609,192	802,235	1,809,075	3,417,373	1,352,479	196,900	15,647	1
504,763	4,258	371,537	524,520	81,427	71,497	130,790	337,087	219,802	54,356	1,098	2
79,893	1,092	40,466	213,370	--------	--------	6,626	83,575	124,842	38,459	334	3
92	5	917	3,029	--------	--------	70	1,080	2,176	617	3	4
79,773	970	39,093	208,160	--------	--------	6,485	81,750	121,311	37,383	324	5
28	117	456	2,181	--------	--------	71	745	1,355	459	7	6
420,703	1,955	320,348	285,320	80,581	70,707	122,226	242,036	79,035	10,364	719	7
238	25	1,173	1,239	206	209	411	1,025	505	53	3	8
266,580	650	225,503	177,506	65,485	49,443	80,903	156,339	46,002	4,479	358	9
153,568	1,109	93,078	105,901	14,731	20,908	40,663	84,209	32,311	5,804	353	10
248	--------	174	94	26	19	56	124	35	6	2	11
69	171	420	580	133	128	193	339	182	22	3	12
558	47	2,027	12,313	--------	--------	156	3,324	7,783	3,069	8	13
--------	--------	34	106	--------	--------	1	42	75	22	--------	14
546	44	1,878	11,889	--------	--------	148	3,150	7,477	2,985	7	15
--------	1	14	80	--------	--------	1	26	48	18	1	16
12	1	49	127	--------	--------	2	51	94	29	--------	17
--------	1	52	111	--------	--------	4	55	89	15	--------	18
73	48	203	162	19	22	53	159	85	22	5	19
--------	--------	1	1	--------	--------	--------	1	1	--------	--------	20
503	111	2,252	7,031	--------	--------	165	2,484	4,824	1,797	13	21
10	3	383	555	--------	--------	31	360	448	97	2	22
30	25	653	2,541	--------	--------	39	719	1,788	644	4	23
462	82	1,191	3,877	--------	--------	89	1,377	2,541	1,054	7	24
--------	--------	7	18	--------	--------	3	14	8	--------	--------	25
1	1	18	40	--------	--------	3	14	39	2	--------	26
2,800	994	4,588	4,111	750	689	1,364	3,906	1,713	263	14	27
1	--------	3	2	--------	--------	--------	2	2	1	--------	28
2,382	603	3,210	2,563	470	452	891	2,621	1,134	198	7	29
69	15	366	754	111	105	192	443	240	27	2	30
348	376	1,009	792	169	132	281	840	337	37	5	31
83	7	131	131	20	26	44	122	48	2	--------	32
--------	--------	2	11	--------	--------	--------	5	5	3	--------	33
--------	--------	1	4	--------	--------	--------	1	3	1	--------	34
--------	--------	1	7	--------	--------	--------	4	2	2	--------	35
150	4	1,519	2,070	57	53	156	1,475	1,466	377	5	36
--------	--------	45	89	--------	1	5	51	65	12	--------	37
--------	--------	2	2	1	--------	--------	2	--------	1	--------	38
--------	--------	3	--------	--------	--------	1	2	--------	--------	--------	39
33	3	824	1,500	--------	8	60	860	1,077	318	1	40
77	1	575	371	53	41	76	493	250	30	3	41
40	--------	70	108	3	3	14	67	74	16	1	42
325	14	1,278	1,440	304	299	510	1,125	405	66	9	43
--------	--------	3	5	--------	--------	--------	4	4	--------	--------	44
--------	--------	2	4	--------	--------	--------	2	4	--------	--------	45
--------	--------	1	1	--------	--------	--------	2	--------	--------	--------	46
1	--------	54	128	--------	--------	7	85	64	23	3	47
--------	--------	8	15	--------	--------	1	12	8	2	--------	48
1	--------	12	29	--------	--------	3	27	11	--------	--------	49
--------	--------	34	84	--------	--------	3	46	45	21	3	50
162	5	764	624	174	141	235	608	207	21	2	51
2	--------	73	63	1	4	27	71	27	6	--------	52
1	1	25	9	--------	2	3	15	13	1	--------	53
31	--------	55	42	6	9	31	39	12	--------	--------	54

TABLE 115.—WOMEN EMPLOYED IN EACH SPECIFIED OCCUPATION, WITH DISTRI

	OCCUPATION	ALL CLASSES		RACE AND NATIVITY:		
				Native white		Foreign-born white
		1920	1910	Native parentage	Foreign or mixed parentage	
	Extraction of minerals—Continued.					
1	Operatives in other and not specified mines	103	74	57	4	7
2	Lead and zinc mine operatives	47	14	42	1	4
3	Other specified mine operatives	47	47	8	3	2
4	Not specified mine operatives	9	13	7		1
5	Quarry operatives	75	43	31	6	17
6	Oil, gas, and salt well operatives	695	327	377	146	92
7	Oil and gas well operatives	234	12	159	10	3
8	Salt well and works operatives	461	315	218	136	89
9	Manufacturing and mechanical industries	1,849,339	1,710,816	741,502	595,460	405,644
10	Apprentices to building and hand trades	52	[1] 16	25	21	4
11	Blacksmiths' apprentices	2	2	1	1	
12	Carpenters' apprentices	7	4	4	2	
13	Electricians' apprentices	4	1		4	
14	Machinists' apprentices [2]	15		5	8	2
15	Painters', glaziers', and varnishers' apprentices.	16	2	9	5	1
16	Paper hangers' apprentices	7	1	6		1
17	Tinsmiths' and coppersmiths' apprentices	1			1	
18	Apprentices to dressmakers and milliners	2,330	5,785	834	1,011	366
19	Dressmakers' apprentices	1,639	2,332	509	746	272
20	Milliners' apprentices	691	3,453	325	265	94
21	Apprentices, other	3,950	1,760	1,638	1,701	568
22	Architects', designers', and draftsmen's apprentices.	253	39	95	118	37
23	Jewelers', watchmakers', goldsmiths', and silversmiths' apprentices.	270	39	91	139	37
24	Printers' and bookbinders' apprentices	969	508	536	369	56
25	Other apprentices	2,458	1,174	916	1,075	438
26	Bakers	4,593	4,774	1,756	1,201	1,285
27	Blacksmiths, forgemen, and hammermen	5	31	3		2
28	Blacksmiths	4	31	2		2
29	Forgemen, hammermen, and welders	1		1		
30	Brick and stone masons	7	15	3	1	
31	Builders and building contractors	79	849	39	26	10
32	Cabinetmakers	8	8	3	4	
33	Carpenters	171	38	97	19	27
34	Compositors, linotypers, and typesetters	11,306	14,025	6,861	3,488	747
35	Coopers	5	7	4		
36	Dressmakers and seamstresses (not in factory)	235,519	446,555	110,245	60,526	37,479
37	Dyers	131	625	32	36	53
38	Electricians	19	86	12	3	4
39	Electrotypers, stereotypers, and lithographers	186	575	99	74	13
40	Electrotypers and stereotypers	10	99	6	3	1
41	Lithographers	176	476	93	71	12
42	Engineers (stationary), cranemen, hoistmen, etc.	44	10	23	16	4
43	Engineers (stationary)	32	10	18	11	2
44	Cranemen, derrickmen, hoistmen, etc	12		5	5	2
45	Engravers	561	533	273	220	64
46	Filers, grinders, buffers, and polishers (metal)	2,413	2,711	938	954	497
47	Buffers and polishers	1,970	2,184	718	814	421
48	Filers	66	164	27	28	10
49	Grinders	377	363	193	112	66
50	Firemen (except locomotive and fire department)	13		9	2	1
51	Forewomen and overseers (manufacturing)	30,171	19,740	12,479	13,199	4,295
52	Furnacemen, smeltermen, heaters, pourers, etc.	6	25	3		2
53	Furnacemen and smeltermen	4	16	3		
54	Heaters	2	9			2

[1] Includes 4 women reported as apprentices to plumbers and 2 as apprentices to roofers and slaters in 1910.

BUTION BY RACE AND NATIVITY, MARITAL CONDITION, AND AGE: 1920—Continued

1920		MARITAL CONDITION: 1920		AGE: 1920							
Negro	All other	Married	Single, widowed, divorced, or unknown	16 and 17 years	18 and 19 years	20 to 24 years	25 to 44 years	45 to 64 years	65 years and over	Not reported	
35	------	58	45	8	6	14	49	16	7	3	1
------	------	27	20	6	4	9	16	7	5	------	2
34	------	27	20	2	2	4	28	7	2	2	3
1	------	4	5	------	------	1	5	2	------	1	4
21	------	46	29	5	6	18	36	7	3	------	5
72	8	200	495	110	131	175	218	55	5	1	6
62	------	112	122	13	30	55	102	30	3	1	7
10	8	88	373	97	101	120	116	25	2	------	8
102,775	3,958	466,663	1,382,676	221,298	214,340	382,765	730,250	271,047	26,986	2,653	9
2	------	5	47	13	33	3	3	------	------	------	10
------	------	1	1	1	------	------	1	------	------	------	11
1	------	1	6	------	7	------	------	------	------	------	12
------	------	------	4	------	3	1	------	------	------	------	13
------	------	2	13	5	8	1	1	------	------	------	14
1	------	1	15	4	10	1	1	------	------	------	15
------	------	------	7	3	4	------	------	------	------	------	16
------	------	------	1	------	1	------	------	------	------	------	17
116	3	39	2,291	1,776	251	193	96	12	2	------	18
109	3	13	1,626	1,398	110	83	40	7	1	------	19
7	------	26	665	378	141	110	56	5	1	------	20
42	1	175	3,775	2,681	727	287	222	30	------	3	21
3	------	3	250	238	6	5	4	------	------	------	22
3	------	4	266	256	6	3	5	------	------	------	23
8	------	39	930	615	226	73	51	4	------	------	24
28	1	129	2,329	1,572	489	206	162	26	------	3	25
337	14	1,809	2,784	------	327	603	2,265	1,246	146	6	26
------	------	2	3	------	------	------	4	1	------	------	27
------	------	1	3	------	------	------	3	1	------	------	28
------	------	1	------	------	------	------	1	------	------	------	29
3	------	4	3	------	------	------	7	------	------	------	30
4	------	27	52	------	------	1	37	36	5	------	31
1	------	5	3	------	------	2	5	1	------	------	32
26	2	93	78	------	------	29	78	56	8	------	33
199	11	2,273	9,033	568	1,449	2,834	5,157	1,189	91	18	34
1	------	4	1	------	------	------	2	3	------	------	35
26,961	308	66,094	169,425	1,597	4,325	17,100	112,496	87,585	12,073	343	36
10	------	49	82	------	------	28	68	31	3	1	37
------	------	8	11	------	------	6	9	4	------	------	38
------	------	32	154	------	------	69	106	11	------	------	39
------	------	1	9	------	------	5	5	------	------	------	40
------	------	31	145	------	------	64	101	11	------	------	41
1	------	16	28	------	------	18	20	6	------	------	42
1	------	14	18	------	------	15	13	4	------	------	43
------	------	2	10	------	------	3	7	2	------	------	44
4	------	82	479	------	------	219	286	51	4	1	45
24	------	509	1,904	322	342	560	933	239	17	------	46
17	------	384	1,586	249	276	450	770	209	16	------	47
1	------	9	57	15	9	19	20	3	------	------	48
6	------	116	261	58	57	91	143	27	1	------	49
1	------	7	6	------	------	7	3	2	1	------	50
194	4	5,807	24,364	------	1,798	6,464	17,363	4,340	164	42	51
1	------	3	3	------	1	------	5	------	------	------	52
1	------	1	3	------	1	------	3	------	------	------	53
------	------	2	------	------	------	------	2	------	------	------	54

¹ Many of the "Machinists' apprentices" probably are machine tenders.

TABLE 115.—WOMEN EMPLOYED IN EACH SPECIFIED OCCUPATION, WITH DISTRI

		ALL CLASSES		RACE AND NATIVITY:		
				Native white		Foreign-born white
	OCCUPATION	1920	1910	Native parentage	Foreign or mixed parentage	
	Manufacturing and mechanical industries—Continued.					
1	Glass blowers_____	89	88	20	39	28
2	Jewelers, watchmakers, goldsmiths, and silversmiths.	1,678	2,477	568	792	303
3	Goldsmiths and silversmiths_____	57	199	17	28	11
4	Jewelers and lapidaries (factory)_____	1,056	1,798	283	573	193
5	Jewelers and watchmakers (not in factory)____	565	480	268	191	99
6	Laborers (n. o. s.³)_____	160,133	80,048	66,787	33,930	26,605
7	Building, general, and not specified laborers____	14,668	15,262	4,519	1,484	1,834
8	Chemical and allied industries_____	3,134	1,855	1,391	870	595
9	Fertilizer factories_____	131	86	5	2	10
10	Paint and varnish factories_____	153	103	58	53	36
11	Powder, cartridge, dynamite, fuse, and fireworks factories.	619	298	342	167	102
12	Soap factories_____	353	230	126	124	89
13	Other chemical factories_____	1,878	1,138	860	524	358
14	Cigar and tobacco factories_____	13,396	4,493	3,939	660	605
15	Clay, glass, and stone industries_____	4,069	2,164	2,438	656	370
16	Brick, tile, and terra cotta factories_____	509	573	288	62	66
17	Glass factories_____	2,295	827	1,297	378	167
18	Lime, cement, and artificial stone factories_	164	150	72	26	42
19	Marble and stone yards_____	23	58	13	5	4
20	Potteries_____	1,078	556	768	185	91
21	Clothing industries_____	5,895	4,307	3,204	1,542	910
22	Corset factories_____	519	484	227	172	119
23	Glove factories_____	798	377	502	232	59
24	Hat factories (felt)_____	151	203	75	50	20
25	Shirt, collar, and cuff factories_____	1,283	1,215	723	398	122
26	Suit, coat, cloak, and overall factories_____	1,667	1,133	953	357	228
27	Other clothing factories_____	1,477	895	724	333	362
28	Food industries_____	15,486	5,649	6,155	3,265	3,028
29	Bakeries_____	1,347	635	624	377	255
30	Butter, cheese, and condensed milk factories.	995	127	596	315	76
31	Candy factories_____	1,983	916	997	581	249
32	Fish curing and packing_____	975	218	238	148	167
33	Flour and grain mills_____	135	88	52	37	23
34	Fruit and vegetable canning, etc._____	3,200	908	1,430	698	791
35	Slaughter and packing houses_____	4,055	1,345	1,241	695	1,163
36	Sugar factories and refineries_____	309	106	113	53	64
37	Other food factories_____	2,487	1,306	864	361	240
38	Harness and saddle industries_____	156	79	121	20	3
39	Helpers in building and hand trades_____	101	78	35	9	21
40	Iron and steel industries_____	12,114	5,781	4,365	3,368	3,282
41	Agricultural implement factories_____	114	113	42	32	34
42	Automobile factories_____	2,419	133	1,115	751	476
43	Blast furnaces and steel rolling mills ⁴____	2,198	1,306	577	457	743
44	Car and railroad shops_____	355	222	107	64	112
45	Ship and boat building_____	272	8	76	42	62
46	Wagon and carriage factories_____	214	154	118	53	15
47	Other iron and steel factories ⁵_____	5,587	3,493	2,052	1,775	1,517
48	Not specified metal industries_____	955	352	278	194	323
49	Other metal industries_____	4,892	2,429	1,791	1,873	1,132
50	Brass mills_____	844	262	205	306	327
51	Clock and watch factories_____	1,143	582	311	664	166
52	Copper factories_____	51	54	15	11	20
53	Gold and silver factories_____	201	163	104	55	42
54	Jewelry factories_____	147	122	35	71	35
55	Lead and zinc factories_____	65	70	34	8	19
56	Tinware, enamelware, etc., factories_____	2,067	779	920	635	456
57	Other metal factories_____	374	397	167	123	67

³ Not otherwise specified.
⁴ Includes tin-plate mills.

BUTION BY RACE AND NATIVITY, MARITAL CONDITION, AND AGE: 1920—Continued

1920		MARITAL CONDITION: 1920		AGE: 1920							
Negro	All other	Married	Single, widowed, divorced, or unknown	16 and 17 years	18 and 19 years	20 to 24 years	25 to 44 years	45 to 64 years	65 years and over	Not reported	
2	------	20	69	--------	--------	55	29	5	--------	--------	1
14	1	334	1,344	--------	224	490	776	166	18	4	2
--------	1	5	52	--------	6	16	27	7	1	--------	3
7	------	156	900	--------	154	346	482	71	1	2	4
7	------	173	392	--------	64	128	267	88	16	2	5
32,582	229	48,863	111,270	24,467	22,969	34,504	56,609	19,007	2,139	438	6
6,765	66	5,642	9,026	780	974	2,115	6,179	3,791	740	89	7
276	2	814	2,320	527	527	683	1,062	298	28	9	8
114	------	59	72	6	13	27	62	18	3	2	9
6	------	45	108	27	27	18	65	15	1	--------	10
8	------	148	471	93	117	165	190	52	2	--------	11
14	------	68	285	81	64	70	104	28	5	1	12
134	2	494	1,384	320	306	403	641	185	17	6	13
8,190	2	5,195	8,201	1,395	1,574	3,040	5,467	1,611	184	125	14
597	8	1,065	3,004	876	701	810	1,245	406	28	3	15
93	------	179	330	75	86	97	181	64	5	1	16
451	2	496	1,799	592	444	454	612	182	11	--------	17
23	1	80	84	12	14	27	77	26	7	1	18
1	------	6	17	8	2	3	7	3	--------	--------	19
29	5	304	774	189	155	229	368	131	5	1	20
235	4	1,201	4,694	1,082	905	1,498	1,823	533	46	8	21
1	------	111	408	98	77	125	151	61	6	1	22
3	2	151	647	160	142	222	211	57	6	--------	23
6	------	28	123	24	16	36	61	13	1	--------	24
40	------	228	1,055	241	207	321	372	134	8	--------	25
128	1	365	1,302	287	242	420	552	143	19	4	26
57	1	318	1,159	272	221	374	476	125	6	3	27
2,977	61	5,298	10,188	2,315	2,142	2,948	5,655	2,190	212	24	28
89	2	320	1,027	308	224	249	400	150	15	1	29
8	------	216	779	153	202	230	322	83	5	--------	30
156	------	363	1,620	522	385	419	498	142	14	3	31
384	38	508	467	79	90	148	396	227	32	3	32
23	------	41	94	19	20	33	43	19	1	--------	33
266	15	1,183	2,017	401	376	471	1,088	768	90	6	34
953	3	1,724	2,331	419	484	777	1,878	453	37	7	35
77	2	96	213	49	44	68	113	33	2	--------	36
1,021	1	847	1,640	365	317	553	917	315	16	4	37
12	------	33	123	32	28	26	49	20	1	--------	38
36	------	43	58	8	13	15	41	24	--------	--------	39
1,089	10	3,917	8,197	1,778	1,756	2,675	4,535	1,233	118	19	40
6	------	40	74	16	22	18	48	9	1	--------	41
76	1	666	1,753	362	403	600	834	199	19	2	42
419	2	925	1,273	270	246	427	941	277	31	6	43
71	1	149	206	19	21	55	189	71	--------	--------	44
92	------	113	159	25	26	63	110	43	5	--------	45
28	------	58	156	36	41	42	79	15	--------	1	46
239	4	1,566	4,021	930	885	1,290	1,908	515	50	9	47
158	2	400	555	120	112	180	426	104	12	1	48
94	2	1,045	3,847	945	867	1,125	1,528	397	23	7	49
6	------	241	603	143	130	169	320	75	6	1	50
2	------	144	999	230	205	330	308	65	1	4	51
3	2	21	30	9	5	6	25	6	--------	--------	52
--------	------	64	137	28	30	49	68	25	1	--------	53
6	------	27	120	31	25	41	41	8	1	--------	54
4	------	27	38	8	10	11	26	10	--------	--------	55
56	------	455	1,612	420	395	427	626	183	14	2	56
17	------	66	308	76	67	92	114	25	--------	--------	57

⁵ Includes iron foundries.

TABLE **115.**—WOMEN EMPLOYED IN EACH SPECIFIED OCCUPATION, WITH DISTRI

	OCCUPATION	ALL CLASSES		RACE AND NATIVITY:		
				Native white		Foreign-born white
		1920	**1910**	Native parentage	Foreign or mixed parentage	
	Manufacturing and mechanical industries—Continued.					
	Laborers (n. o. s.³)—Continued.					
1	Lumber and furniture industries	10,207	3,597	4,460	1,889	840
2	Furniture factories	2,547	477	1,355	590	294
3	Piano and organ factories	685	339	311	261	107
4	Saw and planing mills ⁶	4,140	1,613	1,525	467	212
5	Other woodworking factories	2,835	1,168	1,269	571	227
6	Paper and pulp mills	2,381	1,358	1,130	708	404
7	Printing and publishing	2,379	1,698	1,302	782	196
8	Blank book, envelope, tag, paper bag, etc., factories.	752	426	353	293	84
9	Printing, publishing, and engraving	1,627	1,272	949	489	112
10	Shoe factories	4,740	2,068	2,715	1,386	611
11	Tanneries	743	286	169	212	268
12	Textile industries	30,320	13,465	15,178	5,448	6,204
13	Carpet mills	548	308	186	188	163
14	Cotton mills	15,440	4,744	8,657	1,645	2,618
15	Knitting mills	4,868	2,865	3,122	870	391
16	Lace and embroidery mills	236	191	58	99	73
17	Silk mills	2,381	913	1,102	780	424
18	Textile dyeing, finishing, and printing mills	668	558	282	244	113
19	Woolen and worsted mills	3,713	1,780	999	1,003	1,658
20	Other textile mills	2,466	2,106	772	619	764
21	Hemp and jute mills	135	149	43	8	82
22	Linen mills	80	232	16	27	37
23	Rope and cordage factories	447	602	136	97	188
24	Sail, awning, and tent factories	45	28	27	12	4
25	Not specified textile mills	1,759	1,095	550	475	453
26	Other industries	35,452	15,479	13,875	9,758	6,302
27	Broom and brush factories	367	203	178	110	43
28	Button factories	287	279	95	110	67
29	Charcoal and coke works	29	10	3	5	7
30	Electric light and power plants	155	157	85	43	19
31	Electrical supply factories	3,111	1,308	1,469	1,000	618
32	Gas works	56	15	16	12	17
33	Leather belt, leather case, etc., factories	287	142	122	107	41
34	Liquor and beverage industries	227	529	74	43	25
35	Paper box factories	861	516	364	357	123
36	Petroleum refineries	226	62	95	66	43
37	Rubber factories	3,824	1,203	1,825	1,014	934
38	Straw factories	61	91	26	18	12
39	Trunk factories	205	63	125	48	25
40	Turpentine distilleries	116	47	3	---------	---------
41	Other miscellaneous industries	6,414	2,116	2,364	1,443	854
42	Other not specified industries	19,226	8,738	7,031	5,382	3,474
43	Loom fixers	3	---------	2	1	---------
44	Machinists, millwrights, and toolmakers	8	92	3	1	4
45	Machinists	5	72	3	1	1
46	Toolmakers and die setters and sinkers	3	20	---------	---------	3
47	Managers and superintendents (manufacturing)	4,950	1,462	2,768	1,569	607
48	Manufacturers and officials	8,326	4,699	4,095	2,542	1,682
49	Manufacturers	4,945	4,298	2,111	1,397	1,430
50	Officials	3,381	401	1,984	1,145	252
51	Mechanics (n. o. s. ³)	51	41	32	8	9
52	Gunsmiths, locksmiths, and bellhangers	7	3	4	2	1
53	Other mechanics	44	38	28	6	8
54	Millers (grain, flour, feed, etc.)	7	59	3	3	1
55	Milliners and millinery dealers	69,598	121,446	34,764	24,234	10,006
56	Molders, founders, and casters (metal)	13	⁷ 115	6	3	4
57	Iron molders, founders, and casters	9	51	4	2	3
58	Other molders, founders, and casters	4	61	2	1	1

³ Not otherwise specified.
⁶ Includes box factories (wood).

BUTION BY RACE AND NATIVITY, MARITAL CONDITION, AND AGE: 1920—Continued

1920		MARITAL CONDITION: 1920		AGE: 1920							
Negro	All other	Married	Single, widowed, divorced, or unknown	16 and 17 years	18 and 19 years	20 to 24 years	25 to 44 years	45 to 64 years	65 years and over	Not reported	
2,965	53	3,224	6,983	1,724	1,630	2,190	3,498	1,041	98	26	1
307	1	657	1,890	497	440	495	821	276	16	2	2
6	------	133	552	139	139	160	195	47	4	1	3
1,902	34	1,619	2,521	558	571	918	1,542	471	64	16	4
750	18	815	2,020	530	480	617	940	247	14	7	5
138	1	596	1,785	372	410	563	773	236	23	4	6
96	3	359	2,020	508	468	569	678	138	17	1	7
22	------	133	619	176	153	174	196	45	8	------	8
74	3	226	1,401	332	315	395	482	93	9	1	9
27	1	1,037	3,703	935	822	1,184	1,356	413	23	7	10
94	------	280	463	110	108	158	299	66	2	------	11
3,484	6	9,676	20,644	5,078	4,257	6,721	10,569	3,340	315	40	12
11	------	134	414	90	63	106	196	89	4	------	13
2,518	2	5,796	9,644	2,242	1,988	3,362	5,858	1,789	175	26	14
484	1	1,025	3,843	995	845	1,201	1,267	416	37	7	15
6	------	42	194	56	32	47	81	16	4	------	16
75	------	378	2,003	658	474	544	554	135	15	1	17
28	1	125	543	114	109	163	197	78	6	1	18
52	1	1,395	2,318	525	421	774	1,431	508	52	2	19
316	1	781	1,685	398	325	524	885	309	22	3	20
2	------	60	75	15	11	19	60	29	1	------	21
------	------	28	52	9	7	15	24	20	5	------	22
26	------	166	281	51	55	103	181	52	5	------	23
2	------	12	33	9	4	4	18	9	1	------	24
280	1	515	1,244	314	248	383	602	199	10	3	25
5,507	10	9,438	26,014	6,002	5,787	8,184	11,852	3,270	281	76	26
36	------	100	267	72	54	82	123	34	2	------	27
15	------	72	215	50	36	65	98	36	------	2	28
14	------	15	14	4	1	6	12	6	------	------	29
8	------	34	121	25	32	39	47	11	1	------	30
24	------	664	2,447	595	567	798	961	182	7	1	31
11	------	17	39	5	4	12	26	9	------	------	32
17	------	72	215	42	50	66	99	26	4	------	33
85	------	70	157	22	28	55	95	25	1	1	34
17	------	145	716	229	160	210	197	61	2	2	35
22	------	67	159	31	41	52	78	21	3	------	36
51	------	1,088	2,736	511	665	1,015	1,321	289	20	3	37
5	------	10	51	14	9	14	11	11	2	------	38
7	------	47	158	39	29	53	75	7	2	------	39
113	------	68	48	10	13	21	59	5	------	8	40
1,750	3	1,845	4,569	1,004	950	1,390	2,291	699	64	16	41
3,332	7	5,124	14,102	3,349	3,148	4,306	6,359	1,848	173	43	42
------	------	1	2	------	------	------	3	------	------	------	43
------	------	1	7	------	------	2	6	------	------	------	44
------	------	1	4	------	------	2	3	------	------	------	45
------	------	------	3	------	------	------	3	------	------	------	46
6	------	1,549	3,401	------	------	624	3,093	1,145	76	12	47
6	1	2,632	5,694	------	------	899	4,491	2,593	322	21	48
6	1	2,012	2,933	------	------	232	2,413	2,022	268	10	49
------	------	620	2,761	------	------	667	2,078	571	54	11	50
2	------	23	28	------	------	17	26	8	------	------	51
------	------	4	3	------	------	1	5	1	------	------	52
2	------	19	25	------	------	16	21	7	------	------	53
------	------	2	5	------	------	1	5	1	------	------	54
583	11	12,735	56,863	3,135	4,370	12,735	36,129	12,156	943	130	55
------	------	5	8	------	------	4	8	1	------	------	56
------	------	4	5	------	------	2	6	1	------	------	57
------	------	1	3	------	------	2	2	------	------	------	58

⁷ Includes 3 women reported as brass molders and founders.

TABLE 115.—WOMEN EMPLOYED IN EACH SPECIFIED OCCUPATION, WITH DISTRI

	OCCUPATION	ALL CLASSES		RACE AND NATIVITY:		
				Native white		Foreign-born white
		1920	1910	Native parentage	Foreign or mixed parentage	
	Manufacturing and mechanical industries— Continued.					
1	Oilers of machinery	42	21	17	11	12
2	Painters, glaziers, varnishers, enamelers, etc	3,233	2,412	1,325	1,156	614
3	Enamelers, lacquerers, and japanners	936	958	352	401	175
4	Painters, glaziers, and varnishers (building)	103	379	44	34	17
5	Painters, glaziers, and varnishers (factory)	2,194	1,075	929	721	422
6	Paper hangers	408	797	281	84	31
7	Pattern and model makers	57	531	24	22	9
8	Plasterers	6	6	2	--------	1
9	Plumbers and gas and steam fitters	3	--------	2	1	--------
10	Sawyers	9	19	2	5	1
11	Semiskilled operatives (n. o. s.[3])	1,274,719	955,423	486,407	436,889	307,339
12	Chemical and allied industries	17,391	12,390	7,636	6,992	2,431
13	Fertilizer factories	54	13	6	5	9
14	Paint and varnish factories	791	574	291	346	140
15	Powder, cartridge, dynamite, fuse, and fireworks factories.	2,503	2,208	957	1,054	472
16	Soap factories	2,900	1,731	1,167	1,265	436
17	Other chemical factories	11,143	7,864	5,215	4,322	1,374
18	Cigar and tobacco factories	80,757	66,087	32,620	17,261	17,690
19	Clay, glass, and stone industries	12,396	8,507	7,256	3,221	1,264
20	Brick, tile, and terra cotta factories	586	663	364	151	57
21	Glass factories	6,709	3,445	3,702	1,845	642
22	Lime, cement, and artificial stone factories.	198	122	98	44	46
23	Marble and stone yards	61	137	43	10	8
24	Potteries	4,842	4,140	3,049	1,171	511
25	Clothing industries	256,641	222,479	85,922	82,844	80,272
26	Corset factories	11,035	10,960	4,011	4,681	2,304
27	Glove factories	16,212	13,299	9,029	4,695	2,414
28	Hat factories (felt)	6,162	9,768	2,417	2,617	1,062
29	Shirt, collar, and cuff factories	39,892	43,570	17,751	14,557	6,600
30	Suit, coat, cloak, and overall factories	62,415	57,723	19,029	17,979	23,288
31	Other clothing factories	120,925	87,159	33,685	38,315	44,604
32	Food industries	67,753	32,441	26,648	23,778	12,589
33	Bakeries	10,836	5,200	4,095	4,594	1,966
34	Butter, cheese, and condensed milk factories.	2,666	513	1,562	830	239
35	Candy factories	28,564	14,950	12,284	11,360	4,298
36	Fish curing and packing	3,077	918	845	374	482
37	Flour and grain mills	576	224	239	216	96
38	Fruit and vegetable canning, etc	6,059	2,872	2,565	1,724	1,446
39	Slaughter and packing houses	7,936	2,282	2,079	1,975	2,685
40	Sugar factories and refineries	648	202	208	260	153
41	Other food factories	7,391	5,280	2,771	2,445	1,224
42	Harness and saddle industries	527	652	314	156	35
43	Iron and steel industries	56,009	21,934	21,779	21,804	11,732
44	Agricultural implement factories	579	352	193	209	161
45	Automobile factories	12,582	820	5,610	4,731	2,156
46	Blast furnaces and steel rolling mills [4]	3,955	2,196	1,477	1,474	930
47	Car and railroad shops	956	368	441	262	225
48	Ship and boat building	480	65	236	151	60
49	Wagon and carriage factories	664	1,041	402	173	70
50	Other iron and steel factories [5]	35,014	14,871	12,797	14,100	7,721
51	Not specified metal industries	1,779	2,221	623	704	409
52	Other metal industries	29,086	19,564	10,416	12,645	5,790
53	Brass mills	3,799	2,372	1,059	1,626	1,102
54	Clock and watch factories	7,953	6,235	2,830	3,778	1,337
55	Copper factories	148	50	57	61	29
56	Gold and silver factories	1,724	1,585	676	733	313
57	Jewelry factories	5,662	4,139	1,735	2,672	1,210
58	Lead and zinc factories	256	240	114	107	33
59	Tinware, enamelware, etc., factories	6,882	3,542	3,068	2,400	1,288
60	Other metal factories	2,662	1,401	877	1,268	478

[3] Not otherwise specified.
[4] Includes tin-plate mills.

-BUTION BY RACE AND NATIVITY, MARITAL CONDITION, AND AGE: 1920—Continued

1920		MARITAL CONDITION: 1920		AGE: 1920							
Negro	All other	Married	Single, widowed, divorced, or unknown	16 and 17 years	18 and 19 years	20 to 24 years	25 to 44 years	45 to 64 years	65 years and over	Not reported	
2	------	9	33	8	7	5	16	5	1	------	1
137	1	815	2,418	487	460	734	1,180	338	29	5	2
8	------	190	746	139	135	240	363	57	2	------	3
8	------	48	55	------	------	22	48	26	3	4	4
121	1	577	1,617	348	325	472	769	255	24	1	5
11	1	229	179	------	------	13	175	198	21	1	6
2	------	29	28	------	6	14	26	10	1	------	7
3	------	5	1	------	------	------	6	------	------	------	8
------	------	2	1	------	------	------	2	1	------	------	9
1	------	3	6	------	------	5	4	------	------	------	10
40,779	3,305	312,478	962,241	185,024	174,543	298,003	472,084	133,358	10,148	1,559	11
326	6	3,024	14,367	3,117	2,946	4,083	5,665	1,480	88	12	12
34	------	22	32	3	6	11	24	10	------	------	13
14	------	173	618	153	128	174	264	69	2	1	14
19	1	501	2,002	292	397	693	940	171	8	2	15
31	1	442	2,458	551	611	759	810	156	12	1	16
228	4	1,886	9,257	2,118	1,804	2,446	3,627	1,074	66	8	17
13,176	10	29,382	51,375	9,978	9,827	17,800	33,123	9,040	839	130	18
607	48	2,474	9,922	2,502	2,188	2,615	3,860	1,131	91	9	19
14	------	125	461	103	103	108	195	70	6	1	20
520	------	1,130	5,579	1,586	1,387	1,482	1,757	460	31	6	21
10	------	71	127	30	35	25	79	27	1	1	22
------	------	14	47	11	10	13	17	10	------	------	23
63	48	1,134	3,708	772	653	987	1,812	564	53	1	24
7,525	78	52,906	203,735	26,791	28,445	59,823	103,418	35,201	2,694	269	25
39	------	2,347	8,688	1,133	1,051	2,121	4,541	2,032	146	11	26
64	10	5,693	10,519	1,746	1,849	3,208	6,379	2,640	380	10	27
66	------	1,368	4,794	635	531	1,151	2,580	1,164	96	5	28
976	8	6,897	32,995	5,412	4,981	9,011	14,955	5,096	398	39	29
2,095	24	15,583	46,832	6,598	6,961	14,239	26,463	7,511	574	69	30
4,285	36	21,018	99,907	11,267	13,072	30,093	48,500	16,758	1,100	135	31
4,506	232	16,746	51,007	13,514	10,539	14,528	22,416	6,219	467	70	32
179	2	2,088	8,748	2,734	1,860	2,389	2,966	835	47	5	33
34	1	656	2,010	431	438	642	920	221	14	------	34
609	13	5,142	23,422	6,916	4,965	6,601	8,184	1,772	101	25	35
1,202	174	1,663	1,414	240	280	494	1,482	523	45	13	36
25	------	170	406	65	92	122	217	72	7	1	37
292	32	2,080	3,979	848	698	928	2,216	1,223	139	7	38
1,195	2	2,893	5,043	918	968	1,579	3,656	759	43	13	39
27	------	148	500	95	106	169	221	56	1	------	40
943	8	1,906	5,485	1,267	1,132	1,604	2,554	758	70	6	41
22	------	145	382	68	55	98	211	84	10	1	42
684	10	13,188	42,821	8,076	9,141	14,095	20,284	4,141	229	43	43
16	------	176	403	80	96	155	207	37	3	1	44
82	3	3,068	9,514	1,504	2,065	3,390	4,790	795	29	9	45
74	------	933	3,022	628	672	952	1,397	282	22	2	46
28	------	330	626	76	111	207	398	146	15	3	47
31	2	147	333	40	69	104	206	53	8	------	48
19	------	144	520	116	98	155	225	66	4	------	49
392	4	7,978	27,036	5,325	5,733	8,716	12,456	2,621	135	28	50
42	1	412	1,367	307	297	416	605	141	13	------	51
234	1	5,426	23,660	4,735	4,725	7,098	9,993	2,393	122	20	52
12	------	877	2,922	578	595	958	1,387	272	8	1	53
8	------	1,325	6,628	1,032	1,189	2,013	2,900	769	39	11	54
1	------	24	124	24	28	48	43	5	------	------	55
2	------	309	1,415	247	262	389	586	224	16	------	56
44	1	1,071	4,591	861	797	1,287	2,185	503	27	2	57
2	------	45	211	49	51	51	84	17	4	------	58
126	------	1,425	5,457	1,406	1,271	1,588	2,120	470	23	4	59
39	------	350	2,312	538	532	764	688	133	5	2	60

⁵ Includes iron foundries.

TABLE 115.—WOMEN EMPLOYED IN EACH SPECIFIED OCCUPATION, WITH DISTRI

	OCCUPATION	ALL CLASSES		RACE AND NATIVITY:		
				Native white		Foreign-born white
		1920	1910	Native parent-age	Foreign-or mixed parent-age	
	Manufacturing and mechanical industries—Continued.					
	Semiskilled operatives (n. o. s.[3])—Continued.					
1	Lumber and furniture industries	17,746	12,724	8,384	5,673	2,428
2	Furniture factories	6,588	3,408	3,266	2,023	993
3	Piano and organ factories	2,740	1,440	981	1,271	463
4	Saw and planing mills [6]	3,085	2,119	1,716	879	278
5	Other woodworking factories	5,333	5,757	2,421	1,500	694
6	Paper and pulp mills	12,901	10,046	5,050	5,035	2,483
7	Printing and publishing	39,318	33,916	17,957	17,059	3,506
8	Blank book, envelope, tag, paper bag, etc., factories.	8,153	6,107	3,516	3,573	1,013
9	Printing, publishing, and engraving	31,165	27,809	14,441	13,486	2,493
10	Shoe factories	70,517	55,824	31,825	26,660	11,798
11	Tanneries	3,465	1,759	1,009	1,241	1,019
12	Textile industries	408,280	343,420	158,949	133,274	110,123
13	Carpet mills	10,055	19,043	2,891	3,871	3,199
14	Cotton mills	139,037	121,491	60,463	33,759	43,752
15	Knitting mills	75,250	57,924	40,076	23,374	11,017
16	Lace and embroidery mills	11,980	10,579	2,599	5,067	4,114
17	Silk mills	66,314	44,227	24,862	28,251	12,976
18	Textile dyeing, finishing, and printing mills.	5,303	4,858	1,802	2,327	1,064
19	Woolen and worsted mills	57,923	47,851	13,631	21,815	22,178
20	Other textile mills	42,418	37,447	12,625	14,810	11,823
21	Hemp and jute mills	2,080	2,467	242	372	1,460
22	Linen mills	1,566	1,170	303	617	621
23	Rope and cordage mills	3,578	3,123	1,266	953	1,295
24	Sail, awning, and tent factories	995	999	550	308	126
25	Not specified textile mills	34,199	29,688	10,264	12,560	8,321
26	Other industries	201,932	113,680	70,642	79,246	44,179
27	Broom and brush factories	2,294	1,947	981	887	369
28	Building and hand trades	19	113	4	8	6
29	Button factories	4,911	4,271	1,634	1,900	1,158
30	Charcoal and coke works	30	16	9	6	7
31	Electric light and power plants	326	171	147	125	47
32	Electrical supply factories	26,626	10,467	9,882	11,679	4,961
33	Gas works	163	41	55	76	25
34	Leather belt, leather case, etc., factories	4,115	2,768	1,277	1,637	1,046
35	Liquor and beverage industries	666	1,683	280	226	97
36	Paper box factories	12,171	11,291	4,424	5,705	1,886
37	Petroleum refineries	645	60	256	285	96
38	Rubber factories	18,023	9,747	6,329	6,738	4,864
39	Straw factories	6,091	3,804	1,744	2,319	1,986
40	Trunk factories	756	496	316	290	126
41	Turpentine distilleries	8	8	1		
42	Other miscellaneous industries	43,909	27,223	15,716	16,867	9,807
43	Other not specified industries	81,179	39,574	27,587	30,498	17,698
44	Shoemakers and cobblers (not in factory)	259	776	109	42	78
45	Skilled occupations (n. o. s.[3])	69	457	41	21	7
46	Annealers and temperers (metal)	3	7		3	
47	Piano and organ tuners	40	105	27	10	3
48	Wood carvers	17	60	9	5	3
49	Other skilled occupations	9	[8] 285	5	3	1
50	Stonecutters	3	5	1	1	1
51	Tailoresses	31,828	40,370	7,858	10,752	12,505
52	Tinsmiths and coppersmiths	11	24	2	4	4
53	Coppersmiths	1			1	
54	Tinsmiths and sheet metal workers	10	24	2	3	4
55	Upholsterers	2,267	1,280	1,007	848	372

[3] Not otherwise specified.
[6] Includes box factories (wood).

BUTION BY RACE AND NATIVITY, MARITAL CONDITION, AND AGE: 1920—Continued

1920		MARITAL CONDITION: 1920		AGE: 1920							
Negro	All other	Married	Single, widowed, divorced, or unknown	16 and 17 years	18 and 19 years	20 to 24 years	25 to 44 years	45 to 64 years	65 years and over	Not reported	
900	361	4,538	13,208	2,891	2,794	3,889	5,994	1,956	204	18	1
305	1	1,764	4,824	916	945	1,345	2,415	886	73	8	2
25	------	517	2,223	521	480	727	818	184	9	1	3
210	2	736	2,349	576	538	701	1,008	247	12	3	4
360	358	1,521	3,812	878	831	1,116	1,753	639	110	6	5
331	2	2,891	10,010	1,688	1,888	3,010	4,546	1,642	117	10	6
789	7	5,901	33,417	6,077	5,838	9,827	14,352	2,976	212	36	7
51	------	1,240	6,913	1,469	1,408	2,164	2,546	525	35	6	8
738	7	4,661	26,504	4,608	4,430	7,663	11,806	2,451	177	30	9
229	5	18,907	51,610	8,537	8,278	15,601	28,619	8,846	587	49	10
193	3	1,087	2,378	559	469	728	1,363	332	11	3	11
3,442	2,492	115,777	292,503	63,723	56,288	94,827	150,015	40,131	2,987	309	12
88	6	2,967	7,088	965	950	1,865	4,025	1,813	430	7	13
1,057	6	51,570	87,467	19,688	17,557	31,760	55,167	14,025	711	129	14
777	6	15,297	59,953	12,651	11,629	19,093	24,645	6,547	634	51	15
199	1	1,852	10,128	2,119	1,927	3,283	3,739	838	67	7	16
224	1	11,416	54,898	14,586	11,658	16,569	19,682	3,603	179	37	17
103	7	1,131	4,172	766	727	1,263	1,933	572	39	3	18
144	155	19,567	38,356	7,216	6,759	12,178	24,394	6,987	350	39	19
850	2,310	11,977	30,441	5,732	5,081	8,816	16,430	5,746	577	36	20
6	------	835	1,245	225	190	501	966	190	8	------	21
25	------	362	1,204	243	205	338	548	219	13	------	22
64	------	1,270	2,308	557	493	746	1,384	381	14	3	23
11	------	324	671	54	68	160	452	244	16	1	24
744	2,310	9,186	25,013	4,653	4,125	7,071	13,080	4,712	526	32	25
7,815	50	40,086	161,846	32,746	31,122	49,981	68,225	17,786	1,470	580	26
57	------	507	1,787	376	310	506	850	231	20	1	27
1	------	6	13	1	------	5	9	4	------	------	28
218	1	1,138	3,773	828	771	1,225	1,671	376	35	5	29
8	------	12	18	1	3	7	13	3	3	------	30
7	------	56	270	53	44	103	109	15	1	1	31
103	1	4,308	22,318	4,607	5,185	7,743	7,948	1,083	43	17	32
7	------	44	119	22	10	42	72	15	2	------	33
154	1	677	3,438	749	703	1,087	1,284	271	20	1	34
63	------	158	508	92	86	132	258	87	10	1	35
154	2	1,790	10,381	2,837	2,010	3,012	3,333	915	56	8	36
8	------	81	564	102	138	194	180	28	3	------	37
89	3	4,552	13,471	2,486	2,717	4,609	6,639	1,485	69	18	38
40	2	1,060	5,031	746	753	1,383	2,130	981	87	11	39
23	1	163	593	141	139	167	257	48	3	1	40
7	------	5	3	------	------	2	4	2	------	------	41
1,506	13	8,760	35,149	6,863	6,402	10,436	14,934	4,702	514	58	42
5,370	26	16,769	64,410	12,864	11,851	19,328	28,534	7,540	604	458	43
27	3	137	122	12	9	28	125	74	10	1	44
------	------	20	49	------	------	18	32	17	2	------	45
------	------	3	------	------	------	------	3	------	------	------	46
------	------	9	31	------	------	10	21	9	------	------	47
------	------	5	12	------	------	4	7	4	2	------	48
------	------	3	6	------	------	4	1	4	------	------	49
------	------	------	3	------	------	1	1	1	------	------	50
651	62	9,176	22,652	1,041	2,254	5,699	15,334	6,706	729	65	51
1	------	2	9	------	------	3	7	1	------	------	52
------	------	------	1	------	------	------	1	------	------	------	53
1	------	2	8	------	------	3	6	1	------	------	54
39	1	550	1,717	167	245	488	918	413	33	3	55

⁸ Includes 188 women reported as presswomen and plate printers (printing) and 23 as rollers and roll hands (metal).

TABLE 115.—WOMEN EMPLOYED IN EACH SPECIFIED OCCUPATION, WITH DISTRI

		ALL CLASSES		RACE AND NATIVITY:		
	OCCUPATION			Native white		Foreign-born white
		1920	1910	Native parentage	Foreign or mixed parentage	
1	Transportation	209,759	104,322	124,908	70,505	10,798
2	Water transportation (selected occupations)	380	71	66	57	113
3	Boatmen, canal men, and lock keepers	33	15	21	5	5
4	Captains, masters, mates, and pilots	2		2		
5	Longshoremen and stevedores	320	44	36	49	105
6	Sailors and deck hands	25	12	7	3	3
7	Road and street transportation (selected occupations):	1,868	171	921	427	246
8	Carriage and hack drivers	89	37	72	9	5
9	Chauffeurs	941	32	444	247	137
10	Draymen, teamsters, and expressmen [9]	626	73	260	134	79
11	Foremen of livery and transfer companies	2		1		
12	Garage keepers and managers	207	23	144	37	25
13	Hostlers and stable hands	3	6			
14	Laborers (garage, road, and street)	272	6	54	20	43
15	Garage	107	6	29	12	4
16	Road and street building and repairing	161		25	8	35
17	Street cleaning	4				4
18	Livery stable keepers and managers	72	183	42	18	12
19	Proprietors and managers of transfer companies.	266	230	122	93	34
	Railroad transportation (selected occupations):					
20	Baggagemen and freight agents	30	5	24	5	1
21	Baggagemen	3		1	1	1
22	Freight agents	27	5	23	4	
23	Boiler washers and engine hostlers	34		7	7	5
24	Conductors (street railroad)	253		122	81	49
25	Foremen and overseers	78	240	24	34	16
26	Steam railroad	66	222	19	29	14
27	Street railroad	12	18	5	5	2
28	Laborers	6,953	3,421	1,863	972	1,938
29	Steam railroad	6,488	3,218	1,728	886	1,811
30	Street railroad	465	203	135	86	127
31	Motormen (street railroad)	20		11	6	3
32	Officials and superintendents	51	2	34	15	2
33	Steam railroad	41	2	25	14	2
34	Street railroad	10		9	1	
35	Switchmen, flagmen, and yardmen	565	52	340	104	76
36	Switchmen and flagmen (steam railroad)	558	52	338	99	76
37	Switchmen and flagmen (street railroad)	4		1	3	
38	Yardmen (steam railroad)	3		1	2	
39	Ticket and station agents	2,261	1,206	1,404	624	228
	Express, post, telegraph, and telephone (selected occupations):					
40	Agents (express companies)	100	71	79	17	4
41	Express messengers	9	3	8	1	
42	Mail carriers	1,307	1,009	990	248	43
43	Telegraph and telephone linemen	12	3	11		1
44	Telegraph messengers	359	45	246	88	23
45	Telegraph operators	16,860	8,199	10,696	5,275	867
46	Telephone operators	175,469	86,081	106,403	61,654	6,892
	Other transportation pursuits:					
47	Foremen and overseers (n. o. s.[3])	37	405	21	15	1
48	Road and street building and repairing	1		1		
49	Telegraph and telephone	25	404	14	11	
50	Other transportation	11	1	6	4	1

[3] Not otherwise specified.

BUTION BY RACE AND NATIVITY, MARITAL CONDITION, AND AGE: 1920—Continued

1920 Negro	All other	MARITAL CONDITION: 1920 Married	Single, widowed, divorced, or unknown	AGE: 1920 16 and 17 years	18 and 19 years	20 to 24 years	25 to 44 years	45 to 64 years	65 years and over	Not reported	
3,466	82	26,480	183,279	27,396	39,966	70,702	63,266	7,660	547	222	1
144		185	195	9	27	61	202	69	12		2
2		8	25	1		3	11	15	3		3
		2					1	1			4
130		165	155	6	26	52	175	52	9		5
12		10	15	2	1	6	15	1			6
274		833	1,035	77	151	353	955	290	39	3	7
3		59	30		7	11	49	19	2	1	8
113		415	526	32	92	224	497	91	4	1	9
153		267	359	45	52	103	274	126	25	1	10
1		1	1				1	1			11
1		89	118			14	133	52	8		12
3		2	1			1	1	1			13
153	2	118	154	16	24	57	131	41	3		14
62		42	65	8	6	23	54	14	2		15
91	2	73	88	8	18	34	76	24	1		16
		3	1				1	3			17
		16	56				27	38	7		18
17		67	199			9	152	89	16		19
		11	19			10	16	4			20
		1	2				3				21
		10	17			10	13	4			22
15		13	21			4	26	3	1		23
	1	82	171			83	151	17		2	24
4		26	52			7	51	19	1		25
4		23	43			7	41	17	1		26
		3	9				10	2			27
2,142	38	3,199	3,754	213	377	947	3,896	1,371	119	30	28
2,025	38	3,023	3,465	200	357	900	3,633	1,254	115	29	29
117		176	289	13	20	47	263	117	4	1	30
		13	7			6	13	1			31
		11	40			6	31	12	2		32
		9	32			4	27	8	2		33
		2	8			2	4	4			34
45		201	364			85	341	127	12		35
45		197	361			80	339	127	12		36
		3	1			4					37
		1	2			1	2				38
5		657	1,604	31	96	429	1,189	479	28	9	39
		64	36			20	66	14			40
		2	7			4	5				41
24	2	599	708	50	85	199	678	270	22	3	42
		2	10			3	8	1			43
2		46	313	143	74	54	69	18	1		44
17	5	2,463	14,397	1,443	3,118	6,002	5,359	859	46	33	45
487	33	17,225	158,244	25,279	35,779	61,798	48,673	3,597	205	138	46
		7	30			12	21	4			47
			1				1				48
		4	21			8	13	4			49
		3	8			4	7				50

⁹ Teamsters in agriculture, forestry, and the extraction of minerals are classified with the other workers in those industries, respectively; and drivers for bakeries and laundries are classified with deliverymen in trade.

TABLE 115.—WOMEN EMPLOYED IN EACH SPECIFIED OCCUPATION, WITH DISTRI

		ALL CLASSES		RACE AND NATIVITY:		
				Native white		Foreign-born white
	OCCUPATION	1920	1910	Native parentage	Foreign or mixed parentage	
	Transportation—Continued.					
	Other transportation pursuits—Continued.					
1	Inspectors_____	385	274	203	153	27
2	Steam railroad_____	46	136	24	14	6
3	Street railroad_____	6	3	5	1	_____
4	Telegraph and telephone_____	330	133	173	136	21
5	Other transportation_____	3	2	1	2	_____
6	Laborers (n. o. s.[3])_____	200	253	108	21	17
7	Express companies_____	22	30	11	1	4
8	Pipe lines_____	7	_____	_____	2	4
9	Telegraph and telephone_____	74	61	54	11	6
10	Water transportation_____	3	89	1	_____	_____
11	Other transportation_____	94	73	42	7	3
12	Proprietors, officials, and managers (n. o. s.[3])__	573	1,428	371	177	25
13	Telegraph and telephone_____	544	1,409	357	169	18
14	Other transportation_____	29	19	14	8	7
15	Other occupations (semiskilled)_____	1,345	964	738	393	132
16	Road and street building and repairing____	103	347	90	8	3
17	Steam railroad_____	692	291	383	191	62
18	Street railroad_____	169	39	71	65	28
19	Telegraph and telephone_____	292	205	150	104	32
20	Water transportation_____	21	40	10	9	1
21	Other transportation_____	68	42	34	16	6
22	Trade_____	653,658	455,221	345,432	208,244	88,409
23	Bankers, brokers, and money lenders_____	5,304	2,634	3,675	1,357	263
24	Bankers and bank officials_____	4,226	1,672	3,017	1,071	130
25	Commercial brokers and commission men_____	194	319	108	50	36
26	Loan brokers and loan company officials_____	130	122	82	36	12
27	Pawnbrokers_____	22	41	5	7	10
28	Stockbrokers_____	376	207	236	111	29
29	Brokers not specified and promoters_____	356	273	227	82	46
30	Clerks in stores [10]_____	164,487	106,961	89,024	57,594	15,439
31	Commercial travelers_____	2,806	2,591	1,909	613	234
32	Decorators, drapers, and window dressers_____	1,142	438	552	393	177
33	Deliverymen_____	180	143	61	47	29
34	Bakeries and laundries_____	28	17	15	8	4
35	Stores_____	152	126	46	39	25
36	Floorwalkers, foremen, and overseers_____	4,070	3,075	1,827	1,688	527
37	Floorwalkers and foremen in stores_____	4,039	3,046	1,814	1,675	523
38	Foremen (warehouses, stockyards, etc.)_____	31	29	13	13	4
39	Inspectors, gaugers, and samplers_____	1,031	1,521	467	383	154
40	Insurance agents and officials_____	5,389	2,660	3,323	1,270	341
41	Insurance agents_____	5,083	2,535	3,128	1,183	324
42	Officials of insurance companies_____	306	125	195	87	17
43	Laborers in coal and lumber yards, warehouses, etc.	866	665	227	167	194
44	Coal yards_____	34	8	9	3	4
45	Elevators_____	68	11	40	18	5
46	Lumberyards_____	51	9	11	8	8
47	Stockyards_____	28	7	7	5	6
48	Warehouses_____	685	630	160	133	171
49	Laborers, porters, and helpers in stores_____	7,987	3,865	2,643	1,858	2,052
50	Newsboys_____	133	100	63	31	27
51	Proprietors, officials, and managers (n. o. s.[3])_____	1,061	1,010	477	278	216
52	Employment office keepers_____	669	720	232	166	182
53	Proprietors, etc., elevators_____	22	13	13	8	1
54	Proprietors, etc., warehouses_____	43	25	29	10	4
55	Other proprietors, officials, and managers_____	327	252	203	94	29
56	Real estate agents and officials_____	9,208	2,925	5,457	2,282	1,370

[3] Not otherwise specified.

BUTION BY RACE AND NATIVITY, MARITAL CONDITION, AND AGE: 1920—Continued

1920		MARITAL CONDITION: 1920		AGE: 1920							
Negro	All other	Married	Single, widowed, divorced, or unknown	16 and 17 years	18 and 19 years	20 to 24 years	25 to 44 years	45 to 64 years	65 years and over	Not reported	
2	------	48	337	------	------	141	227	16	1	------	1
2	------	11	35	------	------	10	28	7	1	------	2
------	------	3	3	------	------	------	4	2	------	------	3
------	------	34	296	------	------	130	194	6	------	------	4
------	------	------	3	------	------	1	1	1	------	------	5
54	------	49	151	16	29	49	84	21	1	------	6
6	------	7	15	4	1	7	8	2	------	------	7
1	------	4	3	------	1	1	4	1	------	------	8
3	------	8	66	10	16	18	24	6	------	------	9
2	------	3	------	------	1	1	1	------	------	------	10
42	------	27	67	2	10	22	47	12	1	------	11
------	------	144	429	------	------	87	366	117	3	------	12
------	------	132	412	------	------	85	354	102	3	------	13
------	------	12	17	------	------	2	12	15	------	------	14
81	1	399	946	119	206	276	529	183	28	4	15
2	------	43	60	6	3	5	35	40	14	------	16
56	------	249	443	50	90	144	302	93	9	4	17
5	------	40	129	11	24	37	77	19	1	------	18
5	1	48	244	47	83	75	74	12	1	------	19
1	------	3	18	1	2	4	11	3	------	------	20
12	------	16	52	4	4	11	30	16	3	------	21
10,959	614	156,490	497,168	55,042	67,744	138,915	291,658	91,725	7,408	1,166	22
7	2	1,143	4,161	------	------	1,111	3,245	819	111	18	23
6	2	864	3,362	------	------	1,047	2,662	473	31	13	24
------	------	75	119	------	------	7	107	70	10	------	25
------	------	21	109	------	------	3	68	47	11	1	26
------	------	5	17	------	------	2	13	6	1	------	27
------	------	79	297	------	------	32	228	98	17	1	28
1	------	99	257	------	------	20	167	125	41	3	29
2,277	153	28,486	136,001	21,565	24,672	43,819	61,968	11,777	473	213	30
50	------	902	1,904	------	20	354	1,575	771	76	10	31
20	------	232	910	45	69	205	602	204	10	7	32
43	------	65	115	33	21	27	67	29	3	------	33
1	------	13	15	3	1	5	13	5	1	------	34
42	------	52	100	30	20	22	54	24	2	------	35
28	------	795	3,275	------	223	825	2,323	670	27	2	36
27	------	787	3,252	------	221	818	2,306	665	27	2	37
1	------	8	23	------	2	7	17	5	------	------	38
27	------	262	769	------	170	301	440	107	10	3	39
454	1	1,350	4,039	------	158	565	2,863	1,629	162	12	40
447	1	1,299	3,784	------	158	547	2,672	1,539	156	11	41
7	------	51	255	------	------	18	191	90	6	1	42
278	------	387	479	88	75	149	369	163	15	7	43
18	------	15	19	1	2	8	19	4	------	------	44
5	------	25	43	4	9	12	28	13	2	------	45
24	------	29	22	4	4	5	29	7	2	------	46
10	------	12	16	5	4	4	12	3	------	------	47
221	------	306	379	74	56	120	281	136	11	7	48
1,395	39	3,424	4,563	845	725	1,403	3,470	1,386	138	20	49
12	------	27	106	31	10	11	23	43	15	------	50
89	1	326	735	------	------	46	577	392	43	3	51
88	1	234	435	------	------	34	346	254	34	1	52
------	------	7	15	------	------	2	9	11	------	------	53
------	------	6	37	------	------	1	13	26	3	------	54
1	------	79	248	------	------	9	209	101	6	2	55
93	6	3,449	5,759	------	54	295	4,136	4,104	579	40	56

[10] Many of the "Clerks in stores" probably are "Saleswomen."

TABLE 115.—WOMEN EMPLOYED IN EACH SPECIFIED OCCUPATION, WITH DISTRI

| | OCCUPATION | ALL CLASSES | | RACE AND NATIVITY: | | |
| | | | | Native white | | Foreign-born white |
		1920	1910	Native parentage	Foreign or mixed parentage	
	Trade—Continued.					
1	Retail dealers [11]	78,957	67,010	29,220	19,535	26,939
2	Agricultural implements and wagons	29	108	16	9	4
3	Art stores and artists' materials	657	415	370	179	104
4	Automobiles and accessories	142	52	89	43	10
5	Bicycles	21	46	7	5	8
6	Books	435	322	271	122	40
7	Boots and shoes	763	876	243	238	276
8	Butchers and meat dealers	1,165	1,291	271	292	564
9	Buyers and shippers of grain	17	81	13	3	1
10	Buyers and shippers of livestock	31	170	20	4	7
11	Buyers and shippers of other farm produce	33	58	23	6	4
12	Candy and confectionery	7,723	7,936	2,216	2,277	3,047
13	Cigars and tobacco	1,110	1,353	347	320	415
14	Carpets and rugs	16	85	8	2	6
15	Clothing and men's furnishings	3,213	1,043	1,208	1,004	982
16	Coal and wood	499	524	213	121	77
17	Coffee and tea	278	239	140	83	52
18	Crockery, glassware, and queensware	113	210	34	34	40
19	Curios, antiques, and novelties	760	358	383	192	123
20	Delicatessen stores	768	718	147	232	379
21	Department stores	952	406	502	324	120
22	Drugs and medicines, including druggists and pharmacists.	3,162	2,161	1,715	965	405
23	Dry goods, fancy goods, and notions	7,751	7,962	2,753	2,162	2,764
24	Five and ten cent and variety stores	1,069	1,037	460	289	312
25	Florists (dealers) [12]	962	406	379	335	198
26	Flour and feed	97	106	47	22	27
27	Fruit	1,200	767	329	195	600
28	Furniture	676	470	327	180	150
29	Furs	355	237	121	110	123
30	Gas fixtures and electrical supplies	85	29	45	31	9
31	General stores	3,709	3,325	2,318	719	550
32	Groceries	23,177	18,435	7,443	4,982	9,455
33	Hardware, stoves, and cutlery	691	683	299	204	182
34	Harness and saddlery	21	57	9	7	5
35	Hucksters and peddlers	1,886	3,717	202	102	1,219
36	Ice	37	141	18	11	6
37	Jewelry	781	559	384	230	158
38	Junk	153	140	20	15	96
39	Leather and hides	43	39	12	19	12
40	Lumber	98	253	69	23	5
41	Milk	595	842	251	126	206
42	Music and musical instruments	549	259	337	138	67
43	Newsdealers	666	537	308	162	174
44	Oil, paint, and wall paper	279	222	137	70	72
45	Opticians	889	330	562	233	90
46	Produce and provisions	1,600	1,281	500	330	677
47	Rags	39	166	10	1	16
48	Stationery	691	687	188	176	325
49	Other specified retail dealers	2,726	1,746	1,147	715	700
50	Not specified retail dealers	6,245	4,125	2,309	1,493	2,077
51	Saleswomen	354,390	250,977	198,976	115,198	37,692
52	Auctioneers	3	5	1	---------	2
53	Demonstrators	3,184	3,121	2,063	817	260
54	Sales agents	1,634	4,089	1,073	375	149
55	Saleswomen (stores)	349,569	243,762	195,839	114,006	37,281
56	Undertakers	1,127	813	580	347	94
57	Wholesale dealers, importers, and exporters	794	925	365	257	169
58	Other pursuits (semiskilled)	14,726	6,908	6,586	4,946	2,492
59	Fruit graders and packers	3,020	1,889	2,006	578	318
60	Meat cutters	80	27	20	13	33
61	Packers, wholesale and retail trade	5,582	2,605	2,144	2,381	902
62	Other occupations	6,044	2,387	2,416	1,974	1,239

[11] Includes, also, managers and superintendents of retail stores.

bution by Race and Nativity, Marital Condition, and Age: 1920—Continued

1920		MARITAL CONDITION: 1920		AGE: 1920							
Negro	All other	Married	Single, widowed, divorced, or unknown	16 and 17 years	18 and 19 years	20 to 24 years	25 to 44 years	45 to 64 years	65 years and over	Not reported	
3,128	135	34,801	44,156	90	992	4,872	40,450	28,543	3,858	152	1
----	----	13	16	----	----	2	13	12	2	----	2
1	3	221	436	----	3	27	350	256	20	1	3
----	----	55	87	----	----	10	101	30	1	----	4
----	1	11	10	----	----	2	15	4	----	----	5
2	----	103	332	----	6	38	182	181	25	3	6
5	1	268	495	----	4	58	366	279	54	2	7
38	----	598	567	----	43	110	613	354	40	5	8
----	----	----	17	----	----	----	9	8	----	----	9
----	----	17	14	----	----	1	19	8	2	1	10
----	----	15	18	----	----	2	17	13	1	----	11
176	7	3,811	3,912	33	71	432	4,128	2,668	379	12	12
28	----	476	634	----	11	71	579	385	62	2	13
----	----	6	10	----	----	2	9	4	1	----	14
19	----	1,183	2,030	----	25	188	1,930	990	69	11	15
.87	1	169	330	----	5	31	239	185	36	3	16
2	1	84	194	----	3	27	159	82	5	2	17
3	2	38	75	----	1	4	50	52	6	----	18
56	6	249	511	----	6	40	348	318	47	1	19
9	1	388	380	----	7	34	416	295	15	1	20
5	1	231	721	----	19	104	579	235	15	----	21
73	4	892	2,270	----	103	504	1,692	759	95	9	22
58	14	2,805	4,946	----	51	318	3,834	3,125	416	7	23
7	1	446	623	----	12	57	502	438	57	3	24
46	4	307	655	----	21	81	460	344	53	3	25
1	----	30	67	----	----	2	48	39	8	----	26
65	11	537	663	----	43	194	638	292	32	1	27
19	----	256	420	----	2	43	320	270	40	1	28
----	1	122	233	----	11	40	170	120	14	----	29
----	----	35	50	----	1	4	50	27	3	----	30
113	9	1,628	2,081	----	31	135	1,810	1,513	213	7	31
1,264	33	12,342	10,835	36	185	1,079	11,978	8,734	1,129	36	32
6	----	292	399	----	7	43	329	272	39	1	33
----	----	5	16	----	----	----	8	12	1	----	34
361	2	731	1,155	21	23	73	754	797	215	3	35
2	----	9	28	----	----	1	22	10	4	----	36
8	1	191	590	----	30	108	375	239	27	2	37
22	----	76	77	----	3	5	79	56	10	----	38
----	----	10	33	----	----	----	21	21	1	----	39
1	----	23	75	----	1	5	44	40	8	----	40
12	----	250	345	----	15	43	248	246	43	----	41
7	----	211	338	----	21	71	305	132	18	2	42
21	1	232	434	----	14	64	312	245	31	----	43
----	----	98	181	----	2	13	123	112	28	1	44
4	----	284	605	----	71	170	440	190	14	4	45
85	8	720	880	----	28	108	803	584	76	1	46
12	----	20	19	----	1	2	16	18	2	----	47
2	----	283	408	----	8	47	354	250	30	2	48
159	5	1,000	1,726	----	23	152	1,433	974	132	12	49
349	17	3,030	3,215	----	81	327	3,160	2,325	339	13	50
2,289	235	76,277	278,113	30,072	38,680	81,643	163,078	38,596	1,673	648	51
----	----	2	1	----	----	1	2	----	----	----	52
41	3	917	2,267	----	75	377	1,796	873	59	4	53
37	----	504	1,130	----	51	146	789	541	103	4	54
2,211	232	74,854	274,715	30,072	38,554	81,119	160,491	37,182	1,511	640	55
106	----	514	613	----	----	61	570	448	46	2	56
2	1	249	545	----	----	31	477	257	27	2	57
661	41	3,801	10,925	2,273	1,875	3,197	5,425	1,787	142	27	58
87	31	1,128	1,892	309	376	593	1,295	419	18	10	59
14	----	48	32	----	----	19	45	13	2	1	60
152	3	894	4,688	1,277	893	1,158	1,709	510	29	6	61
408	7	1,731	4,313	687	606	1,427	2,376	845	93	10	62

[12] Growers of flowers are shown under "Agriculture," p. 164.

TABLE 115.—WOMEN EMPLOYED IN EACH SPECIFIED OCCUPATION, WITH DISTRI

	OCCUPATION	ALL CLASSES		RACE AND NATIVITY:		
				Native white		Foreign-born white
		1920	1910	Native parent-age	Foreign or mixed parent-age	
1	Public service (not elsewhere classified)_____	21,749	13,548	14,893	4,854	1,039
2	Guards, watchmen, and doorkeepers_____	399	103	211	99	68
3	Laborers (public service)_____	1,498	725	414	172	189
4	Garbage men and scavengers_____	5	_____	3	2	_____
5	Other laborers_____	1,493	725	411	170	189
6	Marshals, sheriffs, detectives, etc_____	1,246	380	663	434	111
7	Detectives_____	393	187	212	138	43
8	Marshals and constables_____	17	2	10	6	1
9	Probation and truant officers_____	780	188	407	277	58
10	Sheriffs_____	56	3	34	13	9
11	Officials and inspectors (city and county)_____	4,849	2,586	3,389	1,273	180
12	Officials and inspectors (city)_____	1,587	1,011	1,008	489	87
13	Officials and inspectors (county)_____	3,262	1,575	2,381	784	93
14	Officials and inspectors (State and United States)__	12,390	9,533	9,525	2,439	373
15	Officials and inspectors (State)_____	530	540	348	150	31
16	Postmasters_____	11,208	8,718	8,791	2,063	305
17	Other United States officials_____	652	275	386	226	37
18	Policemen_____	236	_____	130	82	17
19	Other pursuits_____	1,131	221	561	355	101
20	Life-savers_____	2	_____	2	_____	_____
21	Lighthouse keepers_____	21	41	11	5	2
22	Other occupations_____	1,108	180	548	350	99
23	Professional service_____	1,015,012	732,381	654,440	250,529	70,485
24	Actresses and showwomen_____	14,220	12,817	7,920	3,800	1,887
25	Actresses_____	13,114	11,750	7,296	3,554	1,727
26	Showwomen_____	1,106	1,067	624	246	160
27	Architects_____	137	302	99	35	3
28	Artists, sculptors, and teachers of art_____	14,566	15,354	9,275	3,767	1,407
29	Authors, editors, and reporters_____	8,735	6,239	6,430	1,742	516
30	Authors_____	3,005	2,058	2,172	558	257
31	Editors and reporters_____	5,730	4,181	4,258	1,184	259
32	Chemists, assayers, and metallurgists_____	1,714	579	1,084	471	150
33	Clergymen_____	1,787	685	1,148	239	171
34	College presidents and professors [13]_____	10,075	2,958	7,428	1,700	448
35	Dentists_____	1,829	1,254	996	505	292
36	Designers, draftsmen, and inventors_____	7,664	3,007	3,408	2,642	1,577
37	Designers_____	5,652	2,572	2,148	2,018	1,450
38	Draftsmen_____	1,985	391	1,243	615	126
39	Inventors_____	27	44	17	9	1
40	Lawyers, judges, and justices_____	1,738	558	1,091	481	162
41	Musicians and teachers of music_____	72,431	83,851	47,382	18,528	4,348
42	Osteopaths_____	1,663	_____	1,100	281	118
43	Photographers_____	7,048	4,917	4,531	1,810	601
44	Physicians and surgeons_____	7,219	9,015	4,561	1,671	912
45	Teachers_____	639,241	477,824	428,611	154,743	26,354
46	Teachers (athletics, dancing, etc.)_____	4,034	1,163	2,628	1,027	322
47	Teachers (school)_____	635,207	476,661	425,983	153,716	26,032
48	Technical engineers_____	41	11	29	9	3
49	Civil engineers and surveyors_____	18	5	11	5	2
50	Electrical engineers_____	12	6	10	2	_____
51	Mechanical engineers [14]_____	11	_____	8	2	1

[13] Probably includes some teachers in schools below collegiate grade.

BUTION BY RACE AND NATIVITY, MARITAL CONDITION, AND AGE: 1920—Continued

1920		MARITAL CONDITION: 1920		AGE: 1920							
Negro	All other	Married	Single, widowed, divorced, or unknown	16 and 17 years	18 and 19 years	20 to 24 years	25 to 44 years	45 to 64 years	65 years and over	Not reported	
947	16	7,542	14,207	94	547	2,929	12,096	5,554	471	58	1
21	------	149	250	------	------	49	164	156	30	------	2
721	2	619	879	61	72	232	693	372	58	10	3
------	------	2	3	1	------	------	3	1	------	------	4
721	2	617	876	60	72	232	690	371	58	10	5
38	------	351	895	------	------	97	753	378	16	2	6
------	------	150	243	------	------	55	273	62	2	1	7
------	------	5	12	------	------	1	12	4	------	------	8
38	------	177	603	------	------	29	447	291	12	1	9
------	------	19	37	------	------	12	21	21	2	------	10
7	------	1,195	3,654	------	------	607	3,083	1,069	71	19	11
3	------	401	1,186	------	------	182	941	425	37	2	12
4	------	794	2,468	------	------	425	2,142	644	34	17	13
43	10	4,883	7,507	------	391	1,733	6,754	3,220	271	21	14
1	------	126	404	------	------	51	321	150	6	2	15
40	9	4,609	6,599	------	391	1,564	6,011	2,968	255	19	16
2	1	148	504	------	------	118	422	102	10	------	17
7	------	66	170	------	------	11	130	88	5	------	18
110	4	279	852	33	84	200	519	271	20	4	19
------	------	2	------	------	------	------	2	------	------	------	20
2	1	11	10	------	------	------	5	13	3	------	21
108	3	266	842	33	84	200	512	258	17	4	22
39,013	545	123,578	891,434	11,449	69,450	298,827	490,894	130,500	10,976	2,916	23
587	26	5,817	8,403	578	1,287	4,259	7,138	855	59	44	24
516	21	5,217	7,897	529	1,193	3,956	6,574	771	48	43	25
71	5	600	506	49	94	303	564	84	11	1	26
------	------	32	105	------	------	20	77	38	2	------	27
107	10	2,880	11,686	296	602	2,573	7,067	3,560	424	44	28
44	3	2,265	6,470	61	286	1,299	4,362	2,312	389	26	29
15	3	956	2,049	6	12	198	1,476	1,072	232	9	30
29	------	1,309	4,421	55	274	1,101	2,886	1,240	157	17	31
8	1	246	1,468	------	------	766	801	135	8	4	32
228	1	841	946	------	------	109	844	695	130	9	33
496	3	1,140	8,935	------	------	1,742	6,186	1,953	142	52	34
35	1	534	1,295	------	------	472	1,070	254	30	3	35
35	2	1,156	6,508	------	540	2,049	4,197	824	41	13	36
34	2	927	4,725	------	305	1,218	3,385	705	28	11	37
1	------	218	1,767	------	235	830	798	111	9	2	38
------	------	11	16	------	------	1	14	8	4	------	39
4	------	594	1,144	------	------	222	991	448	72	5	40
2,138	35	17,830	54,601	1,308	3,286	15,060	39,280	12,247	1,131	119	41
164	------	590	1,073	------	------	84	809	715	49	6	42
100	6	1,829	5,219	384	669	1,540	3,349	1,036	56	14	43
65	10	2,372	4,847	------	------	323	3,209	3,172	493	22	44
29,244	289	62,153	577,088	5,800	49,309	212,065	297,405	68,351	4,552	1,759	45
55	2	670	3,364	72	245	1,324	1,955	396	33	9	46
29,189	287	61,483	573,724	5,728	49,064	210,741	295,450	67,955	4,519	1,750	47
------	------	10	31	------	------	11	25	4	1	------	48
------	------	7	11	------	------	3	11	3	1	------	49
------	------	1	11	------	------	6	6	------	------	------	50
------	------	2	9	------	------	2	8	1	------	------	51

14 Includes, also, all technical engineers not elsewhere classified.

TABLE 115.—WOMEN EMPLOYED IN EACH SPECIFIED OCCUPATION, WITH DISTRI

| | OCCUPATION | ALL CLASSES | | RACE AND NATIVITY: | | |
| | | 1920 | 1910 | Native white | | Foreign-born white |
				Native parentage	Foreign or mixed parentage	
	Professional service—Continued.					
1	Trained nurses	143, 664	76, 481	80, 673	38, 138	21, 556
2	Veterinary surgeons	1	--------	--------	1	--------
3	Other professional pursuits	19, 273	8, 085	13, 703	4, 377	1, 091
4	Aeronauts	8	--------	6	2	--------
5	Librarians	13, 502	5, 828	9, 890	3, 006	559
6	Other occupations	5, 763	2, 257	3, 807	1, 369	532
7	Semiprofessional pursuits	45, 920	20, 370	25, 735	10, 901	7, 919
8	Abstracters, notaries, and justices of peace	1, 483	785	1, 040	377	53
9	Fortune tellers, hypnotists, spiritualists, etc.	691	1, 217	341	140	158
10	Healers (except osteopaths, physicians, and surgeons).	7, 902	4, 669	4, 472	1, 577	1, 482
11	Keepers of charitable and penal institutions	4, 931	2, 245	2, 548	1, 334	995
12	Keepers of pleasure resorts, race tracks, etc.	197	223	111	48	38
13	Officials of lodges, societies, etc.	2, 162	1, 970	1, 435	505	144
14	Religious, charity, and welfare workers	26, 927	8, 877	14, 770	6, 513	4, 866
15	Theatrical owners, managers, and officials	1, 257	295	812	319	114
16	Turfmen and sportsmen	1	1	1	--------	--------
17	Other occupations	369	88	205	88	69
18	Attendants and helpers (professional service)	16, 046	8, 074	9, 236	4, 683	970
19	Dentists' assistants and apprentices	4, 863	1, 472	2, 821	1, 614	290
20	Librarians' assistants and attendants	1, 163	2, 772	757	338	59
21	Physicians' and surgeons' attendants	6, 277	3, 313	3, 673	1, 666	322
22	Stage hands and circus helpers	417	382	180	117	70
23	Theater ushers	2, 203	135	1, 130	598	151
24	Other attendants and helpers	1, 123	--------	675	355	78
25	Domestic and personal service	2, 149, 000	2, 443, 406	637, 250	332, 930	397, 997
26	Barbers, hairdressers, and manicurists	33, 091	22, 011	10, 579	6, 224	3, 531
27	Billiard room, dance hall, skating rink, etc., keepers	242	814	87	50	58
28	Billiard and pool room keepers	73	159	17	9	29
29	Dance hall, skating rink, etc., keepers	169	655	70	41	29
30	Boarding and lodging house keepers	114, 740	142, 392	59, 862	21, 266,	23, 950
31	Bootblacks	30	18	3	2	5
32	Charwomen and cleaners	24, 744	26, 443	4, 250	4, 397	8, 991
33	Elevator tenders	7, 233	25	2, 337	1, 252	604
34	Hotel keepers and managers	14, 134	14, 235	8, 775	2, 932	2, 076
35	Housekeepers and stewardesses	204, 350	173, 280	99, 910	50, 462	40, 232
36	Janitors and sextons	28, 929	21, 357	6, 235	5, 913	11, 329
37	Laborers (domestic and professional service)	1, 631	3, 113	692	306	291
38	Laundresses (not in laundry)	383, 622	513, 586	50, 279	18, 204	32, 763
39	Laundry operatives	78, 548	73, 393	28, 103	17, 366	12, 267
40	Forewomen and overseers	1, 535	1, 397	727	561	201
41	Laborers	6, 288	3, 185	2, 676	1, 098	648
42	Other operatives [15]	70, 725	68, 811	24, 700	15, 707	11, 418
43	Laundry owners, officials, and managers [15]	1, 453	986	578	347	392
44	Managers and officials	584	240	297	171	100
45	Owners and proprietors	869	746	281	176	292
46	Midwives and nurses (not trained)	137, 431	116, 746	67, 105	29, 976	26, 327
47	Midwives	4, 773	6, 205	459	347	2, 476
48	Nurses (not trained)	132, 658	110, 541	66, 646	29, 629	23, 851
49	Porters (except in stores)	480	73	61	72	113
50	Porters, domestic and professional service	277	52	34	37	87
51	Porters, steam railroad	27	1	2	2	--------
52	Other porters (except in stores)	176	20	25	33	26
53	Restaurant, café, and lunch room keepers	15, 644	10, 515	6, 550	2, 889	2, 680
54	Servants	981, 557	1, 234, 758	238, 357	143, 208	207, 811
55	Bell boys, chore boys, etc.	707	580	173	110	80
56	Butlers	1	--------	1	--------	--------
57	Chambermaids	28, 379	38, 113	6, 290	3, 965	8, 016
58	Cooks	268, 618	332, 433	42, 211	18, 536	38, 275
59	Ladies' maids, valets, etc.	4, 464	} 12, 354	{ 2, 034	727	1, 454
60	Nurse maids	8, 357		2, 285	1, 675	1, 536
61	Other servants	671, 031	850, 278	185, 363	118, 195	158, 450

[15] Some owners of hand laundries probably are included with laundry operatives.

BUTION BY RACE AND NATIVITY, MARITAL CONDITION, AND AGE: 1920—Continued

1920		MARITAL CONDITION: 1920		AGE: 1920							
Negro	All other	Married	Single, widowed, divorced, or unknown	16 and 17 years	18 and 19 years	20 to 24 years	25 to 44 years	45 to 64 years	65 years and over	Not reported	
3,199	98	10,706	132,958	937	9,712	43,386	73,556	14,538	968	567	1
---	---	1	---	---	---	---	1	---	---	---	2
93	9	1,803	17,470	45	762	3,580	10,232	4,140	475	39	3
---	---	2	6	---	---	3	5	---	---	---	4
47	---	1,000	12,502	---	532	2,288	7,151	3,145	356	30	5
46	9	801	4,962	45	230	1,289	3,076	995	119	9	6
1,323	42	8,527	37,393	106	647	4,393	24,367	14,325	1,916	166	7
13	---	325	1,158	15	83	243	787	323	28	4	8
48	4	325	366	2	10	19	203	357	95	5	9
360	11	3,056	4,846	---	38	231	3,478	3,697	428	30	10
54	---	618	4,313	---	18	249	2,486	1,946	207	25	11
---	---	74	123	---	1	5	79	86	26	---	12
76	2	525	1,637	8	39	234	1,203	630	45	3	13
755	23	2,995	23,932	68	435	3,231	15,106	6,920	1,071	96	14
11	1	553	704	---	---	137	831	277	9	3	15
---	---	1	---	---	---	---	1	---	---	---	16
6	1	55	314	13	23	44	193	89	7	---	17
1,143	9	2,252	13,794	1,934	2,350	4,874	5,928	898	38	24	18
138	---	545	4,318	359	744	1,653	1,919	181	5	2	19
9	---	78	1,085	245	95	249	434	125	9	6	20
612	4	763	5,514	555	912	1,947	2,433	401	19	10	21
50	---	177	240	28	30	76	181	98	2	2	22
319	5	567	1,636	509	424	580	629	57	1	3	23
15	---	122	1,001	238	145	369	332	36	2	1	24
775,549	5,274	637,675	1,511,325	88,148	118,729	302,226	972,489	568,448	93,135	5,825	25
12,631	126	12,728	20,363	556	1,165	5,408	21,121	4,400	379	62	26
39	8	108	134	---	---	27	139	69	5	2	27
13	5	35	38	---	---	7	50	13	3	---	28
26	3	73	96	---	---	20	89	56	2	2	29
9,536	126	42,431	72,309	---	229	2,217	45,904	56,238	10,016	136	30
20	---	9	21	4	3	7	13	2	1	---	31
7,075	31	10,398	14,346	314	390	1,463	12,050	9,389	1,095	43	32
3,036	4	2,250	4,983	571	1,036	1,956	3,113	505	44	8	33
301	50	6,544	7,590	---	---	302	6,297	6,671	840	24	34
13,250	496	36,688	167,662	---	5,556	16,902	79,577	82,916	19,088	311	35
5,413	39	15,394	13,535	160	236	1,197	14,743	11,197	1,354	42	36
339	3	477	1,154	89	92	247	669	454	67	13	37
281,761	615	187,510	196,112	5,658	9,910	36,539	192,696	118,521	18,835	1,463	38
20,463	349	26,237	52,311	7,028	7,074	13,355	35,703	14,123	1,072	193	39
46	---	462	1,073	---	51	161	945	361	14	3	40
1,834	32	1,982	4,306	667	657	1,176	2,657	1,019	95	17	41
18,583	317	23,793	46,932	6,361	6,366	12,018	32,101	12,743	963	173	42
131	5	633	820	---	---	85	810	516	41	1	43
16	---	222	362	---	---	48	328	197	11	---	44
115	5	411	458	---	---	37	482	319	30	1	45
13,888	135	27,444	109,987	---	3,799	15,434	59,854	49,502	8,424	418	46
1,437	54	2,587	2,186	---	---	45	1,518	2,427	774	9	47
12,451	81	24,857	107,801	---	3,799	15,389	58,336	47,075	7,650	409	48
231	3	179	301	12	18	66	249	116	19	---	49
116	3	108	169	10	13	31	148	65	10	---	50
23	---	8	19	---	1	6	16	3	1	---	51
92	---	63	113	2	4	29	85	48	8	---	52
3,455	70	7,244	8,400	---	176	903	8,809	5,355	356	45	53
389,276	2,905	228,270	753,287	64,642	76,011	175,704	432,165	199,305	30,947	2,783	54
340	4	203	504	102	105	162	272	59	6	1	55
---	---	---	---	---	---	1	---	---	---	---	56
9,993	115	7,649	20,730	1,397	1,818	4,840	14,495	5,256	482	91	57
168,710	886	89,018	179,600	7,334	13,687	41,445	133,167	64,017	7,909	1,059	58
244	5	367	4,097	80	97	315	1,680	1,760	517	15	59
2,848	13	934	7,423	3,690	676	1,055	1,847	902	178	9	60
207,141	1,882	130,099	540,932	52,039	59,628	127,886	280,704	127,311	21,855	1,608	61

TABLE 115.—WOMEN EMPLOYED IN EACH SPECIFIED OCCUPATION, WITH DISTRI

	OCCUPATION	ALL CLASSES		RACE AND NATIVITY:		
				Native white		Foreign-born white
		1920	1910	Native parent-age	Foreign or mixed parent-age	
	Domestic and personal service—Continued.					
1	Waitresses	114,718	83,597	51,180	26,387	23,039
2	Other pursuits	6,423	6,064	2,307	1,677	1,538
3	Bartenders	107	248	11	23	69
4	Bathhouse keepers and attendants	809	1,436	256	209	167
5	Cemetery keepers	44	31	18	13	10
6	Cleaners and renovators (clothing, etc.)	4,533	2,567	1,777	1,182	882
7	Hunters, trappers, and guides	43	47	25	6	4
8	Saloon keepers	523	1,491	36	152	334
9	Umbrella menders and scissors grinders	18	35	1	5	11
10	Other occupations	346	209	183	87	61
11	Clerical occupations	1,405,609	580,645	773,798	533,792	89,574
12	Agents, canvassers, and collectors	15,741	8,754	10,022	3,966	1,213
13	Agents	8,910	2,285	5,755	2,418	682
14	Canvassers	4,124	4,589	2,549	835	359
15	Collectors	2,707	1,880	1,718	713	172
16	Bookkeepers, cashiers, and accountants	356,603	185,299	194,001	132,898	27,979
17	Accountants and auditors	13,378	3,586	8,314	4,353	698
18	Bookkeepers and cashiers	343,225	181,713	185,687	128,545	27,281
19	Clerks (except clerks in stores)	463,570	119,385	262,600	169,747	27,752
20	Shipping clerks	4,624	2,076	2,075	1,851	588
21	Weighers	1,458	555	709	480	186
22	Other clerks	457,488	116,754	259,816	167,416	26,978
23	Messenger, bundle, and office girls [16]	9,947	6,005	4,995	3,446	862
24	Bundle and cash girls	3,243	3,288	1,654	1,197	298
25	Messenger, errand, and office girls	6,704	2,717	3,341	2,249	564
26	Stenographers and typists	559,748	261,202	302,180	223,735	31,768

[16] Except telegraph messengers.

BUTION BY RACE AND NATIVITY, MARITAL CONDITION, AND AGE: 1920—Continued

Negro	All other	Married	Single, widowed, divorced, or unknown	16 and 17 years	18 and 19 years	20 to 24 years	25 to 44 years	45 to 64 years	65 years and over	Not reported	
13,836	276	31,037	83,681	8,933	12,774	29,662	55,200	7,465	409	275	1
868	33	2,094	4,329	181	260	752	3,377	1,704	143	6	2
4	------	53	54	1	2	6	71	26	1	------	3
172	5	270	539	17	28	77	368	301	18	------	4
3	------	12	32	1	------	------	16	24	3	------	5
670	22	1,574	2,959	150	207	603	2,495	985	89	4	6
2	6	13	30	1	3	2	22	14	1	------	7
1	------	88	435	------	------	8	240	256	19	------	8
1	------	9	9	------	------	------	6	9	3	------	9
15	------	75	271	11	20	56	159	89	9	2	10
8,138	307	129,038	1,276,571	124,034	219,663	481,411	518,508	57,338	2,955	1,700	11
537	3	3,905	11,836	340	651	2,300	7,789	3,950	680	31	12
55	------	1,936	6,974	191	408	1,599	4,665	1,800	229	18	13
379	2	1,235	2,889	47	78	243	1,720	1,618	410	8	14
103	1	734	1,973	102	165	458	1,404	532	41	5	15
1,618	107	41,061	315,542	21,436	45,481	115,916	154,970	17,792	587	421	16
13	------	1,662	11,716	--------	1,350	4,099	6,863	980	64	22	17
1,605	107	39,399	303,826	21,436	44,131	111,817	148,107	16,812	523	399	18
3,388	83	46,265	417,305	45,104	68,982	148,493	173,781	25,215	1,377	618	19
108	2	752	3,872	516	702	1,427	1,641	309	27	2	20
83	------	346	1,112	189	209	324	566	155	14	1	21
3,197	81	45,167	412,321	44,399	68,071	¶146,742	171,574	24,751	1,336	615	22
640	4	712	9,235	4,289	1,986	1,978	1,465	200	25	4	23
94	------	250	2,993	1,590	639	477	450	73	14	------	24
546	4	462	6,242	2,699	1,347	1,501	1,015	127	11	4	25
1,955	110	37,095	522,653	52,865	102,563	212,724	180,503	10,181	286	626	26

TABLE **116.**—WOMEN EMPLOYED IN CERTAIN SELECTED

	OCCUPATION	United States	NEW ENGLAND DIVISION				
			Total	Maine	New Hampshire	Vermont	Massachusetts
1	All occupations	8, 202, 901	846, 244	64, 113	48, 778	26, 557	489, 146
2	Agriculture, forestry, and animal husbandry	896, 057	7, 990	2, 083	1, 031	1, 184	1, 758
3	Farmers, general farms	247, 253	5, 223	1, 613	794	761	923
4	Farm laborers (home farms)	403, 009	450	98	33	62	99
5	Farm laborers (working out)	198, 979	859	144	69	99	259
6	All other occupations	46, 816	1, 458	228	135	262	477
7	Extraction of minerals	2, 718	10	3	2	1	3
8	Manufacturing and mechanical industries	1, 849, 339	359, 667	22, 679	24, 604	6, 318	207, 623
9	Dressmakers and seamstresses (not in factory)	235, 519	18, 763	1, 874	977	1, 004	10, 599
10	Forewomen and overseers (manufacturing)	30, 171	4, 920	140	184	53	3, 219
11	Laborers (n. o. s.[1])	160, 133	20, 554	2, 596	2, 702	533	5, 562
12	Food industries	15, 486	619	344	10	40	177
13	Textile industries	30, 320	7, 538	843	1, 585	101	2, 067
14	All other industries	114, 327	12, 397	1, 409	1, 107	392	3, 318
15	Milliners and millinery dealers	69, 598	5, 760	580	349	254	3, 295
16	Semiskilled operatives (n. o. s.[1])	1, 274, 719	300, 803	16, 897	20, 011	4, 250	179, 949
17	Chemical and allied industries	17, 391	2, 750	31	10	13	1, 369
18	Cigar and tobacco factories	80, 757	2, 156	42	218	5	968
19	Clothing industries	256, 641	19, 678	999	618	1, 174	10, 659
20	Electrical supply factories	28, 626	5, 611	1	38		3, 856
21	Food industries	67, 753	6, 834	675	34	198	5, 577
22	Iron and steel industries	56, 009	14, 981	50	716	125	5, 827
23	Other metal industries	29, 086	12, 005	10	13	8	4, 036
24	Lumber and furniture industries	17, 746	2, 388	269	230	167	1, 297
25	Printing and publishing	39, 318	5, 443	362	106	38	4, 392
26	Rubber factories	18, 023	9, 183	2	2		5, 273
27	Shoe factories	70, 517	38, 466	3, 598	4, 988	10	29, 320
28	Textile industries	408, 280	151, 715	9, 500	11, 867	2, 147	88, 101
29	All other industries	186, 572	29, 593	1, 358	1, 171	365	19, 274
30	Tailoresses	31, 828	2, 061	182	95	49	1, 489
31	All other occupations	47, 371	6, 806	410	286	175	3, 510
32	Transportation	209, 759	16, 541	1, 229	699	626	10, 519
33	Telegraph operators	16, 860	1, 034	101	37	26	696
34	Telephone operators	175, 469	14, 649	1, 061	603	546	9, 359
35	All other occupations	17, 430	858	67	59	54	464
36	Trade	653, 658	53, 813	4, 321	2, 431	1, 574	32, 267
37	Clerks in stores	164, 487	13, 041	1, 299	908	391	7, 119
38	Saleswomen (stores)	349, 569	29, 928	2, 172	1, 102	873	18, 938
39	Retail dealers	78, 957	6, 600	579	299	209	3, 761
40	All other occupations	60, 645	4, 244	271	122	101	2, 449
41	Public service (not elsewhere classified)	21, 749	1, 297	268	119	166	543
42	Professional service	1, 015, 012	87, 611	9, 396	5, 080	4, 484	48, 070
43	Musicians and teachers of music	72, 431	6, 974	667	386	284	4, 083
44	Religious, charity, and welfare workers	26, 927	2, 953	175	146	63	1, 979
45	Teachers (school)	655, 207	48, 674	6, 418	3, 093	3, 040	24, 235
46	Trained nurses	143, 664	16, 233	1, 246	886	676	9, 506
47	All other occupations	136, 783	12, 777	890	569	421	8, 267

[1] Not otherwise specified.

OCCUPATIONS, BY DIVISIONS AND STATES: 1920

| | NEW ENGLAND DIVISION—con. | | MIDDLE ATLANTIC DIVISION | | | | EAST NORTH CENTRAL DIVISION | | | | | | |
Rhode Island	Connecticut	Total	New York	New Jersey	Pennsylvania	Total	Ohio	Indiana	Illinois	Michigan	Wisconsin	
76,469	141,181	2,063,007	1,114,831	284,162	664,014	1,535,641	407,081	180,902	527,875	242,120	177,663	1
270	1,664	20,388	9,165	1,845	9,378	45,673	10,496	7,312	9,236	8,548	10,081	2
155	977	10,990	4,693	654	5,643	26,120	6,237	4,422	5,451	4,751	5,259	3
6	152	2,190	728	175	1,287	6,523	925	702	1,017	1,521	2,358	4
28	260	2,056	934	248	874	3,938	842	656	882	833	725	5
81	275	5,152	2,810	768	1,574	9,092	2,492	1,532	1,886	1,443	1,739	6
------	1	817	109	13	695	573	208	42	104	210	9	7
41,610	56,833	654,044	341,843	103,456	208,745	359,575	101,385	43,812	116,945	54,551	42,882	8
1,636	2,673	66,064	37,849	7,391	20,824	49,754	12,989	6,571	16,640	7,532	6,022	9
428	896	13,250	7,061	2,240	3,949	6,702	2,061	706	2,165	995	775	10
2,670	6,491	27,920	11,191	5,735	10,994	42,822	10,767	7,149	10,398	8,182	6,326	11
14	34	1,871	986	183	702	3,832	496	449	1,448	708	731	12
1,760	1,182	5,667	1,834	1,628	2,205	1,982	396	258	412	339	577	13
896	5,275	20,382	8,371	3,924	8,087	37,008	9,875	6,442	8,538	7,135	5,018	14
468	814	22,070	15,090	1,978	5,002	16,312	3,896	1,869	6,489	2,113	1,945	15
34,846	44,850	500,550	254,878	83,274	162,398	220,600	65,160	25,311	71,822	32,456	25,851	16
160	1,167	6,628	3,724	1,597	1,307	4,907	1,336	444	1,681	1,161	285	17
27	896	32,250	8,877	5,187	18,186	16,720	7,739	3,294	1,076	3,532	1,079	18
541	5,687	136,917	98,666	12,764	25,487	48,893	11,475	6,679	21,648	4,318	4,773	19
321	1,395	9,803	3,392	4,146	2,265	9,653	3,034	1,677	3,779	321	842	20
153	197	16,626	9,150	1,822	5,654	17,474	3,679	1,362	7,975	2,293	2,165	21
1,171	7,092	14,802	6,127	3,265	5,410	22,907	6,336	2,228	3,978	8,744	1,421	22
2,710	5,228	5,938	3,102	1,796	1,040	8,215	1,881	567	4,328	813	626	23
26	399	4,363	2,525	402	1,436	6,957	1,152	1,412	1,484	1,890	1,019	24
208	337	13,019	8,686	912	3,421	10,057	2,907	772	4,448	1,045	885	25
1,788	2,118	3,614	1,201	1,413	1,000	4,684	3,390	452	141	141	556	26
227	323	13,286	8,501	894	3,891	10,053	4,471	281	2,554	275	2,472	27
26,245	13,855	154,085	46,166	33,073	74,846	20,863	5,108	2,291	5,010	2,683	5,771	28
1,269	6,156	89,219	54,761	16,003	18,455	39,217	12,452	3,852	13,716	5,240	3,957	29
106	140	10,372	7,611	607	2,154	10,731	3,226	636	5,429	824	616	30
1,456	969	13,818	8,163	2,231	3,424	12,654	3,286	1,570	4,002	2,449	1,347	31
1,188	2,280	56,802	32,720	6,380	17,702	50,423	13,182	5,861	18,947	7,664	4,769	32
41	133	3,869	2,211	334	1,324	3,482	926	304	1,485	499	268	33
1,104	1,976	48,496	28,352	5,336	14,808	43,244	11,560	5,112	15,735	6,568	4,269	34
43	171	4,437	2,157	710	1,570	3,697	696	445	1,727	597	232	35
4,301	8,919	170,076	84,032	19,675	66,369	158,493	43,160	18,424	55,687	24,284	16,938	36
1,028	2,296	42,789	20,012	4,225	18,552	47,116	11,665	5,475	18,838	6,379	4,759	37
2,434	4,409	87,368	43,002	9,656	34,710	81,479	23,815	9,993	25,270	13,320	9,081	38
561	1,191	25,224	11,688	4,107	9,429	16,465	4,564	1,717	6,101	2,310	1,773	39
278	1,023	14,695	9,330	1,687	3,678	13,433	3,116	1,239	5,478	2,275	1,325	40
69	132	3,105	1,679	366	1,060	3,525	730	487	1,184	649	475	41
5,816	14,765	228,872	126,408	28,165	74,299	206,871	51,416	26,187	65,559	35,200	28,509	42
552	1,002	16,784	9,519	2,045	5,220	16,759	4,299	2,111	5,949	2,645	1,755	43
190	400	8,544	5,097	940	2,507	5,665	1,700	889	1,912	669	495	44
3,361	8,527	126,611	63,637	17,070	45,904	129,280	32,139	17,175	36,842	23,093	20,031	45
974	2,945	38,997	21,915	4,180	12,902	27,034	6,654	2,674	9,878	4,505	3,323	46
739	1,891	37,936	26,240	3,930	7,766	28,133	6,624	3,338	10,978	4,288	2,905	47

TABLE 116.—WOMEN EMPLOYED IN CERTAIN SELECTED

	OCCUPATION	United States	NEW ENGLAND DIVISION				
			Total	Maine	New Hampshire	Vermont	Massachusetts
1	Domestic and personal service_____	2, 149, 000	166, 299	16, 359	9, 691	8, 831	94, 017
2	Barbers, hairdressers, and manicurists_____	33, 091	2, 295	114	76	50	1, 520
3	Boarding and lodging house keepers_____	114, 740	10, 217	1, 011	644	502	5, 692
4	Charwomen and cleaners_____	24, 744	1, 984	85	63	42	1, 429
5	Housekeepers and stewardesses_____	204, 350	30, 259	4, 048	2, 772	1, 839	15, 209
6	Janitors and sextons_____	28, 929	828	31	31	26	498
7	Laundresses (not in laundry)_____	383, 622	9, 203	790	475	683	4, 472
8	Laundry operatives_____	78, 548	5, 858	354	273	201	3, 688
9	Midwives and nurses (not trained)_____	137, 431	15, 467	1, 467	862	763	8, 754
10	Restaurant, café, and lunch room keepers_____	15, 644	783	77	37	31	483
11	Servants_____	981, 557	76, 478	7, 140	3, 711	4, 104	44, 096
12	Waitresses_____	114, 718	11, 323	1, 060	640	513	7, 216
13	All other occupations_____	31, 626	1, 604	182	107	77	960
14	Clerical occupations_____	1, 405, 609	153, 016	7, 775	5, 121	3, 373	94, 346
15	Bookkeepers, cashiers, and accountants_____	356, 603	46, 478	2, 880	2, 038	1, 182	30, 125
16	Clerks (except clerks in stores)_____	463, 570	51, 554	1, 842	1, 549	799	30, 420
17	Stenographers and typists_____	559, 748	53, 148	2, 934	1, 461	1, 336	32, 642
18	All other occupations_____	25, 688	1, 836	119	103	56	1, 159

OCCUPATIONS, BY DIVISIONS AND STATES: 1920—Continued

| | NEW ENGLAND DIVISION—con. | MIDDLE ATLANTIC DIVISION | | | | EAST NORTH CENTRAL DIVISION | | | | | | |
Rhode Island	Connecticut	Total	New York	New Jersey	Pennsylvania	Total	Ohio	Indiana	Illinois	Michigan	Wisconsin	
11,831	25,570	488,497	261,877	61,683	164,937	372,439	99,637	46,379	123,392	58,421	44,610	1
174	361	8,412	5,052	1,010	2,350	6,429	1,636	721	2,822	852	398	2
780	1,588	24,236	11,833	3,164	9,239	24,140	6,914	2,929	7,112	4,945	2,240	3
155	210	10,187	6,216	803	3,168	4,886	1,569	302	1,615	491	909	4
2,287	4,104	50,636	23,799	7,086	19,751	45,376	11,854	6,417	13,158	7,762	6,185	5
63	179	14,455	10,453	1,206	2,796	5,182	1,564	581	1,750	968	319	6
812	1,971	43,072	20,551	7,604	14,917	43,276	12,823	7,206	15,152	4,823	3,272	7
499	843	14,903	8,373	1,532	4,998	16,098	3,977	2,013	5,824	3,014	1,270	8
1,003	2,618	35,128	20,811	4,696	9,621	28,061	7,645	3,399	9,043	5,039	2,935	9
46	109	2,814	1,606	327	881	3,418	894	437	1,267	493	327	10
5,300	12,127	249,636	134,010	29,732	85,894	166,674	43,543	19,514	55,594	24,739	23,284	11
619	1,275	29,058	16,087	3,715	9,256	23,079	5,647	2,188	8,278	4,195	2,771	12
93	185	5,960	3,086	808	2,066	5,820	1,571	672	1,777	1,100	700	13
11,384	31,017	440,406	256,998	62,579	120,829	338,069	86,867	32,398	136,821	52,593	29,390	14
3,709	6,544	100,695	59,560	12,056	29,079	85,611	23,998	10,474	28,715	14,115	8,309	15
3,888	13,086	160,357	92,281	24,585	43,491	110,045	26,803	8,432	48,581	17,966	8,263	16
3,653	11,122	173,073	101,769	25,359	45,945	135,861	34,328	12,695	57,114	19,501	12,223	17
134	265	6,281	3,388	579	2,314	6,552	1,738	797	2,411	1,011	595	18

TABLE **116.**—WOMEN EMPLOYED IN CERTAIN SELECTED

	OCCUPATION	Total	WEST NORTH CENTRAL DIVISION				
			Minnesota	Iowa	Missouri	North Dakota	South Dakota
1	All occupations	760,254	162,323	139,681	238,921	27,727	29,269
2	Agriculture, forestry, and animal husbandry	44,314	9,210	7,079	12,938	3,039	2,838
3	Farmers, general farms	25,454	4,996	3,659	7,851	1,765	1,480
4	Farm laborers (home farm)	8,211	2,637	1,516	1,254	764	789
5	Farm laborers (working out)	4,507	835	685	1,530	324	287
6	All other occupations	6,142	742	1,219	2,303	186	282
7	Extraction of minerals	140	19	20	45	2	4
8	Manufacturing and mechanical industries	109,721	23,196	18,068	48,466	1,333	1,967
9	Dressmakers and seamstresses (not in factory)	25,671	5,487	5,555	7,465	819	950
10	Forewomen and overseers (manufacturing)	1,873	423	271	980	2	4
11	Laborers (n. o. s.[1])	9,858	1,683	2,062	3,825	64	142
12	Food industries	2,968	326	815	658	14	59
13	Textile industries	476	247	22	179	1	
14	All other industries	6,414	1,110	1,225	2,988	49	83
15	Milliners and millinery dealers	8,921	1,962	1,455	3,629	157	243
16	Semiskilled operatives (n. o. s.[1])	56,966	12,270	7,634	30,285	175	372
17	Chemical and allied industries	1,264	153	122	747		2
18	Cigar and tobacco factories	2,724	271	584	1,499		41
19	Clothing industries	15,552	2,798	1,836	9,045	65	95
20	Electrical supply factories	1,013	106	13	883		
21	Food industries	8,865	1,892	1,692	3,026	43	139
22	Iron and steel industries	1,121	172	235	608	2	5
23	Other metal industries	683	174	39	429		1
24	Lumber and furniture industries	964	290	236	386		1
25	Printing and publishing	3,814	986	547	1,740	30	38
26	Rubber factories	288	4	33	241		
27	Shoe factories	6,928	710	154	6,026		
28	Textile industries	4,311	2,361	339	1,298	11	19
29	All other industries	9,439	2,353	1,804	4,357	24	31
30	Tailoresses	1,642	416	209	703	20	21
31	All other occupations	4,790	955	882	1,579	96	235
32	Transportation	26,315	5,471	4,584	7,627	945	781
33	Telegraph operators	2,452	513	290	932	122	45
34	Telephone operators	21,841	4,566	3,938	6,116	747	642
35	All other occupations	2,022	392	356	579	76	94
36	Trade	76,729	16,465	14,702	22,909	2,159	2,957
37	Clerks in stores	20,613	4,548	3,615	5,973	713	875
38	Saleswomen (stores)	42,581	9,341	8,824	12,122	1,138	1,626
39	Retail dealers	6,571	1,230	985	2,391	168	249
40	All other occupations	6,964	1,346	1,278	2,423	140	207
41	Public service (not elsewhere classified)	3,792	553	759	729	286	329
42	Professional service	151,336	31,142	32,854	32,012	8,102	8,267
43	Musicians and teachers of music	8,922	1,759	1,936	2,485	253	375
44	Religious, charity, and welfare workers	2,687	645	503	752	50	98
45	Teachers (school)	106,876	20,887	23,484	20,524	6,547	6,467
46	Trained nurses	16,994	4,496	3,544	4,011	784	778
47	All other occupations	15,857	3,355	3,387	4,240	468	549

[1] Not otherwise specified.

OCCUPATIONS, BY DIVISIONS AND STATES: 1920—Continued

	W. N. CENT. DIV.—con.			SOUTH ATLANTIC DIVISION										EAST SOUTH CENTRAL DIVISION	
	Nebraska	Kansas	Total	Delaware	Maryland	Dist. Columbia	Virginia	West Virginia	North Carolina	South Carolina	Georgia	Florida	Total	Kentucky	
70,869	91,464	1,151,407	17,648	133,176	92,027	150,648	55,987	181,480	179,547	258,572	82,322	632,866	127,289	1
3,873	5,337	309,590	508	2,970	19	16,734	5,501	64,142	103,577	102,960	13,179	249,695	17,121	2
2,126	3,577	59,593	241	1,340	5	8,486	3,620	13,370	13,541	16,174	2,816	62,637	10,592	3
735	516	155,283	50	303	1	3,366	884	32,767	58,698	55,726	3,488	136,791	3,750	4
503	343	87,133	134	681	3	3,283	393	17,084	30,515	30,045	4,995	45,891	1,157	5
509	901	7,581	83	646	10	1,599	604	921	823	1,015	1,880	4,376	1,622	6
1	49	361	1	7	------	22	281	4	3	7	36	197	82	7
7,005	9,686	180,484	3,605	34,425	5,686	27,166	8,704	43,208	19,461	27,579	10,650	66,815	24,891	8
2,280	3,115	25,432	574	4,949	1,869	3,864	1,584	2,728	2,259	4,842	2,763	13,044	4,772	9
98	95	1,342	60	656	48	200	81	90	31	151	25	679	321	10
856	1,226	34,311	541	2,392	208	7,501	1,551	12,044	2,943	5,782	1,349	10,945	3,027	11
476	620	2,442	161	634	8	818	19	94	155	448	105	601	168	12
12	15	11,030	38	246	------	903	104	5,023	1,660	3,021	35	2,967	177	13
368	591	20,839	342	1,512	200	5,780	1,428	6,927	1,128	2,313	1,209	7,377	2,682	14
579	896	4,545	126	1,002	224	610	398	586	264	946	389	2,372	1,037	15
2,669	3,561	110,144	2,152	23,559	2,869	14,452	4,663	27,484	13,789	15,362	5,814	36,836	13,859	16
32	208	813	25	420	27	72	71	99	15	62	22	409	140	17
199	130	18,335	198	1,523	31	5,738	518	4,813	397	190	4,927	5,832	5,346	18
684	1,029	16,713	251	10,489	382	2,266	579	561	270	1,748	167	5,934	3,255	19
6	5	64	6	17	------	4	15	2	3	17	------	33	21	20
885	1,188	4,830	48	2,623	97	922	68	98	50	781	143	2,151	852	21
49	50	988	47	430	23	70	278	21	43	54	22	397	239	22
8	32	1,329	17	890	2	45	317	10	------	47	1	198	174	23
14	37	966	25	221	8	147	78	134	45	167	141	692	267	24
207	266	3,550	28	534	2,024	436	77	86	53	252	60	1,001	504	25
1	9	122	20	56	------	1	24	7	2	12	------	8	3	26
20	18	691	------	192	------	336	84	1	------	77	1	794	710	27
107	176	52,795	439	2,858	22	3,483	941	21,206	12,679	11,131	36	17,023	1,292	28
457	413	8,948	1,048	3,306	253	932	1,613	446	232	824	294	2,364	1,056	29
86	187	2,133	40	1,224	190	197	142	73	40	173	54	1,598	1,246	30
437	606	2,577	112	643	278	342	285	203	135	323	256	1,341	629	31
2,747	4,160	15,179	407	2,955	1,888	2,159	1,421	1,488	960	2,849	1,052	8,218	2,792	32
219	331	1,501	18	188	194	228	83	156	70	359	205	722	249	33
2,378	3,454	11,482	349	2,404	1,463	1,634	1,176	1,087	724	2,050	595	6,462	2,256	34
150	375	2,196	40	363	231	297	162	245	166	440	252	1,034	287	35
7,657	9,880	53,624	1,425	11,382	4,129	7,919	5,175	5,837	3,815	8,877	5,065	27,800	9,636	36
2,351	2,538	11,893	291	2,370	1,130	1,942	1,785	1,289	672	1,559	855	5,474	2,064	37
3,960	5,570	29,162	789	5,934	2,179	4,399	2,610	3,535	2,400	5,077	2,239	16,571	5,575	38
597	951	7,942	288	2,117	505	1,049	555	617	524	1,356	931	3,555	1,253	39
749	821	4,627	57	961	315	529	225	396	219	885	1,040	2,200	744	40
428	708	2,794	37	290	429	528	212	344	221	413	320	1,503	532	41
17,371	21,588	100,344	1,653	12,719	6,991	17,807	10,073	16,189	9,626	17,979	7,307	51,599	14,569	42
879	1,235	5,161	115	736	386	825	460	667	367	1,015	590	3,205	956	43
211	428	2,262	51	483	430	341	130	227	175	306	119	826	340	44
12,988	15,979	68,813	1,054	7,254	2,676	12,969	7,726	12,451	7,260	12,814	4,609	38,229	10,412	45
1,651	1,730	14,879	214	2,782	1,735	2,467	1,162	1,983	1,205	2,378	953	4,961	1,411	46
1,642	2,216	9,229	219	1,464	1,764	1,205	595	861	619	1,466	1,036	4,378	1,450	47

6436°—29——14

TABLE **116.**—WOMEN EMPLOYED IN CERTAIN SELECTED

	OCCUPATION	WEST NORTH CENTRAL DIVISION					
		Total	Minnesota	Iowa	Missouri	North Dakota	South Dakota
1	Domestic and personal service------------------	210, 857	43, 974	37, 597	69, 028	8, 747	8, 288
2	Barbers, hairdressers, and manicurists--------------	2, 845	519	440	1, 200	49	70
3	Boarding and lodging house keepers------------------	12, 794	2, 010	2, 127	4, 598	351	424
4	Charwomen and cleaners------------------------------	1, 298	323	255	504	12	22
5	Housekeepers and stewardesses-----------------------	27, 715	6, 413	6, 515	5, 550	1, 804	1, 684
6	Janitors and sextons--------------------------------	2, 052	361	317	837	15	44
7	Laundresses (not in laundry)------------------------	26, 137	2, 331	3, 305	14, 363	418	409
8	Laundry operatives----------------------------------	9, 167	1, 844	1, 203	3, 516	188	292
9	Midwives and nurses (not trained)-------------------	14, 194	2, 760	3, 289	3, 557	475	585
10	Restaurant, café, and lunch room keepers-------------	2, 113	357	437	559	78	79
11	Servants--	92, 391	22, 028	16, 481	28, 734	4, 495	3, 746
12	Waitresses--	15, 853	4, 272	2, 541	4, 137	682	718
13	All other occupations-------------------------------	4, 298	756	687	1, 473	180	215
14	Clerical occupations-----------------------	137, 050	32, 293	24, 018	45, 167	3, 114	3, 838
15	Bookkeepers, cashiers, and accountants--------------	39, 386	8, 669	8, 254	10, 647	937	1, 486
16	Clerks (except clerks in stores)--------------------	36, 637	8, 938	5, 258	13, 624	746	769
17	Stenographers and typists--------------------------	57, 820	13, 972	9, 916	19, 923	1, 373	1, 467
18	All other occupations-------------------------------	3, 207	714	590	973	58	116

OCCUPATIONS, BY DIVISIONS AND STATES: 1920—Continued

W. N. CENT. DIV.—con.			SOUTH ATLANTIC DIVISION									EAST SOUTH CENTRAL DIVISION		
Nebraska	Kansas	Total	Delaware	Maryland	Dist. Columbia	Virginia	West Virginia	North Carolina	South Carolina	Georgia	Florida	Total	Kentucky	
18,520	24,703	366,485	6,252	47,395	29,872	62,242	17,823	42,459	37,424	84,025	38,993	188,681	43,282	1
276	291	4,033	85	540	551	497	155	271	163	1,057	714	2,714	438	2
1,401	1,883	12,596	360	1,295	1,354	1,773	1,645	1,401	1,077	1,940	1,751	6,409	1,728	3
97	85	4,275	33	708	1,857	535	81	326	157	459	119	895	254	4
2,722	3,027	14,320	571	2,530	1,102	2,708	1,827	1,760	1,104	1,578	1,140	6,316	2,352	5
278	200	1,855	74	514	177	334	196	82	81	306	91	933	368	6
1,556	3,755	124,609	1,107	12,381	6,080	19,876	2,491	15,014	14,798	36,429	16,433	71,500	14,981	7
790	1,334	9,369	106	1,316	1,170	1,602	577	1,048	617	2,006	927	4,683	1,278	8
1,538	1,990	13,550	314	2,129	998	2,175	887	1,678	1,249	2,714	1,406	6,118	1,662	9
208	395	1,971	21	271	183	258	122	148	161	454	353	1,011	263	10
7,731	9,176	168,512	3,388	23,741	14,370	30,625	8,977	19,876	17,613	35,701	14,221	83,734	18,676	11
1,493	2,010	8,088	155	1,550	1,590	1,381	520	527	214	844	1,307	2,778	831	12
430	557	3,307	38	420	440	478	345	328	190	537	531	1,590	451	13
13,267	15,353	122,546	3,760	21,033	43,013	16,071	6,797	7,809	4,460	13,883	5,720	38,358	14,384	14
3,962	5,431	21,600	740	4,038	2,319	3,680	1,746	2,305	1,380	3,687	1,705	11,605	4,589	15
3,554	3,748	53,487	1,454	8,116	29,342	5,510	1,753	1,717	854	3,416	1,325	9,028	3,551	16
5,460	5,709	45,431	1,501	8,497	11,008	6,597	3,145	3,617	2,112	6,436	2,518	16,470	5,776	17
291	465	2,028	65	382	344	284	153	170	114	344	172	1,255	468	18

TABLE 116.—WOMEN EMPLOYED IN CERTAIN SELECTED

	OCCUPATION	EAST SOUTH CENTRAL DIVISION—continued			WEST SOUTH CENTRAL DIVISION			
		Tennessee	Alabama	Mississippi	Total	Arkansas	Louisiana	Oklahoma
1	All occupations	142,941	193,315	169,321	608,336	99,762	142,380	88,692
2	Agriculture, forestry, and animal husbandry	29,757	94,381	108,436	189,982	50,918	45,262	16,993
3	Farmers, general farms	10,811	18,588	22,646	44,165	11,827	8,476	5,986
4	Farm laborers (home farm)	12,530	56,486	64,025	91,820	28,325	19,086	6,767
5	Farm laborers (working out)	4,881	18,696	21,157	49,743	9,956	16,956	3,587
6	All other occupations	1,535	611	608	4,254	810	744	653
7	Extraction of minerals	37	73	5	314	4	81	153
8	Manufacturing and mechanical industries	21,587	14,587	5,750	43,564	4,139	13,779	5,417
9	Dressmakers and seamstresses (not in factory)	3,508	2,897	1,867	15,814	1,672	4,948	2,257
10	Forewomen and overseers (manufacturing)	297	52	9	342	18	144	33
11	Laborers (n. o. s.[1])	3,728	2,669	1,521	7,449	970	2,143	802
12	Food industries	148	183	102	926	25	249	134
13	Textile industries	1,422	1,153	215	463	13	281	17
14	All other industries	2,158	1,333	1,204	6,060	932	1,613	651
15	Milliners and millinery dealers	661	412	262	2,925	317	421	632
16	Semiskilled operatives (n. o. s.[1])	12,807	8,244	1,926	14,799	888	5,670	1,237
17	Chemical and allied industries	250	13	6	129	6	61	14
18	Cigar and tobacco factories	460	25	1	1,997	10	1,185	44
19	Clothing industries	1,814	631	234	3,871	358	1,007	446
20	Electrical supply factories	5	7	------	29	------	7	1
21	Food industries	612	251	436	2,410	87	917	287
22	Iron and steel industries	78	77	3	209	19	41	16
23	Other metal industries	11	12	1	201	1	139	1
24	Lumber and furniture industries	294	69	62	399	136	158	18
25	Printing and publishing	380	96	21	674	65	110	102
26	Rubber factories	4	1	------	10	------	5	5
27	Shoe factories	83	------	------	81	------	75	1
28	Textile industries	7,819	6,876	1,036	2,263	57	1,090	43
29	All other industries	997	186	125	2,526	149	875	259
30	Tailoresses	206	98	48	570	52	134	135
31	All other occupations	380	215	117	1,665	222	319	321
32	Transportation	2,646	1,643	1,137	14,958	1,408	2,017	3,777
33	Telegraph operators	238	159	76	1,478	110	210	249
34	Telephone operators	2,078	1,264	864	11,974	1,127	1,454	3,216
35	All other occupations	330	220	197	1,506	171	353	312
36	Trade	7,790	6,407	3,967	41,684	4,592	7,598	8,405
37	Clerks in stores	1,612	947	851	8,952	797	1,693	1,868
38	Saleswomen (stores)	4,580	4,148	2,268	24,624	2,887	3,975	5,068
39	Retail dealers	810	897	595	4,826	556	1,287	820
40	All other occupations	788	415	253	3,282	352	643	649
41	Public service (not elsewhere classified)	288	347	336	2,221	319	332	560
42	Professional service	14,470	12,216	10,344	72,340	9,043	11,119	16,344
43	Musicians and teachers of music	1,078	696	475	4,860	644	602	936
44	Religious, charity, and welfare workers	221	190	75	1,254	168	361	171
45	Teachers (school)	10,136	9,124	8,557	53,141	6,855	7,909	12,327
46	Trained nurses	1,601	1,268	681	6,344	651	1,284	1,144
47	All other occupations	1,434	938	556	6,741	725	963	1,766

[1] Not otherwise specified.

OCCUPATIONS, BY DIVISIONS AND STATES: 1920—Continued

W. S. CENT. DIV.—con.		MOUNTAIN DIVISION								PACIFIC DIVISION				
Texas	Total	Montana	Idaho	Wyoming	Colorado	New Mexico	Arizona	Utah	Nevada	Total	Washington	Oregon	California	
277,502	174,123	28,041	17,322	9,307	61,644	14,475	17,485	21,548	4,301	431,023	92,086	54,118	284,819	1
76,809	12,669	2,213	1,282	802	3,022	1,726	2,584	854	186	15,756	3,729	2,280	9,747	2
17,876	6,731	1,701	892	473	1,619	1,061	342	536	107	6,340	1,879	1,162	3,299	3
37,642	920	131	99	69	349	145	54	72	1	821	292	127	402	4
19,244	3,008	110	80	96	536	198	1,850	99	39	1,844	261	157	1,426	5
2,047	2,010	271	211	164	518	322	338	147	39	6,751	1,297	834	4,620	6
76	211	27	3	23	24	8	97	21	8	95	12	6	77	7
20,229	16,312	1,664	1,299	437	6,072	1,820	2,138	2,624	258	59,157	10,805	7,147	41,205	8
6,937	5,480	778	543	235	2,191	377	461	759	136	15,497	2,932	1,891	10,674	9
147	135	7	7	2	76	-----	2	41	-----	928	123	95	710	10
3,534	948	73	133	37	292	84	64	242	23	5,326	1,393	801	3,132	11
518	319	13	39	-----	109	-----	3	152	3	1,908	440	244	1,224	12
152	15	-----	-----	-----	-----	-----	-----	15	-----	182	24	62	96	13
2,864	614	60	94	37	183	84	61	75	20	3,236	929	495	1,812	14
1,555	1,441	226	185	60	587	58	73	219	33	5,252	882	695	3,675	15
7,004	7,135	409	318	47	2,393	1,246	1,469	1,210	43	26,886	4,464	3,058	19,364	16
48	58	2	1	-----	42	1	1	11	-----	433	37	30	366	17
758	153	10	5	1	118	-----	6	13	-----	590	24	15	551	18
2,060	1,237	152	50	14	679	23	44	256	19	7,846	1,104	806	5,936	19
21	10	-----	-----	-----	8	-----	-----	2	-----	410	20	5	385	20
1,119	1,561	125	116	7	780	2	28	499	4	7,002	1,435	763	4,804	21
133	68	9	8	5	39	1	3	3	-----	536	142	37	357	22
60	13	-----	-----	-----	8	-----	1	4	-----	504	49	67	388	23
87	112	-----	10	1	26	2	53	12	8	905	288	134	483	24
397	398	42	19	6	230	13	15	65	8	1,362	222	118	1,022	25
-------	30	-----	-----	-----	29	-----	-----	1	-----	84	1	9	74	26
5	9	-----	-----	-----	3	-----	-----	6	-----	209	31	11	167	27
1,073	2,762	4	12	8	76	1,148	1,299	214	1	2,463	311	670	1,482	28
1,243	724	65	97	5	355	56	19	124	3	4,542	800	393	3,349	29
249	345	55	23	10	180	9	14	46	8	2,376	482	224	1,670	30
803	828	116	90	46	353	46	55	107	15	2,892	529	383	1,980	31
7,756	5,944	955	638	340	2,285	311	309	942	164	15,379	3,517	2,240	9,622	32
909	983	250	52	57	317	78	61	127	41	1,339	339	227	773	33
6,177	4,368	610	537	246	1,746	177	209	742	101	12,953	2,942	1,832	8,179	34
670	593	95	49	37	222	56	39	73	22	1,087	236	181	670	35
21,089	17,845	2,738	1,934	791	6,552	979	1,502	2,983	366	53,594	11,507	6,382	35,705	36
4,594	4,093	772	440	244	1,384	277	306	573	97	10,516	2,780	1,451	6,285	37
12,694	10,319	1,436	1,172	412	3,712	496	897	2,026	168	27,537	6,083	3,489	17,965	38
2,163	2,069	358	159	98	815	150	187	223	79	5,705	1,132	618	3,955	39
1,638	1,364	172	163	37	641	56	112	161	22	9,836	1,512	824	7,500	40
1,010	1,543	312	222	125	446	58	129	183	68	1,969	473	300	1,196	41
35,834	36,894	6,697	4,383	2,105	12,404	3,099	2,974	4,320	912	79,145	17,066	10,643	51,436	42
2,678	2,369	352	258	106	948	143	175	312	75	7,397	1,459	959	4,979	43
554	689	96	57	24	312	56	70	63	11	2,047	396	179	1,472	44
26,050	24,781	4,900	3,133	1,567	7,304	2,379	2,039	2,894	565	38,802	9,765	6,353	22,684	45
3,265	4,800	790	478	219	2,004	279	394	544	92	13,422	2,558	1,348	9,516	46
3,287	4,255	559	457	189	1,836	242	296	507	169	17,477	2,888	1,804	12,785	47

TABLE **116.**—WOMEN EMPLOYED IN CERTAIN SELECTED

	OCCUPATION	EAST SOUTH CENTRAL DIVISION—continued			WEST SOUTH CENTRAL DIVISION			
		Tennessee	Alabama	Mississippi	Total	Arkansas	Louisiana	Oklahoma
1	Domestic and personal service	54, 103	55, 915	35, 381	185, 642	24, 294	51, 968	24, 249
2	Barbers, hairdressers, and manicurists	957	764	555	2, 878	505	827	354
3	Boarding and lodging house keepers	1, 933	1, 728	1, 020	10, 858	1, 376	2, 197	2, 286
4	Charwomen and cleaners	295	242	104	583	69	182	56
5	Housekeepers and stewardesses	1, 708	1, 396	860	8, 686	1, 199	1, 645	2, 289
6	Janitors and sextons	186	243	136	900	107	204	168
7	Laundresses (not in laundry)	20, 571	23, 248	12, 700	56, 019	7, 333	16, 933	4, 329
8	Laundry operatives	1, 668	1, 136	601	6, 170	558	1, 070	1, 184
9	Midwives and nurses (not trained)	1, 739	1, 814	903	6, 581	712	1, 498	1, 145
10	Restaurant, café, and lunch room keepers	254	271	223	1, 548	218	234	369
11	Servants	23, 378	24, 028	17, 652	81, 365	11, 064	25, 707	9, 150
12	Waitresses	991	600	356	6, 797	691	921	2, 101
13	All other occupations	423	445	271	3, 257	462	550	818
14	Clerical occupations	12, 263	7, 746	3, 965	57, 631	5, 045	10, 224	12, 794
15	Bookkeepers, cashiers, and accountants	3, 425	2, 313	1, 278	15, 474	1, 621	2, 099	4, 036
16	Clerks (except clerks in stores)	2, 849	1, 681	947	14, 227	1, 061	2, 759	2, 960
17	Stenographers and typists	5, 638	3, 462	1, 594	26, 247	2, 184	5, 079	5, 422
18	All other occupations	351	290	146	1, 683	179	287	376

OCCUPATIONS, BY DIVISIONS AND STATES: 1920—Continued.

W. S. CENT. DIV.—con.		MOUNTAIN DIVISION								PACIFIC DIVISION				
Texas	Total	Montana	Idaho	Wyoming	Colorado	New Mexico	Arizona	Utah	Nevada	Total	Washington	Oregon	California	
85,131	54,042	8,951	4,852	3,260	19,253	5,140	5,503	5,372	1,711	116,058	25,694	14,425	75,939	1
1,192	684	99	23	35	354	25	47	84	17	2,801	580	243	1,978	2
4,999	5,187	889	417	356	2,035	328	530	419	213	8,303	1,907	1,131	5,265	3
276	223	21	8	16	71	51	11	44	1	413	77	47	289	4
3,553	6,413	1,349	709	450	2,129	491	479	637	169	14,629	3,386	1,899	9,344	5
421	682	120	40	29	276	22	36	146	13	2,042	505	284	1,253	6
27,424	5,569	412	245	194	1,728	1,284	1,227	280	199	4,237	821	431	2,985	7
3,358	3,093	435	282	188	1,154	206	283	459	86	9,207	2,099	1,079	6,029	8
3,226	4,385	642	462	190	1,723	234	330	657	147	13,947	2,414	1,541	9,992	9
727	665	83	57	39	273	60	88	43	22	1,321	252	153	916	10
35,444	19,913	3,582	1,825	1,228	6,920	1,989	1,812	1,958	599	42,854	8,944	5,271	28,639	11
3,084	5,408	1,005	573	439	1,970	313	499	425	184	12,334	3,635	1,881	6,818	12
1,427	1,820	314	211	96	620	137	161	220	61	3,970	1,074	465	2,431	13
29,568	28,663	4,484	2,709	1,424	11,586	1,334	2,249	4,249	628	89,870	19,283	10,695	59,892	14
7,718	8,634	1,437	979	452	3,364	403	685	1,113	201	27,120	5,763	3,428	17,929	15
7,447	6,060	877	432	362	2,551	275	567	861	135	22,175	4,594	2,549	15,032	16
13,562	13,325	2,077	1,256	588	5,365	617	956	2,177	289	38,373	8,445	4,414	25,514	17
841	644	93	42	22	306	39	41	98	3	2,202	481	304	1,417	18

TABLE **117.**—WOMEN EMPLOYED IN CERTAIN SELECTED OCCU

	OCCUPATION	Total for all cities	NEW ENGLAND DIVISION				
			Total, 11 cities	Boston, Mass.	Bridge-port, Conn.	Cam-bridge, Mass.	Fall River, Mass.
1	All occupations	3,191,006	294,859	102,561	14,986	15,653	19,111
2	Agriculture, forestry, and animal husbandry.	2,786	118	32	4	4	2
3	Extraction of minerals	143	1				
4	Manufacturing and mechanical industries.	839,461	113,305	24,927	6,964	4,670	14,281
5	Dressmakers and seamstresses (not in factory)	96,673	6,970	3,151	239	422	195
6	Forewomen and overseers (manufacturing)	17,494	1,794	689	151	154	32
7	Laborers (n. o. s.[1])	40,135	3,858	416	878	180	87
8	Food industries	5,207	117	44	5	23	
9	Textile industries	3,449	881	21	16	5	81
10	All other industries	31,479	2,860	351	857	152	6
11	Milliners and millinery dealers	36,521	2,091	973	92	75	83
12	Semiskilled operatives (n. o. s.[1])	601,792	94,585	18,063	5,486	3,656	13,832
13	Chemical and allied industries	11,612	1,838	404	578	168	
14	Cigar and tobacco factories	33,215	1,017	227	3	14	2
15	Clothing industries	159,122	9,010	3,387	1,283	347	347
16	Electrical supply factories	12,334	1,970	523	478	80	
17	Food industries	42,969	4,226	3,134	25	619	2
18	Iron and steel industries	27,784	6,531	1,114	460	203	50
19	Metal industries (other than iron and steel)	11,560	3,408	165	280	32	28
20	Lumber and furniture industries	6,372	565	114	14	125	46
21	Printing and publishing	27,319	2,774	858	26	415	25
22	Rubber factories	8,087	3,153	692	96	976	13
23	Shoe factories	19,120	3,355	2,144		103	5
24	Textile industries	128,924	46,667	1,412	344	260	13,152
25	All other industries	113,374	10,071	3,889	1,899	314	162
26	Tailoresses	23,082	1,161	813	18	43	19
27	All other occupations	23,764	2,846	822	100	140	33
28	Transportation	100,886	7,065	3,663	194	542	117
29	Telegraph operators	8,915	383	247	5	33	1
30	Telephone operators	84,514	6,341	3,214	179	487	114
31	All other occupations	7,457	341	202	10	22	2
32	Trade	300,664	23,451	10,280	924	1,032	822
33	Clerks in stores	73,743	5,254	2,232	228	182	196
34	Saleswomen (stores)	156,411	13,728	6,126	547	642	505
35	Retail dealers	37,052	2,437	938	116	109	103
36	All other occupations	33,458	2,032	984	33	99	18
37	Public service (not elsewhere classified)	4,188	223	113	3	18	4
38	Professional service	321,424	27,945	10,743	1,197	1,697	1,309
39	Actresses and showwomen	10,898	330	210	12	18	5
40	Artists, sculptors, and teachers of art	8,939	556	323	13	49	7
41	Librarians	5,610	499	160	19	55	17
42	Musicians and teachers of music	27,881	2,235	998	64	115	54
43	Religious, charity, and welfare workers	14,873	1,413	651	43	113	32
44	Teachers (school)	143,961	12,954	4,030	697	814	893
45	Trained nurses	65,328	6,503	2,772	227	241	241
46	All other occupations	43,934	3,455	1,599	122	292	60

[1] Not otherwise specified.

PATIONS, FOR CITIES OF 100,000 INHABITANTS OR MORE: 1920

			NEW ENGLAND DIVISION—continued					MIDDLE ATLANTIC DIVISION					
Hartford, Conn.	Lowell, Mass.	New bedford, Mass.	New Haven, Conn.	Providence, R. I.	Springfield, Mass.	Worcester, Mass.	Total, 15 cities	Albany, N. Y.	Buffalo, N. Y.	Camden, N. J.	Jersey City, N. J.	New York, N. Y.	
17,228	17,799	19,772	18,281	32,099	16,935	20,434	1,209,534	14,353	48,875	10,349	28,705	677,685	1
21	6	12	14	11	7	5	474	7	13	1	7	330	2
------	------	------	------	------	1	------	37	------	1	------	------	24	3
3,965	12,012	14,725	5,374	13,807	5,279	7,301	371,373	3,425	10,724	4,271	8,996	198,403	4
310	278	235	423	835	370	512	37,889	466	1,728	224	628	22,758	5
67	53	33	109	192	118	196	8,446	83	291	102	303	4,543	6
481	391	136	395	513	168	213	8,240	43	774	225	408	2,711	7
3	------	2	22	10	6	2	568	------	62	40	52	139	8
6	350	121	1	242	26	12	886	------	102	31	15	204	9
472	41	13	372	261	136	199	6,786	43	610	154	341	2,368	10
113	92	106	125	180	97	155	15,769	162	571	58	290	11,479	11
2,824	11,112	14,159	4,155	10,944	4,325	6,029	283,784	2,539	6,477	3,561	7,136	148,643	12
16	292	3	269	75	9	24	4,379	86	366	45	447	2,182	13
486	1	------	82	23	166	13	13,201	170	23	529	955	5,947	14
259	137	61	892	261	766	1,270	89,715	1,138	1,107	177	1,055	66,244	15
285	34	3	97	123	295	52	4,361	7	170	8	175	909	16
13	12	40	88	89	150	54	12,199	42	518	175	541	6,318	17
1,319	177	164	859	881	449	855	7,214	23	493	282	198	2,098	18
40	2	·28	493	2,295	35	10	3,425	18	164	25	349	1,586	19
16	33	------	5	9	13	190	2,060	5	181	25	64	1,113	20
86	24	24	51	103	365	797	10,264	248	293	70	198	6,491	21
54	2	------	644	.526	136	14	1,682	------	56	------	70	877	22
24	324	166	52	10	2	525	6,068	5	132	135	19	2,059	23
43	9,820	13,531	107	5,814	1,050	1,134	63,740	228	1,211	1,009	1,010	14,505	24
183	254	139	516	735	889	1,091	65,476	569	1,763	1,081	2,055	38,314	25
24	23	14	33	65	78	31	8,258	43	495	12	28	3,261	26
146	63	42	134	1,078	123	165	8,987	89	388	89	203	5,008	27
318	153	115	368	676	421	498	37,113	511	1,841	202	1,211	22,397	28
17	6	1	14	23	19	17	2,448	33	238	10	77	1,367	29
290	142	108	316	629	396	466	31,985	438	1,477	142	954	19,494	30
11	5	6	38	24	6	15	2,680	40	126	50	180	1,536	31
1,637	988	708	1,387	2,296	1,668	1,709	103,909	1,264	5,437	888	2,421	52,674	32
396	153	118	304	493	372	580	23,700	328	1,635	165	680	11,444	33
853	668	486	695	1,343	983	875	53,526	712	2,629	449	1,012	26,798	34
88	141	80	272	284	172	134	15,263	156	829	211	394	7,055	35
295	26	24	116	176	141	120	11,420	68	344	63	335	7,377	36
11	8	11	7	15	15	18	1,449	35	70	9	30	843	37
1,727	1,113	942	2,103	2,781	1,877	2,456	117,445	1,775	5,714	701	2,448	67,907	38
16	7	11	14	25	6	6	5,924	25	45	8	49	5,221	39
22	7	3	19	45	35	33	4,001	6	110	11	37	3,100	40
33	10	15	56	50	37	47	2,003	54	67	11	34	1,180	41
121	88	74	129	252	144	196	8,954	118	482	55	177	5,220	42
89	28	46	89	105	88	129	5,945	72	231	20	70	3,577	43
737	682	538	1,030	1,457	944	1,132	52,579	814	3,070	410	1,515	27,546	44
500	214	190	529	569	373	647	22,893	487	1,178	128	321	12,127	45
209	77	65	237	278	250	266	15,146	199	531	58	245	9,936	46

TABLE 117.—WOMEN EMPLOYED IN CERTAIN SELECTED OCCUPA

	OCCUPATION	Total for all cities	NEW ENGLAND DIVISION				
			Total, 11 cities	Boston, Mass.	Bridge-port, Conn.	Cam-bridge, Mass.	Fall River, Mass.
1	Domestic and personal service_____	812,461	59,217	26,882	1,978	3,698	1,377
2	Barbers, hairdressers, and manicurists_____	19,857	1,135	566	40	58	16
3	Boarding and lodging house keepers_____	46,979	4,776	2,346	207	170	57
4	Charwomen and cleaners_____	17,456	1,337	784	21	71	15
5	Housekeepers and stewardesses_____	58,572	6,907	2,686	270	329	318
6	Janitors and sextons_____	20,079	452	197	34	29	3
7	Laundresses (not in laundry)_____	111,056	3,245	1,369	149	271	64
8	Laundry operatives_____	40,304	2,793	1,272	80	176	70
9	Midwives and nurses (not trained)_____	51,542	4,842	1,794	214	267	118
10	Restaurant, café, and lunch room keepers_____	5,901	312	160	15	19	9
11	Servants_____	373,370	27,414	12,073	849	1,929	653
12	Waitresses_____	54,553	5,259	3,234	80	308	48
13	All other occupations_____	12,792	745	401	19	71	6
14	Clerical occupations_____	808,993	63,534	25,921	3,722	3,992	1,199
15	Agents, canvassers, and collectors_____	7,443	482	226	11	41	8
16	Bookkeepers, cashiers, and accountants_____	173,821	17,820	7,501	798	971	475
17	Clerks (except clerks in stores)_____	296,311	23,244	8,714	1,652	1,520	278
18	Messenger, bundle, and office girls_____	5,782	353	189	17	28	1
19	Stenographers and typists_____	325,636	21,635	9,291	1,244	1,432	437

TIONS, FOR CITIES OF 100,000 INHABITANTS OR MORE: 1920—Continued

	NEW ENGLAND DIVISION—continued						MIDDLE ATLANTIC DIVISION						
Hartford, Conn.	Lowell, Mass.	New Bedford, Mass.	New Haven, Conn.	Providence, R. I.	Springfield, Mass.	Worcester, Mass.	Total, 15 cities	Albany, N. Y.	Buffalo, N. Y.	Camden, N. J.	Jersey City, N. J.	New York, N. Y.	
3,633	1,774	1,843	4,002	6,334	3,691	4,005	275,209	3,570	11,228	2,209	4,132	156,196	1
61	23	35	72	112	85	67	6,295	63	236	30	78	3,671	2
281	226	162	340	456	256	275	12,520	299	800	130	256	5,698	3
76	24	29	34	126	25	132	8,420	169	476	25	212	4,817	4
380	307	282	410	847	517	561	20,866	428	1,026	272	547	9,298	5
28	7	11	37	47	34	25	12,040	32	104	48	326	9,605	6
173	48	64	300	436	212	159	21,829	250	965	289	379	10,805	7
191	73	91	177	300	166	197	9,791	97	464	39	324	4,992	8
415	152	174	347	561	430	370	17,634	276	814	125	306	10,078	9
18	4	11	20	22	16	18	1,594	20	82	22	23	860	10
1,792	760	860	2,012	3,009	1,583	1,894	142,890	1,662	5,376	1,055	1,332	84,272	11
199	147	109	207	362	310	255	17,779	249	750	140	272	10,011	12
19	3	15	46	56	57	52	3,551	25	135	34	77	2,089	13
5,916	1,745	1,416	5,026	6,179	3,976	4,442	302,525	3,766	13,847	2,068	9,460	178,911	14
25	13	16	28	48	40	26	2,472	22	131	22	39	1,412	15
859	868	678	1,127	1,897	1,197	1,449	67,217	649	3,106	507	1,376	39,487	16
3,088	419	357	2,079	2,247	1,401	1,489	112,887	1,297	5,518	927	3,647	66,414	17
24	3	6	17	39	12	17	1,626	13	71	10	34	811	18
1,920	442	359	1,775	1,948	1,326	1,461	118,323	1,785	5,021	602	4,364	70,787	19

TABLE **117.**—WOMEN EMPLOYED IN CERTAIN SELECTED OCCUPA

	OCCUPATION	MIDDLE ATLANTIC DIVISION—continued						
		New York city by boroughs					Newark, N. J.	Paterson, N. J.
		Bronx	Brooklyn	Manhattan	Queens	Richmond		
1	All occupations_____	76,080	209,568	337,291	45,329	9,417	40,621	17,999
2	Agriculture, forestry, and animal husbandry.	20	58	59	179	14	6	2
3	Extraction of minerals_____	1	19	4				
4	Manufacturing and mechanical industries.	21,641	63,486	97,335	14,148	1,793	14,774	11,540
5	Dressmakers and seamstresses (not in factory)_	2,456	5,088	13,705	1,230	279	1,010	244
6	Forewomen and overseers (manufacturing)____	685	1,821	1,640	351	46	315	202
7	Laborers (n. o. s.[1])_____	145	1,207	1,073	179	107	476	106
8	Food industries_____	2	61	64	8	4	7	
9	Textile industries_____	5	113	37	13	36	17	58
10	All other industries_____	138	1,033	972	158	67	452	48
11	Milliners and millinery dealers_____	1,859	3,034	5,938	555	93	330	84
12	Semiskilled operatives (n. o. s.[1])_____	15,668	49,172	71,294	11,286	1,223	11,662	10,858
13	Chemical and allied industries_____	138	1,010	690	208	136	130	1
14	Cigar and tobacco factories_____	242	657	4,503	540	5	639	10
15	Clothing industries_____	8,053	19,871	35,100	2,880	340	2,614	733
16	Electrical supply factories_____	76	323	308	200	2	1,770	16
17	Food industries_____	240	2,221	3,104	715	39	264	12
18	Iron and steel industries_____	135	1,233	386	327	17	586	91
19	Metal industries other than iron and steel_	69	975	354	171	17	555	4
20	Lumber and furniture industries_____	126	431	477	67	12	44	6
21	Printing and publishing_____	654	2,709	2,372	718	38	125	12
22	Rubber factories_____	16	138	110	612	1	73	5
23	Shoe factories_____	37	1,399	277	337	9	182	1
24	Textile industries_____	2,217	5,654	4,614	1,937	83	904	9,778
25	All other industries_____	3,665	12,551	19,000	2,574	524	3,776	189
26	Tailoresses_____	254	1,499	1,374	128	6	313	4
27	All other occupations_____	574	1,665	2,311	419	39	668	42
28	Transportation_____	3,276	8,260	8,294	2,121	446	805	159
29	Telegraph operators_____	189	561	457	141	19	26	6
30	Telephone operators_____	2,992	6,991	7,262	1,856	393	694	144
31	All other occupations_____	95	708	575	124	34	85	9
32	Trade_____	6,895	17,544	24,396	3,269	570	3,819	1,009
33	Clerks in stores_____	1,639	3,862	5,108	718	117	741	189
34	Saleswomen (stores)_____	3,696	8,783	12,531	1,544	244	2,135	532
35	Retail dealers_____	759	2,697	2,861	590	148	656	233
36	All other occupations_____	801	2,202	3,896	417	61	287	55
37	Public service (not elsewhere classified)_	109	310	353	60	11	31	5
38	Professional service_____	7,001	18,936	36,258	4,163	1,549	3,494	1,257
39	Actresses and showwomen_____	258	750	4,038	160	15	63	11
40	Artists, sculptors, and teachers of art_____	287	537	2,114	124	38	66	7
41	Librarians_____	102	367	590	98	23	44	14
42	Musicians and teachers of music_____	531	1,363	2,963	288	75	293	57
43	Religious, charity, and welfare workers_____	452	786	2,052	148	139	162	34
44	Teachers (school)_____	3,450	10,164	10,907	2,355	670	1,900	869
45	Trained nurses_____	924	2,840	7,405	496	462	598	196
46	All other occupations_____	997	2,129	6,189	494	127	368	69

[1] Not otherwise specified.

TIONS, FOR CITIES OF 100,000 INHABITANTS OR MORE: 1920—Continued

	MIDDLE ATLANTIC DIVISION—continued							NORTH CENTRAL DIVISIONS					
Phila-delphia, Pa.	Pitts-burgh, Pa.	Read-ing, Pa.	Roch-ester, N.Y.	Scran-ton, Pa.	Syra-cuse, N.Y.	Tren-ton, N.J.	Yon-kers, N.Y.	Total, 19 cities	Akron, Ohio	Chi-cago, Ill.	Cin-cin-nati, Ohio	Cleve-land, Ohio	
210,812	56,784	12,902	36,956	12,864	18,426	11,165	11,038	953,234	15,959	303,085	50,231	73,143	1
67	12	3	13	------	7	1	5	622	7	152	71	34	2
2	1	-----	-----	8	-----	-----	1	50	6	11	-----	7	3
70,975	7,830	7,469	15,496	4,552	4,744	4,568	3,606	229,854	4,490	73,486	14,669	18,660	4
6,455	1,433	406	822	355	758	308	294	26,544	254	8,513	1,641	1,763	5
1,561	190	195	331	116	88	81	45	5,250	91	1,573	303	517	6
1,136	660	99	691	119	325	276	191	16,786	1,350	4,297	449	1,284	7
82	116	3	39	-----	22	1	5	2,833	23	857	62	60	8
180	16	27	11	60	8	21	136	804	1	78	22	118	9
874	528	69	641	59	295	254	50	13,149	1,326	3,362	365	1,106	10
1,687	387	84	228	100	147	54	108	12,101	81	4,341	448	766	11
58,074	4,689	6,507	10,309	3,771	2,901	3,776	2,881	151,990	2,590	47,631	10,116	12,928	12
709	71	16	86	6	214	3	17	4,373	-----	1,187	521	188	13
2,656	686	583	42	78	73	804	6	7,478	1	605	742	413	14
11,119	821	977	1,957	352	488	278	655	39,035	75	15,831	2,684	3,303	15
558	117	-----	222	-----	107	265	37	5,715	4	2,700	66	689	16
2,195	1,109	276	432	42	181	84	10	16,738	65	6,465	1,078	923	17
2,000	398	122	161	8	365	229	160	13,028	37	2,067	361	1,883	18
276	41	-----	48	-----	141	205	13	3,206	2	1,018	254	449	19
269	72	9	131	22	108	4	7	2,664	6	742	410	67	20
2,040	292	15	252	101	106	15	6	9,343	82	3,479	667	481	21
101	1	-----	5	-----	-----	-----	61	3,097	2,197	97	21	167	22
917	1	322	2,009	43	242	-----	1	9,176	5	841	1,699	63	23
25,506	73	3,818	303	2,764	259	699	1,673	11,382	5	2,144	284	1,879	24
9,728	1,007	369	4,661	355	617	757	235	26,755	111	10,455	1,329	2,423	25
782	166	82	2,666	42	347	14	3	9,330	21	4,725	1,272	785	26
1,280	305	96	449	49	178	59	84	7,853	103	2,406	440	617	27
5,428	2,417	147	731	258	572	211	223	34,094	301	11,897	1,501	2,662	28
346	215	2	35	7	54	11	21	3,416	33	1,094	200	199	29
4,767	1,961	137	669	245	493	176	194	28,143	255	9,679	1,180	2,361	30
315	241	8	27	6	25	24	8	2,535	13	1,124	121	102	31
19,667	8,122	932	2,758	1,355	1,990	986	587	102,430	1,626	33,540	4,939	8,391	32
4,006	2,018	147	872	563	629	167	116	30,405	570	12,669	987	1,874	33
10,184	4,659	586	1,321	593	1,028	583	305	50,188	864	13,065	2,797	4,679	34
3,524	1,044	148	352	144	206	202	109	10,938	99	3,909	732	949	35
1,953	401	51	213	55	127	34	57	10,899	93	3,897	423	889	36
288	46	6	25	8	30	18	5	1,107	23	427	32	60	37
17,073	6,081	946	3,642	1,659	2,146	1,178	1,424	94,765	1,394	27,618	4,382	7,038	38
340	71	16	34	2	15	9	15	2,053	8	1,024	72	64	39
415	77	6	82	10	34	8	32	2,454	25	1,087	145	118	40
298	111	14	56	16	52	23	29	1,798	22	443	81	250	41
1,303	448	88	290	91	175	72	85	9,267	114	3,053	395	540	42
1,018	304	44	126	94	78	29	86	4,211	51	1,168	262	446	43
7,756	2,879	489	1,778	1,004	1,010	725	814	43,963	760	11,739	2,110	3,547	44
3,936	1,575	217	815	340	532	210	233	18,144	246	5,004	754	1,268	45
2,007	616	72	461	102	250	102	130	12,875	168	4,100	563	805	46

TABLE 117.—WOMEN EMPLOYED IN CERTAIN SELECTED OCCUPA

	OCCUPATION	MIDDLE ATLANTIC DIVISION—continued						
		New York city by boroughs					New-ark, N. J.	Pat-erson, N. J.
		Bronx	Brook-lyn	Man-hattan	Queens	Rich-mond		
1	Domestic and personal service_____	9,014	32,201	106,153	6,642	2,186	7,252	1,704
2	Barbers, hairdressers, and manicurists_____	308	705	2,479	154	25	187	48
3	Boarding and lodging house keepers_____	139	1,543	3,724	167	125	530	86
4	Charwomen and cleaners_____	150	974	3,547	111	35	197	11
5	Housekeepers and stewardesses_____	728	2,688	4,994	672	216	608	292
6	Janitors and sextons_____	2,371	1,094	5,923	188	29	117	18
7	Laundresses (not in laundry)_____	497	3,187	6,143	720	258	909	149
8	Laundry operatives_____	316	1,163	3,296	207	10	285	67
9	Midwives and nurses (not trained)_____	818	2,592	5,907	580	181	453	182
10	Restaurant, café, and lunch room keepers_____	46	215	544	41	14	42	13
11	Servants_____	3,029	15,794	60,890	3,419	1,140	3,379	744
12	Waitresses_____	476	1,853	7,290	264	128	429	73
13	All other occupations_____	136	393	1,416	119	25	116	21
14	Clerical occupations_____	28,123	68,754	64,439	14,747	2,848	10,440	2,323
15	Agents, canvassers, and collectors_____	113	468	727	86	18	50	13
16	Bookkeepers, cashiers, and accountants_____	6,661	14,762	15,274	2,410	380	1,874	747
17	Clerks (except clerks in stores)_____	8,930	25,329	24,843	6,213	1,099	4,937	637
18	Messenger, bundle, and office girls_____	81	323	352	48	7	59	2
19	Stenographers and typists_____	12,338	27,872	23,243	5,990	1,344	3,520	924

TIONS, FOR CITIES OF 100,000 INHABITANTS OR MORE: 1920—Continued

	MIDDLE ATLANTIC DIVISION—continued								NORTH CENTRAL DIVISIONS					
Phila-del-phia, Pa.	Pitts-burgh, Pa.	Read-ing, Pa.	Roch-ester, N.Y.	Scran-ton, Pa.	Syra-cuse, N.Y.	Tren-ton, N.J.	Yon-kers, N.Y.	Total, 19 cities	Akron, Ohio	Chi-cago, Ill.	Cin-cin-nati, Ohio	Cleve-land, Ohio	
52,902	17,253	1,984	5,724	2,073	4,377	2,152	2,453	222,592	3,333	59,830	14,572	16,016	1
1,243	314	40	161	29	115	42	38	6,046	68	2,145	244	436	2
2,436	1,162	166	325	61	398	141	32	16,780	526	3,677	643	1,266	3
1,572	537	57	135	29	134	32	17	4,065	45	1,275	364	740	4
4,987	1,162	396	688	198	496	286	182	17,801	293	4,982	839	1,136	5
806	603	37	75	67	57	53	92	4,466	44	1,167	394	336	6
4,609	1,933	155	390	126	260	248	362	27,941	167	6,632	2,935	2,140	7
1,973	689	55	296	136	244	87	43	13,667	174	3,837	684	723	8
2,812	775	109	654	141	474	196	239	14,124	222	3,641	751	1,119	9
278	87	14	83	4	47	6	13	2,065	28	590	105	157	10
28,076	8,611	859	2,412	1,155	1,768	860	1,329	94,010	1,328	25,834	6,750	6,426	11
3,577	1,096	80	444	97	300	171	90	17,558	379	5,150	695	1,232	12
533	284	16	61	30	84	30	16	4,069	59	900	168	305	13
44,410	15,022	1,415	8,567	2,951	4,560	2,051	2,734	267,720	4,779	96,124	10,065	20,275	14
430	150	12	71	24	59	18	19	2,627	45	787	119	222	15
10,833	2,742	419	2,314	826	1,381	474	482	55,671	976	16,687	2,482	4,283	16
16,778	5,276	464	3,149	1,155	1,109	583	996	93,257	2,207	36,514	3,089	7,194	17
244	280	12	35	12	19	6	18	2,122	38	645	94	141	18
16,125	6,574	508	2,998	934	1,992	970	1,219	114,043	1,513	41,491	4,281	8,435	19

TABLE 117.—WOMEN EMPLOYED IN CERTAIN SELECTED OCCUPA

	OCCUPATION	NORTH CENTRAL DIVISIONS—continued						
		Co-lum-bus, Ohio	Day-ton, Ohio	Des Moines, Iowa	De-troit, Mich.	Grand Rap-ids, Mich.	In-dian-apolis, Ind.	Kan-sas City, Kans.
1	All occupations	25,396	14,969	15,237	82,843	14,933	35,454	9,041
2	[Agriculture, forestry, and animal husbandry.	24	8	30	31	9	28	11
[3	Extraction of minerals			2	7			1
4	Manufacturing and mechanical industries.	5,263	4,493	1,875	18,298	4,587	8,214	2,551
5	Dressmakers and seamstresses (not in factory).	844	477	398	1,934	471	1,116	209
6	Forewomen and overseers (manufacturing).	137	82	47	438	99	170	51
7	Laborers (n. o. s.[1])	272	146	124	1,589	736	1,001	593
8	Food industries	15	16	16	86	36	191	460
9	Textile industries	6	1	7	15	30	22	10
10	All other industries	251	129	101	1,488	670	788	123
11	Milliners and millinery dealers	252	111	143	688	176	447	78
12	Semiskilled operatives (n. o. s.[1])	3,341	3,437	1,018	12,449	2,801	4,798	1,557
13	Chemical and allied industries	31	54	58	864	43	230	183
14	Cigar and tobacco factories	490	779	13	2,118	441	113	4
15	Clothing industries	510	291	301	1,656	237	1,458	319
16	Electrical supply factories	12	338	1	174	7	81	1
17	Food industries	206	192	158	484	202	542	697
18	Iron and steel industries	249	766	15	4,301	274	794	18
19	Metal industries (other than iron and steel)	42	4	1	421	126	38	5
20	Lumber and furniture industries	55	27	12	96	555	95	13
21	Printing and publishing	140	378	173	486	121	267	75
22	Rubber factories	26	19	2	104	2	119	2
23	Shoe factories	803			36	44	1	2
24	Textile industries	159	16	141	180	300	208	90
25	All other industries	618	573	143	1,529	449	852	148
26	Tailoresses	150	72	23	374	50	331	22
27	All other occupations	267	168	122	826	254	351	41
28	Transportation	774	378	529	3,276	300	1,396	500
29	Telegraph operators	76	16	53	244	29	95	53
30	Telephone operators	648	351	453	2,814	243	1,228	369
31	All other occupations	50	11	23	218	28	73	78
32	Trade	2,804	1,621	1,743	8,739	1,673	3,489	899
33	Clerks in stores	793	411	368	2,238	478	998	188
34	Saleswomen (stores)	1,493	958	1,075	4,743	895	1,822	479
35	Retail dealers	299	122	95	858	146	364	96
36	All other occupations	219	130	205	900	154	305	136
37	Public service (not elsewhere classified).	47	17	21	87	25	43	14
38	Professional service	3,062	1,338	2,311	8,124	1,906	3,468	854
39	Actresses and showwomen	26	16	22	168	24	47	6
40	Artists, sculptors, and teachers of art	48	24	35	123	64	92	12
41	Librarians	49	39	41	190	43	75	6
42	Musicians and teachers of music	355	146	215	743	171	349	93
43	Religious, charity, and welfare workers	116	54	90	272	67	180	24
44	Teachers (school)	1,456	664	1,015	4,150	1,054	1,571	478
45	Trained nurses	577	242	507	1,445	262	643	133
46	All other occupations	435	153	386	1,033	221	511	102

[1] Not otherwise specified.

TIONS, FOR CITIES OF 100,000 INHABITANTS OR MORE: 1920—Continued

| | NORTH CENTRAL DIVISIONS—continued | | | | | | | SOUTHERN DIVISIONS | | | | | |
Kansas City, Mo.	Milwaukee, Wis.	Minneapolis, Minn.	Omaha, Nebr.	St. Louis. Mo.	St. Paul, Minn.	Toledo, Ohio	Youngstown, Ohio	Total, 15 cities	Atlanta, Ga.	Baltimore, Md.	Birmingham, Ala.	Dallas, Tex.	
39,925	49,417	46,444	20,808	96,827	27,863	23,083	8,576	473,853	31,553	89,947	19,737	21,456	1
32	27	28	16	66	23	23	2	801	36	60	40	21	2
3	1	1	------	8	1	2	-------	25	-------	2	11	-------	3
5,619	16,075	8,898	2,882	27,500	5,620	5,682	992	84,151	4,554	25,938	1,717	2,329	4
1,052	1,446	1,500	573	2,696	846	612	199	15,598	908	3,254	566	459	5
114	407	210	71	644	105	156	35	1,347	79	576	15	32	6
469	1,031	632	449	1,570	267	419	108	9,121	400	1,296	296	203	7
193	127	69	337	194	74	17	------	1,123	65	310	53	25	8
5	93	199	10	170	11	5	1	808	94	79	35	23	9
271	811	364	102	1,206	182	397	107	7,190	241	907	208	155	10
504	707	478	127	1,938	581	175	60	2,709	275	667	72	258	11
3,013	11,701	5,562	1,500	19,529	3,524	3,999	496	50,936	2,712	18,499	667	1,235	12
53	177	56	27	647	36	18	------	753	29	372	------	6	13
27	227	71	10	1,171	126	124	3	10,915	10	1,404	1	1	14
755	2,258	1,130	337	5,878	974	966	72	14,756	805	8,830	188	477	15
8	438	90	5	628	5	208	200	52	8	7	5	5	16
767	1,218	794	647	1,453	502	325	20	5,047	433	1,721	111	207	17
71	527	52	26	416	49	1,075	47	722	25	333	43	23	18
45	158	94	6	334	66	100	43	1,085	18	860	------	------	19
23	97	108	9	295	23	22	9	688	42	162	15	12	20
426	566	393	98	1,017	394	81	19	3,718	143	417	46	114	21
25	66	3	1	194	------	11	41	81	3	50	------	------	22
7	1,560	45	20	3,726	324	------	------	390	48	130	------	------	23
141	2,730	1,680	62	995	162	205	1	5,550	770	1,444	191	130	24
665	1,679	1,046	252	2,775	863	804	41	7,179	378	2,769	67	260	25
202	423	210	44	371	101	91	63	2,371	57	1,158	26	50	26
265	360	306	118	752	196	230	31	2,069	123	488	75	92	27
1,649	1,482	1,790	872	2,652	960	854	321	12,252	935	2,061	487	1,249	28
276	89	218	122	449	89	57	24	1,529	187	134	39	311	29
1,204	1,336	1,458	721	2,030	778	750	285	9,448	662	1,698	390	895	30
169	57	114	29	173	93	47	12	1,275	86	229	58	43	31
4,593	5,038	5,019	2,165	8,846	3,323	2,612	1,370	37,324	1,948	8,568	1,565	2,529	32
1,428	1,334	975	646	2,080	1,090	866	412	7,722	217	1,485	281	841	33
2,132	2,617	3,143	1,051	4,668	1,663	1,287	757	20,796	1,278	4,621	975	1,291	34
378	674	374	186	1,034	246	234	143	5,072	173	1,637	168	130	35
655	413	527	282	1,064	324	225	58	3,734	280	825	141	267	36
47	40	47	23	83	41	21	9	919	48	95	15	31	37
4,301	4,867	6,392	2,816	7,916	3,329	2,503	1,146	39,986	2,364	7,372	1,801	2,020	38
206	55	60	23	170	18	39	5	501	35	71	20	36	39
119	86	177	32	143	77	34	13	613	41	125	24	28	40
53	77	130	33	119	79	50	18	637	31	81	20	14	41
506	478	559	198	772	281	214	85	3,035	175	499	134	199	42
168	221	292	103	395	159	83	60	1,939	121	393	72	71	43
1,566	2,506	2,771	1,336	1,634	1,319	608		18,735	1,028	3,452	938	933	44
1,040	873	1,473	731	1,638	613	464	231	9,356	621	1,953	361	462	45
643	571	930	360	1,000	468	300	126	5,170	312	798	232	277	46

6436°—29——15

TABLE 117.—WOMEN EMPLOYED IN CERTAIN SELECTED OCCUPA

	OCCUPATION	NORTH CENTRAL DIVISIONS—continued						
		Co-lum-bus, Ohio	Day-ton, Ohio	Des Moines, Iowa	De-troit, Mich.	Grand Rap-ids, Mich.	In-dian-apolis, Ind.	Kan-sas City, Kans.
1	Domestic and personal service	7,308	3,590	3,685	18,973	3,234	10,086	2,164
2	Barbers, hairdressers, and manicurists	162	96	118	447	64	323	51
3	Boarding and lodging house keepers	522	333	268	2,251	275	770	129
4	Charwomen and cleaners	45	12	19	168	44	54	10
5	Housekeepers and stewardesses	633	313	394	1,829	365	923	156
6	Janitors and sextons	85	62	72	595	52	207	45
7	Laundresses (not in laundry)	1,095	463	275	1,204	184	1,794	544
8	Laundry operatives	341	267	232	1,451	193	660	212
9	Midwives and nurses (not trained)	679	262	286	1,370	312	645	132
10	Restaurant, café, and lunch room keepers	81	24	48	143	48	107	31
11	Servants	3,083	1,529	1,406	7,502	1,445	3,941	678
12	Waitresses	438	135	471	1,631	203	518	136
13	All other occupations	144	94	96	382	49	144	40
14	Clerical occupations	6,114	3,524	5,041	25,308	3,199	8,730	2,047
15	Agents, canvassers, and collectors	85	42	57	191	42	110	22
16	Bookkeepers, cashiers, and accountants	1,649	846	1,232	5,547	935	2,064	466
17	Clerks (except clerks in stores)	1,573	1,126	1,431	9,997	796	2,515	741
18	Messenger, bundle, and office girls	35	13	52	212	43	105	23
19	Stenographers and typists	2,772	1,497	2,269	9,361	1,383	3,936	795

TIONS, FOR CITIES OF 100,000 INHABITANTS OR MORE: 1920—Continued

	NORTH CENTRAL DIVISIONS—continued							SOUTHERN DIVISIONS					
Kansas City, Mo.	Milwaukee, Wis.	Minneapolis, Minn.	Omaha, Nebr.	St. Louis, Mo.	St. Paul, Minn.	Toledo, Ohio	Youngstown, Ohio	Total, 15 cities	Atlanta, Ga.	Baltimore, Md.	Birmingham, Ala.	Dallas, Tex.	
12,025	9,791	11,076	5,163	27,946	6,117	5,359	2,324	189,089	15,647	30,337	11,346	7,456	1
328	178	280	167	641	137	113	48	4,058	433	447	332	184	2
1,171	811	618	587	1,720	429	610	174	7,931	414	891	350	491	3
18	539	128	27	384	93	75	25	3,331	137	553	92	9	4
869	840	947	372	1,607	512	587	204	6,256	253	1,177	338	219	5
156	130	203	164	505	72	118	59	1,641	142	451	56	54	6
1,744	916	539	385	5,877	442	383	222	55,996	5,549	8,056	4,218	2,083	7
983	426	731	322	1,651	436	228	116	8,053	949	1,008	549	522	8
586	620	850	379	1,223	434	439	174	7,374	719	1,234	452	315	9
133	69	127	53	184	54	56	27	1,121	127	209	70	50	10
4,668	4,445	5,271	2,040	11,814	2,628	2,182	1,040	84,711	6,501	14,799	4,575	3,087	11
1,062	638	1,170	520	1,771	759	472	178	6,660	346	1,192	211	338	12
307	179	212	147	569	121	96	57	1,957	77	320	103	104	13
11,656	12,096	13,193	6,871	21,810	8,449	6,027	2,412	109,306	6,021	15,514	2,755	5,821	14
157	126	162	66	224	82	58	30	1,001	72	187	71	63	15
2,751	2,733	3,341	1,469	4,015	1,713	1,675	807	16,157	1,252	3,023	722	949	16
3,525	3,931	3,600	2,194	7,257	3,026	1,877	664	49,693	1,691	5,768	543	1,793	17
97	117	139	54	150	94	45	25	915	34	107	32	64	18
5,126	5,189	5,951	3,088	10,164	3,534	2,372	886	41,540	2,972	6,429	1,387	2,952	19

TABLE **117.**—WOMEN EMPLOYED IN CERTAIN SELECTED OCCUPA

	OCCUPATION	SOUTHERN DIVISIONS—continued						
		Fort Worth, Tex.	Houston, Tex.	Louisville, Ky.	Memphis, Tenn.	Nashville, Tenn.	New Orleans, La.	Norfolk, Va.
1	All occupations	10,570	16,891	33,655	23,784	17,621	48,358	14,384
2	Agriculture, forestry, and animal husbandry.	45	26	12	211	36	189	29
3	Extraction of minerals	4	1	1	2	1	1	1
4	Manufacturing and mechanical industries.	1,467	2,034	10,088	2,972	3,132	9,842	1,747
5	Dressmakers and seamstresses (not in factory).	279	586	1,416	776	562	2,907	444
6	Forewomen and overseers (manufacturing)	21	27	132	51	56	131	19
7	Laborers (n. o. s.[1])	409	473	722	751	388	1,108	239
8	Food industries	220	36	64	37	29	149	28
9	Textile industries		49	36	41	93	261	62
10	All other industries	189	388	622	673	266	698	149
11	Milliners and millinery dealers	56	100	277	99	127	224	55
12	Semiskilled operatives (n. o. s.[1])	611	742	6,870	1,102	1,900	5,152	887
13	Chemical and allied industries	1	2	73	85	46	38	7
14	Cigar and tobacco factories	2	2	3,416	125	248	1,153	252
15	Clothing industries	263	224	1,251	211	464	884	153
16	Electrical supply factories			5			5	
17	Food industries	200	161	450	199	123	835	70
18	Iron and steel industries	13	21	104	6	11	26	9
19	Other metal industries		6	34		3	134	1
20	Lumber and furniture industries	8	3	177	60	30	104	49
21	Printing and publishing	36	63	237	47	212	84	5
22	Rubber factories				4		5	
23	Shoe factories			72	1	56	75	1
24	Textile industries	4	143	536	140	513	1,030	212
25	All other industries	84	117	515	224	194	779	128
26	Tailoresses	14	31	441	98	36	115	56
27	All other occupations	77	75	230	95	63	205	47
28	Transportation	545	654	760	587	447	1,065	191
29	Telegraph operators	46	79	62	79	52	147	28
30	Telephone operators	453	530	613	421	340	745	124
31	All other occupations	46	45	85	87	55	173	39
32	Trade	1,054	1,324	2,879	1,907	1,251	4,354	1,091
33	Clerks in stores	275	180	649	415	224	871	212
34	Saleswomen (stores)	555	870	1,614	1,039	722	2,269	715
35	Retail dealers	88	143	392	171	131	769	91
36	All other occupations	136	131	224	282	174	445	73
37	Public service (not elsewhere classified)	12	17	45	25	7	48	40
38	Professional service	1,080	1,587	2,711	2,073	1,491	4,103	1,127
39	Actresses and showwomen	25	19	52	26	9	75	13
40	Artists, sculptors, and teachers of art	20	22	31	22	27	62	6
41	Librarians	8	11	49	29	28	42	9
42	Musicians and teachers of music	90	177	242	154	157	332	105
43	Religious, charity, and welfare workers	44	48	134	53	54	223	53
44	Teachers (school)	555	849	1,257	992	622	2,198	598
45	Trained nurses	218	247	606	555	334	735	249
46	All other occupations	120	214	340	242	260	436	94

[1] Not otherwise specified.

TIONS, FOR CITIES OF 100,000 INHABITANTS OR MORE: 1920—Continued

	SOUTHERN DIVISIONS—con.				WESTERN DIVISIONS								
Rich-mond, Va.	San An-tonio, Tex.	Wash-ington, D.C.	Wil-ming-ton, Del.	Total, 8 cities	Den-ver, Colo.	Los Ange-les, Calif.	Oak-land, Calif.	Port-land, Oreg.	Salt Lake City, Utah	San Fran-cisco, Calif.	Seat-tle, Wash	Spo-kane, Wash.	
26,017	16,421	92,027	11,432	259,526	28,563	68,061	20,001	28,325	9,995	60,573	32,950	11,058	1
7	66	.19	4	771	71	397	35	73	30	66	62	37	2
------	------	------	1	30	7	9	4	1	------	5	2	2	3
7,602	2,549	5,686	2,494	40,778	3,752	11,533	3,246	4,307	1,299	10,931	4,255	1,455	4
588	656	1,869	328	9,672	1,070	2,976	735	940	336	2,187	973	455	5
89	25	48	46	657	55	185	59	70	24	185	62	17	6
2,223	190	208	215	2,130	132	608	215	274	82	490	227	102	7
66	32	8	1	566	45	199	43	46	45	117	48	23	8
9	2	------	24	70	------	7	29	18	2	13	1	------	9
2,148	156	200	190	1,494	87	402	143	210	35	360	178	79	10
114	97	224	64	3,851	340	1,047	234		102	1,147	426	100	11
4,488	1,486	2,869	1,716	20,497	1,837	5,597	1,705	2,173	667	5,830	2,031	657	12
43	14	27	10	269	35	54	43	27	5	85	16	4	13
3,366	720	31	184	604	107	132	17	6	7	322	8	5	14
239	304	382	81	6,606	502	2,165	338	684	149	1,994	633	141	15
------	11	------	6	236	6	25	126	3	2	58	16	------	16
186	224	97	30	4,759	598	1,229	236	469	312	1,060	550	305	17
13	28	23	44	289	29	64	56	35	1	69	34	1	18
27	------	2	------	436	8	90	73	64	------	153	48	------	19
10	------	8	8	395	23	113	31	89	4	82	33	20	20
234	33	2,024	23	1,220	184	263	103	93	45	377	119	36	21
------	------	------	19	74	25	20	10	8	1	9	1	------	22
4	3	------	------	131	1	12	2	9	6	77	24	------	23
25	18	22	372	1,585	43	229	409	362	55	323	137	27	24
341	131	253	939	3,893	276	1,201	261	324	80	1,221	412	118	25
37	28	190	34	1,962	126	554	138	176	35	586	288	59	26
63	67	278	91	2,009	192	566	160	219	53	506	248	65	27
536	583	1,888	264	10,362	1,166	2,465	739	1,334	482	2,295	1,366	515	28
90	72	194	9	1,139	190	195	58	146	88	278	125	59	29
405	473	1,463	236	8,597	872	2,155	581	1,081	365	1,949	1,171	423	30
41	38	231	19	626	104	115	100	107	29	68	70	33	31
1,671	1,964	4,129	1,090	33,550	3,279	8,836	2,680	3,780	1,272	7,581	4,631	1,491	32
370	376	1,130	196	6,662	701	1,553	447	801	214	1,376	1,215	355	33
934	1,087	2,179	647	18,173	1,772	4,758	1,440	2,095	869	4,050	2,360	829	34
207	267	505	200	3,342	389	865	341	303	96	837	374	137	35
160	234	315	47	5,373	417	1,660	452	581	93	1,318	682	170	36
22	72	429	13	490	56	173	26	39	21	115	38	22	37
1,988	2,321	6,991	957	41,283	4,375	12,167	3,310	4,331	1,761	8,467	5,016	1,856	38
2	70	43	5	2,090	68	1,283	100	67	33	388	124	27	39
15	20	160	10	1,315	148	482	102	93	25	321	108	36	40
14	16	263	22	673	66	175	63	129	28	77	101	34	41
127	182	386	76	4,390	456	1,294	390	521	179	834	528	188	42
92	103	430	48	1,365	135	385	112	116	28	380	169	40	43
924	1,212	2,676	501	15,730	1,885	4,352	1,270	1,829	921	2,492	2,059	922	44
625	494	1,735	161	8,432	905	1,855	734	792	337	2,546	955	308	45
189	224	1,298	134	7,288	712	2,341	539	784	210	1,429	972	301	46

TABLE 117.—WOMEN EMPLOYED IN CERTAIN SELECTED OCCUPA

OCCUPATION	SOUTHERN DIVISIONS—continued						
	Fort Worth, Tex.	Houston, Tex.	Louisville, Ky.	Memphis, Tenn.	Nashville, Tenn.	New Orleans, La.	Norfolk, Va.
1 Domestic and personal service	3,983	7,893	11,460	12,724	8,606	22,040	7,739
2 Barbers, hairdressers, and manicurists	99	168	194	455	197	548	125
3 Boarding and lodging house keepers	271	434	582	698	251	1,011	295
4 Charwomen and cleaners	11	23	135	103	95	95	93
5 Housekeepers and stewardesses	163	153	575	251	205	758	206
6 Janitors and sextons	19	98	181	58	32	103	99
7 Laundresses (not in laundry)	835	2,743	3,978	4,163	3,492	7,282	2,177
8 Laundry operatives	237	367	563	499	446	646	297
9 Midwives and nurses (not trained)	180	270	458	456	303	841	229
10 Restaurant, café, and lunch room keepers	23	45	68	75	43	68	36
11 Servants	1,810	3,193	4,309	5,515	3,254	9,967	3,757
12 Waitresses	233	301	326	384	235	494	356
13 All other occupations	102	98	91	67	53	227	69
14 Clerical occupations	2,380	3,355	5,699	3,283	2,650	6,716	2,419
15 Agents, canvassers, and collectors	18	40	115	43	37	133	20
16 Bookkeepers, cashiers, and accountants	534	626	1,550	764	660	1,121	588
17 Clerks (except clerks in stores)	631	956	1,550	727	682	1,995	702
18 Messenger, bundle, and office girls	23	28	110	53	36	55	13
19 Stenographers and typists	1,174	1,705	2,374	1,696	1,235	3,412	1,096

TIONS, FOR CITIES OF 100,000 INHABITANTS OR MORE: 1920—Continued

	SOUTHERN DIVISIONS—con.			WESTERN DIVISIONS									
Richmond, Va.	San Antonio, Tex.	Washington, D. C.	Wilmington, Del.	Total, 8 cities	Denver, Colo.	Los Angeles, Calif.	Oakland, Calif.	Portland, Oreg.	Salt Lake City, Utah	San Francisco, Calif.	Seattle, Wash.	Spokane, Wash.	
10,029	6,300	29,872	3,657	66,354	8,410	18,082	4,703	7,088	2,485	13,877	8,647	3,062	1
121	135	551	69	2,323	266	656	174	214	65	532	320	96	2
280	322	1,354	287	4,972	785	1,286	512	537	217	773	728	134	3
80	17	1,857	31	303	36	55	54	39	30	51	26	12	4
279	256	1,102	321	6,742	765	1,837	532	702	280	1,346	944	336	5
60	44	177	67	1,480	124	338	71	214	74	353	245	61	6
2,782	1,947	6,080	611	2,045	514	757	115	115	71	244	155	74	7
313	390	1,170	97	6,000	682	1,554	484	647	239	1,290	830	274	8
419	318	998	182	7,568	742	2,337	678	788	259	1,652	805	307	9
48	61	183	15	809	119	273	55	78	21	129	100	34	10
5,232	2,511	14,370	1,831	24,345	3,088	6,769	1,525	2,526	952	5,559	2,782	1,144	11
329	205	1,590	120	7,297	993	1,690	352	984	175	1,331	1,347	425	12
86	94	440	26	2,470	296	530	151	244	102	617	365	165	13
4,162	2,566	43,013	2,952	65,908	7,447	14,399	5,258	7,372	2,645	17,236	8,933	2,618	14
50	33	77	42	861	78	264	69	103	29	185	108	25	15
891	618	2,319	540	16,956	1,775	4,045	1,426	2,079	614	4,059	2,230	728	16
1,443	688	29,342	1,182	17,230	1,780	3,922	1,397	1,913	533	4,803	2,346	536	17
17	62	267	14	766	101	219	28	121	28	119	128	22	18
1,761	1,165	11,008	1,174	30,095	3,713	5,949	2,338	3,156	1,441	8,070	4,121	1,307	19

TABLE **118.**—WOMEN EMPLOYED IN CERTAIN SELECTED OCCUPATIONS, FOR CITIES HAVING FROM 25,000 TO 100,000 INHABITANTS: 1920

OCCUPATION	ALABAMA		ARIZONA	ARKANSAS		CALIFORNIA		
	Mobile	Montgomery	Phoenix	Fort Smith	Little Rock	Alameda	Berkeley	Fresno
All occupations	8,404	7,497	2,601	2,612	8,315	2,408	5,822	4,018
Boarding and lodging house keepers	189	106	70	83	210	28	100	78
Bookkeepers, cashiers, and accountants	231	181	182	127	351	187	351	386
Clerks (except clerks in stores)	278	113	145	77	332	216	424	191
Clerks and saleswomen (in stores)	440	381	267	226	576	195	349	573
Dressmakers and seamstresses (not in factory)	354	258	88	76	277	80	181	108
Housekeepers and stewardesses	67	31	61	44	119	81	175	98
Laundresses (not in laundry)	2,287	2,299	134	327	1,238	6	25	41
Laundry operatives	161	82	88	26	232	36	51	92
Midwives and nurses (not trained)	212	200	78	49	216	87	215	116
Musicians and teachers of music	54	40	48	40	93	59	203	54
Retail dealers	91	103	27	35	73	51	84	51
Semiskilled operatives (manfg.) (n. o. s.[1]):								
Cigar and tobacco factories	1	------	1	3	1	------	1	------
Clothing industries	98	95	15	112	118	33	41	40
Food industries	10	7	18	14	38	29	32	36
Iron and steel industries	5	------	2	7	3	2	20	2
Shoe factories								
Textile industries	12	79	2	1	7	5	44	2
Servants	2,015	1,906	310	393	1,657	219	557	334
Stenographers and typists	511	352	348	208	805	389	647	511
Teachers	395	279	224	202	463	205	855	373
Telephone operators	106	101	26	62	227	78	89	135
Trained nurses	177	152	110	87	204	65	191	157
Waitresses	103	60	72	25	181	16	59	110
All other occupations	607	672	285	388	894	341	1,128	530

OCCUPATION	CALIFORNIA—continued						COLORADO	
	Long Beach	Pasadena	Sacramento	San Diego	San Jose	Stockton	Colorado Springs	Pueblo
All occupations	4,309	5,853	6,485	7,603	3,846	3,212	3,426	3,481
Boarding and lodging house keepers	123	57	234	197	83	137	152	163
Bookkeepers, cashiers, and accountants	267	281	571	445	289	284	180	193
Clerks (except clerks in stores)	170	157	400	247	99	116	75	125
Clerks and saleswomen (in stores)	481	375	786	730	451	325	308	329
Dressmakers and seamstresses (not in factory)	216	343	189	306	161	113	178	124
Housekeepers and stewardesses	143	279	180	270	121	92	99	81
Laundresses (not in laundry)	28	137	35	97	19	30	147	129
Laundry operatives	81	138	165	239	80	76	62	80
Midwives and nurses (not trained)	211	333	193	362	199	178	151	210
Musicians and teachers of music	123	113	96	183	65	50	68	41
Retail dealers	81	58	82	119	52	47	46	44
Semiskilled operatives (manfg.) (n. o. s.[1]):								
Cigar and tobacco factories	1	1	8	16	2	1	------	8
Clothing industries	37	72	67	93	68	37	40	48
Food industries	50	30	152	213	80	77	10	46
Iron and steel industries	3	1	12	7	2	1	2	4
Shoe factories	------	2	------	2	------	------	------	1
Textile industries	49	5	5	4	4	22	4	11
Servants	259	1,271	483	732	261	302	592	436
Stenographers and typists	326	283	831	498	241	347	217	301
Teachers	400	491	493	634	505	218	321	357
Telephone operators	86	143	231	218	106	101	65	84
Trained nurses	146	218	235	324	120	132	177	153
Waitresses	137	236	141	191	76	73	104	116
All other occupations	891	829	896	1,476	762	453	428	397

[1] Not otherwise specified.

TABLE **118.**—WOMEN EMPLOYED IN CERTAIN SELECTED OCCUPATIONS, FOR
CITIES HAVING FROM 25,000 TO 100,000 INHABITANTS: 1920—Continued

OCCUPATION	CONNECTICUT					
	Meriden	New Britain	New London	Norwalk	Stamford	Waterbury
All occupations	3,282	5,645	2,324	3,301	3,402	9,616
Boarding and lodging house keepers	19	37	45	14	29	113
Bookkeepers, cashiers, and accountants	188	221	156	145	131	452
Clerks (except clerks in stores)	368	763	129	118	259	838
Clerks and saleswomen (in stores)	205	267	225	91	168	547
Dressmakers and seamstresses (not in factory)	59	84	70	72	109	113
Housekeepers and stewardesses	107	145	62	69	63	128
Laundresses (not in laundry)	13	20	52	82	175	94
Laundry operatives	16	20	19	25	29	32
Midwives and nurses (not trained)	47	63	63	54	68	115
Musicians and teachers of music	22	31	24	33	27	64
Retail dealers	45	38	25	41	38	82
Semiskilled operatives (manufacturing) (n. o. s.[1]):						
Cigar and tobacco factories	2	3		8	1	
Clothing industries	4	109	45	1,023	179	32
Food industries	7	3	2	4	17	2
Iron and steel industries	167	1,475	8	14	570	344
Shoe factories				67	24	11
Textile industries	3	102	292	133	6	120
Servants	190	312	319	219	437	534
Stenographers and typists	298	554	152	197	245	760
Teachers	208	352	169	176	217	635
Telephone operators	48	52	62	37	52	137
Trained nurses	55	60	68	37	56	222
Waitresses	28	30	44	39	58	42
All other occupations	1,183	904	293	603	444	4,199

OCCUPATION	FLORIDA				GEORGIA			
	Jacksonville	Miami	Pensacola	Tampa	Augusta	Columbus	Macon	Savannah
All occupations	13,131	4,028	3,307	7,622	8,705	5,495	8,608	12,608
Boarding and lodging house keepers	383	109	79	184	134	67	87	239
Bookkeepers, cashiers, and accountants	362	167	111	158	157	114	204	307
Clerks (except clerks in stores)	378	84	70	86	166	60	104	342
Clerks and saleswomen (in stores)	591	191	217	246	379	225	379	504
Dressmakers and seamstresses (not in factory)	546	189	144	253	306	151	325	630
Housekeepers and stewardesses	134	85	29	76	65	34	64	88
Laundresses (not in laundry)	3,292	902	1,009	1,369	2,562	963	2,452	3,022
Laundry operatives	282	99	48	113	79	46	161	241
Midwives and nurses (not trained)	236	105	76	109	133	83	143	274
Musicians and teachers of music	88	32	27	45	40	29	61	62
Retail dealers	146	53	51	81	100	51	89	253
Semiskilled operatives (manfg.) (n. o. s.[1]):								
Cigar and tobacco factories	80	3	2	2,657	4	3	1	106
Clothing industries	63	14	13	15	25	36	140	165
Food industries	60	2	4	7	23	7	35	30
Iron and steel industries	7			5	2	3	2	6
Shoe factories								
Textile industries	10	3	1	6	763	1,720	460	62
Servants	3,147	1,045	657	939	1,871	943	1,955	3,238
Stenographers and typists	772	183	175	294	298	169	363	694
Teachers	464	154	167	268	290	179	338	411
Telephone operators	162	32	38	14	84	42	110	138
Trained nurses	254	64	52	99	185	50	152	279
Waitresses	232	100	43	73	70	23	39	105
All other occupations	1,442	412	294	525	969	497	944	1,412

[1] Not otherwise specified.

TABLE 118.—WOMEN EMPLOYED IN CERTAIN SELECTED OCCUPATIONS, FOR
CITIES HAVING FROM 25,000 TO 100,000 INHABITANTS: 1920—Continued

OCCUPATION	ILLINOIS							
	Aurora	Bloomington	Cicero town	Danville	Decatur	East St. Louis	Elgin	Evanston
All occupations	3,614	2,946	3,954	3,231	3,986	5,720	3,998	5,095
Boarding and lodging house keepers	52	44	7	76	82	219	13	53
Bookkeepers, cashiers, and accountants	253	203	122	242	302	231	191	249
Clerks (except clerks in stores)	327	133	662	152	135	511	208	316
Clerks and saleswomen (in stores)	288	391	216	406	456	539	196	247
Dressmakers and seamstresses (not in factory)	99	116	36	113	162	102	56	178
Housekeepers and stewardesses	104	83	34	112	137	115	50	92
Laundresses (not in laundry)	68	66	53	226	134	359	37	352
Laundry operatives	42	52	6	29	85	70	17	109
Midwives and nurses (not trained)	69	90	23	61	85	47	123	162
Musicians and teachers of music	53	40	16	43	55	38	44	86
Retail dealers	28	25	54	36	33	87	19	51
Semiskilled operatives (mangf.) (n. o. s.¹):								
Cigar and tobacco factories	5	1	50	4	9	8	10	-----
Clothing industries	391	74	347	161	198	112	60	67
Food industries	6	68	40	16	11	315	10	6
Iron and steel industries	32	3	53	17	50	23	7	4
Shoe factories	-----	-----	5	-----	5	28	21	-----
Textile industries	81	2	17	3	10	37	52	2
Servants	289	370	74	468	425	504	181	1,523
Stenographers and typists	420	286	399	213	340	667	204	305
Teachers	248	256	74	223	224	334	214	394
Telephone operators	74	78	72	63	126	103	49	106
Trained nurses	73	98	9	99	78	52	98	158
Waitresses	42	69	39	87	102	137	11	74
All other occupations	570	398	1,546	381	742	1,082	2,127	561

OCCUPATION	ILLINOIS—continued							
	Joliet	Moline	Oak Park village	Peoria	Quincy	Rock Island	Rockford	Springfield
All occupations	3,376	2,610	4,393	8,436	3,976	3,333	7,134	6,762
Boarding and lodging house keepers	46	80	12	175	108	85	110	140
Bookkeepers, cashiers, and accountants	228	130	295	593	212	238	574	453
Clerks (except clerks in stores)	203	242	682	569	151	295	512	417
Clerks and saleswomen (in stores)	388	267	242	1,072	448	410	549	587
Dressmakers and seamstresses (not in factory)	129	87	109	232	146	116	202	208
Housekeepers and stewardesses	58	63	99	218	97	90	143	182
Laundresses (not in laundry)	71	49	32	174	144	84	100	161
Laundry operatives	29	60	4	115	92	41	88	123
Midwives and nurses (not trained)	70	43	87	106	72	57	132	96
Musicians and teachers of music	45	26	104	93	59	35	80	66
Retail dealers	43	43	40	98	37	47	60	63
Semiskilled operatives (mangf.) (n. o. s.¹):								
Cigar and tobacco factories	6	3	-----	69	7	31	5	5
Clothing industries	127	22	55	342	252	44	180	95
Food industries	13	41	9	124	39	42	32	22
Iron and steel industries	20	78	5	43	18	48	339	85
Shoe factories	-----	-----	1	-----	108	-----	15	99
Textile industries	2	3	5	75	32	19	606	5
Servants	351	285	692	1,066	560	329	514	711
Stenographers and typists	352	402	654	983	350	438	622	815
Teachers	375	164	476	491	230	246	395	456
Telephone operators	67	74	63	234	83	123	178	190
Trained nurses	54	89	155	253	108	50	182	246
Waitresses	66	56	19	162	45	64	124	130
All other occupations	635	303	553	1,149	578	401	1,392	1,407

¹ Not otherwise specified.

TABLE 118.—WOMEN EMPLOYED IN CERTAIN SELECTED OCCUPATIONS, FOR CITIES HAVING FROM 25,000 TO 100,000 INHABITANTS: 1920—Continued

INDIANA

OCCUPATION	Anderson	East Chicago	Evansville	Fort Wayne	Gary	Hammond	Kokomo	Muncie
All occupations	2,923	1,186	9,717	9,974	2,351	2,147	2,156	3,341
Boarding and lodging house keepers	36	35	161	181	47	34	64	110
Bookkeepers, cashiers, and accountants	214	63	449	496	152	129	173	270
Clerks (except clerks in stores)	200	93	218	687	172	320	141	143
Clerks and saleswomen (in stores)	197	87	744	780	282	232	249	377
Dressmakers and seamstresses (not in factory)	78	13	264	255	40	39	85	106
Housekeepers and stewardesses	71	24	210	173	91	56	54	95
Laundresses (not in laundry)	67	23	415	157	42	22	46	124
Laundry operatives	22	21	177	82	42	1	32	49
Midwives and nurses (not trained)	45	14	165	183	58	32	40	36
Musicians and teachers of music	24	5	74	84	25	30	35	57
Retail dealers	25	26	85	55	41	44	14	46
Semiskilled operatives (manfg.) (n. o. s.[1]):								
Cigar and tobacco factories		3	2,377	12		3	3	
Clothing industries	29	35	244	413	12	14	36	82
Food industries	4	39	34	110	7	18	4	14
Iron and steel industries	112	12	78	44	50	36	67	177
Shoe factories								
Textile industries	41		120	731		1	3	1
Servants	198	111	1,109	1,062	321	169	214	297
Stenographers and typists	200	122	650	1,003	171	284	176	178
Teachers	136	115	450	432	233	128	111	173
Telephone operators	62	38	167	207	63	77	46	87
Trained nurses	21	7	201	200	63	29	31	48
Waitresses	23	51	77	167	111	57	35	54
All other occupations	1,118	249	1,248	2,460	328	392	497	812

OCCUPATION	INDIANA—con.			IOWA				
	Richmond	South Bend	Terre Haute	Cedar Rapids	Council Bluffs	Davenport	Dubuque	Sioux City	Waterloo
All occupations	2,543	6,360	6,155	4,763	3,361	5,759	4,404	7,395	3,374
Boarding and lodging house keepers	64	75	124	80	38	174	39	174	87
Bookkeepers, cashiers, and accountants	194	448	388	361	316	402	230	748	318
Clerks (except clerks in stores)	79	495	206	194	267	431	210	368	210
Clerks and saleswomen (in stores)	249	565	799	520	340	600	453	928	328
Dressmakers and seamstresses (not in factory)	108	142	158	163	81	213	121	162	130
Housekeepers and stewardesses	81	140	208	107	78	192	115	139	71
Laundresses (not in laundry)	98	68	328	67	62	113	101	91	72
Laundry operatives	26	65	87	58	56	70	31	94	75
Midwives and nurses (not trained)	62	81	86	104	59	109	106	166	90
Musicians and teachers of music	42	49	90	64	35	70	65	88	61
Retail dealers	29	48	72	33	28	45	32	58	30
Semiskilled operatives (manfg.) (n. o. s.[1]):									
Cigar and tobacco factories		88	3	6	1	215	55	9	4
Clothing industries	300	704	201	136	39	108	209	126	91
Food industries	26	75	120	229	153	134	87	277	39
Iron and steel industries	32	258	39	2	4	53	34	7	21
Shoe factories		40	1				8		
Textile industries	35	132	8	13	8	4	3	5	3
Servants	255	408	746	489	259	538	480	650	315
Stenographers and typists	188	540	488	481	560	656	445	879	429
Teachers	155	359	574	418	271	392	365	581	284
Telephone operators	17	122	142	107	89	147	76	125	88
Trained nurses	21	52	92	145	130	118	155	312	79
Waitresses	22	46	105	71	52	135	58	263	80
All other occupations	460	1,360	1,090	915	435	840	926	1,145	469

[1] Not otherwise specified.

TABLE 118.—WOMEN EMPLOYED IN CERTAIN SELECTED OCCUPATIONS, FOR CITIES HAVING FROM 25,000 TO 100,000 INHABITANTS: 1920—Continued

OCCUPATION	KANSAS		KENTUCKY			LOUISIANA	MAINE		
	Topeka	Wichita	Covington	Lexington	Newport	Shreveport	Bangor	Lewiston	Portland
All occupations	5,514	6,963	6,807	6,461	3,458	6,253	3,021	5,419	8,131
Boarding and lodging house keepers	104	200	41	122	11	119	47	49	264
Bookkeepers, cashiers, and accountants	370	572	373	311	192	185	217	193	615
Clerks (except clerks in stores)	717	325	398	93	205	130	75	85	380
Clerks and saleswomen (in stores)	476	654	709	422	312	289	286	245	825
Dressmakers and seamstresses (not in factory)	145	225	317	272	129	206	126	77	250
Housekeepers and stewardesses	155	155	110	90	55	60	136	129	401
Laundresses (not in laundry)	227	144	378	1,061	140	1,491	34	19	66
Laundry operatives	88	180	48	161	46	161	38	10	107
Midwives and nurses (not trained)	101	163	59	164	36	92	79	74	237
Musicians and teachers of music	74	102	48	51	31	46	38	25	107
Retail dealers	57	75	112	43	57	48	32	29	63
Semiskilled operatives (manfg.) (n. o. s.[1]):									
Cigar and tobacco factories	38	2	114	363	106	3	21	2	4
Clothing industries	70	126	644*	79	370	38	35	199	248
Food industries	55	74	156	6	91	10	9	31	105
Iron and steel industries	3	4	29		17	4	3		26
Shoe factories		3	147	2	130		28	926	96
Textile industries	9	3	36	3	31	4	6	1,994	15
Servants	521	694	489	1,410	168	1,730	602	236	1,016
Stenographers and typists	731	881	726	326	341	456	354	93	906
Teachers	414	536	256	304	155	240	193	231	567
Telephone operators	140	285	181	81	68	106	77	56	182
Trained nurses	158	228	38	129	21	208	149	51	315
Waitresses	87	255	77	42	34	111	74	53	268
All other occupations	774	1,077	1,321	926	712	516	362	612	1,068

OCCUPATION	MARYLAND		MASSACHUSETTS					
	Cumberland	Hagerstown	Brockton	Brookline town	Chelsea	Chicopee	Everett	Fitchburg
All occupations	2,522	2,475	9,896	7,522	3,965	3,960	3,791	5,409
Boarding and lodging house keepers	55	43	117	66	37	22	9	56
Bookkeepers, cashiers, and accountants	84	103	647	290	346	138	368	308
Clerks (except clerks in stores)	189	74	732	389	310	227	389	192
Clerks and saleswomen (in stores)	321	203	457	285	300	73	355	304
Dressmakers and seamstresses (not in factory)	124	103	130	168	76	22	94	88
Housekeepers and stewardesses	86	71	266	198	102	93	160	177
Laundresses (not in laundry)	50	93	42	136	31	3	31	19
Laundry operatives	60	35	40	36	18	8	27	33
Midwives and nurses (not trained)	60	52	115	262	40	27	54	95
Musicians and teachers of music	22	21	85	100	34	13	40	47
Retail dealers	28	18	52	56	58	17	33	29
Semiskilled operatives (manfg.) (n. o. s.[1]):								
Cigar and tobacco factories	1	3			24	37	7	
Clothing industries	51	147	31	38	172	14	109	271
Food industries	4	3	39	13	153	3	78	2
Iron and steel industries	25	2	90	8	6	223	24	46
Shoe factories		50	4,691	13	335		259	29
Textile industries	227	324	135	2	232	1,533	59	1,835
Servants	304	364	456	3,427	174	79	112	364
Stenographers and typists	157	163	385	425	296	134	493	242
Teachers	132	124	374	370	195	171	195	296
Telephone operators	54	50	146	148	84	22	96	60
Trained nurses	85	54	126	223	114	13	48	63
Waitresses	49	33	65	201	50	21	43	48
All other occupations	354	342	675	668	778	1,067	708	805

[1] Not otherwise specified.

TABLE 118.—WOMEN EMPLOYED IN CERTAIN SELECTED OCCUPATIONS, FOR CITIES HAVING FROM 25,000 TO 100,000 INHABITANTS: 1920—Continued

MASSACHUSETTS—continued

OCCUPATION	Haverhill	Holyoke	Lawrence	Lynn	Malden	Medford	Newton
All occupations	8,631	9,757	15,377	14,428	5,889	4,148	6,499
Boarding and lodging house keepers	80	40	117	180	47	11	9
Bookkeepers, cashiers, and accountants	634	314	522	1,064	646	415	308
Clerks (except clerks in stores)	201	434	313	967	501	534	381
Clerks and saleswomen (in stores)	366	322	494	732	425	358	144
Dressmakers and seamstresses (not in factory)	151	110	138	304	126	121	132
Housekeepers and stewardesses	277	183	221	423	177	101	282
Laundresses (not in laundry)	47	31	19	77	53	32	106
Laundry operatives	50	40	44	119	42	20	39
Midwives and nurses (not trained)	116	130	73	208	112	76	200
Musicians and teachers of music	59	50	53	114	60	62	81
Retail dealers	39	54	101	130	46	36	31
Semiskilled operatives (manfg.) (n. o. s.[1]):							
Cigar and tobacco factories	2	6	1		12	32	1
Clothing industries	59	51	46	83	142	91	64
Food industries	12	3	8	19	64	85	4
Iron and steel industries	3	68	25	26	11	21	17
Shoe factories	4,445	1	223	4,484	77	23	3
Textile industries	121	3,772	11,008	20	156	121	574
Servants	409	441	282	770	335	273	1,900
Stenographers and typists	190	465	288	864	686	615	598
Teachers	317	448	489	520	323	197	459
Telephone operators	99	81	93	147	160	190	110
Trained nurses	138	164	127	202	98	56	213
Waitresses	49	66	58	126	72	52	136
All other occupations	767	2,483	634	2,849	1,518	626	707

MASSACHUSETTS—continued

OCCUPATION	Pittsfield	Quincy	Revere	Salem	Somerville	Taunton	Waltham
All occupations	5,171	4,030	2,326	5,575	10,733	4,323	5,031
Boarding and lodging house keepers	59	40	4	50	56	22	23
Bookkeepers, cashiers, and accountants	268	350	198	437	1,141	278	349
Clerks (except clerks in stores)	408	423	272	239	1,227	155	268
Clerks and saleswomen (in stores)	318	264	250	383	893	218	162
Dressmakers and seamstresses (not in factory)	104	85	44	118	344	75	98
Housekeepers and stewardesses	98	103	41	176	297	169	137
Laundresses (not in laundry)	48	83	6	34	54	21	96
Laundry operatives	14	29	9	54	68	38	34
Midwives and nurses (not trained)	88	99	28	81	196	93	203
Musicians and teachers of music	30	48	19	50	135	43	47
Retail dealers	34	60	24	79	116	31	21
Semiskilled operatives (manfg.) (n. o. s.[1]):							
Cigar and tobacco factories			8		11	6	2
Clothing industries	43	77	93	31	268	45	90
Food industries	3	23	117	2	470	2	4
Iron and steel industries	8	207	8	60	58	50	70
Shoe factories		286	127	904	109	14	2
Textile industries	710	2	33	667	87	1,357	406
Servants	441	364	69	502	449	322	424
Stenographers and typists	395	514	242	345	1,499	232	384
Teachers	281	278	117	284	563	225	213
Telephone operators	86	115	104	84	346	48	54
Trained nurses	209	84	12	94	144	97	133
Waitresses	43	34	27	62	139	36	56
All other occupations	1,483	462	474	839	2,063	746	1,755

[1] Not otherwise specified.

TABLE **118.**—WOMEN EMPLOYED IN CERTAIN SELECTED OCCUPATIONS, FOR CITIES HAVING FROM 25,000 TO 100,000 INHABITANTS: 1920—Continued

OCCUPATION	MICHIGAN								
	Battle Creek	Bay City	Flint	Hamtramck (village)	Highland Park	Jackson	Kalamazoo	Lansing	Muskegon
All occupations	4,254	4,127	6,912	1,509	3,420	4,573	5,672	5,085	3,321
Boarding and lodging house keepers	69	69	143	7	118	64	71	103	90
Bookkeepers, cashiers, and accountants	274	260	498	14	270	324	291	354	202
Clerks (except clerks in stores)	337	226	686	54	470	390	271	539	226
Clerks and saleswomen (in stores)	307	407	564	102	265	443	369	455	310
Dressmakers and seamstresses (not in factory)	140	168	130	32	71	131	278	122	86
Housekeepers and stewardesses	135	130	208	28	65	158	154	162	101
Laundresses (not in laundry)	60	117	89	83	17	88	109	61	47
Laundry operatives	88	27	96	50	5	44	83	81	38
Midwives and nurses (not trained)	102	105	136	8	62	96	160	116	30
Musicians and teachers of music	49	37	73		53	39	44	59	35
Retail dealers	32	77	30	17	30	36	35	31	35
Semiskilled operatives (manfg.) (n. o. s.[1]):									
Cigar and tobacco factories	18	185	33	182	2	12	3	6	6
Clothing industries	27	67	32	15	42	448	348	32	15
Food industries	266	30	24	12	10	35	25	30	36
Iron and steel industries	99	62	1,152	290	221	317	74	434	143
Shoe factories	1			1			1		
Textile industries		211	4	3	2	10	42	5	168
Servants	296	426	613	133	353	311	500	418	278
Stenographers and typists	360	328	625	24	451	448	409	649	260
Teachers	264	312	469	33	275	245	368	313	275
Telephone operators	88	98	144	12	132	112	113	116	23
Trained nurses	313	92	122	1	56	97	160	83	93
Waitresses	122	64	194	93	46	61	111	131	51
All other occupations	807	629	847	315	404	664	1,653	785	773

OCCUPATION	MICHIGAN—con.			MINNESOTA	MISSOURI			MONTANA	NEBRASKA
	Pontiac	Port Huron	Saginaw	Duluth	Joplin	St. Joseph	Springfield	Butte	Lincoln
All occupations	2,559	1,886	5,543	9,957	2,660	8,953	3,749	3,473	6,171
Boarding and lodging house keepers	50	24	116	160	127	243	72	255	105
Bookkeepers, cashiers, and accountants	177	147	411	708	193	480	222	301	531
Clerks (except clerks in stores)	263	141	369	571	55	394	259	91	308
Clerks and saleswomen (in stores)	247	232	434	1,088	275	800	354	401	674
Dressmakers and seamstresses (not in factory)	58	55	199	233	97	252	162	86	194
Housekeepers and stewardesses	60	37	150	240	136	190	99	120	141
Laundresses (not in laundry)	19	24	90	122	142	378	321	35	215
Laundry operatives	77	44	69	167	56	172	74	76	110
Midwives and nurses (not trained)	123	41	108	190	57	384	97	89	148
Musicians and teachers of music	34	31	56	118	36	92	60	54	108
Retail dealers	12	29	53	83	28	111	31	77	42
Semiskilled operatives (manfg.) (n. o. s.[1]):									
Cigar and tobacco factories	4	2	22	9	113	2	3		14
Clothing industries	10	65	228	182	94	479	280	31	177
Food industries	3	25	76	110	32	549	36	21	80
Iron and steel industries	178	36	115	16	2	6	3		13
Shoe factories				39		103			
Textile industries		103	4	296	3	8			6
Servants	260	139	593	1,267	293	771	317	461	540
Stenographers and typists	274	149	527	1,331	213	824	403	326	777
Teachers	172	158	395	769	177	469	269	356	513
Telephone operators	90	63	173	377	89	261	111	82	135
Trained nurses	27	55	145	250	48	310	102	116	170
Waitresses	66	33	87	383	72	175	66	114	153
All other occupations	355	253	1,123	1,248	322	1,500	408	381	1,017

[1] Not otherwise specified.

TABLE 118.—WOMEN EMPLOYED IN CERTAIN SELECTED OCCUPATIONS, FOR CITIES HAVING FROM 25,000 TO 100,000 INHABITANTS: 1920—Continued

| OCCUPATION | NEW HAMPSHIRE | | NEW JERSEY | | | | | | |
	Manchester	Nashua	Atlantic City	Bayonne	Clifton	East Orange	Elizabeth	Hoboken	Irvington
All occupations	13, 609	3, 907	7, 304	5, 104	2, 685	5, 699	7, 820	6, 746	1, 970
Boarding and lodging house keepers	115	29	202	48	3	83	124	173	10
Bookkeepers, cashiers, and accountants	589	211	247	264	62	209	390	327	172
Clerks (except clerks in stores)	465	113	213	506	135	848	717	578	295
Clerks and saleswomen (in stores)	510	113	489	236	42	211	387	391	131
Dressmakers and seamstresses (not in factory)	190	63	334	85	23	169	168	167	45
Housekeepers and stewardesses	298	93	307	65	24	125	133	137	32
Laundresses (not in laundry)	37	13	526	82	7	154	272	70	17
Laundry operatives	51	21	86	22	2	25	54	39	13
Midwives and nurses (not trained)	135	56	168	65	18	146	139	46	34
Musicians and teachers of music	67	15	63	37	13	85	63	29	16
Retail dealers	62	36	112	121	24	36	147	126	28
Semiskilled operatives (manfg.) (n. o. s.[1]):									
Cigar and tobacco factories	209	1		74	7	8	85	22	12
Clothing industries	70	30	78	379	68	87	472	426	107
Food industries	9		20	50	2	9	13	191	14
Iron and steel industries	178	5	3	116	3	11	542	69	35
Shoe factories	1, 824	597		1		6	3	1	4
Textile industries	5, 242	1, 305	34	554	1, 393	11	44	215	30
Servants	457	206	2, 151	292	58	1, 130	773	353	96
Stenographers and typists	367	92	206	736	180	647	1, 073	844	224
Teachers	423	178	235	400	84	625	503	398	90
Telephone operators	103	44	182	116	34	75	150	144	61
Trained nurses	204	85	85	62	13	101	157	40	10
Waitresses	95	32	871	24	3	54	60	86	13
All other occupations	1, 909	569	692	769	487	844	1, 351	1, 874	481

| OCCUPATION | NEW JERSEY—continued | | | | | | | | |
	Kearny (town)	Montclair (town)	New Bruns-wick	Orange	Passaic	Perth Amboy	Plainfield	West Hoboken (town)	West New York (town)
All occupations	2, 729	3, 600	3, 600	3, 945	7, 595	2, 850	3, 189	4, 000	2, 660
Boarding and lodging house keepers	10	37	27	15	35	26	70	5	2
Bookkeepers, cashiers, and accountants	121	84	101	128	175	127	142	154	110
Clerks (except clerks in stores)	513	201	157	466	475	153	239	277	186
Clerks and saleswomen (in stores)	68	90	146	100	208	144	158	179	155
Dressmakers and seamstresses (not in factory)	40	111	59	115	87	50	128	105	105
Housekeepers and stewardesses	31	97	75	59	62	54	69	27	26
Laundresses (not in laundry)	13	189	96	148	84	50	237	21	26
Laundry operatives	2	10	5	54	21	3	9	6	9
Midwives and nurses (not trained)	27	172	25	104	65	28	119	33	32
Musicians and teachers of music	15	50	19	25	41	13	38	16	15
Retail dealers	21	18	26	35	60	60	31	74	48
Semiskilled operatives (manfg.) (n. o. s.[1]):									
Cigar and tobacco factories	4		637	14	130	487	6	6	3
Clothing industries	26	15	53	255	544	107	106	237	133
Food industries	4		9	6	2	1	4	20	12
Iron and steel industries	58	3	113	22	18	8	36	16	7
Shoe factories	2		5					1	1
Textile industries	475	5	115	21	2, 679	2	47	1, 369	848
Servants	92	1, 454	301	893	312	223	781	141	55
Stenographers and typists	336	225	313	286	444	176	272	456	250
Teachers	129	252	158	204	365	192	198	104	90
Telephone operators	57	44	58	101	75	44	41	48	62
Trained nurses	34	73	62	106	73	52	112	16	7
Waitresses	12	90	27	43	13	16	84	13	10
All other occupations	639	380	1, 013	745	1, 627	834	262	676	468

[1] Not otherwise specified.

TABLE 118.—WOMEN EMPLOYED IN CERTAIN SELECTED OCCUPATIONS, FOR CITIES HAVING FROM 25,000 TO 100,000 INHABITANTS: 1920—Continued

OCCUPATION	NEW YORK							
	Amsterdam	Auburn	Binghamton	Elmira	Jamestown	Kingston	Mount Vernon	New Rochelle
All occupations	5,183	4,262	9,259	4,888	4,702	3,421	4,895	4,303
Boarding and lodging house keepers	35	24	108	87	71	23	17	43
Bookkeepers, cashiers, and accountants	128	256	428	295	230	137	247	188
Clerks (except clerks in stores)	89	175	423	347	265	40	503	201
Clerks and saleswomen (in stores)	156	255	607	452	352	188	203	194
Dressmakers and seamstresses (not in factory)	65	161	240	180	148	105	191	141
Housekeepers and stewardesses	46	142	175	180	86	107	97	97
Laundresses (not in laundry)	16	47	130	67	33	67	188	397
Laundry operatives	13	53	95	62	45	11	40	29
Midwives and nurses (not trained)	41	132	288	122	74	83	112	113
Musicians and teachers of music	23	44	103	57	56	26	53	47
Retail dealers	19	46	67	67	44	55	56	42
Semiskilled operatives (manfg.) (n. o. s.[1]):								
Cigar and tobacco factories			1,210	52	1	620	1	
Clothing industries	105	69	369	61	60	779	411	119
Food industries		3	67	69	19		3	2
Iron and steel industries	16	44	22	73	83		18	28
Shoe factories		296	1,541		3		1	
Textile industries	3,233	625	249	368	1,329	51	25	9
Servants	202	342	718	540	409	342	921	1,237
Stenographers and typists	162	267	509	463	329	156	519	202
Teachers	172	232	407	290	224	211	430	315
Telephone operators	39	70	152	97	72	56	81	93
Trained nurses	52	115	173	162	100	101	77	93
Waitresses	10	79	96	97	59	70	20	62
All other occupations	501	785	1,022	700	619	193	681	561

OCCUPATION	NEW YORK—continued							
	Newburgh	Niagara Falls	Poughkeepsie	Rome	Schenectady	Troy	Utica	Watertown
All occupations	3,499	3,824	4,268	2,351	8,244	11,903	12,049	3,615
Boarding and lodging house keepers	74	100	94	25	156	71	137	52
Bookkeepers, cashiers, and accountants	140	206	171	179	288	344	587	199
Clerks (except clerks in stores)	142	444	207	101	991	456	360	143
Clerks and saleswomen (in stores)	297	303	305	169	537	520	766	336
Dressmakers and seamstresses (not in factory)	97	69	153	80	216	310	350	163
Housekeepers and stewardesses	86	90	125	89	268	247	239	121
Laundresses (not in laundry)	73	61	126	47	82	88	125	61
Laundry operatives	21	32	37	42	41	83	93	48
Midwives and nurses (not trained)	53	54	114	96	166	196	314	105
Musicians and teachers of music	24	33	40	24	85	99	95	62
Retail dealers	56	55	49	31	83	118	116	46
Semiskilled operatives (manfg.) (n. o. s.[1]):								
Cigar and tobacco factories	89	2	192	1		6	9	1
Clothing industries	636	61	597	13	147	5,699	429	170
Food industries	1	104	13	2	20	6	14	8
Iron and steel industries	2	25	96	43	13	10	140	33
Shoe factories	1	2	1					
Textile industries	357	24	66	250	8	279	3,948	203
Servants	262	387	489	227	712	777	797	475
Stenographers and typists	243	418	265	132	1,134	647	722	303
Teachers	219	254	200	207	571	500	545	234
Telephone operators	64	95	84	39	143	161	206	85
Trained nurses	81	108	109	63	171	234	299	144
Waitresses	39	72	44	43	79	76	133	51
All other occupations	437	825	691	448	2,333	976	1,625	567

[1] Not otherwise specified.

TABLE 118.—WOMEN EMPLOYED IN CERTAIN SELECTED OCCUPATIONS, FOR CITIES HAVING FROM 25,000 TO 100,000 INHABITANTS: 1920—Continued

OCCUPATION	NORTH CAROLINA				OHIO				
	Asheville	Charlotte	Wilmington	Winston-Salem	Canton	East Cleveland	Hamilton	Lakewood	Lima
All occupations	3,432	6,567	4,335	9,193	6,505	2,787	3,285	3,579	3,641
Boarding and lodging house keepers	86	56	71	150	273	9	95	18	66
Bookkeepers, cashiers, and accountants	121	166	79	206	459	228	189	309	271
Clerks (except clerks in stores)	77	203	208	118	479	379	137	466	126
Clerks and saleswomen (in stores)	184	334	152	277	783	208	353	252	435
Dressmakers and seamstresses (not in factory)	93	177	125	108	128	70	84	77	93
Housekeepers and stewardesses	62	76	52	61	222	35	100	70	94
Laundresses (not in laundry)	434	1,154	1,146	481	48	11	51	79	66
Laundry operatives	117	128	79	86	84	1	30	2	45
Midwives and nurses (not trained)	86	133	120	86	99	53	18	71	66
Musicians and teachers of music	32	25	15	27	58	42	29	63	44
Retail dealers	14	25	25	31	79	20	51	28	27
Semiskilled operatives (manfg.) (n. o. s.[1]):									
Cigar and tobacco factories		5		2,463	2		61	4	883
Clothing industries	19	102	5	18	133	37	28	40	60
Food industries	4	7	5	7	26	4	13	16	58
Iron and steel industries	2	5	2	2	410	16	91	28	11
Shoe factories							1	1	
Textile industries	77	689	191	533	3	10	244	5	2
Servants	1,051	1,384	1,069	649	503	319	292	348	289
Stenographers and typists	155	573	272	277	680	468	234	566	273
Teachers	205	264	201	197	366	311	223	393	237
Telephone operators	62	115	42	31	189	72	80	152	75
Trained nurses	203	186	113	80	131	51	59	56	85
Waitresses	71	60	36	19	122	14	41	16	43
All other occupations	277	700	327	3,286	1,228	429	781	519	292

OCCUPATION	OHIO—continued								
	Lorain	Mansfield	Marion	Newark	Portsmouth	Springfield	Steubenville	Warren	Zanesville
All occupations	1,508	2,605	2,128	2,346	3,037	5,769	1,941	2,004	2,765
Boarding and lodging house keepers	56	41	36	39	64	99	77	29	49
Bookkeepers, cashiers, and accountants	142	161	189	219	169	300	129	138	220
Clerks (except clerks in stores)	75	111	87	97	151	663	104	141	71
Clerks and saleswomen (in stores)	264	247	264	287	259	432	255	146	251
Dressmakers and seamstresses (not in factory)	21	82	101	90	72	181	55	55	115
Housekeepers and stewardesses	47	75	68	75	108	162	51	59	75
Laundresses (not in laundry)	23	37	62	78	115	180	37	41	78
Laundry operatives	31	24	29	36	45	55	30	26	46
Midwives and nurses (not trained)	24	49	52	51	31	97	44	42	49
Musicians and teachers of music	20	25	20	39	32	76	20	32	39
Retail dealers	37	20	18	29	19	70	27	9	21
Semiskilled operatives (manfg.) (n. o. s.[1]):									
Cigar and tobacco factories		185	75	155		43	1		31
Clothing industries	20	75	29	65	41	70	11	9	213
Food industries		53	19	7		5	3	3	36
Iron and steel industries	33	6	10	23	7	100	17	38	14
Shoe factories		1		40	960	3			1
Textile industries	25	35	226	6	25				1
Servants	129	244	200	179	212	582	256	170	286
Stenographers and typists	139	262	144	167	209	480	143	248	153
Teachers	169	159	170	158	187	344	156	176	148
Telephone operators	21	76	20	28	46	150	46	32	63
Trained nurses	20	36	8	37	20	108	52	43	62
Waitresses	37	51	57	32	37	41	28	40	17
All other occupations	175	550	244	409	228	1,528	399	527	726

[1] Not otherwise specified.

6436°—29——16

TABLE 118.—WOMEN EMPLOYED IN CERTAIN SELECTED OCCUPATIONS, FOR CITIES HAVING FROM 25,000 TO 100,000 INHABITANTS: 1920—Continued

OCCUPATION	OKLAHOMA			PENNSYLVANIA				
	Muskogee	Oklahoma City	Tulsa	Allentown	Altoona	Bethlehem	Chester	Easton
All occupations	2,807	10,976	7,794	7,609	4,823	3,732	4,563	3,474
Boarding and lodging house keepers	53	291	318	66	79	73	109	68
Bookkeepers, cashiers, and accountants	164	734	512	254	323	100	234	200
Clerks (except clerks in stores)	164	814	463	288	575	368	333	157
Clerks and saleswomen (in stores)	264	862	593	663	722	208	270	347
Dressmakers and seamstresses (not in factory)	108	287	161	191	141	102	85	110
Housekeepers and stewardesses	64	186	180	170	168	106	137	105
Laundresses (not in laundry)	287	499	364	46	115	45	156	61
Laundry operatives	63	256	128	27	34	22	36	28
Midwives and nurses (not trained)	55	180	142	45	64	58	65	82
Musicians and teachers of music	29	143	82	47	56	19	23	28
Retail dealers	33	64	71	84	63	32	76	54
Semiskilled operatives (manfg.) (n. o. s.[1]):								
Cigar and tobacco factories				964		516	34	1
Clothing industries	19	132	44	219	107	21	7	94
Food industries	15	206	15	9	14		6	8
Iron and steel industries		9	1	36	13	25	52	18
Shoe factories				210	3			
Textile industries	3	10	2	1,971	478	663	1,161	881
Servants	401	1,373	1,457	626	502	428	588	302
Stenographers and typists	342	1,506	1,112	451	279	287	352	217
Teachers	228	669	528	310	338	203	201	157
Telephone operators	123	506	379	104	108	46	74	49
Trained nurses	58	243	184	150	76	27	68	56
Waitresses	51	359	273	83	94	52	50	33
All other occupations	283	1,647	785	595	474	328	446	328

OCCUPATION	PENNSYLVANIA—continued							
	Erie	Harrisburg	Hazleton	Johnstown	Lancaster	McKeesport	New Castle	Norristown Borough
All occupations	7,538	7,759	2,817	4,229	7,226	2,753	2,788	3,715
Boarding and lodging house keepers	136	156	36	101	83	98	75	25
Bookkeepers, cashiers, and accountants	388	314	151	229	294	157	241	147
Clerks (except clerks in stores)	663	676	85	154	200	197	197	169
Clerks and saleswomen (in stores)	823	693	283	764	556	446	403	176
Dressmakers and seamstresses (not in factory)	258	239	75	108	255	69	89	165
Housekeepers and stewardesses	157	349	63	110	141	63	70	105
Laundresses (not in laundry)	124	110	35	76	101	57	61	71
Laundry operatives	95	128	27	38	62	3	24	101
Midwives and nurses (not trained)	144	108	32	86	77	32	47	41
Musicians and teachers of music	89	66	21	39	59	32	28	30
Retail dealers	100	82	29	47	70	48	44	75
Semiskilled operatives (manfg.) (n. o. s.[1]):								
Cigar and tobacco factories	6	440		66	983			222
Clothing industries	206	173	231	59	92	19	40	159
Food industries	27	41	3	27	307	27	1	7
Iron and steel industries	197	41		8	127	50	91	28
Shoe factories		135	1					
Textile industries	155	331	825	51	1,077		34	698
Servants	970	1,156	286	564	593	339	279	390
Stenographers and typists	762	884	106	476	319	360	210	244
Teachers	447	400	231	452	288	261	224	152
Telephone operators	123	141	42	121	94	79	101	53
Trained nurses	294	135	58	186	115	84	71	136
Waitresses	81	127	15	81	63	29	49	96
All other occupations	1,293	834	182	386	1,270	303	409	425

[1] Not otherwise specified.

TABLE **118.**—WOMEN EMPLOYED IN CERTAIN SELECTED OCCUPATIONS, FOR CITIES HAVING FROM 25,000 TO 100,000 INHABITANTS: 1920—Continued

OCCUPATION	PENNSYLVANIA—contd.			RHODE ISLAND			
	Wilkes-Barre	Williamsport	York	Cranston	Newport	Pawtucket	Woonsocket
All occupations	6, 563	4, 136	5, 709	2, 828	2, 843	9, 293	6, 483
Boarding and lodging house keepers	59	78	77	5	69	68	40
Bookkeepers, cashiers, and accountants	371	160	117	198	219	363	225
Clerks (except clerks in stores)	257	217	179	200	83	391	169
Clerks and saleswomen (in stores)	868	334	413	119	264	397	284
Dressmakers and seamstresses (not in factory)	235	149	159	84	160	119	85
Housekeepers and stewardesses	159	154	126	149	125	183	123
Laundresses (not in laundry)	136	74	154	15	164	14	16
Laundry operatives	49	32	46	50	65	39	4
Midwives and nurses (not trained)	110	98	59	83	86	53	29
Musicians and teachers of music	53	40	47	24	37	52	41
Retail dealers	89	37	46	24	35	64	22
Semiskilled operatives (manfg.) (n. o. s.[1]):							
Cigar and tobacco factories	20		845			3	1
Clothing industries	130	64	259	7	20	55	77
Food industries	110	24	88	7	45	4	3
Iron and steel industries	53	25	178	62	8	72	51
Shoe factories		60				6	1
Textile industries	1, 143	444	616	561	2	5, 279	3, 169
Servants	850	414	455	284	532	284	177
Stenographers and typists	409	309	296	252	166	345	165
Teachers	411	178	196	116	189	349	253
Telephone operators	135	61	50	34	80	118	44
Trained nurses	184	66	72	43	110	77	32
Waitresses	94	36	38	24	58	43	25
All other occupations	638	1, 082	1, 193	487	326	915	1, 442

OCCUPATION	SOUTH CAROLINA		SOUTH DA-KOTA	TENNESSEE		TEXAS		
	Charleston	Columbia	Sioux Falls	Chattanooga	Knoxville	Austin	Beaumont	El Paso
All occupations	10, 319	4, 992	2, 645	8, 014	8, 645	4, 013	4, 168	6, 914
Boarding and lodging house keepers	118	146	31	197	144	100	129	113
Bookkeepers, cashiers, and accountants	187	106	207	360	307	113	136	332
Clerks (except clerks in stores)	238	130	105	357	157	151	96	306
Clerks and saleswomen (in stores)	365	225	305	432	575	270	341	646
Dressmakers and seamstresses (not in factory)	558	151	75	207	237	161	149	239
Housekeepers and stewardesses	92	56	54	83	119	77	46	126
Laundresses (not in laundry)	2, 822	1, 058	29	1, 225	888	665	737	504
Laundry operatives	113	105	61	172	151	71	141	196
Midwives and nurses (not trained)	239	147	59	107	129	145	56	101
Musicians and teachers of music	62	23	48	46	85	46	46	59
Retail dealers	134	49	23	53	38	39	51	136
Semiskilled operatives (manfg.) (n. o. s.[1]):								
Cigar and tobacco factories	282		2				1	20
Clothing industries	87	21	30	149	390	29	22	105
Food industries	26	1	99	112	51	12	3	40
Iron and steel industries	12			25	11	1	6	5
Shoe factories				2	1			
Textile industries	152	297	2	465	1, 729		10	4
Servants	2, 643	1, 121	234	1, 745	1, 159	691	1, 120	1, 653
Stenographers and typists	583	358	347	598	521	306	279	649
Teachers	410	253	247	328	414	487	236	423
Telephone operators	84	67	82	144	128	66	77	177
Trained nurses	193	259	94	164	146	89	59	162
Waitresses	51	30	87	127	51	61	87	176
All other occupations	868	389	424	916	1, 214	433	340	742

[1] Not otherwise specified.

TABLE 118.—WOMEN EMPLOYED IN CERTAIN SELECTED OCCUPATIONS, FOR CITIES HAVING FROM 25,000 TO 100,000 INHABITANTS: 1920—Continued

OCCUPATION	TEXAS—contd.			UTAH	VIRGINIA				
	Galveston	Waco	Wichita Falls	Ogden	Lynchburg	Newport News	Petersburg	Portsmouth	Roanoke
All occupations	4,722	3,723	2,845	2,233	5,183	3,198	4,885	5,342	4,550
Boarding and lodging house keepers	306	78	107	39	43	109	29	65	96
Bookkeepers, cashiers, and accountants	122	161	189	148	140	143	138	171	219
Clerks (except clerks in stores)	215	102	138	90	112	160	69	495	337
Clerks and saleswomen (in stores)	263	394	284	283	317	185	170	268	366
Dressmakers and seamstresses (not in factory)	227	129	42	72	96	61	106	143	111
Housekeepers and stewardesses	86	51	45	64	49	51	46	65	61
Laundresses (not in laundry)	726	474	152	21	608	554	680	1,241	482
Laundry operatives	101	114	49	81	91	143	64	90	49
Midwives and nurses (not trained)	100	67	36	67	67	37	66	45	83
Musicians and teachers of music	44	60	22	37	34	36	24	35	55
Retail dealers	58	36	23	25	32	26	33	55	19
Semiskilled operatives (manfg.) (n. o. s.[1]):									
Cigar and tobacco factories	1	1	----	5	267	1	799	4	2
Clothing industries	77	72	14	68	757	8	25	36	154
Food industries	22	24	5	80	38	----	105	77	15
Iron and steel industries	----	5	3	2	6	11	----	4	9
Shoe factories	----	----	2	----	277	----	----	----	1
Textile industries	2	16	----	38	192	3	14	85	267
Servants	977	687	542	153	900	925	731	1,218	832
Stenographers and typists	344	262	330	268	311	234	165	303	385
Teachers	269	318	135	226	225	134	198	276	206
Telephone operators	101	94	97	70	58	36	36	57	75
Trained nurses	99	24	49	60	96	64	69	73	164
Waitresses	64	62	118	43	45	64	22	62	35
All other occupations	518	492	463	293	422	213	1,296	474	437

OCCUPATION	WASHINGTON			WEST VIRGINIA			
	Bellingham	Everett	Tacoma	Charleston	Clarksburg	Huntington	Wheeling
All occupations	1,965	2,115	8,148	3,794	1,975	3,991	5,153
Boarding and lodging house keepers	43	80	164	104	63	71	58
Bookkeepers, cashiers, and accountants	136	165	553	196	107	164	304
Clerks (except clerks in stores)	50	65	427	259	61	142	254
Clerks and saleswomen (in stores)	237	219	955	344	233	383	636
Dressmakers and seamstresses (not in factory)	62	83	306	113	65	150	146
Housekeepers and stewardesses	50	68	265	102	53	72	130
Laundresses (not in laundry)	18	26	72	219	95	226	109
Laundry operatives	45	71	223	76	34	63	62
Midwives and nurses (not trained)	64	70	219	87	54	89	110
Musicians and teachers of music	39	43	152	34	27	38	42
Retail dealers	27	39	131	35	28	30	64
Semiskilled operatives (manfg.) (n. o. s.[1]):							
Cigar and tobacco factories	1	----	4	----	4	207	166
Clothing industries	16	18	143	59	14	103	95
Food industries	32	32	181	2	3	6	29
Iron and steel industries	1	----	11	33	20	8	41
Shoe factories	1	----	4	----	----	17	----
Textile industries	1	2	5	29	----	4	10
Servants	191	226	728	763	256	580	740
Stenographers and typists	146	167	830	465	184	377	447
Teachers	320	243	655	247	204	321	367
Telephone operators	44	37	262	107	61	83	135
Trained nurses	77	68	274	80	76	125	144
Waitresses	81	78	298	36	18	63	35
All other occupations	283	315	1,286	404	317	669	1,029

[1] Not otherwise specified.

TABLE **118.**—WOMEN EMPLOYED IN CERTAIN SELECTED OCCUPATIONS, FOR CITIES HAVING FROM 25,000 TO 100,000 INHABITANTS: 1920—Continued

OCCUPATION	Green Bay	Kenosha	La Crosse	Madison	Oshkosh	Racine	Sheboygan	Superior
	WISCONSIN							
All occupations	3,116	3,053	3,470	4,880	3,508	5,252	2,658	3,002
Boarding and lodging house keepers	28	44	54	95	34	112	13	67
Bookkeepers, cashiers and accountants	218	145	134	267	174	291	175	198
Clerks (except clerks in stores)	96	251	134	393	104	451	102	130
Clerks and saleswomen (in stores)	308	222	260	371	342	354	327	327
Dressmakers and seamstresses (not in factory)	123	49	116	139	103	116	83	86
Housekeepers and stewardesses	57	64	76	131	86	97	33	96
Laundresses (not in laundry)	119	27	60	91	50	60	46	20
Laundry operatives	20	44	42	51	29	62	14	83
Midwives and nurses (not trained)	76	39	26	80	78	72	22	73
Musicians and teachers of music	43	26	38	82	37	58	18	40
Retail dealers	26	29	28	28	39	57	26	52
Semiskilled operatives (manfg.) (n. o. s.[1]):								
Cigar and tobacco factories	3	2	70	54	12	6	3	6
Clothing industries	62	142	188	39	339	332	139	34
Food industries	63	4	112	46	51	55	8	12
Iron and steel industries	4	151	55	19	12	176	18	5
Shoe factories		10	10	87		181	60	1
Textile industries	19	477	119	2	93	20	174	10
Servants	439	230	328	593	349	417	205	351
Stenographers and typists	267	233	247	666	221	614	190	269
Teachers	265	216	278	337	298	335	196	479
Telephone operators	98	68	56	139	70	106	39	83
Trained nurses	85	57	183	124	97	87	41	66
Waitresses	79	66	53	115	44	79	19	132
All other occupations	618	457	803	931	846	1,114	707	382

[1] Not otherwise specified.

TABLE 119.—WOMEN 16 YEARS OF AGE AND OVER ENGAGED IN GAINFUL
NATIVITY, MARITAL CONDITION, AND

	DIVISION AND STATE	ALL CLASSES		RACE AND NATIVITY: 1920				
				Native white		Foreign-born white	Negro	All other
		1920	1910	Native parentage	Foreign or mixed parentage			
1	UNITED STATES	8,202,901	7,438,686	3,596,397	2,042,804	1,102,697	1,445,935	15,068
	GEOGRAPHIC DIVISIONS:							
2	New England	846,244	749,308	276,850	319,283	235,944	13,915	252
3	Middle Atlantic	2,063,007	1,759,218	819,665	679,431	447,418	115,867	626
4	East North Central	1,535,641	1,239,353	746,036	513,449	203,396	72,066	694
5	West North Central	760,254	668,995	403,679	248,123	66,593	41,312	547
6	South Atlantic	1,151,407	1,191,755	493,943	50,405	23,477	582,824	758
7	East South Central	632,866	793,970	252,161	19,034	4,426	357,106	139
8	West South Central	608,336	622,391	288,975	39,408	27,246	251,424	1,283
9	Mountain	174,123	136,420	96,579	46,675	22,920	3,602	4,347
10	Pacific	431,023	277,276	218,509	126,996	71,277	7,819	6,422
	NEW ENGLAND:							
11	Maine	64,113	61,566	37,620	14,481	11,752	172	88
12	New Hampshire	48,778	46,803	20,483	15,041	13,173	72	9
13	Vermont	26,557	27,710	16,669	6,797	3,021	67	3
14	Massachusetts	489,146	430,728	138,508	193,051	149,398	8,084	105
15	Rhode Island	76,469	67,213	18,730	32,677	23,325	1,719	18
16	Connecticut	141,181	115,288	44,840	57,236	35,275	3,801	29
	MIDDLE ATLANTIC:							
17	New York	1,114,831	957,949	361,022	397,775	306,460	49,046	528
18	New Jersey	284,162	228,721	101,278	100,491	60,905	21,446	42
19	Pennsylvania	664,014	572,548	357,365	181,165	80,053	45,375	56
	EAST NORTH CENTRAL:							
20	Ohio	407,081	335,772	241,261	101,677	39,718	24,393	32
21	Indiana	180,902	149,726	134,186	28,389	6,778	11,531	18
22	Illinois	527,875	416,758	201,591	202,854	94,461	28,888	81
23	Michigan	242,120	181,402	105,682	89,502	40,012	6,648	276
24	Wisconsin	177,663	155,695	63,316	91,027	22,427	606	287
	WEST NORTH CENTRAL:							
25	Minnesota	162,323	141,948	48,205	87,604	25,066	1,255	193
26	Iowa	139,681	127,906	84,270	43,920	9,208	2,271	12
27	Missouri	238,921	203,235	146,185	50,270	13,158	29,276	32
28	North Dakota	27,727	27,623	8,583	13,967	5,065	45	67
29	South Dakota	29,269	27,458	13,527	12,176	3,333	94	139
30	Nebraska	70,869	61,864	38,846	23,487	6,618	1,866	52
31	Kansas	91,464	78,961	64,063	16,699	4,145	6,505	52
	SOUTH ATLANTIC:							
32	Delaware	17,648	16,643	9,282	2,655	1,209	4,502	------
33	Maryland	133,176	122,449	64,013	20,325	8,334	40,489	15
34	District of Columbia	92,027	52,489	48,357	11,480	3,876	28,295	19
35	Virginia	150,648	154,025	71,466	3,454	1,627	74,068	33
36	West Virginia	55,987	50,846	44,734	3,842	1,540	5,869	2
37	North Carolina	181,480	220,007	93,089	797	542	86,413	639
38	South Carolina	179,547	216,963	51,704	983	374	126,464	22
39	Georgia	258,572	293,055	86,550	2,485	1,188	168,335	14
40	Florida	82,322	65,333	24,748	4,384	4,787	48,389	14.
	EAST SOUTH CENTRAL:							
41	Kentucky	127,289	136,757	76,956	12,494	1,947	35,877	15
42	Tennessee	142,941	153,377	74,953	3,123	1,050	63,811	4
43	Alabama	193,315	253,744	63,480	2,206	901	126,706	22
44	Mississippi	169,321	250,092	36,772	1,211	528	130,712	98
	WEST SOUTH CENTRAL:							
45	Arkansas	99,762	129,652	44,221	2,307	934	52,294	6
46	Louisiana	142,380	156,707	41,917	8,294	2,728	89,395	46
47	Oklahoma	88,692	67,525	66,313	5,421	1,628	14,238	1,092
48	Texas	277,502	268,507	136,524	23,386	21,956	95,497	139
	MOUNTAIN:							
49	Montana	28,041	18,535	12,999	10,227	4,469	205	141
50	Idaho	17,322	12,764	11,172	4,484	1,499	79	88
51	Wyoming	9,307	5,902	5,760	2,351	946	205	45
52	Colorado	61,644	52,460	37,176	15,859	6,612	1,912	85
53	New Mexico	14,475	14,215	9,893	1,632	1,160	301	1,489
54	Arizona	17,485	10,213	7,567	2,660	4,571	670	2,017
55	Utah	21,548	18,007	9,960	8,210	3,105	154	119
56	Nevada	4,301	4,324	2,052	1,252	558	76	363
	PACIFIC:							
57	Washington	92,086	65,084	46,831	28,421	14,777	918	1,139
58	Oregon	54,118	39,938	32,652	14,649	6,179	315	323
59	California	284,819	172,254	139,026	83,926	50,321	6,586	4,960

OCCUPATIONS IN 1920 AND 1910, WITH DISTRIBUTION FOR 1920 BY RACE AND AGE, FOR DIVISIONS AND STATES

MARITAL CONDITION: 1920		AGE: 1920							
Married	Single, widowed, divorced, or unknown	16 and 17 years	18 and 19 years	20 to 24 years	25 to 44 years	45 to 64 years	65 years and over	Not reported	
1,920,281	6,282,620	609,192	802,235	1,809,075	3,417,373	1,352,479	196,900	15,647	1
175,568	670,676	59,700	77,197	185,147	355,609	147,646	20,023	922	2
348,128	1,714,879	188,580	220,958	473,555	823,751	313,107	40,750	2,306	3
282,285	1,253,356	119,488	168,758	357,045	615,258	238,656	34,130	2,306	4
137,368	622,886	44,905	77,263	189,619	310,982	118,688	17,092	1,705	5
394,664	756,743	84,799	103,386	237,687	492,344	196,250	33,930	3,011	6
225,222	407,644	44,882	52,351	118,686	271,196	121,413	22,901	1,437	7
201,013	407,323	42,125	56,025	127,585	265,645	100,006	14,747	2,203	8
43,152	130,971	7,876	15,253	37,941	77,114	31,578	3,843	518	9
112,881	318,142	16,837	31,044	81,810	205,474	85,135	9,484	1,239	10
16,288	47,825	3,580	5,430	13,504	25,277	13,493	2,721	108	11
13,308	35,470	3,135	4,123	10,015	19,653	9,902	1,853	97	12
6,011	20,546	1,517	2,330	5,341	10,029	6,031	1,267	42	13
96,496	392,650	32,083	43,119	106,596	212,130	84,869	9,937	412	14
15,530	60,939	6,958	7,404	16,777	31,729	12,109	1,445	47	15
27,935	113,246	12,427	14,791	32,914	56,791	21,242	2,800	216	16
194,305	920,526	92,714	112,512	257,234	458,725	171,254	21,203	1,189	17
50,451	233,711	29,740	32,496	66,294	110,389	40,053	4,890	300	18
103,372	560,642	66,126	75,950	150,027	254,637	101,800	14,657	817	19
76,655	330,426	26,685	44,109	90,712	166,130	68,458	10,612	375	20
34,848	146,054	14,339	19,209	39,031	69,255	33,006	5,680	382	21
96,448	431,427	43,994	55,874	122,992	219,386	75,816	8,815	998	22
52,097	190,023	19,862	27,390	56,894	95,486	36,729	5,416	343	23
22,237	155,426	14,608	22,176	47,416	65,001	24,647	3,607	208	24
20,170	142,153	9,946	17,812	46,235	65,539	19,989	2,554	248	25
24,200	115,481	7,161	13,752	35,559	56,497	23,108	3,375	229	26
50,414	188,507	16,521	22,391	49,944	100,685	42,170	6,666	544	27
3,910	23,817	1,446	3,383	8,746	10,262	3,377	413	100	28
5,231	24,038	1,329	3,129	8,502	11,659	3,993	503	154	29
13,967	56,902	3,911	7,751	18,557	29,118	10,171	1,185	176	30
19,476	71,988	4,591	9,045	22,076	37,222	15,880	2,396	254	31
4,413	13,235	1,315	1,659	3,562	7,125	3,338	585	64	32
32,262	100,914	11,400	12,926	26,271	54,448	24,130	3,880	121	33
22,871	69,156	2,823	5,609	20,002	45,853	15,469	1,874	397	34
41,555	109,093	9,529	13,415	31,756	61,226	28,388	5,803	531	35
10,499	45,488	4,096	6,180	13,026	21,306	9,214	2,022	143	36
60,112	120,529	16,200	18,391	39,766	71,501	29,285	5,808	529	37
79,526	100,021	15,387	16,731	36,669	77,240	28,366	4,867	287	38
107,275	151,297	19,800	22,528	51,762	113,817	43,214	6,956	495	39
35,312	47,010	4,249	5,947	14,873	39,828	14,846	2,135	444	40
31,280	96,009	7,199	9,750	22,999	52,293	28,723	6,078	247	41
44,262	98,679	9,204	11,869	27,675	61,660	26,879	5,297	357	42
72,733	120,582	15,978	17,017	36,085	82,437	35,124	6,285	389	43
76,947	92,374	12,501	13,715	31,927	74,806	30,687	5,241	444	44
36,919	62,843	7,927	9,112	18,990	42,933	17,913	2,619	268	45
50,112	92,268	9,704	11,830	26,851	63,182	25,978	4,263	572	46
26,953	61,739	5,241	9,168	20,904	37,898	13,670	1,570	241	47
87,029	190,473	19,253	25,915	60,840	121,632	42,445	6,295	1,122	48
6,508	21,533	1,063	2,455	6,274	13,015	4,674	480	80	49
4,408	12,914	762	1,684	4,321	7,256	2,954	320	25	50
2,666	6,641	371	752	2,077	4,426	1,439	184	58	51
14,462	47,182	2,796	4,871	12,575	27,256	12,488	1,499	159	52
3,715	10,760	700	1,207	2,859	6,228	3,007	443	31	53
6,174	11,311	761	1,321	3,363	8,719	2,878	332	111	54
3,779	17,769	1,309	2,719	5,737	8,111	3,195	436	41	55
1,440	2,861	114	244	735	2,103	943	149	13	56
24,172	67,914	3,991	7,723	19,839	42,543	16,031	1,629	330	57
15,155	38,963	2,258	4,453	11,201	24,939	10,111	1,072	84	58
73,554	211,265	10,588	18,868	50,770	137,992	58,993	6,783	825	59

TABLE 120.—PERCENTAGE OF WOMEN ENGAGED IN ALL OCCUPATIONS AND IN NONAGRICULTURAL PURSUITS, FOR DIVISIONS AND STATES: 1920, 1910, AND 1900

DIVISION AND STATE	WOMEN 16 YEARS OF AGE AND OVER							
	Total number: 1920	Engaged in gainful occupations				Per cent engaged in nonagricultural pursuits		
		Number: 1920	Per cent					
			1920	1910	1900	1920	1910	1900
UNITED STATES	34,241,749	8,202,901	24.0	25.5	20.6	21.3	20.7	17.3
GEOGRAPHIC DIVISIONS:								
New England	2,621,950	846,244	32.3	31.9	27.8	32.0	31.5	27.3
Middle Atlantic	7,579,969	2,063,007	27.2	26.8	22.6	26.9	26.4	22.1
East North Central	7,147,542	1,535,641	21.5	20.6	16.8	20.8	19.6	15.8
West North Central	4,045,923	760,254	18.8	18.6	15.3	17.7	17.0	13.9
South Atlantic	4,280,480	1,151,407	26.9	32.5	25.0	19.7	19.2	16.8
East South Central	2,701,751	632,866	23.4	31.8	23.1	14.2	14.6	12.4
West South Central	3,021,712	608,336	20.1	25.2	17.9	13.8	13.0	10.1
Mountain	971,112	174,123	17.9	18.7	15.5	16.6	17.0	14.0
Pacific	1,871,310	431,023	23.0	21.5	17.6	22.2	20.4	16.4
NEW ENGLAND:								
Maine	265,315	64,113	24.2	23.9	20.5	23.4	22.9	19.2
New Hampshire	157,778	48,778	30.9	30.3	26.6	30.3	29.4	25.6
Vermont	121,006	26,557	21.9	22.7	18.4	21.0	21.6	17.2
Massachusetts	1,395,044	489,146	35.1	35.0	30.8	34.9	34.7	30.6
Rhode Island	214,279	76,469	35.7	34.9	31.4	35.6	34.7	31.2
Connecticut	468,528	141,181	30.1	29.7	26.2	29.8	29.2	25.8
MIDDLE ATLANTIC:								
New York	3,688,676	1,114,831	30.2	29.8	25.0	30.0	29.4	24.5
New Jersey	1,067,476	284,162	26.6	26.5	22.4	26.4	26.2	22.1
Pennsylvania	2,823,817	664,014	23.5	23.1	19.5	23.2	22.6	19.0
EAST NORTH CENTRAL:								
Ohio	1,946,617	407,081	20.9	20.6	16.9	20.4	19.9	15.8
Indiana	997,347	180,902	18.1	16.6	13.8	17.4	15.7	12.6
Illinois	2,189,680	527,875	24.1	22.5	18.2	23.7	21.9	17.4
Michigan	1,169,258	242,120	20.7	19.7	16.5	20.0	18.6	15.4
Wisconsin	844,640	177,663	21.0	21.3	17.4	19.8	19.3	16.1
WEST NORTH CENTRAL:								
Minnesota	752,838	162,323	21.6	22.9	18.7	20.3	21.0	17.4
Iowa	798,958	139,681	17.5	17.9	15.1	16.6	16.6	13.9
Missouri	1,155,999	238,921	20.7	19.0	15.4	19.5	17.6	13.8
North Dakota	174,561	27,727	15.8	18.4	17.0	14.1	15.7	14.9
South Dakota	184,915	29,269	15.8	16.9	13.7	14.3	14.1	11.9
Nebraska	407,323	70,869	17.4	17.2	14.8	16.4	15.8	13.4
Kansas	570,939	91,464	16.0	15.1	12.3	15.1	13.9	10.9
SOUTH ATLANTIC:								
Delaware	75,327	17,648	23.4	24.5	19.8	22.8	23.2	19.1
Maryland	494,321	133,176	26.9	27.8	23.3	26.3	26.8	22.5
District of Columbia	185,640	92,027	49.6	39.8	37.0	49.6	39.7	37.0
Virginia	707,824	150,648	21.3	24.6	20.6	18.9	19.9	17.0
West Virginia	417,841	55,987	13.4	14.7	10.6	12.1	12.5	8.7
North Carolina	741,844	181,480	24.5	34.3	23.3	15.8	15.5	13.5
South Carolina	485,225	179,547	37.0	49.9	37.9	15.7	16.0	15.2
Georgia	868,749	258,572	29.8	38.5	28.8	17.9	17.7	17.0
Florida	303,709	82,322	27.1	29.9	22.8	22.8	20.9	15.8
EAST SOUTH CENTRAL:								
Kentucky	747,136	127,289	17.0	19.5	15.5	14.7	16.0	12.9
Tennessee	725,417	142,941	19.7	23.2	17.5	15.6	15.8	13.0
Alabama	695,111	193,315	27.8	40.8	30.4	14.2	14.0	12.3
Mississippi	534,087	169,321	31.7	48.6	33.4	11.4	12.0	10.8
WEST SOUTH CENTRAL:								
Arkansas	506,193	99,762	19.7	29.5	17.7	9.6	10.5	8.0
Louisiana	551,425	142,380	25.8	32.2	27.8	17.6	17.9	14.7
Oklahoma	573,732	88,692	15.5	15.3	9.9	12.5	10.4	6.4
Texas	1,390,362	277,502	20.0	24.5	15.1	14.4	12.8	9.6
MOUNTAIN:								
Montana	156,262	28,041	17.9	19.3	16.9	16.5	17.6	15.9
Idaho	119,285	17,322	14.5	15.2	11.5	13.4	13.4	9.7
Wyoming	52,799	9,307	17.6	17.3	14.5	16.1	15.7	13.4
Colorado	299,744	61,646	20.6	21.1	17.2	19.6	19.6	16.5
New Mexico	99,819	14,475	14.5	15.9	11.1	12.8	12.5	9.6
Arizona	92,850	17,485	18.8	19.5	20.3	16.0	18.1	14.1
Utah	129,124	21,548	16.7	17.3	13.6	16.0	16.5	12.3
Nevada	21,229	4,301	20.3	21.0	17.6	19.4	20.0	16.4
PACIFIC:								
Washington	427,710	92,086	21.5	20.0	15.3	20.7	18.9	13.9
Oregon	255,562	54,118	21.2	20.2	15.6	20.3	18.9	14.3
California	1,188,038	284,819	24.0	22.4	18.7	23.2	21.5	17.6

TABLE 121.—PERCENTAGE OF NATIVE WHITE WOMEN OF NATIVE PARENTAGE ENGAGED IN ALL OCCUPATIONS AND IN NONAGRICULTURAL PURSUITS, FOR DIVISIONS AND STATES: 1920, 1910, AND 1900

DIVISION AND STATE	NATIVE WHITE WOMEN OF NATIVE PARENTAGE 16 YEARS OF AGE AND OVER								
	Total number: 1920	Engaged in gainful occupations					Per cent engaged in nonagricultural pursuits		
		Number: 1920	Per cent						
			1920	1910	1900		1920	1910	1900
UNITED STATES	17,969,950	3,596,397	20.0	18.9	14.6		18.3	15.9	12.4
GEOGRAPHIC DIVISIONS:									
New England	983,854	276,850	28.1	25.3	20.3		27.6	24.6	19.4
Middle Atlantic	3,207,246	819,665	25.6	22.7	18.0		25.1	22.0	17.3
East North Central	3,660,289	746,036	20.4	18.0	14.3		19.7	17.2	13.2
West North Central	2,189,038	403,679	18.4	16.8	13.2		17.5	15.6	11.8
South Atlantic	2,659,052	493,943	18.6	19.2	14.1		15.2	12.3	9.8
East South Central	1,795,743	252,161	14.0	16.2	11.1		10.0	8.6	6.4
West South Central	1,980,052	288,975	14.6	15.0	9.7		11.3	8.6	5.6
Mountain	545,622	96,579	17.7	17.4	13.9		16.6	15.6	12.8
Pacific	949,054	218,509	23.0	20.1	15.8		22.3	19.2	14.6
NEW ENGLAND:									
Maine	172,531	37,620	21.8	21.2	17.9		20.8	20.0	16.3
New Hampshire	81,309	20,483	25.2	24.2	20.4		24.2	22.8	18.8
Vermont	76,673	16,669	21.7	21.5	16.9		20.6	20.1	15.4
Massachusetts	437,325	138,508	31.7	28.2	22.2		31.5	27.8	21.9
Rhode Island	58,967	18,730	31.8	27.5	21.9		31.5	27.1	21.6
Connecticut	157,049	44,840	28.6	24.0	19.2		28.1	23.3	18.4
MIDDLE ATLANTIC:									
New York	1,249,547	361,022	28.9	24.9	19.3		28.5	24.2	18.5
New Jersey	404,287	101,278	25.1	21.9	16.7		24.8	21.4	16.3
Pennsylvania	1,553,412	357,365	23.0	21.1	17.3		22.5	20.4	16.6
EAST NORTH CENTRAL:									
Ohio	1,198,745	241,261	20.1	18.6	14.7		19.5	17.7	13.5
Indiana	769,870	134,186	17.4	15.3	12.3		16.7	14.4	11.1
Illinois	943,828	201,591	21.4	18.5	14.8		20.8	17.7	13.7
Michigan	489,178	105,682	21.6	18.3	14.9		21.0	17.4	13.6
Wisconsin	258,668	63,316	24.5	23.1	17.2		23.7	21.8	16.2
WEST NORTH CENTRAL:									
Minnesota	199,249	48,205	24.2	23.9	18.0		23.5	23.1	17.3
Iowa	456,830	84,270	18.4	18.0	14.3		17.8	17.0	13.3
Missouri	803,013	146,185	18.2	15.6	12.0		17.0	14.1	10.1
North Dakota	44,554	8,583	19.3	18.6	17.3		18.2	16.7	15.6
South Dakota	74,188	13,527	18.2	18.0	15.4		17.3	15.9	14.3
Nebraska	210,892	38,846	18.4	17.3	14.4		17.7	16.3	13.3
Kansas	400,312	64,063	16.0	14.6	11.5		15.2	13.6	10.2
SOUTH ATLANTIC:									
Delaware	47,776	9,282	19.4	18.5	14.5		18.7	17.1	13.7
Maryland	294,273	64,013	21.8	20.3	16.9		21.2	19.3	16.0
District of Columbia	101,891	48,357	47.5	28.2	23.4		47.5	28.2	23.3
Virginia	468,700	71,466	15.2	14.2	11.6		13.4	11.2	8.7
West Virginia	353,639	44,734	12.6	13.3	9.5		11.2	10.8	7.3
North Carolina	512,001	93,089	18.2	23.3	15.4		12.9	10.4	8.8
South Carolina	231,622	51,704	22.3	26.3	20.2		14.5	12.3	10.3
Georgia	486,529	86,550	17.8	19.8	13.3		12.6	9.8	7.9
Florida	162,621	24,748	15.2	14.8	11.1		13.2	9.9	7.5
EAST SOUTH CENTRAL:									
Kentucky	601,600	76,956	12.8	13.9	10.2		10.2	9.8	7.1
Tennessee	554,838	74,953	13.5	13.7	9.9		10.7	8.7	6.4
Alabama	399,071	63,480	15.9	21.6	13.4		9.5	7.4	5.7
Mississippi	240,234	36,772	15.3	19.3	13.0		8.9	7.2	6.0
WEST SOUTH CENTRAL:									
Arkansas	341,794	44,221	12.9	16.8	10.2		7.7	6.8	4.9
Louisiana	270,944	41,917	15.5	15.6	11.9		13.2	10.8	7.6
Oklahoma	465,940	66,313	14.2	13.1	8.9		11.7	9.2	5.7
Texas	901,374	136,524	15.1	14.9	9.0		11.9	8.4	5.4
MOUNTAIN:									
Montana	72,370	12,999	18.0	18.5	16.1		16.6	16.7	15.1
Idaho	75,132	11,172	14.9	15.3	11.7		14.0	13.6	10.0
Wyoming	32,049	5,760	18.0	17.3	14.2		16.5	15.7	13.0
Colorado	184,178	37,176	20.2	19.6	15.6		19.3	18.3	14.8
New Mexico	75,693	9,893	13.1	13.7	9.9		11.2	10.1	8.5
Arizona	41,667	7,567	18.2	15.7	12.8		17.2	14.4	11.6
Utah	54,880	9,960	18.1	17.5	13.4		17.6	16.8	12.2
Nevada	9,653	2,052	21.3	19.1	16.0		20.6	18.4	14.8
PACIFIC:									
Washington	215,928	46,831	21.7	18.9	14.6		20.9	18.0	13.5
Oregon	156,694	32,652	20.8	19.2	14.5		20.0	18.0	13.2
California	576,432	139,026	24.1	21.0	16.7		23.5	20.2	15.5

TABLE **122.**—PERCENTAGE OF NATIVE WHITE WOMEN OF FOREIGN OR MIXED PARENTAGE ENGAGED IN ALL OCCUPATIONS AND IN NONAGRICULTURAL PURSUITS, FOR DIVISIONS AND STATES: 1920, 1910, AND 1900

DIVISION AND STATE	NATIVE WHITE WOMEN OF FOREIGN OR MIXED PARENTAGE 16 YEARS OF AGE AND OVER							
	Total number: 1920	Engaged in gainful occupations				Per cent engaged in nonagricultural pursuits		
		Number: 1920	Per cent					
			1920	1910	1900	1920	1910	1900
UNITED STATES	6,990,685	2,042,804	29.2	28.8	25.4	28.6	27.8	24.8
GEOGRAPHIC DIVISIONS:								
New England	725,971	319,283	44.0	43.0	39.7	43.8	42.8	39.5
Middle Atlantic	1,951,208	679,431	34.8	32.9	29.5	34.6	32.6	29.2
East North Central	1,949,781	513,449	26.3	26.6	23.0	25.7	25.6	22.3
West North Central	1,173,171	248,123	21.1	22.8	20.4	20.0	21.2	19.6
South Atlantic	181,354	50,405	27.8	25.3	21.6	27.3	24.6	20.9
East South Central	83,794	19,034	22.7	23.8	20.7	21.8	22.3	19.7
West South Central	214,654	39,408	18.4	22.5	13.9	14.6	13.8	11.4
Mountain	229,847	46,675	20.3	20.6	16.9	19.3	19.5	16.3
Pacific	480,905	126,996	26.4	25.2	21.7	25.8	24.5	21.1
NEW ENGLAND:								
Maine	43,946	14,481	33.0	33.1	28.5	32.5	32.6	27.8
New Hampshire	34,300	15,041	43.9	43.4	40.0	43.6	43.0	39.7
Vermont	25,337	6,797	26.8	28.4	25.0	26.1	27.5	24.3
Massachusetts	418,652	193,051	46.1	45.0	41.5	46.0	44.9	41.5
Rhode Island	68,392	32,677	47.8	46.4	45.1	47.7	46.3	45.0
Connecticut	135,344	57,236	42.3	41.7	39.5	42.1	41.5	39.3
MIDDLE ATLANTIC:								
New York	1,070,086	397,775	37.2	34.7	31.3	37.0	34.4	31.0
New Jersey	288,129	100,491	34.9	33.1	30.0	34.8	32.9	29.9
Pennsylvania	592,993	181,165	30.6	29.5	26.1	30.3	29.2	25.7
EAST NORTH CENTRAL:								
Ohio	410,902	101,677	24.7	25.9	23.1	24.3	25.3	22.4
Indiana	138,714	28,389	20.5	21.0	18.7	19.6	20.0	17.8
Illinois	650,035	202,854	31.2	29.9	24.6	30.8	29.3	24.1
Michigan	363,298	89,502	24.6	25.1	22.0	23.9	24.1	21.3
Wisconsin	386,832	91,027	23.5	25.7	23.2	22.4	23.7	22.3
WEST NORTH CENTRAL:								
Minnesota	346,344	87,604	25.3	28.0	24.4	24.1	26.3	23.7
Iowa	239,969	43,920	18.3	20.7	19.3	17.2	19.3	18.5
Missouri	207,543	50,270	24.2	23.8	21.3	23.4	22.7	20.5
North Dakota	74,897	13,967	18.6	22.5	22.7	17.1	20.2	21.4
South Dakota	71,805	12,176	17.0	19.8	18.0	15.2	16.7	16.6
Nebraska	127,810	23,487	18.4	19.8	18.4	17.3	18.2	17.4
Kansas	104,803	16,699	15.9	16.1	14.4	14.7	14.8	13.3
SOUTH ATLANTIC:								
Delaware	9,554	2,655	27.8	28.9	27.0	27.6	28.5	26.8
Maryland	73,318	20,325	27.7	27.9	23.8	27.4	27.5	23.5
District of Columbia	25,118	11,480	45.7	29.3	26.4	45.7	29.3	26.3
Virginia	15,429	3,454	22.4	19.2	15.2	21.6	18.2	14.3
West Virginia	20,391	3,842	18.8	20.0	16.8	18.2	19.2	15.8
North Carolina	3,722	797	21.4	19.1	16.9	20.2	16.5	13.7
South Carolina	4,354	983	22.6	21.6	18.7	21.4	20.0	16.6
Georgia	10,391	2,485	23.9	22.9	18.2	23.0	21.4	16.9
Florida	19,077	4,384	23.0	18.7	14.1	22.4	17.9	13.1
EAST SOUTH CENTRAL:								
Kentucky	50,551	12,494	24.7	26.4	23.7	24.1	25.3	23.1
Tennessee	14,723	3,123	21.2	20.6	17.4	20.4	19.5	16.3
Alabama	11,663	2,206	18.9	19.3	14.1	17.7	16.2	12.1
Mississippi	6,857	1,211	17.7	16.9	13.8	15.4	14.0	10.9
WEST SOUTH CENTRAL:								
Arkansas	13,247	2,307	17.4	21.7	14.5	14.4	15.6	11.1
Louisiana	41,708	8,294	19.9	19.5	15.7	19.4	18.7	15.2
Oklahoma	34,008	5,421	15.9	14.8	10.8	14.4	12.7	8.5
Texas	125,691	23,386	18.6	26.2	13.3	13.0	11.8	9.6
MOUNTAIN:								
Montana	47,068	10,227	21.7	22.8	20.3	20.5	21.3	19.7
Idaho	29,241	4,484	15.3	16.1	12.2	14.2	14.5	11.0
Wyoming	12,113	2,351	19.4	18.5	18.1	18.1	17.1	17.4
Colorado	65,013	15,859	24.4	24.7	20.2	23.6	23.6	19.7
New Mexico	8,159	1,632	20.0	18.2	12.6	18.7	15.9	11.9
Arizona	14,312	2,660	18.6	16.4	13.0	17.5	15.7	12.4
Utah	48,041	8,210	17.1	18.1	14.3	16.4	17.5	13.6
Nevada	5,900	1,252	21.2	20.5	17.3	20.5	20.0	16.8
PACIFIC:								
Washington	111,568	28,421	25.5	24.0	18.1	24.8	23.3	17.4
Oregon	57,794	14,649	25.3	24.8	20.3	24.6	23.7	19.4
California	311,543	83,926	26.9	25.7	22.7	26.4	25.1	22.2

DETAILED TABLES **235**

TABLE 123.—PERCENTAGE OF FOREIGN-BORN WHITE WOMEN ENGAGED IN ALL OCCUPATIONS AND IN NONAGRICULTURAL PURSUITS, FOR DIVISIONS AND STATES: 1920, 1910, AND 1900

		FOREIGN-BORN WHITE WOMEN 16 YEARS OF AGE AND OVER							
DIVISION AND STATE	Total number: 1920	Engaged in gainful occupations				Per cent engaged in nonagricultural pursuits		
		Number: 1920	Per cent					
			1920	1910	1900	1920	1910	1900
UNITED STATES	5,872,366	1,102,697	18.8	22.1	19.1	18.1	21.1	18.1
GEOGRAPHIC DIVISIONS:								
New England	883,012	235,944	26.7	31.5	30.4	26.5	31.2	30.2
Middle Atlantic	2,192,814	447,418	20.4	25.4	22.0	20.3	25.2	21.7
East North Central	1,350,733	203,396	15.1	16.7	14.0	14.4	15.6	12.9
West North Central	572,441	66,593	11.6	13.9	12.6	10.0	11.5	10.4
South Atlantic	123,858	23,477	19.0	20.0	17.0	18.5	19.2	16.1
East South Central	28,671	4,426	15.4	15.6	12.7	14.1	13.3	11.1
West South Central	167,455	27,246	16.3	20.0	12.6	12.3	11.1	9.3
Mountain	163,640	22,920	14.0	16.6	14.5	11.7	14.7	13.2
Pacific	389,742	71,277	18.3	19.1	16.3	17.3	17.8	14.9
NEW ENGLAND:								
Maine	48,126	11,752	24.4	26.9	26.8	24.0	26.5	26.3
New Hampshire	41,972	13,173	31.4	35.2	35.3	31.1	34.9	35.1
Vermont	18,831	3,021	16.0	20.5	16.6	15.3	19.7	15.7
Massachusetts	522,080	149,398	28.6	33.6	32.4	28.5	33.4	32.3
Rhode Island	83,332	23,325	28.0	31.8	30.2	27.9	31.5	30.0
Connecticut	168,671	35,275	20.9	25.9	24.7	20.6	25.5	24.4
MIDDLE ATLANTIC:								
New York	1,284,865	306,460	23.9	29.1	24.8	23.7	28.9	24.5
New Jersey	331,391	60,905	18.4	23.4	21.1	18.2	23.0	20.9
Pennsylvania	576,558	80,053	13.9	18.2	16.5	13.7	17.9	16.3
EAST NORTH CENTRAL:								
Ohio	273,178	39,718	14.5	17.1	13.6	14.2	16.5	12.7
Indiana	59,900	6,778	11.3	14.9	11.3	10.7	10.8	9.5
Illinois	527,551	94,461	17.9	19.4	16.5	17.7	19.0	15.8
Michigan	295,285	40,012	13.6	15.2	13.5	12.6	13.7	12.1
Wisconsin	194,819	22,427	11.5	13.0	11.1	9.8	10.2	9.0
WEST NORTH CENTRAL:								
Minnesota	201,601	25,066	12.4	15.9	14.1	10.7	13.2	12.1
Iowa	95,597	9,208	9.6	11.3	10.9	8.3	9.2	8.7
Missouri	79,965	13,158	16.5	16.3	14.1	15.8	14.9	12.5
North Dakota	53,636	5,065	9.4	14.8	14.7	6.8	11.1	12.3
South Dakota	33,726	3,333	9.9	12.7	10.2	7.4	9.1	7.4
Nebraska	63,094	6,618	10.5	12.2	11.4	9.0	9.9	9.2
Kansas	45,122	4,145	9.2	9.6	9.4	7.2	7.3	6.5
SOUTH ATLANTIC:								
Delaware	8,046	1,209	15.0	18.6	17.6	14.8	18.2	17.1
Maryland	45,735	8,334	18.2	21.5	18.1	17.9	20.8	17.2
District of Columbia	12,965	3,876	29.9	26.7	22.6	29.9	26.6	22.4
Virginia	11,038	1,627	14.7	14.6	14.1	13.8	12.8	12.4
West Virginia	18,212	1,540	8.5	12.3	9.9	8.2	11.8	8.6
North Carolina	2,596	542	20.9	17.6	14.7	19.9	14.8	12.1
South Carolina	2,192	374	17.1	19.6	16.5	16.3	18.4	14.9
Georgia	5,899	1,188	20.1	14.5	13.7	19.5	13.6	13.0
Florida	17,115	4,787	27.9	24.4	16.3	27.0	23.7	15.7
EAST SOUTH CENTRAL:								
Kentucky	12,974	1,947	15.0	15.2	12.9	14.4	13.9	11.6
Tennessee	6,179	1,050	17.0	15.6	12.5	15.6	13.7	10.8
Alabama	6,641	901	13.6	14.5	10.8	12.2	11.2	9.2
Mississippi	2,877	528	18.4	20.2	15.6	13.9	13.3	11.3
WEST SOUTH CENTRAL:								
Arkansas	5,181	934	18.0	18.6	12.6	13.3	11.9	9.0
Louisiana	17,243	2,728	15.8	15.8	12.1	14.7	13.4	10.9
Oklahoma	14,066	1,628	11.6	10.4	8.0	9.1	7.6	5.1
Texas	130,965	21,956	16.8	22.5	13.2	12.2	11.0	9.2
MOUNTAIN:								
Montana	32,967	4,469	13.6	18.3	17.1	11.7	16.3	16.1
Idaho	13,344	1,499	11.2	13.4	11.3	9.4	10.9	8.5
Wyoming	7,663	946	12.3	13.9	12.6	10.2	11.9	11.1
Colorado	45,345	6,612	14.6	18.7	16.5	12.8	16.0	15.7
New Mexico	9,911	1,160	11.7	13.0	9.5	10.9	11.6	8.8
Arizona	26,136	4,571	17.5	14.9	11.9	11.4	14.4	11.2
Utah	24,449	3,105	12.7	14.6	12.9	11.9	13.5	10.7
Nevada	3,825	558	14.6	19.6	13.7	13.3	18.0	11.9
PACIFIC:								
Washington	91,142	14,777	16.2	17.7	13.6	15.0	16.4	12.3
Oregon	37,799	6,179	16.3	17.9	14.5	15.3	16.4	12.8
California	260,801	50,321	19.3	19.8	17.3	18.4	18.7	16.0

TABLE **124.**—PERCENTAGE OF NEGRO WOMEN ENGAGED IN ALL OCCUPATIONS
AND IN NONAGRICULTURAL PURSUITS, FOR DIVISIONS AND STATES: 1920, 1910,
AND 1900

DIVISION AND STATE	Total number: 1920	NEGRO WOMEN 16 YEARS OF AGE AND OVER				Per cent engaged in nonagricultural pursuits		
		Engaged in gainful occupations						
		Number: 1920	Per cent					
			1920	1910	1900	1920	1910	1900
UNITED STATES	3,312,081	1,445,935	43.7	58.2	43.2	28.4	30.9	26.5
GEOGRAPHIC DIVISIONS:								
New England	28,311	13,915	49.2	55.4	48.4	49.0	55.2	48.3
Middle Atlantic	226,075	115,867	51.3	57.4	47.9	51.2	57.2	47.8
East North Central	181,947	72,066	39.6	43.2	32.7	39.4	42.7	32.3
West North Central	100,157	41,312	41.2	45.5	34.9	40.5	44.9	34.2
South Atlantic	1,312,669	582,824	44.4	58.5	44.3	27.8	30.9	28.1
East South Central	793,083	357,106	45.0	63.9	46.1	22.8	25.7	22.5
West South Central	643,608	251,424	39.1	55.1	38.3	22.1	25.1	19.8
Mountain	8,650	3,602	41.6	49.1	41.0	41.0	48.8	40.7
Pacific	17,581	7,819	44.5	46.4	35.7	43.8	46.0	35.2
NEW ENGLAND:								
Maine	435	172	39.5	42.4	37.4	39.3	41.4	36.5
New Hampshire	180	72	40.0	60.3	56.3	38.3	58.8	55.9
Vermont	160	67	41.9	37.6	41.0	40.6	37.0	40.2
Massachusetts	16,622	8,084	48.6	55.5	46.7	48.5	55.2	46.6
Rhode Island	3,536	1,719	48.6	56.5	52.5	48.5	56.4	52.4
Connecticut	7,378	3,801	51.5	56.6	50.2	51.2	56.5	50.0
MIDDLE ATLANTIC:								
New York	81,873	49,046	59.9	61.9	55.2	59.9	61.8	55.1
New Jersey	43,545	21,446	49.3	57.4	48.0	49.1	57.2	47.9
Pennsylvania	100,657	45,375	45.1	53.8	42.4	45.0	53.7	42.4
EAST NORTH CENTRAL:								
Ohio	63,672	24,393	38.3	44.1	31.2	38.1	43.8	30.8
Indiana	28,808	11,531	40.0	43.9	35.0	39.9	43.7	34.7
Illinois	67,983	28,888	42.5	43.2	33.3	42.3	42.5	32.9
Michigan	19,828	6,648	33.5	34.6	30.2	33.3	33.8	29.6
Wisconsin	1,656	606	36.6	41.3	27.1	35.8	39.9	26.4
WEST NORTH CENTRAL:								
Minnesota	3,124	1,255	40.2	40.1	34.9	39.9	39.7	34.8
Iowa	6,397	2,271	35.5	36.3	26.3	35.0	35.6	26.0
Missouri	65,684	29,276	44.6	50.3	38.0	43.6	49.7	37.3
North Dakota	137	45	32.8	47.0	(1)	30.7	40.4	(1)
South Dakota	228	94	41.2	35.3	42.4	38.6	32.5	41.6
Nebraska	4,561	1,866	40.9	43.3	41.4	40.8	43.1	40.7
Kansas	20,026	6,505	32.5	34.2	26.0	32.0	33.5	25.4
SOUTH ATLANTIC:								
Delaware	9,950	4,502	45.2	51.1	37.1	43.9	49.1	36.6
Maryland	80,962	40,489	50.0	56.3	44.1	48.9	54.1	43.1
District of Columbia	45,606	28,295	62.0	66.4	63.6	62.0	66.4	63.6
Virginia	212,429	74,068	34.9	45.8	37.2	31.2	37.5	32.0
West Virginia	25,588	5,869	22.9	34.6	26.2	22.8	34.0	25.8
North Carolina	220,605	86,413	39.2	58.2	39.5	22.6	26.5	23.0
South Carolina	246,970	126,464	51.2	70.2	51.5	16.7	19.0	18.7
Georgia	365,895	168,335	46.0	61.4	46.9	24.8	27.0	27.5
Florida	104,664	48,389	46.2	49.7	37.1	37.1	33.9	25.2
EAST SOUTH CENTRAL:								
Kentucky	81,988	35,877	43.8	50.8	38.7	42.6	49.3	37.6
Tennessee	149,653	63,811	42.6	54.3	40.1	33.4	38.6	32.3
Alabama	277,643	126,706	45.6	65.9	50.6	20.9	22.0	19.8
Mississippi	283,799	130,712	46.1	71.1	48.0	13.4	15.4	14.1
WEST SOUTH CENTRAL:								
Arkansas	145,929	52,294	35.8	59.2	35.8	13.7	18.2	14.9
Louisiana	221,207	89,395	40.4	52.4	44.5	22.9	25.1	20.7
Oklahoma	44,774	14,238	31.8	40.5	20.8	23.2	24.8	14.7
Texas	231,698	95,497	41.2	58.0	34.6	26.3	29.4	22.1
MOUNTAIN:								
Montana	542	205	37.8	50.0	44.1	36.7	49.5	43.4
Idaho	262	79	30.2	51.5	(1)	29.8	50.5	(1)
Wyoming	423	205	48.5	50.6	24.0	48.2	50.5	23.6
Colorado	4,306	1,912	44.4	48.7	42.5	44.0	48.5	42.3
New Mexico	864	301	34.8	46.5	30.4	34.5	45.3	30.1
Arizona	1,641	670	40.8	54.8	47.6	39.3	54.7	47.0
Utah	490	154	31.4	37.7	46.7	31.0	37.7	46.7
Nevada	122	76	62.3	55.9	(1)	62.3	54.5	(1)
PACIFIC:								
Washington	2,296	918	40.0	40.9	30.6	39.6	40.0	30.2
Oregon	742	315	42.5	47.2	43.5	41.8	45.6	44.8
California	14,543	6,586	45.3	47.7	35.7	44.5	47.4	35.2

¹ Per cent not shown where base is less than 100.

TABLE 125.—PERCENTAGE OF WOMEN ENGAGED IN GAINFUL OCCUPATIONS, FOR CITIES OF 100,000 INHABITANTS OR MORE AND FOR AREAS OUTSIDE OF SUCH CITIES, BY DIVISIONS AND STATES: 1920, 1910, AND 1900

DIVISION AND STATE	WOMEN 16 YEARS OF AGE AND OVER									
	In cities having 100,000 inhabitants or more					In balance of State				
	Total number: 1920	Engaged in gainful occupations				Total number: 1920	Engaged in gainful occupations			
		Number: 1920	Per cent				Number: 1920	Per cent		
			1920	1910	1900			1920	1910	1900
UNITED STATES	9,803,818	3,191,006	32.5	32.3	28.0	24,437,931	5,011,895	20.5	23.2	18.6
GEOGRAPHIC DIVISIONS:										
New England	795,166	294,859	37.1	37.3	33.3	1,826,784	551,385	30.2	30.1	26.5
Middle Atlantic	3,721,840	1,209,534	32.5	32.8	28.1	3,858,129	853,473	22.1	21.7	18.4
East North Central	2,332,883	697,089	29.9	29.7	25.3	4,814,659	838,552	17.4	17.1	14.3
West North Central	795,539	256,145	32.2	30.9	27.2	3,250,384	504,109	15.5	16.3	13.3
South Atlantic	676,203	265,360	39.2	38.3	33.0	3,604,277	886,047	24.6	31.7	24.2
East South Central	264,412	94,797	35.9	36.9	32.9	2,437,339	538,069	22.1	31.3	22.6
West South Central	346,148	113,696	32.8	33.5	26.2	2,675,564	494,640	18.5	24.8	17.4
Mountain	135,610	38,558	28.4	28.4	24.8	835,502	135,565	16.2	17.5	14.3
Pacific	736,017	220,968	30.0	26.9	24.4	1,135,293	210,055	18.5	18.1	15.7
NEW ENGLAND:										
Maine						265,315	64,113	24.2	23.9	20.5
New Hampshire						157,778	48,778	30.9	30.3	26.6
Vermont						121,006	26,557	21.9	22.7	18.4
Massachusetts	554,397	212,265	38.3	38.6	34.0	840,647	276,881	32.9	33.1	29.6
Rhode Island	87,447	32,099	36.7	36.4	33.5	126,832	44,370	35.0	33.8	29.7
Connecticut	153,322	50,495	32.9	32.0	28.0	315,206	90,686	28.8	29.1	26.0
MIDDLE ATLANTIC:										
New York	2,414,126	807,333	33.4	33.6	28.8	1,274,550	307,498	24.1	23.7	20.4
New Jersey	366,929	108,839	29.7	29.4	25.8	700,547	175,323	25.0	25.3	21.0
Pennsylvania	940,785	293,362	31.2	31.9	27.4	1,883,032	370,652	19.7	19.0	15.9
EAST NORTH CENTRAL:										
Ohio	750,913	211,357	28.1	29.1	25.5	1,195,704	195,724	16.4	16.9	14.1
Indiana	119,505	35,454	29.7	28.1	24.8	877,842	145,448	16.6	15.4	12.9
Illinois	937,411	303,085	32.3	30.8	25.1	1,252,269	224,790	18.0	17.0	14.3
Michigan	363,829	97,776	26.9	28.6	25.4	805,429	144,344	17.9	17.3	15.2
Wisconsin	161,225	49,417	30.7	29.2	25.6	683,415	128,246	18.8	19.6	15.9
WEST NORTH CENTRAL:										
Minnesota	227,806	74,307	32.6	33.1	28.8	525,032	88,016	16.8	18.6	15.4
Iowa	47,449	15,237	32.1			751,509	124,444	16.6	17.9	15.1
Missouri	419,010	136,752	32.6	29.9	26.3	736,989	102,169	13.9	13.9	10.7
North Dakota						174,951	27,727	15.8	18.4	17.0
South Dakota						184,915	29,269	15.8	16.9	13.7
Nebraska	67,135	20,808	31.0	30.0	28.4	340,188	50,061	14.7	15.4	13.0
Kansas	34,139	9,041	26.5			536,800	82,423	15.4	15.1	12.3
SOUTH ATLANTIC:										
Delaware	37,935	11,432	30.1			37,392	6,216	16.6	24.5	19.8
Maryland	268,739	89,947	33.5	35.3	30.6	225,582	43,229	19.2	21.0	16.8
District of Columbia	185,640	92,027	49.6	39.8	37.0					
Virginia	107,292	40,401	37.7	41.6		600,532	110,247	18.4	23.1	20.6
West Virginia						417,841	55,987	13.4	14.7	10.6
North Carolina						741,844	181,480	24.5	34.3	23.3
South Carolina						485,225	179,547	37.0	49.9	37.9
Georgia	76,597	31,553	41.2	42.8		792,152	227,019	28.7	38.1	28.8
Florida						303,709	82,322	27.1	29.9	22.8
EAST SOUTH CENTRAL:										
Kentucky	92,799	33,655	36.3	35.7	29.2	654,337	93,634	14.3	17.3	13.6
Tennessee	108,978	41,405	38.0	39.6	40.8	616,439	101,536	16.5	20.6	16.0
Alabama	62,635	19,737	31.5	34.0		632,476	173,578	27.4	41.4	30.4
Mississippi						534,087	169,321	31.7	48.6	33.4
WEST SOUTH CENTRAL:										
Arkansas						506,193	99,762	19.7	29.5	17.7
Louisiana	143,058	48,358	33.8	33.5	26.2	408,367	94,022	23.0	31.8	28.3
Oklahoma						573,732	88,692	15.5	15.3	9.9
Texas	203,090	65,338	32.2			1,187,272	212,164	17.9	24.5	15.1
MOUNTAIN:										
Montana						156,262	28,041	17.9	19.3	16.9
Idaho						119,285	17,322	14.5	15.2	11.5
Wyoming						52,799	9,307	17.6	17.3	14.5
Colorado	95,339	28,563	30.0	28.4	24.8	204,405	33,081	16.2	17.6	13.9
New Mexico						99,819	14,475	14.5	15.9	11.1
Arizona						92,850	17,485	18.8	19.5	20.3
Utah	40,271	9,995	24.8			88,853	11,553	13.0	17.3	13.6
Nevada						21,229	4,301	20.3	21.0	17.6
PACIFIC:										
Washington	150,008	44,008	29.3	25.4		277,702	48,078	17.3	17.2	15.3
Oregon	94,783	28,325	29.9	28.7		160,779	25,793	16.0	15.7	15.6
California	491,226	148,635	30.3	27.0	24.4	696,812	136,184	19.5	19.2	15.8

TABLE 126.—PERCENTAGE OF NATIVE WHITE WOMEN OF NATIVE PARENTAGE ENGAGED IN GAINFUL OCCUPATIONS, FOR CITIES OF 100,000 INHABITANTS OR MORE AND FOR AREAS OUTSIDE OF SUCH CITIES, BY DIVISIONS AND STATES: 1920, 1910, AND 1900

	NATIVE WHITE WOMEN OF NATIVE PARENTAGE 16 YEARS OF AGE AND OVER									
	In cities having 100,000 inhabitants or more					In balance of State				
DIVISION AND STATE	Total number: 1920	Engaged in gainful occupations				Total number: 1920	Engaged in gainful occupations			
		Number: 1920	Per cent				Number: 1920	Per cent		
			1920	1910	1900			1920	1910	1900
UNITED STATES	3,345,797	1,110,218	33.2	29.4	24.6	14,624,153	2,486,179	17.0	17.2	13.4
GEOGRAPHIC DIVISIONS:										
New England	196,482	71,954	36.6	32.2	26.4	787,372	204,896	26.0	24.1	19.5
Middle Atlantic	992,406	344,756	34.7	31.0	25.1	2,214,840	474,909	21.4	19.8	15.9
East North Central	747,592	243,012	32.5	29.7	24.8	2,912,697	503,024	17.3	16.0	13.1
West North Central	341,905	115,335	33.7	30.1	25.1	1,847,133	288,344	15.6	15.2	12.0
South Atlantic	358,697	123,557	34.4	27.6	23.8	2,300,355	370,386	16.1	18.3	13.4
East South Central	137,786	38,861	28.2	24.1	21.5	1,657,957	213,300	12.9	15.7	10.8
West South Central	181,029	51,707	28.6	24.7	17.8	1,799,023	237,268	13.2	14.7	9.5
Mountain	66,145	19,769	29.9	27.4	22.9	479,477	76,810	16.0	16.3	12.7
Pacific	323,755	101,267	31.3	26.2	22.8	625,299	117,242	18.7	17.3	14.7
NEW ENGLAND:										
Maine						172,531	37,620	21.8	21.2	17.9
New Hampshire						81,309	20,483	25.2	24.2	20.4
Vermont						76,673	16,669	21.7	21.5	16.9
Massachusetts	130,170	48,490	37.3	34.1	27.7	307,155	90,018	29.3	26.4	21.0
Rhode Island	23,193	8,394	36.2	32.1	25.8	35,774	10,336	28.9	24.5	19.5
Connecticut	43,119	15,070	34.9	24.0	20.5	113,930	29,770	26.1	24.0	19.1
MIDDLE ATLANTIC:										
New York	529,345	194,033	36.7	31.6	24.9	720,202	166,989	23.2	21.2	17.0
New Jersey	108,107	35,280	32.6	30.2	24.0	296,180	65,998	22.3	20.0	15.2
Pennsylvania	354,954	115,443	32.5	30.3	25.6	1,198,458	241,922	20.2	18.9	15.3
EAST NORTH CENTRAL:										
Ohio	323,329	98,380	30.4	29.4	25.3	875,416	142,881	16.3	16.1	13.3
Indiana	80,510	23,350	29.0	25.9	22.7	689,360	110,836	16.1	14.4	11.7
Illinois	197,705	73,262	37.1	31.1	24.8	746,123	128,329	17.2	15.8	12.8
Michigan	110,451	33,917	30.7	28.6	24.0	378,727	71,765	18.9	16.7	14.3
Wisconsin	35,597	14,103	39.6	35.4	29.2	223,071	49,213	22.1	21.5	16.1
WEST NORTH CENTRAL:										
Minnesota	65,144	22,382	34.4	31.1	24.0	134,105	25,823	19.3	20.0	15.4
Iowa	30,424	9,971	32.8			426,406	74,299	17.4	18.0	14.3
Missouri	199,297	68,829	34.5	29.8	25.1	603,716	77,356	12.8	12.2	9.5
North Dakota						44,554	8,583	19.3	18.6	17.3
South Dakota						74,188	13,527	18.2	18.0	15.4
Nebraska	28,506	9,325	32.7	29.8	27.2	182,386	29,521	16.2	15.9	13.1
Kansas	18,534	4,828	26.0			381,778	59,235	15.5	14.6	11.5
SOUTH ATLANTIC:										
Delaware	19,895	5,629	28.3			27,881	3,653	13.1	18.5	14.5
Maryland	131,486	38,881	29.6	28.8	24.1	162,787	25,132	15.4	15.3	12.8
District of Columbia	101,891	48,357	47.5	28.2	23.4					
Virginia	59,225	16,639	28.1	25.8		409,475	54,827	13.4	13.5	11.6
West Virginia						353,639	44,734	12.6	13.3	9.5
North Carolina						512,001	93,089	18.2	23.3	15.4
South Carolina						231,622	51,704	22.3	26.3	20.2
Georgia	46,200	14,051	30.4	24.6		440,329	72,499	16.5	19.4	13.3
Florida						162,621	24,748	15.2	14.8	11.1
EAST SOUTH CENTRAL:										
Kentucky	49,071	15,623	31.8	29.8	22.6	552,529	61,333	11.1	12.7	9.4
Tennessee	57,377	16,311	28.4	22.6	18.8	497,461	58,642	11.8	12.9	9.7
Alabama	31,338	6,927	22.1	17.1		367,733	56,553	15.4	21.9	13.4
Mississippi						240,234	36,772	15.3	19.3	13.0
WEST SOUTH CENTRAL:										
Arkansas						341,794	44,221	12.9	16.8	10.2
Louisiana	62,335	17,990	28.9	24.7	17.8	208,609	23,927	11.5	13.2	10.6
Oklahoma						465,940	66,313	14.2	13.1	8.9
Texas	118,694	33,717	28.4			782,680	102,807	13.1	14.9	9.0
MOUNTAIN:										
Montana						72,370	12,999	18.0	18.5	16.1
Idaho						75,132	11,172	14.9	15.3	11.7
Wyoming						32,049	5,760	18.0	17.3	14.2
Colorado	50,586	15,520	30.7	27.4	22.9	133,592	21,656	16.2	16.8	13.0
New Mexico						75,693	9,893	13.1	13.7	9.9
Arizona						41,667	7,567	18.2	15.7	12.8
Utah	15,559	4,249	27.3			39,321	5,711	14.5	17.5	13.4
Nevada						9,653	2,052	21.3	19.1	16.0
PACIFIC:										
Washington	68,706	20,794	30.3	24.0		147,222	26,037	17.7	16.7	14.6
Oregon	49,213	15,342	31.2	28.5		107,481	17,310	16.1	15.6	14.5
California	205,836	65,131	31.6	26.5	22.8	370,596	73,895	19.9	18.3	14.9

TABLE 127.—PERCENTAGE OF NATIVE WHITE WOMEN OF FOREIGN OR MIXED PARENTAGE ENGAGED IN GAINFUL OCCUPATIONS, FOR CITIES OF 100,000 INHABITANTS OR MORE AND FOR AREAS OUTSIDE OF SUCH CITIES, BY DIVISIONS AND STATES: 1920, 1910, AND 1900

	NATIVE WHITE WOMEN OF FOREIGN OR MIXED PARENTAGE 16 YEARS OF AGE AND OVER									
	In cities having 100,000 inhabitants or more					In balance of State				
DIVISION AND STATE	Total number: 1920	Engaged in gainful occupations				Total number: 1920	Engaged in gainful occupations			
		Number: 1920	Per cent				Number: 1920	Per cent		
			1920	1910	1900			1920	1910	1900
UNITED STATES	2,860,668	1,068,872	37.4	36.3	32.4	4,130,017	973,932	23.6	24.3	21.8
GEOGRAPHIC DIVISIONS:										
New England	252,206	120,302	47.7	46.7	42.6	473,765	198,981	42.0	41.4	38.7
Middle Atlantic	1,145,278	449,666	39.3	36.9	32.8	805,930	229,765	28.5	27.5	25.4
East North Central	761,383	271,503	35.7	36.8	32.5	1,188,398	241,946	20.4	21.3	19.1
West North Central	258,338	89,105	34.5	34.5	31.4	914,833	159,018	17.4	19.8	17.6
South Atlantic	98,154	33,395	34.0	30.6	26.8	83,200	17,010	20.4	20.4	17.4
East South Central	32,030	8,537	26.7	27.2	26.1	51,764	10,497	20.3	21.6	18.3
West South Central	56,135	13,031	23.2	21.2	17.0	158,519	26,377	16.6	22.9	12.9
Mountain	41,099	12,494	30.4	32.1	27.8	188,748	34,181	18.1	19.0	15.5
Pacific	216,045	70,839	32.8	30.4	28.4	264,860	56,157	21.2	21.0	18.9
NEW ENGLAND:										
Maine						43,946	14,481	33.0	33.1	28.5
New Hampshire						34,300	15,041	43.9	43.4	40.2
Vermont						25,337	6,797	26.8	28.4	25.0
Massachusetts	177,081	86,243	48.7	47.5	42.2	241,571	106,808	44.2	43.5	41.2
Rhode Island	28,553	13,749	48.2	46.7	45.9	39,839	18,928	47.5	46.1	44.3
Connecticut	46,572	20,310	43.6	42.6	39.5	88,772	36,926	41.6	41.4	39.5
MIDDLE ATLANTIC:										
New York	764,427	309,405	40.5	37.4	33.2	305,659	88,370	28.9	29.1	28.2
New Jersey	115,151	44,304	38.5	37.0	33.7	172,978	56,187	32.5	30.7	27.4
Pennsylvania	265,700	95,957	36.1	35.7	31.8	327,293	85,208	26.0	24.2	21.1
EAST NORTH CENTRAL:										
Ohio	212,944	65,959	31.0	33.4	31.7	197,958	35,718	18.0	19.8	17.9
Indiana	18,479	5,087	27.5	28.4	27.7	120,235	23,302	19.4	20.0	17.6
Illinois	337,498	135,837	40.2	39.6	33.0	312,537	67,017	21.4	20.8	18.6
Michigan	114,830	37,376	32.5	36.5	33.1	248,468	52,126	21.0	21.4	20.0
Wisconsin	77,632	27,244	35.1	36.6	34.6	309,200	63,783	20.6	23.3	21.0
WEST NORTH CENTRAL:										
Minnesota	98,769	38,819	39.3	42.0	37.9	247,575	48,785	19.7	22.8	20.4
Iowa	10,177	3,488	34.3			229,792	40,432	17.6	20.7	19.3
Missouri	123,392	37,679	30.5	29.8	28.5	84,151	12,591	15.0	15.7	11.7
North Dakota						74,897	13,967	18.6	22.5	22.7
South Dakota						71,805	12,176	17.0	19.8	18.0
Nebraska	20,113	7,339	36.5	36.5	35.0	107,697	16,148	15.0	17.4	16.2
Kansas	5,887	1,780	30.2			98,916	14,919	15.1	16.1	14.4
SOUTH ATLANTIC:										
Delaware	7,386	2,312	31.3			2,168	343	15.8	28.9	27.0
Maryland	56,699	17,238	30.4	31.7	27.0	16,619	3,087	18.6	18.9	16.0
District of Columbia	25,118	11,480	45.7	29.3	26.4					
Virginia	6,049	1,587	26.2	22.8		9,380	1,867	19.9	18.0	15.2
West Virginia						20,391	3,842	18.8	20.0	16.8
North Carolina						3,722	797	21.4	19.1	16.9
South Carolina						4,354	983	22.6	21.6	18.7
Georgia	2,902	778	26.8	27.9		7,489	1,707	22.8	21.1	18.2
Florida						19,077	4,384	23.0	18.7	14.1
EAST SOUTH CENTRAL:										
Kentucky	21,232	5,927	27.9	29.2	27.0	29,319	6,567	22.4	24.3	21.3
Tennessee	7,803	1,902	24.4	22.8	20.7	6,920	1,221	17.6	18.0	16.2
Alabama	2,995	708	23.6	22.3		8,668	1,498	17.3	18.4	14.1
Mississippi						6,857	1,211	17.7	16.9	13.8
WEST SOUTH CENTRAL:										
Arkansas						13,247	2,307	17.4	21.7	14.5
Louisiana	30,720	6,763	22.0	21.2	17.0	10,988	1,531	13.9	13.9	11.1
Oklahoma						34,008	5,421	15.9	14.8	10.8
Texas	25,415	6,268	24.7			100,276	17,118	17.1	26.2	13.3
MOUNTAIN:										
Montana						47,068	10,227	21.7	22.8	20.3
Idaho						29,241	4,484	15.3	16.1	12.2
Wyoming						12,113	2,351	19.4	18.5	18.1
Colorado	26,065	8,605	33.0	32.1	27.8	38,948	7,254	18.6	19.8	15.9
New Mexico						8,159	1,632	20.0	18.2	12.6
Arizona						14,312	2,660	18.6	16.4	13.0
Utah	15,034	3,889	25.9			33,007	4,321	13.1	18.1	14.3
Nevada						5,900	1,252	21.2	20.5	17.3
PACIFIC:										
Washington	42,629	14,077	33.0	29.1		68,939	14,344	20.8	21.0	18.1
Oregon	25,735	8,610	33.5	33.1		32,059	6,039	18.8	18.7	20.3
California	147,681	48,152	32.6	30.3	28.4	163,862	35,774	21.8	21.4	18.7

TABLE 128.—PERCENTAGE OF FOREIGN-BORN WHITE WOMEN ENGAGED IN GAINFUL OCCUPATIONS, FOR CITIES OF 100,000 INHABITANTS OR MORE AND FOR AREAS OUTSIDE OF SUCH CITIES, BY DIVISIONS AND STATES: 1920, 1910, AND 1900

	FOREIGN-BORN WHITE WOMEN 16 YEARS OF AGE AND OVER									
	In cities having 100,000 inhabitants or more					In balance of State				
DIVISION AND STATE	Total number: 1920	Engaged in gainful occupations				Total number: 1920	Engaged in gainful occupations			
		Number: 1920	Per cent				Number: 1920	Per cent		
			1920	1910	1900			1920	1910	1900
UNITED STATES	2,927,767	655,349	22.4	26.6	23.2	2,944,599	447,348	15.2	18.2	16.1
GEOGRAPHIC DIVISIONS:										
New England	328,768	93,833	28.5	33.0	31.3	554,244	142,111	25.6	30.8	30.0
Middle Atlantic	1,434,632	333,495	23.2	28.9	24.9	758,182	113,923	15.0	18.9	16.9
East North Central	711,712	132,936	18.7	21.4	18.5	639,021	70,460	11.0	12.5	11.0
West North Central	141,747	26,540	18.7	21.0	20.0	430,694	40,053	9.3	12.0	10.8
South Atlantic	63,945	13,388	20.9	23.2	20.0	59,913	10,089	16.8	17.2	14.3
East South Central	11,517	1,887	16.4	15.5	14.1	17,154	2,539	14.8	15.7	12.1
West South Central	34,298	6,999	20.4	17.8	13.5	133,157	20,247	15.2	20.2	12.4
Mountain	25,447	4,944	19.4	22.9	22.3	138,193	17,976	13.0	15.7	13.5
Pacific	175,701	41,327	23.5	23.0	21.4	214,041	29,950	14.0	15.7	14.0
NEW ENGLAND:										
Maine						48,126	11,752	24.4	26.9	26.8
New Hampshire						41,972	13,173	31.4	35.2	35.3
Vermont						18,831	3,021	16.0	20.5	16.6
Massachusetts	235,490	71,924	30.5	34.6	32.2	286,590	77,474	27.0	32.9	32.5
Rhode Island	33,642	8,881	26.4	30.8	30.3	49,690	14,444	29.1	32.5	30.1
Connecticut	59,636	13,028	21.8	25.9	24.4	109,035	22,247	20.4	26.0	24.8
MIDDLE ATLANTIC:										
New York	1,050,880	261,541	24.9	30.6	26.3	233,985	44,919	19.2	23.1	19.9
New Jersey	129,477	22,972	17.7	21.6	19.7	201,914	37,933	18.8	24.4	22.0
Pennsylvania	254,275	48,982	19.3	25.2	22.1	322,283	31,071	9.6	12.2	10.8
EAST NORTH CENTRAL:										
Ohio	173,992	29,348	16.9	20.1	16.7	99,186	10,370	10.5	13.2	10.4
Indiana	7,390	1,135	15.4	17.6	15.3	52,510	5,643	10.7	11.0	10.7
Illinois	358,754	73,319	20.4	22.7	19.5	168,797	21,142	12.5	12.9	11.6
Michigan	124,369	21,357	17.2	21.1	20.2	170,916	18,655	10.9	12.6	11.8
Wisconsin	47,207	7,777	16.5	16.6	15.6	147,612	14,650	9.9	12.0	10.0
WEST NORTH CENTRAL:										
Minnesota	61,148	11,977	19.6	23.9	24.1	140,453	13,089	9.3	12.8	11.1
Iowa	4,819	917	19.0			90,778	8,291	9.1	11.3	10.9
Missouri	56,564	10,463	18.5	18.3	16.4	23,101	2,695	11.7	12.1	9.7
North Dakota						53,636	5,065	9.4	14.8	14.7
South Dakota						33,726	3,333	9.9	12.7	10.2
Nebraska	14,826	2,570	17.3	20.5	22.7	48,268	4,048	8.4	10.6	9.5
Kansas	4,390	613	14.0			40,732	3,532	8.7	9.6	9.4
SOUTH ATLANTIC:										
Delaware	6,643	1,027	15.5			1,403	182	13.0	18.6	17.6
Maryland	38,368	7,362	19.2	22.8	19.3	7,367	972	13.2	17.2	14.3
District of Columbia	12,965	3,876	29.9	26.7	22.6					
Virginia	4,037	779	19.3	17.5		7,001	848	12.1	14.0	14.1
West Virginia						18,212	1,540	8.5	12.3	9.9
North Carolina						2,596	542	20.9	17.6	14.7
South Carolina						2,192	374	17.1	19.6	16.5
Georgia	1,932	344	17.8	14.5		3,967	844	21.3	14.5	13.7
Florida						17,175	4,787	27.9	24.4	16.3
EAST SOUTH CENTRAL:										
Kentucky	5,630	935	16.6	15.9	13.8	7,344	1,012	13.8	14.6	12.2
Tennessee	3,456	641	18.5	16.6	15.5	2,723	409	15.0	14.4	11.2
Alabama	2,431	311	12.8	12.0		4,210	590	14.0	15.8	10.8
Mississippi						2,877	528	18.4	20.2	15.6
WEST SOUTH CENTRAL:										
Arkansas						5,181	934	18.0	18.6	12.6
Louisiana	10,000	1,791	17.9	17.8	13.5	7,243	937	12.9	12.7	9.1
Oklahoma						14,006	1,628	11.6	10.4	8.0
Texas	24,298	5,208	21.4			106,667	16,748	15.7	22.5	13.2
MOUNTAIN:										
Montana						32,967	4,469	13.6	18.3	17.1
Idaho						13,344	1,499	11.2	13.4	11.3
Wyoming						7,663	946	12.3	13.9	12.6
Colorado	16,142	3,228	20.0	22.9	22.3	29,203	3,384	11.6	16.2	13.4
New Mexico						9,911	1,160	11.7	13.0	9.5
Arizona						26,136	4,571	17.5	14.9	11.9
Utah	9,305	1,716	18.4			15,144	1,389	9.2	14.6	12.9
Nevada						3,825	558	14.6	19.6	13.7
PACIFIC:										
Washington	35,157	8,002	22.8	23.6		55,985	6,775	12.1	14.3	13.6
Oregon	18,660	4,008	21.5	23.6		19,139	2,171	11.3	12.7	14.5
California	121,884	29,317	24.1	22.8	21.4	138,917	21,004	15.1	17.0	14.1

TABLE 129.—PERCENTAGE OF NEGRO WOMEN ENGAGED IN GAINFUL OCCUPATIONS, FOR CITIES OF 100,000 INHABITANTS OR MORE AND FOR AREAS OUTSIDE OF SUCH CITIES, BY DIVISIONS AND STATES: 1920, 1910, AND 1900

DIVISION AND STATE	NEGRO WOMEN 16 YEARS OF AGE AND OVER								
	In cities having 100,000 inhabitants or more					In balance of State			
	Total number: 1920	Engaged in gainful occupations				Total number: 1920	Engaged in gainful occupations		
		Number: 1920	Per cent				Number: 1920	Per cent		
			1920	1910	1900			1920	1910	1900
UNITED STATES	658,189	353,619	53.7	61.8	53.7	2,653,892	1,092,316	41.2	57.6	42.0
GEOGRAPHIC DIVISIONS:										
New England	17,514	8,717	49.8	58.1	51.7	10,797	5,198	48.1	52.9	46.6
Middle Atlantic	148,632	81,362	54.7	61.0	52.0	77,443	34,505	44.6	52.5	43.2
East North Central	111,805	49,507	44.3	50.7	42.0	70,142	22,559	32.2	37.1	27.4
West North Central	53,406	25,121	47.0	55.4	48.1	46,751	16,191	34.6	39.9	28.5
South Atlantic	155,304	94,977	61.2	69.3	62.9	1,157,365	487,847	42.2	57.3	43.0
East South Central	83,063	45,498	54.8	63.6	58.2	710,020	311,608	43.9	64.0	45.5
West South Central	74,607	41,931	56.2	60.8	49.3	569,001	209,493	36.8	54.7	37.6
Mountain	2,716	1,301	47.9	53.0	48.2	5,934	2,301	38.8	47.5	37.5
Pacific	11,142	5,205	46.7	45.7	39.0	6,439	2,614	40.6	47.5	34.3
NEW ENGLAND:										
Maine						435	172	39.5	42.4	37.4
New Hampshire						180	72	40.0	60.3	56.3
Vermont						160	67	41.9	37.6	41.0
Massachusetts	11,506	5,568	48.4	58.3	51.6	5,116	2,516	49.2	51.9	43.2
Rhode Island	2,039	1,070	52.5	58.8	51.8	1,497	649	43.4	53.2	53.4
Connecticut	3,969	2,079	52.4	56.8	51.7	3,409	1,722	50.5	56.6	49.8
MIDDLE ATLANTIC:										
New York	68,732	42,146	61.3	64.3	58.2	13,141	6,900	52.5	54.3	48.5
New Jersey	14,161	6,270	44.3	48.6	43.3	29,384	15,176	51.6	59.5	49.0
Pennsylvania	65,739	32,946	50.1	59.6	47.9	34,918	12,429	35.6	44.5	34.5
EAST NORTH CENTRAL:										
Ohio	40,578	17,647	43.5	52.6	42.1	23,094	6,746	29.2	36.6	25.4
Indiana	13,121	5,877	44.8	51.4	43.0	15,687	5,654	36.0	38.9	31.3
Illinois	43,250	20,608	47.6	49.9	42.5	24,733	8,280	33.5	37.6	27.1
Michigan	14,081	5,090	36.1	41.4	36.6	5,747	1,558	27.1	30.0	27.5
Wisconsin	775	285	36.8	43.5	31.5	881	321	36.4	39.8	24.5
WEST NORTH CENTRAL:										
Minnesota	2,685	1,113	41.5	40.2	34.0	439	142	32.3	40.0	38.3
Iowa	2,025	857	42.3			4,372	1,414	32.3	36.3	26.3
Missouri	39,705	19,762	49.8	57.0	49.1	25,979	9,514	36.6	44.1	29.8
North Dakota						137	45	32.8	47.0	(¹)
South Dakota						228	94	41.2	35.3	42.4
Nebraska	3,673	1,573	42.8	46.7	44.5	888	293	33.0	37.8	36.7
Kansas	5,318	1,816	34.1			14,708	4,689	31.9	34.2	26.0
SOUTH ATLANTIC:										
Delaware	4,010	2,464	61.4			5,940	2,038	34.3	51.1	37.1
Maryland	42,163	26,454	62.7	70.2	62.1	38,799	14,035	36.2	44.7	30.3
District of Columbia	45,606	28,295	62.0	66.4	63.6					
Virginia	37,965	21,387	56.3	67.9		174,464	52,681	30.2	43.6	37.2
West Virginia						25,588	5,869	22.9	34.6	26.2
North Carolina						220,605	86,413	39.2	58.2	39.5
South Carolina						246,970	126,464	51.2	70.2	51.5
Georgia	25,560	16,377	64.1	74.4		340,335	151,958	44.6	60.5	46.9
Florida						104,664	48,389	46.2	49.7	37.1
EAST SOUTH CENTRAL:										
Kentucky	16,859	11,161	66.2	68.1	54.4	65,129	24,716	37.9	46.8	35.5
Tennessee	40,334	22,549	55.9	65.2	61.4	109,319	41,262	37.7	54.7	37.6
Alabama	25,870	11,788	45.6	56.5		251,773	114,918	45.6	66.6	50.6
Mississippi						283,799	130,712	46.1	71.1	48.0
WEST SOUTH CENTRAL:										
Arkansas						145,929	52,294	35.8	59.2	35.8
Louisiana	39,971	21,803	54.5	60.8	49.3	181,236	67,592	37.3	50.8	43.6
Oklahoma						44,774	14,238	31.8	40.5	20.8
Texas	34,636	20,128	58.1			197,062	75,369	38.2	58.0	34.6
MOUNTAIN:										
Montana						542	205	37.8	50.0	44.1
Idaho						262	79	30.2	51.5	(¹)
Wyoming						423	205	48.5	50.6	24.0
Colorado	2,443	1,191	48.8	53.0	48.2	1,863	721	38.7	44.2	35.5
New Mexico						864	301	34.8	46.5	30.4
Arizona						1,641	670	40.8	54.8	47.5
Utah	273	110	40.3			217	44	20.3	37.7	46.7
Nevada						122	76	62.3	55.9	(¹)
PACIFIC:										
Washington	1,289	582	45.2	39.8		1,007	336	33.4	42.2	30.6
Oregon	589	250	42.4	46.5		153	65	42.5	49.6	45.7
California	9,264	4,373	47.2	46.9	39.0	5,279	2,213	41.9	48.8	33.7

¹ Per cent not shown where base is less than 100.

TABLE 130.—PERCENTAGE OF MARRIED WOMEN ENGAGED IN ALL OCCUPATIONS
AND IN NONAGRICULTURAL PURSUITS, FOR DIVISIONS AND STATES: 1920, 1910,
AND 1900

DIVISION AND STATE	MARRIED WOMEN 16 YEARS OF AGE AND OVER								
	Total number: 1920	Engaged in gainful occupations				Per cent engaged in nonagricultural pursuits		
		Number: 1920	Per cent					
			1920	1910	1900	1920	1910	1900
UNITED STATES	21,306,099	1,920,281	9.0	10.7	5.6	7.3	6.8	3.9
GEOGRAPHIC DIVISIONS:								
New England	1,485,098	175,568	11.8	10.7	6.7	11.7	10.5	6.5
Middle Atlantic	4,517,251	348,128	7.7	7.4	4.0	7.6	7.2	3.8
East North Central	4,544,269	282,285	6.2	5.2	2.5	6.0	4.8	2.3
West North Central	2,555,048	137,368	5.4	5.0	2.6	5.0	4.4	2.2
South Atlantic	2,651,025	394,664	14.9	21.3	11.8	9.6	9.8	6.8
East South Central	1,722,120	225,222	13.1	22.4	10.7	6.5	9.9	4.7
West South Central	1,985,926	201,013	10.1	15.6	7.1	6.1	6.2	3.6
Mountain	654,080	43,152	6.6	7.4	4.9	6.0	6.5	4.2
Pacific	1,191,282	112,881	9.5	7.6	4.5	9.0	7.0	4.0
NEW ENGLAND:								
Maine	162,547	16,288	10.0	9.1	5.6	9.8	8.8	5.3
New Hampshire	92,340	13,308	14.4	13.5	9.2	14.2	13.2	9.0
Vermont	74,488	6,011	8.1	8.9	4.6	7.7	8.4	4.3
Massachusetts	758,794	96,496	12.7	11.6	7.3	12.6	11.5	7.3
Rhode Island	118,749	15,530	13.1	11.1	6.9	13.0	10.9	6.8
Connecticut	278,180	27,935	10.0	8.4	5.0	9.8	8.1	4.9
MIDDLE ATLANTIC:								
New York	2,134,287	194,305	9.1	8.7	4.7	9.0	8.5	4.6
New Jersey	653,461	50,451	7.7	7.4	4.1	7.6	7.1	4.0
Pennsylvania	1,729,503	103,372	6.0	5.9	2.9	5.9	5.6	2.8
EAST NORTH CENTRAL:								
Ohio	1,241,194	76,655	6.2	5.4	2.5	6.0	5.2	2.3
Indiana	649,984	34,848	5.4	4.6	2.3	5.2	4.3	2.1
Illinois	1,352,860	96,448	7.1	5.4	2.7	7.0	5.2	2.5
Michigan	782,534	52,097	6.7	5.3	2.9	6.3	4.8	2.5
Wisconsin	517,697	22,237	4.3	4.7	2.0	3.8	3.4	1.6
WEST NORTH CENTRAL:								
Minnesota	450,730	20,170	4.5	4.7	2.4	4.1	3.6	2.0
Iowa	505,169	24,200	4.8	4.5	2.3	4.5	4.0	2.0
Missouri	724,457	50,414	7.0	6.1	3.1	6.6	5.5	2.7
North Dakota	113,828	3,910	3.4	4.6	2.6	3.0	3.4	9.0
South Dakota	121,390	5,231	4.3	4.3	2.2	3.8	3.5	1.7
Nebraska	263,843	13,967	5.3	4.5	2.5	5.0	3.9	2.1
Kansas	375,631	19,476	5.2	4.7	2.5	4.9	4.2	2.0
SOUTH ATLANTIC:								
Delaware	47,452	4,413	9.3	10.4	5.3	9.0	9.4	5.1
Maryland	293,956	32,262	11.0	12.4	7.2	10.7	11.6	6.9
District of Columbia	88,584	22,871	25.8	21.3	17.5	25.8	21.3	17.5
Virginia	432,195	41,555	9.6	12.5	7.4	8.7	9.6	6.2
West Virginia	280,506	10,499	3.7	5.1	2.0	3.4	4.0	1.5
North Carolina	460,164	60,951	13.2	22.4	11.8	7.7	7.9	5.2
South Carolina	298,337	79,526	26.7	41.9	23.9	8.7	9.5	8.3
Georgia	550,333	107,275	19.5	28.9	15.2	10.3	10.6	8.6
Florida	199,498	35,312	17.7	21.2	11.2	14.9	14.2	7.8
EAST SOUTH CENTRAL:								
Kentucky	480,166	31,280	6.5	8.7	4.6	5.8	6.9	4.1
Tennessee	461,121	44,262	9.6	13.3	6.1	7.4	8.0	4.8
Alabama	439,426	72,733	16.6	31.1	16.1	7.1	7.8	5.7
Mississippi	341,407	76,947	22.5	41.9	19.3	5.4	6.5	4.6
WEST SOUTH CENTRAL:								
Arkansas	343,633	36,919	10.7	20.3	6.0	4.1	5.1	2.7
Louisiana	338,405	50,112	14.8	22.0	15.7	8.1	9.2	6.1
Oklahoma	402,249	26,953	6.7	7.3	2.6	5.2	4.5	1.7
Texas	901,639	87,029	9.7	14.8	5.0	6.4	6.2	3.4
MOUNTAIN:								
Montana	108,098	6,508	6.0	6.6	4.5	5.6	5.7	4.0
Idaho	84,522	4,408	5.2	6.1	3.4	4.8	5.1	2.7
Wyoming	38,163	2,666	7.0	6.9	3.9	6.4	6.3	3.3
Colorado	195,096	14,462	7.4	7.6	4.8	6.9	6.7	4.5
New Mexico	66,476	3,715	5.6	8.0	3.8	5.2	6.4	3.3
Arizona	63,576	6,174	9.7	11.7	13.2	7.5	10.9	8.3
Utah	83,692	3,779	4.5	5.3	3.7	4.3	4.9	3.1
Nevada	14,457	1,440	10.0	11.7	8.3	9.6	11.1	7.9
PACIFIC:								
Washington	287,797	24,172	8.4	6.7	4.3	8.0	6.1	3.6
Oregon	170,027	15,155	8.9	7.2	3.9	8.5	6.5	3.4
California	733,458	73,554	10.0	8.2	4.7	9.5	7.5	4.3

TABLE 131.—PERCENTAGE OF WOMEN WHO WERE NOT MARRIED ENGAGED IN ALL OCCUPATIONS AND IN NONAGRICULTURAL PURSUITS, FOR DIVISIONS AND STATES: 1920, 1910, AND 1900

SINGLE, WIDOWED, OR DIVORCED WOMEN [1] 16 YEARS OF AGE AND OVER

DIVISION AND STATE	Total number: 1920	Engaged in gainful occupations				Per cent engaged in nonagricultural pursuits		
		Number: 1920	1920	1910	1900	1920	1910	1800
UNITED STATES	12,935,650	6,282,620	48.6	48.2	42.0	44.5	42.5	36.4
GEOGRAPHIC DIVISIONS:								
New England	1,136,852	670,676	59.0	57.7	52.2	58.5	57.0	51.3
Middle Atlantic	3,062,718	1,714,879	56.0	53.1	46.4	55.5	52.4	45.6
East North Central	2,603,273	1,253,356	48.1	45.0	38.7	46.8	43.3	36.5
West North Central	1,490,875	622,886	41.8	40.9	36.3	39.4	38.0	33.1
South Atlantic	1,629,455	756,743	46.4	49.6	42.5	36.1	33.4	30.0
East South Central	979,631	407,644	41.6	47.4	41.0	27.7	26.7	23.2
West South Central	1,035,786	407,323	39.3	43.5	36.0	28.8	25.7	23.3
Mountain	317,032	130,971	41.3	41.0	36.0	38.6	37.8	33.2
Pacific	680,028	318,142	46.8	44.1	37.1	45.4	42.4	34.9
NEW ENGLAND:								
Maine	102,768	47,825	46.5	46.5	41.8	44.9	44.5	39.1
New Hampshire	65,438	35,470	54.2	53.6	49.2	53.0	51.8	47.1
Vermont	46,518	20,546	44.2	45.4	40.3	42.2	43.1	37.6
Massachusetts	636,260	392,650	61.7	60.6	55.1	61.5	60.3	54.8
Rhode Island	95,530	60,939	63.8	62.3	57.8	63.6	62.0	57.5
Connecticut	190,348	113,246	59.5	56.8	51.5	58.9	56.1	50.6
MIDDLE ATLANTIC:								
New York	1,554,389	920,526	59.2	56.3	49.7	58.8	55.7	48.8
New Jersey	414,015	233,711	56.4	53.8	46.8	56.2	53.3	46.3
Pennsylvania	1,094,314	560,642	51.2	48.3	42.0	50.6	47.4	41.0
EAST NORTH CENTRAL:								
Ohio	705,423	330,426	46.8	44.4	37.5	45.6	42.9	35.3
Indiana	347,363	146,054	42.0	38.0	32.8	40.3	36.0	30.0
Illinois	836,820	431,427	51.6	48.3	41.0	50.6	47.2	39.4
Michigan	386,724	190,023	49.1	45.0	40.3	47.6	43.0	37.8
Wisconsin	326,943	155,426	47.5	45.8	41.1	45.2	42.7	38.4
WEST NORTH CENTRAL:								
Minnesota	302,108	142,153	47.1	48.0	44.2	44.6	45.1	41.5
Iowa	293,789	115,481	39.3	39.5	35.9	37.4	37.0	33.3
Missouri	431,542	188,507	43.7	40.0	34.1	41.3	37.4	30.5
North Dakota	61,123	23,817	39.0	44.7	46.0	34.7	39.1	40.9
South Dakota	63,525	24,038	37.8	40.2	36.1	34.3	33.7	31.9
Nebraska	143,480	56,902	39.7	39.6	37.3	37.5	36.7	34.3
Kansas	195,308	71,988	36.9	35.0	30.2	34.6	32.3	26.8
SOUTH ATLANTIC:								
Delaware	27,875	13,235	47.5	45.6	39.9	46.3	43.9	38.5
Maryland	200,365	100,914	50.4	47.8	42.2	49.3	46.4	40.8
District of Columbia	97,056	69,156	71.3	58.0	53.8	71.2	57.9	53.7
Virginia	275,629	109,093	39.6	41.5	36.5	35.0	34.3	30.1
West Virginia	137,335	45,488	33.1	32.9	24.5	29.9	28.5	20.2
North Carolina	281,680	120,529	42.8	52.2	38.4	29.1	27.0	24.2
South Carolina	186,888	100,021	53.5	62.3	57.4	26.8	26.0	24.7
Georgia	318,416	151,297	47.5	54.3	48.2	31.1	29.4	29.1
Florida	104,211	47,010	45.1	46.6	42.0	37.8	33.8	29.1
EAST SOUTH CENTRAL:								
Kentucky	266,970	96,009	36.0	37.4	31.4	30.8	31.1	25.9
Tennessee	264,296	98,679	37.3	39.3	33.4	29.9	28.5	24.4
Alabama	255,685	120,582	47.2	57.0	50.5	26.5	24.1	21.7
Mississippi	192,680	92,374	47.9	60.0	53.7	22.1	21.2	19.7
WEST SOUTH CENTRAL:								
Arkansas	162,560	62,843	38.7	47.6	37.9	21.4	21.0	17.3
Louisiana	213,020	92,268	43.3	47.3	43.8	32.8	30.7	26.2
Oklahoma	171,483	61,739	36.0	35.7	28.0	29.6	25.7	17.8
Texas	488,723	190,473	39.0	42.5	32.3	29.2	24.9	20.1
MOUNTAIN:								
Montana	48,164	21,533	44.7	40.6	43.8	41.1	41.4	41.7
Idaho	34,763	12,914	37.1	36.4	31.4	34.4	32.8	26.6
Wyoming	14,636	6,641	45.4	42.7	39.7	41.4	39.0	37.2
Colorado	104,648	47,182	45.1	44.7	39.8	43.2	42.9	38.3
New Mexico	33,343	10,760	32.3	33.1	28.6	27.9	25.8	24.5
Arizona	29,274	11,311	38.6	34.6	34.6	34.7	33.4	25.8
Utah	45,432	17,769	39.1	38.0	29.8	37.6	36.6	27.4
Nevada	6,772	2,861	42.2	41.1	32.4	40.3	39.4	30.0
PACIFIC:								
Washington	139,913	67,914	48.5	45.5	38.4	46.8	43.7	35.5
Oregon	85,535	38,963	45.6	44.0	36.1	43.7	41.7	33.3
California	454,580	211,265	46.5	43.6	37.0	45.2	42.2	35.1

1 Including women whose marital condition was not reported.

TABLE 132.—NUMBER AND PERCENTAGE OF NATIVE WHITE WOMEN OF NATIVE
PARENTAGE ENGAGED IN GAINFUL OCCUPATIONS, BY MARITAL CONDITION,
FOR DIVISIONS AND STATES: 1920

DIVISION AND STATE	NATIVE WHITE WOMEN OF NATIVE PARENTAGE 16 YEARS OF AGE AND OVER: 1920					
	Married			Single, widowed, divorced, or unknown		
	Total number	Engaged in gainful occupations		Total number	Engaged in gainful occupations	
		Number	Per cent		Number	Per cent
UNITED STATES	11,187,355	707,503	6.3	6,782,595	2,888,894	42.6
GEOGRAPHIC DIVISIONS:						
New England	534,556	53,955	10.1	449,298	222,895	49.6
Middle Atlantic	1,851,965	128,914	7.0	1,355,281	690,751	51.0
East North Central	2,291,442	131,837	5.8	1,368,847	614,199	44.9
West North Central	1,378,732	75,291	5.5	810,306	328,388	40.5
South Atlantic	1,667,783	111,538	6.7	991,269	382,405	38.6
East South Central	1,171,928	54,980	4.7	623,815	197,181	31.6
West South Central	1,329,458	68,620	5.2	650,594	220,355	33.9
Mountain	364,341	23,592	6.5	181,281	72,987	40.3
Pacific	597,150	58,776	9.8	351,904	159,733	45.4
NEW ENGLAND:						
Maine	105,338	9,793	9.3	67,193	27,827	41.4
New Hampshire	46,861	5,270	11.2	34,448	15,213	44.2
Vermont	46,294	3,870	8.4	30,379	12,799	42.1
Massachusetts	220,904	24,173	10.9	216,421	114,335	52.8
Rhode Island	30,370	3,136	10.3	28,597	15,594	54.5
Connecticut	84,789	7,713	9.1	72,260	37,127	51.4
MIDDLE ATLANTIC:						
New York	692,186	62,953	9.1	557,361	298,069	53.5
New Jersey	233,415	13,866	5.9	170,872	87,412	51.2
Pennsylvania	926,364	52,095	5.6	627,048	305,270	48.7
EAST NORTH CENTRAL:						
Ohio	756,333	41,093	5.4	442,412	200,168	45.2
Indiana	502,830	24,839	4.9	267,040	109,347	40.9
Illinois	573,021	34,380	6.0	370,807	167,211	45.1
Michigan	319,304	24,690	7.7	169,874	80,992	47.7
Wisconsin	139,954	6,835	4.9	118,714	56,481	47.6
WEST NORTH CENTRAL:						
Minnesota	109,135	6,292	5.8	90,114	41,913	46.5
Iowa	284,097	15,533	5.5	172,733	68,737	39.8
Missouri	511,354	27,915	5.5	291,659	118,270	40.6
North Dakota	27,721	1,494	5.4	16,833	7,089	42.1
South Dakota	47,379	2,745	5.8	26,809	10,782	40.2
Nebraska	135,075	8,003	5.9	75,817	30,843	40.7
Kansas	263,971	13,309	5.0	136,341	50,754	37.2
SOUTH ATLANTIC:						
Delaware	30,283	1,709	5.6	17,493	7,573	43.3
Maryland	174,854	8,979	5.1	119,419	55,034	46.1
District of Columbia	46,051	8,558	18.6	55,840	39,799	71.3
Virginia	289,745	12,236	4.2	178,955	59,230	33.1
West Virginia	236,135	7,281	3.1	117,504	37,453	31.9
North Carolina	323,994	24,327	7.5	188,007	68,762	36.6
South Carolina	145,496	17,215	11.8	86,126	34,489	40.0
Georgia	312,942	24,432	7.8	173,587	62,118	35.8
Florida	108,283	6,801	6.3	54,338	17,947	33.0
EAST SOUTH CENTRAL:						
Kentucky	397,140	13,636	3.4	204,460	63,320	31.0
Tennessee	358,608	15,157	4.2	196,230	59,796	30.5
Alabama	261,756	16,483	6.3	137,315	46,997	34.2
Mississippi	154,424	9,704	6.3	85,810	27,068	31.5
WEST SOUTH CENTRAL:						
Arkansas	235,796	11,674	5.0	105,998	32,547	30.7
Louisiana	168,607	7,030	4.2	102,337	34,887	34.1
Oklahoma	329,970	18,359	5.6	135,970	47,954	35.3
Texas	595,085	31,557	5.3	306,289	104,967	34.3
MOUNTAIN:						
Montana	50,016	3,391	6.8	22,354	9,608	43.0
Idaho	52,323	2,888	5.5	22,809	8,284	36.3
Wyoming	23,035	1,692	7.3	9,014	4,068	45.1
Colorado	120,184	9,006	7.5	63,994	28,170	44.0
New Mexico	50,436	2,149	4.3	25,257	7,744	30.7
Arizona	28,739	2,153	7.5	12,928	5,414	41.9
Utah	33,185	1,671	5.0	21,695	8,289	38.2
Nevada	6,423	642	10.0	3,230	1,410	43.7
PACIFIC:						
Washington	144,122	13,044	9.1	71,806	33,787	47.1
Oregon	104,534	9,796	9.4	52,160	22,856	43.8
California	348,494	35,936	10.3	227,938	103,090	45.2

TABLE 133.—NUMBER AND PERCENTAGE OF NATIVE WHITE WOMEN OF FOREIGN OR MIXED PARENTAGE ENGAGED IN GAINFUL OCCUPATIONS, BY MARITAL CONDITION, FOR DIVISIONS AND STATES: 1920

DIVISION AND STATE	NATIVE WHITE WOMEN OF FOREIGN OR MIXED PARENTAGE 16 YEARS OF AGE AND OVER: 1920					
	Married			Single, widowed, divorced, or unknown		
	Total number	Engaged in gainful occupations		Total number	Engaged in gainful occupations	
		Number	Per cent		Number	Per cent
UNITED STATES	3, 889, 982	245, 311	6. 3	3, 100, 703	1, 797, 493	58. 0
GEOGRAPHIC DIVISIONS:						
New England	330, 898	40, 863	12. 3	395, 073	278, 420	70. 5
Middle Atlantic	986, 838	62, 990	6. 4	964, 370	616, 441	63. 9
East North Central	1, 156, 072	60, 811	5. 3	793, 709	452. 638	57. 0
West North Central	702, 820	29, 359	4. 2	470, 351	218, 764	46. 5
South Atlantic	98, 389	6, 754	6. 9	82, 965	43, 651	52. 6
East South Central	46, 334	2, 205	4. 8	37, 460	16, 829	44. 9
West South Central	130, 824	7, 991	6. 1	83, 830	31, 417	37. 5
Mountain	150, 577	8, 760	5. 8	79, 270	37, 915	47. 8
Pacific	287, 230	25, 578	8. 9	193, 675	101, 418	52. 4
NEW ENGLAND:						
Maine	23, 172	2, 665	11. 5	20, 774	11, 816	56. 9
New Hampshire	16, 662	2, 844	17. 1	17, 638	12, 197	69. 2
Vermont	14, 751	1, 292	8. 8	10, 586	5, 505	52. 0
Massachusetts	181, 954	23, 522	12. 9	236, 698	169, 529	71. 6
Rhode Island	30, 255	4, 208	13. 9	38, 137	28, 469	74. 6
Connecticut	64, 104	6, 332	9. 9	71, 240	50, 904	71. 5
MIDDLE ATLANTIC:						
New York	528, 862	40, 166	7. 6	541, 224	357, 609	66. 1
New Jersey	149, 309	9, 012	6. 0	138, 820	91, 479	65. 9
Pennsylvania	308, 667	13, 812	4. 5	284, 326	167, 353	58. 9
EAST NORTH CENTRAL:						
Ohio	242, 569	11, 589	4. 8	168, 333	90, 088	53. 5
Indiana	86, 275	3, 494	4. 0	52, 439	24, 895	47. 5
Illinois	364, 388	23, 372	6. 4	285, 647	179, 482	62. 8
Michigan	226, 350	13, 009	5. 7	136, 948	76, 493	55. 9
Wisconsin	236, 490	9, 347	4. 0	150, 342	81, 680	54. 3
WEST NORTH CENTRAL:						
Minnesota	193, 515	8, 339	4. 3	152, 829	79, 265	51. 9
Iowa	151, 054	5, 637	3. 7	88, 915	38, 283	43. 1
Missouri	123, 161	6, 521	5. 3	84, 382	43, 749	51. 8
North Dakota	43, 318	1, 476	3. 4	31, 579	12, 491	39. 6
South Dakota	45, 424	1, 710	3. 8	26, 381	10, 466	39. 7
Nebraska	79, 322	3, 208	4. 0	48, 488	20, 279	41. 8
Kansas	67, 026	2, 468	3. 7	37, 777	14, 231	37. 7
SOUTH ATLANTIC:						
Delaware	5, 215	295	5. 7	4, 339	2, 360	54. 4
Maryland	39, 629	2, 042	5. 2	33, 689	18, 283	54. 3
District of Columbia	11, 196	1, 651	14. 7	13, 922	9, 829	70. 6
Virginia	8, 646	537	6. 2	6, 783	2, 917	43. 0
West Virginia	11, 950	396	3. 3	8, 441	3, 446	40. 8
North Carolina	2, 040	135	6. 6	1, 682	662	39. 4
South Carolina	2, 255	127	5. 6	2, 099	856	40. 8
Georgia	5, 634	386	6. 9	4, 757	2, 099	44. 1
Florida	11, 824	1, 185	10. 0	7, 253	3, 199	44. 1
EAST SOUTH CENTRAL:						
Kentucky	27, 567	1, 174	4. 3	22, 984	11, 320	49. 3
Tennessee	8, 212	433	5. 3	6, 511	2, 690	41. 3
Alabama	6, 632	349	5. 3	5, 031	1, 857	36. 9
Mississippi	3, 923	249	6. 3	2, 934	962	32. 8
WEST SOUTH CENTRAL:						
Arkansas	8, 413	448	5. 3	4, 834	1, 859	38. 5
Louisiana	21, 653	1, 054	4. 9	20, 055	7, 240	36. 1
Oklahoma	23, 100	1, 306	5. 7	10, 908	4, 115	37. 7
Texas	77, 658	5, 183	6. 7	48, 033	18, 203	37. 9
MOUNTAIN:						
Montana	30, 504	1, 845	6. 0	16, 564	8, 382	50. 6
Idaho	20, 945	984	4. 7	8, 296	3, 500	42. 2
Wyoming	8, 387	538	6. 4	3, 726	1, 813	48. 7
Colorado	39, 196	2, 797	7. 1	25, 817	13, 062	50. 6
New Mexico	5, 121	314	6. 1	3, 038	1, 318	43. 4
Arizona	9, 451	665	7. 0	4, 861	1, 995	41. 0
Utah	32, 967	1, 259	3. 8	15, 074	6, 951	46. 1
Nevada	4, 006	358	8. 9	1, 894	894	47. 2
PACIFIC:						
Washington	69, 304	5, 782	8. 3	42, 264	22, 639	53. 6
Oregon	36, 057	3, 206	8. 9	21, 737	11, 443	52. 6
California	181, 869	16, 590	9. 1	129, 674	67, 336	51. 9

TABLE **134.**—NUMBER AND PERCENTAGE OF FOREIGN-BORN WHITE WOMEN ENGAGED IN GAINFUL OCCUPATIONS, BY MARITAL CONDITION, FOR DIVISIONS AND STATES: 1920

DIVISION AND STATE	FOREIGN-BORN WHITE WOMEN 16 YEARS OF AGE AND OVER: 1920					
	Married			Single, widowed, divorced, or unknown		
	Total number	Engaged in gainful occupations		Total number	Engaged in gainful occupations	
		Number	Per cent		Number	Per cent
UNITED STATES	4,122,932	296,126	7.2	1,749,434	806,571	46.1
GEOGRAPHIC DIVISIONS:						
New England	603,222	75,446	12.5	279,790	160,498	57.4
Middle Atlantic	1,541,678	107,143	6.9	651,136	340,275	52.3
East North Central	974,117	56,092	5.8	376,616	147,304	39.1
West North Central	404,084	14,434	3.6	168,357	52,159	31.0
South Atlantic	86,306	6,986	8.1	37,552	16,491	43.9
East South Central	17,902	1,243	6.9	10,769	3,183	29.6
West South Central	109,847	7,664	7.0	57,608	19,582	34.0
Mountain	117,463	6,649	5.7	46,177	16,271	35.2
Pacific	268,313	20,469	7.6	121,429	50,808	41.8
NEW ENGLAND:						
Maine	33,637	3,742	11.1	14,489	8,010	55.3
New Hampshire	28,699	5,172	18.0	13,273	8,001	60.3
Vermont	13,352	822	6.2	5,479	2,199	40.1
Massachusetts	346,569	45,935	13.3	175,511	103,463	58.9
Rhode Island	56,185	7,624	13.6	27,147	15,701	57.8
Connecticut	124,780	12,151	9.7	43,891	23,124	52.7
MIDDLE ATLANTIC:						
New York	866,317	70,860	8.2	418,548	235,600	56.3
New Jersey	244,664	18,708	7.6	86,727	42,197	48.7
Pennsylvania	430,697	17,575	4.1	145,861	62,478	42.8
EAST NORTH CENTRAL:						
Ohio	199,493	12,120	6.1	73,685	27,598	37.5
Indiana	42,614	1,605	3.8	17,286	5,173	29.9
Illinois	372,419	25,758	6.9	155,132	68,703	44.3
Michigan	221,192	10,872	4.9	74,093	29,140	39.3
Wisconsin	138,399	5,737	4.1	56,420	16,690	29.6
WEST NORTH CENTRAL:						
Minnesota	144,326	4,921	3.4	57,275	20,145	35.2
Iowa	65,632	1,978	3.0	29,965	7,230	24.1
Missouri	50,136	3,154	6.3	29,529	10,004	33.9
North Dakota	41,525	916	2.2	12,111	4,149	34.3
South Dakota	25,051	697	2.8	8,675	2,636	30.4
Nebraska	45,618	1,758	3.9	17,476	4,860	27.8
Kansas	31,796	1,010	3.2	13,326	3,135	23.5
SOUTH ATLANTIC:						
Delaware	5,958	308	5.2	2,088	901	43.2
Maryland	30,755	1,955	6.4	14,980	6,379	42.6
District of Columbia	7,616	877	11.5	5,349	2,999	56.1
Virginia	8,199	495	6.0	2,839	1,132	39.9
West Virginia	14,797	485	3.3	3,415	1,055	30.9
North Carolina	1,733	123	7.1	863	419	48.6
South Carolina	1,467	137	9.3	725	237	32.7
Georgia	3,932	337	8.6	1,967	851	43.3
Florida	11,849	2,269	19.1	5,326	2,518	47.3
EAST SOUTH CENTRAL:						
Kentucky	7,146	366	5.1	5,828	1,581	27.1
Tennessee	3,996	306	7.7	2,183	744	34.1
Alabama	4,762	298	6.3	1,879	603	32.1
Mississippi	1,998	273	13.7	879	255	29.0
WEST SOUTH CENTRAL:						
Arkansas	3,461	247	7.1	1,720	687	39.9
Louisiana	10,736	742	6.9	6,507	1,986	30.5
Oklahoma	10,620	508	4.8	3,446	1,120	32.5
Texas	85,030	6,167	7.3	45,935	15,789	34.4
MOUNTAIN:						
Montana	24,802	1,145	4.6	8,165	3,324	40.7
Idaho	10,092	446	4.4	3,252	1,053	32.4
Wyoming	6,009	305	5.1	1,654	641	38.8
Colorado	32,392	1,842	5.7	12,953	4,770	36.8
New Mexico	7,040	261	3.7	2,871	899	31.3
Arizona	18,002	1,753	9.7	8,134	2,818	34.6
Utah	16,293	686	4.2	8,156	2,419	29.7
Nevada	2,833	211	7.4	992	347	35.0
PACIFIC:						
Washington	67,299	4,096	6.1	23,843	10,681	44.8
Oregon	27,188	1,788	6.6	10,611	4,391	41.4
California	173,826	14,585	8.4	86,975	35,736	41.1

TABLE 135.—NUMBER AND PERCENTAGE OF NEGRO WOMEN ENGAGED IN GAIN-
FUL OCCUPATIONS, BY MARITAL CONDITION, FOR DIVISIONS AND STATES: 1920

DIVISION AND STATE	NEGRO WOMEN 16 YEARS OF AGE AND OVER: 1920					
	Married			Single, widowed, divorced, or unknown		
	Total number	Engaged in gainful occupations		Total number	Engaged in gainful occupations	
		Number	Per cent		Number	Per cent
UNITED STATES	2,036,419	662,684	32.5	1,275,662	783,251	61.4
GEOGRAPHIC DIVISIONS:						
New England	15,949	5,205	32.6	12,362	8,710	70.5
Middle Atlantic	135,135	48,833	36.1	90,940	67,034	73.7
East North Central	119,534	33,328	27.9	62,413	38,738	62.1
West North Central	62,005	18,112	29.2	38,152	23,200	60.8
South Atlantic	796,137	269,074	33.8	516,532	313,750	60.7
East South Central	485,654	166,730	34.3	307,429	190,376	61.9
West South Central	405,552	116,388	28.7	238,056	135,036	56.7
Mountain	5,639	1,600	28.4	3,011	2,002	66.5
Pacific	10,814	3,414	31.6	6,767	4,405	65.1
NEW ENGLAND:						
Maine	228	43	18.9	207	129	62.3
New Hampshire	108	17	15.7	72	55	(1)
Vermont	88	25	(1)	72	42	(1)
Massachusetts	9,156	2,831	30.9	7,466	5,253	·70.4
Rhode Island	1,912	558	29.2	1,624	1,161	71.5
Connecticut	4,457	1,731	38.8	2,921	2,070	70.9
MIDDLE ATLANTIC:						
New York	45,496	20,112	44.2	36,377	28,934	79.5
New Jersey	25,992	8,850	34.0	17,553	12,596	71.8
Pennsylvania	63,647	19,871	31.2	37,010	25,504	68.9
EAST NORTH CENTRAL:						
Ohio	42,722	11,835	27.7	20,950	12,558	59.9
Indiana	18,240	4,907	26.9	10,568	6,624	62.7
Illinois	42,842	12,906	30.1	25,141	15,982	63.6
Michigan	14,619	3,427	23.4	5,209	3,221	61.8
Wisconsin	1,111	253	22.8	545	353	64.8
WEST NORTH CENTRAL:						
Minnesota	2,061	553	26.8	1,063	702	66.0
Iowa	4,275	1,046	24.5	2,122	1,225	57.7
Missouri	39,746	12,811	32.2	25,938	16,465	63.5
North Dakota	84	11	(1)	53	34	(1)
South Dakota	146	43	29.5	82	51	(1)
Nebraska	3,122	979	31.4	1,439	887	61.6
Kansas	12,571	2,669	21.2	7,455	3,836	51.5
SOUTH ATLANTIC:						
Delaware	5,995	2,101	35.0	3,955	2,401	60.7
Maryland	48,698	19,281	39.6	32,264	21,208	65.7
District of Columbia	23,683	11,779	49.7	21,923	16,516	75.3
Virginia	125,456	28,278	22.5	86,973	45,790	52.6
West Virginia	17,615	2,335	13.3	7,973	3,534	44.3
North Carolina	130,399	36,095	27.7	90,206	50,318	55.8
South Carolina	149,060	62,039	41.6	97,910	64,425	65.8
Georgia	227,798	82,114	36.0	138,097	86,221	62.4
Florida	67,433	25,052	37.2	37,231	23,337	62.7
EAST SOUTH CENTRAL:						
Kentucky	48,300	16,098	33.3	33,688	19,779	58.7
Tennessee	90,290	28,365	31.4	59,363	35,446	59.7
Alabama	166,221	55,600	33.4	111,422	71,106	63.8
Mississippi	180,843	66,667	36.9	102,956	64,045	62.2
WEST SOUTH CENTRAL:						
Arkansas	95,938	24,549	25.6	49,991	27,745	55.5
Louisiana	137,213	41,274	30.1	83,994	48,121	57.3
Oklahoma	28,972	6,495	22.4	15,802	7,743	49.0
Texas	143,429	44,070	30.7	88,269	51,427	58.3
MOUNTAIN:						
Montana	347	68	19.6	195	137	70.3
Idaho	189	36	19.0	73	43	(1)
Wyoming	279	103	36.9	144	102	70.8
Colorado	2,574	765	29.7	1,732	1,147	66.2
New Mexico	647	172	26.6	217	129	59.4
Arizona	1,158	336	29.0	483	334	69.2
Utah	368	81	22.0	122	73	59.8
Nevada	77	39	(1)	45	37	(1)
PACIFIC:						
Washington	1,545	441	28.5	751	477	63.5
Oregon	511	168	32.9	231	147	63.6
California	8,758	2,805	32.0	5,785	3,781	65.4

1 Per cent not shown where base is less than 100.

TABLE 136.—AGE DISTRIBUTION OF MARRIED WOMEN ENGAGED IN GAINFUL OCCUPATIONS, FOR DIVISIONS AND STATES: 1920

DIVISION AND STATE	MARRIED WOMEN 16 YEARS OF AGE AND OVER ENGAGED IN GAINFUL OCCUPATIONS: 1920						
	Total number	16 to 19 years of age	20 to 24 years of age	25 to 34 years of age	35 to 44 years of age	45 years and over	Age unknown
UNITED STATES	1,920,281	74,305	283,870	627,580	516,126	414,436	3,964
GEOGRAPHIC DIVISIONS:							
New England	175,568	4,101	23,347	58,444	48,693	40,769	214
Middle Atlantic	348,128	8,757	45,649	117,139	98,291	77,863	429
East North Central	282,285	8,374	39,216	93,627	75,643	64,942	483
West North Central	137,368	4,117	18,211	43,201	37,127	34,408	304
South Atlantic	394,664	22,006	69,652	127,175	100,557	74,224	1,050
East South Central	225,222	12,534	36,436	69,949	58,283	47,556	464
West South Central	201,013	10,847	33,706	67,586	51,575	36,673	626
Mountain	43,152	1,193	5,030	13,969	12,402	10,452	106
Pacific	112,881	2,376	12,623	36,490	33,555	27,549	288
NEW ENGLAND:							
Maine	16,288	400	2,085	4,655	4,454	4,674	20
New Hampshire	13,308	324	1,606	4,174	3,545	3,532	37
Vermont	6,011	143	625	1,517	1,664	2,050	12
Massachusetts	96,496	2,074	12,721	32,971	27,159	21,488	83
Rhode Island	15,530	437	2,340	5,459	4,162	3,122	10
Connecticut	27,935	723	3,880	9,668	7,709	5,903	52
MIDDLE ATLANTIC:							
New York	194,305	4,055	23,415	65,522	56,732	44,364	217
New Jersey	50,451	1,355	7,183	17,511	14,099	10,238	65
Pennsylvania	103,372	3,347	15,051	34,106	27,460	23,261	147
EAST NORTH CENTRAL:							
Ohio	76,655	2,325	10,942	25,221	20,626	17,460	81
Indiana	34,848	1,310	4,741	10,143	9,107	9,471	76
Illinois	96,448	2,587	13,351	34,180	26,477	19,620	233
Michigan	52,097	1,678	7,607	17,263	13,230	12,263	56
Wisconsin	22,237	474	2,575	6,820	6,203	6,128	37
WEST NORTH CENTRAL:							
Minnesota	20,170	413	2,665	6,650	5,562	4,838	42
Iowa	24,200	685	3,261	7,250	6,228	6,742	34
Missouri	50,414	1,718	6,670	16,161	13,773	11,987	105
North Dakota	3,910	107	594	1,272	1,015	915	7
South Dakota	5,231	139	760	1,651	1,398	1,257	26
Nebraska	13,967	463	1,895	4,508	3,710	3,353	38
Kansas	19,476	592	2,366	5,709	5,441	5,316	52
SOUTH ATLANTIC:							
Delaware	4,413	168	613	1,324	1,151	1,133	24
Maryland	32,262	1,071	4,591	10,297	8,754	7,504	45
District of Columbia	22,871	613	3,449	7,914	6,654	4,151	90
Virginia	41,555	1,549	6,490	12,815	11,278	9,304	119
West Virginia	10,499	425	1,523	3,161	2,788	2,578	24
North Carolina	60,951	3,987	11,445	19,165	14,873	11,322	159
South Carolina	79,526	5,098	15,661	25,582	19,570	13,502	113
Georgia	107,275	7,597	20,333	34,820	25,704	18,589	232
Florida	35,312	1,498	5,547	12,097	9,785	6,141	244
EAST SOUTH CENTRAL:							
Kentucky	31,280	1,109	3,769	9,194	8,619	8,501	88
Tennessee	44,262	2,427	7,184	13,989	11,656	8,876	130
Alabama	72,733	3,864	11,829	22,757	19,009	15,162	112
Mississippi	76,947	5,134	13,654	24,009	18,999	15,017	134
WEST SOUTH CENTRAL:							
Arkansas	36,919	2,453	6,184	12,034	9,422	6,775	51
Louisiana	50,112	2,334	7,818	16,438	13,364	9,975	183
Oklahoma	26,953	1,328	4,510	8,950	6,880	5,227	58
Texas	87,029	4,732	15,194	30,164	21,909	14,696	334
MOUNTAIN:							
Montana	6,508	97	665	2,353	1,889	1,494	10
Idaho	4,408	108	546	1,389	1,230	1,129	6
Wyoming	2,666	56	330	1,029	745	502	4
Colorado	14,462	349	1,570	4,278	4,257	3,959	49
New Mexico	3,715	134	448	1,222	1,033	873	5
Arizona	6,174	300	877	2,137	1,746	1,094	20
Utah	3,779	124	465	1,102	1,066	1,012	10
Nevada	1,440	25	129	459	436	389	2
PACIFIC:							
Washington	24,172	589	2,896	7,781	7,111	5,720	75
Oregon	15,155	364	1,717	4,635	4,459	3,967	13
California	73,554	1,423	8,010	24,074	21,985	17,862	200

TABLE 137.—PERCENTAGE DISTRIBUTION, BY AGE, OF GAINFULLY OCCUPIED MARRIED WOMEN AND OF WOMEN WHO WERE NOT MARRIED, FOR DIVISIONS AND STATES: 1920

DIVISION AND STATE	PER CENT OF TOTAL MARRIED							PER CENT OF TOTAL NOT MARRIED				
	16 to 19 years of age	20 to 24 years of age	25 to 34 years of age	35 to 44 years of age	25 to 44 years of age	45 years and over	Age un-known	16 to 19 years of age	20 to 24 years of age	25 to 44 years of age	45 years and over	Age un-known
UNITED STATES	3.9	14.8	32.7	26.9	59.6	21.6	0.2	21.3	24.3	36.2	18.1	0.2
GEOGRAPHIC DIVISIONS:												
New England	2.3	13.3	33.3	27.7	61.0	23.2	0.1	19.8	24.1	37.0	18.9	0.1
Middle Atlantic	2.5	13.1	33.6	28.2	61.9	22.4	0.1	23.4	25.0	35.5	16.1	0.1
East North Central	3.0	13.9	33.2	26.8	60.0	23.0	0.2	22.3	25.4	35.6	16.6	0.1
West North Central	3.0	13.3	31.4	27.0	58.5	25.0	0.2	19.0	27.5	37.0	16.3	0.2
South Atlantic	5.6	17.6	32.2	25.5	57.7	18.8	0.3	22.0	22.2	35.0	20.6	0.3
East South Central	5.6	16.2	31.1	25.9	56.9	21.1	0.2	20.8	20.2	35.1	23.7	0.2
West South Central	5.4	16.8	33.6	25.7	59.3	18.2	0.3	21.4	23.0	36.0	19.2	0.4
Mountain	2.8	11.7	32.4	28.7	61.1	24.2	0.2	16.7	25.1	38.7	19.1	0.3
Pacific	2.1	11.2	32.3	29.7	62.1	24.4	0.3	14.3	21.7	42.6	21.1	0.3
NEW ENGLAND:												
Maine	2.5	12.8	28.6	27.3	55.9	28.7	0.1	18.0	23.9	33.8	24.1	0.2
New Hampshire	2.4	12.7	31.4	26.6	58.0	26.5	0.3	19.5	23.5	33.6	23.2	0.2
Vermont	2.4	10.4	25.2	27.7	52.9	34.1	0.2	18.0	23.0	33.3	25.5	0.1
Massachusetts	2.1	13.2	34.2	28.1	62.3	22.3	0.1	18.6	23.9	38.7	18.7	0.1
Rhode Island	2.8	15.1	35.2	26.8	62.0	20.1	0.1	22.9	23.7	36.3	17.1	0.1
Connecticut	2.6	13.9	34.6	27.6	62.2	21.1	0.2	23.4	25.6	34.8	16.0	0.1
MIDDLE ATLANTIC:												
New York	2.1	12.1	33.7	29.2	62.9	22.8	0.1	21.9	25.4	36.6	16.1	0.1
New Jersey	2.7	14.2	34.7	27.9	62.7	20.3	0.1	26.0	25.3	33.7	14.8	0.1
Pennsylvania	3.2	14.6	33.0	26.6	59.6	22.5	0.1	24.7	24.1	34.4	16.6	0.1
EAST NORTH CENTRAL:												
Ohio	3.0	14.3	32.9	26.9	59.8	22.8	0.1	20.7	24.1	36.4	18.6	0.1
Indiana	3.8	13.6	29.1	26.1	55.2	27.2	0.2	22.1	23.5	34.2	20.0	0.2
Illinois	2.7	13.8	35.4	27.5	62.9	20.3	0.2	22.5	25.4	36.8	15.1	0.2
Michigan	3.2	14.6	33.1	25.4	58.5	23.5	0.1	24.0	25.9	34.2	15.7	0.2
Wisconsin	2.1	11.6	30.7	27.9	58.6	27.6	0.2	23.4	28.9	33.4	14.2	0.1
WEST NORTH CENTRAL:												
Minnesota	2.0	13.2	33.0	27.6	60.5	24.0	0.2	19.2	30.7	37.5	12.5	0.1
Iowa	2.8	13.5	30.0	25.7	55.7	27.9	0.1	17.5	28.0	37.3	17.1	0.2
Missouri	3.4	13.2	32.1	27.3	59.4	23.8	0.2	19.7	23.0	37.5	19.5	0.2
North Dakota	2.7	15.2	32.5	26.0	58.5	23.4	0.2	19.8	34.2	33.5	12.1	0.4
South Dakota	2.7	14.5	31.6	26.7	58.3	24.0	0.5	18.0	32.2	35.8	13.5	0.5
Nebraska	3.3	13.6	32.3	26.6	58.8	24.0	0.3	19.7	29.3	36.7	14.1	0.2
Kansas	3.0	12.1	29.3	27.9	57.2	27.3	0.3	18.1	27.4	36.2	18.0	0.3
SOUTH ATLANTIC:												
Delaware	3.8	13.9	30.0	26.1	56.1	25.7	0.5	21.2	22.3	35.1	21.1	0.3
Maryland	3.3	14.2	31.9	27.1	59.1	23.3	0.1	23.0	21.5	35.1	20.3	0.1
District of Columbia	2.7	15.1	34.6	29.1	63.7	18.1	0.4	11.3	23.9	45.2	19.1	0.4
Virginia	3.7	15.6	30.8	27.1	58.0	22.4	0.3	19.6	23.2	34.0	22.8	0.4
West Virginia	4.0	14.5	30.1	26.6	56.7	24.6	0.2	21.7	25.3	33.8	19.0	0.3
North Carolina	6.5	18.8	31.4	24.4	55.8	18.6	0.3	25.4	23.5	31.1	19.7	0.3
South Carolina	6.4	19.7	32.2	24.6	56.8	17.0	0.1	27.0	21.0	32.1	19.7	0.2
Georgia	7.1	19.0	32.5	24.0	56.4	17.3	0.2	23.0	20.8	35.2	20.9	0.2
Florida	4.2	15.7	34.3	27.7	62.0	17.4	0.7	18.5	19.8	38.2	23.1	0.4
EAST SOUTH CENTRAL:												
Kentucky	3.5	12.0	29.4	27.6	56.9	27.2	0.3	16.5	20.0	35.9	27.4	0.2
Tennessee	5.5	16.2	31.6	26.3	57.9	20.1	0.3	18.9	20.8	36.5	23.6	0.2
Alabama	5.3	16.3	31.3	26.1	57.4	20.8	0.2	24.2	20.1	33.7	21.8	0.2
Mississippi	6.7	17.7	31.2	24.7	55.9	19.5	0.2	22.8	19.8	34.4	22.6	0.3
WEST SOUTH CENTRAL:												
Arkansas	6.6	16.8	32.6	25.5	58.1	18.4	0.1	23.2	20.4	34.2	21.9	0.3
Louisiana	4.7	15.6	32.8	26.7	59.5	19.9	0.4	20.8	20.6	36.2	22.0	0.4
Oklahoma	4.9	16.7	33.2	25.5	58.7	19.4	0.2	21.2	26.6	35.7	16.2	0.3
Texas	5.4	17.5	34.7	25.2	59.8	16.9	0.4	21.2	24.0	36.5	17.9	0.4
MOUNTAIN:												
Montana	1.5	10.2	36.2	29.0	65.2	23.0	0.2	15.9	26.0	40.7	17.0	0.3
Idaho	2.5	12.4	31.5	27.9	59.4	25.6	0.1	18.1	29.2	35.9	16.6	0.1
Wyoming	2.1	12.4	38.6	27.9	66.5	18.8	0.2	16.1	26.3	39.9	16.9	0.8
Colorado	2.4	10.9	29.6	29.4	59.0	27.4	0.3	15.5	23.3	39.7	21.3	0.2
New Mexico	3.6	12.1	32.9	27.8	60.7	23.5	0.1	16.5	22.4	36.9	24.0	0.2
Arizona	4.9	14.2	34.6	28.3	62.9	17.7	0.3	16.2	22.0	42.8	18.7	0.8
Utah	3.3	12.3	29.2	28.2	57.4	26.8	0.3	22.0	29.7	33.4	14.7	0.2
Nevada	1.7	9.0	31.9	30.3	62.2	27.0	0.1	11.6	21.2	42.2	24.6	0.4
PACIFIC:												
Washington	2.4	12.0	32.2	29.4	61.6	23.7	0.3	16.4	24.9	40.7	17.6	0.4
Oregon	2.4	11.3	30.6	29.4	60.0	26.2	0.1	16.3	24.3	40.7	18.5	0.2
California	1.9	10.9	32.7	29.9	62.6	24.3	0.3	13.3	20.2	43.5	22.7	0.3

TABLE 138.—PERCENTAGE OF MARRIED WOMEN ENGAGED IN GAINFUL OCCUPATIONS, FOR CITIES OF 100,000 INHABITANTS OR MORE AND FOR AREAS OUTSIDE OF SUCH CITIES, BY DIVISIONS AND STATES: 1920, 1910, AND 1900

DIVISION AND STATE	MARRIED WOMEN 16 YEARS OF AGE AND OVER							
	In cities having 100,000 inhabitants or more			In balance of State				
	Total number: 1920	Engaged in gainful occupations		Total number: 1920	Engaged in gainful occupations			
		Number: 1920	Per cent: 1920		Number: 1920	Per cent		
						1920	1910	1900
UNITED STATES____	5,667,010	626,764	11.1	15,639,089	1,293,517	8.3	11.0	5.6
GEOGRAPHIC DIVISIONS:								
New England_____	425,579	54,720	12.9	1,059,519	120,848	11.4	10.5	6.6
Middle Atlantic_____	2,120,668	192,414	9.1	2,396,583	155,714	6.5	3.6	
East North Central___	1,431,192	137,478	9.6	3,113,077	144,807	4.7	4.5	2.3
West North Central__	460,682	49,922	10.8	2,094,366	87,446	4.2	4.5	2.3
South Atlantic_____	369,061	69,689	18.9	2,281,964	324,975	14.2	21.5	11.7
East South Central___	150,061	27,665	18.4	1,572,059	197,557	12.6	22.6	10.6
West South Central__	196,848	32,418	16.5	1,789,025	168,595	9.4	15.5	6.9
Mountain_____	79,360	7,973	10.0	574,720	35,179	6.1	7.2	4.7
Pacific_____	433,559	54,485	12.6	757,723	58,396	7.7	7.1	4.1
NEW ENGLAND:								
Maine_____				162,547	16,288	10.0	9.1	5.6
New Hampshire_____				92,340	13,308	14.4	13.5	9.2
Vermont_____				74,488	6,011	8.1	8.9	4.6
Massachusetts_____	289,570	39,591	13.7	469,224	56,905	12.1	11.3	7.3
Rhode Island_____	46,221	5,433	11.8	72,528	10,097	13.9	12.0	7.2
Connecticut_____	89,788	9,696	10.8	188,392	18,239	9.7	8.3	5.1
MIDDLE ATLANTIC:								
New York_____	1,362,294	126,374	9.3	771,993	67,931	8.8	8.4	4.7
New Jersey_____	219,939	17,687	8.0	433,522	32,764	7.6	7.8	4.3
Pennsylvania_____	538,435	48,353	9.0	1,191,068	55,019	4.6	4.8	2.4
EAST NORTH CENTRAL:								
Ohio_____	463,642	43,644	9.4	777,552	33,011	4.2	4.5	2.1
Indiana_____	73,556	8,876	12.1	576,428	25,972	4.5	4.1	2.1
Illinois_____	560,572	58,438	10.4	792,288	38,010	4.8	4.4	2.2
Michigan_____	239,390	20,150	8.4	543,144	31,947	5.9	5.1	2.9
Wisconsin_____	94,032	6,370	6.8	423,665	15,867	3.7	4.7	1.9
WEST NORTH CENTRAL:								
Minnesota_____	127,974	10,140	7.9	322,756	10,030	3.0	4.4	2.0
Iowa_____	28,252	3,554	12.6	476,917	20,646	4.3	4.5	2.3
Missouri_____	241,020	28,970	12.0	483,437	21,444	4.4	4.8	2.2
North Dakota_____				113,828	3,910	3.4	4.6	2.6
South Dakota_____				121,390	5,231	4.3	4.3	2.2
Nebraska_____	40,707	4,759	11.7	223,136	9,208	4.1	4.1	2.3
Kansas_____	22,729	2,499	11.0	352,902	16,977	4.8	4.7	2.5
SOUTH ATLANTIC:								
Delaware_____	23,010	2,636	11.5	24,442	1,777	7.3	10.4	5.3
Maryland_____	152,645	20,957	13.7	141,311	11,305	8.0	10.2	5.0
District of Columbia_	88,584	22,871	25.8					
Virginia_____	60,445	12,113	20.0	371,750	29,442	7.9	11.8	7.4
West Virginia_____				280,506	10,499	3.7	5.1	2.0
North Carolina_____				460,164	60,951	13.2	22.4	11.8
South Carolina_____				298,337	79,526	26.7	41.9	23.9
Georgia_____	44,377	11,112	25.0	505,956	96,163	19.0	29.0	15.2
Florida_____				199,498	35,312	17.7	21.2	11.2
EAST SOUTH CENTRAL:								
Kentucky_____	49,667	8,078	16.3	430,499	23,202	5.4	8.0	4.2
Tennessee_____	61,380	13,064	21.3	399,741	31,198	7.8	11.9	5.6
Alabama_____	39,014	6,523	16.7	400,412	66,210	16.5	31.9	16.1
Mississippi_____				341,407	76,947	22.5	41.9	19.3
WEST SOUTH CENTRAL:								
Arkansas_____				343,633	36,919	10.7	20.3	6.0
Louisiana_____	74,783	12,375	16.5	263,622	37,737	14.3	22.9	16.7
Oklahoma_____				402,249	26,953	6.7	7.3	2.6
Texas_____	122,065	20,043	16.4	779,574	66,986	8.6	14.8	5.0
MOUNTAIN:								
Montana_____				108,098	6,508	6.0	6.6	4.5
Idaho_____				84,522	4,408	5.2	6.1	3.4
Wyoming_____				38,163	2,666	7.0	6.9	3.9
Colorado_____	54,983	6,205	11.3	140,113	8,257	5.9	6.7	4.0
New Mexico_____				66,476	3,715	5.6	8.0	3.8
Arizona_____				63,576	6,174	9.7	11.7	13.2
Utah_____	24,377	1,768	7.3	59,315	2,011	3.4	5.3	3.7
Nevada_____				14,457	1,440	10.0	11.7	8.3
PACIFIC:								
Washington_____	93,482	10,879	11.6	194,315	13,293	6.8	6.4	4.3
Oregon_____	58,542	7,423	12.7	111,485	7,732	6.9	6.5	3.9
California_____	281,535	36,183	12.9	451,923	37,371	8.3	7.6	4.1

TABLE 139.—NUMBER AND PERCENTAGE OF NATIVE WHITE MARRIED WOMEN OF NATIVE PARENTAGE ENGAGED IN GAINFUL OCCUPATIONS, FOR CITIES OF 100,000 INHABITANTS OR MORE AND FOR AREAS OUTSIDE OF SUCH CITIES, BY DIVISIONS AND STATES: 1920

	NATIVE WHITE MARRIED WOMEN OF NATIVE PARENTAGE 16 YEARS OF AGE AND OVER: 1920					
DIVISION AND STATE	In cities having 100,000 inhabitants or more			In balance of State		
	Total number	Engaged in gainful occupations		Total number	Engaged in gainful occupations	
		Number	Per cent		Number	Per cent
UNITED STATES	1,836,468	192,287	10.5	9,350,887	515,216	5.5
GEOGRAPHIC DIVISIONS:						
New England	93,082	11,428	12.3	441,474	42,527	9.6
Middle Atlantic	514,789	46,771	9.1	1,337,176	82,143	6.1
East North Central	435,551	44,858	10.3	1,855,891	86,979	4.7
West North Central	194,884	22,082	11.3	1,183,848	53,209	4.5
South Atlantic	191,438	20,334	10.6	1,476,345	91,204	6.2
East South Central	79,271	6,901	8.7	1,092,657	48,079	4.4
West South Central	103,374	9,831	9.5	1,226,084	58,789	4.8
Mountain	37,861	4,347	11.5	326,480	19,245	5.9
Pacific	186,218	25,735	13.8	410,932	33,041	8.0
NEW ENGLAND:						
Maine				105,338	9,793	9.3
New Hampshire				46,861	5,270	11.2
Vermont				46,294	3,870	8.4
Massachusetts	59,757	7,495	12.5	161,147	16,678	10.3
Rhode Island	10,945	1,300	11.9	19,425	1,836	9.5
Connecticut	22,380	2,633	11.8	62,409	5,080	8.1
MIDDLE ATLANTIC:						
New York	264,149	26,078	9.9	428,037	36,875	8.6
New Jersey	59,032	4,599	7.8	174,383	9,267	5.3
Pennsylvania	191,608	16,094	8.4	734,756	36,001	4.9
EAST NORTH CENTRAL:						
Ohio	192,314	17,888	9.3	564,019	23,205	4.1
Indiana	50,007	5,307	10.6	452,823	19,532	4.3
Illinois	106,167	12,905	12.2	466,854	21,475	4.6
Michigan	69,460	7,368	10.6	249,844	17,322	6.9
Wisconsin	17,603	1,390	7.9	122,351	5,445	4.5
WEST NORTH CENTRAL:						
Minnesota	34,584	3,344	9.7	74,551	2,948	4.0
Iowa	18,010	2,357	13.1	266,087	13,176	5.0
Missouri	113,030	13,051	11.5	398,324	14,864	3.7
North Dakota				27,721	1,494	5.4
South Dakota				47,379	2,745	5.8
Nebraska	16,892	2,146	12.7	118,183	5,857	5.0
Kansas	12,368	1,184	9.6	251,603	12,125	4.8
SOUTH ATLANTIC:						
Delaware	11,939	964	8.1	18,344	745	4.1
Maryland	73,020	4,970	6.8	101,834	4,009	3.9
District of Columbia	46,051	8,558	18.6			
Virginia	33,310	2,564	7.7	256,435	9,672	3.8
West Virginia				236,135	7,281	3.1
North Carolina				323,994	24,327	7.5
South Carolina				145,496	17,215	11.8
Georgia	27,118	3,278	12.1	285,824	21,154	7.4
Florida				108,283	6,801	6.3
EAST SOUTH CENTRAL:						
Kentucky	26,846	2,385	8.9	370,294	11,251	3.0
Tennessee	32,857	3,214	9.8	325,751	11,943	3.7
Alabama	19,568	1,302	6.7	242,188	15,181	6.3
Mississippi				154,424	9,704	6.3
WEST SOUTH CENTRAL:						
Arkansas				235,796	11,674	5.0
Louisiana	32,170	1,996	6.2	136,437	5,034	3.7
Oklahoma				329,970	18,359	5.6
Texas	71,204	7,835	11.0	523,881	23,722	4.5
MOUNTAIN:						
Montana				50,016	3,391	6.8
Idaho				52,323	2,888	5.5
Wyoming				23,035	1,692	7.3
Colorado	28,912	3,566	12.3	91,272	5,440	6.0
New Mexico				50,436	2,149	4.3
Arizona				28,739	2,153	7.5
Utah	8,949	781	8.7	24,236	890	3.7
Nevada				6,423	642	10.0
PACIFIC:						
Washington	41,934	5,421	12.9	102,188	7,623	7.5
Oregon	30,125	4,404	14.6	74,409	5,392	7.2
California	114,159	15,910	13.9	234,335	20,026	8.5

TABLE 140.—NUMBER AND PERCENTAGE OF NATIVE WHITE MARRIED WOMEN OF FOREIGN OR MIXED PARENTAGE ENGAGED IN GAINFUL OCCUPATIONS, FOR CITIES OF 100,000 INHABITANTS OR MORE AND FOR AREAS OUTSIDE OF SUCH CITIES, BY DIVISIONS AND STATES: 1920

DIVISION AND STATE	NATIVE WHITE MARRIED WOMEN OF FOREIGN OR MIXED PARENTAGE 16 YEARS OF AGE AND OVER: 1920					
	In cities having 100,000 inhabitants or more			In balance of State		
	Total number	Engaged in gainful occupations		Total number	Engaged in gainful occupations	
		Number	Per cent		Number	Per cent
UNITED STATES	1,444,899	116,028	8.0	2,445,083	129,283	5.3
GEOGRAPHIC DIVISIONS:						
New England	106,318	13,226	12.4	224,580	27,637	12.3
Middle Atlantic	546,099	39,100	7.2	440,739	23,890	5.4
East North Central	412,630	30,983	7.5	743,442	29,828	4.0
West North Central	139,284	10,599	7.6	563,536	18,760	3.3
South Atlantic	49,626	3,927	7.9	48,763	2,827	5.8
East South Central	16,662	875	5.3	29,672	1,330	4.5
West South Central	30,383	1,900	6.3	100,441	6,091	6.1
Mountain	23,520	1,959	8.3	127,057	6,801	5.4
Pacific	120,377	13,459	11.2	166,853	12,119	7.3
NEW ENGLAND:						
Maine				23,172	2,665	11.5
New Hampshire				16,662	2,844	17.1
Vermont				14,751	1,292	8.8
Massachusetts	72,610	9,594	13.2	109,344	13,928	12.7
Rhode Island	11,959	1,486	12.4	18,296	2,722	14.9
Connecticut	21,749	2,146	9.9	42,355	4,186	9.9
MIDDLE ATLANTIC:						
New York	358,523	27,157	7.6	170,339	13,009	7.6
New Jersey	56,941	3,890	6.8	92,368	5,122	5.5
Pennsylvania	130,635	8,053	6.2	178,032	5,759	3.2
EAST NORTH CENTRAL:						
Ohio	117,676	7,359	6.3	124,893	4,230	3.4
Indiana	10,621	708	6.7	75,654	2,786	3.7
Illinois	173,752	15,522	8.9	190,636	7,850	4.1
Michigan	67,459	4,803	7.1	158,891	8,206	5.2
Wisconsin	43,122	2,591	6.0	193,368	6,756	3.5
WEST NORTH CENTRAL:						
Minnesota	50,776	3,956	7.8	142,739	4,383	3.1
Iowa	5,702	564	9.9	145,352	5,073	3.5
Missouri	68,316	4,721	6.9	54,845	1,800	3.3
North Dakota				43,318	1,476	3.4
South Dakota				45,424	1,710	3.8
Nebraska	10,958	1,076	9.8	68,364	2,132	3.1
Kansas	3,532	282	8.0	63,494	2,186	3.4
SOUTH ATLANTIC:						
Delaware	3,887	249	6.4	1,328	46	3.5
Maryland	29,720	1,681	5.7	9,909	361	3.6
District of Columbia	11,196	1,651	14.7			
Virginia	3,208	229	7.1	5,438	308	5.7
West Virginia				11,950	396	3.3
North Carolina				2,040	135	6.6
South Carolina				2,255	127	5.6
Georgia	1,615	117	7.2	4,019	269	6.7
Florida				11,824	1,185	10.0
EAST SOUTH CENTRAL:						
Kentucky	10,903	547	5.0	16,664	627	3.8
Tennessee	4,091	241	5.9	4,121	192	4.7
Alabama	1,668	87	5.2	4,964	262	5.3
Mississippi				3,923	249	6.3
WEST SOUTH CENTRAL:						
Arkansas				8,413	448	5.3
Louisiana	15,377	802	5.2	6,276	252	4.0
Oklahoma				23,100	1,306	5.7
Texas	15,006	1,098	7.3	62,652	4,085	6.5
MOUNTAIN:						
Montana				30,504	1,845	6.0
Idaho				20,945	984	4.7
Wyoming				8,387	538	6.4
Colorado	14,198	1,394	9.8	24,998	1,403	5.6
New Mexico				5,121	314	6.1
Arizona				9,451	665	7.0
Utah	9,322	565	6.1	23,645	694	2.9
Nevada				4,006	358	8.9
PACIFIC:						
Washington	24,784	2,744	11.1	44,520	3,038	6.8
Oregon	14,916	1,745	11.7	21,141	1,461	6.9
California	80,677	8,970	11.1	101,192	7,620	7.5

TABLE 141.—NUMBER AND PERCENTAGE OF FOREIGN-BORN WHITE MARRIED WOMEN ENGAGED IN GAINFUL OCCUPATIONS, FOR CITIES OF 100,000 INHABITANTS OR MORE AND FOR AREAS OUTSIDE OF SUCH CITIES, BY DIVISIONS AND STATES: 1920

DIVISION AND STATE	FOREIGN-BORN WHITE MARRIED WOMEN 16 YEARS OF AGE AND OVER: 1920					
	In cities having 100,000 inhabitants or more			In balance of State		
	Total number	Engaged in gainful occupations		Total number	Engaged in gainful occupations	
		Number	Per cent		Number	Per cent
UNITED STATES	1,986,572	159,489	8.0	2,136,360	136,637	6.4
GEOGRAPHIC DIVISIONS:						
New England	216,023	26,674	12.3	387,199	48,772	12.6
Middle Atlantic	970,609	71,496	7.4	571,069	35,647	6.2
East North Central	508,750	37,662	7.4	465,367	18,430	4.0
West North Central	93,266	6,032	6.5	310,818	8,402	2.7
South Atlantic	42,388	3,197	7.5	43,918	3,789	8.6
East South Central	6,846	436	6.4	11,056	807	7.3
West South Central	20,260	1,550	7.7	89,587	6,114	6.8
Mountain	16,194	1,092	6.7	101,269	5,557	5.5
Pacific	112,236	11,350	10.1	156,077	9,119	5.8
NEW ENGLAND:						
Maine				33,637	3,742	11.1
New Hampshire				28,699	5,172	18.0
Vermont				13,352	822	6.2
Massachusetts	150,627	20,434	13.6	195,942	25,501	13.0
Rhode Island	22,212	2,283	10.3	33,973	5,341	15.7
Connecticut	43,184	3,957	9.2	81,596	8,194	10.0
MIDDLE ATLANTIC:						
New York	700,892	55,704	7.9	165,425	15,156	9.2
New Jersey	94,830	6,460	6.8	149,834	12,248	8.2
Pennsylvania	174,887	9,332	5.3	255,810	8,243	3.2
EAST NORTH CENTRAL:						
Ohio	126,010	9,318	7.4	73,483	2,802	3.8
Indiana	4,690	287	6.1	37,924	1,318	3.5
Illinois	253,431	20,521	8.1	118,988	5,237	4.4
Michigan	91,861	5,277	5.7	129,331	5,595	4.3
Wisconsin	32,758	2,259	6.9	105,641	3,478	3.3
WEST NORTH CENTRAL:						
Minnesota	40,813	2,345	5.7	103,513	2,576	2.5
Iowa	3,204	214	6.7	62,428	1,764	2.8
Missouri	35,593	2,542	7.1	14,543	612	4.2
North Dakota				41,525	916	2.2
South Dakota				25,051	697	2.8
Nebraska	10,317	695	6.7	35,301	1,063	3.0
Kansas	3,339	236	7.1	28,457	774	2.7
SOUTH ATLANTIC:						
Delaware	4,915	279	5.7	1,043	29	2.8
Maryland	25,688	1,736	6.8	5,067	219	4.3
District of Columbia	7,616	877	11.5			
Virginia	2,841	221	7.8	5,358	274	5.1
West Virginia				14,797	485	3.3
North Carolina				1,733	123	7.1
South Carolina				1,467	137	9.3
Georgia	1,328	84	6.3	2,604	253	9.7
Florida				11,849	2,269	19.1
EAST SOUTH CENTRAL:						
Kentucky	2,935	174	5.9	4,211	192	4.6
Tennessee	2,137	163	7.6	1,859	143	7.7
Alabama	1,774	99	5.6	2,988	199	6.7
Mississippi				1,998	273	13.7
WEST SOUTH CENTRAL:						
Arkansas				3,461	247	7.1
Louisiana	5,307	397	7.5	5,429	345	6.4
Oklahoma				10,620	508	4.8
Texas	14,953	1,153	7.7	70,077	5,014	7.2
MOUNTAIN:						
Montana				24,802	1,145	4.6
Idaho				10,092	446	4.4
Wyoming				6,009	305	5.1
Colorado	10,366	751	7.2	22,026	1,091	5.0
New Mexico				7,040	261	3.7
Arizona				18,002	1,753	9.7
Utah	5,828	341	5.9	10,465	345	3.3
Nevada				2,833	211	7.4
PACIFIC:						
Washington	23,923	2,027	8.5	43,376	2,069	4.8
Oregon	12,599	1,066	8.5	14,589	722	4.9
California	75,714	8,257	10.9	98,112	6,328	6.4

TABLE 142.—NUMBER AND PERCENTAGE OF NEGRO MARRIED WOMEN ENGAGED IN GAINFUL OCCUPATIONS, FOR CITIES OF 100,000 INHABITANTS OR MORE AND FOR AREAS OUTSIDE OF SUCH CITIES, BY DIVISIONS AND STATES: 1920

DIVISION AND STATE	NEGRO MARRIED WOMEN 16 YEARS OF AGE AND OVER: 1920					
	In cities having 100,000 inhabitants or more			In balance of State		
	Total number	Engaged in gainful occupations		Total number	Engaged in gainful occupations	
		Number	Per cent		Number	Per cent
UNITED STATES	389,779	157,062	40.3	1,646,640	505,622	30.7
GEOGRAPHIC DIVISIONS:						
New England	10,029	3,376	33.7	5,920	1,829	30.9
Middle Atlantic	88,578	34,946	39.5	46,557	13,887	29.8
East North Central	73,999	23,920	32.3	45,535	9,408	20.7
West North Central	33,152	11,190	33.8	28,853	6,922	24.0
South Atlantic	85,545	42,219	49.4	710,592	226,855	31.9
East South Central	47,274	19,449	41.1	438,380	147,281	33.6
West South Central	42,776	19,125	44.7	362,776	97,263	26.8
Mountain	1,613	540	33.5	4,026	1,060	26.3
Pacific	6,813	2,297	33.7	4,001	1,117	27.9
NEW ENGLAND:						
Maine				228	43	18.9
New Hampshire				108	17	15.7
Vermont				88	25	(1)
Massachusetts	6,476	2,055	31.7	2,680	776	29.0
Rhode Island	1,093	362	33.1	819	196	23.9
Connecticut	2,460	959	39.0	1,997	772	38.7
MIDDLE ATLANTIC:						
New York	38,234	17,350	45.4	7,262	2,762	38.0
New Jersey	9,118	2,735	30.0	16,874	6,115	36.2
Pennsylvania	41,226	14,861	36.0	22,421	5,010	22.3
EAST NORTH CENTRAL:						
Ohio	27,600	9,069	32.9	15,122	2,766	18.3
Indiana	8,236	2,572	31.2	10,004	2,335	23.3
Illinois	27,072	9,463	35.0	15,770	3,443	21.8
Michigan	10,550	2,689	25.5	4,069	738	18.1
Wisconsin	541	127	23.5	570	126	22.1
WEST NORTH CENTRAL:						
Minnesota	1,759	488	27.7	302	65	21.5
Iowa	1,335	418	31.3	2,940	628	21.4
Missouri	24,048	8,647	36.0	15,698	4,164	26.5
North Dakota				84	11	(1)
South Dakota				146	43	29.5
Nebraska	2,525	841	33.3	597	138	23.1
Kansas	3,485	796	22.8	9,086	1,873	20.6
SOUTH ATLANTIC:						
Delaware	2,268	1,144	50.4	3,727	957	25.7
Maryland	24,202	12,566	51.9	24,496	6,715	27.4
District of Columbia	23,683	11,779	49.7			
Virginia	21,076	9,097	43.2	104,380	19,181	18.4
West Virginia				17,615	2,335	13.3
North Carolina				130,399	36,095	27.7
South Carolina				149,060	62,039	41.6
Georgia	14,316	7,633	53.3	213,482	74,481	34.9
Florida				67,433	25,052	37.2
EAST SOUTH CENTRAL:						
Kentucky	8,980	4,969	55.3	39,320	11,129	28.3
Tennessee	22,290	9,445	42.4	68,000	18,920	27.8
Alabama	16,004	5,035	31.5	150,217	50,565	33.7
Mississippi				180,843	66,667	36.9
WEST SOUTH CENTRAL:						
Arkansas				95,938	24,549	25.6
Louisiana	21,910	9,178	41.9	115,303	32,096	27.8
Oklahoma				28,972	6,495	22.4
Texas	20,866	9,947	47.7	122,563	34,123	27.8
MOUNTAIN:						
Montana				347	68	19.6
Idaho				189	36	19.0
Wyoming				279	103	36.9
Colorado	1,426	485	34.0	1,148	280	24.4
New Mexico				647	172	26.6
Arizona				1,158	336	29.0
Utah	187	55	29.4	181	26	14.4
Nevada				77	39	(1)
PACIFIC:						
Washington	877	296	33.8	668	145	21.7
Oregon	414	134	32.4	97	34	(1)
California	5,522	1,867	33.8	3,236	938	29.0

1 Per cent not shown, base being less than 100.

TABLE **143.**—PERCENTAGE DISTRIBUTION, BY RACE AND NATIVITY, OF WOMEN ENGAGED IN GAINFUL OCCUPATIONS, CLASSIFIED BY AGE, FOR DIVISIONS AND STATES: 1920

	WOMEN 16 TO 24 YEARS OF AGE ENGAGED IN GAINFUL OCCUPATIONS: 1920										
DIVISION AND STATE	Number						Per cent				
	Total	Native white		Foreign-born white	Negro	All other	Native white		Foreign-born white	Negro	All other
		Native parentage	Foreign or mixed parentage				Native parentage	Foreign or mixed parentage			
UNITED STATES	3,220,502	1,498,460	973,413	306,196	438,204	4,229	46.5	30.2	9.5	13.6	0.1
GEOGRAPHIC DIVISIONS:											
New England	322,044	96,243	160,723	61,689	3,324	65	29.9	49.9	19.2	1.0	(1)
Middle Atlantic	883,093	352,971	355,877	143,609	30,444	192	40.0	40.3	16.3	3.4	(1)
East North Central	645,291	330,016	241,889	55,664	17,518	204	51.1	37.5	8.6	2.7	(1)
West North Central	311,787	179,323	109,798	13,427	9,097	142	57.5	35.2	4.3	2.9	(1)
South Atlantic	425,872	209,633	20,364	5,932	189,680	263	49.2	4.8	1.4	44.5	0.1
East South Central	215,919	101,538	5,560	729	108,031	61	47.0	2.6	0.3	50.0	(1)
West South Central	225,735	124,520	15,446	7,275	78,134	360	55.2	6.8	3.2	34.6	0.2
Mountain	61,070	35,737	18,831	4,619	614	1,269	58.5	30.8	7.6	1.0	2.1
Pacific	129,691	68,479	44,925	13,252	1,362	1,673	52.8	34.6	10.2	1.1	1.3
NEW ENGLAND:											
Maine	22,514	11,537	7,356	3,568	33	20	51.2	32.7	15.8	0.1	0.1
New Hampshire	17,273	5,966	7,906	3,382	16	3	34.5	45.8	19.6	0.1	(1)
Vermont	9,188	5,889	2,536	753	10		64.1	27.6	8.2	0.1	
Massachusetts	181,798	47,739	95,103	37,002	1,924	30	26.3	52.3	20.4	1.1	(1)
Rhode Island	31,139	7,059	17,042	6,629	405	4	22.7	54.7	21.3	1.3	(1)
Connecticut	60,132	18,053	30,780	10,355	936	8	30.0	51.2	17.2	1.6	(1)
MIDDLE ATLANTIC:											
New York	462,460	147,594	202,664	99,428	12,610	164	31.9	43.8	21.5	2.7	(1)
New Jersey	128,530	46,290	57,359	19,383	5,490	8	36.0	44.6	15.1	4.3	(1)
Pennsylvania	292,103	159,087	95,854	24,798	12,344	20	54.5	32.8	8.5	4.2	(1)
EAST NORTH CENTRAL:											
Ohio	161,506	102,954	41,172	11,449	5,943	8	63.7	25.5	7.1	3.7	(1)
Indiana	72,579	57,961	10,156	1,678	2,779	5	79.9	14.0	2.3	3.8	(1)
Illinois	222,860	87,630	102,226	26,226	6,754	24	39.3	45.9	11.8	3.0	(1)
Michigan	104,146	46,245	44,433	11,499	1,896	73	44.4	42.7	11.0	1.8	0.1
Wisconsin	84,200	35,226	43,902	4,832	146	94	41.8	52.1	5.7	0.2	0.1
WEST NORTH CENTRAL:											
Minnesota	73,993	24,403	44,143	5,118	275	59	33.0	59.7	6.9	0.4	0.1
Iowa	56,472	37,262	17,090	1,573	545	2	66.0	30.3	2.8	1.0	(1)
Missouri	88,856	62,149	17,187	3,202	6,315	3	69.9	19.3	3.6	7.1	(1)
North Dakota	13,575	4,573	7,904	1,073	6	19	33.7	58.2	7.9	(1)	0.1
South Dakota	12,960	6,406	5,969	536	22	27	49.4	46.1	4.1	0.2	0.2
Nebraska	30,219	17,326	11,074	1,334	470	15	57.3	36.6	4.4	1.6	(1)
Kansas	35,712	27,204	6,431	596	1,464	17	76.2	18.0	1.7	4.1	(1)
SOUTH ATLANTIC:											
Delaware	6,536	3,832	1,227	330	1,147		58.6	18.8	5.0	17.5	
Maryland	50,597	28,043	9,081	2,503	10,965	5	55.4	17.9	4.9	21.7	(1)
Dist. of Columbia	28,434	17,055	3,786	737	6,851	5	60.0	13.3	2.6	24.1	(1)
Virginia	54,700	30,025	1,462	416	22,789	8	54.9	2.7	0.8	41.7	(1)
West Virginia	23,302	19,724	1,446	410	1,722		84.6	6.2	1.8	7.4	
North Carolina	74,357	42,720	315	111	30,976	235	57.5	0.4	0.1	41.7	0.3
South Carolina	68,787	22,873	313	57	45,541	3	33.3	0.5	0.1	66.2	(1)
Georgia	94,090	36,830	875	294	56,086	5	39.1	0.9	0.3	59.6	(1)
Florida	25,069	8,531	1,859	1,074	13,603	2	34.0	7.4	4.3	54.3	(1)
EAST SOUTH CENTRAL:											
Kentucky	39,948	28,881	3,393	242	7,429	3	72.3	8.5	0.6	18.6	(1)
Tennessee	48,748	29,764	1,006	210	17,768		61.1	2.1	0.4	36.4	
Alabama	69,080	28,023	833	181	40,035	8	40.6	1.2	0.3	58.0	(1)
Mississippi	58,143	14,870	328	96	42,799	50	25.6	0.6	0.2	73.6	0.1
WEST SOUTH CENTRAL:											
Arkansas	36,029	17,943	870	112	17,101	3	49.8	2.4	0.3	47.5	(1)
Louisiana	48,385	18,351	2,253	419	27,349	13	37.9	4.7	0.9	56.5	(1)
Oklahoma	35,313	28,239	1,998	291	4,488	297	80.0	5.7	0.8	12.7	0.8
Texas	106,008	59,987	10,325	6,453	29,196	47	56.6	9.7	6.1	27.5	(1)
MOUNTAIN:											
Montana	9,792	4,634	4,325	777	26	30	47.3	44.2	7.9	0.3	0.3
Idaho	6,767	4,689	1,788	259	13	18	69.3	26.4	3.8	0.2	0.3
Wyoming	3,200	2,033	954	178	28	7	63.5	29.8	5.6	0.9	0.2
Colorado	20,242	12,597	6,245	1,047	337	16	62.2	30.9	5.2	1.7	0.1
New Mexico	4,766	3,399	564	247	61	495	71.3	11.8	5.2	1.3	10.4
Arizona	5,445	2,481	897	1,357	113	597	45.6	16.5	24.9	2.1	11.0
Utah	9,765	5,315	3,697	691	29	33	54.4	37.9	7.1	0.3	0.3
Nevada	1,093	589	361	63	7	73	53.9	33.0	5.8	0.6	6.7
PACIFIC:											
Washington	31,553	16,319	11,706	3,074	130	324	51.7	37.1	9.7	0.4	1.0
Oregon	17,912	10,911	5,638	1,235	48	80	60.9	31.5	6.9	0.3	0.4
California	80,226	41,249	27,581	8,943	1,184	1,269	51.4	34.4	11.1	1.5	1.6

[1] Less than one-tenth of 1 per cent.

TABLE 143.—PERCENTAGE DISTRIBUTION, BY RACE AND NATIVITY, OF WOMEN ENGAGED IN GAINFUL OCCUPATIONS, CLASSIFIED BY AGE, FOR DIVISIONS AND STATES: 1920—Continued

DIVISION AND STATE	PER CENT OF WOMEN 25 TO 44 YEARS OF AGE GAINFULLY OCCUPIED [1]					PER CENT OF WOMEN 45 TO 64 YEARS OF AGE GAINFULLY OCCUPIED					PER CENT OF WOMEN 65 YEARS OF AGE AND OVER GAINFULLY OCCUPIED				
	Native white Native parentage	Native white Foreign or mixed par.	Foreign-born white	Negro	All other	Native white Native parentage	Native white Foreign or mixed par.	Foreign-born white	Negro	All other	Native white Native parentage	Native white Foreign or mixed par.	Foreign-born white	Negro	All other
UNITED STATES	42.1	22.6	14.8	20.2	0.2	41.3	20.1	18.5	20.0	0.2	47.2	11.0	19.5	21.9	0.3
GEOGRAPHIC DIVISIONS:															
New England	32.0	33.1	32.9	2.0	(²)	37.5	25.7	34.8	2.1	(²)	56.1	12.7	28.7	2.4	0.1
Middle Atlantic	39.4	28.2	24.7	7.7	(²)	38.7	26.7	28.2	6.3	(²)	48.9	17.2	28.9	5.0	0.1
East North Central	47.1	31.7	14.7	6.5	(²)	45.1	29.2	20.1	5.5	0.1	51.5	17.1	27.0	4.3	0.1
West North Central	51.2	33.2	8.5	7.0	0.1	46.9	27.1	18.3	7.5	0.1	50.2	13.0	28.6	7.9	0.3
South Atlantic	39.6	4.0	2.2	54.2	0.1	38.0	4.7	2.8	54.4	0.1	40.6	3.0	3.2	53.1	0.1
East South Central	35.7	3.0	0.7	60.6	(²)	36.3	4.0	1.2	58.6	(²)	40.7	2.1	1.9	55.3	(²)
West South Central	43.7	6.1	4.5	45.5	0.2	41.6	6.9	6.6	44.7	0.2	39.4	4.5	9.0	46.5	0.6
Mountain	55.2	26.3	13.3	2.6	2.5	51.1	21.9	21.6	2.7	2.7	48.6	13.4	29.3	2.1	6.6
Pacific	49.9	29.1	17.0	2.2	1.9	49.3	24.1	23.6	2.1	0.9	52.4	14.6	30.1	1.9	1.1
NEW ENGLAND:															
Maine	58.8	20.3	20.4	0.3	0.2	66.8	13.2	19.5	0.3	0.2	78.5	7.1	13.9	0.4	0.2
New Hampshire	40.3	27.0	32.6	0.2	(²)	52.5	16.9	30.3	0.2	(²)	73.7	7.2	18.8	0.2	___
Vermont	62.0	25.3	12.4	0.3	(²)	60.6	25.1	13.9	0.3	(²)	69.4	16.1	14.4	0.2	___
Massachusetts	27.8	34.5	35.7	2.0	(²)	31.7	27.2	39.0	2.0	(²)	48.0	14.6	35.0	2.3	0.1
Rhode Island	24.5	37.3	35.7	2.4	(²)	26.9	29.5	39.8	3.6	(²)	42.3	14.0	36.7	6.9	0.1
Connecticut	31.7	34.9	30.0	3.4	(²)	34.1	29.2	32.8	3.8	(²)	52.7	13.0	29.6	4.6	0.1
MIDDLE ATLANTIC:															
New York	32.6	30.5	30.7	6.1	0.1	31.9	29.5	34.1	4.4	0.1	41.8	19.2	35.3	3.5	0.1
New Jersey	35.2	29.6	25.3	10.0	(²)	34.6	24.3	30.1	11.0	(²)	45.0	13.8	30.9	10.2	0.1
Pennsylvania	53.5	23.4	13.5	9.5	(²)	51.9	22.8	17.6	7.8	(²)	60.3	15.3	19.0	5.4	(²)
EAST NORTH CENTRAL:															
Ohio	57.4	23.7	10.8	8.0	(²)	53.2	27.8	12.4	6.7	(²)	59.6	18.6	16.8	5.1	(²)
Indiana	71.9	15.8	3.8	8.5	(²)	67.1	19.8	5.6	7.6	(²)	70.6	13.0	10.3	6.1	(²)
Illinois	37.0	35.1	20.3	7.6	(²)	37.6	29.0	27.0	6.5	(²)	45.3	15.8	33.7	5.3	(²)
Michigan	43.2	35.4	17.4	3.9	0.1	42.4	28.0	26.9	2.5	0.3	45.8	16.3	35.6	1.9	0.4
Wisconsin	34.1	52.6	12.7	0.5	0.2	20.7	48.6	30.0	0.5	0.2	21.5	23.7	54.0	0.4	0.5
WEST NORTH CENTRAL:															
Minnesota	28.6	54.3	15.9	1.1	0.1	22.2	37.0	39.4	1.1	0.2	21.5	13.9	63.4	0.7	0.5
Iowa	58.4	33.5	6.1	2.0	(²)	52.0	31.7	14.1	2.1	(²)	55.3	15.3	26.9	2.4	0.1
Missouri	57.6	21.7	5.1	15.6	(²)	51.9	24.4	9.0	14.7	(²)	58.0	12.7	15.0	14.2	(²)
North Dakota	30.4	49.5	19.7	0.2	0.2	29.2	25.9	50.3	0.4	0.4	21.3	14.0	62.5	0.5	1.7
South Dakota	46.0	42.0	11.2	0.4	0.4	38.0	29.6	30.8	0.6	1.0	33.6	14.1	47.3	0.4	4.6
Nebraska	53.8	33.7	8.8	3.6	0.1	50.8	23.6	22.5	3.0	0.1	50.4	11.3	35.9	2.1	0.3
Kansas	68.1	19.5	4.0	8.4	0.1	62.3	17.1	10.2	10.3	0.1	60.4	9.9	18.2	11.3	0.2
SOUTH ATLANTIC:															
Delaware	49.6	13.2	7.7	29.4	___	47.5	13.1	8.1	31.3	___	50.6	7.2	9.2	33.0	___
Maryland	45.2	12.7	6.0	36.0	(²)	40.2	15.9	8.7	35.3	(²)	40.8	11.8	12.1	35.3	(²)
District of Columbia	51.4	11.8	4.3	32.5	(²)	43.5	13.3	6.2	37.0	(²)	42.9	9.7	9.6	37.8	___
Virginia	43.4	2.1	1.2	53.3	(²)	42.4	2.1	1.4	54.1	(²)	45.1	1.4	1.2	52.2	0.1
West Virginia	75.9	6.9	3.4	13.8	(²)	76.6	8.9	3.5	11.0	___	82.1	5.4	4.4	8.2	___
North Carolina	47.5	0.5	0.4	51.3	0.3	45.5	0.5	0.4	53.2	0.4	49.2	0.3	0.3	49.7	0.5
South Carolina	27.0	0.6	0.2	72.2	(²)	23.9	0.8	0.4	74.9	(²)	23.2	0.4	0.6	75.7	(²)
Georgia	30.8	0.9	0.5	67.8	(²)	28.9	1.1	0.7	69.3	(²)	29.4	0.7	0.7	69.2	___
Florida	26.5	4.3	6.4	62.9	(²)	32.3	4.8	6.9	55.9	(²)	35.8	3.6	5.9	54.8	___
EAST SOUTH CENTRAL:															
Kentucky	55.1	10.1	1.3	33.4	(²)	53.6	12.0	2.6	31.8	(²)	61.1	5.2	4.7	29.0	(²)
Tennessee	47.3	2.2	0.8	49.7	(²)	48.4	2.5	1.1	48.0	(²)	53.1	1.3	1.3	44.3	___
Alabama	29.3	1.1	0.5	69.1	(²)	27.1	1.1	0.7	71.0	(²)	26.7	0.8	0.8	71.7	(²)
Mississippi	19.6	0.7	0.3	79.4	(²)	19.8	1.1	0.5	78.6	(²)	21.2	1.0	0.6	77.2	0.1
WEST SOUTH CENTRAL:															
Arkansas	40.0	2.2	1.0	56.8	(²)	43.4	2.5	1.9	52.2	___	47.2	1.2	2.3	49.2	(²)
Louisiana	26.0	5.3	1.9	66.8	(²)	22.7	9.2	3.2	64.8	(²)	25.0	6.8	6.1	62.0	0.1
Oklahoma	71.8	6.3	1.9	18.7	1.3	70.7	7.0	3.9	16.9	1.6	64.4	5.0	5.8	19.9	4.9
Texas	45.5	7.9	7.9	38.7	0.1	42.9	7.3	11.6	38.1	0.1	39.6	4.1	14.6	41.5	0.1
MOUNTAIN:															
Montana	47.5	34.7	16.4	0.8	0.6	44.1	27.1	29.4	1.4	0.7	44.2	18.1	34.8	1.9	1.0
Idaho	63.7	26.7	8.3	0.7	0.6	56.8	23.8	18.3	0.5	0.6	51.6	14.1	30.3	0.3	3.8
Wyoming	62.2	24.0	10.4	2.9	0.6	58.0	20.3	18.0	3.1	0.7	57.6	15.8	22.8	2.7	1.1
Colorado	60.8	24.9	10.4	3.7	0.2	56.6	20.6	18.6	4.1	0.1	55.4	15.1	26.1	2.9	0.5
New Mexico	65.5	12.0	8.8	3.1	10.7	70.0	9.6	10.2	1.5	8.6	65.7	6.8	12.4	0.9	14.2
Arizona	43.8	15.1	9.4	4.8	10.1	39.0	14.4	28.4	4.3	14.0	28.0	5.7	26.5	3.0	36.7
Utah	43.1	40.7	14.3	1.1	0.8	31.6	35.6	31.3	0.9	0.7	28.2	13.5	56.7	0.9	0.7
Nevada	49.1	29.5	11.9	2.1	7.4	40.2	26.1	21.5	2.3	9.9	30.2	13.4	26.8	2.0	27.5
PACIFIC:															
Washington	50.6	30.2	16.4	1.3	1.5	49.8	22.1	25.9	1.4	0.8	51.6	13.4	32.2	1.1	1.6
Oregon	59.7	27.1	11.7	0.7	0.7	60.4	20.5	17.8	0.8	0.5	63.7	13.4	21.3	0.3	1.3
California	47.9	29.1	18.1	2.7	2.2	47.3	25.2	24.0	2.6	1.0	50.7	15.1	31.0	2.3	0.9

[1] Includes women of unknown age.   [2] Less than one-tenth of 1 per cent.

TABLE 144.—PERCENTAGE OF WOMEN ENGAGED IN GAINFUL OCCUPATIONS, CLASSIFIED BY AGE, FOR DIVISIONS AND STATES: 1920 AND 1900

DIVISION AND STATE	Total number	Engaged in gainful occupations Number	Per cent	20 to 24 years of age 1920	16 to 24 years of age 1920	16 to 24 years of age 1900	25 to 44 years of age 1920	25 to 44 years of age[1] 1900	45 to 64 years of age 1920	45 to 64 years of age 1900	65 years and over 1920	65 years and over 1900
UNITED STATES	3,820,998	1,411,427	36.9	38.1	37.6	31.6	22.4	18.1	17.1	14.1	8.0	9.1
GEOGRAPHIC DIVISIONS:												
New England	239,554	136,897	57.1	57.1	57.1	50.3	31.4	26.8	21.5	14.4	8.6	7.2
Middle Atlantic	743,908	409,538	55.1	47.1	50.5	41.4	24.0	19.2	17.0	12.3	7.5	7.1
East North Central	721,490	288,246	40.0	38.6	39.2	30.1	19.4	14.0	13.7	9.5	6.1	6.3
West North Central	461,290	122,168	26.5	34.0	30.6	25.2	17.6	12.6	12.6	9.5	5.5	6.2
South Atlantic	573,987	188,185	32.8	35.2	34.1	31.0	26.4	23.0	22.4	22.1	12.3	16.1
East South Central	372,466	97,233	26.1	28.4	27.3	26.6	23.2	21.5	21.7	22.3	13.0	17.4
West South Central	432,268	98,150	22.7	26.2	24.5	19.9	19.5	16.3	17.5	18.7	9.3	14.1
Mountain	112,211	23,129	20.6	27.9	24.6	19.5	16.7	14.0	15.1	14.7	7.6	9.1
Pacific	163,824	47,881	29.2	37.1	33.7	25.6	23.6	16.4	17.9	12.7	6.9	7.8
NEW ENGLAND:												
Maine	25,637	9,010	35.1	43.6	39.8	36.7	24.3	19.7	18.4	12.8	8.7	7.9
New Hampshire	14,341	7,258	50.6	54.7	52.9	48.2	31.6	26.6	22.4	15.5	10.1	9.0
Vermont	11,652	3,847	33.0	40.2	36.9	34.1	21.4	17.3	17.8	12.0	8.5	7.2
Massachusetts	123,990	75,202	60.7	61.4	61.1	54.0	34.5	29.9	23.3	12.6	8.6	6.6
Rhode Island	20,327	14,362	70.7	61.0	65.1	58.5	33.8	28.4	21.6	15.1	8.7	6.9
Connecticut	43,607	27,218	62.4	54.2	57.6	50.6	26.9	23.4	18.4	13.5	7.6	7.5
MIDDLE ATLANTIC:												
New York	339,429	205,226	60.5	52.4	55.7	46.1	27.3	21.6	18.9	13.7	8.0	7.4
New Jersey	104,169	62,236	59.7	47.2	52.5	42.7	22.4	18.3	15.6	12.2	6.8	6.9
Pennsylvania	300,310	142,076	47.3	40.2	43.4	35.4	20.3	16.3	14.9	10.6	7.1	6.7
EAST NORTH CENTRAL:												
Ohio	187,801	70,794	37.7	36.7	37.2	29.8	19.3	14.5	14.1	9.9	6.5	7.2
Indiana	102,328	33,548	32.8	31.8	32.2	21.9	16.5	12.0	12.7	9.6	6.3	6.9
Illinois	219,390	99,868	45.5	42.3	43.7	32.2	21.8	15.3	14.6	9.7	5.9	5.6
Michigan	117,152	47,252	40.3	37.4	38.7	31.1	18.1	13.2	13.2	9.0	5.9	6.2
Wisconsin	94,819	36,784	38.8	41.8	40.4	34.8	17.9	12.6	12.1	8.2	5.3	4.9
WEST NORTH CENTRAL:												
Minnesota	88,306	27,758	31.4	42.2	37.4	34.1	19.8	14.5	11.8	9.0	4.9	5.2
Iowa	86,618	20,913	24.1	33.3	29.2	26.8	16.7	12.3	11.8	8.2	4.8	5.0
Missouri	125,616	38,912	31.0	33.1	32.1	22.1	20.0	13.5	14.9	11.5	7.4	8.3
North Dakota	24,481	4,829	19.7	32.0	26.2	30.7	12.8	11.4	10.0	10.4	6.0	6.5
South Dakota	23,260	4,458	19.2	30.6	25.4	24.6	14.0	9.8	10.4	8.3	4.5	4.8
Nebraska	47,604	11,662	24.5	31.8	28.5	24.8	16.2	11.7	11.2	8.6	4.0	5.2
Kansas	65,405	13,636	20.8	28.9	25.2	18.8	15.2	10.5	11.8	8.7	4.9	6.0
SOUTH ATLANTIC:												
Delaware	7,512	2,974	39.6	36.2	37.7	32.0	22.1	17.6	17.4	13.3	9.3	9.2
Maryland	52,741	24,326	46.1	39.9	42.7	34.9	25.3	20.9	19.8	17.2	10.2	10.8
Dist. of Columbia	15,053	8,432	56.0	68.7	64.4	44.7	52.4	38.0	37.5	31.5	15.7	15.0
Virginia	92,775	22,944	24.7	29.5	27.3	24.2	20.2	19.1	18.7	19.8	11.7	15.8
West Virginia	56,170	10,276	18.3	20.3	19.4	13.4	11.6	9.2	10.8	9.9	7.6	8.8
North Carolina	109,029	34,591	31.7	32.5	32.1	29.9	22.7	20.0	20.2	21.0	11.9	17.0
South Carolina	75,122	32,118	42.8	42.9	42.8	45.5	36.5	34.9	33.1	33.1	18.5	25.6
Georgia	127,351	42,328	33.2	35.7	34.5	33.4	29.9	27.3	26.5	26.5	13.8	18.3
Florida	38,234	10,196	26.7	32.5	29.8	23.4	29.0	22.6	23.7	23.4	11.6	16.9
EAST SOUTH CENTRAL:												
Kentucky	94,279	16,949	18.0	21.6	19.9	17.3	16.5	14.5	16.7	15.5	10.9	12.6
Tennessee	97,499	21,073	21.6	25.1	23.5	18.8	19.6	16.4	17.5	18.3	11.0	16.4
Alabama	101,324	32,995	32.6	31.9	32.2	35.2	27.0	28.3	26.5	28.8	15.2	22.1
Mississippi	79,364	26,116	33.0	36.4	34.8	38.2	32.0	31.5	30.4	30.9	16.8	23.8
WEST SOUTH CENTRAL:												
Arkansas	74,446	17,039	22.9	24.0	23.5	20.0	19.0	15.6	18.3	18.8	9.4	14.1
Louisiana	77,673	21,534	27.7	29.8	28.8	31.1	25.6	26.1	24.8	27.7	14.2	19.8
Oklahoma	83,931	14,409	17.2	22.7	20.1	11.5	14.6	8.2	12.5	11.4	5.7	9.5
Texas	196,218	45,168	23.0	26.8	25.1	16.6	19.3	14.0	16.4	15.9	8.5	11.4
MOUNTAIN:												
Montana	16,607	3,518	21.2	30.4	26.3	24.5	16.3	14.5	14.5	13.4	7.6	7.3
Idaho	14,684	2,446	16.7	25.2	21.3	15.5	12.9	9.1	11.8	11.7	5.4	9.6
Wyoming	5,518	1,123	20.4	26.7	24.0	21.6	16.0	11.4	12.0	9.3	7.6	7.6
Colorado	31,377	7,667	24.4	32.2	28.8	21.9	19.8	16.5	17.2	14.8	8.1	7.3
New Mexico	13,700	1,907	13.9	18.5	16.5	10.5	13.8	9.9	14.5	14.7	9.3	12.6
Arizona	11,190	2,082	18.6	23.8	21.5	18.7	18.9	19.3	17.1	15.3	8.2	20.1
Utah	17,270	4,028	23.3	29.8	26.4	19.1	14.1	11.1	11.9	12.5	5.5	6.7
Nevada	1,865	358	19.2	29.2	24.9	19.4	19.3	17.0	20.3	17.4	11.8	15.1
PACIFIC:												
Washington	42,322	11,714	27.7	36.3	32.5	23.5	21.1	13.8	15.8	10.9	6.3	7.3
Oregon	25,309	6,711	26.5	35.3	31.4	24.0	21.4	13.6	15.9	10.4	5.9	6.6
California	96,193	29,456	30.6	37.8	34.8	26.7	25.1	18.1	19.0	13.7	7.3	8.1

[1] Includes age unknown.

6436°—29——18

TABLE 145.—PERCENTAGE OF NATIVE WHITE WOMEN OF NATIVE PARENTAGE ENGAGED IN GAINFUL OCCUPATIONS, CLASSIFIED BY AGE, FOR DIVISIONS AND STATES: 1920 AND 1900

NATIVE WHITE WOMEN OF NATIVE PARENTAGE 16 YEARS OF AGE AND OVER

DIVISION AND STATE	16–19 yrs 1920 Total number	Engaged in gainful occ. Number	Per cent	20–24 yrs 1920	16–24 1920	16–24 1900	25–44[1] 1920	25–44 1900	45–64 1920	45–64 1900	65+ 1920	65+ 1900
UNITED STATES	2,241,771	642,514	28.7	32.5	30.8	21.0	18.5	12.9	14.4	11.3	6.8	7.8
GEOGRAPHIC DIVISIONS:												
New England	88,420	37,566	42.5	51.9	47.8	34.6	29.9	22.0	20.8	14.0	8.3	7.2
Middle Atlantic	351,285	158,499	53.7	44.2	44.6	31.4	23.4	15.8	16.3	10.8	7.1	6.7
East North Central	444,517	143,452	32.3	35.1	43.5	22.6	18.2	12.6	13.5	9.5	6.1	6.7
West North Central	296,006	71,663	24.2	32.0	28.4	19.8	16.9	11.3	12.4	9.0	5.5	6.2
South Atlantic	350,323	93,657	26.7	28.6	27.7	18.3	16.9	11.9	13.4	13.2	7.3	11.1
East South Central	251,305	46,171	18.4	20.2	19.3	12.3	12.5	9.3	11.8	12.7	7.7	11.5
West South Central	292,660	53,793	18.4	21.9	20.2	10.3	13.1	8.2	11.4	11.9	5.6	8.6
Mountain	72,265	13,021	18.0	26.8	22.7	16.0	16.6	13.0	15.5	13.7	7.2	8.5
Pacific	94,990	24,692	26.0	36.2	31.7	21.1	23.9	15.3	18.4	12.1	6.8	7.4
NEW ENGLAND:												
Maine	15,670	4,293	27.4	38.7	33.6	30.2	23.2	18.1	18.3	12.6	8.7	8.1
New Hampshire	6,485	2,302	35.5	46.2	41.3	34.4	27.6	22.5	21.2	15.0	10.0	9.0
Vermont	7,952	2,425	30.5	39.1	35.0	31.1	21.5	15.9		11.7	8.5	7.5
Massachusetts	38,279	18,125	47.3	57.9	53.4	36.2	34.4	25.5	23.0	15.2	8.1	6.2
Rhode Island	5,439	3,054	56.2	57.1	56.7	41.4	32.8	22.6	21.3	13.6	8.2	6.2
Connecticut	14,595	7,367	50.5	55.1	53.1	35.5	28.5	19.4	18.4	13.2	7.3	7.4
MIDDLE ATLANTIC:												
New York	130,324	62,700	48.1	49.1	48.7	33.1	27.4	18.0	19.2	12.1	7.7	7.0
New Jersey	43,328	21,498	49.6	45.5	47.3	30.3	22.1	14.6	14.6	10.2	6.2	6.0
Pennsylvania	177,633	74,301	41.8	39.8	40.7	30.4	20.5	14.4	14.4	9.8	6.9	6.5
EAST NORTH CENTRAL:												
Ohio	134,075	44,013	32.8	35.2	34.2	24.0	18.2	12.6	13.4	9.5	6.3	7.5
Indiana	87,866	26,813	30.5	30.4	30.5	18.9	15.3	10.5	11.9	9.0	6.0	6.8
Illinois	118,247	37,509	31.7	35.5	33.8	21.7	19.4	13.7	14.5	10.0	5.9	6.1
Michigan	58,658	20,421	34.8	36.4	35.7	25.3	19.4	13.3	14.7	9.5	6.1	6.2
Wisconsin	45,671	14,696	32.2	41.3	36.9	27.9	19.6	14.5	14.0	9.1	5.6	5.2
WEST NORTH CENTRAL:												
Minnesota	33,634	8,995	26.7	40.9	34.2	28.0	21.9	16.6	14.1	9.6	5.2	4.8
Iowa	61,144	14,045	23.0	32.9	28.3	23.8	17.2	12.3	12.5	8.2	5.1	5.0
Missouri	102,112	27,588	27.0	29.7	28.5	16.3	16.6	10.2	12.5	10.1	6.6	8.1
North Dakota	7,730	1,574	20.4	36.9	28.8	28.9	15.4	12.6	11.5	11.4	5.8	5.8
South Dakota	11,470	2,196	19.1	32.3	26.1	25.0	16.0	12.2	12.3	9.6	5.0	6.1
Nebraska	29,057	6,739	23.2	31.9	27.8	22.6	17.0	12.2	12.4	8.5	4.2	4.8
Kansas	50,859	10,526	20.7	29.0	25.1	17.3	14.9	10.0	11.3	8.0	4.5	5.3
SOUTH ATLANTIC:												
Delaware	4,854	1,732	35.7	34.1	34.8	24.5	17.6	12.1	13.1	10.2	6.7	7.6
Maryland	33,615	13,884	41.3	34.8	37.7	26.4	19.1	14.5	14.2	11.7	7.0	7.9
Dist. of Columbia	8,272	4,684	56.6	71.4	66.6	30.2	49.4	24.3	31.8	18.1	11.5	8.2
Virginia	60,547	12,662	20.9		23.1	12.9	13.4	10.0	11.7	12.3	7.4	12.1
West Virginia	49,740	8,742	17.6	19.9	18.8	11.6	10.6	7.9	9.8	9.4	7.2	8.9
North Carolina	71,830	20,512	28.6	27.7	28.1	20.4	15.6	11.9	12.8	15.1	7.9	14.1
South Carolina	32,812	10,816	33.0	32.7	32.8	28.0	20.3	16.2	15.3	16.9	7.7	13.5
Georgia	68,329	17,138	25.1	25.9	25.5	16.1	16.4	11.4	13.0	13.4	6.3	10.1
Florida	20,324	3,487	17.2	21.7	19.6	10.9	14.9	10.3	13.5	13.3	6.5	10.4
EAST SOUTH CENTRAL:												
Kentucky	82,500	12,861	15.6	17.7	16.7	11.0	11.3	8.6	11.9	11.8	8.8	11.7
Tennessee	76,151	13,397	17.6	19.6	18.6	10.0	12.3	8.6	11.0	12.2	7.4	11.4
Alabama	58,064	13,782	23.7	22.6	23.1	16.5	13.8	10.7	12.4	14.2	6.6	11.3
Mississippi	34,590	6,131	17.7	23.3	20.6	14.5	14.1	11.2	12.8	14.3	6.9	11.2
WEST SOUTH CENTRAL:												
Arkansas	50,787	8,736	17.2	17.9	17.5	10.4	11.4	8.5	11.6	13.4	6.0	10.1
Louisiana	41,213	7,985	19.4	22.0	20.8	12.9	13.5	10.3	12.7	13.8	8.1	10.9
Oklahoma	69,957	11,695	16.7	21.8	19.4	10.6	12.9	7.1	11.2	10.2	4.7	8.0
Texas	130,703	25,377	19.4	23.4	21.5	9.4	13.6	7.8	11.1	11.2	5.1	7.3
MOUNTAIN:												
Montana	8,821	1,563	17.7	28.3	23.6	21.1	16.8	14.5	15.0	13.6	7.7	10.0
Idaho	10,832	1,729	16.0	24.4	20.4	14.8	13.2	9.5	12.3	11.7	4.8	10.4
Wyoming	3,723	702	18.9	26.6	23.0	20.1	16.4	11.7	16.4	11.2	9.6	9.5
Colorado	21,039	4,543	21.6	31.1	26.8	18.3	19.5	15.4	17.3	14.1	7.6	7.1
New Mexico	10,761	1,329	12.4	17.2	14.9	8.9	12.1	8.5	13.5	14.2	8.4	11.5
Arizona	5,016	810	16.1	26.1	21.7	13.3	18.3	12.7	15.1	13.6	5.7	6.6
Utah	11,003	2,147	19.5	28.7	24.1	15.5	14.7	12.3	14.3	13.3	6.4	6.2
Nevada	1,070	198	18.5	28.7	24.2	16.0	21.1	16.5	20.3	15.8	10.5	12.8
PACIFIC:												
Washington	24,324	6,041	24.8	34.4	30.1	21.0	21.5	13.0	16.8	10.3	6.3	6.8
Oregon	17,367	4,041	23.3	33.1	28.6	20.7	21.2	13.1	16.6	10.2	6.1	6.5
California	53,299	14,610	27.4	37.8	33.3	21.4	25.6	17.0	19.4	13.2	7.0	7.8

[1] Includes age unknown.

TABLE 146.—PERCENTAGE OF NATIVE WHITE WOMEN OF FOREIGN OR MIXED PARENTAGE ENGAGED IN GAINFUL OCCUPATIONS, CLASSIFIED BY AGE, FOR DIVISIONS AND STATES: 1920 AND 1900

NATIVE WHITE WOMEN OF FOREIGN OR MIXED PARENTAGE 16 YEARS OF AGE AND OVER

DIVISION AND STATE	16 to 19 years of age: 1920 Total number	Engaged in gainful occupations Number	Per cent	20 to 24 years of age: 1920	16 to 24 years of age 1920	16 to 24 years of age 1900	25 to 44 years of age [1] 1920	25 to 44 years of age [1] 1900	45 to 64 years of age 1920	45 to 64 years of age 1900	65 years and over 1920	65 years and over 1900
UNITED STATES	881,660	452,396	51.3	48.8	50.0	39.0	24.6	19.6	16.7	12.5	8.3	7.7
GEOGRAPHIC DIVISIONS:												
New England	116,175	75,118	64.7	65.3	65.0	56.5	38.1	33.2	25.8	17.8	11.7	8.6
Middle Atlantic	281,990	181,382	64.3	54.6	59.2	47.9	28.3	22.6	18.6	13.5	9.0	8.0
East North Central	214,499	112,115	52.3	47.6	49.7	37.4	21.9	16.6	14.3	10.5	7.2	7.4
West North Central	139,520	41,322	29.6	38.0	34.3	30.3	18.3	14.6	12.8	9.8	6.4	5.8
South Atlantic	18,502	9,272	50.1	46.8	48.3	32.3	26.2	19.0	17.6	13.8	9.3	9.3
East South Central	5,535	2,257	40.8	43.2	42.2	30.6	23.1	17.9	16.2	13.5	8.9	8.9
West South Central	27,597	6,915	25.1	27.2	26.2	17.1	16.7	11.7	14.0	13.7	9.9	9.3
Mountain	27,716	7,178	25.9	33.8	30.3	21.2	17.6	14.1	14.9	14.6	9.6	8.8
Pacific	50,126	16,837	33.6	42.3	38.5	29.5	25.4	18.1	18.5	13.5	8.3	7.8
NEW ENGLAND:												
Maine	7,526	3,248	43.2	51.7	47.6	42.6	28.8	23.9	20.8	14.7	9.7	7.5
New Hampshire	6,104	3,669	60.1	62.5	61.4	54.7	37.2	33.9	27.3	19.8	13.8	12.2
Vermont	2,865	1,123	39.2	46.6	43.0	38.6	25.8	22.0	19.9	13.9	13.8	12.2
Massachusetts	66,369	43,446	65.5	67.8	66.7	57.4	40.7	35.4	27.5	19.1	12.4	8.4
Rhode Island	11,124	8,373	75.3	67.6	71.2	64.4	39.9	36.3	27.4	19.1	12.2	8.2
Connecticut	22,187	15,259	68.8	63.8	66.2	59.1	34.5	30.7	22.5	16.4	12.2	9.8
MIDDLE ATLANTIC:												
New York	147,333	99,693	67.7	58.7	62.8	50.1	30.9	24.1	20.2	14.8	9.8	8.5
New Jersey	44,060	30,131	68.4	55.1	61.4	49.2	26.0	21.3	16.1	12.4	7.8	7.1
Pennsylvania	90,597	51,558	56.9	46.9	51.8	43.4	24.7	20.2	16.8	11.7	8.1	7.7
EAST NORTH CENTRAL:												
Ohio	37,170	19,174	51.6	46.4	48.7	40.1	22.7	18.1	15.1	10.7	7.5	8.0
Indiana	9,816	4,731	48.2	42.6	45.0	31.5	19.3	15.4	13.3	10.1	7.0	6.8
Illinois	77,583	48,110	62.0	53.3	57.1	39.1	25.3	17.3	15.1	10.7	7.1	6.8
Michigan	45,981	20,668	44.9	43.0	43.9	34.1	19.5	15.4	13.7	10.5	6.9	7.6
Wisconsin	43,949	19,432	44.2	44.0	44.1	37.0	18.8	14.8	12.3	9.8	7.2	6.8
WEST NORTH CENTRAL:												
Minnesota	49,641	16,513	33.3	43.7	39.1	34.2	21.0	16.6	12.8	10.4	6.5	6.0
Iowa	22,939	6,022	26.3	34.7	31.2	29.6	16.6	13.9	12.0	9.0	5.6	4.3
Missouri	14,692	7,498	51.0	46.4	48.3	34.2	23.3	16.0	15.2	11.0	8.2	7.1
North Dakota	14,492	2,802	19.3	32.8	26.3	31.4	14.1	13.6	11.3	11.9	9.5	(2)
South Dakota	10,382	2,028	19.5	30.8	25.7	25.8	13.6	11.5	10.7	8.8	5.7	4.2
Nebraska	16,483	4,162	25.3	31.8	29.0	25.8	15.2	12.8	11.1	9.3	4.3	6.8
Kansas	10,891	2,297	21.9	29.3	25.7	20.2	14.4	11.5	11.2	8.6	5.2	6.1
SOUTH ATLANTIC:												
Delaware	1,153	624	54.1	41.5	47.1	45.9	24.8	22.0	16.7	12.7	8.2	5.2
Maryland	7,656	4,747	62.0	46.6	53.6	39.0	23.6	19.6	17.2	13.5	9.9	8.9
Dist. of Columbia	1,698	1,051	61.9	74.1	70.3	34.2	48.3	25.7	28.9	18.8	13.7	7.2
Virginia	1,708	613	35.9	40.4	38.4	18.9	20.3	14.7	14.0	10.9	9.2	13.4
West Virginia	2,189	716	32.7	32.2	32.4	26.3	18.1	14.7	12.9	10.1	7.3	7.7
North Carolina	392	106	27.0	37.8	33.3	20.1	20.5	15.8	14.7	15.3	6.1	16.3
South Carolina	391	132	33.8	38.1	36.1	23.5	23.7	18.0	16.0	15.9	6.6	11.8
Georgia	976	339	34.7	41.0	38.3	23.4	23.3	17.0	17.0	16.0	7.7	8.4
Florida	2,339	944	40.4	35.8	38.0	13.9	21.3	15.0	14.5	13.1	7.0	8.9
EAST SOUTH CENTRAL:												
Kentucky	2,604	1,397	53.6	50.2	51.7	37.5	25.7	19.7	17.4	13.2	9.3	9.8
Tennessee	1,119	357	31.9	42.3	37.9	23.0	21.0	15.6	14.4	13.7	8.1	8.8
Alabama	1,266	379	29.9	30.6	30.3	16.6	18.3	13.1	12.6	13.7	7.0	8.7
Mississippi	546	124	22.7	30.1	26.8	15.7	17.4	12.9	14.9	14.7	9.8	6.3
WEST SOUTH CENTRAL:												
Arkansas	1,431	368	25.7	30.1	28.1	18.9	16.1	11.8	12.6	13.7	4.9	12.0
Louisiana	3,608	1,005	27.9	30.4	29.2	19.0	20.1	14.6	16.6	14.6	10.1	9.2
Oklahoma	3,999	742	18.7	26.2	22.7	13.5	14.9	9.0	12.2	11.2	5.7	8.9
Texas	18,559	4,800	25.9	26.6	26.2	16.7	16.3	10.2	13.2	13.5	7.6	8.7
MOUNTAIN:												
Montana	6,152	1,583	25.7	36.5	31.7	27.5	18.2	16.3	16.5	16.6	10.9	(2)
Idaho	3,283	610	18.6	28.5	24.1	16.3	12.9	9.2	11.7	10.7	6.7	(2)
Wyoming	1,389	330	23.8	30.9	28.0	23.8	16.7	14.4	14.4	14.9	12.4	(2)
Colorado	8,011	2,483	31.0	38.4	35.0	25.3	22.3	18.1	17.8	16.2	10.4	8.0
New Mexico	1,089	213	19.6	28.4	24.3	12.4	19.5	12.7	16.4	13.6	12.9	(2)
Arizona	1,965	430	21.9	27.4	24.5	21.3	11.7	18.0	13.2	17.0	6.8	(2)
Utah	5,349	1,508	28.2	32.2	30.4	19.3	13.6	10.0	10.6	10.5	7.4	(2)
Nevada	478	103	21.5	36.5	30.5	20.3	19.0	15.6	19.5	12.1	11.9	(2)
PACIFIC:												
Washington	14,260	4,330	30.4	41.0	36.3	25.2	23.4	14.4	16.9	12.4	7.4	6.5
Oregon	6,332	2,096	33.1	41.7	38.0	23.7	18.1	14.7	16.2	11.3	7.1	7.8
California	29,534	10,411	35.3	43.0	39.7	30.4	26.4	19.3	19.3	14.1	8.7	8.1

[1] Includes age unknown. [2] Per cent not shown where base is less than 100.

TABLE 147.—PERCENTAGE OF FOREIGN-BORN WHITE WOMEN ENGAGED IN GAINFUL OCCUPATIONS, CLASSIFIED BY AGE, FOR DIVISIONS AND STATES: 1920 AND 1900

	FOREIGN-BORN WHITE WOMEN 16 YEARS OF AGE AND OVER											
DIVISION AND STATE	16 to 19 years of age: 1920			Per cent engaged in gainful occupations								
	Total number	Engaged in gainful occupations		20 to 24 years of age: 1920	16 to 24 years of age		25 to 44 years of age[1]		45 to 64 years of age		65 years and over	
		Number	Per cent		1920	1900	1920	1900	1920	1900	1920	1900
UNITED STATES___	227,053	129,166	56.9	37.7	43.9	48.8	18.6	16.7	13.9	10.9	5.9	6.2
GEOGRAPHIC DIVISIONS:												
New England_____	32,423	22,946	70.8	50.8	56.8	64.6	27.2	27.1	19.1	14.3	7.6	6.8
Middle Atlantic____	90,359	59,378	65.7	40.4	48.1	52.8	18.5	18.5	14.4	12.4	6.6	6.8
East North Central_	46,042	26,633	57.8	31.3	40.1	42.9	15.1	11.8	11.2	8.1	5.0	5.2
West North Central	14,783	6,002	40.6	29.6	33.7	36.2	13.1	10.4	9.9	8.5	4.4	5.4
South Atlantic____	5,361	2,699	50.3	31.9	38.3	37.6	18.6	16.1	15.6	13.7	7.8	8.0
East South Central_	880	332	37.7	27.1	31.1	29.5	17.8	13.9	14.7	10.8	6.8	6.8
West South Central	14,073	3,541	25.2	20.1	22.3	18.2	16.8	10.8	14.5	13.2	7.6	9.4
Mountain_____	8,414	2,146	25.5	20.1	22.4	26.8	13.9	12.7	13.3	13.2	6.6	7.5
Pacific_____	14,718	5,489	37.3	31.2	33.5	35.1	19.9	16.0	15.6	12.6	6.4	7.6
NEW ENGLAND:												
Maine_____	2,371	1,452	61.2	49.9	54.0	58.0	24.0	22.3	17.3	12.9	8.1	6.3
New Hampshire____	1,731	1,277	73.8	59.0	63.9	68.1	33.2	30.9	22.2	16.2	9.2	8.2
Vermont_____	823	298	36.2	33.5	34.5	40.8	15.2	15.4	14.4	11.3	7.0	5.6
Massachusetts_____	17,911	12,923	72.2	54.9	59.9	66.8	29.7	29.4	20.6	15.3	7.8	6.9
Rhode Island_____	3,449	2,753	79.8	53.3	61.9	67.1	29.2	26.1	18.1	13.8	7.4	6.7
Connecticut_____	6,138	4,243	69.1	38.5	47.0	58.7	19.7	20.7	14.9	11.9	6.5	6.7
MIDDLE ATLANTIC:												
New York_____	55,238	38,929	70.5	46.9	54.0	58.0	22.1	21.0	16.3	13.9	7.2	7.2
New Jersey_____	12,616	8,564	67.9	35.9	45.4	53.3	16.6	16.8	12.9	11.9	5.8	6.9
Pennsylvania_____	22,505	11,885	52.8	26.2	34.6	40.5	11.7	13.8	11.2	9.6	5.8	6.0
EAST NORTH CENTRAL:												
Ohio_____	10,801	5,554	51.4	26.4	34.6	42.9	13.9	11.8	11.2	8.8	5.2	5.7
Indiana_____	1,919	960	50.0	20.2	30.8	36.2	10.5	10.4	10.3	8.6	5.2	6.1
Illinois_____	17,961	12,034	67.0	37.8	47.3	47.3	18.2	14.0	12.4	8.3	4.9	4.6
Michigan_____	10,664	5,530	51.9	27.2	35.2	38.3	12.7	10.7	10.5	7.7	5.2	5.8
Wisconsin_____	4,697	2,555	54.4	30.2	39.5	39.9	12.3	8.3	10.0	7.4	4.7	4.7
WEST NORTH CENTRAL:												
Minnesota_____	4,486	2,136	47.6	37.1	40.9	41.1	14.1	11.4	10.0	8.4	4.5	5.2
Iowa_____	1,923	665	34.6	27.9	30.4	35.5	11.8	9.1	8.8	7.7	3.8	5.0
Missouri_____	2,690	1,643	61.3	35.0	44.8	42.4	18.2	14.5	13.8	9.7	6.0	6.1
North Dakota_____	2,007	444	22.1	18.6	19.9	32.4	8.7	10.2	9.0	10.0	4.3	6.3
South Dakota_____	807	217	26.9	24.9	25.7	26.9	10.8	7.2	9.1	8.1	4.1	4.2
Nebraska_____	1,556	610	39.2	28.2	32.3	31.5	12.4	8.7	8.8	7.9	3.5	5.3
Kansas_____	1,314	287	21.8	14.4	17.2	25.3	10.5	7.3	9.3	8.2	4.3	6.1
SOUTH ATLANTIC:												
Delaware_____	315	156	49.5	22.9	30.7	45.5	14.0	15.9	12.1	10.4	7.2	6.9
Maryland_____	1,906	1,252	62.0	36.2	46.7	45.0	16.7	15.9	14.2	13.9	7.7	8.4
Dist. of Columbia __	438	231	52.7	47.3	48.9	44.0	33.2	25.7	24.9	19.1	11.4	7.8
Virginia_____	466	181	38.8	26.9	31.1	21.2	13.5	13.1	12.6	14.3	6.6	9.9
West Virginia_____	952	216	22.7	11.2	15.3	24.3	6.8	9.4	8.9	7.7	6.2	5.3
North Carolina____	99	32	(²)	32.9	32.7	24.1	23.0	13.4	16.5	14.0	7.4	11.9
South Carolina____	71	23	(²)	17.2	21.2	32.9	18.3	17.7	17.6	14.7	8.9	10.0
Georgia_____	275	129	46.9	33.9	38.6	27.1	20.3	13.6	16.7	11.9	7.2	6.9
Florida_____	839	479	57.1	45.4	50.0	21.8	31.8	16.4	19.5	14.4	7.4	7.5
EAST SOUTH CENTRAL:												
Kentucky_____	241	95	39.4	33.1	35.3	41.9	18.9	15.2	15.7	9.9	7.1	6.0
Tennessee_____	229	102	44.5	30.7	36.1	20.2	18.7	13.2	14.7	11.5	6.7	7.2
Alabama_____	271	83	30.6	21.6	25.0	12.5	14.5	10.5	11.3	11.3	6.2	8.3
Mississippi_____	139	52	37.4	20.2	26.9	22.5	20.5	13.5	18.0	17.4	6.7	12.3
WEST SOUTH CENTRAL:												
Arkansas_____	147	58	39.5	25.5	31.2	22.7	21.6	9.9	16.8	13.1	7.1	8.6
Louisiana_____	672	191	28.4	19.7	22.9	13.4	17.7	11.3	15.7	13.7	8.1	9.4
Oklahoma_____	580	113	19.5	19.0	19.2	13.8	12.6	6.1	10.6	8.5	4.9	7.2
Texas_____	12,674	3,179	25.1	20.1	22.3	19.3	17.0	11.3	14.7	13.4	7.9	9.7
MOUNTAIN:												
Montana_____	1,200	350	29.2	23.8	26.0	31.9	12.7	13.9	12.9	14.3	7.0	8.0
Idaho_____	428	101	23.5	23.5	23.5	20.3	10.8	8.5	10.9	12.5	5.7	9.5
Wyoming_____	324	85	26.2	18.3	21.4	25.2	11.5	8.5	12.0	12.8	7.1	6.6
Colorado_____	1,912	509	26.6	20.4	23.0	30.8	14.7	15.0	14.2	13.7	7.8	7.1
New Mexico_____	906	118	13.0	10.1	11.3	11.9	11.4	8.0	13.4	11.1	8.9	9.3
Arizona_____	2,776	595	21.4	19.3	20.2	11.1	17.3	11.4	16.8	14.0	7.1	8.3
Utah_____	770	361	46.9	28.5	35.8	28.9	13.6	11.3	11.3	12.5	4.8	6.7
Nevada_____	98	27	(²)	14.3	18.1	18.0	12.8	11.1	19.5	14.9	8.4	15.1
PACIFIC:												
Washington_____	3,041	1,218	40.1	35.2	37.0	30.1	16.7	11.8	13.1	9.9	5.9	5.8
Oregon_____	1,218	537	44.1	35.5	38.7	37.7	18.2	12.8	13.0	9.8	4.8	5.7
California_____	10,459	3,734	35.7	29.5	23.5	36.4	21.2	17.9	17.0	13.5	6.8	8.1

[1] Includes age unknown.   [2] Per cent not shown where base is less than 100.

TABLE 148.—PERCENTAGE OF NEGRO WOMEN ENGAGED IN GAINFUL OCCUPATIONS, CLASSIFIED BY AGE, FOR DIVISIONS AND STATES: 1920 AND 1900

NEGRO WOMEN 16 YEARS OF AGE AND OVER

DIVISION AND STATE	16 to 19 years of age: 1920 Total number	Engaged in gainful occupations Number	Per cent	20 to 24 years of age: 1920	16 to 24 years of age 1920	16 to 24 years of age 1900	25 to 44 years of age[1] 1920	25 to 44 years of age[1] 1900	45 to 64 years of age 1920	45 to 64 years of age 1900	65 years and over 1920	65 years and over 1900
UNITED STATES	458,780	185,787	40.5	44.5	42.7	47.9	45.2	41.6	45.7	41.8	27.1	28.5
GEOGRAPHIC DIVISIONS:												
New England	2,452	1,245	50.8	53.7	52.5	55.9	49.5	47.1	49.7	46.1	30.2	26.8
Middle Atlantic	19,964	10,198	51.1	55.4	53.9	57.6	51.6	45.1	51.1	42.7	26.5	24.8
East North Central	15,846	5,958	37.6	40.8	39.6	36.5	41.2	33.0	39.7	29.9	19.0	18.0
West North Central	9,383	3,132	33.4	43.1	39.1	37.8	43.4	34.5	43.3	34.9	23.4	20.9
South Atlantic	199,265	82,443	41.4	45.5	43.6	49.4	46.0	42.5	46.3	42.4	28.2	28.9
East South Central	114,682	48,447	42.2	44.6	43.7	50.5	46.7	44.7	48.0	45.0	29.8	31.6
West South Central	95,251	33,747	35.4	39.5	37.6	41.5	40.7	36.8	41.2	38.4	23.9	26.8
Mountain	652	199	30.5	37.5	34.9	35.5	42.8	42.8	48.5	47.2	23.7	18.8
Pacific	1,285	418	32.5	46.5	41.1	35.8	46.8	36.6	46.1	36.0	22.4	23.6
NEW ENGLAND:												
Maine	39	8	(2)	(2)	(2)	48.7	40.6	37.6	43.8	28.6	(2)	(2)
New Hampshire	18	9	(2)	(2)	(2)	(2)	(2)	55.2	(2)	(2)	(2)	(2)
Vermont	12	1	(2)	(2)	(2)	(2)	(2)	38.9	(2)	(2)	(2)	(2)
Massachusetts	1,385	697	50.3	54.6	53.0	54.4	49.3	45.9	47.9	43.1	26.6	21.6
Rhode Island	314	182	58.0	55.9	56.8	54.9	46.0	54.2	50.3	51.9	37.4	30.9
Connecticut	684	348	50.9	51.9	51.5	59.4	52.5	45.9	53.8	50.8	33.1	33.0
MIDDLE ATLANTIC:												
New York	6,252	3,828	61.2	65.2	64.0	63.9	60.6	53.2	57.0	50.0	29.9	30.5
New Jersey	4,159	2,041	49.1	53.4	51.7	58.9	49.0	44.7	51.3	42.9	27.7	24.8
Pennsylvania	9,553	4,329	45.3	48.2	47.2	52.5	45.0	39.4	46.4	37.0	23.3	20.7
EAST NORTH CENTRAL:												
Ohio	5,740	2,051	35.7	39.1	37.9	35.6	40.0	31.1	39.0	28.0	18.3	17.0
Indiana	2,721	1,042	38.3	41.2	40.0	39.0	40.8	34.8	42.4	32.9	23.3	20.4
Illinois	5,579	2,209	39.6	44.8	42.9	35.6	44.7	34.0	40.5	31.3	17.7	18.1
Michigan	1,665	594	35.7	34.5	34.8	39.1	33.9	29.5	33.0	25.5	16.8	14.9
Wisconsin	141	62	44.0	34.6	38.0	27.1	36.0	27.2	39.7	·27.8	22.6	(2)
WEST NORTH CENTRAL:												
Minnesota	224	95	42.4	45.5	44.4	35.3	41.6	33.9	36.3	41.7	16.4	(2)
Iowa	596	180	30.2	39.1	35.6	30.5	36.0	24.4	37.1	26.8	24.2	16.4
Missouri	6,116	2,180	35.6	45.1	41.3	40.4	47.1	37.8	47.1	38.7	26.1	23.0
North Dakota	7	2	(2)	(2)	(2)	(2)	(2)	(2)	(2)	(2)	(2)	(2)
South Dakota	14	8	(2)	(2)	(2)	(2)	39.3	(2)	(2)	(2)	(2)	(2)
Nebraska	383	147	38.4	46.2	43.4	43.4	41.4	42.6	39.9	38.0	18.0	(2)
Kansas	2,043	520	25.5	36.1	31.4	30.4	33.9	24.7	35.7	25.1	17.7	15.9
SOUTH ATLANTIC:												
Delaware	1,190	462	38.8	46.8	43.2	44.7	47.5	36.1	46.6	32.1	32.2	21.9
Maryland	9,562	4,441	46.4	52.6	49.9	51.9	52.1	41.9	50.9	41.0	30.1	26.1
Dist. of Columbia	4,639	2,465	53.1	62.7	58.9	64.5	65.8	65.2	63.2	65.2	33.8	35.5
Virginia	30,019	9,482	31.6	37.6	34.9	42.5	35.4	35.6	37.0	35.3	24.0	24.2
West Virginia	3,288	602	18.3	22.6	20.9	29.1	23.1	24.5	28.2	26.1	18.8	20.1
North Carolina	36,250	13,838	38.2	41.9	40.1	46.2	39.7	36.6	40.3	35.7	25.0	24.9
South Carolina	41,838	21,146	50.5	50.9	50.7	57.0	52.4	49.0	53.9	49.0	33.8	37.3
Georgia	57,765	24,721	42.8	46.6	44.9	51.2	48.0	45.4	47.6	46.1	28.7	30.1
Florida	14,705	5,286	35.9	44.6	40.8	36.6	46.9	39.7	44.9	41.2	30.0	27.1
EAST SOUTH CENTRAL:												
Kentucky	8,930	2,594	29.0	41.3	36.0	38.6	47.3	40.1	49.4	40.1	30.6	24.0
Tennessee	19,999	7,217	36.1	42.7	39.8	42.8	45.4	39.6	44.7	39.7	28.4	26.6
Alabama	41,711	18,747	44.9	44.4	44.6	55.5	46.4	48.6	49.5	49.7	31.4	35.9
Mississippi	44,042	19,889	45.2	46.6	45.9	53.6	47.3	45.6	47.8	45.6	28.7	33.3
WEST SOUTH CENTRAL:												
Arkansas	22,074	7,876	35.7	36.4	36.1	41.0	36.2	32.5	37.7	34.6	22.2	24.9
Louisiana	32,113	12,344	38.4	39.7	39.1	48.8	41.7	42.8	43.8	44.7	24.4	29.9
Oklahoma	6,850	1,738	25.3	35.0	30.5	21.2	34.2	20.5	31.3	21.9	16.8	16.4
Texas	34,197	11,789	34.5	42.0	38.6	36.2	43.9	48.1	42.8	34.5	25.7	24.4
MOUNTAIN:												
Montana	27	11	(2)	(2)	(2)	34.7	34.1	46.6	16.8	(2)	(2)	
Idaho	20	4	(2)	(2)	(2)	(2)	36.0	(2)	(2)	(2)	(2)	
Wyoming	28	5	(2)	(2)	(2)	(2)	50.6	23.5	(2)	(2)	(2)	(2)
Colorado	345	125	36.2	44.0	40.7	38.2	45.3	43.8	49.7	48.7	21.7	(2)
New Mexico	75	12	(2)	29.9	25.5	26.8	39.0	31.8	39.8	(2)	(2)	(2)
Arizona	119	32	26.9	31.3	28.2	(2)	42.6	49.8	53.0	(2)	(2)	(2)
Utah	28	5	(2)	(2)	(2)	31.7	(2)	(2)	(2)	(2)	(2)	
Nevada	10	5	(2)	(2)	(2)	(2)	(2)	(2)	(2)	(2)	(2)	
PACIFIC:												
Washington	164	36	22.0	40.7	32.9	31.3	42.6	31.2	43.1	(2)	18.0	(2)
Oregon	44	13	(2)	(2)	43.2	(2)	44.2	50.0	43.3	(2)	(2)	(2)
California	1,077	369	34.3	47.1	42.2	36.2	47.6	36.3	46.8	36.4	23.7	24.2

[1] Includes age unknown.   [2] Per cent not shown where base is less than 100.

TABLE 149.—PERCENTAGE OF WOMEN 16 TO 24 YEARS OF AGE ENGAGED IN
GAINFUL OCCUPATIONS, FOR CITIES OF 100,000 INHABITANTS OR MORE AND FOR
AREAS OUTSIDE OF SUCH CITIES, BY DIVISIONS AND STATES: 1920 AND 1900

DIVISION AND STATE	WOMEN 16 TO 24 YEARS OF AGE							
	In cities having 100,000 inhabitants or more				In balance of State			
	Total number: 1920	Engaged in gainful occupations			Total number: 1920	Engaged in gainful occupations		
		Number: 1920	Per cent 1920	Per cent 1900		Number: 1920	Per cent 1920	Per cent 1900
UNITED STATES____	2,314,415	1,280,026	55.3	48.6	6,256,559	1,940,476	31.0	27.5
GEOGRAPHIC DIVISIONS:								
New England_____	178,780	112,874	63.1	57.0	385,161	209,170	54.3	48.6
Middle Atlantic_____	892,361	527,486	59.1	51.2	856,398	355,607	41.5	33.5
East North Central__	549,455	293,844	53.5	47.1	1,097,898	351,447	32.0	25.1
West North Central__	188,088	101,325	53.9	45.5	830,323	210,462	25.3	21.8
South Atlantic_____	168,880	93,362	55.3	45.9	1,080,822	332,510	30.8	29.8
East South Central___	68,134	31,127	45.7	43.9	721,839	184,792	25.6	25.8
West South Central__	93,236	40,263	43.2	29.4	826,913	185,472	22.4	19.4
Mountain_____	30,193	13,554	44.9	34.0	217,978	47,516	21.8	18.0
Pacific_____	145,288	66,191	45.6	37.6	239,227	63,500	26.5	22.4
NEW ENGLAND:								
Maine_____	_____	_____	_____	_____	56,624	22,514	39.8	36.7
New Hampshire_____	_____	___	_____	_____	32,644	17,273	52.9	48.2
Vermont_____	_____	_____	_____	_____	24,928	9,188	36.9	34.1
Massachusetts_____	123,527	78,959	63.9	57.0	174,029	102,839	59.1	52.8
Rhode Island_____	18,657	12,045	64.6	59.7	29,182	19,094	65.4	57.6
Connecticut_____	36,596	21,870	59.8	53.1	67,754	38,262	56.5	50.3
MIDDLE ATLANTIC:								
New York_____	582,742	354,900	60.9	52.2	247,716	107,560	43.4	37.1
New Jersey_____	90,600	51,890	57.3	51.2	154,065	76,640	49.7	33.8
Pennsylvania_____	219,019	120,696	55.1	48.9	454,617	171,407	37.7	29.3
EAST NORTH CENTRAL:								
Ohio_____	174,832	84,042	48.1	46.4	259,857	77,464	29.8	24.1
Indiana_____	26,775	12,846	48.0	38.5	198,401	59,733	30.1	20.6
Illinois_____	217,582	129,543	59.5	47.3	292,293	93,317	31.9	23.6
Michigan_____	90,693	43,748	48.2	48.5	178,607	60,398	33.8	28.4
Wisconsin_____	39,573	23,665	59.8	52.3	168,740	60,535	35.9	31.5
WEST NORTH CENTRAL:								
Minnesota_____	55,593	32,082	57.7	50.3	142,382	41,911	29.4	28.9
Iowa_____	11,765	5,866	49.9	_____	181,494	50,606	27.9	26.8
Missouri_____	95,897	51,252	53.4	43.6	180,518	37,604	20.8	13.5
North Dakota_____	_____	_____	_____	_____	51,826	13,575	26.2	30.7
South Dakota_____	_____	_____	_____	_____	51,047	12,960	25.4	24.6
Nebraska_____	16,285	8,382	51.5	44.9	89,683	21,837	24.3	22.4
Kansas_____	8,548	3,743	43.8	_____	133,373	31,969	24.0	18.8
SOUTH ATLANTIC:								
Delaware_____	9,187	4,517	49.2	_____	8,166	2,019	24.7	32.0
Maryland_____	64,323	34,565	53.7	46.6	54,269	16,032	29.5	24.8
District of Columbia__	44,159	28,434	64.4	44.7				
Virginia_____	29,671	14,922	50.3	_____	170,874	39,778	23.3	24.2
West Virginia_____	_____	_____	_____	_____	120,326	23,302	19.4	13.4
North Carolina_____	_____	_____	_____	_____	231,570	74,357	32.1	29.9
South Carolina_____	_____	_____	_____	_____	160,648	68,787	42.8	45.5
Georgia_____	21,540	10,924	50.7	_____	250,954	83,166	33.1	33.4
Florida_____	_____	_____	_____	_____	84,015	25,069	29.8	23.4
EAST SOUTH CENTRAL:								
Kentucky_____	21,082	11,074	52.5	41.6	179,912	28,874	16.0	14.4
Tennessee_____	28,386	13,096	46.1	48.4	179,301	35,652	19.9	17.1
Alabama_____	18,666	6,957	37.3	_____	195,656	62,123	31.8	35.2
Mississippi_____	_____	_____	_____	_____	166,970	58,143	34.8	38.2
WEST SOUTH CENTRAL:								
Arkansas_____	_____	_____	_____	_____	153,445	36,029	23.5	20.0
Louisiana_____	36,665	16,227	44.3	29.4	131,134	32,158	24.5	31.6
Oklahoma_____	_____	_____	_____	_____	175,842	35,313	20.1	11.5
Texas_____	56,571	24,036	42.5	_____	366,492	81,972	22.4	16.6
MOUNTAIN:								
Montana_____	_____	_____	_____	_____	37,234	9,792	26.3	24.5
Idaho_____	_____	_____	_____	_____	31,826	6,767	21.3	15.5
Wyoming_____	_____	_____	_____	_____	13,311	3,200	24.0	21.6
Colorado_____	19,924	9,319	46.8	34.0	50,482	10,923	21.6	17.2
New Mexico_____	_____	_____	_____	_____	29,126	4,766	16.4	10.5
Arizona_____	_____	_____	_____	_____	25,343	5,445	21.5	18.7
Utah_____	10,269	4,235	41.2	_____	26,275	5,530	21.0	19.1
Nevada_____	_____	_____	_____	_____	4,381	1,093	24.9	19.4
PACIFIC:								
Washington_____	32,419	14,444	44.6	_____	64,548	17,109	26.5	23.5
Oregon_____	20,106	9,395	46.7	_____	36,913	8,517	23.1	24.0
California_____	92,763	42,352	45.7	37.6	137,766	37,874	27.5	21.3

TABLE 150.—PERCENTAGE OF WOMEN 25 TO 44 YEARS OF AGE ENGAGED IN GAINFUL OCCUPATIONS, FOR CITIES OF 100,000 INHABITANTS OR MORE AND FOR AREAS OUTSIDE OF SUCH CITIES, BY DIVISIONS AND STATES: 1920 AND 1900

DIVISION AND STATE	WOMEN 25 TO 44 YEARS OF AGE AND UNKNOWN							
	In cities having 100,000 inhabitants or more				In balance of State			
	Total number: 1920	Engaged in gainful occupations			Total number: 1920	Engaged in gainful occupations		
		Number: 1920	Per cent 1920	Per cent 1900		Number: 1920	Per cent 1920	Per cent 1900
UNITED STATES	4,689,077	1,399,650	29.8	23.8	10,616,349	2,033,370	19.2	16.4
GEOGRAPHIC DIVISIONS:								
New England	363,985	128,428	35.3	31.1	772,324	228,103	29.5	25.6
Middle Atlantic	1,766,119	498,645	28.2	22.9	1,675,105	327,412	19.5	16.0
East North Central	1,147,905	303,538	26.4	20.4	2,042,116	314,026	15.4	11.8
West North Central	380,407	116,009	30.5	23.3	1,392,988	196,678	14.1	10.5
South Atlantic	315,773	123,495	39.1	31.7	1,562,376	371,860	23.8	22.0
East South Central	125,990	45,616	36.2	31.6	1,050,443	227,017	21.6	20.9
West South Central	167,000	54,778	32.8	25.8	1,205,104	213,070	17.7	15.7
Mountain	63,433	17,483	27.6	24.6	400,284	60,149	15.0	12.6
Pacific	358,465	111,658	31.1	23.2	515,609	95,055	18.4	14.5
NEW ENGLAND:								
Maine					104,285	25,385	24.3	19.7
New Hampshire					62,541	19,750	31.6	26.6
Vermont					47,158	10,071	21.4	17.3
Massachusetts	252,761	93,649	37.1	31.9	363,794	118,893	32.7	29.1
Rhode Island	39,169	13,892	35.5	31.1	54,816	17,884	32.6	26.4
Connecticut	72,055	20,887	29.0	24.4	139,730	36,120	25.8	23.3
MIDDLE ATLANTIC:								
New York	1,159,075	335,103	28.9	23.1	527,968	124,811	23.6	19.4
New Jersey	171,165	41,772	24.4	19.6	322,078	68,917	21.4	17.8
Pennsylvania	435,879	121,770	27.9	23.5	825,059	133,684	16.2	12.6
EAST NORTH CENTRAL:								
Ohio	362,336	93,169	25.7	21.3	500,542	73,336	14.7	12.1
Indiana	56,242	15,873	28.2	23.8	366,757	53,764	14.7	10.9
Illinois	467,492	132,872	28.4	19.9	542,411	87,512	16.1	12.2
Michigan	186,345	42,119	22.6	20.5	343,388	53,710	15.6	12.0
Wisconsin	75,490	19,505	25.8	17.8	289,018	45,704	15.8	11.6
WEST NORTH CENTRAL:								
Minnesota	108,746	33,105	30.4	23.9	224,040	32,682	14.6	10.9
Iowa	22,211	7,044	31.7		318,131	49,682	15.6	12.3
Missouri	201,032	62,463	31.1	22.7	306,037	38,766	12.7	8.9
North Dakota					81,060	10,362	12.8	11.4
South Dakota					84,522	11,813	14.0	9.8
Nebraska	32,554	9,589	29.5	25.4	148,752	19,705	13.2	9.7
Kansas	15,864	3,808	24.0		230,446	33,668	14.6	10.5
SOUTH ATLANTIC:								
Delaware	17,221	4,760	27.6		15,296	2,429	15.9	17.6
Maryland	121,783	38,241	31.4	27.9	93,939	16,328	17.4	14.1
District of Columbia	88,301	46,250	52.4	38.0				
Virginia	50,953	18,622	36.5		254,485	43,135	16.9	19.1
West Virginia					185,219	21,449	11.6	9.2
North Carolina					316,924	72,030	22.7	20.0
South Carolina					212,550	77,527	36.5	34.9
Georgia	37,515	15,622	41.6		345,225	98,690	28.6	27.3
Florida					138,738	40,272	29.0	22.6
EAST SOUTH CENTRAL:								
Kentucky	41,723	15,259	36.6	28.3	276,540	37,281	13.5	12.5
Tennessee	52,756	20,476	38.8	38.6	263,309	41,541	15.8	14.8
Alabama	31,511	9,881	31.4		275,440	72,945	26.5	28.3
Mississippi					235,154	75,250	32.0	31.5
WEST SOUTH CENTRAL:								
Arkansas					227,143	43,200	19.0	15.6
Louisiana	66,432	22,435	33.8	25.8	182,557	41,319	22.6	26.2
Oklahoma					261,268	38,139	14.6	8.2
Texas	100,568	32,343	32.2		534,136	90,411	16.9	14.0
MOUNTAIN:								
Montana					80,463	13,095	16.3	14.5
Idaho					56,533	7,281	12.9	9.1
Wyoming					28,076	4,484	16.0	11.4
Colorado	44,850	13,366	29.8	24.6	93,334	14,049	15.1	12.8
New Mexico					45,204	6,259	13.8	9.9
Arizona					46,603	8,830	18.9	19.3
Utah	18,583	4,117	22.2		39,124	4,035	10.3	11.1
Nevada					10,947	2,116	19.3	17.0
PACIFIC:								
Washington	75,060	22,116	29.5		128,421	20,757	16.2	13.3
Oregon	45,987	13,873	30.2		70,819	11,150	15.7	13.6
California	237,418	75,669	31.9	23.2	316,569	63,148	19.9	15.3

TABLE **151.**—PERCENTAGE OF WOMEN 45 YEARS OF AGE AND OVER ENGAGED IN GAINFUL OCCUPATIONS, FOR CITIES OF 100,000 INHABITANTS OR MORE AND FOR AREAS OUTSIDE OF SUCH CITIES, BY DIVISIONS AND STATES: 1920 AND 1900

	WOMEN 45 YEARS OF AGE AND OVER							
	In cities having 100,000 inhabitants or more				In balance of State			
DIVISION AND STATE	Total number: 1920	Engaged in gainful occupations			Total number: 1920	Engaged in gainful occupations		
		Number: 1920	Per cent			Number: 1920	Per cent	
			1920	1900			1920	1900
UNITED STATES	2,800,326	511,330	18.3	13.7	7,565,023	1,038,049	13.7	12.8
GEOGRAPHIC DIVISIONS:								
New England	252,401	53,557	21.2	15.5	669,299	114,112	17.0	12.2
Middle Atlantic	1,063,360	183,403	17.2	13.2	1,326,626	170,454	12.8	9.8
East North Central	635,523	99,707	15.7	10.0	1,674,645	173,079	10.3	8.4
West North Central	227,044	38,811	17.1	11.7	1,027,073	96,969	9.4	8.3
South Atlantic	191,550	48,503	25.3	22.5	961,079	181,677	18.9	20.5
East South Central	70,288	18,054	25.7	22.2	665,057	126,260	19.0	21.1
West South Central	85,912	18,655	21.7	23.6	643,547	96,098	14.9	17.4
Mountain	41,984	7,521	17.9	15.9	217,240	27,900	12.8	13.3
Pacific	232,264	43,119	18.6	14.0	380,457	51,500	13.5	11.0
NEW ENGLAND:								
Maine					104,406	16,214	15.5	11.3
New Hampshire					62,593	11,755	18.8	13.5
Vermont					48,920	7,298	14.9	10.5
Massachusetts	178,109	39,657	22.3	16.0	302,824	55,149	18.2	12.7
Rhode Island	29,621	6,162	20.8	15.2	42,834	7,392	17.3	11.8
Connecticut	44,671	7,738	17.3	12.8	107,722	16,304	15.1	11.8
MIDDLE ATLANTIC:								
New York	672,309	117,330	17.5	13.6	498,866	75,127	15.1	11.0
New Jersey	105,164	15,177	14.4	11.0	224,404	29,766	13.3	10.9
Pennsylvania	285,887	50,896	17.8	13.0	603,356	65,561	10.9	8.2
EAST NORTH CENTRAL:								
Ohio	213,745	34,146	16.0	11.0	435,305	44,924	10.3	8.7
Indiana	36,488	6,735	18.5	12.8	312,684	31,951	10.2	8.6
Illinois	252,337	40,670	16.1	9.6	417,565	43,961	10.5	8.4
Michigan	86,791	11,909	13.7	8.9	283,434	30,236	10.7	8.3
Wisconsin	46,162	6,247	13.5	7.2	225,657	22,007	9.8	7.4
WEST NORTH CENTRAL:								
Minnesota	63,467	9,120	14.4	10.2	158,610	13,423	8.5	7.5
Iowa	13,473	2,327	17.3		251,884	24,156	9.6	7.4
Missouri	122,081	23,037	18.9	12.3	250,434	25,799	10.3	10.3
North Dakota					42,065	3,790	9.0	9.6
South Dakota					49,346	4,496	9.1	7.6
Nebraska	18,296	2,837	15.5	11.9	101,753	8,519	8.4	7.4
Kansas	9,727	1,490	15.3		172,981	16,786	9.7	8.1
SOUTH ATLANTIC:								
Delaware	11,527	2,155	18.7		13,930	1,768	12.7	12.4
Maryland	82,633	17,141	20.7	19.2	77,374	10,869	14.0	12.9
District of Columbia	53,180	17,343	32.6	28.0				
Virginia	26,668	6,857	25.7		175,173	27,334	15.6	18.9
West Virginia					112,296	11,236	10.0	9.7
North Carolina					193,350	35,093	18.1	20.1
South Carolina					112,027	33,233	29.7	31.4
Georgia	17,542	5,007	28.5		195,973	45,163	23.0	24.7
Florida					80,956	16,981	21.0	22.1
EAST SOUTH CENTRAL:								
Kentucky	29,994	7,322	24.4	17.6	197,885	27,479	13.9	14.5
Tennessee	27,836	7,833	28.1	34.3	173,829	24,343	14.0	16.6
Alabama	12,458	2,899	23.3		161,380	38,510	23.9	27.3
Mississippi					131,963	35,928	27.2	29.4
WEST SOUTH CENTRAL:								
Arkansas					125,605	20,532	16.3	18.0
Louisiana	39,961	9,696	24.3	23.6	94,676	20,545	21.7	27.0
Oklahoma					136,622	15,240	11.2	11.1
Texas	45,951	8,959	19.5		286,644	39,781	13.9	15.0
MOUNTAIN:								
Montana					38,565	5,154	13.4	12.4
Idaho					30,926	3,274	10.6	11.4
Wyoming					11,412	1,623	14.2	11.3
Colorado	30,565	5,878	19.2	15.9	60,589	8,109	13.4	12.5
New Mexico					25,489	3,450	13.5	14.3
Arizona					20,904	3,210	15.4	24.4
Utah	11,419	1,643	14.4		23,454	1,988	8.5	11.0
Nevada					5,901	1,092	18.5	16.9
PACIFIC:								
Washington	42,529	7,448	17.5		84,933	10,212	12.0	10.2
Oregon	28,690	5,057	17.6		53,047	6,126	11.5	9.6
California	161,045	30,614	19.0	14.0	242,477	35,162	14.5	11.7

Table 152.—Percentage of Native White Women of Native Parentage 16 to 24 Years of Age Engaged in Gainful Occupations, for Cities of 100,000 Inhabitants or More and for Areas Outside of Such Cities, by Divisions and States: 1920 and 1900

	NATIVE WHITE WOMEN OF NATIVE PARENTAGE 16 TO 24 YEARS OF AGE							
	In cities having 100,000 inhabitants or more				In balance of State			
DIVISION AND STATE	Total number: 1920	Engaged in gainful occupations			Total number: 1920	Engaged in gainful occupations		
		Number: 1920	Per cent 1920	Per cent 1900		Number: 1920	Per cent 1920	Per cent 1900
UNITED STATES	898,814	463,332	51.5	38.1	3,972,846	1,035,128	26.1	18.9
GEOGRAPHIC DIVISIONS:								
New England	45,022	25,957	57.7	40.8	156,470	70,286	44.9	33.7
Middle Atlantic	268,548	151,936	56.6	41.3	522,859	201,035	38.4	28.0
East North Central	209,267	105,284	50.3	37.8	766,625	224,732	29.3	20.7
West North Central	98,665	51,050	51.7	37.8	533,721	128,273	24.0	17.9
South Atlantic	94,278	50,471	53.5	35.4	661,352	159,162	24.1	17.1
East South Central	39,176	16,838	43.0	31.5	486,851	84,700	17.4	11.7
West South Central	55,354	23,188	41.9	20.5	560,308	101,332	18.1	10.0
Mountain	16,692	7,138	42.8	28.6	140,359	28,599	20.4	14.8
Pacific	71,812	31,470	43.8	30.7	144,301	37,009	25.6	19.8
NEW ENGLAND:								
Maine					34,383	11,537	33.6	30.2
New Hampshire					14,424	5,966	41.4	34.4
Vermont					16,817	5,889	35.0	31.1
Massachusetts	29,635	16,850	56.9	40.4	59,808	30,889	51.6	35.1
Rhode Island	4,827	2,911	60.3	44.5	7,623	4,148	54.4	39.3
Connecticut	10,560	6,196	58.7	37.1	23,415	11,857	50.6	35.3
MIDDLE ATLANTIC:								
New York	148,301	85,997	58.0	40.0	154,751	61,597	39.8	29.4
New Jersey	30,528	17,197	56.3	43.5	67,298	29,093	43.2	27.1
Pennsylvania	89,719	48,742	54.3	42.5	300,810	110,345	36.7	27.4
EAST NORTH CENTRAL:								
Ohio	89,284	42,118	47.2	30.5	212,017	60,836	28.7	21.6
Indiana	20,139	9,534	47.3	34.0	170,046	48,427	28.5	18.0
Illinois	54,402	30,656	56.4	36.1	205,084	56,974	27.8	19.0
Michigan	32,193	15,246	47.4	39.3	97,335	30,999	31.8	24.2
Wisconsin	13,249	7,730	58.3	41.9	82,143	27,496	33.5	26.3
WEST NORTH CENTRAL:								
Minnesota	19,429	10,211	52.6	35.2	51,895	14,192	27.3	25.2
Iowa	8,345	4,077	48.9		123,305	33,185	26.9	23.8
Missouri	57,985	30,680	52.9	38.4	160,420	31,469	19.6	11.7
North Dakota					15,862	4,573	28.8	28.9
South Dakota					24,514	6,406	26.1	25.0
Nebraska	7,717	3,795	49.2	38.2	54,506	13,531	24.8	21.1
Kansas	5,189	2,287	44.1		103,219	24,917	24.1	17.3
SOUTH ATLANTIC:								
Delaware	5,046	2,508	49.7		5,970	1,324	22.2	24.5
Maryland	34,473	17,335	50.3	38.1	39,835	10,708	26.9	19.1
District of Columbia	25,610	17,055	66.6	30.2				
Virginia	16,312	7,640	46.8		113,643	22,385	19.7	12.9
West Virginia					104,945	19,724	18.8	11.6
North Carolina					152,120	42,720	28.1	20.4
South Carolina					69,724	22,873	32.8	28.0
Georgia	12,837	5,933	46.2		131,573	30,897	23.5	16.1
Florida					43,542	8,531	19.6	10.9
EAST SOUTH CENTRAL:								
Kentucky	14,097	6,878	48.8	33.4	158,997	22,003	13.8	9.6
Tennessee	15,972	6,853	42.9	26.5	143,780	22,911	15.9	9.5
Alabama	9,107	3,107	34.1		112,045	24,916	22.2	16.5
Mississippi					72,029	14,870	20.6	14.5
WEST SOUTH CENTRAL:								
Arkansas					102,539	17,943	17.5	10.4
Louisiana	20,254	8,570	42.3	20.5	68,035	9,781	14.4	11.1
Oklahoma					145,911	28,239	19.4	10.6
Texas	35,100	14,618	41.6		243,823	45,369	18.6	9.4
MOUNTAIN:								
Montana					19,661	4,634	23.6	21.1
Idaho					22,962	4,689	20.4	14.8
Wyoming					8,828	2,033	23.0	20.1
Colorado	11,411	5,111	44.8	28.6	35,543	7,486	21.1	15.2
New Mexico					22,764	3,399	14.9	8.9
Arizona					11,419	2,481	21.7	13.3
Utah	5,281	2,027	38.4		16,748	3,288	19.6	15.5
Nevada					2,434	589	24.2	16.0
PACIFIC:								
Washington	16,382	6,951	42.4		37,856	9,368	24.7	21.0
Oregon	11,396	5,058	44.4		26,725	5,853	21.9	20.7
California	44,034	19,461	44.2	30.7	79,720	21,788	27.3	18.6

TABLE 153.—PERCENTAGE OF NATIVE WHITE WOMEN OF FOREIGN OR MIXED PARENTAGE 16 TO 24 YEARS OF AGE ENGAGED IN GAINFUL OCCUPATIONS, FOR CITIES OF 100,000 INHABITANTS OR MORE AND FOR AREAS OUTSIDE OF SUCH CITIES, BY DIVISIONS AND STATES: 1920 AND 1900

	NATIVE WHITE WOMEN OF FOREIGN OR MIXED PARENTAGE 16 TO 24 YEARS OF AGE						
DIVISION AND STATE	In cities having 100,000 inhabitants or more				In balance of State		
	Total number: 1920	Engaged in gainful occupations			Total number: 1920	Engaged in gainful occupations		
		Number: 1920	Per cent 1920	Per cent 1900		Number: 1920	Per cent 1920	Per cent 1900
UNITED STATES	851,062	526,858	61.9	50.5	1,097,618	446,555	40.7	33.0
GEOGRAPHIC DIVISIONS:								
New England	88,177	60,573	68.7	59.2	159,121	100,150	62.9	55.6
Middle Atlantic	375,145	241,077	64.3	52.3	226,217	114,800	50.7	41.9
East North Central	223,476	136,451	61.1	50.7	263,687	105,438	40.0	31.2
West North Central	63,200	37,897	60.0	48.9	256,575	71,901	28.0	26.1
South Atlantic	23,760	13,891	58.5	42.6	18,443	6,473	35.1	24.5
East South Central	5,249	2,681	51.1	41.9	7,939	2,879	36.3	25.4
West South Central	11,184	4,312	38.6	21.4	47,767	11,134	23.3	16.2
Mountain	10,843	5,199	47.9	36.8	51,318	13,632	26.6	19.6
Pacific	50,028	24,777	49.5	39.8	66,551	20,148	30.3	25.0
NEW ENGLAND:								
Maine					15,469	7,356	47.6	42.6
New Hampshire					12,878	7,906	61.4	54.7
Vermont					5,900	2,536	43.0	38.6
Massachusetts	62,476	43,050	68.9	57.5	80,104	52,053	65.0	57.4
Rhode Island	9,377	6,599	70.4	66.2	14,575	10,443	71.7	62.9
Connecticut	16,324	10,924	66.9	60.3	30,195	19,856	65.8	58.9
MIDDLE ATLANTIC:								
New York	256,985	168,370	65.5	52.1	65,796	34,294	52.1	46.0
New Jersey	38,793	24,961	64.3	54.6	54,671	32,398	59.3	45.1
Pennsylvania	79,367	47,746	60.2	51.8	105,750	48,108	45.5	36.0
EAST NORTH CENTRAL:								
Ohio	52,169	28,754	55.1	50.7	32,420	12,418	38.3	31.7
Indiana	2,982	1,701	57.0	44.1	19,581	8,455	43.2	29.8
Illinois	111,251	72,700	65.3	49.9	67,871	29,526	43.5	29.6
Michigan	35,424	19,570	55.2	51.4	65,869	24,863	37.7	30.9
Wisconsin	21,650	13,726	63.4	55.4	77,946	30,176	38.7	33.3
WEST NORTH CENTRAL:								
Minnesota	30,177	18,276	62.1	54.8	82,671	25,417	30.7	28.9
Iowa	2,455	1,353	55.1		52,408	15,737	30.0	29.6
Missouri	22,911	13,453	58.7	45.9	12,650	3,734	29.5	17.4
North Dakota					30,065	7,904	26.3	31.4
South Dakota					23,193	5,969	25.7	25.8
Nebraska	6,053	3,482	57.5	49.7	32,196	7,592	23.6	23.0
Kansas	1,604	883	55.0		23,392	5,548	23.7	20.2
SOUTH ATLANTIC:								
Delaware	2,196	1,111	50.6		411	116	28.2	45.9
Maryland	14,012	8,015	57.2	45.4	2,945	1,066	36.2	23.4
District of Columbia	5,387	3,786	70.3	34.2				
Virginia	1,453	663	45.6		2,354	799	33.9	18.9
West Virginia					4,459	1,446	32.4	26.3
North Carolina					945	315	33.3	20.1
South Carolina					866	313	36.1	23.5
Georgia	712	316	44.4		1,571	559	35.6	23.4
Florida					4,892	1,859	38.0	13.9
EAST SOUTH CENTRAL:								
Kentucky	2,964	1,732	58.4	44.2	3,597	1,661	46.2	32.5
Tennessee	1,322	600	45.4	29.7	1,331	406	30.5	20.6
Alabama	963	349	36.2		1,788	484	27.1	16.6
Mississippi					1,223	328	26.8	15.7
WEST SOUTH CENTRAL:								
Arkansas					3,099	870	28.1	18.9
Louisiana	4,644	1,736	37.4	21.4	3,062	517	16.9	11.6
Oklahoma					8,784	1,998	22.7	13.5
Texas	6,540	2,576	39.4		32,822	7,749	23.6	16.7
MOUNTAIN:								
Montana					13,656	4,325	31.7	27.5
Idaho					7,416	1,788	24.1	16.3
Wyoming					3,409	954	28.0	23.8
Colorado	6,760	3,429	50.7	36.8	11,058	2,816	25.5	19.1
New Mexico					2,324	564	24.3	12.4
Arizona					4,204	897	21.3	11.7
Utah	4,083	1,770	43.4		8,066	1,927	23.9	19.3
Nevada					1,185	361	30.5	20.3
PACIFIC:								
Washington	11,429	5,463	47.8		20,824	6,243	30.0	25.2
Oregon	6,517	3,340	51.3		8,306	2,298	27.7	29.6
California	32,082	15,974	49.8	39.8	37,421	11,607	31.0	23.7

TABLE 154.—PERCENTAGE OF FOREIGN-BORN WHITE WOMEN 16 TO 24 YEARS OF AGE ENGAGED IN GAINFUL OCCUPATIONS, FOR CITIES OF 100,000 INHABITANTS OR MORE AND FOR AREAS OUTSIDE OF SUCH CITIES, BY DIVISIONS AND STATES: 1920 AND 1900

	FOREIGN-BORN WHITE WOMEN 16 TO 24 YEARS OF AGE							
	In cities having 100,000 inhabitants or more				In balance of State			
DIVISION AND STATE	Total number: 1920	Engaged in gainful occupations			Total number: 1920	Engaged in gainful occupations		
		Number: 1920	Per cent			Number: 1920	Per cent	
			1920	1900			1920	1900
UNITED STATES	392,488	199,159	50.7	55.8	304,421	107,037	35.2	42.8
GEOGRAPHIC DIVISIONS:								
New England	41,687	24,281	58.2	65.1	66,924	37,408	55.9	64.5
Middle Atlantic	211,403	112,816	53.4	57.4	87,349	30,793	35.3	42.7
East North Central	89,267	39,905	44.7	50.6	49,627	15,759	31.8	35.3
West North Central	14,150	6,797	48.0	53.4	25,737	6,630	25.8	31.4
South Atlantic	8,131	3,731	45.9	47.1	7,356	2,201	29.9	28.6
East South Central	936	348	37.2	44.6	1,411	381	27.0	22.3
West South Central	6,071	1,920	31.6	20.5	26,584	5,355	20.1	18.0
Mountain	2,095	970	46.3	44.6	18,564	3,649	19.7	24.7
Pacific	18,748	8,391	44.8	46.7	20,869	4,861	23.3	30.3
NEW ENGLAND:								
Maine					6,610	3,568	54.0	58.0
New Hampshire					5,296	3,382	63.9	68.1
Vermont					2,181	753	34.5	40.8
Massachusetts	28,936	17,804	61.5	65.5	32,852	19,198	58.4	67.5
Rhode Island	4,043	2,273	56.2	65.8	6,673	4,356	65.3	68.0
Connecticut	8,708	4,204	48.3	58.6	13,312	6,151	46.2	58.7
MIDDLE ATLANTIC:								
New York	160,526	89,512	55.8	59.0	23,746	9,916	41.8	53.0
New Jersey	17,571	7,969	45.4	52.7	25,153	11,414	45.4	53.6
Pennsylvania	33,306	15,335	46.0	52.9	38,450	9,463	24.6	27.9
EAST NORTH CENTRAL:								
Ohio	23,128	8,798	38.0	49.1	9,946	2,631	26.5	33.4
Indiana	553	227	41.0	48.5	4,921	1,451	29.5	33.9
Illinois	42,072	21,340	50.7	50.9	13,390	4,886	36.5	37.6
Michigan	19,010	7,400	38.9	50.6	13,634	4,099	30.1	34.4
Wisconsin	4,504	2,140	47.5	52.3	7,736	2,692	34.8	35.8
WEST NORTH CENTRAL:								
Minnesota	5,442	2,896	53.2	57.9	7,068	2,217	31.4	33.9
Iowa	443	204	46.0		4,730	1,369	28.9	35.5
Missouri	6,073	2,848	46.9	49.0	1,072	354	33.0	20.7
North Dakota					5,381	1,073	19.9	32.4
South Dakota					2,088	536	25.7	26.9
Nebraska	1,639	703	42.9	49.9	2,488	631	25.4	26.7
Kansas	553	146	26.4		2,910	450	15.5	25.3
SOUTH ATLANTIC:								
Delaware	942	300	31.8		134	30	22.4	45.5
Maryland	4,819	2,336	48.5	47.8	539	167	31.0	33.4
District of Columbia	1,507	737	48.9	44.0				
Virginia	577	231	40.0		762	185	24.3	21.2
West Virginia					2,687	410	15.3	24.3
North Carolina					339	111	32.7	24.1
South Carolina					269	57	21.2	32.9
Georgia	286	127	44.4		476	167	35.1	27.1
Florida					2,150	1,074	50.0	21.8
EAST SOUTH CENTRAL:								
Kentucky	261	131	50.2	49.0	424	111	26.2	34.1
Tennessee	356	142	39.9	26.0	225	68	30.2	17.9
Alabama	319	75	23.5		405	106	26.2	12.5
Mississippi					357	96	26.9	22.5
WEST SOUTH CENTRAL:								
Arkansas					359	112	31.2	22.7
Louisiana	1,002	296	29.5	20.5	825	123	14.9	7.7
Oklahoma					1,516	291	19.2	13.8
Texas	5,069	1,624	32.0		23,884	4,829	20.2	19.3
MOUNTAIN:								
Montana					2,991	777	26.0	31.9
Idaho					1,101	259	23.5	20.3
Wyoming					833	178	21.4	25.2
Colorado	1,269	563	44.4	44.6	3,285	484	14.7	24.1
New Mexico					2,182	247	11.3	11.9
Arizona					6,721	1,357	20.2	11.1
Utah	826	407	49.3		1,102	284	25.8	28.9
Nevada					349	63	18.1	18.0
PACIFIC:								
Washington	3,727	1,762	47.3		4,585	1,312	28.6	30.1
Oregon	1,934	920	47.6		1,252	315	25.2	37.7
California	13,087	5,709	43.6	46.7	15,032	3,234	21.5	27.8

TABLE 155.—PERCENTAGE OF NEGRO WOMEN 16 TO 24 YEARS OF AGE ENGAGED IN GAINFUL OCCUPATIONS, FOR CITIES OF 100,000 INHABITANTS OR MORE AND FOR AREAS OUTSIDE OF SUCH CITIES, BY DIVISIONS AND STATES: 1920 AND 1900

DIVISION AND STATE	NEGRO WOMEN 16 TO 24 YEARS OF AGE						
	In cities having 100,000 inhabitants or more			In balance of State			
	Total number: 1920	Engaged in gainful occupations			Total number: 1920	Engaged in gainful occupations		
		Number: 1920	Per cent			Number: 1920	Per cent	
			1920	1900			1920	1900
UNITED STATES	168,828	89,846	53.2	58.1	857,630	348,358	40.6	46.9
GEOGRAPHIC DIVISIONS:								
New England	3,827	2,044	53.4	55.2	2,499	1,280	51.2	56.2
Middle Atlantic	36,994	21,567	58.3	61.1	19,518	8,877	45.5	53.8
East North Central	27,328	12,162	44.5	45.9	16,864	5,356	31.8	32.0
West North Central	12,033	5,569	46.3	50.8	11,205	3,528	31.5	32.0
South Atlantic	42,681	25,257	59.2	65.7	392,537	164,423	41.9	48.4
East South Central	22,771	11,258	49.4	60.4	225,488	96,773	42.9	50.0
West South Central	20,608	10,833	52.6	48.7	187,032	67,301	36.0	41.1
Mountain	512	234	45.7	44.2	1,247	380	30.5	31.4
Pacific	2,074	922	44.5	40.0	1,240	440	35.5	34.1
NEW ENGLAND:								
Maine					96	33	(¹)	48.7
New Hampshire					39	16	(¹)	(¹)
Vermont					30	10	(¹)	(¹)
Massachusetts	2,423	1,240	51.2	56.8	1,208	684	56.6	52.9
Rhode Island	408	260	63.7	52.3	305	145	47.5	57.4
Connecticut	996	544	54.6	53.2	821	392	47.7	60.5
MIDDLE ATLANTIC:								
New York	16,699	10,947	65.6	65.4	3,015	1,663	55.2	60.6
New Jersey	3,703	1,759	47.5	56.4	6,919	3,731	53.9	59.4
Pennsylvania	16,592	8,861	53.4	58.0	9,584	3,483	36.3	44.6
EAST NORTH CENTRAL:								
Ohio	10,229	4,366	42.7	46.9	5,461	1,577	28.9	29.7
Indiana	3,099	1,382	44.6	44.9	3,843	1,397	36.4	36.6
Illinois	9,799	4,826	49.2	45.3	5,935	1,928	32.5	30.6
Michigan	4,035	1,521	37.7	48.3	1,407	375	26.7	35.4
Wisconsin	166	67	40.4	(¹)	218	79	36.2	24.0
WEST NORTH CENTRAL:								
Minnesota	525	242	46.1	35.1	95	33	(¹)	(¹)
Iowa	521	231	44.3		1,009	314	31.1	30.5
Missouri	8,918	4,269	47.9	51.9	6,370	2,046	32.1	32.6
North Dakota					16	6	(¹)	(¹)
South Dakota					46	22	(¹)	(¹)
Nebraska	868	401	46.2	44.6	214	69	32.2	41.7
Kansas	1,201	426	35.5		3,455	1,038	30.0	30.4
SOUTH ATLANTIC:								
Delaware	1,003	598	59.6		1,651	549	33.3	44.7
Maryland	11,014	6,876	62.4	67.1	10,948	4,089	37.3	40.6
District of Columbia	11,638	6,851	58.9	64.5				
Virginia	11,323	6,385	56.4		54,055	16,404	30.3	42.5
West Virginia					8,234	1,722	20.9	29.1
North Carolina					77,194	30,976	40.1	46.2
South Carolina					89,763	45,541	50.7	57.0
Georgia	7,703	4,547	59.0		117,321	51,539	43.9	51.2
Florida					33,371	13,603	40.8	36.6
EAST SOUTH CENTRAL:								
Kentucky	3,759	2,331	62.0	52.8	16,890	5,098	30.2	35.9
Tennessee	10,735	5,501	51.2	66.3	33,964	12,267	36.1	39.7
Alabama	8,277	3,426	41.4		81,388	36,609	45.0	55.5
Mississippi					93,246	42,799	45.9	53.6
WEST SOUTH CENTRAL:								
Arkansas					47,430	17,101	36.1	41.0
Louisiana	10,758	5,623	52.3	48.7	59,106	21,726	36.8	48.8
Oklahoma					14,713	4,488	30.5	21.2
Texas	9,850	5,210	52.9		65,783	23,986	36.5	36.2
MOUNTAIN:								
Montana					68	26	(¹)	34.7
Idaho					50	13	(¹)	(¹)
Wyoming					81	28	(¹)	(¹)
Colorado	462	213	46.1	44.2	365	124	34.0	31.7
New Mexico					239	61	25.5	26.8
Arizona					378	113	29.9	(¹)
Utah	50	21	(¹)		49	8	(¹)	(¹)
Nevada					17	7	(¹)	(¹)
PACIFIC:								
Washington	216	88	40.7		179	42	23.5	31.3
Oregon	85	38	(¹)		26	10	(¹)	(¹)
California	1,773	796	44.9	40.0	1,035	388	37.5	34.1

¹ Per cent not shown where base is less than 100.

DETAILED TABLES 269

TABLE 156.—Percentage of Women Engaged in Gainful Occupations, Classified by Marital Condition, for Cities of 100,000 Inhabitants or More: 1920, 1910, and 1900

		WOMEN 16 YEARS OF AGE AND OVER											
	Total					Married					Not married—Per cent in gainful occupations		
CITY	Number: 1920	Engaged in gainful occupations				Number: 1920	Engaged in gainful occupations						
		Number: 1920	Per cent 1920	1910	1900		Number: 1920	Per cent 1920	1910	1900	1920	1910	1900
NEW ENGLAND DIV.:													
Boston, Mass	275,352	102,561	37.2	38.0	33.1	137,835	13,583	9.9	10.6	6.0	64.7	63.7	57.7
Bridgeport, Conn	47,431	14,986	31.6	32.6	29.2	29,738	3,669	12.3	9.9	5.7	64.0	64.0	58.6
Cambridge, Mass	41,616	15,653	37.6	36.1	32.1	20,657	2,220	10.7	9.6	5.5	64.1	61.5	56.2
Fall River, Mass	41,779	19,111	45.7	45.8	44.7	22,374	5,489	24.5	24.2	20.1	70.2	69.9	70.1
Hartford, Conn	49,304	17,228	34.9	-----	30.2	27,882	3,183	11.4	-----	4.8	65.6	-----	57.2
Lowell, Mass	41,252	17,799	43.1	45.4	45.1	21,351	4,458	20.9	20.5	16.5	67.0	69.2	69.9
New Bedford, Mass	42,846	19,772	46.1	-----	35.9	24,587	7,200	29.3	-----	14.6	68.9	-----	60.9
New Haven, Conn	56,587	18,281	32.3	31.6	28.0	32,168	2,844	8.8	7.5	4.2	63.2	60.5	54.8
Providence, R. I	87,447	32,099	36.7	36.4	33.5	46,221	5,433	11.8	9.7	6.5	64.7	64.3	59.9
Springfield, Mass	48,098	16,935	35.2	-----	28.4	27,345	3,768	13.8	-----	5.5	63.4	-----	52.9
Worcester, Mass	63,454	20,434	32.2	32.1	28.8	35,421	2,873	8.1	6.6	4.3	62.6	60.5	55.9
MID. ATLANTIC DIV.:													
Albany, N. Y	45,337	14,353	31.7	31.4	27.5	22,526	1,311	5.8	6.0	2.9	57.2	54.7	48.3
Buffalo, N. Y	178,176	48,875	27.4	27.6	23.1	104,337	5,166	5.0	4.6	2.8	59.2	55.9	48.8
Camden, N. J	38,599	10,349	26.8	-----	23.6	25,121	2,217	8.8	-----	5.1	60.3	-----	51.6
Jersey City, N. J	99,894	28,705	28.7	26.9	22.8	58,543	3,467	5.9	4.2	2.8	61.0	56.6	49.0
New York, N. Y	1,983,862	677,635	34.2	34.2	29.3	1,115,531	107,315	9.6	9.4	4.9	65.7	63.1	56.4
Bronx Bor	254,290	76,030	29.9	27.4	-----	152,161	9,485	6.2	6.1	-----	62.0	57.0	-----
Brooklyn Bor	690,971	209,568	30.3	29.2	-----	399,460	26,717	6.7	6.5	3.2	62.7	57.7	-----
Manhattan Bor	839,067	337,291	40.2	40.2	-----	441,520	63,012	14.3	12.9	6.2	69.0	68.4	-----
Queens Bor	162,744	45,329	27.9	24.2	-----	100,669	7,063	7.0	5.4	3.1	61.6	53.7	-----
Richmond Bor	36,790	9,417	25.6	24.2	-----	21,712	1,038	4.8	5.0	3.6	55.6	49.0	-----
Newark, N. J	140,208	40,621	29.0	29.2	26.2	84,056	5,728	6.8	6.6	3.6	62.1	59.9	54.1
Paterson, N. J	48,415	17,999	37.2	35.2	30.6	27,880	4,243	15.2	11.0	5.7	67.0	65.7	61.7
Philadelphia, Pa	653,787	210,812	32.2	33.7	29.3	353,613	37,402	10.0	9.8	5.1	61.9	60.3	51.7
Pittsburgh, Pa	201,782	56,784	28.1	27.6	¹22.2	115,373	6,968	6.0	6.2	2.8	57.7	53.6	¹45.7
Reading, Pa	38,931	12,902	33.1	-----	25.6	23,645	3,312	14.0	-----	4.3	62.7	-----	54.0
Rochester, N. Y	109,019	36,956	33.9	33.8	31.5	62,517	7,537	12.1	9.3	5.0	63.2	57.4	51.5
Scranton, Pa	46,285	12,864	27.8	25.8	24.1	25,804	671	2.6	2.9	1.9	59.5	55.2	51.5
Syracuse, N. Y	62,848	18,426	29.3	30.1	26.2	37,452	3,369	9.0	8.4	4.5	59.3	57.2	51.7
Trenton, N. J	39,813	11,165	28.0	-----	22.3	24,339	2,032	8.3	-----	4.2	59.0	-----	47.0
Yonkers, N. Y	34,884	11,038	31.6	-----	-----	19,931	1,626	8.2	-----	-----	62.9	-----	-----
NORTH CENT. DIVS.:													
Akron, Ohio	61,668	15,959	25.9	-----	-----	42,722	4,282	10.0	-----	-----	61.6	-----	-----
Chicago, Ill	937,411	303,085	32.3	30.8	25.1	560,572	58,438	10.4	7.1	3.5	64.9	62.3	54.4
Cincinnati, Ohio	158,201	50,231	31.8	33.0	29.4	84,712	8,403	9.9	9.2	4.4	56.9	56.8	52.5
Cleveland, Ohio	260,964	73,143	28.0	27.9	23.4	168,121	16,153	9.6	7.1	3.3	61.4	56.4	54.7
Columbus, Ohio	89,247	25,396	28.5	28.0	24.5	52.353	5,445	10.4	8.2	4.1	54.1	53.4	48.3
Dayton, Ohio	55,511	14,969	27.0	26.2	24.1	34,900	3,140	9.0	7.2	3.2	57.4	53.9	50.5
Des Moines, Iowa	47,449	15,237	32.1	-----	23.2	28,252	3,554	12.6	-----	4.0	60.9	-----	49.0
Detroit, Mich	314,078	82,843	26.4	29.1	25.4	209,193	17,105	8.2	8.6	2.8	62.7	60.6	52.5
Grand Rapids,Mich	49,751	14,933	30.0	26.8	24.5	30,197	3,045	10.1	5.9	4.0	60.8	56.7	54.1
Indianapolis, Ind	119,505	35,454	29.7	28.1	24.8	73,556	8,876	12.1	9.2	5.2	57.8	54.5	49.8
Kansas City, Kans	34,139	9,041	26.5	-----	18.8	22,729	2,499	11.0	-----	4.2	57.3	-----	44.5
Kansas City, Mo	125,288	39,925	31.9	30.0	26.8	75,224	10,347	13.8	11.7	7.2	59.1	55.3	52.1
Milwaukee, Wis	161,225	49,417	30.7	29.2	25.6	94,032	6,370	6.8	4.9	2.4	64.1	60.0	55.5
Minneapolis, Minn	142,158	46,444	32.7	32.3	28.1	80,164	6,441	8.0	5.8	3.8	64.5	62.2	58.5
Omaha, Nebr	67,135	20,808	31.0	30.0	28.4	40,707	4,759	11.7	7.8	5.0	60.7	57.6	57.3
St. Louis, Mo	293,722	96,827	33.0	29.8	25.5	165,796	18,623	11.2	8.4	4.9	61.1	55.0	48.2
St. Paul, Minn	85,648	27,863	32.5	34.3	29.6	47,810	3,699	7.7	5.4	3.5	63.9	63.7	57.8
Toledo, Ohio	85,006	23,832	28.0	27.3	22.3	53,859	4,834	9.0	7.0	3.4	58.6	56.8	49.3
Youngstown, Ohio	40,316	8,576	21.3	-----	-----	26,975	1,387	5.1	-----	-----	53.9	-----	-----
THE SOUTH:													
Atlanta, Ga	76,597	31,553	41.2	42.8	42.1	44,377	11,112	25.0	27.5	23.0	63.4	61.5	59.0
Baltimore, Md	268,739	89,497	33.5	35.3	30.6	152,645	20,957	13.7	15.2	10.2	59.4	56.9	50.9
Birmingham, Ala	62,635	19,737	31.5	34.0	-----	39,014	6,523	16.7	19.7	-----	55.9	55.7	-----
Dallas, Tex	59,289	21,456	36.2	-----	-----	35,123	6,845	19.5	-----	-----	60.5	-----	-----
Fort Worth, Tex	36,577	10,760	29.4	-----	-----	23,239	3,418	14.7	-----	-----	53.7	-----	-----
Houston, Tex	50,660	16,891	33.3	-----	-----	31,191	5,787	18.6	-----	-----	57.0	-----	-----
Louisville, Ky	92,799	33,653	36.3	35.7	29.2	49,667	8,316	16.3	15.3	9.0	58.9	57.1	47.8
Memphis, Tenn	63,049	23,784	37.7	40.4	40.8	36,253	7,717	21.3	25.5	18.1	60.0	58.8	61.9
Nashville, Tenn	45,929	17,621	38.4	38.6	36.7	25,127	5,347	21.3	21.4	20.2	59.0	56.6	51.5
New Orleans, La	143,058	48,358	33.8	33.5	26.2	74,783	12,375	16.5	18.5	11.8	52.7	47.8	38.5

¹ Includes Allegheny.

TABLE **156.**—PERCENTAGE OF WOMEN ENGAGED IN GAINFUL OCCUPATIONS, CLASSIFIED BY MARITAL CONDITION, FOR CITIES OF 100,000 INHABITANTS OR MORE: 1920, 1910, AND 1900—Continued

	WOMEN 16 YEARS OF AGE AND OVER												
	Total					Married					Not married—Per cent in gainful occupations		
CITY	Number: 1920	Engaged in gainful occupations				Number: 1920	Engaged in gainful occupations						
		Number: 1920	Per cent				Number: 1920	Per cent					
			1920	1910	1900			1920	1910	1900	1920	1910	1900
THE SOUTH—Con.													
Norfolk, Va	40,742	14,384	35.3	----	----	25,287	5,128	20.3	----	----	59.9	----	----
Richmond, Va	66,550	26,017	39.1	41.6	36.9	35,158	6,985	19.9	22.6	16.7	60.6	59.0	52.1
San Antonio, Tex	56,564	16,421	29.0	----	21.9	32,512	4,003	12.3	----	9.7	51.6	----	35.9
Washington, D. C	185,640	92,027	49.6	39.8	37.0	88,584	22,871	25.8	21.3	17.5	71.3	58.0	53.8
Wilmington, Del	37,935	11,432	30.1	----	27.0	23,010	2,636	11.5	----	6.8	58.9	----	51.3
THE WEST:													
Denver, Colo	95,339	28,563	30.0	28.4	24.8	54,983	6,205	11.3	10.0	6.9	55.4	53.3	48.1
Los Angeles, Calif	230,476	68,061	29.5	26.2	21.8	132,869	18,174	13.7	9.8	6.2	51.1	48.7	40.8
Oakland, Calif	78,420	20,001	25.5	23.0	20.9	47,866	4,820	10.1	6.9	4.5	49.7	45.2	39.3
Portland, Oreg	94,783	28,325	29.9	28.7	26.2	58,542	7,423	12.7	8.6	5.7	57.7	56.0	51.0
Salt Lake City, Utah	40,271	9,995	24.8	----	21.5	24,377	1,768	7.3	----	4.6	51.8	----	41.4
San Francisco, Calif	182,830	60,573	33.2	29.3	25.2	100,800	13,189	13.1	9.2	5.9	58.1	52.9	45.2
Seattle, Wash	111,615	32,950	29.5	25.8	22.8	70,042	8,203	11.7	7.1	7.0	59.5	53.8	47.7
Spokane, Wash	38,393	11,058	28.8	24.6	----	23,440	2,676	11.4	8.1	----	56.1	52.9	----

TABLE **157.**—PERCENTAGE OF NATIVE WHITE WOMEN OF NATIVE PARENTAGE ENGAGED IN GAINFUL OCCUPATIONS, FOR CITIES OF 100,000 INHABITANTS OR MORE: 1920, 1910, AND 1900, WITH MARITAL CONDITION FOR 1920

	NATIVE WHITE WOMEN OF NATIVE PARENTAGE 16 YEARS OF AGE AND OVER								Per cent not married and gainfully occupied: 1920
CITY	Total					Married			
	Number: 1920	Engaged in gainful occupations				Number: 1920	Engaged in gainful occupations		
		Number: 1920	Per cent				Number: 1920	Per cent: 1920	
			1920	1910	1900				
NEW ENGLAND DIV.:									
Boston, Mass	63,193	25,074	39.7	36.3	28.8	26,838	3,401	12.7	59.6
Bridgeport, Conn	12,351	4,234	34.3	30.1	24.4	6,958	918	13.2	61.5
Cambridge, Mass	10,977	3,902	35.5	31.0	24.0	4,605	483	10.5	53.7
Fall River, Mass	5,452	2,181	40.0	33.6	28.2	2,403	334	13.9	60.6
Hartford, Conn	14,850	5,471	36.8	----	23.0	7,397	948	12.8	60.7
Lowell, Mass	8,093	2,964	36.6	34.4	34.2	3,840	546	14.2	57.0
New Bedford, Mass	7,136	2,390	33.5	----	22.3	3,617	495	13.7	53.9
New Haven, Conn	15,918	5,365	33.7	19.7	20.5	8,025	767	9.6	58.3
Providence, R. I	23,193	8,394	36.2	32.1	25.8	10,945	1,300	11.9	57.9
Springfield, Mass	17,923	6,172	34.4	----	22.4	9,673	1,369	14.2	58.2
Worcester, Mass	17,396	5,807	33.4	28.1	22.9	8,781	867	9.9	57.3
MIDDLE ATLANTIC DIV.:									
Albany, N. Y	20,992	7,274	34.7	31.6	24.7	9,981	640	6.4	60.2
Buffalo, N. Y	52,255	16,745	32.0	30.7	24.3	28,319	1,726	6.1	62.7
Camden, N. J	18,618	5,143	27.6	----	22.0	11,618	928	8.0	60.2
Jersey City, N. J	25,345	8,774	34.6	28.3	20.6	13,171	815	6.2	65.4
New York, N. Y	378,908	143,207	37.8	37.8	28.8	183,537	18,558	10.1	63.8
Bronx Borough	38,934	14,714	37.8	30.6	------	19,942	1,616	8.1	69.0
Brooklyn Borough	144,621	52,761	36.5	39.2	------	71,393	5,924	8.3	64.0
Manhattan Borough	142,866	58,804	41.2	35.0	------	63,200	9,148	14.5	62.3
Queens Borough	41,609	13,693	32.9	25.0	------	23,264	1,587	6.8	66.0
Richmond Borough	10,878	3,235	29.7	21.9	------	5,738	283	4.9	57.4

TABLE 157.—PERCENTAGE OF NATIVE WHITE WOMEN OF NATIVE PARENTAGE ENGAGED IN GAINFUL OCCUPATIONS, FOR CITIES OF 100,000 INHABITANTS OR MORE: 1920, 1910, AND 1900, WITH MARITAL CONDITION FOR 1920—Continued

CITY	NATIVE WHITE WOMEN OF NATIVE PARENTAGE 16 YEARS OF AGE AND OVER								Per cent not married and gainfully occupied: 1920
	Total					Married			
	Number: 1920	Engaged in gainful occupations				Number: 1920	Engaged in gainful occupations		
		Number: 1920	Per cent				Number: 1920	Per cent: 1920	
			1920	1910	1900				
MIDDLE ATLANTIC DIV.—Con.									
Newark, N. J	37,680	12,623	33.5	30.3	24.8	19,942	1,467	7.4	62.9
Paterson, N. J	10,687	4,118	38.5	34.2	28.1	5,463	717	13.1	65.1
Philadelphia, Pa	240,382	79,069	32.9	31.3	26.4	128,704	11,054	8.6	60.9
Pittsburgh, Pa	69,801	21,350	30.6	27.1	1 23.1	37,323	2,135	5.7	59.2
Reading, Pa	30,087	10,277	34.2	----	26.0	18,050	2,648	14.7	63.4
Rochester, N. Y	39,025	14,742	37.8	34.5	30.5	20,843	2,989	14.3	64.6
Scranton, Pa	14,684	4,747	32.3	27.5	22.2	7,531	257	3.4	62.8
Syracuse, N. Y	28,368	9,018	31.8	29.6	23.4	16,295	1,831	11.2	59.5
Trenton, N. J	15,777	4,622	29.3	----	20.6	8,838	672	7.6	56.9
Yonkers, N. Y	9,797	3,047	31.1	----	----	5,174	334	6.5	58.7
NORTH CENTRAL DIVS.:									
Akron, Ohio	37,078	10,575	28.5	----	----	24,967	2,658	10.6	65.4
Chicago, Ill	197,705	73,262	37.1	31.1	24.8	106,167	12,905	12.2	65.9
Cincinnati, Ohio	69,913	23,522	33.6	34.9	30.5	37,522	3,072	8.2	63.1
Cleveland, Ohio	67,650	22,545	33.3	28.8	23.3	39,391	4,252	10.8	64.7
Columbus, Ohio	58,269	16,509	28.3	27.1	23.5	33,896	3,048	9.0	55.2
Dayton, Ohio	35,110	9,551	27.2	25.9	23.2	22,042	1,701	7.7	60.1
Des Moines, Iowa	30,424	9,971	32.8	----	21.1	18,010	2,357	13.1	61.3
Detroit, Mich	91,994	27,938	30.4	29.1	24.0	58,695	5,926	10.1	66.1
Grand Rapids, Mich	18,457	5,979	32.4	27.3	24.1	10,765	1,442	13.4	59.0
Indianapolis, Ind	80,510	23,350	29.0	25.9	22.7	50,007	5,307	10.6	59.2
Kansas City, Kans	18,534	4,828	26.0	----	16.8	12,368	1,184	9.6	59.1
Kansas City, Mo	78,894	24,743	31.4	26.9	22.6	47,378	6,099	12.9	59.2
Milwaukee, Wis	35,597	14,103	39.6	35.4	29.2	17,603	1,390	7.9	70.7
Minneapolis, Minn	42,914	14,410	33.6	29.0	22.6	22,963	2,215	9.6	61.1
Omaha, Nebr	28,506	9,325	32.7	29.8	27.2	16,892	2,146	12.7	61.8
St. Louis, Mo	120,403	44,086	36.6	31.8	25.2	65,652	6,952	10.6	67.8
St. Paul, Minn	22,230	7,972	35.9	34.8	26.4	11,621	1,129	9.7	64.5
Toledo, Ohio	40,905	12,027	29.4	27.3	21.4	25,476	2,604	10.2	61.1
Youngstown, Ohio	14,404	3,651	25.3	----	----	9,020	553	6.1	57.5
THE SOUTH:									
Atlanta, Ga	46,200	14,051	30.4	24.6	21.7	27,118	3,278	12.1	56.5
Baltimore, Md	131,486	38,881	29.6	28.8	24.1	73,020	4,970	6.8	58.0
Birmingham, Ala	31,338	6,927	22.1	17.1	----	19,568	1,302	6.7	47.8
Dallas, Tex	41,644	13,496	32.4	----	----	24,340	3,336	13.7	58.7
Fort Worth, Tex	25,812	6,511	25.2	----	----	16,379	1,641	10.0	51.6
Houston, Tex	25,344	6,877	27.1	----	----	15,462	1,525	9.9	54.2
Louisville, Ky	49,071	15,623	31.8	29.8	22.6	26,846	2,385	8.9	59.6
Memphis, Tenn	30,324	8,526	28.1	22.5	18.8	17,586	1,731	9.8	53.3
Nashville, Tenn	27,053	7,785	28.8	22.8	19.0	15,271	1,483	9.7	53.5
New Orleans, La	62,335	17,990	28.9	24.7	17.8	32,170	1,996	6.2	53.0
Norfolk, Va	20,317	4,908	24.2	----	----	12,731	1,053	8.3	50.8
Richmond, Va	38,908	11,731	30.2	25.8	21.1	20,579	1,511	7.3	55.8
San Antonio, Tex	25,894	6,833	26.4	----	16.1	15,023	1,333	8.9	50.6
Washington, D. C	101,891	48,357	47.5	----	28.2	24,051	8,558	18.6	71.3
Wilmington, Del	19,895	5,629	28.3	----	21.4	11,939	964	8.1	58.6
THE WEST:									
Denver, Colo	50,586	15,520	30.7	27.4	22.9	28,912	3,566	12.3	55.2
Los Angeles, Calif	118,893	35,508	29.9	24.9	22.0	66,602	9,263	13.9	50.2
Oakland, Calif	31,229	8,623	27.6	21.9	18.3	18,253	2,057	11.3	50.6
Portland, Oreg	49,213	15,342	31.2	28.5	26.2	30,125	4,404	14.6	57.3
Salt Lake City, Utah	15,559	4,249	27.3	----	18.6	8,949	781	8.7	52.5
San Francisco, Calif	55,714	21,000	37.7	32.1	24.6	29,304	4,590	15.7	62.1
Seattle, Wash	48,826	14,897	30.5	24.3	22.6	29,919	3,903	13.0	58.1
Spokane, Wash	19,880	5,897	29.7	23.4	----	12,015	1,518	12.6	55.7

1 Includes Allegheny.

TABLE 158.—PERCENTAGE OF NATIVE WHITE WOMEN OF FOREIGN OR MIXED PARENTAGE ENGAGED IN GAINFUL OCCUPATIONS, FOR CITIES OF 100,000 INHABITANTS OR MORE: 1920, 1910, AND 1900, WITH MARITAL CONDITION FOR 1920

CITY	NATIVE WHITE WOMEN OF FOREIGN OR MIXED PARENTAGE 16 YEARS OF AGE AND OVER								
	Total					Married			Per cent not married and gain-fully occu-pied: 1920
	Number: 1920	Engaged in gainful occupations				Number: 1920	Engaged in gainful occupations		
		Number: 1920	Per cent				Number: 1920	Per cent: 1920	
			1920	1910	1900				
NEW ENGLAND DIV.:									
Boston, Mass	88,749	41,632	46.9	44.9	39.7	34,917	3,302	9.5	71.2
Bridgeport, Conn	14,102	6,014	42.6	42.9	40.1	6,935	769	11.1	73.2
Cambridge, Mass	12,390	6,233	50.3	45.1	39.8	4,782	498	10.4	75.4
Fall River, Mass	15,193	8,816	58.0	59.3	58.4	6,199	1,537	24.8	80.9
Hartford, Conn	14,666	6,592	44.9	40.3		6,702	726	10.8	73.7
Lowell, Mass	14,263	7,601	53.3	55.5	54.8	5,601	1,066	19.0	75.4
New Bedford, Mass	11,057	6,223	56.3		48.2	4,923	1,346	27.3	79.5
New Haven, Conn	17,804	7,704	43.3	42.4	39.5	8,112	651	8.0	72.8
Providence, R. I	28,553	13,749	48.2	46.7	45.9	11,959	1,486	12.4	73.9
Springfield, Mass	14,394	6,300	43.8		39.0	7,111	996	14.0	72.8
Worcester, Mass	21,035	9,438	44.9	45.4	42.3	9,077	849	9.4	71.8
MIDDLE ATLANTIC DIV.:									
Albany, N. Y	15,527	5,272	34.0	35.2	34.6	7,285	389	5.3	59.2
Buffalo, N. Y	70,130	22,723	32.4	33.3	27.8	37,217	1,546	4.2	64.3
Camden, N. J	8,298	2,563	30.9		26.1	4,864	306	6.3	65.7
Jersey City, N. J	37,187	13,739	36.9	33.9	30.5	18,392	949	5.2	68.1
New York, N. Y	610,087	255,511	41.9	37.8	33.4	278,583	21,928	7.9	70.5
Bronx Borough	87,000	35,802	41.2	33.1		41,429	2,554	6.2	73.0
Brooklyn Borough	229,513	90,787	39.6	34.8		107,205	6,871	6.4	68.6
Manhattan Borough	215,596	103,479	48.0	43.8		85,974	9,968	11.6	72.1
Queens Borough	66,013	21,592	32.7	28.3		37,784	2,247	5.9	68.5
Richmond Borough	11,965	3,851	32.2	27.3		6,191	288	4.7	61.7
Newark, N. J	43,736	16,580	37.9	36.4	33.6	21,508	1,220	5.7	69.1
Paterson, N. J	16,208	7,795	48.1	41.6		7,356	1,086	14.8	75.8
Philadelphia, Pa	177,010	66,064	37.3	37.4	34.0	87,152	6,298	7.2	66.5
Pittsburgh, Pa	65,630	21,509	32.8	31.1	1 25.5	32,208	1,199	3.7	60.8
Reading, Pa	4,634	1,719	37.1		30.5	2,477	314	12.7	65.1
Rochester, N. Y	36,915	14,254	38.6	39.6	38.6	19,158	2,065	10.8	68.6
Scranton, Pa	18,426	6,665	36.2	35.8	33.9	8,798	242	2.8	66.7
Syracuse, N. Y	19,726	6,779	34.4	36.4	34.1	10,708	854	8.0	65.7
Trenton, N. J	9,722	3,627	37.3		29.8	4,821	329	6.8	67.3
Yonkers, N. Y	12,042	4,866	40.4			5,572	375	6.7	69.4
NORTH CENTRAL DIVS.:									
Akron, Ohio	10,735	2,870	26.7			6,769	458	6.8	60.8
Chicago, Ill	337,498	135,837	40.2	39.6	33.0	173,752	15,522	8.9	73.5
Cincinnati, Ohio	56,225	16,809	29.9	32.8	33.0	28,507	1,499	5.3	55.2
Cleveland, Ohio	79,980	27,886	34.9	36.1	31.6	44,064	3,153	7.2	68.9
Columbus, Ohio	16,431	4,470	27.2		28.8	9,066	553	6.1	53.2
Dayton, Ohio	11,728	3,021	25.8	27.2	28.5	6,843	304	4.4	55.6
Des Moines, Iowa	10,177	3,488	34.3		30.0	5,702	564	9.9	65.3
Detroit, Mich	96,732	30,813	31.9	36.7	33.1	57,444	3,951	6.9	68.4
Grand Rapids, Mich	18,098	6,653	36.3	35.5	33.4	10,015	852	8.5	70.7
Indianapolis, Ind	18,479	5,087	27.5	28.4	27.7	10,621	708	6.7	55.7
Kansas City, Kans	5,887	1,780	30.2		19.8	3,532	282	8.0	63.6
Kansas City, Mo	22,514	6,842	30.4	30.1	27.5	12,953	1,135	8.8	59.7
Milwaukee, Wis	77,632	27,244	35.1	36.6	34.6	43,122	2,591	6.0	71.4
Minneapolis, Minn	59,369	23,575	39.7	40.9	36.9	30,466	2,481	8.1	73.0
Omaha, Nebr	20,113	7,339	36.5	36.5	35.0	10,958	1,076	9.8	68.4
St. Louis, Mo	100,878	30,837	30.6	29.7	28.4	55,363	3,586	6.5	59.9
St. Paul, Minn	39,400	15,244	38.7	43.2	39.1	20,310	1,475	7.3	72.1
Toledo, Ohio	26,408	7,908	29.9	33.2	29.6	15,764	1,137	7.2	63.6
Youngstown, Ohio	11,437	2,995	26.2			6,663	255	3.8	57.4
THE SOUTH:									
Atlanta, Ga	2,902	778	26.8	27.9	22.6	1,615	117	7.2	51.4
Baltimore, Md	56,699	17,238	30.4	31.7	27.0	29,720	1,681	5.7	57.7
Birmingham, Ala	2,995	708	23.6	22.3		1,668	87	5.2	46.8
Dallas, Tex	4,966	1,393	28.1			2,902	270	9.3	54.4
Fort Worth, Tex	2,467	579	23.5			1,535	112	7.3	50.1
Houston, Tex	7,205	1,637	22.7			4,373	285	6.5	47.7
Louisville, Ky	21,232	5,927	27.9	29.2	27.0	10,903	547	5.0	52.1
Memphis, Tenn	4,922	1,175	23.9	21.9	20.7	2,678	165	6.2	45.0
Nashville, Tenn	2,881	727	25.2	24.2	23.4	1,413	76	5.4	44.3
New Orleans, La	30,720	6,763	22.0	21.2	17.0	15,377	802	5.2	38.9
Norfolk, Va	2,211	588	26.6			1,249	121	9.7	48.5
Richmond, Va	3,838	999	26.0	22.8		1,959	108	5.5	47.4
San Antonio, Tex	10,777	2,659	24.7		17.4	6,196	431	7.0	48.6
Washington, D. C	25,118	11,480	45.7	29.3	26.4	11,196	1,651	14.7	70.6
Wilmington, Del	7,386	2,312	31.3		29.9	3,887	249	6.4	59.0

1 Includes Allegheny.

TABLE 158.—PERCENTAGE OF NATIVE WHITE WOMEN OF FOREIGN OR MIXED PARENTAGE ENGAGED IN GAINFUL OCCUPATIONS, FOR CITIES OF 100,000 INHABITANTS OR MORE: 1920, 1910, AND 1900, WITH MARITAL CONDITION FOR 1920—Continued

	NATIVE WHITE WOMEN OF FOREIGN OR MIXED PARENTAGE 16 YEARS OF AGE AND OVER							
CITY	Total				Married			Per cent not married and gainfully occupied: 1920
	Number: 1920	Engaged in gainful occupations			Number: 1920	Engaged in gainful occupations		
		Number: 1920	Per cent			Number: 1920	Per cent: 1920	
			1920	1910	1900				
THE WEST:								
Denver, Colo	26,065	8,605	33.0	32.1	27.8	14,198	1,394	9.8	60.8
Los Angeles, Calif	54,018	16,955	31.4	28.8	24.2	29,956	3,659	12.2	55.3
Oakland, Calif	25,304	7,084	28.0	26.8	26.6	15,007	1,308	8.7	56.1
Portland, Oreg	25,735	8,610	33.5	33.1	31.3	14,916	1,745	11.7	63.5
Salt Lake City, Utah	15,034	3,889	25.9		24.4	9,322	565	6.1	58.2
San Francisco, Calif	68,359	24,113	35.3	32.3	29.2	35,714	4,003	11.2	61.6
Seattle, Wash	31,416	10,543	33.6	29.6	24.6	18,279	2,057	11.3	64.6
Spokane, Wash	11,213	3,534	31.5	28.0		6,505	687	10.6	60.5

TABLE 159.—PERCENTAGE OF FOREIGN-BORN WHITE WOMEN ENGAGED IN GAINFUL OCCUPATIONS, FOR CITIES OF 100,000 INHABITANTS OR MORE: 1920, 1910, AND 1900, WITH MARITAL CONDITION FOR 1920

	FOREIGN-BORN WHITE WOMEN 16 YEARS OF AGE AND OVER							
CITY	Total				Married			Per cent not married and gainfully occupied: 1920
	Number: 1920	Engaged in gainful occupations			Number: 1920	Engaged in gainful occupations		
		Number: 1920	Per cent			Number: 1920	Per cent: 1920	
			1920	1910	1900				
NEW ENGLAND DIV.:								
Boston, Mass	116,890	32,622	27.9	33.5	31.0	72,521	5,743	7.9	60.6
Bridgeport, Conn	20,205	4,372	21.6	26.7	24.1	15,330	1,792	11.7	52.9
Cambridge, Mass	16,196	4,597	28.4	32.4	32.0	10,123	940	9.3	60.2
Fall River, Mass	21,009	8,030	38.2	41.4	42.8	13,702	3,583	26.1	60.9
Hartford, Conn	18,281	4,329	23.7		29.1	12,836	1,097	8.5	59.4
Lowell, Mass	18,841	7,208	38.3	44.0	45.6	11,875	2,840	23.9	62.7
New Bedford, Mass	23,261	10,623	45.7		40.0	15,154	5,123	33.8	67.8
New Haven, Conn	21,150	4,327	20.5	25.3	24.4	15,018	1,068	7.1	53.1
Providence, R. I	33,642	8,881	26.4	30.8	30.3	22,212	2,293	10.3	57.7
Springfield, Mass	14,753	3,895	26.4		28.1	9,967	1,142	11.5	57.5
Worcester, Mass	24,540	4,949	20.2	25.1	24.9	17,285	1,063	6.1	53.6
MIDDLE ATLANTIC DIV.:								
Albany, N. Y	8,338	1,614	19.4	23.0	19.6	5,006	228	4.6	41.6
Buffalo, N. Y	54,132	8,760	16.2	19.0	18.0	37,673	1,625	4.3	43.4
Camden, N. J	8,712	1,334	15.3		16.6	6,736	419	6.2	46.3
Jersey City, N. J	34,499	5,072	14.7	18.6	16.6	25,119	1,270	5.1	40.5
New York, N. Y	929,485	238,488	25.7	31.7	27.2	617,178	50,134	8.1	60.3
Bronx Borough	126,531	24,622	19.5	21.2		89,824	4,999	5.6	53.5
Brooklyn Borough	303,676	58,602	19.3	23.6		213,604	11,233	5.3	52.6
Manhattan Borough	432,948	144,392	33.4	38.5		265,801	30,716	11.6	68.0
Queens Borough	52,927	8,830	16.7	18.4		38,465	2,796	7.3	41.7
Richmond Borough	13,403	2,042	15.2	22.0		9,484	390	4.1	42.2
Newark, N. J	52,541	8,636	16.4	21.2	19.5	38,521	1,794	4.7	48.8
Paterson, N. J	20,886	5,710	27.3	27.6	24.8	14,708	2,288	15.6	55.4
Philadelphia, Pa	184,324	38,043	20.6	27.4	24.5	125,714	7,502	6.0	52.1
Pittsburgh, Pa	53,065	8,773	16.5	21.6	[1]17.1	36,900	1,385	3.8	45.7
Reading, Pa	3,909	786	20.1		13.9	2,920	296	10.1	49.5
Rochester, N. Y	32,390	7,608	23.5	25.8	24.0	22,113	2,382	10.8	50.9
Scranton, Pa	12,977	1,380	10.6	13.1	15.8	9,353	149	1.6	34.0
Syracuse, N. Y	14,278	2,430	17.0	22.0	20.0	10,152	597	5.9	44.4
Trenton, N. J	12,839	2,220	17.3		17.3	9,746	689	7.1	49.5
Yonkers, N. Y	12,257	2,641	21.5			8,770	738	8.4	54.6

[1] Includes Allegheny.

6436°—29——19

TABLE 159.—PERCENTAGE OF FOREIGN-BORN WHITE WOMEN ENGAGED IN GAINFUL OCCUPATIONS, FOR CITIES OF 100,000 INHABITANTS OR MORE: 1920, 1910, AND 1900, WITH MARITAL CONDITION FOR 1920—Continued

	FOREIGN-BORN WHITE WOMEN 16 YEARS OF AGE AND OVER							
CITY	Total				Married			Per cent not married and gainfully occupied: 1920
	Number: 1920	Engaged in gainful occupations			Number: 1920	Engaged in gainful occupations		
		Number: 1920	Per cent			Number: 1920	Per cent: 1920	
			1920	1910	1900				
NORTH CENTRAL DIVS.:									
Akron, Ohio	12,256	1,896	15.5			9,787	803	8.2	44.3
Chicago, Ill	358,754	73,319	20.4	22.7	19.5	253,431	20,521	8.1	50.1
Cincinnati, Ohio	20,463	3,996	19.5	21.8	18.0	11,294	882	7.8	34.0
Cleveland, Ohio	101,071	17,618	17.4	20.3	16.8	75,954	5,993	7.9	46.3
Columbus, Ohio	6,668	1,152	17.3	17.8	15.1	4,220	245	5.8	37.1
Dayton, Ohio	5,456	914	16.8	18.3	15.1	3,824	341	8.9	35.1
Des Moines, Iowa	4,819	917	19.0		21.1	3,204	214	6.7	43.5
Detroit, Mich	111,579	19,119	17.1	22.0	20.2	82,705	4,588	5.5	50.3
Grand Rapids, Mich	12,790	2,238	17.5	16.1	17.2	9,156	689	7.5	42.6
Indianapolis, Ind	7,390	1,135	15.4	17.6	15.3	4,690	287	6.1	31.4
Kansas City, Kans	4,390	613	14.0		11.0	3,339	236	7.1	35.9
Kansas City, Mo	11,270	1,977	17.5	19.9	20.8	7,464	470	6.3	39.6
Milwaukee, Wis	47,207	7,777	16.5	16.6	15.6	32,758	2,259	6.9	38.2
Minneapolis, Minn	38,382	7,812	20.4	25.3	25.1	25,770	1,462	5.7	50.3
Omaha, Nebr	14,826	2,570	17.3	17.9	15.4	10,317	695	6.7	41.6
St. Louis, Mo	45,294	8,486	18.7	17.9	15.4	28,129	2,072	7.4	37.4
St. Paul, Minn	22,766	4,165	18.3	21.9	22.9	15,043	883	5.9	42.5
Toledo, Ohio	15,701	2,381	15.2	18.0	14.1	11,203	695	6.2	37.5
Youngstown, Ohio	12,377	1,391	11.2			9,728	359	3.7	39.0
THE SOUTH:									
Atlanta, Ga	1,932	344	17.8	14.5	13.6	1,328	84	6.3	43.0
Baltimore, Md	38,368	7,362	19.2	22.8	19.3	25,688	1,736	6.8	44.4
Birmingham, Ala	2,431	311	12.8	12.0		1,774	99	5.6	32.3
Dallas, Tex	3,266	625	19.1			2,201	171	7.8	42.6
Fort Worth, Tex	2,212	365	16.5			1,555	118	7.6	37.6
Houston, Tex	4,671	732	15.7			3,197	207	6.5	35.6
Louisville, Ky	5,630	935	16.6	15.9	13.8	2,935	174	5.9	28.2
Memphis, Tenn	2,397	463	19.3	17.6	15.5	1,525	113	7.4	40.1
Nashville, Tenn	1,059	178	16.8	14.6	14.2	612	50	8.2	28.6
New Orleans, La	10,000	1,791	17.9	17.8	13.5	5,307	397	7.5	29.7
Norfolk, Va	2,026	355	17.5			1,556	132	8.5	47.4
Richmond, Va	2,011	424	21.1	17.5	17.5	1,285	89	6.9	46.1
San Antonio, Tex	14,149	3,486	24.6		15.0	8,000	657	8.2	46.0
Washington, D. C	12,965	3,876	29.9	26.7	22.6	7,616	877	11.5	56.1
Wilmington, Del	6,643	1,027	15.5		18.4	4,915	279	5.7	43.3
THE WEST:									
Denver, Colo	16,142	3,228	20.0	22.9	22.3	10,366	751	7.2	42.9
Los Angeles, Calif	48,102	11,545	24.0	23.5	20.6	29,800	3,188	10.7	45.7
Oakland, Calif	18,828	3,381	18.0	18.7	17.9	12,475	1,013	8.1	37.3
Portland, Oreg	18,660	4,008	21.5	23.6	20.7	12,599	1,066	8.5	48.5
Salt Lake City, Utah	9,305	1,716	18.4		20.5	5,828	341	5.9	39.5
San Francisco, Calif	54,954	14,391	26.2	23.7	21.5	33,439	4,056	12.1	48.0
Seattle, Wash	28,182	6,507	23.1	24.0	20.3	19,229	1,625	8.5	54.5
Spokane, Wash	6,975	1,495	21.4	22.4		4,694	402	8.6	47.9

TABLE 160.—PERCENTAGE OF NEGRO WOMEN ENGAGED IN GAINFUL OCCUPATIONS, FOR CITIES OF 100,000 INHABITANTS OR MORE: 1920, 1910, AND 1900, WITH MARITAL CONDITION FOR 1920

CITY	Total Number: 1920	Total Engaged Number: 1920	Per cent 1920	Per cent 1910	Per cent 1900	Married Number: 1920	Married Engaged Number: 1920	Married Per cent: 1920	Per cent not married and gainfully occupied: 1920
NEW ENGLAND DIV.:									
Boston, Mass	6,426	3,211	50.0	62.0	51.3	3,495	1,131	32.4	71.0
Bridgeport, Conn	771	365	47.3	56.8	48.5	514	190	37.0	68.1
Cambridge, Mass	2,040	915	44.9	48.0	37.9	1,139	296	26.0	68.7
Fall River, Mass	120	82	68.3	75.7	76.5	68	34	(1)	(1)
Hartford, Conn	1,494	830	55.6		47.2	941	412	43.8	75.6
Lowell, Mass	52	26	(1)	(1)	(1)	32	6	(1)	(1)
New Bedford, Mass	1,385	533	38.5		31.7	890	236	26.5	60.0
New Haven, Conn	1,704	884	51.9	56.8	51.7	1,005	357	35.5	75.4
Providence, R. I	2,039	1,070	52.5	58.8	51.8	1,093	362	33.1	74.8
Springfield, Mass	1,018	566	55.6		47.0	588	260	44.2	71.2
Worcester, Mass	465	235	50.5	48.4	45.3	264	92	34.8	71.1
MIDDLE ATLANTIC DIV.:									
Albany, N. Y	478	193	40.4	60.3	42.9	252	54	21.4	61.5
Buffalo, N. Y	1,620	627	38.7	37.8	41.1	1,104	263	23.8	70.5
Camden, N. J	2,969	1,308	44.1		44.0	1,902	564	29.7	69.7
Jersey City, N. J	2,858	1,119	39.2	37.9	33.7	1,858	433	23.3	68.6
New York, N. Y	64,723	40,315	62.3	65.0	59.0	35,787	16,623	46.4	81.9
Bronx Borough	1,807	936	51.8	42.6		954	312	32.7	73.2
Brooklyn Borough	13,086	7,397	56.5	61.5		7,210	2,680	37.2	80.3
Manhattan Borough	47,125	30,484	64.7	68.2		26,188	13,122	50.1	82.9
Queens Borough	2,162	1,210	56.0	57.0		1,137	433	38.1	75.8
Richmond Borough	543	288	53.0	56.0		298	76	25.5	86.5
Newark, N. J	6,234	2,773	44.5	51.3	45.0	4,074	1,244	30.5	70.8
Paterson, N. J	629	374	59.5	68.5	59.3	351	152	43.3	79.9
Philadelphia, Pa	51,978	27,606	53.1	63.0	52.3	31,982	12,538	39.2	75.4
Pittsburgh, Pa	13,262	5,148	38.8	46.6	2 30.6	8,924	2,246	25.2	66.9
Reading, Pa	301	120	39.9		40.1	198	54	27.3	64.1
Rochester, N. Y	672	335	49.9	60.4	46.3	398	149	37.4	67.9
Scranton, Pa	198	72	36.4	37.9	31.4	122	23	18.9	(1)
Syracuse, N. Y	456	194	42.5	55.1	39.1	282	84	29.8	63.2
Trenton, N. J	1,471	696	47.3		39.9	933	342	36.7	65.8
Yonkers, N. Y	783	482	61.6			411	177	43.1	82.0
NORTH CENTRAL DIVS.:									
Akron, Ohio	1,597	618	38.7			1,198	363	30.3	63.9
Chicago, Ill	43,250	20,608	47.6	49.9	42.5	27,072	9,463	35.0	68.9
Cincinnati, Ohio	11,585	5,896	50.9	59.7	47.2	7,381	2,947	39.9	70.1
Cleveland, Ohio	12,237	5,088	41.6	47.3	36.5	8,695	2,752	31.7	66.0
Columbus, Ohio	7,870	3,260	41.4	48.1	38.2	5,165	1,598	30.9	61.4
Dayton, Ohio	3,208	1,482	46.2	48.2	38.7	2,187	793	36.3	67.5
Des Moines, Iowa	2,025	857	42.3		33.5	1,335	418	31.3	63.6
Detroit, Mich	13,685	4,941	36.1	42.6	36.6	10,293	2,627	25.5	68.2
Grand Rapids, Mich	396	149	37.6	31.0	34.3	257	62	24.1	62.6
Indianapolis, Ind	13,121	5,877	44.8	51.4	43.0	8,236	2,572	31.2	67.7
Kansas City, Kans	5,318	1,816	34.1		32.8	3,485	796	22.8	55.6
Kansas City, Mo	12,589	6,357	50.5	59.0	52.2	7,416	2,639	35.6	71.9
Milwaukee, Wis	775	285	36.8	43.5	31.5	541	127	23.5	67.5
Minneapolis, Minn	1,456	637	43.8	42.5	37.0	941	279	29.6	69.5
Omaha, Nebr	3,673	1,573	42.8	46.7	44.5	2,525	841	33.3	63.8
St. Louis, Mo	27,116	13,405	49.4	56.0	46.7	16,632	6,008	36.1	70.6
St. Paul, Minn	1,229	476	38.7	38.1	31.7	818	209	25.6	65.0
Toledo, Ohio	1,985	764	38.5	40.5	34.4	1,411	396	28.1	64.1
Youngstown, Ohio	2,096	539	25.7			1,563	221	14.1	59.8
THE SOUTH:									
Atlanta, Ga	25,560	16,377	64.1	74.4	68.0	14,316	7,633	53.3	77.8
Baltimore, Md	42,163	26,454	62.7	70.2	62.1	24,202	12,566	51.9	77.3
Birmingham, Ala	25,870	11,788	45.6	56.5		16,004	5,035	31.5	68.4
Dallas, Tex	9,401	5,936	63.1			5,671	3,065	54.0	77.0
Fort Worth, Tex	6,080	3,114	51.2			3,764	1,536	40.8	68.1
Houston, Tex	13,431	7,639	56.9			8,151	3,765	46.2	73.4
Louisville, Ky	16,859	11,161	66.2	68.1	54.4	8,980	4,969	55.3	78.6
Memphis, Tenn	25,399	13,618	53.2	64.1	61.4	14,459	5,707	39.5	72.3
Nashville, Tenn	14,935	8,931	59.8	66.7	61.7	7,831	3,738	47.7	73.1
New Orleans, La	39,971	21,803	54.5	60.8	49.3	21,910	9,178	41.9	69.9
Norfolk, Va	16,181	8,530	52.7			9,745	3,821	39.2	73.2
Richmond, Va	21,784	12,857	59.0	67.9	60.7	11,331	5,276	46.6	72.5
San Antonio, Tex	5,724	3,439	60.1		59.2	3,280	1,516	46.2	76.0
Washington, D. C	45,606	28,295	62.0	66.4	63.6	23,683	11,779	49.7	75.3
Wilmington, Del	4,010	2,464	61.4		54.0	2,268	1,144	50.4	75.8

1 Per cent not shown where base is less than 100.   2 Includes Allegheny.

TABLE 160.—PERCENTAGE OF NEGRO WOMEN ENGAGED IN GAINFUL OCCUPATIONS, FOR CITIES OF 100,000 INHABITANTS OR MORE: 1920, 1910, AND 1900, WITH MARITAL CONDITION FOR 1920—Continued

CITY	NEGRO WOMEN 16 YEARS OF AGE AND OVER								
	Total				Married			Per cent not married and gainfully occupied: 1920
	Number: 1920	Engaged in gainful occupations			Number: 1920	Engaged in gainful occupations		
		Number: 1920	Per cent			Number: 1920	Per cent: 1920	
			1920	1910	1900				
THE WEST:									
Denver, Colo	2,443	1,191	48.8	53.0	48.2	1,426	485	34.0	69.4
Los Angeles, Calif	6,438	3,254	50.5	50.0	38.4	3,800	1,430	37.6	69.1
Oakland, Calif	1,944	632	32.5	36.8	29.4	1,229	238	19.4	55.1
Portland, Oreg	589	250	42.4	46.5	49.0	414	134	32.4	66.3
Salt Lake City, Utah	273	110	40.3	----	(1)	187	55	29.4	(1)
San Francisco, Calif	882	487	55.2	51.9	39.7	493	199	40.4	74.0
Seattle, Wash	1,017	464	45.6	40.4	49.0	695	236	34.0	70.8
Spokane, Wash	272	118	43.4	38.4	----	182	60	33.0	(1)

1 Per cent not shown where base is less than 100.

TABLE 161.—PERCENTAGE OF WOMEN ENGAGED IN GAINFUL OCCUPATIONS, CLASSIFIED BY AGE GROUPS, FOR CITIES OF 100,000 INHABITANTS OR MORE: 1920 AND 1900

CITY	WOMEN 16 YEARS OF AGE AND OVER											
	16 to 24 years of age				25 to 44 years of age [1]				45 years of age and over			
	Total number: 1920	Engaged in gainful occupations			Total number: 1920	Engaged in gainful occupations			Total number: 1920	Engaged in gainful occupations		
		Number: 1920	Per cent			Number: 1920	Per cent			Number: 1920	Per cent	
			1920	1900			1920	1900			1920	1900
NEW ENGLAND DIV.:												
Boston, Mass	59,417	36,610	61.6	54.1	126,152	45,083	35.7	31.5	89,783	20,868	23.2	17.1
Bridgeport, Conn	11,663	6,755	57.9	54.2	23,124	6,289	27.2	24.5	12,644	1,942	15.4	8.9
Cambridge, Mass	9,131	5,674	62.1	54.0	18,373	6,933	37.7	30.5	14,112	3,046	21.6	15.5
Fall River, Mass	10,574	7,975	75.4	73.1	18,035	8,010	44.4	40.9	13,170	3,126	23.7	16.0
Hartford, Conn	11,739	7,248	61.7	52.7	23,206	7,318	31.5	27.3	14,359	2,662	18.5	15.1
Lowell, Mass	9,455	6,487	68.6	71.5	18,455	7,938	43.0	43.4	13,342	3,374	25.3	21.3
New Bedford, Mass	10,506	7,906	75.3	63.8	19,666	9,054	46.0	34.1	12,674	2,812	22.2	14.0
New Haven, Conn	13,194	7,867	59.6	53.1	25,725	7,280	28.3	24.4	17,668	3,134	17.7	12.8
Providence, R. I	18,657	12,045	64.6	59.7	39,169	13,892	35.5	31.1	29,621	6,162	20.8	15.2
Springfield, Mass	10,296	6,015	58.4	49.7	22,870	7,910	34.6	28.2	14,932	3,010	20.2	12.5
Worcester, Mass	14,148	8,292	58.6	53.6	29,210	8,721	29.9	26.4	20,096	3,421	17.0	10.8
MIDDLE ATLANTIC DIV.:												
Albany, N. Y	9,127	5,094	55.8	49.5	20,405	6,374	31.2	25.5	15,805	2,885	18.3	11.9
Buffalo, N. Y	41,386	22,154	53.5	44.5	83,309	19,487	23.4	18.6	53,481	7,234	13.5	8.9
Camden, N. J	9,436	4,745	50.3	44.9	17,815	3,901	21.9	18.4	11,348	1,703	15.0	13.1
Jersey City, N. J	24,935	14,460	58.0	45.8	46,888	10,697	22.8	16.5	28,071	3,548	12.6	9.8
New York, N. Y	487,390	301,544	61.9	52.8	959,472	280,850	29.3	23.2	537,000	95,291	17.7	14.2
Bronx Borough	65,790	41,026	62.4	----	125,193	27,981	22.4	----	63,307	7,073	11.2	----
Brooklyn Borough	176,025	106,360	60.4	----	322,088	76,085	23.6	----	192,858	27,123	14.1	----
Manhattan Borough	199,494	126,813	63.6	----	415,180	156,201	37.6	----	224,393	54,277	24.2	----
Queens Borough	37,711	22,960	60.9	----	79,446	17,019	21.4	----	45,587	5,350	11.7	----
Richmond Borough	8,370	4,385	52.4	----	17,565	3,564	20.3	----	10,855	1,468	13.5	----
Newark, N. J	34,501	19,440	56.3	51.5	66,444	15,514	23.3	20.2	39,263	5,667	14.4	11.6
Paterson, N. J	11,962	8,036	67.2	60.6	21,848	7,431	34.0	23.9	14,605	2,532	17.3	11.5
Philadelphia, Pa	149,644	84,410	56.4	52.4	301,206	87,855	29.2	25.7	202,937	38,547	19.0	14.4
Pittsburgh, Pa	48,855	24,239	49.6	[2]39.3	96,112	23,960	24.9	[2]17.9	56,815	8,639	15.2	[2]9.3
Reading, Pa	8,322	5,118	61.5	50.9	17,329	5,363	30.9	19.7	13,280	2,421	18.2	10.3
Rochester, N. Y	23,331	14,420	61.8	58.5	50,601	16,018	31.7	28.6	35,087	6,518	18.6	14.1
Scranton, Pa	12,198	6,929	56.8	48.2	21,232	4,646	21.9	17.0	12,855	1,289	10.0	6.5
Syracuse, N. Y	13,369	6,861	51.3	47.5	28,575	7,819	27.4	24.1	20,904	3,746	17.9	11.7
Trenton, N. J	9,766	5,209	53.3	42.3	18,170	4,229	23.3	18.2	11,877	1,727	14.5	11.0
Yonkers, N. Y	8,139	4,827	59.3	----	16,713	4,555	27.3	----	10,032	1,656	16.5	----

1 Includes women of unknown age.   2 Includes Allegheny.

TABLE 161.—PERCENTAGE OF WOMEN ENGAGED IN GAINFUL OCCUPATIONS, CLASSIFIED BY AGE GROUPS, FOR CITIES OF 100,000 INHABITANTS OR MORE: 1920 AND 1900—Continued

	WOMEN 16 YEARS OF AGE AND OVER											
	16 to 24 years of age				25 to 44 years of age [1]				45 years of age and over			
CITY	Total number: 1920	Engaged in gainful occupations			Total number: 1920	Engaged in gainful occupations			Total number: 1920	Engaged in gainful occupations		
		Number: 1920	Per cent			Number: 1920	Per cent			Number: 1920	Per cent	
			1920	1900			1920	1900			1920	1900
NORTH CENTRAL DIVS.:												
Akron, Ohio	17,854	7,526	42.2	____	30,983	6,910	22.3	____	12,831	1,523	11.9	____
Chicago, Ill	217,582	129,543	59.5	47.3	467,492	132,872	28.4	19.9	252,337	40,670	16.1	9.6
Cincinnati, Ohio	32,138	17,154	53.4	51.6	70,946	22,082	31.1	26.0	55,117	10,995	19.9	13.5
Cleveland, Ohio	63,376	31,967	50.4	45.1	132,360	32,313	24.4	17.7	65,228	8,863	13.6	9.2
Columbus, Ohio	19,395	8,366	43.1	39.7	41,412	11,827	28.6	23.1	28,440	5,203	18.3	11.4
Dayton, Ohio	12,280	5,678	46.2	44.1	25,707	6,529	25.4	21.1	17,524	2,762	15.8	10.2
Des Moines, Iowa	11,765	5,866	49.9	38.0	22,211	7,044	31.7	21.8	13,473	2,327	17.3	8.9
Detroit, Mich	79,391	37,483	47.2	48.5	163,889	35,983	22.0	20.5	70,798	9,377	13.2	8.9
Grand Rapids, Mich	11,302	6,265	55.4	46.6	22,456	6,136	27.3	19.8	15,993	2,532	15.8	9.5
Indianapolis, Ind	26,775	12,846	48.0	38.5	56,242	15,873	28.2	23.8	36,488	6,735	18.5	12.8
Kansas City, Kans	8,548	3,743	43.8	31.8	15,864	3,808	24.0	14.8	9,727	1,490	15.3	11.2
Kansas City, Mo	28,126	13,363	47.5	38.3	62,234	20,118	32.3	25.4	34,928	6,444	18.4	15.0
Milwaukee, Wis	39,573	23,665	59.8	52.3	75,490	19,505	25.8	17.8	46,162	6,247	13.5	7.2
Minneapolis, Minn	34,601	19,736	57.0	48.4	68,615	21,078	30.7	24.0	38,942	5,630	14.5	10.7
Omaha, Nebr	16,285	8,382	51.5	44.9	32,554	9,589	29.5	25.4	18,296	2,837	15.5	11.9
St. Louis, Mo	67,771	37,889	55.9	43.7	138,798	42,345	30.5	21.7	87,153	16,593	19.0	11.7
St. Paul, Minn	20,992	12.346	58.8	52.6	40,131	12,027	30.0	23.9	24,525	3,490	14.2	9.4
Toledo, Ohio	19,600	9,518	48.6	43.1	40,198	9,819	24.4	17.5	25,208	3,746	14.9	8.4
Youngstown, Ohio	10,189	3,833	37.6	____	20,730	3,689	17.8	____	9,397	1,054	11.2	____
THE SOUTH:												
Atlanta, Ga	21,540	10,924	50.7	46.8	37,515	15,622	41.6	43.1	17,542	5,007	28.5	33.3
Baltimore, Md	64,323	34,565	53.7	46.6	121,783	38,241	31.4	27.9	82,633	17,141	20.7	19.2
Birmingham, Ala	18,666	6,957	37.3	____	31,511	9,881	31.4	____	12,458	2,899	23.3	____
Dallas, Tex	16,617	8,049	48.4	____	29,689	10,795	36.4	____	12,983	2,612	20.1	____
Fort Worth, Tex	10,518	3,993	38.0	____	18,545	5,274	28.4	____	7,514	1,303	17.3	____
Houston, Tex	13,855	5,989	43.2	____	25,425	8,490	33.4	____	11,380	2,412	21.2	____
Louisville, Ky	21,082	11,074	52.5	41.6	41,723	15,259	36.6	28.3	29,994	7,322	24.4	17.6
Memphis, Tenn	16,259	7,362	45.3	48.4	31,912	12,176	38.2	38.6	14,878	4,246	28.5	34.3
Nashville, Tenn	12,127	5,734	47.3	39.1	20,844	8,300	39.8	38.3	12,958	3,587	27.7	30.7
New Orleans, La	36,665	16,227	44.3	29.4	66,432	22,435	33.8	25.8	39,961	9,696	24.3	23.6
Norfolk, Va	11,330	5,025	44.4	____	20,317	7,027	34.6	____	9,095	2,332	25.6	____
Richmond, Va	18,341	9,897	54.0	45.9	30,636	11,595	37.8	36.2	17,573	4,525	25.7	27.7
San Antonio, Tex	15,581	6,005	38.5	26.5	26,909	7,784	28.9	21.1	14,074	2,632	18.7	16.6
Washington, D. C.	44,159	28,434	64.4	44.7	88,301	46,250	52.4	38.0	53,180	17,343	32.6	28.0
Wilmington, Del	9,187	4,517	49.2	46.7	17,221	4,760	27.6	23.8	11,527	2,155	18.7	13.9
THE WEST:												
Denver, Colo	19,924	9,319	46.8	34.0	44,850	13,366	29.8	24.6	30,565	5,878	19.2	15.9
Los Angeles, Calif	41,619	17,294	41.6	30.6	107,589	35,017	32.5	22.5	81,268	15,750	19.4	13.4
Oakland, Calif	15,439	6,409	41.5	32.1	37,737	9,600	25.4	21.1	25,244	3,992	15.8	11.5
Portland, Oreg	20,106	9,395	46.7	42.5	45,987	13,873	30.2	22.8	28,690	5,057	17.6	12.0
Salt Lake City, Utah	10,269	4,235	41.2	32.7	18,583	4,117	22.2	18.9	11,419	1,643	14.4	12.8
San Francisco, Calif	35,705	18,649	52.2	39.7	92,092	31,052	33.7	23.4	54,533	10,872	19.9	14.2
Seattle, Wash	23,746	10,556	44.5	35.6	57,115	16,881	29.6	20.9	30,754	5,513	17.9	11.3
Spokane, Wash	8,673	3,888	44.8	____	17,945	5,235	29.2	____	11,775	1,935	16.4	____

[1] Includes women of unknown age.

TABLE 162.—PERCENTAGE OF NATIVE WHITE WOMEN OF NATIVE PARENTAGE ENGAGED IN GAINFUL OCCUPATIONS, CLASSIFIED BY AGE GROUPS, FOR CITIES OF 100,000 INHABITANTS OR MORE: 1920 AND 1900

	NATIVE WHITE WOMEN OF NATIVE PARENTAGE											
	16 to 24 years of age				25 to 44 years of age [1]				45 years of age and over			
CITY	Total number: 1920	Engaged in gainful occupations			Total number: 1920	Engaged in gainful occupations			Total number: 1920	Engaged in gainful occupations		
		Number: 1920	Per cent 1920	Per cent 1900		Number: 1920	Per cent 1920	Per cent 1900		Number: 1920	Per cent 1920	Per cent 1900
NEW ENGLAND DIV.:												
Boston, Mass	14,547	8,350	57.4	40.2	26,755	11,412	42.7	33.0	21,891	5,312	24.3	17.4
Bridgeport, Conn	3,058	1,745	57.1	45.7	5,736	1,869	32.6	23.0	3,557	620	17.4	11.7
Cambridge, Mass	2,439	1,302	53.4	34.8	4,270	1,735	40.6	29.5	4,268	865	20.3	13.5
Fall River, Mass	1,590	1,021	64.2	44.6	2,075	839	40.4	29.8	1,787	321	18.0	13.3
Hartford, Conn	3,611	2,204	61.0	36.8	6,407	2,386	37.2	24.4	4,832	881	18.2	13.5
Lowell, Mass	1,795	1,023	57.0	54.7	3,334	1,310	39.3	38.6	2,964	631	21.3	19.0
New Bedford, Mass	1,350	833	61.7	40.0	2,778	1,000	36.0	25.3	3,008	557	18.5	12.0
New Haven, Conn	3,891	2,247	57.7	37.1	6,677	2,220	33.2	21.3	5,350	898	16.8	10.8
Providence, R. I	4,827	2,911	60.3	44.5	9,834	3,798	38.6	27.3	8,532	1,685	19.7	13.6
Springfield, Mass	3,851	2,092	54.3	38.3	7,915	2,884	36.4	25.5	6,157	1,196	19.4	11.5
Worcester, Mass	4,063	2,229	54.9	39.4	7,039	2,410	34.2	25.5	6,294	1,168	18.6	11.9
MIDDLE ATLANTIC DIV.:												
Albany, N. Y	5,507	2,999	54.5	41.3	9,799	3,219	32.9	21.9	5,686	1,056	18.6	11.2
Buffalo, N. Y	14,861	7,916	53.3	38.3	26,678	7,040	26.4	20.3	10,716	1,789	16.7	9.7
Camden, N. J	4,681	2,396	51.2	41.9	8,313	1,921	23.1	17.4	5,624	826	14.7	11.0
Jersey City, N. J	8,599	4,996	58.1	37.3	11,533	3,034	26.3	15.5	5,213	744	14.3	8.1
New York, N. Y	108,407	64,200	59.2	39.6	183,618	61,680	33.6	21.7	86,883	17,327	19.9	11.6
Bronx Borough	12,681	7,886	62.2		19,525	5,732	29.4		6,728	1,006	16.3	
Brooklyn Borough	43,418	26,186	60.3		67,534	20,692	30.6		33,669	5,883	17.5	
Manhattan Borough	35,844	20,455	57.1		70,787	29,339	41.4		36,235	9,010	24.9	
Queens Borough	13,342	8,031	60.2		20,795	4,683	22.5		7,472	979	13.1	
Richmond Borough	3,122	1,642	52.6		4,977	1,234	24.8		2,779	359	12.9	
Newark, N. J	10,381	5,868	56.5	44.7	17,693	5,203	29.4	21.1	9,606	1,552	16.2	10.6
Paterson, N. J	3,001	1,894	63.1	53.3	4,679	1,663	35.6	23.4	3,007	558	18.6	9.8
Philadelphia, Pa	58,958	32,787	55.6	45.4	110,927	33,154	29.9	23.3	70,497	13,128	18.6	12.9
Pittsburgh, Pa	19,463	9,294	47.8	[2]33.8	34,167	9,278	27.2	[2]20.4	16,171	2,778	17.2	[2]10.8
Reading, Pa	6,492	4,008	61.7	50.4	13,394	4,352	32.5	19.8	10,201	1,917	18.8	10.8
Rochester, N. Y	10,087	6,084	60.3	50.3	18,957	6,566	34.6	28.7	9,981	2,092	21.0	13.1
Scranton, Pa	4,806	2,653	55.2	39.2	6,738	1,710	25.4	17.0	3,140	384	12.2	9.2
Syracuse, N. Y	6,857	3,416	49.8	37.7	13,311	3,954	29.7	22.6	8,200	1,648	20.1	12.6
Trenton, N. J	3,866	2,043	52.8	35.9	6,852	1,865	27.2	18.1	5,059	714	14.1	11.1
Yonkers, N. Y	2,582	1,382	53.5		4,605	1,271	27.6		2,610	394	15.1	
NORTH CENTRAL DIVS.:												
Akron, Ohio	12,086	5,245	43.4		18,134	4,446	24.5		6,858	884	12.9	
Chicago, Ill	54,402	30,656	56.4	36.1	99,271	32,990	33.2	24.5	44,032	9,616	21.8	11.5
Cincinnati, Ohio	20,118	10,432	51.9	45.7	34,652	9,955	28.7	25.0	15,143	3,135	20.7	13.9
Cleveland, Ohio	18,765	9,544	50.9	36.2	34,474	10,442	30.3	21.4	14,411	2,559	17.8	11.4
Columbus, Ohio	14,097	6,015	42.7	36.1	27,634	7,594	27.5	21.9	16,538	2,900	17.5	10.9
Dayton, Ohio	9,018	4,070	45.1	39.1	16,824	4,068	24.2	19.7	9,268	1,413	15.2	10.6
Des Moines, Iowa	8,345	4,077	48.9	31.8	13,994	4,463	32.0	21.1	8,125	1,431	17.6	8.7
Detroit, Mich	27,478	12,927	47.0	39.3	48,202	12,360	25.6	22.1	16,314	2,651	16.2	9.6
Grand Rapids, Mich	4,715	2,319	49.2	38.8	8,248	2,602	31.5	23.1	5,494	1,058	19.3	11.8
Indianapolis, Ind	20,139	9,534	47.3	34.0	38,182	9,938	26.0	21.4	22,189	3,878	17.5	12.3
Kansas City, Kans	5,189	2,287	44.1	29.0	8,323	1,866	22.4	13.1	5,022	675	13.4	8.0
Kansas City, Mo	19,286	9,139	47.4	32.9	34,883	12,063	31.0	21.4	20,725	3,541	17.1	11.4
Milwaukee, Wis	13,249	7,730	58.3	41.9	17,811	5,521	31.0	24.2	4,537	852	18.8	10.1
Minneapolis, Minn	12,346	6,390	51.8	32.3	20,031	6,315	31.5	23.6	10,537	1,705	16.2	11.3
Omaha, Nebr	7,717	3,795	49.2	38.2	14,016	4,360	31.1	27.0	6,773	1,170	17.3	11.7
St. Louis, Mo	38,699	21,541	55.7	37.1	59,229	17,860	30.2	20.9	22,475	4,685	20.8	12.3
St. Paul, Minn	7,083	3,821	53.9	39.3	10,731	3,434	32.0	24.6	4,416	717	16.2	10.2
Toledo, Ohio	11,113	5,149	46.3	35.5	19,682	5,150	26.2	18.6	10,110	1,728	17.1	9.9
Youngstown, Ohio	4,087	1,663	40.7		7,218	1,564	21.7		3,099	424	13.7	
THE SOUTH:												
Atlanta, Ga	12,837	5,933	46.2	30.8	22,336	6,490	29.1	20.3	11,027	1,628	14.8	13.1
Baltimore, Md	34,473	17,335	50.3	38.1	61,004	15,718	25.8	21.2	36,009	5,828	16.2	12.6
Birmingham, Ala	9,107	3,107	34.1		15,752	3,083	19.8		6,659	737	11.1	
Dallas, Tex	12,301	5,860	47.6		20,423	6,263	30.7		8,920	1,373	15.4	
Fort Worth, Tex	7,591	2,828	37.3		12,852	3,002	23.4		5,369	681	12.7	
Houston, Tex	7,395	3,045	41.2		12,531	3,094	24.7		5,418	738	13.6	
Louisville, Ky	14,097	6,878	48.8	33.4	22,938	6,455	28.1	20.0	12,036	2,290	19.0	11.4
Memphis, Tenn	8,310	3,493	42.0	26.5	14,949	3,945	26.4	16.7	5,065	1,088	15.4	12.2
Nashville, Tenn	7,662	3,360	43.9	24.5	12,169	3,334	27.4	19.6	7,222	1,091	15.1	12.0
New Orleans, La	20,254	8,570	42.3	20.5	29,999	7,241	24.1	17.1	12,082	2,179	18.0	14.1

[1] Includes women of unknown age.   [2] Includes Allegheny.

TABLE 162.—PERCENTAGE OF NATIVE WHITE WOMEN OF NATIVE PARENTAGE ENGAGED IN GAINFUL OCCUPATIONS, CLASSIFIED BY AGE GROUPS, FOR CITIES OF 100,000 INHABITANTS OR MORE: 1920 AND 1900—Continued

	NATIVE WHITE WOMEN OF NATIVE PARENTAGE										
	16 to 24 years of age			25 to 44 years of age [1]			45 years of age and over				
CITY	Total number: 1920	Engaged in gainful occupations		Total number: 1920	Engaged in gainful occupations		Total number: 1920	Engaged in gainful occupations			
		Number: 1920	Per cent		Number: 1920	Per cent		Number: 1920	Per cent		
			1920	1900			1920	1900			1920	1900
THE SOUTH—Con.											
Norfolk, Va	5,461	2,159	39.5	____	9,831	2,132	21.7	____	5,025	617	12.3	____
Richmond, Va	10,851	5,481	50.5	34.0	17,530	4,710	26.9	18.7	10,527	1,540	14.6	11.6
San Antonio, Tex	7,813	2,885	36.9	19.1	12,512	3,094	24.7	15.6	5,569	854	15.3	12.4
Washington, D. C	25,610	17,055	66.6	30.2	48,112	23,765	49.4	24.3	28,169	7,537	26.8	16.0
Wilmington, Del	5,046	2,508	49.7	39.9	9,012	2,221	24.6	17.1	5,837	900	15.4	10.5
THE WEST:											
Denver, Colo	11,411	5,111	44.8	28.6	24,630	7,439	30.2	24.0	14,545	2,970	20.4	15.1
Los Angeles, Calif	22,381	9,174	41.0	26.9	54,164	18,134	33.5	22.4	42,348	8,200	19.4	12.8
Oakland, Calif	7,243	2,897	40.0	24.2	14,700	4,066	27.7	20.2	9,286	1,660	17.9	11.1
Portland, Oreg	11,396	5,058	44.4	37.9	23,581	7,480	31.7	24.8	14,236	2,804	19.7	12.7
Salt Lake City, Utah	5,281	2,027	38.4	23.2	7,243	1,683	23.2	18.8	3,035	539	17.8	11.7
San Francisco, Calif	14,410	7,390	51.3	33.3	28,697	10,566	36.8	24.2	12,607	3,044	24.1	15.1
Seattle, Wash	11,283	4,738	42.0	33.2	24,535	7,618	31.0	21.9	13,008	2,541	19.5	11.0
Spokane, Wash	5,099	2,213	43.4	____	9,290	2,773	29.8	____	5,491	911	16.6	____

[1] Includes women of unknown age.

TABLE 163.—PERCENTAGE OF NATIVE WHITE WOMEN OF FOREIGN OR MIXED PARENTAGE ENGAGED IN GAINFUL OCCUPATIONS, CLASSIFIED BY AGE GROUPS, FOR CITIES OF 100,000 INHABITANTS OR MORE: 1920 AND 1900

	NATIVE WHITE WOMEN OF FOREIGN OR MIXED PARENTAGE										
	16 to 24 years of age			25 to 44 years of age [1]			45 years of age and over				
CITY	Total number: 1920	Engaged in gainful occupations		Total number: 1920	Engaged in gainful occupations		Total number: 1920	Engaged in gainful occupations			
		Number: 1920	Per cent		Number: 1920	Per cent		Total number: 1920	Per cent		
			1920	1900			1920	1900			1920	1900
NEW ENGLAND DIV.:											
Boston, Mass	30,406	20,229	66.5	53.7	38,084	15,789	41.5	34.6	20,259	5,614	27.7	19.6
Bridgeport, Conn	5,194	3,447	66.4	61.0	6,036	2,039	33.8	31.4	2,872	528	18.4	14.8
Cambridge, Mass	4,373	3,075	70.3	54.3	5,244	2,424	46.2	33.3	2,773	734	26.5	22.1
Fall River, Mass	6,130	4,798	78.3	75.9	6,621	3,262	49.3	46.0	2,442	756	31.0	21.8
Hartford, Conn	5,000	3,391	67.8	59.2	6,405	2,462	38.4	32.4	3,261	739	22.7	16.0
Lowell, Mass	5,260	3,803	72.3	71.7	6,205	2,949	47.5	48.1	2,798	849	30.3	28.6
New Bedford, Mass	4,816	3,685	76.5	69.1	4,637	2,123	45.8	36.8	1,604	415	25.9	18.3
New Haven, Conn	6,130	4,086	66.7	60.3	7,536	2,672	35.5	30.0	4,138	946	22.9	16.5
Providence, R. I	9,377	6,599	70.4	66.2	12,363	5,261	42.6	38.0	6,813	1,889	27.7	18.8
Springfield, Mass	4,345	2,810	64.7	55.5	6,670	2,611	39.1	33.5	3,379	879	26.0	16.6
Worcester, Mass	7,146	4,650	65.1	57.1	9,584	3,753	39.2	35.7	4,305	1,035	24.0	14.7
MIDDLE ATLANTIC DIV.:											
Albany, N. Y	2,659	1,662	62.5	54.5	6,857	2,373	34.6	29.0	6,011	1,237	20.6	15.0
Buffalo, N. Y	20,214	11,739	58.1	46.3	30,778	8,154	26.5	20.8	19,138	2,830	14.8	11.8
Camden, N. J	2,754	1,508	54.8	49.5	3,446	765	22.2	17.6	2,098	290	13.8	12.9
Jersey City, N. J	11,739	7,625	65.0	49.5	16,868	4,828	28.6	20.3	8,580	1,286	15.0	10.7

[1] Includes women of unknown age.

TABLE 163.—PERCENTAGE OF NATIVE WHITE WOMEN OF FOREIGN OR MIXED PARENTAGE ENGAGED IN GAINFUL OCCUPATIONS, CLASSIFIED BY AGE GROUPS, FOR CITIES OF 100,000 INHABITANTS OR MORE: 1920 AND 1900—Continued

CITY	NATIVE WHITE WOMEN OF FOREIGN OR MIXED PARENTAGE											
	16 to 24 years of age				25 to 44 years of age [1]				45 years of age and over			
	Total number: 1920	Engaged in gainful occupations			Total number: 1920	Engaged in gainful occupations			Total number: 1920	Engaged in gainful occupations		
		Number: 1920	Per cent			Number: 1920	Per cent			Number: 1920	Per cent	
			1920	1900			1920	1900			1920	1900
MIDDLE ATLANTIC DIV.--Con.												
New York, N. Y.	216,652	143,606	66.3	52.1	263,926	86,143	32.6	24.0	129,509	25,762	19.9	15.1
Bronx Borough	32,979	21,918	66.5	----	38,761	11,470	29.6	----	15,260	2,414	15.8	----
Brooklyn Borough	81,419	52,910	65.0	----	96,636	28,877	29.9	----	51,458	9,000	17.5	----
Manhattan Borough	79,387	54,328	68.4	----	90,882	37,088	40.8	----	45,327	12,063	26.6	----
Queens Borough	19,133	12,327	64.4	----	32,445	7,458	23.0	----	14,435	1,807	12.5	----
Richmond Borough	3,734	2,123	56.9	----	5,202	1,250	24.0	----	3,029	478	15.8	----
Newark, N. J.	14,800	9,351	63.2	55.1	18,745	5,435	29.0	23.7	10,191	1,794	17.6	13.6
Paterson, N. J.	6,012	4,325	71.9	64.4	7,083	2,809	39.7	28.6	3,113	661	21.2	12.3
Philadelphia, Pa.	52,119	32,153	61.7	56.5	73,235	23,216	31.7	27.1	51,656	10,695	20.7	15.2
Pittsburgh, Pa.	19,891	11,007	55.3	[2]41.2	28,633	7,817	27.3	[2]19.1	17,106	2,685	15.7	[2]11.0
Reading, Pa.	1,188	801	67.4	56.9	1,836	615	33.5	22.5	1,610	303	18.8	11.6
Rochester, N. Y.	8,650	5,919	68.4	62.0	16,399	5,783	35.3	31.6	11,866	2,552	21.5	17.7
Scranton, Pa.	6,169	3,785	61.4	51.9	8,251	2,341	28.4	22.5	4,006	539	13.5	8.1
Syracuse, N. Y.	4,741	2,749	58.0	53.7	8,427	2,690	31.9	28.3	6,558	1,340	20.4	15.5
Trenton, N. J.	3,488	2,152	61.7	50.4	3,904	1,061	27.2	21.2	2,330	414	17.8	12.9
Yonkers, N. Y.	4,069	2,695	66.2	----	5,257	1,645	31.3	----	2,716	526	19.4	----
NORTH CENTRAL DIVS.:												
Akron, Ohio	2,980	1,381	46.3	----	5,145	1,158	22.5	----	2,610	331	12.7	----
Chicago, Ill.	111,251	72,700	65.3	49.9	165,793	51,663	31.2	22.3	60,454	11,474	19.0	12.3
Cincinnati, Ohio	7,919	4,712	59.5	55.0	23,414	7,173	30.6	26.0	24,892	4,924	19.8	14.4
Cleveland, Ohio	26,561	15,227	57.3	48.0	37,943	10,272	27.1	21.4	15,476	2,387	15.4	11.7
Columbus, Ohio	2,676	1,300	48.6	46.4	6,960	1,946	28.0	24.5	6,795	1,224	18.0	12.4
Dayton, Ohio	1,915	1,014	53.0	51.9	4,811	1,211	25.2	22.8	5,002	796	15.9	11.5
Des Moines, Iowa	2,455	1,353	55.1	45.3	5,175	1,681	32.5	24.2	2,547	454	17.8	9.0
Detroit, Mich.	30,075	16,262	54.1	51.4	49,037	11,886	24.2	22.9	17,620	2,665	15.1	11.4
Grand Rapids, Mich.	5,349	3,308	61.8	51.6	8,761	2,512	28.7	22.9	3,988	743	18.6	14.2
Indianapolis, Ind.	2,982	1,701	57.0	44.1	8,244	2,222	27.0	23.0	7,253	1,164	16.0	11.5
Kansas City, Kans.	1,604	883	55.0	33.8	2,716	685	25.2	14.0	1,567	212	13.5	6.6
Kansas City, Mo.	4,738	2,399	50.6	41.1	11,301	3,370	29.8	23.1	6,475	1,073	16.6	12.8
Milwaukee, Wis.	21,650	13,726	63.4	55.4	37,771	10,481	29.7	21.9	18,211	3,037	16.7	10.1
Minneapolis, Minn.	18,359	11,279	61.4	53.5	30,585	10,497	34.3	26.9	10,425	1,799	17.3	13.2
Omaha, Nebr.	6,053	3,482	57.5	49.7	10,086	3,152	31.3	26.4	3,974	705	17.7	16.9
St. Louis, Mo.	18,173	11,054	60.8	46.1	46,882	13,434	28.7	20.5	35,823	6,349	17.7	11.8
St. Paul, Minn.	11,818	7,447	63.0	56.3	19,815	6,446	32.5	28.8	7,767	1,351	17.4	11.8
Toledo, Ohio	6,426	3,556	55.3	48.5	12,598	3,183	25.3	20.6	7,384	1,169	15.8	10.9
Youngstown, Ohio	3,692	1,564	42.4	----	5,460	1,145	21.0	----	2,285	286	12.5	----
THE SOUTH:												
Atlanta, Ga.	712	316	44.4	29.7	1,360	329	24.2	20.8	830	133	16.0	12.8
Baltimore, Md.	14,012	8,015	57.2	45.4	22,661	5,841	25.8	21.8	20,026	3,382	16.9	13.8
Birmingham, Ala.	963	349	36.2	----	1,386	298	21.5	----	646	61	9.4	----
Dallas, Tex.	1,239	549	44.3	----	2,524	648	25.7	----	1,203	196	16.3	----
Fort Worth, Tex.	606	217	35.8	----	1,269	280	22.1	----	592	82	13.9	----
Houston, Tex.	1,827	722	39.5	----	3,536	706	20.0	----	1,842	209	11.3	----
Louisville, Ky.	2,964	1,732	58.4	44.2	8,715	2,515	28.9	21.8	9,553	1,680	17.6	13.0
Memphis, Tenn.	879	391	44.5	29.7	2,309	540	23.4	17.4	1,734	244	14.1	12.6
Nashville, Tenn.	443	209	47.2	28.3	1,283	347	27.0	23.0	1,155	171	14.8	14.4
New Orleans, La.	4,644	1,736	37.4	21.4	12,367	2,770	22.4	15.8	13,709	2,257	16.5	14.4
Norfolk, Va.	669	274	41.0	----	995	241	24.2	----	547	73	13.3	----
Richmond, Va.	784	389	49.6	29.0	1,612	399	24.8	17.6	1,442	211	14.6	9.1
San Antonio, Tex.	2,868	1,088	37.9	22.3	5,041	1,169	23.2	14.7	2,868	402	14.0	13.2
Washington, D. C.	5,387	3,786	70.3	34.2	11,289	5,454	48.3	25.7	8,442	2,240	26.5	18.0
Wilmington, Del.	2,196	1,111	50.6	51.1	2,939	819	27.9	23.7	2,251	382	17.0	12.0
THE WEST:												
Denver, Colo.	6,760	3,429	50.7	36.8	12,410	3,802	30.6	24.8	6,895	1,374	19.9	17.6
Los Angeles, Calif.	11,087	4,950	44.6	33.4	26,006	8,653	33.1	22.7	16,865	3,370	20.0	13.9
Oakland, Calif.	5,854	2,633	45.0	35.8	13,147	3,403	25.9	22.6	6,303	1,048	16.6	12.8
Portland, Oreg.	6,517	3,340	51.3	46.0	13,270	4,195	31.6	23.2	5,948	1,075	18.1	13.4
Salt Lake City, Utah	4,083	1,770	43.4	33.7	7,661	1,661	21.7	17.6	3,290	458	13.9	10.4
San Francisco, Calif.	15,141	8,391	55.4	40.8	35,500	11,963	33.7	23.0	17,718	3,759	21.2	14.9
Seattle, Wash.	8,562	4,125	48.2	35.3	16,332	5,178	31.7	19.2	6,552	1,240	19.0	15.9
Spokane, Wash.	2,867	1,338	46.7	----	5,522	1,681	30.4	----	2,824	515	18.2	----

[1] Includes women of unknown age.   [2] Includes Allegheny.

TABLE 164.—PERCENTAGE OF FOREIGN-BORN WHITE WOMEN ENGAGED IN GAINFUL OCCUPATIONS, CLASSIFIED BY AGE GROUPS, FOR CITIES OF 100,000 INHABITANTS OR MORE: 1920 AND 1900

CITY	FOREIGN-BORN WHITE WOMEN											
	16 to 24 years of age				25 to 44 years of age [1]				45 years of age and over			
	Total number: 1920	Engaged in gainful occupations			Total number: 1920	Engaged in gainful occupations			Total number: 1920	Engaged in gainful occupations		
		Number: 1920	Per cent 1920	Per cent 1900		Number: 1920	Per cent 1920	Per cent 1900		Total number: 1920	Per cent 1920	Per cent 1900
NEW ENGLAND DIV.:												
Boston, Mass	13,120	7,376	56.2	62.7	57,723	16,029	27.8	28.2	46,047	9,217	20.0	15.5
Bridgeport, Conn	3,231	1,472	45.6	53.5	10,928	2,188	20.0	18.9	6,046	712	11.8	10.4
Cambridge, Mass	1,877	1,075	57.3	66.3	7,783	2,293	29.5	28.9	6,536	1,229	18.8	14.4
Fall River, Mass	2,837	2,146	75.6	77.5	9,273	3,863	41.7	40.7	8,899	2,021	22.7	16.0
Hartford, Conn	2,667	1,390	52.1	59.8	9,672	2,056	21.3	24.9	5,942	883	14.9	14.6
Lowell, Mass	2,386	1,656	69.4	77.4	8,891	3,667	41.2	43.0	7,564	1,885	24.9	21.4
New Bedford, Mass	4,039	3,231	80.0	72.6	11,508	5,667	49.2	37.5	7,714	1,725	22.4	14.4
New Haven, Conn	2,810	1,342	47.8	58.6	10,641	1,944	18.3	20.4	7,699	1,041	13.5	11.1
Providence, R. I	4,043	2,273	56.2	65.8	15,956	4,347	27.2	27.1	13,643	2,261	16.6	13.7
Springfield, Mass	1,862	974	52.3	59.0	7,734	2,110	27.3	25.9	5,157	811	15.7	11.4
Worcester, Mass	2,815	1,346	47.8	60.8	12,379	2,458	19.9	20.7	9,346	1,145	12.3	8.3
MIDDLE ATLANTIC DIV.:												
Albany, N. Y	857	386	45.0	60.4	3,501	692	19.8	22.0	3,980	536	13.5	10.5
Buffalo, N. Y	5,895	2,339	39.7	47.9	24,903	3,932	15.8	15.0	23,334	2,489	10.7	7.5
Camden, N. J	1,271	490	38.6	46.6	4,516	547	12.1	12.6	2,925	297	10.2	9.7
Jersey City, N. J	3,899	1,535	39.4	47.4	16,989	2,254	13.3	12.8	13,611	1,283	9.4	9.6
New York, N. Y	146,345	83,186	56.8	59.7	473,591	109,141	23.0	21.6	309,549	46,161	14.9	13.8
Bronx Borough	19,667	10,908	55.5	-----	65,975	10,317	15.6	-----	40,889	3,397	8.3	-----
Brooklyn Borough	47,994	25,229	52.6	-----	150,634	22,495	14.9	-----	105,048	10,878	10.4	-----
Manhattan Borough	72,626	44,249	60.9	-----	224,805	71,136	31.6	-----	135,517	29,007	21.4	-----
Queens Borough	4,710	2,278	48.4	-----	25,073	4,256	17.0	-----	23,144	2,296	9.9	-----
Richmond Borough	1,348	522	38.7	-----	7,104	937	13.2	-----	4,951	583	11.8	-----
Newark, N. J	7,621	3,396	44.6	52.1	26,556	3,384	12.7	14.6	18,364	1,856	10.1	10.2
Paterson, N. J	2,797	1,714	61.3	60.0	9,753	2,760	28.3	20.4	8,336	1,236	14.8	11.3
Philadelphia, Pa	25,311	11,983	47.3	56.5	87,892	16,077	18.3	22.4	71,121	9,983	14.0	12.9
Pittsburgh, Pa	6,247	2,602	41.7	[2]44.9	25,829	3,977	15.4	[2]12.9	20,989	2,194	10.5	[2]6.9
Reading, Pa	564	276	48.9	44.5	1,933	326	16.9	11.4	1,412	184	13.0	6.1
Rochester, N. Y	4,435	2,315	52.2	64.4	14,875	3,480	23.4	23.9	13,080	1,813	13.9	10.3
Scranton, Pa	1,184	474	40.0	49.3	6,132	557	9.1	11.3	5,661	349	6.2	5.0
Syracuse, N. Y	1,681	648	38.5	56.5	6,569	1,064	16.2	18.6	6,028	718	11.9	9.1
Trenton, N. J	1,983	834	42.1	45.0	6,688	938	14.0	13.5	4,168	448	10.7	8.3
Yonkers, N .Y	1,313	638	48.6	-----	6,432	1,376	21.4	-----	4,512	627	13.9	-----
NORTH CENTRAL DIVS.:												
Akron, Ohio	2,310	733	31.7	-----	6,777	918	13.5	-----	3,169	245	7.7	-----
Chicago, Ill	42,072	21,340	50.7	50.9	177,005	35,721	20.2	15.4	139,677	16,258	11.6	7.8
Cincinnati, Ohio	1,421	720	50.7	58.2	6,509	1,597	24.5	20.7	12,533	1,679	13.4	10.9
Cleveland, Ohio	14,767	5,798	39.3	47.6	52,822	8,553	16.2	12.1	33,482	3,267	9.8	7.5
Columbus, Ohio	662	258	39.0	45.3	2,621	476	18.2	16.3	3,385	418	12.3	7.5
Dayton, Ohio	597	249	41.7	55.2	2,333	420	18.0	14.5	2,526	245	9.7	7.3
Des Moines, Iowa	443	204	46.0	57.1	2,047	448	21.9	19.7	2,329	265	11.4	6.9
Detroit, Mich	17,846	6,800	38.1	50.6	58,509	8,773	15.0	17.5	35,224	3,546	10.1	7.6
Grand Rapids, Mich	1,164	600	51.5	49.2	5,233	944	18.0	13.5	6,393	694	10.9	6.1
Indianapolis, Ind	553	227	41.0	48.5	2,894	531	18.3	16.5	3,943	377	9.6	7.0
Kansas City, Kans	553	146	26.4	33.7	2,091	310	14.8	7.4	1,746	157	9.0	7.1
Kansas City, Mo	1,328	483	36.4	48.8	4,784	897	18.8	20.5	5,158	597	11.6	9.8
Milwaukee, Wis	4,504	2,140	47.5	52.3	19,421	3,326	17.1	11.4	23,282	2,311	9.9	6.2
Minneapolis, Minn	3,578	1,918	53.6	56.9	17,131	3,869	22.6	21.8	17,673	2,025	11.5	9.3
Omaha, Nebr	1,639	703	42.9	49.9	6,319	1,164	18.4	19.9	6,868	703	10.2	8.9
St. Louis, Mo	4,745	2,365	49.8	48.6	17,415	3,294	18.9	16.2	23,134	2,827	12.2	7.9
St. Paul, Minn	1,864	978	52.5	59.1	8,882	1,874	21.1	18.6	12,020	1,313	10.9	8.2
Toledo, Ohio	1,554	595	38.3	47.0	6,776	1,037	15.3	10.6	7,371	749	10.2	5.9
Youngstown, Ohio	1,817	445	24.5	-----	6,825	674	9.9	-----	3,735	272	7.3	-----
THE SOUTH:												
Atlanta, Ga	286	127	44.4	29.9	910	138	15.2	12.6	736	79	10.7	8.7
Baltimore, Md	4,819	2,336	48.5	47.8	16,606	2,902	17.5	16.3	16,943	2,124	12.5	12.8
Birmingham, Ala	319	75	23.5	-----	1,173	163	13.9	-----	939	73	7.8	-----
Dallas, Tex	510	182	35.7	-----	1,497	327	21.8	-----	1,259	116	9.2	-----
Fort Worth, Tex	475	98	20.6	-----	1,095	185	16.9	-----	642	82	12.8	-----
Houston, Tex	827	212	25.6	-----	2,135	341	16.0	-----	1,709	179	10.5	-----
Louisville, Ky	261	131	50.2	49.0	1,472	319	21.7	17.0	3,897	485	12.4	7.4
Memphis, Tenn	256	111	43.4	36.6	1,085	209	19.3	16.3	1,056	143	13.5	12.8
Nashville, Tenn	100	31	31.0	33.6	370	84	22.7	18.3	589	63	10.7	9.2
New Orleans, La	1,002	296	29.5	20.5	3,629	763	21.0	14.6	5,369	732	13.6	12.4

[1] Includes women of unknown age. [2] Includes Allegheny.

TABLE 164.—PERCENTAGE OF FOREIGN-BORN WHITE WOMEN ENGAGED IN GAINFUL OCCUPATIONS, CLASSIFIED BY AGE GROUPS, FOR CITIES OF 100,000 INHABITANTS OR MORE: 1920 AND 1900—Continued

	FOREIGN-BORN WHITE WOMEN											
	16 to 24 years of age				25 to 44 years of age [1]				45 years of age and over			
CITY	Total number: 1920	Engaged in gainful occupations			Total number: 1920	Engaged in gainful occupations			Total number: 1920	Engaged in gainful occupations		
		Number: 1920	Per cent			Number: 1920	Per cent			Number: 1920	Per cent	
			1920	1900			1920	1900			1920	1900
THE SOUTH—Con.												
Norfolk, Va	330	120	36.4	----	1,112	178	16.0	----	584	57	9.8	----
Richmond, Va	247	111	44.9	26.8	925	183	19.8	16.3	839	130	15.5	16.6
San Antonio, Tex	3,257	1,135	34.8	24.2	6,334	1,615	25.5	15.4	4,558	736	16.1	10.9
Washington, D. C	1,507	737	48.9	44.0	6,039	2,003	33.2	25.7	5,419	1,136	21.0	15.8
Wilmington, Del	942	300	31.8	48.1	3,308	469	14.2	16.0	2,393	258	10.8	9.3
THE WEST:												
Denver, Colo	1,269	563	44.4	44.6	6,436	1,460	22.7	21.9	8,437	1,205	14.3	13.8
Los Angeles, Calif	6,039	2,370	39.2	39.5	21,812	5,827	26.7	21.9	20,251	3,348	16.5	12.9
Oakland, Calif	1,712	693	40.5	40.5	8,105	1,588	19.6	20.0	9,011	1,100	12.2	11.0
Portland, Oreg	1,934	920	47.6	52.0	8,447	1,988	23.5	17.8	8,279	1,100	13.3	10.3
Salt Lake City, Utah	826	407	49.3	46.1	3,458	694	20.1	19.8	5,021	615	12.2	13.3
San Francisco, Calif	5,336	2,646	49.6	48.3	25,911	7,843	30.3	23.2	23,707	3,902	16.5	13.5
Seattle, Wash	3,081	1,444	46.9	40.8	14,247	3,478	24.4	19.3	10,854	1,585	14.6	9.8
Spokane, Wash	646	318	49.2	----	2,962	708	23.9	----	3,367	469	13.9	----

[1] Includes women of unknown age.

TABLE 165.—PERCENTAGE OF NEGRO WOMEN ENGAGED IN GAINFUL OCCUPATIONS, CLASSIFIED BY AGE GROUPS, FOR CITIES OF 100,000 INHABITANTS OR MORE: 1920 AND 1900

	NEGRO WOMEN											
	16 to 24 years of age				25 to 44 years of age [1]				45 years of age and over			
CITY	Total number: 1920	Engaged in gainful occupations			Total number: 1920	Engaged in gainful occupations			Total number: 1920	Engaged in gainful occupations		
		Number: 1920	Per cent			Number: 1920	Per cent			Number: 1920	Per cent	
			1920	1900			1920	1900			1920	1900
NEW ENGLAND DIV.:												
Boston, Mass	1,304	645	49.5	56.6	3,544	1,844	52.0	50.3	1,578	722	45.8	47.3
Bridgeport, Conn	179	91	50.8	56.3	423	192	45.4	47.5	169	82	48.5	40.0
Cambridge, Mass	437	220	50.3	44.5	1,070	479	44.8	37.3	533	216	40.5	31.0
Fall River, Mass	15	10	----	----	64	44	----	----	41	28	----	----
Hartford, Conn	457	261	57.1	59.9	719	414	57.6	42.2	318	155	48.7	43.2
Lowell, Mass	13	5	----	----	23	12	----	----	16	9	----	----
New Bedford, Mass	298	155	52.0	38.7	743	264	35.5	32.3	344	114	33.1	25.9
New Haven, Conn	360	192	53.3	53.2	866	443	51.2	49.3	478	249	52.1	54.2
Providence, R. I	408	260	63.7	52.3	1,008	485	48.1	52.6	623	325	52.2	50.0
Springfield, Mass	234	139	59.4	46.8	548	305	55.7	49.0	236	122	51.7	43.8
Worcester, Mass	122	66	54.1	45.1	201	99	49.3	43.6	142	70	49.3	48.6
MIDDLE ATLANTIC DIV.:												
Albany, N. Y	104	47	45.2	50.4	246	90	36.6	40.6	128	56	43.8	38.6
Buffalo, N. Y	401	150	37.4	46.8	930	352	37.8	40.2	289	125	43.3	36.8
Camden, N. J	729	350	48.0	51.5	1,539	668	43.4	40.0	701	290	41.4	43.5
Jersey City, N. J	696	304	43.7	46.3	1,498	581	38.8	27.1	664	234	35.2	34.6
New York, N. Y	15,784	10,496	66.5	66.2	37,940	23,792	62.7	56.5	10,999	6,027	54.8	53.5
Bronx Bor	458	313	68.3	----	923	498	49.6	----	426	165	38.7	----
Brooklyn Bor	3,170	2,027	63.9	----	7,245	4,012	55.4	----	2,671	1,358	50.8	----
Manhattan Bor	11,477	7,736	67.4	----	28,372	18,560	65.4	----	7,276	4,188	57.6	----
Queens Bor	513	322	62.8	----	1,119	620	55.4	----	530	268	50.6	----
Richmond Bor	166	98	59.0	----	281	142	50.5	----	96	48	----	----

[1] Includes women of unknown age.

TABLE 165.—PERCENTAGE OF NEGRO WOMEN ENGAGED IN GAINFUL OCCUPATIONS, CLASSIFIED BY AGE GROUPS, FOR CITIES OF 100,000 INHABITANTS OR MORE: 1920 AND 1900—Continued

NEGRO WOMEN

| CITY | 16 to 24 years of age | | | | 25 to 44 years of age [1] | | | | 45 years of age and over | | | |
	Total number: 1920	Engaged in gainful occupations Number: 1920	Per cent 1920	Per cent 1900	Total number: 1920	Engaged in gainful occupations Number: 1920	Per cent 1920	Per cent 1900	Total number: 1920	Engaged in gainful occupations Number: 1920	Per cent 1920	Per cent 1900
MIDDLE ATLANTIC DIV.—Continued.												
Newark, N. J......	1,699	823	48.4	57.4	3,437	1,488	43.3	39.4	1,098	462	42.1	39.1
Paterson, N. J......	151	102	67.5	75.3	330	195	59.1	53.4	148	77	52.0	-----
Philadelphia, Pa....	13,229	7,476	56.5	62.6	29,107	15,399	52.9	48.8	9,642	4,731	49.1	43.7
Pittsburgh, Pa......	3,246	1,335	41.1	[2]39.0	7,470	2,833	37.9	[2]27.6	2,546	980	38.5	[2]25.0
Reading, Pa.......	78	33	-----	-----	166	70	42.2	-----	57	17	-----	-----
Rochester, N. Y....	151	95	62.9	-----	362	182	50.3	41.2	159	58	36.5	-----
Scranton, Pa.......	39	17	-----	-----	111	38	34.2	-----	48	17	-----	-----
Syracuse, N. Y.....	87	48	-----	40.2	253	107	42.3	44.0	116	39	33.6	-----
Trenton, N. J......	428	180	42.1	44.1	725	365	50.3	38.3	318	151	47.5	38.5
Yonkers, N. Y......	172	111	64.5	-----	419	263	62.8	-----	192	108	56.3	-----
NORTH CENTRAL DIVS.:												
Akron, Ohio........	477	167	35.0	-----	926	388	41.9	-----	194	63	32.5	-----
Chicago, Ill.......	9,799	4,826	49.2	45.3	25,298	12,471	49.3	42.3	8,153	3,311	40.6	39.2
Cincinnati, Ohio....	2,676	1,287	48.1	51.9	6,362	3,353	52.7	45.9	2,547	1,256	49.3	44.2
Cleveland, Ohio.....	3,276	1,398	42.7	39.8	7,105	3,040	42.8	36.0	1,856	650	35.0	32.6
Columbus, Ohio.....	1,957	792	40.5	44.6	4,193	1,809	43.1	37.6	1,720	659	38.3	31.0
Dayton, Ohio.......	747	344	46.1	45.9	1,733	830	47.9	38.8	728	308	42.3	27.8
Des Moines, Iowa...	521	231	44.3	39.9	1,034	451	43.6	29.2	470	175	37.2	33.6
Detroit, Mich.......	3,965	1,486	37.5	48.3	8,096	2,949	36.4	34.3	1,624	506	31.2	29.2
Grand Rapids,Mich.	70	35	-----	-----	209	78	37.3	34.7	117	36	30.8	-----
Indianapolis, Ind...	3,099	1,382	44.6	44.9	6,921	3,180	45.9	45.0	3,101	1,315	42.4	36.3
Kansas City, Kans..	1,201	426	35.5	38.5	2,731	945	34.6	30.4	1,386	445	32.1	31.2
Kansas City, Mo....	2,767	1,341	48.5	52.4	7,257	3,783	52.1	51.8	2,565	1,233	48.1	53.0
Milwaukee, Wis....	166	67	40.4	-----	478	171	35.8	29.8	131	47	35.9	-----
Minneapolis, Minn.	304	143	47.0	36.4	850	394	46.4	36.5	302	100	33.1	-----
Omaha, Nebr.......	868	401	46.2	44.6	2,124	913	43.0	46.5	681	259	38.0	38.6
St. Louis, Mo.......	6,151	2,928	47.6	49.1	15,249	7,748	50.8	46.1	5,716	2,729	47.7	44.7
St. Paul, Minn.....	221	99	44.8	34.0	689	268	38.9	29.6	319	109	34.2	35.9
Toledo, Ohio.......	504	217	43.1	39.8	1,139	447	39.2	34.0	342	100	29.2	27.4
Youngstown, Ohio..	592	161	27.2	-----	1,226	306	25.0	-----	278	72	25.9	-----
THE SOUTH:												
Atlanta, Ga........	7,703	4,547	59.0	64.8	12,909	8,664	67.1	71.4	4,948	3,166	64.0	65.6
Baltimore, Md......	11,014	6,876	62.4	67.1	21,500	13,773	64.1	60.6	9,649	5,805	60.2	57.9
Birmingham, Ala....	8,277	3,426	41.4	-----	13,380	6,337	47.4	-----	4,213	2,025	48.1	-----
Dallas, Tex........	2,563	1,456	56.8	-----	5,238	3,553	67.8	-----	1,600	927	57.9	-----
Fort Worth, Tex....	1,844	849	46.0	-----	3,325	1,807	54.3	-----	911	458	50.3	-----
Houston, Tex......	3,804	2,009	52.8	-----	7,217	4,346	60.2	-----	2,410	1,284	53.3	-----
Louisville, Ky......	3,759	2,331	62.0	52.8	8,594	5,966	69.4	57.0	4,506	2,864	63.6	50.8
Memphis, Tenn.....	6,813	3,367	49.4	66.3	13,564	7,480	55.1	59.2	5,022	2,771	55.2	58.7
Nashville, Tenn.....	3,922	2,134	54.4	57.6	7,021	4,535	64.6	65.0	3,992	2,262	56.7	61.0
New Orleans, La....	10,758	5,623	52.3	48.7	20,421	11,653	57.1	48.9	8,792	4,527	51.5	50.5
Norfolk, Va........	4,867	2,472	50.8	-----	8,375	4,474	53.4	-----	2,939	1,584	53.9	-----
Richmond, Va......	6,456	3,913	60.6	61.3	10,566	6,302	59.6	61.8	4,762	2,642	55.5	57.4
San Antonio, Tex...	1,639	896	54.7	52.9	3,008	1,904	63.3	55.2	1,077	639	59.3	50.4
Washington, D. C...	11,638	6,851	58.9	64.5	22,822	15,017	65.8	65.2	11,146	6,427	57.7	59.4
Wilmington, Del....	1,003	598	59.6	62.3	1,961	1,251	63.8	53.8	1,046	615	58.8	42.9
THE WEST:												
Denver, Colo.......	462	213	46.1	44.2	1,301	651	50.0	50.9	680	327	48.1	45.9
Los Angeles, Calif...	1,276	598	46.9	40.3	3,539	1,889	53.4	37.8	1,623	767	47.3	38.0
Oakland, Calif.....	341	115	33.7	-----	1,106	369	33.4	-----	497	148	29.8	27.5
Portland, Oreg.....	85	38	-----	-----	339	151	44.5	54.4	165	61	37.0	-----
Salt Lake City, Utah	50	21	-----	-----	158	62	39.2	-----	65	27	-----	-----
San Francisco, Calif.	156	83	53.2	39.5	525	304	57.9	41.1	201	100	49.8	36.8
Seattle, Wash......	169	72	42.6	-----	622	293	47.1	-----	226	99	43.8	-----
Spokane, Wash.....	47	16	-----	-----	138	64	46.4	-----	87	38	-----	-----

[1] Includes women of unknown age.   [2] Includes Allegheny.

TABLE **166.**—NUMBER AND PERCENTAGE OF WOMEN ENGAGED IN GAINFUL
OCCUPATIONS, FOR CITIES HAVING FROM 25,000 TO 100,000 INHABITANTS:
1920

CITY	WOMEN 16 YEARS OF AGE AND OVER: 1920			CITY	WOMEN 16 YEARS OF AGE AND OVER: 1920		
	Total number	Engaged in gainful occupations			Total number	Engaged in gainful occupations	
		Number	Per cent			Number	Per cent
ALABAMA				**ILLINOIS**—continued			
Mobile	22,805	8,404	36.9	Quincy	14,172	3,976	28.1
Montgomery	16,931	7,497	44.3	Rock Island	12,698	3,333	26.2
				Rockford	23,580	7,134	30.3
ARIZONA				Springfield	22,235	6,762	30.4
Phoenix	10,038	2,601	25.9	**INDIANA**			
ARKANSAS				Anderson	10,598	2,923	27.6
				East Chicago	8,349	1,186	14.2
Fort Smith	10,078	2,612	25.9	Evansville	32,306	9,717	30.1
Little Rock	24,785	8,315	33.5	Fort Wayne	32,394	9,974	30.8
				Gary	14,381	2,351	16.3
CALIFORNIA				Hammond	10,549	2,147	20.4
				Kokomo	10,235	2,156	21.1
Alameda	11,014	2,408	21.9	Muncie	12,988	3,341	25.7
Berkeley	23,069	5,822	25.2	Richmond	9,916	2,543	25.6
Fresno	15,504	4,018	25.9	South Bend	23,167	6,360	27.5
Long Beach	23,795	4,309	18.1	Terre Haute	24,262	6,155	25.4
Pasadena	20,917	5,853	28.0				
Sacramento	23,482	6,485	27.6	**IOWA**			
San Diego	29,829	7,603	25.5				
San Jose	15,126	3,846	25.4	Cedar Rapids	17,138	4,763	27.8
Stockton	13,966	3,212	23.0	Council Bluffs	12,856	3,361	26.1
				Davenport	21,016	5,759	27.4
COLORADO				Dubuque	14,896	4,404	29.6
				Sioux City	24,228	7,395	30.5
Colorado Springs	12,681	3,426	27.0	Waterloo	13,002	3,374	25.9
Pueblo	14,552	3,481	23.9				
				KANSAS			
CONNECTICUT				Topeka	19,394	5,514	28.4
Meriden	10,435	3,282	31.5	Wichita	26,908	6,963	25.9
New Britain	18,017	5,645	31.3				
New London	9,249	2,324	25.1	**KENTUCKY**			
Norwalk	10,189	3,301	32.4				
Stamford	11,665	3,402	29.2	Covington	21,969	6,807	31.0
Waterbury	29,795	9,616	32.3	Lexington	16,617	6,461	38.9
				Newport	11,316	3,458	30.6
FLORIDA							
Jacksonville	33,832	13,131	38.8	**LOUISIANA**			
Miami	10,587	4,028	38.0	Shreveport	16,202	6,253	38.6
Pensacola	10,446	3,307	31.7				
Tampa	17,274	7,622	44.1	**MAINE**			
				Bangor	10,525	3,021	28.7
GEORGIA				Lewiston	11,734	5,419	46.2
				Portland	26,920	8,131	30.2
Augusta	20,129	8,705	43.2				
Columbus	11,653	5,495	47.2	**MARYLAND**			
Macon	19,909	8,608	43.2				
Savannah	31,078	12,608	40.6	Cumberland	10,322	2,522	24.4
				Hagerstown	9,923	2,475	24.9
ILLINOIS							
				MASSACHUSETTS			
Aurora	13,333	3,614	27.1				
Bloomington	11,341	2,946	26.0	Brockton	24,314	9,896	40.7
Cicero town	13,439	3,954	29.4	Brookline town	18,658	7,522	40.3
Danville	12,326	3,231	26.2	Chelsea	13,407	3,965	29.6
Decatur	16,097	3,986	24.8	Chicopee	10,873	3,960	36.4
East St. Louis	21,712	5,720	26.3	Everett	13,897	3,791	27.3
Elgin	11,701	3,998	34.2	Fitchburg	14,244	5,409	38.0
Evanston	14,969	5,095	34.0	Haverhill	20,131	8,631	42.9
Joliet	13,010	3,376	25.9	Holyoke	21,986	9,757	44.4
Moline	10,511	2,610	24.8	Lawrence	32,331	15,377	47.6
Oak Park village	15,950	4,393	27.5	Lynn	36,752	14,428	39.3
Peoria	29,007	8,436	29.1	Malden	18,371	5,889	32.1

TABLE **166.**—NUMBER AND PERCENTAGE OF WOMEN ENGAGED IN GAINFUL OCCUPATIONS, FOR CITIES HAVING FROM 25,000 TO 100,000 INHABITANTS: 1920—Continued

CITY	WOMEN 16 YEARS OF AGE AND OVER: 1920			CITY	WOMEN 16 YEARS OF AGE AND OVER: 1920		
	Total number	Engaged in gainful occupations			Total number	Engaged in gainful occupations	
		Number	Per cent			Number	Per cent
MASSACHUSETTS—con.				**NEW YORK**			
Medford	14,743	4,148	28.1	Amsterdam	11,946	5,183	43.
Newton	19,054	6,499	34.1	Auburn	13,123	4,262	32.4
Pittsfield	15,144	5,171	34.1	Binghamton	25,661	9,259	36.5
Quincy	16,235	4,030	24.8	Elmira	17,212	4,888	28.1
Revere	9,347	2,326	24.9	Jamestown	14,609	4,702	32.4
Salem	15,254	5,575	36.5	Kingston	10,742	3,421	31.2
Somerville	35,534	10,733	30.2	Mount Vernon	15,946	4,895	30.8
Taunton	13,398	4,323	32.3	New Rochelle	13,114	4,303	32.7
Waltham	12,284	5,031	41.0	Newburgh	11,591	3,499	30.8
MICHIGAN				Niagara Falls	15,513	3,824	24.2
				Poughkeepsie	13,457	4,268	31.7
				Rome	8,452	2,351	27.7
Battle Creek	13,938	4,254	30.5	Schenectady	30,660	8,244	26.9
Bay City	15,955	4,127	25.9	Troy	30,278	11,903	39.3
Flint	27,872	6,912	24.8	Utica	34,410	12,049	35.0
Hamtramck village	10,750	1,509	14.0	Watertown	12,031	3,615	30.0
Highland Park	15,057	3,420	22.7				
Jackson	16,875	4,573	27.1	**NORTH CAROLINA**			
Kalamazoo	18,058	5,672	31.4				
Lansing	19,791	5,085	25.7	Asheville	10,658	3,432	32.2
Muskegon	12,266	3,321	27.1	Charlotte	16,401	6,567	40.0
Pontiac	11,169	2,559	22.9	Wilmington	11,764	4,335	36.8
Port Huron	9,075	1,886	20.8	Winston-Salem	16,946	9,193	54.2
Saginaw	21,677	5,543	25.6				
MINNESOTA				**OHIO**			
				Canton	28,144	6,505	23.1
Duluth	32,527	9,957	30.6	East Cleveland	11,120	2,787	25.1
				Hamilton	13,773	3,285	23.9
MISSOURI				Lakewood	15,544	3,579	23.0
				Lima	14,711	3,641	24.8
Joplin	10,978	2,660	24.2	Lorain	10,183	1,508	14.8
St. Joseph	28,917	8,953	31.0	Mansfield	10,210	2,605	25.5
Springfield	14,950	3,749	25.1	Marion	9,863	2,128	21.6
				Newark	9,907	2,346	23.7
MONTANA				Portsmouth	11,632	3,037	26.1
				Springfield	22,013	5,769	26.2
Butte	13,528	3,473	25.7	Steubenville	9,052	1,941	21.4
				Warren	9,040	2,004	22.2
NEBRASKA				Zanesville	11,226	2,765	24.6
Lincoln	20,764	6,171	29.7				
				OKLAHOMA			
NEW HAMPSHIRE				Muskogee	10,793	2,807	26.0
				Oklahoma City	32,851	10,976	33.4
Manchester	28,749	13,609	47.3	Tulsa	24,946	7,794	31.2
Nashua	10,000	3,907	39.1				
				PENNSYLVANIA			
NEW JERSEY							
Atlantic City	20,308	7,304	36.0	Allentown	25,991	7,609	29.3
Bayonne	22,021	5,104	23.2	Altoona	21,134	4,823	22.8
Clifton	8,316	2,685	32.3	Bethlehem	16,037	3,732	23.3
East Orange	21,229	5,699	26.8	Chester	18,018	4,563	25.3
Elizabeth	30,259	7,820	25.8	Easton	12,617	3,474	27.5
Hoboken	22,171	6,746	30.4	Erie	31,494	7,538	23.9
Irvington town	9,040	1,970	21.8	Harrisburg	29,098	7,759	26.7
Kearny town	8,996	2,729	30.3	Hazleton	10,330	2,817	27.3
Montclair town	11,535	3,600	31.2	Johnstown	20,333	4,229	20.8
New Brunswick	11,135	3,600	32.3	Lancaster	20,914	7,226	34.6
Orange	11,733	3,945	33.6	McKeesport	14,155	2,753	19.4
Passaic	20,186	7,595	37.6	New Castle	14,332	2,788	19.5
Perth Amboy	11,731	2,850	24.3	Norristown borough	12,441	3,715	29.9
Plainfield	10,351	3,189	30.8	Wilkes-Barre	24,884	6,563	26.4
West Hoboken town	14,075	4,000	28.4	Williamsport	14,019	4,136	29.5
West New York town	9,949	2,660	26.7	York	17,771	5,709	32.1

TABLE **166.**—NUMBER AND PERCENTAGE OF WOMEN ENGAGED IN GAINFUL OCCUPATIONS, FOR CITIES HAVING FROM 25,000 TO 100,000 INHABITANTS: 1920—Continued

CITY	WOMEN 16 YEARS OF AGE AND OVER: 1920			CITY	WOMEN 16 YEARS OF AGE AND OVER: 1920		
	Total number	Engaged in gainful occupations			Total number	Engaged in gainful occupations	
		Num- ber	Per cent			Num- ber	Per cent
RHODE ISLAND				VIRGINIA			
Cranston	10,461	2,828	27.0	Lynchburg	11,625	5,183	44.6
Newport	10,067	2,843	28.2	Newport News	10,928	3,198	29.3
Pawtucket	23,474	9,293	39.6	Petersburg	11,729	4,885	41.6
Woonsocket	15,140	6,483	42.8	Portsmouth	18,281	5,342	29.2
				Roanoke	17,661	4,550	25.8
SOUTH CAROLINA							
Charleston	25,264	10,319	40.8	WASHINGTON			
Columbia	14,277	4,992	35.0	Bellingham	8,769	1,965	22.4
				Everett	9,255	2,115	22.9
SOUTH DAKOTA				Tacoma	32,726	8,148	24.9
Sioux Falls	8,916	2,645	29.7	WEST VIRGINIA			
				Charleston	13,758	3,794	27.6
TENNESSEE				Clarksburg	9,079	1,975	21.8
Chattanooga	21,482	8,014	37.3	Huntington	17,127	3,991	23.3
Knoxville	27,764	8,645	31.1	Wheeling	20,530	5,153	25.1
TEXAS				WISCONSIN			
Austin	13,628	4,013	29.4				
Beaumont	13,552	4,168	30.8	Green Bay	10,945	3,116	28.5
El Paso	27,498	6,914	25.1	Kenosha	11,688	3,053	26.1
Galveston	15,107	4,722	31.3	La Crosse	11,639	3,470	29.8
Waco	13,919	3,723	26.7	Madison	15,034	4,880	32.5
Wichita Falls	11,289	2,845	25.2	Oshkosh	12,328	3,508	28.5
				Racine	18,764	5,252	28.0
UTAH				Sheboygan	10,357	2,658	25.7
Ogden	10,667	2,233	20.9	Superior	12,289	3,002	24.4

TABLE 167.—FAMILY RELATIONSHIP OF GAINFULLY OCCUPIED WOMEN, BY RACE, NATIVITY, AND MARITAL CONDITION, FOR THE 11 SELECTED CITIES COMBINED: 1920

RACE AND NATIVITY AND MARITAL CONDITION	GAINFULLY EMPLOYED WOMEN 16 YEARS OF AGE AND OVER: 1920							
	Total	Living at home					Board-ing or lodg-ing	Liv-ing with em-ploy-er
		Heads of fami-lies	Living with—					
			Father	Mother	Hus-band	Other rela-tive		

ELEVEN SELECTED CITIES

Number

All classes[1]	373, 204	56, 659	96, 281	44, 360	53, 411	42, 502	50, 297	29, 694
Single (including unknown)	224, 428	13, 883	87, 571	37, 968	--------	30, 748	31, 826	22, 432
Married	85, 642	8, 129	5, 568	3, 269	53, 411	3, 722	9, 033	2, 510
Widowed or divorced	63, 134	34, 647	3, 142	3, 123	--------	8, 032	9, 438	4, 752
Native white—Native parentage	156, 686	18, 997	46, 183	20, 939	16, 202	17, 847	26, 588	9, 930
Single (including unknown)	104, 182	5, 106	41, 789	18, 183	--------	13, 631	17, 880	7, 593
Married	28, 606	2, 435	2, 608	1, 315	16, 202	1, 284	4, 074	688
Widowed or divorced	23, 898	11, 456	1, 786	1, 441	--------	2, 932	4, 634	1, 649
Native white—Foreign or mixed parentage	102, 064	11, 770	37, 008	16, 215	7, 275	13, 248	8, 906	7, 642
Single (including unknown)	78, 234	4, 372	34, 945	14, 769	--------	11, 057	6, 632	6, 459
Married	12, 457	1, 191	1, 352	710	7, 275	646	983	300
Widowed or divorced	11, 373	6, 207	711	736	--------	1, 545	1, 291	883
Foreign-born white	44, 572	7, 467	8, 264	2, 495	10, 210	4, 474	4, 329	7, 333
Single (including unknown)	23, 104	1, 585	7, 415	2, 092	--------	3, 104	2, 829	6, 079
Married	13, 713	1, 122	615	251	10, 210	495	670	350
Widowed or divorced	7, 755	4, 760	234	152	--------	875	830	904
Negro	69, 808	18, 417	4, 822	4, 698	19, 707	6, 931	10, 462	4, 771
Single (including unknown)	18, 869	2, 817	3, 418	2, 915	--------	2, 956	4, 476	2, 287
Married	30, 844	3, 379	993	993	19, 707	1, 296	3, 305	1, 171
Widowed or divorced	20, 095	12, 221	411	790	--------	2, 679	2, 681	1, 313

Per cent

All classes	100. 0	15. 2	25. 8	11. 9	14. 3	11. 4	13. 5	8. 0
Single (including unknown)	100. 0	6. 2	39. 0	16. 9	--------	13. 7	14. 2	10. 0
Married	100. 0	9. 5	6. 5	3. 8	62. 4	4. 3	10. 5	2. 9
Widowed or divorced	100. 0	54. 9	5. 0	4. 9	--------	12. 7	14. 9	7. 5
Native white—Native parentage	100. 0	12. 1	29. 5	13. 4	10. 3	11. 4	17. 0	6. 3
Single (including unknown)	100. 0	4. 9	40. 1	17. 5	--------	13. 1	17. 2	7. 3
Married	100. 0	8. 5	9. 1	4. 6	56. 6	4. 5	14. 2	2. 4
Widowed or divorced	100. 0	47. 9	7. 5	6. 0	--------	12. 3	19. 4	6. 9
Native white—Foreign or mixed parentage	100. 0	11. 5	36. 3	15. 9	7. 1	13. 0	8. 7	7. 5
Single (including unknown)	100. 0	5. 6	44. 7	18. 9	--------	14. 1	8. 5	8. 3
Married	100. 0	9. 6	10. 9	5. 7	58. 4	5. 2	7. 9	2. 4
Widowed or divorced	100. 0	54. 6	6. 3	6. 5	--------	13. 6	11. 4	7. 8
Foreign-born white	100. 0	16. 8	18. 5	5. 6	22. 9	10. 0	9. 7	16. 5
Single (including unknown)	100. 0	6. 9	32. 1	9. 1	--------	13. 4	12. 2	26. 3
Married	100. 0	8. 2	4. 5	1. 8	74. 5	3. 6	4. 9	2. 6
Widowed or divorced	100. 0	61. 4	3. 0	2. 0	--------	11. 3	10. 7	11. 7
Negro	100. 0	26. 4	6. 9	6. 7	28. 2	9. 9	15. 0	6. 8
Single (including unknown)	100. 0	14. 9	18. 1	15. 4	--------	15. 7	23. 7	12. 1
Married	100. 0	11. 0	3. 2	3. 2	63. 9	4. 2	10. 7	3. 8
Widowed or divorced	100. 0	60. 8	2. 0	3. 9	--------	13. 3	13. 3	6. 5

[1] Total includes 74 Indians, Chinese, Japanese, and other races—classes for which figures are not shown separately or in detail in the table.

TABLE 168.—FAMILY RELATIONSHIP OF GAINFULLY OCCUPIED WOMEN, BY RACE, NATIVITY, AND MARITAL CONDITION, FOR 11 SELECTED CITIES: 1920

RACE AND NATIVITY AND MARITAL CONDITION	GAINFULLY EMPLOYED WOMEN 16 YEARS OF AGE AND OVER							
		Living at home					Board-ing or lodg-ing	Liv-ing with em-ploy-er
			Living with—					
	Total	Heads of fami-lies	Father	Mother	Hus-band	Other rela-tive		
FALL RIVER, MASS								
Number								
All classes [1]	19,111	1,881	7,063	2,298	4,022	1,928	921	998
Single (including unknown)	12,142	612	6,551	1,999		1,534	606	840
Married	5,489	363	427	231	4,022	193	203	50
Widowed or divorced	1,480	906	85	68		201	112	108
Native white—Native parentage	2,181	172	935	346	225	234	111	158
Single (including unknown)	1,686	70	883	311		207	88	127
Married	334	22	33	22	225	12	12	8
Widowed or divorced	161	80	19	13		15	11	23
Native white—Foreign or mixed parentage	8,816	542	4,492	1,395	1,033	848	229	277
Single (including unknown)	6,893	236	4,265	1,250		730	172	240
Married	1,537	87	188	113	1,033	70	35	11
Widowed or divorced	386	219	39	32		48	22	26
Foreign-born white	8,030	1,142	1,630	550	2,744	841	580	543
Single (including unknown)	3,535	303	1,398	435		594	345	460
Married	3,583	248	205	93	2,744	110	156	27
Widowed or divorced	912	591	27	22		137	79	56
Negro	82	25	6	6	19	5	1	20
Single (including unknown)	27	3	5	2		3	1	13
Married	34	6	1	3	19	1		4
Widowed or divorced	21	16		1		1		3
Per cent [2]								
All classes	100.0	9.8	37.0	12.0	21.0	10.1	4.8	5.2
Single (including unknown)	100.0	5.0	54.0	16.5		12.6	5.0	6.9
Married	100.0	6.6	7.8	4.2	73.3	3.5	3.7	0.9
Widowed or divorced	100.0	61.2	5.7	4.6		13.6	7.6	7.3
Native white—Native parentage	100.0	7.9	42.9	15.9	10.3	10.7	5.1	7.2
Single (including unknown)	100.0	4.2	52.4	18.4		12.3	5.2	7.5
Married	100.0	6.6	9.9	6.6	67.4	3.6	3.6	2.4
Widowed or divorced	100.0	49.7	11.8	8.1		9.3	6.8	14.3
Native white—Foreign or mixed parentage	100.0	6.1	51.0	15.8	11.7	9.6	2.6	3.1
Single (including unknown)	100.0	3.4	61.9	18.1		10.6	2.5	3.5
Married	100.0	5.7	12.2	7.4	67.2	4.6	2.3	0.7
Widowed or divorced	100.0	56.7	10.1	8.3		12.4	5.7	6.7
Foreign-born white	100.0	14.2	20.3	6.8	34.2	10.5	7.2	6.8
Single (including unknown)	100.0	8.6	39.5	12.3		16.8	9.8	13.0
Married	100.0	6.9	5.7	2.6	76.6	3.1	4.4	0.8
Widowed or divorced	100.0	64.8	3.0	2.4		15.0	8.7	6.1

[1] Includes Indians.   [2] Per cent not shown where base is less than 100.

TABLE 168.—FAMILY RELATIONSHIP OF GAINFULLY OCCUPIED WOMEN, BY RACE, NATIVITY, AND MARITAL CONDITION, FOR 11 SELECTED CITIES: 1920—Con.

RACE AND NATIVITY AND MARITAL CONDITION	GAINFULLY EMPLOYED WOMEN 16 YEARS OF AGE AND OVER							
	Total	Living at home					Board-ing or lodg-ing	Liv-ing with em-ploy-er
		Heads of fami-lies	Living with—					
			Father	Mother	Hus-band	Other rela-tive		
PROVIDENCE, R. I.								
Number								
All classes [1]	32,099	3,732	10,187	4,272	3,254	3,894	3,366	3,394
Single (including unknown)	22,813	1,224	9,520	3,853	-------	3,174	2,264	2,778
Married	5,433	499	476	230	3,254	290	522	162
Widowed or divorced	3,853	2,009	191	189	-------	430	580	454
Native white—Native parentage	8,394	967	2,604	1,253	659	985	1,364	562
Single (including unknown)	5,953	363	2,394	1,111	-------	796	905	384
Married	1,300	127	140	76	659	66	194	38
Widowed or divorced	1,141	477	70	66	-------	123	265	140
Native white—Foreign or mixed parentage	13,749	1,114	5,899	2,436	772	1,830	997	701
Single (including unknown)	11,233	481	5,629	2,244	-------	1,608	699	572
Married	1,486	118	196	109	772	92	170	29
Widowed or divorced	1,030	515	74	83	-------	130	128	100
Foreign-born white	8,881	1,342	1,565	504	1,598	980	899	1,993
Single (including unknown)	5,205	318	1,394	438	-------	717	597	1,741
Married	2,283	198	127	36	1,598	114	138	72
Widowed or divorced	1,393	826	44	30	-------	149	164	180
Negro	1,070	309	118	79	223	99	104	138
Single (including unknown)	419	62	102	60	-------	53	61	81
Married	362	56	13	9	223	18	20	23
Widowed or divorced	289	191	3	10	-------	28	23	34
Per cent								
All classes	100.0	11.6	31.7	13.3	10.1	12.1	10.5	10.6
Single (including unknown)	100.0	5.4	41.7	16.9	-------	13.9	9.9	12.2
Married	100.0	9.2	8.8	4.2	59.9	5.3	9.6	3.0
Widowed or divorced	100.0	52.1	5.0	4.9	-------	11.2	15.1	11.8
Native white—Native parentage	100.0	11.5	31.0	14.9	7.9	11.7	16.2	6.7
Single (including unknown)	100.0	6.1	40.2	18.7	-------	13.4	15.2	6.5
Married	100.0	9.8	10.8	5.8	50.7	5.1	14.9	2.9
Widowed or divorced	100.0	41.8	6.1	5.8	-------	10.8	23.2	12.3
Native white—Foreign or mixed parentage	100.0	8.1	42.9	17.7	5.6	13.3	7.3	5.1
Single (including unknown)	100.0	4.3	50.1	20.0	-------	14.3	6.2	5.1
Married	100.0	7.9	13.2	7.3	52.0	6.2	11.4	2.0
Widowed or divorced	100.0	50.0	7.2	8.1	-------	12.6	12.4	9.7
Foreign-born white	100.0	15.1	17.6	5.7	18.0	11.0	10.1	22.4
Single (including unknown)	100.0	6.1	26.8	8.4	-------	13.8	11.5	33.4
Married	100.0	8.7	5.6	1.6	70.0	5.0	6.0	3.2
Widowed or divorced	100.0	59.3	3.2	2.2	-------	10.7	11.8	12.9
Negro	100.0	28.9	11.0	7.4	20.8	9.3	9.7	12.9
Single (including unknown)	100.0	14.8	24.3	14.3	-------	12.6	14.6	19.3
Married	100.0	15.5	3.6	2.5	61.6	5.0	5.5	6.4
Widowed or divorced	100.0	66.1	1.0	3.5	-------	9.7	8.0	11.8

[1] Includes Indians and Chinese.

6436°—29——20

TABLE 168.—FAMILY RELATIONSHIP OF GAINFULLY OCCUPIED WOMEN, BY RACE, NATIVITY, AND MARITAL CONDITION, FOR 11 SELECTED CITIES: 1920—Con.

RACE AND NATIVITY AND MARITAL CONDITION	Total	GAINFULLY EMPLOYED WOMEN 16 YEARS OF AGE AND OVER						
		Living at home					Board-ing or lodg-ing	Liv-ing with em-ploy-er
		Heads of fami-lies	Living with—					
			Father	Mother	Hus-band	Other rela-tive		
ROCHESTER, N. Y.								
Number								
All classes [1]	36,956	3,897	11,349	4,409	4,683	4,319	5,289	3,010
Single (including unknown)	25,255	1,280	10,403	3,971		3,338	3,928	2,335
Married	7,587	583	733	269	4,683	414	702	203
Widowed or divorced	4,114	2,034	213	169,		567	659	472
Native white—Native parentage	14,742	1,484	4,426	1,861	1,664	1,565	2,826	916
Single (including unknown)	10,176	506	4,003	1,662		1,195	2,122	688
Married	2,989	237	331	127	1,664	162	388	80
Widowed or divorced	1,577	741	92	72		208	316	148
Native white—Foreign or mixed parentage	14,254	1,330	5,286	2,128	1,184	1,889	1,481	956
Single (including unknown)	10,886	538	4,936	1,949		1,572	1,135	756
Married	2,065	167	266	105	1,184	127	161	55
Widowed or divorced	1,303	625	84	74		190	185	145
Foreign-born white	7,608	1,039	1,605	399	1,744	835	923	1,063
Single (including unknown)	4,048	223	1,439	348		559	641	838
Married	2,382	170	130	34	1,744	112	134	58
Widowed or divorced	1,178	646	36	17		164	148	167
Negro	335	44	31	14	89	30	56	71
Single (including unknown)	133	13	24	8		12	27	49
Married	149	9	6	3	89	13	19	10
Widowed or divorced	53	22	1	3		5	10	12
Per cent [2]								
All classes	100.0	10.5	30.7	11.9	12.7	11.7	14.3	8.1
Single (including unknown)	100.0	5.1	41.2	15.7		13.2	15.6	9.2
Married	100.0	7.7	9.7	3.5	61.7	5.5	9.3	2.7
Widowed or divorced	100.0	49.4	5.2.	4.1		13.8	16.0	11.5
Native white—Native parentage	100.0	10.1	30.0	12.6	11.3	10.6	19.2	6.2
Single (including unknown	100.0	5.0	39.3	16.3		11.7	20.9	6.8
Married	10v.0	7.9	11.1	4.2	55.7	5.4	13.0	2.7
Widowed or divorced	1 J.0	47.0	5.8	4.6		13.2	20.0	9.4
Native white—Foreign or mixed parentage	100.0	9.3	37.1	14.9	8.3	13.3	10.4	6.7
Single (including unknown)	100.0	4.9	45.3	17.9		14.4	10.4	6.9
Married	100.0	8.1	12.9	5.1	57.3	6.2	7.8	2.7
Widowed or divorced	100.0	48.0	6.4	5.7		14.6	14.2	11.1
Foreign-born white	100.0	13.7	21.1	5.2	22.9	11.0	12 1	14.0
Single (including unknown	100 0	5.5	35.5	8.6		13.8	15.8	20.7
Married	100.0	7.1	5.5	1.4	73.2	4.7	5.6	2.4
Widowed or divorced	100.0	54.8	3.1	1.4		13.9	12.6	14.2
Negro	100.0	13.1	9.3	4.2	26.6	9.0	16.7	21.2
Single (including unknown)	100.0	9.8	18.0	6.0		9.0	20.3	36.8
Married	100.0	6.0	4.0	2.0	59.7	8.7	12.8	6.7
Widowed or divorced								

[1] Includes Indians and Japanese.   [2] Per cent not shown where base is less than 100.

TABLE **168.**—FAMILY RELATIONSHIP OF GAINFULLY OCCUPIED WOMEN, BY RACE, NATIVITY, AND MARITAL CONDITION, FOR 11 SELECTED CITIES: 1920—Con.

RACE AND NATIVITY AND MARITAL CONDITION	GAINFULLY EMPLOYED WOMEN 16 YEARS OF AGE AND OVER							
			Living at home					
	Total	Heads of families	Living with—				Boarding or lodging	Living with employer
			Father	Mother	Husband	Other relative		
PATERSON, N. J.								
Number								
All classes [1]	17,999	1,856	6,976	2,298	2,973	1,861	1,223	812
Single (including unknown)	11,990	496	6,528	2,030	_____	1,507	849	580
Married	4,243	303	347	177	2,973	146	210	87
Widowed or divorced	1,766	1,057	101	91	_____	208	164	145
Native white—Native parentage	4,118	432	1,596	619	399	509	420	143
Single (including unknown)	2,976	139	1,482	556	_____	415	290	94
Married	717	57	87	35	399	40	81	18
Widowed or divorced	425	236	27	28	_____	54	49	31
Native white—Foreign or mixed parentage	7,795	532	4,015	1,296	633	750	369	200
Single (including unknown)	6,267	204	3,801	1,159	_____	656	289	158
Married	1,086	86	168	97	633	39	49	14
Widowed or divorced	442	242	46	40	_____	55	31	28
Foreign-born white	5,710	817	1,335	358	1,849	573	394	384
Single (including unknown)	2,603	137	1,226	295	_____	419	249	277
Married	2,288	141	83	42	1,849	61	73	39
Widowed or divorced	819	539	26	21	_____	93	72	68
Negro	374	75	30	25	92	29	40	83
Single (including unknown)	142	16	19	20	_____	17	21	49
Married	152	19	9	3	92	6	7	16
Widowed or divorced	80	40	2	2	_____	6	12	18
Per cent [2]								
All classes	100.0	10.3	38.8	12.8	16.5	10.3	6.8	4.5
Single (including unknown)	100.0	4.1	54.4	16.9	_____	12.6	7.1	4.8
Married	100.0	7.1	8.2	4.2	70.1	3.4	4.9	2.1
Widowed or divorced	100.0	59.9	5.7	5.2	_____	11.8	9.3	8.2
Native white—Native parentage	100.0	10.5	38.8	15.0	9.7	12.4	10.2	3.5
Single (including unknown)	100.0	4.7	49.8	18.7	_____	13.9	9.7	3.2
Married	100.0	7.9	12.1	4.9	55.6	5.6	11.3	2.5
Widowed or divorced	100.0	55.5	6.4	6.6	_____	12.7	11.5	7.3
Native white—Foreign or mixed parentage	100.0	6.8	51.5	16.6	8.1	9.6	4.7	2.6
Single (including unknown)	100.0	3.3	60.7	18.5	_____	10.5	4.6	2.5
Married	100.0	7.9	15.5	8.9	58.3	3.6	4.5	1.3
Widowed or divorced	100.0	54.8	10.4	9.0	_____	12.4	7.0	6.3
Foreign-born white	100.0	14.3	23.4	6.3	32.4	10.0	6.9	6.7
Single (including unknown)	100.0	5.3	47.1	11.3	_____	16.1	9.6	10.6
Married	100.0	6.2	3.6	1.8	80.8	2.7	3.2	1.7
Widowed or divorced	100.0	65.8	3.2	2.6	_____	11.4	8.8	8.3
Negro	100.0	20.1	8.0	6.7	24.6	7.8	10.7	22.2
Single (including unknown)	100.0	11.3	13.4	14.1	_____	12.0	14.8	34.5
Married	100.0	12.5	5.9	2.0	60.5	3.9	4.6	10.5
Widowed or divorced	_____	_____	_____	_____	_____	_____	_____	_____

[1] Includes Indians.   [2] Per cent not shown where base is less than 100.

TABLE **168.**—FAMILY RELATIONSHIP OF GAINFULLY OCCUPIED WOMEN, BY RACE, NATIVITY, AND MARITAL CONDITION, FOR 11 SELECTED CITIES: 1920—Con.

GAINFULLY EMPLOYED WOMEN 16 YEARS OF AGE AND OVER

RACE AND NATIVITY AND MARITAL CONDITION	Total	Living at home					Boarding or lodging	Living with employer
		Heads of families	Living with—					
			Father	Mother	Husband	Other relative		
CINCINNATI, OHIO								
Number								
All classes [1]	50,231	8,852	14,074	7,206	5,077	5,500	4,121	5,401
Single (including unknown)	33,735	2,648	13,186	6,475	--------	4,326	2,651	4,449
Married	8,403	1,152	461	304	5,077	314	770	325
Widowed or divorced	8,093	5,052	427	427	--------	860	700	627
Native white—Native parentage	23,522	3,174	8,317	3,769	1,664	2,300	2,229	2,069
Single (including unknown)	17,321	922	7,823	3,408	--------	1,874	1,530	1,764
Married	3,072	430	250	153	1,664	123	350	102
Widowed or divorced	3,129	1,822	244	208	--------	303	349	203
Native white—Foreign or mixed parentage	16,809	3,125	4,836	2,948	866	2,434	811	1,789
Single (including unknown)	12,736	1,228	4,584	2,728	--------	2,043	611	1,542
Married	1,499	257	112	67	866	77	59	61
Widowed or divorced	2,574	1,640	140	153	--------	314	141	186
Foreign-born white	3,996	1,032	543	177	647	318	229	1,050
Single (including unknown)	2,108	210	508	150	--------	212	168	860
Married	882	121	12	9	647	27	15	51
Widowed or divorced	1,006	701	23	18	--------	79	46	139
Negro	5,896	1,519	378	311	1,898	448	849	493
Single (including unknown)	1,566	287	271	188	--------	197	340	283
Married	2,947	343	87	75	1,898	87	346	111
Widowed or divorced	1,383	889	20	48	--------	164	163	99
Per cent								
All classes	100.0	17.6	28.0	14.3	10.1	10.9	8.2	10.8
Single (including unknown)	100.0	7.8	39.1	19.2	--------	12.8	7.9	13.2
Married	100.0	13.7	5.5	3.6	60.4	3.7	9.2	3.9
Widowed or divorced	100.0	62.4	5.3	5.3	--------	10.6	8.6	7.7
Native white—Native parentage	100.0	13.5	35.4	16.0	7.1	9.8	9.5	8.8
Single (including unknown)	100.0	5.3	45.2	19.7	--------	10.8	8.8	10.2
Married	100.0	14.0	8.1	5.0	54.2	4.0	11.4	3.3
Widowed or divorced	100.0	58.2	7.8	6.6	--------	9.7	11.2	6.5
Native white—Foreign or mixed parentage	100.0	18.6	28.8	17.5	5.2	14.5	4.8	10.6
Single (including unknown)	100.0	9.6	36.0	21.4	--------	16.1	4.8	12.1
Married	100.0	17.1	7.5	4.5	57.8	5.1	3.9	4.1
Widowed or divorced	100.0	63.7	5.4	5.9	--------	12.2	5.5	7.2
Foreign-born white	100.0	25.8	13.6	4.4	16.2	8.0	5.7	26.3
Single (including unknown)	100.0	10.0	24.1	7.1	--------	10.1	8.0	40.8
Married	100.0	13.7	1.4	1.0	73.4	3.1	1.7	5.8
Widowed or divorced	100.0	69.7	2.3	1.8	--------	7.9	4.6	13.8
Negro	100.0	25.8	6.4	5.3	32.2	7.6	14.4	8.4
Single (including unknown)	100.0	18.3	17.3	12.0	--------	12.6	21.7	18.1
Married	100.0	11.6	3.0	2.5	64.4	3.0	11.7	3.8
Widowed or divorced	100.0	64.3	1.4	3.5	--------	11.9	11.8	7.2

[1] Includes Indians, Chinese, and Japanese.

TABLE 168.—FAMILY RELATIONSHIP OF GAINFULLY OCCUPIED WOMEN, BY RACE, NATIVITY, AND MARITAL CONDITION, FOR 11 SELECTED CITIES: 1920—Con.

RACE AND NATIVITY AND MARITAL CONDITION	GAINFULLY EMPLOYED WOMEN 16 YEARS OF AGE AND OVER							
		Living at home					Board-ing or lodg-ing	Liv-ing with em-ploy-er
	Total	Heads of fami-lies	Living with—					
			Father	Mother	Hus-band	Other rela-tive		
INDIANAPOLIS, IND.								
Number								
All classes [1]	35,454	5,557	9,009	3,511	5,526	4,021	5,442	2,388
Single (including unknown)	19,511	1,235	7,769	2,857	------	2,664	3,368	1,618
Married	8,876	689	785	323	5,526	382	938	233
Widowed or divorced	7,067	3,633	455	331	------	975	1,136	537
Native white—Native parentage	23,350	3,188	6,740	2,311	3,247	2,582	3,877	1,405
Single (including unknown)	13,805	741	5,823	1,886	------	1,798	2,579	978
Married	5,307	378	573	213	3,247	227	562	107
Widowed or divorced	4,238	2,069	344	212	------	557	736	320
Native white—Foreign or mixed parentage	5,087	706	1,587	754	432	731	478	399
Single (including unknown)	3,600	253	1,455	681	------	567	336	308
Married	708	62	86	29	432	36	42	21
Widowed or divorced	779	391	46	44	------	128	100	70
Foreign-born white	1,135	225	163	54	213	115	133	232
Single (including unknown)	576	45	138	48	------	69	91	185
Married	287	28	11	4	213	11	10	10
Widowed or divorced	272	152	14	2	------	35	32	37
Negro	5,877	1,437	518	392	1,632	593	953	352
Single (including unknown)	1,527	195	352	242	------	230	361	147
Married	2,572	221	115	77	1,632	108	324	95
Widowed or divorced	1,778	1,021	51	73	------	255	268	110
Per cent								
All classes	100.0	15.7	25.4	9.9	15.6	11.3	15.3	6.7
Single (including unknown)	100.0	6.3	39.8	14.6	------	13.7	17.3	8.3
Married	100.0	7.8	8.8	3.6	62.3	4.3	10.6	2.6
Widowed or divorced	100.0	51.4	6.4	4.7	------	13.8	16.1	7.6
Native white—Native parentage	100.0	13.7	28.9	9.9	13.9	11.1	16.6	6.0
Single (including unknown)	100.0	5.4	42.2	13.7	------	13.0	18.7	7.1
Married	100.0	7.1	10.8	4.0	61.2	4.3	10.6	2.0
Widowed or divorced	100.0	48.8	8.1	5.0	------	13.1	17.4	7.6
Native white—Foreign or mixed parentage	100.0	13.9	31.2	14.8	8.5	14.4	9.4	7.8
Single (including unknown)	100.0	7.0	40.4	18.9	------	15.8	9.3	8.6
Married	100.0	8.8	12.1	4.1	61.0	5.1	5.9	3.0
Widowed or divorced	100.0	50.2	5.9	5.6	------	16.4	12.8	9.0
Foreign-born white	100.0	19.8	14.4	4.8	18.8	10.1	11.7	20.4
Single (including unknown)	100.0	7.8	24.0	8.3	------	12.0	15.8	32.1
Married	100.0	9.8	3.8	1.4	74.2	3.8	3.5	3.5
Widowed or divorced	100.0	55.9	5.1	0.7	------	12.9	11.8	13.6
Negro	100.0	24.5	8.8	6.7	27.8	10.1	16.2	6.0
Single (including unknown)	100.0	12.8	23.1	15.8	------	15.1	23.6	9.6
Married	100.0	8.6	4.5	3.0	63.5	4.2	12.6	3.7
Widowed or divorced	100.0	57.4	2.9	4.1	------	14.3	15.1	6.2

[1] Includes Chinese.

TABLE **168.**—FAMILY RELATIONSHIP OF GAINFULLY OCCUPIED WOMEN, BY RACE, NATIVITY, AND MARITAL CONDITION, FOR 11 SELECTED CITIES: 1920—Con.

RACE AND NATIVITY AND MARITAL CONDITION	GAINFULLY EMPLOYED WOMEN 16 YEARS OF AGE AND OVER							
		Living at home					Board-ing or lodg-ing	Liv-ing with em-ploy er
	Total	Heads of fami-lies	Living with—					
			Father	Mother	Hus-band	Other rela-tive		
ST. PAUL, MINN.								
Number								
All classes [1]	27,863	2,765	8,908	3,418	2,310	2,750	4,625	3,087
Single (including unknown)	21,223	857	8,450	3,159		2,334	3,677	2,746
Married	3,699	327	273	121	2,310	139	432	97
Widowed or divorced	2,941	1,581	185	138		277	516	244
Native white—Native parentage	7,972	682	2,470	1,074	662	761	1,720	603
Single (including unknown)	6,057	238	2,315	981		658	1,334	531
Married	1,129	79	93	43	662	34	197	21
Widowed or divorced	786	365	62	50		69	189	51
Native white—Foreign or mixed parentage	15,244	1,183	5,675	2,085	868	1,556	2,284	1,593
Single (including unknown)	12,638	457	5,436	1,966		1,379	1,933	1,467
Married	1,475	131	146	59	868	67	166	38
Widowed or divorced	1,131	595	93	60		110	185	88
Foreign-born white	4,165	803	716	229	628	385	541	863
Single (including unknown)	2,400	155	666	191		277	379	732
Married	883	102	27	16	628	30	48	32
Widowed or divorced	882	546	23	22		78	114	99
Negro	476	97	46	30	150	47	80	26
Single (including unknown)	125	7	32	21		20	31	14
Married	209	15	7	3	150	7	21	6
Widowed or divorced	142	75	7	6		20	28	6
Per cent								
All classes	100.0	9.9	32.0	12.3	8.3	9.9	16.6	11.1
Single (including unknown)	100.0	4.0	39.8	14.9		11.0	17.3	12.9
Married	100.0	8.8	7.4	3.3	62.4	3.8	11.7	2.6
Widowed or divorced	100.0	53.8	6.3	4.7		9.4	17.5	8.3
Native white—Native parentage	100.0	8.6	31.0	13.5	8.3	9.5	21.6	7.6
Single (including unknown)	100.0	3.9	38.2	16.2		10.9	22.0	8.8
Married	100.0	7.0	8.2	3.8	58.6	3.0	17.4	1.9
Widowed or divorced	100.0	46.4	7.9	6.4		8.8	24.0	6.5
Native white—Foreign or mixed parentage	100.0	7.8	37.2	13.7	5.7	10.2	15.0	10.5
Single (including unknown)	100.0	3.6	43.0	15.6		10.9	15.3	11.6
Married	100.0	8.9	9.9	4.0	58.8	4.5	11.3	2.6
Widowed or divorced	100.0	52.6	8.2	5.3		9.7	16.4	7.8
Foreign-born white	100.0	19.3	17.2	5.5	15.1	9.2	13.0	20.7
Single (including unknown)	100.0	6.5	27.8	8.0		11.5	15.8	30.5
Married	100.0	11.6	3.1	1.8	71.1	3.4	5.4	3.6
Widowed or divorced	100.0	61.9	2.6	2.5		8.8	12.9	11.2
Negro	100.0	20.4	9.7	6.3	31.5	9.9	16.8	5.5
Single (including unknown)	100.0	5.6	25.6	16.8		16.0	24.8	11.2
Married	100.0	7.2	3.3	1.4	71.8	3.3	10.0	2.9
Widowed or divorced	100.0	52.8	4.9	4.2		14.1	19.7	4.2

[1] Includes Indians and Japanese.

TABLE **168.**—FAMILY RELATIONSHIP OF GAINFULLY OCCUPIED WOMEN, BY RACE, NATIVITY, AND MARITAL CONDITION, FOR 11 SELECTED CITIES: 1920—Con.

	GAINFULLY EMPLOYED WOMEN 16 YEARS OF AGE AND OVER							
RACE AND NATIVITY AND MARITAL CONDITION	Total	Living at home					Board-ing or lodg-ing	Liv-ing with em-ploy-er
		Heads of fami-lies	Living with—					
			Father	Mother	Hus-band	Other rela-tive		
KANSAS CITY, MO.								
Number								
All classes [1]	39,925	5,824	7,704	3,671	6,279	3,766	9,442	3,239
Single (including unknown)	21,389	1,267	6,712	3,009		2,540	5,666	2,195
Married	10,347	760	556	292	6,279	364	1,723	373
Widowed or divorced	8,189	3,797	436	370		862	2,053	671
Native white—Native parentage	24,743	3,111	5,268	2,432	3,667	2,422	6,453	1,390
Single (including unknown)	13,896	716	4,540	2,007		1,645	4,039	949
Married	6,099	391	410	191	3,667	238	1,084	118
Widowed or divorced	4,748	2,004	318	234		539	1,330	323
Native white—Foreign or mixed parentage	6,842	817	1,847	842	690	779	1,190	677
Single (including unknown)	4,661	246	1,705	756		614	787	553
Married	1,135	84	71	37	690	41	176	36
Widowed or divorced	1,046	487	71	49		124	227	88
Foreign-born white	1,977	346	297	78	325	146	314	471
Single (including unknown)	1,060	71	270	63		101	188	367
Married	470	42	11	9	325	10	45	28
Widowed or divorced	447	233	16	6		35	81	76
Negro	6,357	1,549	292	319	1,595	419	1,484	699
Single (including unknown)	1,771	234	197	183		180	652	325
Married	2,639	242	64	55	1,595	75	418	190
Widowed or divorced	1,947	1,073	31	81		164	414	184
Per cent								
All classes	100.0	14.6	19.3	9.2	15.7	9.4	23.6	8.1
Single (including unknown)	100.0	5.9	31.4	14.1		11.9	26.5	10.3
Married	100.0	7.4	5.4	2.8	60.7	3.5	16.7	3.6
Widowed or divorced	100.0	46.4	5.3	4.5		10.5	25.1	8.2
Native white—Native parentage	100.0	12.6	21.3	9.8	14.8	9.8	26.1	5.6
Single (including unknown)	100.0	5.2	32.7	14.4		11.8	29.1	6.8
Married	100.0	6.4	6.7	3.1	60.1	3.9	17.8	1.9
Widowed or divorced	100.0	42.2	6.7	4.9		11.4	28.0	6.8
Native white—Foreign or mixed parentage	100.0	11.9	27.0	12.3	10.1	11.4	17.4	9.9
Single (including unknown)	100.0	5.3	36.6	16.2		13.2	16.9	11.9
Married	100.0	7.4	6.3	3.3	60.8	3.6	15.5	3.2
Widowed or divorced	100.0	46.6	6.8	4.7		11.9	21.7	8.4
Foreign-born white	100.0	17.5	15.0	3.9	16.4	7.4	15.9	23.8
Single (including unknown)	100.0	6.7	25.5	5.9		9.5	17.7	34.6
Married	100.0	8.9	2.3	1.9	69.1	2.1	9.6	6.0
Widowed or divorced	100.0	52.1	3.6	1.3		7.8	18.1	17.0
Negro	100.0	24.4	4.6	5.0	25.1	6.6	23.3	11.0
Single (including unknown)	100.0	13.2	11.1	10.3		10.2	36.8	18.4
Married	100.0	9.2	2.4	2.1	60.4	2.8	15.8	7.2
Widowed or divorced	100.0	55.1	1.6	4.2		8.4	21.3	9.5

[1] Includes Indians.

TABLE **168.**—FAMILY RELATIONSHIP OF GAINFULLY OCCUPIED WOMEN, BY RACE, NATIVITY, AND MARITAL CONDITION, FOR 11 SELECTED CITIES: 1920—Con.

RACE AND NATIVITY AND MARITAL CONDITION	Total	GAINFULLY EMPLOYED WOMEN 16 YEARS OF AGE AND OVER					Board-ing or lodg-ing	Liv-ing with em-ploy-er
		Living at home						
		Heads of fami-lies	Living with—					
			Father	Mother	Hus-band	Other rela-tive		
ATLANTA, GA.								
Number								
All classes [1]	31,553	6,677	4,380	3,064	7,130	3,241	5,324	1,737
Single (including unknown)	12,659	968	3,628	2,193		1,920	3,134	816
Married	11,112	1,084	468	472	7,130	353	1,151	454
Widowed or divorced	7,782	4,625	284	399		968	1,039	467
Native white—Native parentage	14,051	1,741	3,080	1,761	1,793	1,658	3,490	528
Single (including unknown)	8,344	392	2,648	1,387		1,223	2,346	348
Married	3,278	225	254	207	1,793	129	608	62
Widowed or divorced	2,429	1,124	178	167		306	536	118
Native white—Foreign or mixed parentage	778	94	248	113	60	103	133	27
Single (including unknown)	543	30	232	101		80	78	22
Married	117	10	11	3	60	8	25	
Widowed or divorced	118	54	5	9		15	30	5
Foreign-born white	344	47	93	19	53	31	67	34
Single (including unknown)	183	6	88	16		18	29	26
Married	84	9	1	1	53	3	15	2
Widowed or divorced	77	32	4	2		10	23	6
Negro	16,377	4,795	959	1,171	5,224	1,449	1,634	1,145
Single (including unknown)	3,588	540	660	689		599	681	419
Married	7,633	840	202	261	5,224	213	503	390
Widowed or divorced	5,156	3,415	97	221		637	450	336
Per cent [2]								
All classes	100.0	21.2	13.9	9.7	22.6	10.3	16.9	5.5
Single (including unknown)	100.0	7.6	28.7	17.3		15.2	24.8	6.4
Married	100.0	9.8	4.2	4.2	64.2	3.2	10.4	4.1
Widowed or divorced	100.0	59.4	3.6	5.1		12.4	13.4	6.0
Native white—Native parentage	100.0	12.4	21.9	12.5	12.8	11.8	24.8	3.8
Single (including unknown)	100.0	4.7	31.7	16.6		14.7	28.1	4.2
Married	100.0	6.9	7.7	6.3	54.7	3.9	18.5	1.9
Widowed or divorced	100.0	46.3	7.3	6.9		12.6	22.1	4.9
Native white—Foreign or mixed parentage	100.0	12.1	31.9	14.5	7.7	13.2	17.1	3.5
Single (including unknown)	100.0	5.5	42.7	18.6		14.7	14.4	4.1
Married	100.0	8.5	9.4	2.6	51.3	6.8	21.4	
Widowed or divorced	100.0	45.8	4.2	7.6		12.7	25.4	4.2
Foreign-born white	100.0	13.7	27.0	5.5	15.4	9.0	19.5	9.9
Single (including unknown)	100.0	3.3	48.1	8.7		9.8	15.8	14.2
Married								
Widowed or divorced								
Negro	100.0	29.3	5.9	7.2	31.9	8.8	10.0	7.0
Single (including unknown)	100.0	15.1	18.4	19.2		16.7	19.0	11.7
Married	100.0	11.0	2.6	3.4	68.4	2.8	6.6	5.1
Widowed or divorced	100.0	66.2	1.9	4.3		12.4	8.7	6.5

[1] Includes Indians.　　[2] Per cent not shown where base is less than 100.

TABLE 168.—FAMILY RELATIONSHIP OF GAINFULLY OCCUPIED WOMEN, BY RACE, NATIVITY, AND MARITAL CONDITION, FOR 11 SELECTED CITIES: 1920—Con.

RACE AND NATIVITY AND MARITAL CONDITION	GAINFULLY EMPLOYED WOMEN 16 YEARS OF AGE AND OVER							
	Total	Living at home					Board-ing or lodg-ing	Liv-ing with em-ploy-er
		Heads of fami-lies	Living with—					
			Father	Mother	Hus-band	Other rela-tive		
LOUISVILLE, KY.								
Number								
All classes [1]	33,655	6,469	7,505	4,185	5,144	3,882	4,118	2,352
Single (including unknown)	18,429	1,542	6,656	3,483		2,609	2,376	1,763
Married	8,078	865	447	306	5,144	342	809	165
Widowed or divorced	7,148	4,062	402	396		931	933	424
Native white—Native parentage	15,623	2,032	4,953	2,264	1,350	1,810	2,005	1,209
Single (including unknown)	10,646	512	4,477	1,979		1,387	1,311	980
Married	2,385	224	233	109	1,350	111	292	66
Widowed or divorced	2,592	1,296	243	176		312	402	163
Native white—Foreign or mixed parentage	5,927	937	1,692	1,121	321	1,005	380	471
Single (including unknown)	4,403	330	1,580	1,016		809	272	396
Married	547	66	51	34	321	29	35	11
Widowed or divorced	977	541	61	71		167	73	64
Foreign-born white	935	252	129	35	125	97	86	211
Single (including unknown)	486	48	119	30		58	58	173
Married	174	21	3	2	125	7	7	9
Widowed or divorced	275	183	7	3		32	21	29
Negro	11,161	3,246	731	762	3,346	970	1,645	461
Single (including unknown)	2,891	652	480	456		355	734	214
Married	4,969	554	160	161	3,346	195	474	79
Widowed or divorced	3,301	2,040	91	145		420	437	168
Per cent								
All classes	100.0	19.2	22.3	12.4	15.3	11.5	12.4	7.0
Single (including unknown)	100.0	8.4	36.1	18.9		14.2	12.9	9.6
Married	100.0	10.7	5.5	3.8	63.7	4.2	10.0	2.0
Widowed or divorced	100.0	56.8	5.6	5.5		13.0	13.1	5.9
Native white—Native parentage	100.0	13.0	31.7	14.5	8.6	11.6	12.8	7.7
Single (including unknown)	100.0	4.8	42.1	18.6		13.0	12.3	9.2
Married	100.0	9.4	9.8	4.6	56.6	4.7	12.2	2.8
Widowed or divorced	100.0	50.0	9.4	6.8		12.0	15.5	6.3
Native white—Foreign or mixed parentage	100.0	15.8	28.5	18.9	5.4	17.0	6.4	7.9
Single (including unknown)	100.0	7.5	35.9	23.1		18.4	6.2	9.0
Married	100.0	12.1	9.3	6.2	58.7	5.3	6.4	2.0
Widowed or divorced	100.0	55.4	6.2	7.3		17.1	7.5	6.6
Foreign-born white	100.0	27.0	13.8	3.7	13.4	10.4	9.2	22.6
Single (including unknown)	100.0	9.9	24.5	6.2		11.9	11.9	35.6
Married	100.0	12.1	1.7	1.1	71.8	4.0	4.0	5.2
Widowed or divorced	100.0	66.5	2.5	1.1		11.6	7.6	10.5
Negro	100.0	29.1	6.5	6.8	30.0	8.7	14.7	4.1
Single (including unknown)	100.0	22.6	16.6	15.8		12.3	25.4	7.4
Married	100.0	11.1	3.2	3.2	67.3	3.9	9.5	1.6
Widowed or divorced	100.0	61.8	2.8	4.4		12.7	13.2	5.1

[1] Includes Indians.

TABLE 168.—FAMILY RELATIONSHIP OF GAINFULLY OCCUPIED WOMEN, BY RACE, NATIVITY, AND MARITAL CONDITION, FOR 11 SELECTED CITIES: 1920—Con.

RACE AND NATIVITY AND MARITAL CONDITION	GAINFULLY EMPLOYED WOMEN 16 YEARS OF AGE AND OVER							
		Living at home					Board-ing or lodg-ing	Liv-ing with em-ploy-er
	Total	Heads of fami-lies	Living with—					
			Father	Mother	Hus-band	Other rela-tive		
NEW ORLEANS, LA.								
Number								
All classes [1]	48,358	9,149	9,126	6,028	7,013	7,340	6,426	3,276
Single (including unknown)	25,282	1,754	8,168	4,939	------	4,802	3,307	2,312
Married	12,375	1,504	595	544	7,013	785	1,573	361
Widowed or divorced	10,701	5,891	363	545	------	1,753	1,546	603
Native white—Native parentage	17,990	2,014	5,794	3,249	872	3,021	2,093	947
Single (including unknown)	13,322	507	5,401	2,895	------	2,433	1,336	750
Married	1,996	265	204	139	872	142	306	68
Widowed or divorced	2,672	1,242	189	215	------	446	451	129
Native white—Foreign or mixed parentage	6,763	1,390	1,431	1,097	416	1,323	554	552
Single (including unknown)	4,374	369	1,322	919	------	999	320	445
Married	802	123	57	57	416	60	65	24
Widowed or divorced	1,587	898	52	121	------	264	169	83
Foreign-born white	1,791	422	188	92	284	153	163	489
Single (including unknown)	900	69	169	78	------	80	84	420
Married	397	42	5	5	284	10	29	22
Widowed or divorced	494	311	14	9	------	63	50	47
Negro	21,803	5,321	1,713	1,589	5,439	2,842	3,616	1,283
Single (including unknown)	6,680	808	1,276	1,046	------	1,290	1,567	693
Married	9,178	1,074	329	343	5,439	573	1,173	247
Widowed or divorced	5,945	3,439	108	200	------	979	876	343
Per cent								
All classes	100.0	18.9	18.9	12.5	14.5	15.2	13.3	6.8
Single (including unknown)	100.0	6.9	32.3	19.5	------	19.0	13.1	9.1
Married	100.0	12.2	4.8	4.4	56.7	6.3	12.7	2.9
Widowed or divorced	100.0	55.1	3.4	5.1	------	16.4	14.4	5.6
Native white—Native parentage	100.0	11.2	32.2	18.1	4.8	16.8	11.6	5.3
Single (including unknown)	100.0	3.8	40.5	21.7	------	18.3	10.0	5.6
Married	100.0	13.3	10.2	7.0	43.7	7.1	15.3	3.4
Widowed or divorced	100.0	46.5	7.1	8.0	------	16.7	16.9	4.8
Native white—Foreign or mixed parentage	100.0	20.6	21.2	16.2	6.2	19.6	8.2	8.2
Single (including unknown)	100.0	8.4	30.2	21.0	------	22.8	7.3	10.2
Married	100.0	15.3	7.1	7.1	51.9	7.5	8.1	3.0
Widowed or divorced	100.0	56.6	3.3	7.6	------	16.6	10.6	5.2
Foreign-born white	100.0	23.6	10.5	5.1	15.9	8.5	9.1	27.3
Single (including unknown)	100.0	7.7	18.8	8.7	------	8.9	9.3	46.7
Married	100.0	10.6	1.3	1.3	71.5	2.5	7.3	5.5
Widowed or divorced	100.0	63.0	2.8	1.8	------	12.8	10.1	9.5
Negro	100.0	24.4	7.9	7.3	24.9	13.0	16.6	5.9
Single (including unknown)	100.0	12.1	19.1	15.7	------	19.3	23.5	10.4
Married	100.0	11.7	3.6	3.7	59.3	6.2	12.8	2.7
Widowed or divorced	100.0	57.8	1.8	3.4	------	16.5	14.7	5.8

[1] Includes Indians, Chinese, Japanese, and other races.

TABLE 169.—FAMILY RELATIONSHIP OF GAINFULLY EMPLOYED WOMEN, BY SPECIFIED OCCUPATIONS, FOR THE 11 SELECTED CITIES COMBINED: 1920

OCCUPATION	Total	GAINFULLY EMPLOYED WOMEN 16 YEARS OF AGE AND OVER							
		Living at home						Boarding or lodging	Living with employer
		Total	Heads of families	Living with—					
				Father	Mother	Husband	Other relative		
All occupations	373,204	293,213	56,659	96,281	44,360	53,411	42,502	50,297	29,694
Actresses and showwomen [1]	452	232	25	79	44	62	22	220	
Agents [2]	467	369	80	126	58	47	58	91	7
Artists, sculptors, and teachers of art [2]	622	514	76	195	87	80	76	100	8
Attendants and helpers (professional service) [3]	771	642	53	266	169	59	95	126	3
Barbers, hairdressers, and manicurists [4]	2,480	2,050	504	308	229	753	256	425	5
Boarding and lodging house keepers	5,944	5,870	4,343	23	41	1,388	75	57	17
Bookkeepers, accountants, and cashiers	18,366	15,735	1,029	7,912	3,556	1,031	2,207	2,582	49
Charwomen and cleaners [3]	1,139	1,017	501	41	51	325	99	99	23
Clerks (except clerks in stores)	23,702	20,343	1,300	10,479	4,392	1,288	2,884	3,289	70
Compositors, linotypers, and typesetters [1]	335	274	34	103	49	47	41	61	
Dressmakers and seamstresses (not in factory)	11,982	9,976	3,720	1,255	1,055	2,096	1,850	1,531	475
Elevator tenders [5]	289	226	35	64	36	51	40	58	5
Forewomen and overseers (manufacturing) [6]	1,759	1,567	224	460	344	210	329	190	2
Housekeepers and stewardesses	6,874	3,164	1,289	275	167	506	927	846	2,864
Janitors and sextons [3]	1,330	1,220	587	44	49	431	109	81	29
Laborers (manufacturing) (n. o. s.[7])	5,813	4,799	951	1,454	568	1,111	715	1,000	14
Laborers, porters, and helpers in stores [1]	361	318	48	75	41	106	48	40	3
Laborers, steam and street railroad [8]	449	407	167	36	27	128	49	42	
Laundresses (not in laundry)	24,763	22,093	9,325	727	915	9,179	1,947	2,296	374
Laundry operatives	5,654	4,598	1,260	803	554	1,258	723	930	126
Librarians [3]	485	395	42	180	92	14	67	87	3
Manufacturers, officials, and managers [3]	667	583	184	115	68	119	97	82	2
Messenger, bundle, and office girls [8]	555	511	16	329	90	17	59	43	1
Midwives and nurses (not trained)	5,949	3,354	1,050	437	321	591	955	1,309	1,286
Milliners and millinery dealers	3,331	2,680	370	911	527	358	514	649	2
Musicians and teachers of music	2,933	2,552	406	988	400	442	316	336	45
Religious, charity, and welfare workers [6]	1,510	737	214	195	100	129	99	275	498
Restaurant, café, and lunch room keepers [8]	745	659	288	32	37	239	63	82	4
Retail dealers	4,026	3,791	1,535	341	231	1,343	341	210	25
Saleswomen and clerks in stores	25,266	21,394	2,292	8,760	3,652	3,284	3,406	3,848	24
Semiskilled operatives (manufacturing) (n. o. s.[7])	82,128	73,473	9,681	27,961	11,404	14,059	10,368	8,614	41
Servants	45,582	22,459	7,528	2,293	2,211	6,515	3,912	6,661	16,462
Stenographers and typists	31,942	27,009	1,087	15,234	6,012	1,124	3,552	4,900	33
Tailoresses [4]	5,250	4,731	875	1,284	682	1,103	787	514	5
Teachers (school)	16,361	11,384	1,550	4,634	2,408	706	2,086	2,172	2,805
Telegraph operators [2]	1,056	847	51	427	171	75	123	208	1
Telephone operators	7,966	6,655	290	3,559	1,537	282	987	1,273	38
Trained nurses	6,833	2,041	464	582	309	221	465	1,290	3,502
Waitresses	5,127	2,702	723	454	348	774	403	1,932	493
All other occupations	11,940	9,842	2,462	2,840	1,328	1,860	1,352	1,748	350

[1] Includes only 5 cities.
[2] Includes only 7 cities.
[3] Includes only 8 cities.
[4] Includes only 9 cities.
[5] Includes only 4 cities.
[6] Includes only 10 cities.
[7] Not otherwise specified.
[8] Includes only 6 cities.

TABLE 170.—FAMILY RELATIONSHIP OF GAINFULLY EMPLOYED WOMEN, BY MARITAL CONDITION AND SPECIFIED OCCUPATION, FOR 11 SELECTED CITIES: 1920

OCCUPATION AND MARITAL CONDITION	GAINFULLY EMPLOYED WOMEN 16 YEARS OF AGE AND OVER							
			Living at home					
				Living with—				
	Total	Heads of families	Father	Mother	Husband	Other relative	Boarding or lodging	Living with employer
FALL RIVER, MASS.								
ALL CLASSES								
All occupations	19,111	1,881	7,063	2,298	4,022	1,928	921	998
Boarding and lodging house keepers	57	36	1	----	20	----	----	----
Bookkeepers, cashiers, and accountants	475	12	306	72	19	52	12	2
Clerks (except clerks in stores)	278	6	173	55	18	19	7	----
Clerks in stores	196	6	102	40	26	14	7	1
Dressmakers and seamstresses (not in factory)	195	60	29	22	32	29	8	15
Housekeepers and stewardesses	318	44	17	12	19	66	26	134
Laborers (manufacturing) (n. o. s.¹)	87	9	28	1	33	13	2	----
Cotton mills	63	8	18	----	25	11	1	----
All other industries	24	1	11	1	8	2	1	----
Laundresses (not in laundry)	64	35	1	6	12	4	2	4
Laundry operatives	70	12	20	6	6	11	11	4
Midwives and nurses (not trained)	118	17	26	11	11	19	14	20
Milliners and millinery dealers	83	7	25	26	10	14	1	----
Musicians and teachers of music	54	6	27	6	7	6	1	1
Retail dealers	103	45	4	2	39	12	1	----
Saleswomen (stores)	505	29	236	94	65	65	15	1
Semiskilled operatives (manufacturing) (n. o. s.¹)	13,832	1,325	5,170	1,628	3,597	1,378	733	1
Clothing industries—								
Hat factories (felt)	178	5	68	21	61	15	8	----
Shirt, collar, and cuff factories	53	2	36	2	7	6	----	----
All other clothing factories	116	12	41	16	22	17	8	----
Iron and steel industries	50	4	26	9	4	6	1	----
Textile industries—								
Cotton mills	12,562	1,254	4,538	1,437	3,417	1,244	672	----
Rope and cordage factories	50	2	29	7	5	5	2	----
Textile dyeing, finishing, and printing mills	288	10	165	60	20	24	9	----
All other textile mills	252	13	123	42	28	29	17	----
All other industries	283	23	144	34	33	32	16	1
Servants	653	90	24	25	39	33	24	418
Stenographers and typists	437	4	319	74	9	26	5	----
Teachers (school)	893	66	338	134	4	108	24	219
Telephone operators	114	3	61	30	5	10	5	----
Trained nurses	241	8	57	7	1	12	10	146
All other occupations	338	61	98	47	50	37	13	32
SINGLE (INCLUDING UNKNOWN)								
All occupations	12,142	612	6,551	1,999	----	1,534	606	840
Boarding and lodging house keepers	5	4	1	----	----	----	----	----
Bookkeepers, cashiers, and accountants	435	9	296	66	----	50	12	2
Clerks (except clerks in stores)	251	5	165	55	----	19	7	----
Clerks in stores	148	----	94	36	----	12	5	1
Dressmakers and seamstresses (not in factory)	114	20	28	20	----	25	7	14
Housekeepers and stewardesses	151	14	16	10	----	39	6	66
Laborers (manufacturing) (n. o. s.¹)	34	----	26	1	----	6	1	----
Cotton mills	20	----	15	----	----	5	----	----
All other industries	14	----	11	1	----	1	1	----
Laundresses (not in laundry)	10	2	1	1	----	3	----	3
Laundry operatives	49	4	19	6	----	8	8	4
Midwives and nurses (not trained)	74	5	21	10	----	13	8	17
Milliners and millinery dealers	65	3	24	24	----	13	1	----
Musicians and teachers of music	42	5	24	5	----	6	1	1
Retail dealers	20	8	3	----	----	8	1	----
Saleswomen (stores)	390	13	222	85	----	58	11	1

¹ Not otherwise specified.

TABLE 170.—FAMILY RELATIONSHIP OF GAINFULLY EMPLOYED WOMEN, BY MARITAL CONDITION AND SPECIFIED OCCUPATION, FOR 11 SELECTED CITIES: 1920—Continued

OCCUPATION AND MARITAL CONDITION	Total	Heads of families	Living at home — Living with—				Boarding or lodging	Living with employer
			Father	Mother	Husband	Other relative		

FALL RIVER, MASS.—Continued

OCCUPATION AND MARITAL CONDITION	Total	Heads of families	Father	Mother	Husband	Other relative	Boarding or lodging	Living with employer
SINGLE (INCLUDING UNKNOWN)—continued								
Semiskilled operatives (manufacturing) (n. o. s.[1])	8,096	415	4,743	1,389	------	1,070	478	1
Clothing industries—								
Hat factories (felt)	101	------	65	20	------	9	7	------
Shirt, collar, and cuff factories	40	------	33	2	------	5	------	------
All other clothing factories	77	2	40	15	------	15	5	------
Iron and steel industries	45	3	26	9	------	6	1	------
Textile industries—								
Cotton mills	7,140	396	4,135	1,210	------	962	437	------
Rope and cordage factories	38	------	27	7	------	3	1	------
Textile dyeing, finishing, and printing mills	246	1	161	55	------	21	8	------
All other textile mills	190	3	118	39	------	21	9	------
All other industries	219	10	138	32	------	28	10	1
Servants	438	21	21	19	------	24	8	345
Stenographers and typists	407	2	310	67	------	23	5	------
Teachers (school)	873	57	334	132	------	108	23	219
Telephone operators	102	1	60	27	------	9	5	------
Trained nurses	219	4	53	7	------	10	10	135
All other occupations	219	20	90	39	------	30	9	31
MARRIED								
All occupations	5,489	363	427	231	4,022	193	203	50
Boarding and lodging house keepers	23.	3.	------	------	20	------	------	------
Bookkeepers, cashiers, and accountants	30	1	5	4	19	1	------	------
Clerks (except clerks in stores)	23	------	5	------	18	------	------	------
Clerks in stores	42	3	7	3	26	2	1	------
Dressmakers and seamstresses (not in factory)	46	11	------	2	32	1	------	------
Housekeepers and stewardesses	55	5	1	1	19	6	5	18
Laborers (manufacturing) (n. o. s.[1])	41	1	3	------	33	4	------	------
Cotton mills	33	1	3	------	25	4	------	------
All other industries	8	------	------	------	8	------	------	------
Laundresses (not in laundry)	23	7	------	4	12	------	------	------
Laundry operatives	9	------	------	------	6	2	1	------
Midwives and nurses (not trained)	16	2	------	------	11	------	2	1
Milliners and millinery dealers	14	1	1	1	10	1	------	------
Musicians and teachers of music	11	1	2	1	7	------	------	------
Retail dealers	45	4	------	1	39	1	------	------
Saleswomen (stores)	89	4	10	5	65	4	1	------
Semiskilled operatives (manufacturing) (n. o. s.[1])	4,794	288	369	193	3,597	161	186	------
Clothing industries—								
Hat factories (felt)	70	1	2	1	61	4	1	------
Shirt, collar, and cuff factories	11	1	2	------	7	1	------	------
All other clothing factories	29	3	------	------	22	1	3	------
Iron and steel industries	4	------	------	------	4	------	------	------
Textile industries—								
Cotton mills	4,544	271	353	182	3,417	149	172	------
Rope and cordage factories	8	1	2	------	5	------	------	------
Textile dyeing, finishing, and printing mills	33	3	3	5	20	2	------	------
All other textile mills	45	4	3	3	28	2	5	------
All other industries	50	4	4	2	33	2	5	------
Servants	92	13	3	3	39	5	6	23
Stenographers and typists	24	------	9	4	9	2	------	------
Teachers (school)	12	5	2	1	4	------	------	------
Telephone operators	10	1	1	3	5	------	------	------
Trained nurses	12	1	3	------	1	------	------	7
All other occupations	78	12	6	5	50	3	1	1
WIDOWED OR DIVORCED								
All occupations	1,480	906	85	68	4	201	112	108
Boarding and lodging house keepers	29	29	------	------	------	------	------	------
Bookkeepers, cashiers, and accountants	10	2	5	2	------	1	------	------
Clerks (except clerks in stores)	4	1	3	------	------	------	------	------

[1] Not otherwise specified.

TABLE 170.—FAMILY RELATIONSHIP OF GAINFULLY EMPLOYED WOMEN, BY MARITAL CONDITION AND SPECIFIED OCCUPATION, FOR 11 SELECTED CITIES: 1920—Continued

OCCUPATION AND MARITAL CONDITION	GAINFULLY EMPLOYED WOMEN 16 YEARS OF AGE AND OVER							
			Living at home					
			Living with—					
	Total	Heads of families	Father	Mother	Husband	Other relative	Boarding or lodging	Living with employer
FALL RIVER, MASS.—Continued								
WIDOWED OR DIVORCED—continued								
Clerks in stores	6	3	1	1			1	
Dressmakers and seamstresses (not in factory)	35	29	1			3	1	1
Housekeepers and stewardesses	112	25			1	21	15	50
Laborers (manufacturing) (n. o. s.[1])	12	8				3	1	
Cotton mills	10	7				2	1	
All other industries	2	1				1		
Laundresses (not in laundry)	31	26		1		1	2	1
Laundry operatives	12	8	1			1	2	
Midwives and nurses (not trained)	28	10	5	1		6	4	2
Milliners and millinery dealers	4	3		1				
Musicians and teachers of music	1		1					
Retail dealers	38	33	1	1		3		
Saleswomen (stores)	26	12	4	4		3	3	
Semiskilled operatives (manufacturing) (n. o. s.[1])	942	622	58	46		147	69	
Clothing industries—								
Hat factories (felt)	7	4	1			2		
Shirt, collar, and cuff factories	2	1	1					
All other clothing factories	10	7	1	1		1		
Iron and steel industries	1	1						
Textile industries—								
Cotton mills	878	587	50	45		133	63	
Rope and cordage factories	4	1				2	1	
Textile dyeing, finishing, and printing mills	9	6	1			1	1	
All other textile mills	17	6	2			6	3	
All other industries	14	9	2			2	1	
Servants	123	56		3		4	10	50
Stenographers and typists	6	2		3		1		
Teachers (school)	8	4	2	1			1	
Telephone operators	2	1				1		
Trained nurses	10	3	1			2		4
All other occupations	41	29	2	3		4	3	
PROVIDENCE, R. I.								
ALL CLASSES								
All occupations	32,099	3,732	10,187	4,272	3,254	3,894	3,366	3,394
Attendants and helpers (professional service)	68	10	20	18	6	7	6	1
Barbers, hairdressers, and manicurists	112	12	21	18	8	20	32	1
Boarding and lodging house keepers	456	321	4	1	119	4	7	
Bookkeepers, cashiers, and accountants	1,897	93	913	380	68	243	197	3
Buffers, polishers, and grinders (metal)	113	13	30	18	13	19	20	
Charwomen and cleaners	126	64	2	2	34	11	7	6
Clerks (except clerks in stores)	2,247	92	1,069	465	85	294	233	9
Clerks in stores	493	32	195	69	54	63	79	1
Dressmakers and seamstresses (not in factory)	835	284	107	74	101	136	111	22
Enamelers, lacquerers, and japanners	152	9	67	35	12	19	10	
Forewomen and overseers (manufacturing)	192	22	49	39	17	42	23	
Housekeepers and stewardesses	847	142	24	13	67	114	113	374
Jewelers and lapidaries (factory)	519	33	229	112	37	77	31	
Jewelers', watchmakers', goldsmiths', and silversmiths' apprentices	85		68	11		5	1	
Laborers (manufacturing) (n. o. s.[1])	513	33	238	43	88	76	35	
Iron and steel industries	79	4	39	7	6	13	10	
Jewelry factories	54	1	32	8	3	5	5	
Textile industries—								
Cotton mills	68	2	38	2	13	10	3	
Woolen and worsted mills	85	3	31	4	22	17	3	
All other textile mills	89	9	38	6	21	14	1	
All other industries	138	9	60	16	23	17	13	
Laundresses (not in laundry)	436	205	8	14	104	29	33	43

[1] Not otherwise specified.

TABLE 170.—FAMILY RELATIONSHIP OF GAINFULLY EMPLOYED WOMEN, BY MARITAL CONDITION AND SPECIFIED OCCUPATION, FOR 11 SELECTED CITIES: 1920—Continued

OCCUPATION AND MARITAL CONDITION	GAINFULLY EMPLOYED WOMEN 16 YEARS OF AGE AND OVER							
		Living at home					Boarding or lodging	Living with employer
	Total	Heads of families	Living with—					
			Father	Mother	Husband	Other relative		
PROVIDENCE, R. I.—Continued								
ALL CLASSES—Continued								
Laundry operatives	300	66	50	29	61	40	47	7
Librarians	50	4	19	12	---	5	10	---
Manufacturers, officials, and managers	62	15	10	9	14	9	4	1
Midwives and nurses (not trained)	561	85	55	36	41	91	138	115
Milliners and millinery dealers	180	28	45	34	22	24	27	---
Musicians and teachers of music	252	23	115	40	33	19	21	1
Religious, charity, and welfare workers	105	19	13	5	6	6	20	36
Retail dealers	284	104	28	15	96	30	9	2
Saleswomen (stores)	1,343	151	404	202	187	199	200	---
Semiskilled operatives (manufacturing) (n. o. s.[1])	10,944	1,071	4,069	1,594	1,559	1,586	1,061	4
Chemical and allied industries	75	6	33	14	4	13	5	---
Clothing industries	261	46	63	34	29	55	34	---
Electrical supply factories	123	5	55	17	13	21	12	---
Food industries	89	10	31	12	14	13	9	---
Gold and silver factories	51	5	24	5	3	4	10	---
Iron and steel industries	881	82	329	159	80	141	89	1
Jewelry factories	2,211	184	901	342	207	301	276	---
Paper box factories	132	13	49	18	11	27	14	---
Printing and publishing	103	7	37	11	12	14	22	---
Rubber factories	526	55	202	93	53	79	44	---
Textile industries—								
Cotton mills	843	93	268	98	179	119	85	1
Knitting mills	274	23	93	56	22	49	31	---
Lace and embroidery mills	61	4	25	9	12	8	3	---
Silk mills	377	27	169	45	65	39	32	---
Textile dyeing, finishing, and printing mills	180	12	72	29	26	24	17	---
Woolen and worsted mills	3,208	321	1,137	436	604	474	236	---
All other textile mills	871	108	319	108	147	123	66	---
All other industries	678	70	262	108	78	82	76	2
Servants	3,009	320	54	45	169	119	227	2,075
Stenographers and typists	1,948	49	1,121	387	32	186	171	2
Tailoresses	65	12	12	7	13	12	9	---
Teachers (school)	1,457	127	497	245	24	187	155	222
Telephone operators	629	14	337	157	6	72	39	4
Trained nurses	569	28	55	24	6	21	82	353
Waitresses	362	46	25	22	45	24	102	98
All other occupations	888	205	234	97	127	105	106	14
SINGLE (INCLUDING UNKNOWN)								
All occupations	22,813	1,224	9,520	3,853	---	3,174	2,264	2,778
Attendants and helpers (professional service)	50	4	17	16	---	7	5	1
Barbers, hairdressers, and manicurists	84	6	18	16	---	19	25	---
Boarding and lodging house keepers	84	76	2	1	---	2	3	---
Bookkeepers, cashiers, and accountants	1,665	58	871	355	---	229	149	3
Buffers, polishers, and grinders (metal)	77	2	28	15	---	15	17	---
Charwomen and cleaners	19	8	---	---	---	2	3	6
Clerks (except clerks in stores)	1,953	54	1,016	434	---	266	176	7
Clerks in stores	371	13	181	63	---	57	56	1
Dressmakers and seamstresses (not in factory)	431	95	93	64	---	98	66	15
Enamelers, lacquerers, and japanners	116	4	56	32	---	19	5	---
Forewomen and overseers (manufacturing)	138	6	46	35	---	39	12	---
Housekeepers and stewardesses	360	42	19	8	---	74	48	169
Jewelers and lapidaries (factory)	416	11	212	102	---	68	23	---
Jewelers', watchmakers', goldsmiths', and silversmiths' apprentices	85	---	68	11	---	5	1	---
Laborers (manufacturing) (n. o. s.[1])	350	7	223	39	---	60	21	---
Iron and steel industries	59	---	37	6	---	10	6	---
Jewelry factories	48	---	31	8	---	4	5	---
Textile industries—								
Cotton mills	51	1	37	2	---	8	3	---
Woolen and worsted mills	46	3	26	4	---	12	1	---
All other textile mills	55	1	36	6	---	12	---	---
All other industries	91	2	56	13	---	14	6	---

[1] Not otherwise specified.

TABLE **170.**—FAMILY RELATIONSHIP OF GAINFULLY EMPLOYED WOMEN, BY MARITAL CONDITION AND SPECIFIED OCCUPATION, FOR 11 SELECTED CITIES: 1920—Continued

OCCUPATION AND MARITAL CONDITION	Total	Heads of families	Living at home					Boarding or lodging	Living with employer
			Living with—						
			Father	Mother	Husband	Other relative			

PROVIDENCE, R. I.—Continued

OCCUPATION AND MARITAL CONDITION	Total	Heads of families	Father	Mother	Husband	Other relative	Boarding or lodging	Living with employer
SINGLE (INCLUDING UNKNOWN)—continued								
Laundresses (not in laundry)	110	29	6	9		16	18	32
Laundry operatives	140	12	44	25		31	23	5
Librarians	42	3	16	12		4	7	
Manufacturers, officials, and managers	31	3	10	8		7	3	
Midwives and nurses (not trained)	354	28	45	26		53	104	98
Milliners and millinery dealers	124	14	40	31		21	18	
Musicians and teachers of music	184	14	107	32		18	12	1
Religious, charity, and welfare workers	88	14	13	5		4	16	36
Retail dealers	91	28	22	14		21	4	2
Saleswomen (stores)	863	53	370	169		161	110	
Semiskilled operatives (manufacturing) (n. o. s.[1])	7,463	325	3,746	1,416		1,276	698	2
Chemical and allied industries	60	2	29	11		13	5	
Clothing industries	155	14	55	28		38	20	
Electrical supply factories	98	1	54	15		20	8	
Food industries	54	3	30	8		9	4	
Gold and silver factories	40	1	24	5		4	6	
Iron and steel industries	648	20	298	141		117	71	1
Jewelry factories	1,609	44	835	307		242	181	
Paper box factories	99	8	45	16		22	8	
Printing and publishing	73	3	33	8		12	17	
Rubber factories	398	22	192	84		65	35	
Textile industries—								
Cotton mills	483	25	243	88		88	39	
Knitting mills	209	10	89	46		41	23	
Lace and embroidery mills	43		24	9		8	2	
Silk mills	239	4	155	39		25	16	
Textile dyeing, finishing, and printing mills	130	4	68	26		22	10	
Woolen and worsted mills	2,092	116	1,039	394		384	159	
All other textile mills	569	35	291	98		103	42	
All other industries	464	13	242	93		63	52	1
Servants	2,075	80	47	28		60	114	1,746
Stenographers and typists	1,809	32	1,091	374		176	134	2
Tailoresses	33	3	10	7		8	5	
Teachers (school)	1,364	100	488	236		176	143	221
Telephone operators	588	10	325	149		66	34	4
Trained nurses	514	15	54	20		16	75	334
Waitresses	208	7	20	15		17	66	83
All other occupations	533	68	216	86		83	70	10
MARRIED								
All occupations	5,433	499	476	230	3,254	290	522	162
Attendants and helpers (professional service)	12	2	2	2	6			
Barbers, hairdressers, and manicurists	16	3	2		8		3	
Boarding and lodging house keepers	174	53	1		119		1	
Bookkeepers, cashiers, and accountants	146	4	32	13	68	6	23	
Buffers, polishers, and grinders (metal)	21	2	1	2	13	1	2	
Charwomen and cleaners	53	11	2	1	34	3	2	
Clerks (except clerks in stores)	188	10	43	16	85	9	25	
Clerks in stores	81	2	7	4	54	2	12	
Dressmakers and seamstresses (not in factory)	155	24	9		101	10	7	4
Enamelers, lacquerers, and japanners	26	2	6	2	12		4	
Forewomen and overseers (manufacturing)	29	2	2	4	17	2	2	
Housekeepers and stewardesses	145	14	3	3	67	6	17	35
Jewelers and lapidaries (factory)	67	4	12	4	37	5	5	
Laborers (manufacturing) (n. o. s.[1])	125	6	12	4	88	7	8	
Iron and steel industries	14	2	1	1	6		4	
Jewelry factories	5		1		3	1		
Textile industries—								
Cotton mills	15		1		13	1		
Woolen and worsted mills	31		4		22	3	2	
All other textile mills	25	1	1		21	1	1	
All other industries	35	3	4	3	23	1	1	

[1] Not otherwise specified.

TABLE 170.—FAMILY RELATIONSHIP OF GAINFULLY EMPLOYED WOMEN, BY MARITAL CONDITION AND SPECIFIED OCCUPATION, FOR 11 SELECTED CITIES: 1920—Continued

OCCUPATION AND MARITAL CONDITION	Total	Heads of families	Living at home — Living with—				Boarding or lodging	Living with employer
			Father	Mother	Husband	Other relative		
PROVIDENCE, R. I.—Continued								
MARRIED—continued								
Laundresses (not in laundry)	148	27	2	2	104	1	5	7
Laundry operatives	98	13	3	3	61	2	15	1
Librarians	4		3			1		
Manufacturers, officials, and managers	17	2			14			1
Midwives and nurses (not trained)	78	2	6	2	41	11	12	4
Milliners and millinery dealers	36	4	3	2	22	2	3	
Musicians and teachers of music	50	1	7	4	33	1	4	
Religious, charity, and welfare workers	9				6		3	
Retail dealers	111	8	3		96	2	2	
Saleswomen (stores)	318	26	23	20	187	16	46	
Semiskilled operatives (manufacturing) (n. o. s.[1])	2,458	183	233	107	1,559	164	211	1
Chemical and allied industries	11	2	3	2	4			
Clothing industries	48	4	7	2	29	3	3	
Electrical supply factories	18		1	1	13		3	
Food industries	25	1	1	3	14	3	3	
Gold and silver factories	8	3			3		2	
Iron and steel industries	142	16	19	7	80	14	6	
Jewelry factories	408	34	49	25	207	36	57	
Paper box factories	23	1	3	2	11	3	3	
Printing and publishing	22	1	2	2	12	1	3	
Rubber factories	89	8	5	5	53	9	9	
Textile industries—								
Cotton mills	273	20	22	6	179	16	29	1
Knitting mills	43	2	4	6	22	5	4	
Lace and embroidery mills	12				12			
Silk mills	100	7	8	3	65	9	8	
Textile dyeing, finishing, and printing mills	35	2	3	1	26		3	
Woolen and worsted mills	856	57	71	29	604	46	49	
All other textile mills	213	16	19	5	147	11	15	
All other industries	132	9	16	7	78	8	14	
Servants	371	40	4	7	169	14	45	92
Stenographers and typists	100	6	23	12	32	5	22	
Tailoresses	18	2	1		13	1	1	
Teachers (school)	49	6	5		24	5	8	1
Telephone operators	26	2	9	4	6	3	2	
Trained nurses	24		2	2	6	4	2	8
Waitresses	92	9	3	3	45	2	23	7
All other occupations	188	27	14	3	127	5	11	1
WIDOWED OR DIVORCED								
All occupations	3,853	2,009	191	189		430	580	454
Attendants and helpers (professional service)	6	4	1				1	
Barbers, hairdressers, and manicurists	12	3	1	2			4	1
Boarding and lodging house keepers	198	192	1			1	4	
Bookkeepers, cashiers, and accountants	86	31	10	12		8	25	
Buffers, polishers, and grinders (metal)	15	9	1	1		3	1	
Charwomen and cleaners	54	45		1		6	2	
Clerks (except clerks in stores)	106	28	10	15		19	32	2
Clerks in stores	41	17	7	2		4	11	
Dressmakers and seamstresses (not in factory)	249	165	5	10		28	38	3
Enamelers, lacquerers, and japanners	10	3	5	1			1	
Forewomen and overseers (manufacturing)	25	14	1			1	9	
Housekeepers and stewardesses	342	86	2	2		34	48	170
Jewelers and lapidaries (factory)	36	18	5	6		4	3	
Laborers (manufacturing) (n. o. s.[1])	38	20	3			9	6	
Iron and steel industries	6	2	1			1	2	
Jewelry factories	1	1						
Textile industries—								
Cotton mills	2	1				1		
Woolen and worsted mills	8	5	1				2	
All other textile mills	9	7	1				1	
All other industries	12	4	1			1	6	

[1] Not otherwise specified.

6436°—29——21

TABLE **170.**—FAMILY RELATIONSHIP OF GAINFULLY EMPLOYED WOMEN, BY MARITAL CONDITION AND SPECIFIED OCCUPATION, FOR 11 SELECTED CITIES: 1920—Continued

OCCUPATION AND MARITAL CONDITION	Total	Heads of families	Father	Mother	Husband	Other relative	Boarding or lodging	Living with employer

GAINFULLY EMPLOYED WOMEN 16 YEARS OF AGE AND OVER — Living at home — Living with—

PROVIDENCE, R. I.—Continued

WIDOWED OR DIVORCED—continued								
Laundresses (not in laundry)	178	149		3		12	10	4
Laundry operatives	62	41	3	1		7	9	1
Librarians	4	1					3	
Manufacturers, officials, and managers	14	10		1		2	1	
Midwives and nurses (not trained)	129	55	4	8		27	22	13
Milliners and millinery dealers	20	10	2	1		1	6	
Musicians and teachers of music	18	8	1	4			5	
Religious, charity, and welfare workers	8	5				2	1	
Retail dealers	82	68	3	1		7	3	
Saleswomen (stores)	162	72	11	13		22	44	
Semiskilled operatives (manufacturing) (n. o. s.[1])	1,023	563	90	71		146	152	1
Chemical and allied industries	4	2	1	1				
Clothing industries	58	28	1	4		14	11	
Electrical supply factories	7	4		1		1	1	
Food industries	10	6		1		1	2	
Gold and silver factories	3	1					2	
Iron and steel industries	91	46	12	11		10	12	
Jewelry factories	194	106	17	10		23	38	
Paper box factories	10	4	1			2	3	
Printing and publishing	8	3	2			1	2	
Rubber factories	39	25	5	4		5		
Textile industries—								
Cotton mills	87	48	3	4		15	17	
Knitting mills	22	11		4		3	4	
Lace and embroidery mills	6	4	1				1	
Silk mills	38	16	6	3		5	8	
Textile dyeing, finishing, and printing mills	15	6	1	2		2	4	
Woolen and worsted mills	260	148	27	13		44	28	
All other textile mills	89	57	9	5		9	9	
All other industries	82	48	4	8		11	10	1
Servants	563	200	3	10		45	68	237
Stenographers and typists	39	11	7	1		5	15	
Tailoresses	14	7	1			3	3	
Teachers (school)	44	21	4	5		6	8	
Telephone operators	15	2	3	4		3	3	
Trained nurses	31	11	1	2		1	5	11
Waitresses	62	30	2	4		5	13	8
All other occupations	167	110	4	8		17	25	3

ROCHESTER, N. Y.

ALL CLASSES								
All occupations	36,956	3,897	11,349	4,409	4,683	4,319	5,289	3,010
Agents	50	9	16	5	2	4	14	
Artists, sculptors, and teachers of art	82	14	19	15	11	7	14	2
Attendants and helpers (professional service)	85	7	27	21	8	8	14	
Barbers, hairdressers, and manicurists	161	25	29	21	28	20	37	1
Boarding and lodging house keepers	325	216	1	5	100	3		
Bookkeepers, cashiers, and accountants	2,314	121	1,027	489	105	267	304	1
Charwomen and cleaners	135	62	3	5	40	13	11	1
Clerks (except clerks in stores)	3,149	142	1,552	530	152	359	408	6
Clerks in stores	872	76	327	108	147	89	124	1
Compositors, linotypers, and typesetters	80	9	24	13	12	12	10	
Dressmakers and seamstresses (not in factory)	822	230	83	71	125	144	155	14
Forewomen and overseers (manufacturing)	331	44	73	63	41	68	42	
Housekeepers and stewardesses	688	90	33	10	45	111	72	327
Janitors and sextons	75	34	4	2	24	7	4	
Laborers (manufacturing) (n. o. s.[1])	691	68	218	67	98	78	162	
Shoe factories	65	6	22	9	8	12	8	
All other industries	626	62	196	58	90	66	154	

[1] Not otherwise specified.

TABLE 170.—FAMILY RELATIONSHIP OF GAINFULLY EMPLOYED WOMEN, BY MARITAL CONDITION AND SPECIFIED OCCUPATION, FOR 11 SELECTED CITIES: 1920—Continued

OCCUPATION AND MARITAL CONDITION	Total	Heads of families	Living at home				Boarding or lodging	Living with employer
			Living with—					
			Father	Mother	Husband	Other relative		
ROCHESTER, N. Y.—Continued								
ALL CLASSES—Continued								
Laundresses (not in laundry)	390	157	5	7	124	30	46	21
Laundry operatives	296	63	36	10	85	49	50	3
Librarians	56	8	20	9	1	7	11	----
Manufacturers, officials, and managers	82	16	20	5	18	15	7	1
Midwives and nurses (not trained)	654	80	45	33	60	104	171	161
Milliners and millinery dealers	228	23	68	40	33	27	37	----
Musicians and teachers of music	290	44	104	36	40	32	30	4
Photographers	53	7	9	8	2	8	19	----
Religious, charity, and welfare workers	126	20	32	15	11	17	20	11
Restaurant, café, and lunch room keepers	83	26	2	6	14	21	14	----
Retail dealers	352	113	48	25	112	28	25	1
Saleswomen (stores)	1,321	146	345	152	257	181	240	----
Semiskilled operatives (manufacturing) (n. o. s.¹)	10,309	911	3,671	1,266	1,658	1,313	1,482	8
Button factories	406	26	119	51	84	53	73	----
Chemical and allied industries	86	13	14	3	30	7	18	1
Clothing industries—								
Shirt, collar, and cuff factories	196	12	67	26	34	24	33	----
Suit, coat, cloak, and overall factories	1,422	117	521	134	394	151	104	1
All other clothing factories	339	64	55	40	57	61	62	----
Electrical supply factories	222	15	96	23	25	30	33	----
Food industries—								
Candy factories	202	24	68	19	51	22	18	----
Fruit and vegetable canning, etc	131	32	17	6	49	15	12	----
All other food factories	99	14	21	6	24	17	17	----
Iron and steel industries	161	11	42	21	38	20	29	----
Lumber and furniture industries	131	24	34	22	18	17	16	----
Paper box factories	281	16	125	35	40	26	39	----
Petroleum refineries	52	3	13	2	12	7	15	----
Printing and publishing	252	26	90	39	27	28	42	----
Shoe factories	2,009	192	689	274	308	297	248	1
Textile industries—								
Knitting mills	159	20	36	28	19	33	22	1
All other textile mills	144	15	33	17	32	18	29	----
All other industries	4,017	287	1,631	520	416	487	672	4
Servants	2,412	248	50	36	165	120	221	1,572
Stenographers and typists	2,998	89	1,589	544	83	316	369	8
Tailoresses	2,666	286	749	276	725	359	270	1
Teachers (school)	1,778	187	432	207	78	220	297	357
Telephone operators	669	28	291	115	31	86	115	3
Trained nurses	815	51	65	48	40	65	154	392
Waitresses	444	71	21	16	75	24	167	70
All other occupations	1,074	176	311	130	133	107	173	44
SINGLE (INCLUDING UNKNOWN)								
All occupations	25,255	1,280	10,403	3,971	----	3,338	3,928	2,335
Agents	37	4	15	5	----	4	9	----
Artists, sculptors, and teachers of art	53	7	17	11	----	6	10	2
Attendants and helpers (professional service)	67	2	25	20	----	7	13	----
Barbers, hairdressers, and manicurists	98	13	24	18	----	14	28	1
Boarding and lodging house keepers	49	41	1	4	----	3	----	----
Bookkeepers, cashiers, and accountants	2,013	77	979	459	----	241	256	1
Charwomen and cleaners	19	9	2	1	----	1	5	1
Clerks (except clerks in stores)	2,725	74	1,468	501	----	321	355	6
Clerks in stores	569	22	298	95	----	68	85	1
Compositors, linotypers, and typesetters	47	4	18	9	----	9	7	----
Dressmakers and seamstresses (not in factory)	406	69	70	59	----	96	104	8
Forewomen and overseers (manufacturing)	209	17	62	51	----	44	35	----
Housekeepers and stewardesses	277	24	27	8	----	59	25	134
Janitors and sextons	12	5	3	1	----	2	1	----
Laborers (manufacturing) (n. o. s.¹)	433	7	202	56	----	54	114	----
Shoe factories	43	2	19	8	----	8	6	----
All other industries	390	5	183	48	----	46	108	----

¹ Not otherwise specified.

TABLE 170.—FAMILY RELATIONSHIP OF GAINFULLY EMPLOYED WOMEN, BY MARITAL CONDITION AND SPECIFIED OCCUPATION, FOR 11 SELECTED CITIES: 1920—Continued

	GAINFULLY EMPLOYED WOMEN 16 YEARS OF AGE AND OVER							
OCCUPATION AND MARITAL CONDITION	Total	Heads of families	Living at home				Boarding or lodging	Living with employer
			Living with—					
			Father	Mother	Husband	Other relative		
ROCHESTER, N. Y.—Continued								
SINGLE (INCLUDING UNKNOWN)—continued								
Laundresses (not in laundry)	57	18	2	3		6	15	13
Laundry operatives	105	17	29	10		32	16	1
Librarians	54	8	20	8		7	11	
Manufacturers, officials, and managers	48	8	18	5		12	4	1
Midwives and nurses (not trained)	360	19	35	31		60	112	103
Milliners and millinery dealers	173	16	67	37		24	29	
Musicians and teachers of music	199	19	96	31		26	23	4
Photographers	41	2	9	8		7	15	
Religious, charity, and welfare workers	96	10	31	15		11	18	11
Restaurant, café, and lunch room keepers	40	11	2	4		11	12	
Retail dealers	113	23	38	17		20	14	1
Saleswomen (stores)	750	38	289	126		135	162	
Semiskilled operatives (manufacturing) (n. o. s.[1])	6,765	271	3,280	1,111		1,001	1,097	5
Button factories	250	8	103	44		39	56	
Chemical and allied industries	33		13	3		5	11	1
Clothing industries—								
Shirt, collar, and cuff factories	131	3	56	24		20	28	
Suit, coat, cloak, and overall factories	811	24	472	114		122	78	1
All other clothing factories	191	28	49	32		41	41	
Electrical supply factories	160	5	81	21		25	28	
Food industries—								
Candy factories	103	3	62	17		12	9	
Fruit and vegetable canning, etc.	27	2	12	5		2	6	
All other food factories	34	3	16	3		5	7	
Iron and steel industries	85	1	36	18		8	22	
Lumber and furniture industries	82	5	31	21		14	11	
Paper box factories	193	6	112	30		20	25	
Petroleum refineries	27		11	1		4	11	
Printing and publishing	167	9	79	30		21	28	
Shoe factories	1,310	74	593	244		234	164	1
Textile industries—								
Knitting mills	111	8	33	26		27	16	1
All other textile mills	85	4	30	17		13	21	
All other industries	2,965	88	1,491	461		389	535	1
Servants	1,498	45	34	27		65	103	1,224
Stenographers and typists	2,767	58	1,540	524		304	336	5
Tailoresses	1,395	62	648	239		259	187	
Teachers (school)	1,590	144	414	201		206	270	355
Telephone operators	589	16	275	107		83	105	3
Trained nurses	689	37	61	44		56	135	356
Waitresses	198	19	12	6		10	90	61
All other occupations	714	64	292	119		74	127	38
MARRIED								
All occupations	7,587	583	733	269	4,683	414	702	203
Agents	3		1		2			
Artists, sculptors, and teachers of art	19	1	1	3	11	1	2	
Attendants and helpers (professional service)	10			1	8	1		
Barbers, hairdressers, and manicurists	45	3	5	3	28	2	4	
Boarding and lodging house keepers	132	31		1	100			
Bookkeepers, cashiers, and accountants	215	14	36	16	105	17	27	
Charwomen and cleaners	54	8		1	40	2	3	
Clerks (except clerks in stores)	313	16	69	20	152	22	34	
Clerks in stores	218	11	21	10	147	12	17	
Compositors, linotypers, and typesetters	27	4	4	3	12	1	3	
Dressmakers and seamstresses (not in factory)	204	35	9	3	125	14	16	2
Forewomen and overseers (manufacturing)	75	5	9	4	41	12	4	
Housekeepers and stewardesses	129	11	2		45	13	16	42
Janitors and sextons	39	10	1	1	24	1	2	
Laborers (manufacturing) (n. o. s.[1])	174	19	10	10	98	13	24	
Shoe factories	14		1	1	8	1	1	
All other industries	160	19	9	9	90	10	23	

[1] Not otherwise specified.

TABLE 170.—FAMILY RELATIONSHIP OF GAINFULLY EMPLOYED WOMEN, BY MARITAL CONDITION AND SPECIFIED OCCUPATION, FOR 11 SELECTED CITIES: 1920—Continued

		GAINFULLY EMPLOYED WOMEN 16 YEARS OF AGE AND OVER						
		Living at home					Boarding or lodging	Living with employer
OCCUPATION AND MARITAL CONDITION	Total	Heads of families	Living with—					
			Father	Mother	Husband	Other relative		

ROCHESTER, N. Y.—Continued

MARRIED—continued								
Laundresses (not in laundry)	174	27	2	1	124	5	13	2
Laundry operatives	120	10	5		85	5	15	
Librarians	1				1			
Manufacturers, officials, and managers	26	3	1		18	2	2	
Midwives and nurses (not trained)	120	9	7		60	9	17	17
Milliners and millinery dealers	39			1	33	3	2	
Musicians and teachers of music	58	5	6	4	40	2	1	
Photographers	6	1			2		3	
Religious, charity, and welfare workers	16	2	1		11	2		
Restaurant, café, and lunch room keepers	21	2		1	14	4		
Retail dealers	145	17	6	2	112	3	5	
Saleswomen (stores)	399	25	38	15	257	20	44	
Semiskilled operatives (manufacturing) (n. o. s.[1])	2,609	145	323	98	1,658	158	226	1
Button factories	120	4	12	7	84	7	6	
Chemical and allied industries	38	3	1		30	1	3	
Clothing industries—								
Shirt, collar, and cuff factories	52	2	9	1	34	2	4	
Suit, coat, cloak, and overall factories	492	14	41	10	394	17	16	
All other clothing factories	86	6	5	5	57	6	7	
Electrical supply factories	46	3	9	1	25	4	4	
Food industries—								
Candy factories	72	5	5	1	51	4	6	
Fruit and vegetable canning, etc	64	5	3	1	49	4	2	
All other food factories	51	8	4	2	24	6	7	
Iron and steel industries	63	5	5	2	38	10	3	
Lumber and furniture industries	34	8	3	1	18	1	3	
Paper box factories	67		12	3	40	3	9	
Petroleum refineries	16	1			12	2	1	
Printing and publishing	58	6	11	5	27	2	7	
Shoe factories	509	27	79	15	308	30	50	
Textile industries—								
Knitting mills	29	2	3	1	19		4	
All other textile mills	46	2	3		32	3	6	
All other industries	766	44	118	43	416	56	88	1
Servants	409	50	8	4	165	19	53	110
Stenographers and typists	180	8	41	17	83	8	20	3
Tailoresses	962	55	79	22	725	39	41	1
Teachers (school)	127	12	11	4	78	5	17	
Telephone operators	63	4	12	6	31	2	8	
Trained nurses	79	4	3	3	40	1	10	18
Waitresses	162	15	7	6	75	5	50	4
All other occupations	214	21	15	8	133	11	23	3
WIDOWED OR DIVORCED								
All occupations	4,114	2,034	213	169		567	659	472
Agents	10	5					5	
Artists, sculptors, and teachers of art	10	6	1	1			2	
Attendants and helpers (professional service)	8	5	2				1	
Barbers, hairdressers, and manicurists	18	9				4	5	
Boarding and lodging house keepers	144	144						
Bookkeepers, cashiers, and accountants	86	30	12	14		9	21	
Charwomen and cleaners	62	45	1	3		10	3	
Clerks (except clerks in stores)	111	52	15	9		16	19	
Clerks in stores	85	43	8	3		9	22	
Compositors, linotypers, and typesetters	6	1	2	1		2		
Dressmakers and seamstresses (not in factory)	212	126	4	9		34	35	4
Forewomen and overseers (manufacturing)	47	22	2	8		12	3	
Housekeepers and stewardesses	282	55	4	2		39	31	151
Janitors and sextons	24	19				4	1	
Laborers (manufacturing) (n. o. s.[1])	84	42	6	1		11	24	
Shoe factories	8	4	2			1	1	
All other industries	76	38	4	1		10	23	

[1] Not otherwise specified.

TABLE 170.—FAMILY RELATIONSHIP OF GAINFULLY EMPLOYED WOMEN, BY MARITAL CONDITION AND SPECIFIED OCCUPATION, FOR 11 SELECTED CITIES: 1920—Continued

OCCUPATION AND MARITAL CONDITION	Total	Heads of families	Living at home				Boarding or lodging	Living with employer
			Living with—					
			Father	Mother	Husband	Other relative		

ROCHESTER, N. Y.—Continued

WIDOWED OR DIVORCED—continued

OCCUPATION AND MARITAL CONDITION	Total	Heads of families	Father	Mother	Husband	Other relative	Boarding or lodging	Living with employer
Laundresses (not in laundry)	159	112	1	3		19	18	6
Laundry operatives	71	36	2			12	19	2
Librarians	1				1			
Manufacturers, officials, and managers	8	5	1			1	1	
Midwives and nurses (not trained)	174	52	3	1		35	42	41
Milliners and millinery dealers	16	7	1	2			6	
Musicians and teachers of music	33	20	2	1		4	6	
Photographers	6	4				1	1	
Religious, charity, and welfare workers	14	8				4	2	
Restaurant, café, and lunch room keepers	22	13		1		6	2	
Retail dealers	94	73	4	6		5	6	
Saleswomen (stores)	172	83	18	11		26	34	
Semiskilled operatives (manufacturing) (n. o. s.[1])	935	495	68	57		154	159	2
Button factories	36	14	4			7	11	
Chemical and allied industries	15	10				1	4	
Clothing industries—								
Shirt, collar, and cuff factories	13	7	2	1		2	1	
Suit, coat, cloak, and overall factories	119	79	8	10		12	10	
All other clothing factories	62	30	1	3		14	14	
Electrical supply factories	16	7	6	1		1	1	
Food industries—								
Candy factories	27	16	1	1		6	3	
Fruit and vegetable canning, etc	40	25	2			9	4	
All other food factories	14	3	1	1		6	3	
Iron and steel industries	13	5	1	1		2	4	
Lumber and furniture industries	15	11				2	2	
Paper box factories	21	10	1	2		3	5	
Petroleum refineries	9	2	2	1		1	3	
Printing, publishing, and engraving	27	11		4		5	7	
Shoe factories	190	91	17	15		33	34	
Textile industries—								
Knitting mills	19	10		1		6	2	
All other textile mills	13	9				2	2	
All other industries	286	155	22	16		42	49	2
Servants	505	153	8	5		36	65	238
Stenographers and typists	51	23	8	3		4	13	
Tailoresses	309	169	22	15		61	42	
Teachers (school)	61	31	7	2		9	10	2
Telephone operators	17	8	4	2		1	2	
Trained nurses	47	10	1	1		8	9	18
Waitresses	84	37	2	4		9	27	5
All other occupations	146	91	4	3		22	23	3

PATERSON, N. J.

ALL CLASSES

OCCUPATION AND MARITAL CONDITION	Total	Heads of families	Father	Mother	Husband	Other relative	Boarding or lodging	Living with employer
All occupations	17,999	1,856	6,976	2,298	2,973	1,861	1,223	812
Boarding and lodging house keepers	86	64			21			
Bookkeepers, cashiers, and accountants	747	15	473	142	21	69	26	1
Clerks (except clerks in stores)	637	20	362	138	15	67	34	1
Clerks in stores	189	8	93	34	28	16	10	
Dressmakers and seamstresses (not in factory)	244	65	45	26	39	42	22	5
Forewomen and overseers (manufacturing)	202	25	60	52	19	32	13	1
Housekeepers and stewardesses	292	74	19	7	18	32	25	117
Laborers (manufacturing) (n. o. s.[1])	106	12	28	9	41	3	13	
Textile industries	58	7	18	5	21	3	4	
All other industries	48	5	10	4	20		9	
Laundresses (not in laundry)	149	66	5	4	48	11	12	3
Laundry operatives	67	13	14	6	18	10	2	4
Midwives and nurses (not trained)	182	40	29	15	10	45	28	15

[1] Not otherwise specified.

TABLE 170.—FAMILY RELATIONSHIP OF GAINFULLY EMPLOYED WOMEN, BY MARITAL CONDITION AND SPECIFIED OCCUPATION, FOR 11 SELECTED CITIES: 1920—Continued

OCCUPATION AND MARITAL CONDITION	GAINFULLY EMPLOYED WOMEN 16 YEARS OF AGE AND OVER							
	Total	Living at home					Boarding or lodging	Living with employer
		Heads of families	Living with—					
			Father	Mother	Husband	Other relative		

PATERSON, N. J.—Continued

ALL CLASSES—Continued								
Milliners and millinery dealers	84	7	31	21	9	14	2	
Musicians and teachers of music	57	3	29	5	8	6	5	1
Retail dealers	233	78	10	8	121	13	2	1
Saleswomen (stores)	532	39	239	87	63	58	45	1
Semiskilled operatives (manufacturing) (n. o. s.[1])	10,858	1,053	4,241	1,336	2,331	1,154	737	6
Clothing industries—								
Shirt, collar, and cuff factories	603	71	206	83	118	80	45	
Suit, coat, cloak, and overall factories	55	1	8	3	33	9	1	
All other clothing factories	75	10	20	10	19	12	4	
Iron and steel industries	91	8	31	6	32	8	6	
Textile industries—								
Hemp and jute mills	201	43	36	9	75	25	13	
Knitting mills	84	3	43	16	6	6	10	
Linen mills	297	52	76	24	79	31	35	
Silk mills	8,813	806	3,574	1,107	1,801	924	595	6
Textile dyeing, finishing, and printing mills	113	10	44	10	37	8	4	
All other textile mills	270	17	114	34	70	26	9	
All other industries	256	32	89	34	61	25	15	
Servants	744	76	27	18	64	28	54	477
Stenographers and typists	924	17	634	167	13	72	21	
Teachers (school)	869	55	390	150	9	115	64	86
Telephone operators	144	1	101	30		8	3	1
Trained nurses	196	21	46	12	5	13	39	60
Waitresses	73	10	9	5	5	6	18	20
All other occupations	384	94	91	26	67	46	48	12
SINGLE (INCLUDING UNKNOWN)								
All occupations	11,990	496	6,528	2,030		1,507	849	580
Boarding and lodging house keepers	5	5						
Bookkeepers, cashiers, and accountants	689	10	458	135		65	20	1
Clerks (except clerks in stores)	581	10	351	129		63	27	1
Clerks in stores	141	3	87	28		16	7	
Dressmakers and seamstresses (not in factory)	132	21	41	21		33	15	1
Forewomen and overseers (manufacturing)	153	13	57	44		27	11	1
Housekeepers and stewardesses	127	13	16	6		14	10	68
Laborers (manufacturing) (n. o. s.[1])	42	1	26	7		1	7	
Textile industries	23		17	3		1	2	
All other industries	19	1	9	4			5	
Laundresses (not in laundry)	24	6	2	3		7	5	1
Laundry operatives	25	2	13	2		6	1	1
Midwives and nurses (not trained)	111	10	26	12		27	25	11
Milliners and millinery dealers	66	1	29	20		14	2	
Musicians and teachers of music	41	1	25	4		6	4	1
Retail dealers	33	8	9	5		8	2	1
Saleswomen (stores)	399	12	230	74		51	32	
Semiskilled operatives (manufacturing) (n. o. s.[1])	6,745	267	3,902	1,156		912	503	5
Clothing industries—								
Shirt, collar, and cuff factories	396	21	196	80		63	36	
Suit, coat, cloak, and overall factories	13		6	1		6		
All other clothing factories	43	5	18	8		10	2	
Iron and steel industries	48		30	6		8	4	
Textile industries—								
Hemp and jute mills	70	9	30	7		17	7	
Knitting mills	65	1	38	14		4	8	
Linen mills	137	10	66	20		21	20	
Silk mills	5,604	215	3,288	952		740	404	5
Textile dyeing, finishing, and printing mills	62		43	9		6	4	
All other textile mills	164	4	108	28		17	7	
All other industries	143	2	79	31		20	11	
Servants	410	14	21	14		13	22	326
Stenographers and typists	878	12	618	161		71	16	

[1] Not otherwise specified.

TABLE 170.—FAMILY RELATIONSHIP OF GAINFULLY EMPLOYED WOMEN, BY MARITAL CONDITION AND SPECIFIED OCCUPATION, FOR 11 SELECTED CITIES: 1920—Continued

OCCUPATION AND MARITAL CONDITION	GAINFULLY EMPLOYED WOMEN 16 YEARS OF AGE AND OVER								
	Total	Heads of families	Living at home					Boarding or lodging	Living with employer
			Living with—						
			Father	Mother	Husband	Other relative			

PATERSON, N. J.—Continued

SINGLE (INCLUDING UNKNOWN)—continued									
Teachers (school)	836	49	383	146			113	60	85
Telephone operators	140	1	99	28			8	3	1
Trained nurses	166	10	45	11			12	35	53
Waitresses	39	2	6	3			3	9	16
All other occupations	207	25	84	21			37	33	7
MARRIED									
All occupations	4,243	303	347	177	2,973	146	210	87	
Boarding and lodging house keepers	32	11			21				
Bookkeepers, cashiers, and accountants	44	1	11	3	21	3	5		
Clerks (except clerks in stores)	39	5	8	6	15	1	4		
Clerks in stores	38	2	4	4	28				
Dressmakers and seamstresses (not in factory)	54	7	1	2	39	2	3		
Forewomen and overseers (manufacturing)	36	4	3	6	19	3	1		
Housekeepers and stewardesses	48	5	3		18	7	3	12	
Laborers (manufacturing) (n. o. s.[1])	48	1	1		41	1	4		
Textile industries	24	1			21	1	1		
All other industries	24		1		20		3		
Laundresses (not in laundry)	73	21	1	1	48	1	1		
Laundry operatives	27	3	1	2	18	2		1	
Midwives and nurses (not trained)	25	5	3	1	10	2	1	3	
Milliners and millinery dealers	15	3	2	1	9				
Musicians and teachers of music	11	1	2		8				
Retail dealers	135	10	1	1	121	2			
Saleswomen (stores)	93	4	6	6	63	4	9	1	
Semiskilled operatives (manufacturing) (n. o. s.[1])	3,170	193	267	130	2,331	105	144		
Clothing industries—									
Shirt, collar, and cuff factories	153	10	10	1	118	8	6		
Suit, coat, cloak, and overall factories	39		2	2	33	2			
All other clothing factories	23		1	2	19	1			
Iron and steel industries	38	4			32		2		
Textile industries—									
Hemp and jute mills	100	8	4	2	75	5	6		
Knitting mills	16		5	1	6	2	2		
Linen mills	108	8	7	4	79	3	7		
Silk mills	2,483	148	226	111	1,801	79	118		
Textile dyeing, finishing, and printing mills	47	6	1	1	37	2			
All other textile mills	84	3	5	5	70		1		
All other industries	79	6	6	1	61	3	2		
Servants	165	10	5	2	64	5	14	65	
Stenographers and typists	35		14	3	13		5		
Teachers (school)	19		5	3	9	2			
Telephone operators	3		2	1					
Trained nurses	9		1	1	5		2		
Waitresses	20	3	1	1	5	1	6	3	
All other occupations	104	14	5	3	67	5	8	2	
WIDOWED OR DIVORCED									
All occupations	1,766	1,057	101	91		208	164	145	
Boarding and lodging house keepers	49	48				1			
Bookkeepers, cashiers, and accountants	14	4	4	4		1	1		
Clerks (except clerks in stores)	17	5	3	3		3	3		
Clerks in stores	10	3	2	2			3		
Dressmakers and seamstresses (not in factory)	58	37	3	3		7	4	4	
Forewomen and overseers (manufacturing)	13	8		2			3		
Housekeepers and stewardesses	117	56		1		11	12	37	
Laborers (manufacturing) (n. o. s.[1])	16	10	1	2		1	2		
Textile industries	11	6	1	2		1	1		
All other industries	5	4					1		

[1] Not otherwise specified.

TABLE 170.—FAMILY RELATIONSHIP OF GAINFULLY EMPLOYED WOMEN, BY MARITAL CONDITION AND SPECIFIED OCCUPATION, FOR 11 SELECTED CITIES: 1920—Continued

OCCUPATION AND MARITAL CONDITION	GAINFULLY EMPLOYED WOMEN 16 YEARS OF AGE AND OVER							
	Total	Heads of families	Living at home				Boarding or lodging	Living with employer
			Living with—					
			Father	Mother	Husband	Other relative		

PATERSON, N. J.—Continued

WIDOWED OR DIVORCED—continued

Laundresses (not in laundry)	52	39	2			3	6	2
Laundry operatives	15	8		2		2	1	2
Midwives and nurses (not trained)	46	25		2		16	2	1
Milliners and millinery dealers	3	3						
Musicians and teachers of music	5	1	2	1			1	
Retail dealers	65	60		2		3		
Saleswomen (stores)	40	23	3	7		3	4	
Semiskilled operatives (manufacturing) (n. o. s.[1])	943	593	72	50		137	90	1
Clothing industries—								
Shirt, collar, and cuff factories	54	40		2		9	3	
Suit, coat, cloak, and overall factories	3	1				1	1	
All other clothing factories	9	5	1			1	2	
Iron and steel industries	5	4	1					
Textile industries—								
Hemp and jute mills	31	26	2			3		
Knitting mills	3	2		1				
Linen mills	52	34	3			7	8	
Silk mills	726	443	60	44		105	73	1
Textile dyeing, finishing, and printing mills	4	4						
All other textile mills	22	10	1	1		9	1	
All other industries	34	24	4	2		2	2	
Servants	169	52	1	2		10	18	86
Stenographers and typists	11	5	2	3		1		
Teachers (school)	14	6	2	1			4	1
Telephone operators	1			1				
Trained nurses	21	11				1	2	7
Waitresses	14	5	2	1		2	3	1
All other occupations	73	55	2	2		4	7	3

CINCINNATI, OHIO

ALL CLASSES

All occupations	50,231	8,852	14,074	7,206	5,077	5,500	4,121	5,401
Actresses and showwomen	72	7	18	11	10	2	24	
Agents	62	11	17	16	4	3	10	1
Artists, sculptors, and teachers of art	145	16	51	25	8	12	31	2
Attendants and helpers (professional service)	124	8	39	33	4	19	20	1
Bakers	54	15	9	5	8	6	9	2
Barbers, hairdresses, and manicurists	244	71	26	29	63	23	32	
Boarding and lodging house keepers	643	451	3	5	158	12	11	3
Bookkeepers, cashiers, and accountants	2,482	151	1,210	586	72	294	161	8
Charwomen and cleaners	364	179	11	11	105	27	28	3
Cleaners and renovators (clothing, etc.)	73	17	22	6	6	15	5	3
Clerks (except clerks in stores)	3,089	204	1,524	697	70	364	218	12
Clerks in stores	987	75	430	189	81	139	71	2
Compositors, linotypers, and typesetters	59	7	21	12	9	6	4	
Dressmakers and seamstresses (not in factory)	1,641	529	242	171	166	288	124	121
Forewomen and overseers (manufacturing)	303	36	99	68	26	59	15	
Housekeepers and stewardesses	839	170	47	31	47	144	78	322
Janitors and sextons	394	195	15	15	124	24	14	7
Laborers (manufacturing) (n. o. s.[1])	449	90	106	64	70	54	64	1
Food industries	62	11	11	9	13	9	9	
All other industries	387	79	95	55	57	45	55	1
Laborers, porters, and helpers in stores	68	13	16	7	23	5	4	
Laborers, steam railroad	89	38	3	2	32	7	7	
Laundresses (not in laundry)	2,935	1,200	82	90	1,060	189	228	86
Laundry operatives	684	243	80	72	141	84	60	4
Librarians	81	8	28	23		10	10	2
Manufacturers, officials, and managers	124	36	21	16	17	23	11	

[1] Not otherwise specified.

TABLE **170.**—FAMILY RELATIONSHIP OF GAINFULLY EMPLOYED WOMEN, BY MARITAL CONDITION AND SPECIFIED OCCUPATION, FOR 11 SELECTED CITIES: 1920—Continued

			GAINFULLY EMPLOYED WOMEN 16 YEARS OF AGE AND OVER					
				Living at home				
OCCUPATION AND MARITAL CONDITION	Total	Heads of families		Living with—			Boarding or lodging	Living with employer
			Father	Mother	Husband	Other relative		

CINCINNATI, OHIO—Continued

ALL CLASSES—Continued

OCCUPATION AND MARITAL CONDITION	Total	Heads of families	Father	Mother	Husband	Other relative	Boarding or lodging	Living with employer
Messenger, bundle, and office girls	94	3	62	13	4	10	1	1
Midwives and nurses (not trained)	751	160	54	42	37	96	114	248
Milliners and millinery dealers	448	59	134	97	27	74	56	1
Musicians and teachers of music	395	59	153	63	39	37	31	13
Physicians and surgeons	56	25	3	5	8	4	7	4
Religious, charity, and welfare workers	262	29	41	17	21	17	39	98
Restaurant, café, and lunch room keepers	105	41	6	8	36	6	7	1
Retail dealers	732	322	61	58	201	56	25	9
Saleswomen (stores)	2,797	350	1,143	484	162	392	262	4
Semiskilled operatives, manufacturing (n. o. s.)[1]	10,116	1,705	3,520	1,955	968	1,299	664	5
Chemical and allied industries—								
Soap factories	336	34	190	53	18	27	14	_____
All other chemical factories	185	29	66	37	23	17	13	_____
Cigar and tobacco factories	742	183	146	158	115	92	48	_____
Clay, glass, and stone industries—								
Glass factories	91	9	39	15	9	11	8	_____
All other clay, glass, and stone industries	32	5	15	4	1	5	2	_____
Clothing industries—								
Shirt, collar, and cuff factories	381	56	140	70	39	45	31	_____
Suit, coat, cloak, and overall factories	1,379	259	477	264	131	167	81	_____
All other clothing factories	924	200	260	156	76	148	82	2
Electrical supply factories	66	8	30	13	3	10	2	_____
Food industries—								
Bakeries	204	39	63	40	21	25	16	_____
Candy factories	509	88	195	90	45	54	37	_____
Fruit and vegetable canning, etc	146	35	23	22	35	21	10	_____
Slaughter and packing houses	100	27	28	6	20	11	7	1
All other food factories	119	15	51	14	19	11	9	_____
Iron and steel industries—								
Automobile factories	83	21	21	25	4	8	4	_____
All other iron and steel industries	278	67	85	40	40	29	17	_____
Lumber and furniture industries—								
Furniture factories	186	21	82	21	27	24	11	_____
Piano and organ factories	125	20	52	29	10	10	4	_____
Saw and planing mills	60	14	16	14	7	8	1	_____
Other woodworking factories	39	2	20	9	2	5	1	_____
Paper and pulp mills	113	16	44	19	10	17	7	_____
Paper box factories	169	20	79	38	6	22	4	_____
Printing and publishing—								
Blank book, envelope, tag, paper bag, etc., factories	236	19	113	47	7	42	8	_____
Printing, publishing, and engraving	431	44	187	90	16	68	26	_____
Shoe factories	1,699	234	611	411	126	220	97	_____
Textile industries—								
Cotton mills	59	16	10	5	9	11	8	_____
All other textile mills	225	42	64	38	35	36	9	1
Tinware, enamelware, etc., factories	118	20	40	18	17	15	8	_____
All other industries	1,081	162	373	209	97	140	99	1
Servants	6,750	1,116	330	224	724	422	612	3,322
Stenographers and typists	4,281	118	2,470	960	40	416	273	4
Tailoresses	1,272	294	340	240	159	180	58	1
Teachers (school)	2,110	225	453	273	81	267	211	600
Telegraph operators	200	10	97	46	5	28	13	1
Telephone operators	1,180	54	605	265	16	147	85	8
Trained nurses	754	54	89	47	12	46	107	399
Waitresses	695	154	81	59	94	53	196	58
All other occupations	1,228	304	312	167	139	141	121	44

[1] Not otherwise specified.

TABLE 170.—FAMILY RELATIONSHIP OF GAINFULLY EMPLOYED WOMEN, BY MARITAL CONDITION AND SPECIFIED OCCUPATION, FOR 11 SELECTED CITIES: 1920—Continued

	GAINFULLY EMPLOYED WOMEN 16 YEARS OF AGE AND OVER							
OCCUPATION AND MARITAL CONDITION	Total	Living at home					Boarding or lodging	Living with employer
		Heads of families	Living with—					
			Father	Mother	Husband	Other relative		

CINCINNATI, OHIO—Continued

SINGLE (INCLUDING UNKNOWN)								
All occupations	33,735	2,648	13,186	6,475		4,326	2,651	4,449
Actresses and showwomen	23		7	7		2	7	
Agents	42	3	16	13		2	7	1
Artists, sculptors, and teachers of art	120	10	50	25		11	22	2
Attendants and helpers (professional service)	98	6	37	28		15	11	1
Bakers	18		7	4		3	3	1
Barbers, hairdressers, and manicurists	103	20	22	25		13	23	
Boarding and lodging house keepers	111	94	1	4		8	2	2
Bookkeepers, cashiers, and accountants	2,218	80	1,159	553		279	139	8
Charwomen and cleaners	50	18	5	5		13	9	
Cleaners and renovators (clothing, etc.)	43	3	20	5		11	1	3
Clerks (except clerks in stores)	2,777	104	1,470	671		340	182	10
Clerks in stores	779	29	402	174		115	57	2
Compositors, linotypers, and typesetters	42	4	18	12		5	3	
Dressmakers and seamstresses (not in factory)	1,024	217	227	155		239	76	110
Forewomen and overseers (manufacturing)	217	11	92	60		44	10	
Housekeepers and stewardesses	413	46	37	23		89	40	178
Janitors and sextons	56	23	9	10		6	5	3
Laborers (manufacturing) (n. o. s.[1])	237	19	90	49		42	36	1
Food industries	26	1	9	6		6	4	
All other industries	211	18	81	43		36	32	1
Laborers, porters, and helpers in stores	26	2	14	4		4	2	
Laborers, steam railroad	15	6	2			3	4	
Laundresses (not in laundry)	417	166	37	43		51	67	53
Laundry operatives	248	42	71	61		46	25	3
Librarians	73	5	26	23		9	9	1
Manufacturers, officials, and managers	66	11	14	16		19	6	
Messenger, bundle, and office girls	84	1	60	13		9		1
Midwives and nurses (not trained)	435	41	50	36		45	77	186
Milliners and millinery dealers	352	27	127	88		68	41	1
Musicians and teachers of music	304	36	141	53		33	28	13
Physicians and surgeons	29	11	3	5		3	5	2
Religious, charity, and welfare workers	209	21	37	14		12	28	97
Restaurant, café, and lunch room keepers	31	11	5	7		3	5	
Retail dealers	231	73	48	51		39	12	8
Saleswomen (stores)	2,132	134	1,067	428		326	174	3
Semiskilled operatives (manufacturing) (n. o. s.[1])	6,978	527	3,260	1,711		1,053	423	4
Chemical and allied industries—								
Soap factories	265	4	179	50		24	8	
All other chemical factories	120	6	62	32		14	6	
Cigar and tobacco factories	391	54	127	122		62	26	
Clay, glass, and stone industries—								
Glass factories	66	2	38	12		9	5	
All other clay, glass, and stone industries	26	2	14	3		5	2	
Clothing industries—								
Shirt, collar, and cuff factories	283	24	132	64		40	23	
Suit, coat, cloak, and overall factories	971	89	441	247		135	59	
All other clothing factories	659	90	252	131		129	55	2
Electrical supply factories	48	1	29	10		7	1	
Food industries—								
Bakeries	127	9	59	31		17	11	
Candy factories	328	17	179	70		45	17	
Fruit and vegetable canning, etc.	52	4	13	16		16	3	
Slaughter and packing houses	51	5	27	5		10	4	
All other food factories	78	2	46	14		9	7	
Iron and steel industries—								
Automobile factories	51	4	18	20		6	3	
All other iron and steel industries	159	11	78	37		20	13	

[1] Not otherwise specified.

TABLE 170.—FAMILY RELATIONSHIP OF GAINFULLY EMPLOYED WOMEN, BY MARITAL CONDITION AND SPECIFIED OCCUPATION, FOR 11 SELECTED CITIES: 1920—Continued

		GAINFULLY EMPLOYED WOMEN 16 YEARS OF AGE AND OVER						
			Living at home					
OCCUPATION AND MARITAL CONDITION	Total			Living with—			Boarding or lodging	Living with employer
		Heads of families	Father	Mother	Husband	Other relative		
CINCINNATI, OHIO—Continued								
SINGLE (INCLUDING UNKNOWN)—continued								
Semiskilled operatives (manfg.) (n. o. s.¹)—Con.								
Lumber and furniture industries—								
Furniture factories	129	4	80	17			19	9	
Piano and organ factories	92	5	51	27		5	4	
Saw and planing mills	47	11	15	12		8	1	
Other woodworking factories	28	1	15	8		4		
Paper and pulp mills	73	2	40	18		10	3	
Paper box factories	142	8	76	38		19	1	
Printing and publishing—								
Blank book, envelope, tag, paper bag, etc., factories	210	10	111	46		37	6	
Printing, publishing, and engraving	358	18	177	87		59	17	
Shoe factories	1,259	82	554	368		188	67	
Textile industries—								
Cotton mills	36	8	10	3		11	4	
All other textile mills	136	11	59	35		26	4	1
Tinware, enamelware, etc., factories	67	3	36	10		11	7	
All other industries	726	40	342	178		108	57	1
Servants	3,907	275	261	155		223	290	2,703
Stenographers and typists	4,075	78	2,423	936		395	242	1
Tailoresses	853	129	323	219		145	37	
Teachers (school)	1,919	174	433	265		256	197	594
Telegraph operators	178	6	92	43		28	8	1
Telephone operators	1,076	28	581	248		138	73	8
Trained nurses	662	33	85	42		38	97	367
Waitresses	336	47	65	42		34	99	49
All other occupations	728	77	292	149		109	69	32
MARRIED								
All occupations	8,403	1,152	461	304	5,077	314	770	325
Actresses and showwomen	40	3	9	3	10		15	
Agents	9	3	1	1	4			
Artists, sculptors, and teachers of art	16		1		8		7	
Attendants and helpers (professional service)	13		1	3	4	1	4	
Bakers	17	4	1	1	8	1	2	
Barbers, hairdressers, and manicurists	93	18	2	2	63	3	5	
Boarding and lodging house keepers	236	71			158		6	1
Bookkeepers, cashiers, and accountants	142	16	23	17	72	5	9	
Charwomen and cleaners	150	24	5	4	105	5	6	1
Cleaners and renovators (clothing, etc.)	11	2	1		6		2	
Clerks (except clerks in stores)	164	22	32	9	70	8	22	1
Clerks in stores	125	7	12	9	81	6	10	
Compositors, linotypers, and typesetters	11	1	1		9			
Dressmakers and seamstresses (not in factory)	252	50	6	4	166	8	13	5
Forewomen and overseers (manufacturing)	41	4	1	4	26	4	2	
Housekeepers and stewardesses	114	18	4	1	47	7	10	27
Janitors and sextons	159	23	2		124	4	4	2
Laborers (manufacturing) (n. o. s.¹)	130	11	10	11	70	6	22	
Food industries	24	2	2	2	13	2	3	
All other industries	106	9	8	9	57	4	19	
Laborers, porters, and helpers in stores	29	1	2	1	23	1	1	
Laborers, steam railroad	42	5	1	1	32	1	2	
Laundresses (not in laundry)	1,447	188	32	24	1,060	31	93	19
Laundry operatives	215	40	4	4	141	9	16	1
Librarians	4	1	2			1		
Manufacturers, officials, and managers	28	5	3		17		3	
Messenger, bundle, and office girls	7		2		4		1	
Midwives and nurses (not trained)	83	8	2	1	37	5	11	19
Milliners and millinery dealers	43	5	3	2	27		6	
Musicians and teachers of music	48	1	4	2	39	2		
Physicians and surgeons	11	1			8		1	1
Religious, charity, and welfare workers	30	2	3		21	1	3	1

¹ Not otherwise specified.

TABLE 170.—FAMILY RELATIONSHIP OF GAINFULLY EMPLOYED WOMEN, BY MARITAL CONDITION AND SPECIFIED OCCUPATION, FOR 11 SELECTED CITIES: 1920—Continued

OCCUPATION AND MARITAL CONDITION	GAINFULLY EMPLOYED WOMEN 16 YEARS OF AGE AND OVER								
	Total	Heads of families	Living at home				Boarding or lodging	Living with employer
			Living with—					
			Father	Mother	Husband	Other relative		
CINCINNATI, OHIO—Continued								
MARRIED—continued								
Restaurant, café, and lunch room keepers	42	4			36		1	1
Retail dealers	249	27	6	4	201	2	8	1
Saleswomen (stores)	313	35	31	21	162	20	44	
Semiskilled operatives (manufacturing) (n. o. s.[1])	1,675	265	139	97	968	76	130	
Chemical and allied industries—								
Soap factories	28	2	4	2	18		2	
All other chemical factories	36	6		2	23	2	3	
Cigar and tobacco factories	189	25	7	14	115	15	13	
Clay, glass, and stone industries—								
Glass factories	15	2	1		9		3	
All other clay, glass, and stone industries	2	1			1			
Clothing industries—								
Shirt, collar, and cuff factories	61	11	4	1	39	1	5	
Suit, coat, cloak, and overall factories	211	36	20	7	131	8	9	
All other clothing factories	124	23	5	5	76	3	12	
Electrical supply factories	7	2		1	3	1		
Food industries—								
Bakeries	40	7	1	4	21	3	4	
Candy factories	103	20	10	11	45	1	16	
Fruit and vegetable canning, etc	62	9	5	4	35	3	6	
Slaughter and packing houses	32	9	1		20		2	
All other food factories	27	4	2		19	1	1	
Iron and steel industries—								
Automobile factories	10	3	2	1	4			
All other iron and steel industries	65	13	5	2	40	4	1	
Lumber and furniture industries—								
Furniture factories	38	3	2	4	27	2		
Piano and organ factories	18	6		1	10	1		
Saw and planing mills	9		1	1	7			
Other woodworking factories	4		1		2		1	
Paper and pulp mills	20	2	4	1	10	2	1	
Paper box factories	10	2	2		6			
Printing and publishing—								
Blank book, envelope, tag, paper bag, etc., factories	13	1	1		7	3	1	
Printing, publishing, and engraving	33	3	6		16	4	4	
Shoe factories	238	38	31	18	126	9	16	
Textile industries—								
Cotton mills	11				9		2	
All other textile mills	51	4	4		35	5	3	
Tinware, enamelware, etc., factories	31	7	2	3	17	2		
All other industries	187	26	18	15	97	6	25	
Servants	1,441	164	41	30	724	59	196	227
Stenographers and typists	110	8	24	11	40	8	18	1
Tailoresses	218	25	6	6	159	10	11	1
Teachers (school)	124	11	12	7	81	6	3	4
Telegraph operators	10	1	2	1	5		1	
Telephone operators	45	4	8	5	16	7	5	
Trained nurses	26		3	1	12	2	4	4
Waitresses	204	26	10	10	94	3	57	4
All other occupations	236	48	9	7	139	10	18	5
WIDOWED OR DIVORCED								
All occupations	8,093	5,052	427	427		860	700	627
Actresses and showwomen	9	4	2	1			2	
Agents	11	5		2			3	1
Artists, sculptors, and teachers of art	9	6				1	2	
Attendants and helpers (professional service)	13	2	1	2			5	
Bakers	19	11	1			3	5	
Barbers, hairdressers, and manicurists	48	33	2	2		2	4	1
Boarding and lodging house keepers	296	286	2	1		4	3	
Bookkeepers, cashiers, and accountants	122	55	28	16		10	13	
Charwomen and cleaners	164	137	1	2		9	13	2

[1] Not otherwise specified.

TABLE 170.—FAMILY RELATIONSHIP OF GAINFULLY EMPLOYED WOMEN, BY MARITAL CONDITION AND SPECIFIED OCCUPATION, FOR 11 SELECTED CITIES: 1920—Continued

OCCUPATION AND MARITAL CONDITION	GAINFULLY EMPLOYED WOMEN 16 YEARS OF AGE AND OVER							
		Living at home					Boarding or lodging	Living with employer
	Total	Heads of families	Living with—					
			Father	Mother	Husband	Other rel alive		
CINCINNATI, OHIO—Continued								
WIDOWED OR DIVORCED—continued								
Cleaners and renovators (clothing, etc.)	19	12	1			2	4	
Clerks (except clerks in stores)	148	78	22	17		16	14	1
Clerks in stores	83	39	16	6		18	4	
Compositors, linotypers, and typesetters	6	2	2			1	1	
Dressmakers and seamstresses (not in factory)	365	262	9	12		41	35	6
Forewomen and overseers (manufacturing)	45	21	6	4		11	3	
Housekeepers and stewardesses	312	106	6	7		48	23	117
Janitors and sextons	179	149	4	5		14	5	2
Laborers (manufacturing) (n. o. s.[1])	82	60	6	4		6	6	
Food industries	12	8		1		1	2	
All other industries	70	52	6	3		5	4	
Laborers, porters, and helpers in stores	13	10		2			1	
Laborers, steam railroad	32	27		1		3	1	
Laundresses (not in laundry)	1,071	846	13	23		107	68	14
Laundry operatives	221	161	5	7		29	19	
Librarians	4	2					1	1
Manufacturers, officials, and managers	30	20	4			4	2	
Messenger, bundle, and office girls	3	2				1		
Midwives and nurses (not trained)	233	111	2	5		46	26	43
Milliners and millinery dealers	53	27	4	7		6	9	
Musicians and teachers of music	43	22	8	8		2	3	
Physicians and surgeons	16	13				1	1	1
Religious, charity, and welfare workers	23	6	1	3		4	8	1
Restaurant, café, and lunch room keepers	32	26	1	1		3	1	
Retail dealers	252	222	7	3		15	5	
Saleswomen (stores)	352	181	45	35		46	44	1
Semiskilled operatives (manufacturings) (n. o. s.[1])	1,463	913	121	147		170	111	1
Chemical and allied industries—								
Soap factories	43	28	7	1		3	4	
All other chemical factories	29	17	4	3		1	4	
Cigar and tobacco factories	162	104	12	22		15	9	
Clay, glass, and stone industries—								
Glass factories	10	5		3		2		
All other clay, glass, and stone industries	4	2	1	1				
Clothing industries—								
Shirt, collar, and cuff factories	37	21	4	5		4	3	
Suit, coat, cloak, and overall factories	197	134	16	10		24	13	
All other clothing factories	141	87	3	20		16	15	
Electrical supply factories	11	5	1	2		2	1	
Food industries—								
Bakeries	37	23	3	5		5	1	
Candy factories	78	51	6	9		8	4	
Fruit and vegetable canning, etc	32	22	5	2		2	1	
Slaughter and packing houses	17	13		1		1	1	1
All other food factories	14	9	3			1	1	
Iron and steel industries—								
Automobile factories	22	14	1	4		2	1	
All other iron and steel industries	54	43	2	1		5	3	
Lumber and furniture industries—								
Furniture factories	19	14				3	2	
Piano and organ factories	15	9	1	1		4		
Saw and planing mills	4	3		1				
Other woodworking factories	7	1	4	1		1		
Paper and pulp mills	20	12				5	3	
Paper box factories	17	10	1			3	3	
Printing and publishing—								
Blank book, envelope, tag, paper bag, etc., factories	13	8	1	1		2	1	
Printing, publishing, and engraving	40	23	4	3		5	5	
Shoe factories	202	114	26	25		23	14	
Textile industries—								
Cotton mills	12	8		2			2	
All other textile mills	38	27	1	3		5	2	
Tinware, enamelware, etc., factories	20	10	2	5		2	1	
All other industries	168	96	13	16		26	17	

[1] Not otherwise specified.

TABLE **170.**—FAMILY RELATIONSHIP OF GAINFULLY EMPLOYED WOMEN, BY MARITAL CONDITION AND SPECIFIED OCCUPATION, FOR 11 SELECTED CITIES: 1920—Continued

			GAINFULLY EMPLOYED WOMEN 16 YEARS OF AGE AND OVER						
				Living at home					
					Living with—				
OCCUPATION AND MARITAL CONDITION	Total	Heads of families	Father	Mother	Husband	Other relative	Boarding or lodging	Living with employer

CINCINNATI, OHIO—Continued

WIDOWED OR DIVORCED—continued

Servants	1,402	677	28	39		140	126	392
Stenographers and typists	96	32	23	13		13	13	2
Tailoresses	201	140	11	15		25	10	
Teachers (school)	67	40	8	1		5	11	2
Telegraph operators	12	3	3	2			4	
Telephone operators	59	22	16	12		2	7	
Trained nurses	66	21	1	4		6	6	28
Waitresses	155	81	6	7		16	40	5
All other occupations	264	179	11	11		22	34	7

INDIANAPOLIS, IND.

ALL CLASSES

All occupations	35,454	5,557	9,009	3,511	5,526	4,021	5,442	2,383
Agents, canvassers, and collectors	119	31	16	16	12	16	19	
Artists, sculptors, and teachers of art	92	9	30	12	19	12	9	1
Attendants and helpers (professional service)	91	7	35	17	4	12	16	
Bakers	53	10	9	4	15	4	11	
Barbers, hairdressers, and manicurists	323	66	45	22	104	28	57	1
Boarding and lodging house keepers	770	614	2	6	133	12		3
Bookkeepers, cashiers, and accountants	2,064	148	806	336	172	230	367	5
Charwomen and cleaners	54	16	4	4	15	9	5	1
Clerks (except clerks in stores)	2,515	153	1,113	371	218	294	364	2
Clerks in stores	998	68	392	113	187	107	130	1
Compositors, linotypers, and typesetters	52	6	12	7	10	8	9	
Dressmakers and seamstresses (not in factory)	1,116	370	83	73	239	150	167	34
Elevator tenders	60	6	16	7	9	9	13	
Forewomen and overseers (manufacturing)	170	24	37	17	34	37	21	
Healers (except osteopaths, physicians, and surgeons)	71	23	9	1	20	4	14	
Housekeepers and stewardesses	923	176	29	13	63	124	120	398
Janitors and sextons	207	82	4	5	87	18	7	4
Laborers (manufacturing) (n. o. s.)[1]	1,001	139	249	95	203	125	190	
Building, general, and not specified laborers	75	16	9	4	17	9	20	
Chemical and allied industries	75	11	27	3	16	8	10	
Food industries—								
Slaughter and packing houses	119	13	26	5	32	11	32	
All other food factories	72	6	17	4	15	20	10	
Iron and steel industries—								
Automobile factories	53	8	13	8	9	7	8	
All other iron and steel industries	143	26	36	21	20	23	17	
Rubber factories	52	10	3	7	11	6	15	
All other industries	412	49	118	43	83	41	78	
Laborers, porters, and helpers in stores	56	8	15	6	17	4	6	
Laundresses (not in laundry)	1,794	662	58	61	654	136	168	55
Laundry operatives	660	130	80	54	165	104	109	18
Librarians	75	9	28	13	7	9	9	
Manufacturers, officials, and managers	106	26	12	11	24	12	21	
Messenger, bundle, and office girls	105		68	13	2	9	13	
Midwives and nurses (not trained)	645	113	28	15	57	128	171	133
Milliners and millinery dealers	447	51	114	59	76	65	82	
Musicians and teachers of music	349	38	128	46	78	29	29	1
Religious, charity, and welfare workers	180	23	29	14	18	12	40	44
Restaurant, café, and lunch room keepers	107	42	6	4	37	10	8	
Retail dealers	364	137	35	24	125	30	12	1
Saleswomen (stores)	1,822	231	536	186	368	186	313	2

[1] Not otherwise specified.

TABLE 170.—FAMILY RELATIONSHIP OF GAINFULLY EMPLOYED WOMEN, BY MARITAL CONDITION AND SPECIFIED OCCUPATION, FOR 11 SELECTED CITIES: 1920—Continued

OCCUPATION AND MARITAL CONDITION	Total	GAINFULLY EMPLOYED WOMEN 16 YEARS OF AGE AND OVER						
			Living at home				Boarding or lodging	Living with employer
		Heads of families	Living with—					
			Father	Mother	Husband	Other relative		
INDIANAPOLIS, IND.—Continued								
ALL CLASSES—Continued								
Semiskilled operatives (manufacturing) (n. o. s.¹)___	4,798	663	1,392	483	878	669	709	4
Chemical and allied industries___	230	19	94	30	32	32	23	___
Cigar and tobacco factories___	113	22	25	6	23	16	21	___
Clothing industries—								
Glove factories___	139	15	54	17	21	16	16	___
Suit, coat, cloak, and overall factories___	513	75	129	49	105	80	75	___
All other clothing factories___	806	160	171	61	156	128	130	___
Electrical supply factories___	81	9	22	11	9	11	19	___
Food industries—								
Bakeries___	150	15	53	14	34	23	11	___
Candy factories___	169	13	86	19	15	18	18	___
Fruit and vegetable canning, etc___	55	7	15	9	10	9	4	1
Slaughter and packing houses___	138	18	35	15	37	13	19	1
All other food factories___	30	3	13	5	3	5	1	___
Iron and steel industries—								
Automobile factories___	321	43	73	32	73	50	50	___
All other iron and steel industries___	473	62	134	46	93	61	76	1
Lumber and furniture industries___	95	14	26	8	21	16	10	___
Printing and publishing___	267	13	109	38	36	30	41	___
Rubber factories___	119	14	27	12	29	13	24	___
Textile industries—								
Cotton mills___	75	15	19	4	12	12	13	___
All other textile mills___	133	19	55	13	17	12	17	___
All other industries___	891	127	252	94	152	124	141	1
Servants___	3,941	681	253	177	635	395	646	1,154
Stenographers and typists___	3,936	171	1,863	628	219	423	628	4
Tailoresses___	331	78	55	29	71	51	47	___
Teachers (school)___	1,571	171	481	224	170	172	218	135
Telegraph operators___	95	6	44	13	10	7	15	___
Telephone operators___	1,228	43	575	188	60	157	201	4
Trained nurses___	643	45	43	20	25	48	134	328
Waitresses___	518	71	57	40	85	46	187	32
All other occupations___	1,013	210	218	84	201	120	157	23
SINGLE (INCLUDING UNKNOWN)								
All occupations___	19,511	1,235	7,769	2,857	___	2,664	3,368	1,618
Agents, canvassers, and collectors___	54	6	11	14	___	11	12	___
Artists, sculptors, and teachers of art___	56	2	26	12	___	9	6	1
Attendants and helpers (professional service)___	68	2	31	15	___	8	12	___
Bakers___	18	2	6	2	___	3	5	___
Barbers, hairdressers, and manicurists___	103	15	32	11	___	16	29	___
Boarding and lodging house keepers___	66	59	1	3	___	3	___	___
Bookkeepers, cashiers, and accountants___	1,548	80	712	294	___	198	260	4
Charwomen and cleaners___	15	4	3	2	___	1	4	1
Clerks (except clerks in stores)___	1,900	64	996	319	___	246	273	2
Clerks in stores___	589	22	332	85	___	72	78	___
Compositors, linotypers, and typesetters___	28	2	12	5	___	4	5	___
Dressmakers and seamstresses (not in factory)___	369	83	59	50	___	86	80	11
Elevator tenders___	28	2	8	4	___	7	7	___
Forewomen and overseers (manufacturing)___	85	11	26	13	___	21	14	___
Healers (except osteopaths, physicians, and surgeons)	20	8	7	1	___	___	4	___
Housekeepers and stewardesses___	322	28	15	7	___	54	44	174
Janitors and sextons___	20	4	2	3	___	6	3	2
Laborers (manufacturing) (n .o. s.¹)___	458	19	194	70	___	70	105	___
Building, general, and not specified laborers___	25	5	4	4	___	4	8	___
Chemical and allied industries___	45	2	24	3	___	8	8	___
Food industries—								
Slaughter and packing houses___	43	1	18	2	___	4	18	___
All other food factories___	34	___	14	3	___	11	6	___
Iron and steel industries—								
Automobile factories___	22	1	8	6	___	3	4	___
All other iron and steel industries___	69	2	27	16	___	13	11	___
Rubber factories___	19	1	2	3	___	4	9	___
All other industries___	201	7	97	33	___	23	41	___

¹ Not otherwise specified.

TABLE 170.—FAMILY RELATIONSHIP OF GAINFULLY EMPLOYED WOMEN, BY MARITAL CONDITION AND SPECIFIED OCCUPATION, FOR 11 SELECTED CITIES: 1920—Continued

OCCUPATION AND MARITAL CONDITION	GAINFULLY EMPLOYED WOMEN 16 YEARS OF AGE AND OVER							
	Total	Heads of families	Living at home				Boarding or lodging	Living with employer
			Living with—					
			Father	Mother	Husband	Other relative		

INDIANAPOLIS, IND.—Continued

SINGLE (INCLUDING UNKNOWN)—continued								
Laborers, porters, and helpers in stores	23	2	12	4		2	3	
Laundresses (not in laundry)	189	51	20	31		25	47	15
Laundry operatives	241	23	79	38		60	48	13
Librarians	57	6	27	10		6	8	
Manufacturers, officials, and managers	43	3	10	8		6	16	
Messenger, bundle, and office girls	98		67	13		9	9	
Midwives and nurses (not trained)	322	28	21	12		44	117	100
Milliners and millinery dealers	247	19	87	48		40	53	
Musicians and teachers of music	202	17	111	37		22	14	1
Religious, charity, and welfare workers	132	8	27	13		8	32	44
Restaurant, café, and lunch room keepers	17	4	5	3		4	1	
Retail dealers	93	18	32	18		19	6	
Saleswomen (stores)	979	60	454	150		139	174	2
Semiskilled operatives (manufacturing) (n. o. s.[1])	2,487	111	1,136	370		447	421	2
Chemical and allied industries	153	4	75	24		30	20	
Cigar and tobacco factories	46	6	12	5		9	14	
Clothing industries—								
Glove factories	94	3	49	16		13	13	
Suit, coat, cloak, and overall factories	251	17	107	34		52	41	
All other clothing factories	363	29	141	45		77	71	
Electrical supply factories	53	2	21	10		8	12	
Food industries—								
Bakeries	75	2	43	10		16	4	
Candy factories	105		64	16		11	14	
Fruit and vegetable canning, etc.	26	1	11	5		5	3	1
Slaughter and packing houses	61	4	27	12		7	11	
All other food factories	20		12	3		5		
Iron and steel industries—								
Automobile industries	150	5	54	21		41	29	
All other iron and steel industries	230	7	111	31		35	45	1
Lumber and furniture industries	40		20	7		9	4	
Printing and publishing	183	3	94	32		27	27	
Rubber factories	66	2	22	12		10	20	
Textile industries—								
Cotton mills	29	1	15	4		2	7	
All other textile mills	83	5	51	9		10	8	
All other industries	459	20	207	74		80	78	
Servants	1,548	101	182	98		158	243	766
Stenographers and typists	3,349	100	1,736	569		396	544	4
Tailoresses	143	22	45	20		27	29	
Teachers (school)	1,280	129	458	214		158	191	130
Telegraph operators	69	2	39	10		6	12	
Telephone operators	1,010	19	514	168		145	160	4
Trained nurses	539	25	38	16		32	124	304
Waitresses	205	15	38	25		26	79	22
All other occupations	491	59	178	72		70	96	16
MARRIED								
All occupations	8,876	689	785	323	5,526	382	938	233
Agents, canvassers, and collectors	21	3	2	1	12	2	1	
Artists, sculptors, and teachers of art	24		4		19		1	
Attendants and helpers (professional service)	13	2	3	1	4	1	2	
Bakers	23	2	2	2	15		2	
Barbers, hairdressers, and manicurists	145	10	8	3	104	4	16	
Boarding and lodging house keepers	207	72			133	1		1
Bookkeepers, cashiers, and accountants	315	8	58	20	172	10	47	
Charwomen and cleaners	23	1	1	2	15	3	1	
Clerks (except clerks in stores)	392	21	70	24	218	18	41	
Clerks in stores	284	5	37	13	187	13	28	1
Compositors, linotypers, and typesetters	14	1			10	2	1	
Dressmakers and seamstresses (not in factory)	335	29	13	8	239	8	25	13
Elevator tenders	22	2	7	2	9		2	

[1] Not otherwise specified.

6436°—29——22

TABLE 170.—FAMILY RELATIONSHIP OF GAINFULLY EMPLOYED WOMEN, BY MARITAL CONDITION AND SPECIFIED OCCUPATION, FOR 11 SELECTED CITIES: 1920—Continued

OCCUPATION AND MARITAL CONDITION	Total	GAINFULLY EMPLOYED WOMEN 16 YEARS OF AGE AND OVER						
		Heads of families	Living at home				Boarding or lodging	Living with employer
			Living with—					
			Father	Mother	Husband	Other relative		

INDIANAPOLIS, IND.—Continued

MARRIED—continued								
Forewomen and overseers (manufacturing)	53	2	7	2	34	7	1	-----
Healers (except osteopaths, physicians, and surgeons)	26	2	1	-----	20	-----	3	-----
Housekeepers and stewardesses	164	23	4	2	63	16	21	35
Janitors and sextons	102	9	-----	-----	87	4	2	-----
Laborers (manufacturing) (n. o. s.¹)	357	30	38	15	203	24	47	-----
Building, general, and not specified laborers	29	1	4	-----	17	1	6	-----
Chemical and allied industries	20	1	1	-----	16	-----	2	-----
Food industries—								
Slaughter and packing houses	52	3	5	2	32	4	6	-----
All other food factories	26	1	3	1	15	4	2	-----
Iron and steel industries—								
Automobile factories	17	-----	3	1	9	1	3	-----
All other iron and steel industries	46	11	5	1	20	6	3	-----
Rubber factories	24	3	1	4	11	-----	5	-----
All other industries	143	10	16	6	83	8	20	-----
Laborers, porters, and helpers in stores	23	1	2	1	17	1	1	-----
Laundresses (not in laundry)	896	86	25	11	654	30	57	33
Laundry operatives	254	24	12	6	165	10	36	1
Librarians	11	-----	1	1	7	2	-----	-----
Manufacturers, officials, and managers	37	7	1	1	24	2	2	-----
Messenger, bundle, and office girls	6	-----	1	-----	2	-----	3	-----
Midwives and nurses (not trained)	91	8	4	-----	57	10	8	4
Milliners and millinery dealers	113	3	16	1	76	6	11	-----
Musicians and teachers of music	108	2	11	5	78	3	9	-----
Religious, charity, and welfare workers	25	-----	2	1	18	2	2	-----
Restaurant, café, and lunch room keepers	45	3	-----	-----	37	2	3	-----
Retail dealers	155	18	2	2	125	4	4	-----
Saleswomen (stores)	532	30	43	19	368	13	59	-----
Semiskilled operatives (manufacturing) (n. o. s.¹)	1,389	92	171	56	878	63	129	-----
Chemical and allied industries	50	1	12	3	32	1	1	-----
Cigar and tobacco factories	43	3	11	-----	23	5	1	-----
Clothing industries—								
Glove factories	27	1	4	-----	21	1	-----	-----
Suit, coat, cloak, and overall factories	149	10	13	5	105	4	12	-----
All other clothing factories	220	9	18	7	156	9	21	-----
Electrical supply factories	18	2	1	1	9	2	3	-----
Food industries—								
Bakeries	54	3	6	3	34	6	2	-----
Candy factories	43	4	15	3	15	4	2	-----
Fruit and vegetable canning, etc	13	-----	2	1	10	-----	-----	-----
Slaughter and packing houses	54	4	4	2	37	2	5	-----
All other food factories	4	-----	1	-----	3	-----	-----	-----
Iron and steel industries—								
Automobile factories	116	10	16	4	73	1	12	-----
All other iron and steel industries	153	13	17	5	93	10	15	-----
Lumber and furniture industries	37	7	4	1	21	2	2	-----
Printing and publishing	66	2	10	6	36	1	11	-----
Rubber factories	38	1	4	-----	29	1	3	-----
Textile industries—								
Cotton mills	21	2	3	-----	12	1	3	-----
All other textile mills	28	3	3	1	17	-----	4	-----
All other industries	255	17	27	14	152	13	32	-----
Servants	1,217	113	47	45	635	62	188	127
Stenographers and typists	416	12	88	35	219	12	50	-----
Tailoresses	96	6	5	3	71	5	6	-----
Teachers (school)	214	5	16	5	170	5	12	1
Telegraph operators	19	-----	4	2	10	-----	3	-----
Telephone operators	150	6	39	14	60	6	25	-----
Trained nurses	43	3	2	1	25	4	2	6
Waitresses	204	21	11	10	85	12	57	8
All other occupations	312	27	27	9	201	15	30	3

¹ Not otherwise specified.

TABLE 170.—FAMILY RELATIONSHIP OF GAINFULLY EMPLOYED WOMEN, BY MARITAL CONDITION AND SPECIFIED OCCUPATION, FOR 11 SELECTED CITIES: 1920—Continued

OCCUPATION AND MARITAL CONDITION	Total	GAINFULLY EMPLOYED WOMEN 16 YEARS OF AGE AND OVER						
		Heads of families	Living at home				Boarding or lodging	Living with employer
			Living with—					
			Father	Mother	Husband	Other relative		

INDIANAPOLIS, IND.—Continued

OCCUPATION AND MARITAL CONDITION	Total	Heads of families	Father	Mother	Husband	Other relative	Boarding or lodging	Living with employer
WIDOWED OR DIVORCED								
All occupations	7,067	3,633	455	331	.....	975	1,136	537
Agents, canvassers, and collectors	35	22	3	1	.....	3	6	.....
Artists, sculptors, and teachers of art	12	7	---	---	.....	3	2	.....
Attendants and helpers (professional service)	10	3	1	1	.....	3	2	.....
Bakers	12	6	1	---	.....	1	4	.....
Barbers, hairdressers, and manicurists	75	41	5	8	.....	8	12	1
Boarding and lodging house keepers	497	483	1	3	.....	8	---	2
Bookkeepers, cashiers, and accountants	201	60	36	22	.....	22	60	1
Charwomen and cleaners	16	11	---	---	.....	5	---	.....
Clerks (except clerks in stores)	223	68	47	28	.....	30	50	.....
Clerks in stores	125	41	23	15	.....	22	24	.....
Compositors, linotypers, and typesetters	10	3	---	---	.....	2	3	.....
Dressmakers and seamstresses (not in factory)	412	258	11	15	.....	56	62	10
Elevator tenders	10	2	1	1	.....	2	4	.....
Forewomen and overseers (manufacturing)	32	11	4	2	.....	9	6	.....
Healers (except osteopaths, physicians, and surgeons)	25	13	1	---	.....	4	7	.....
Housekeepers and stewardesses	437	125	10	4	.....	54	55	189
Janitors and sextons	85	69	2	2	.....	8	2	2
Laborers (manufacturing) (n. o. s.)[1]	186	90	17	10	.....	31	38	.....
Building, general, and not specified laborers	21	10	1	---	.....	4	6	.....
Chemical and allied industries	10	8	2	---	.....	---	---	.....
Food industries—								
Slaughter and packing houses	24	9	3	1	.....	3	8	.....
All other food factories	12	5	---	---	.....	5	2	.....
Iron and steel industries—								
Automobile factories	14	7	2	1	.....	3	1	.....
All other iron and steel industries	28	13	4	4	.....	4	3	.....
Rubber factories	9	6	---	---	.....	2	1	.....
All other industries	68	32	5	4	.....	10	17	.....
Laborers, porters, and helpers in stores	10	5	1	1	.....	1	2	.....
Laundresses (not in laundry)	709	525	13	19	.....	81	64	7
Laundry operatives	165	83	9	10	.....	34	25	4
Librarians	7	3	---	2	.....	1	1	.....
Manufacturers, officials, and managers	26	16	1	2	.....	4	3	.....
Messenger, bundle, and office girls	1	---	---	---	.....	---	1	.....
Midwives and nurses (not trained)	232	77	3	3	.....	74	46	29
Milliners and millinery dealers	87	29	11	10	.....	19	18	.....
Musicians and teachers of music	39	19	6	4	.....	4	6	.....
Religious, charity, and welfare workers	23	15	---	---	.....	2	6	.....
Restaurant, café, and lunch room keepers	45	35	1	1	.....	4	4	.....
Retail dealers	116	101	1	4	.....	7	2	1
Saleswomen (stores)	311	141	39	17	.....	34	80	.....
Semiskilled operatives (manufacturing) (n. o. s.)[1]	922	460	85	57	.....	159	159	2
Chemical and allied industries	27	14	7	3	.....	1	2	.....
Cigar and tobacco factories	24	13	2	1	.....	2	6	.....
Clothing industries—								
Glove factories	18	11	1	1	.....	2	3	.....
Suit, coat, cloak, and overall factories	113	48	9	10	.....	24	22	.....
All other clothing factories	223	122	12	9	.....	42	38	.....
Electrical supply factories	10	5	---	---	.....	1	4	.....
Food industries—								
Bakeries	21	10	4	1	.....	1	5	.....
Candy factories	21	9	7	---	.....	3	2	.....
Fruit and vegetable canning, etc.	16	6	2	3	.....	4	1	.....
Slaughter and packing houses	23	10	4	1	.....	4	3	1
All other food factories	6	3	---	2	.....	---	1	.....
Iron and steel industries—								
Automobile factories	55	28	3	7	.....	8	9	.....
All other iron and steel industries	90	42	6	10	.....	16	16	.....

[1] Not otherwise specified.

TABLE 170.—FAMILY RELATIONSHIP OF GAINFULLY EMPLOYED WOMEN, BY MARITAL CONDITION AND SPECIFIED OCCUPATION, FOR 11 SELECTED CITIES: 1920—Continued

OCCUPATION AND MARITAL CONDITION	GAINFULLY EMPLOYED WOMEN 16 YEARS OF AGE AND OVER							
			Living at home					
				Living with—				
	Total	Heads of families	Father	Mother	Husband	Other relative	Boarding or lodging	Living with employer

INDIANAPOLIS, IND.—Continued

WIDOWED OR DIVORCED—continued								
Semiskilled operatives (manfg.) (n. o. s.¹)—Contd.								
Lumber and furniture industries	18	7	2			5	4	
Printing and publishing	18	8	5			2	3	
Rubber factories	15	11	1			2	1	
Textile industries—								
Cotton mills	25	12	1			9	3	
All other textile mills	22	11	1	3		2	5	
All other industries	177	90	18	6		31	31	1
Servants	1,176	467	24	34		175	215	261
Stenographers and typists	171	59	39	24		15	34	
Tailoresses	92	50	5	6		19	12	
Teachers (school)	77	37	7	5		9	15	4
Telegraph operators	7	4	1	1		1		
Telephone operators	68	18	22	6		6	16	
Trained nurses	61	17	3	3		12	8	18
Waitresses	109	35	8	5		8	51	2
All other occupations	210	124	13	3		35	31	4

ST. PAUL, MINN.

ALL CLASSES								
All occupations	27,863	2,765	8,908	3,418	2,310	2,750	4,625	3,087
Agents	58	11	23	3	5	6	9	1
Artists, sculptors, and teachers of art	77	5	37	7	7	10	10	1
Attendants and helpers (professional service)	124	4	47	30	9	12	22	
Barbers, hairdressers, and manicurists	137	17	31	17	21	12	39	
Boarding and lodging house keepers	429	276	2	5	137	6		3
Bookkeepers, cashiers, and accountants	1,713	76	809	297	87	181	258	5
Charwomen and cleaners	93	43	3	6	24	3	9	5
Clerks (except clerks in stores)	3,026	141	1,503	594	97	288	383	20
Clerks in stores	1,090	37	530	162	83	122	156	
College presidents and professors	82	8	15	7	1	1	13	37
Compositors, linotypers, and typesetters	72	6	29	8	3	8	18	
Dressmakers and seamstresses (not in factory)	846	232	102	55	117	100	160	80
Elevator tenders	59	7	13	4	12	6	13	4
Floorwalkers and forewomen in stores	51	5	17	7	8	7	7	
Forewomen and overseers (manufacturing)	105	12	35	18	10	11	19	
Housekeepers and stewardesses	512	88	22	12	36	54	74	226
Janitors and sextons	72	24	3	1	32	5	5	2
Laborers (manufacturing) (n. o. s.¹)	267	41	83	16	50	28	47	2
Food industries	74	16	27	6	10	8	7	
All other industries	193	25	56	10	40	20	40	2
Laborers, steam and street railroad	74	15	9	3	35	5	7	
Laundresses (not in laundry)	442	191	5	10	133	24	26	53
Laundry operatives	436	51	117	50	70	42	85	21
Librarians	79	3	31	14	3	8	20	
Manufacturers, officials, and managers	51	15	9	6	9	5	7	
Messenger, bundle, and office girls	94		68	10	2	6	8	
Midwives and nurses (not trained)	434	66	61	31	44	63	128	41
Milliners and millinery dealers	581	45	186	81	28	81	160	
Musicians and teachers of music	281	39	103	42	32	26	34	5
Packers, wholesale and retail trade	66	5	36	10	2	4	9	
Religious, charity, and welfare workers	159	17	19	8	9	6	31	69
Restaurant, café, and lunch room keepers	54	22	1	3	16	2	9	1
Retail dealers	246	85	28	19	70	15	23	6
Saleswomen (stores)	1,663	172	486	200	216	207	382	

¹ Not otherwise specified.

TABLE 170.—FAMILY RELATIONSHIP OF GAINFULLY EMPLOYED WOMEN, BY MARITAL CONDITION AND SPECIFIED OCCUPATION, FOR 11 SELECTED CITIES: 1920—Continued

OCCUPATION AND MARITAL CONDITION	GAINFULLY EMPLOYED WOMEN 16 YEARS OF AGE AND OVER							
	Total	Heads of families	Living at home				Boarding or lodging	Living with employer
			Living with—					
			Father	Mother	Husband	Other relative		

ST. PAUL, MINN.—Continued

ALL CLASSES—Continued

Semiskilled operatives (manufacturing) (n. o. s.¹)	3,524	278	1,387	506	324	462	567	----
Cigar and tobacco factories	126	5	43	19	31	14	14	----
Clothing industries—								
Shirt, collar, and cuff factories	137	20	42	24	18	15	18	----
Suit, coat, cloak, and overall factories	288	24	110	46	25	36	47	----
All other clothing factories	549	71	155	73	64	79	107	----
Food industries—								
Bakeries	55	3	31	5	5	5	6	----
Candy factories	256	13	129	39	18	20	37	----
Slaughter and packing houses	111	14	33	11	18	10	25	----
All other food factories	80	4	35	11	9	10	11	----
Paper box factories	50	1	31	4	----	8	6	----
Printing and publishing	394	6	217	65	13	44	49	----
Shoe factories	324	20	125	61	17	47	54	----
Textile industries—								
Carpet mills	82	5	44	14	7	11	1	----
All other textile mills	80	7	24	7	16	13	13	----
Tinware, enamelware, etc., factories	60	2	20	8	5	8	17	----
All other industries	932	83	348	119	78	142	162	----
Servants	2,628	209	63	39	207	106	294	1,710
Stenographers and typists	3,534	106	1,789	623	78	392	543	3
Tailoresses	101	16	19	8	19	15	23	1
Teachers (school)	1,634	115	473	220	43	163	303	317
Telegraph operators	89	5	40	12	5	11	16	----
Telephone operators	778	22	378	141	19	77	134	7
Trained nurses	613	26	67	30	4	40	98	348
Waitresses	759	68	56	34	82	66	351	102
All other occupations	730	161	173	69	121	64	125	17
SINGLE (INCLUDING UNKNOWN)								
All occupations	21,223	857	8,450	3,159	----	2,334	3,677	2,746
Agents	40	5	21	3	----	4	6	1
Artists, sculptors, and teachers of art	65	3	36	7	----	8	10	1
Attendants and helpers (professional service)	106	1	45	30	----	12	18	----
Barbers, hairdressers, and manicurists	77	4	27	14	----	7	25	----
Boarding and lodging house keepers	63	54	1	2	----	5	----	1
Bookkeepers, cashiers, and accountants	1,489	49	777	277	----	163	218	5
Charwomen and cleaners	16	3	1	4	----	1	3	4
Clerks (except clerks in stores)	2,717	75	1,451	565	----	267	342	17
Clerks in stores	899	17	507	144	----	106	125	----
College presidents and professors	75	7	14	6	----	1	10	37
Compositors, linotypers, and typesetters	59	----	27	7	----	8	17	----
Dressmakers and seamstresses (not in factory)	485	71	92	47	----	77	120	78
Elevator tenders	36	3	12	3	----	5	9	4
Floorwalkers and forewomen in stores	34	1	17	5	----	5	6	----
Forewomen and overseers (manufacturing)	78	6	33	15	----	9	15	----
Housekeepers and stewardesses	234	16	16	9	----	31	34	128
Janitors and sextons	5	----	----	1	----	2	1	1
Laborers (manufacturing) (n. o. s.¹)	171	10	79	15	----	25	40	2
Food industries	51	5	26	6	----	7	7	----
All other industries	120	5	53	9	----	18	33	2
Laborers, steam and street railroad	18	3	8	2	----	1	4	----
Laundresses (not in laundry)	88	13	1	5	----	10	8	51
Laundry operatives	244	5	98	40	----	28	55	18
Librarians	70	1	30	14	----	7	18	----
Manufacturers, officials, and managers	25	5	7	6	----	2	5	----
Messenger, bundle, and office girls	88	----	64	10	----	6	8	----
Midwives and nurses (not trained)	281	23	53	28	----	43	101	33

¹ Not otherwise specified.

TABLE 170.—FAMILY RELATIONSHIP OF GAINFULLY EMPLOYED WOMEN, BY MARITAL CONDITION AND SPECIFIED OCCUPATION, FOR 11 SELECTED CITIES: 1920—Continued

OCCUPATION AND MARITAL CONDITION	GAINFULLY EMPLOYED WOMEN 16 YEARS OF AGE AND OVER							
	Total	Heads of families	Living at home				Boarding or lodging	Living with employer
			Living with—					
			Father	Mother	Husband	Other relative		

ST. PAUL, MINN.—Continued

OCCUPATION AND MARITAL CONDITION	Total	Heads of families	Father	Mother	Husband	Other relative	Boarding or lodging	Living with employer
SINGLE (INCLUDING UNKNOWN)—continued								
Milliners and millinery dealers	487	23	178	76	___	71	139	___
Musicians and teachers of music	207	19	96	39	___	21	27	5
Packers, wholesale and retail trade	53	___	32	8	___	4	9	___
Religious, charity, and welfare workers	135	9	17	8	___	5	28	68
Restaurant, café, and lunch room keepers	12	2	1	2	___	2	4	1
Retail dealers	84	18	21	16	___	10	14	5
Saleswomen (stores)	1,104	44	440	174	___	163	283	___
Semiskilled operatives (manufacturing) (n. o. s.[1])	2,707	75	1,316	462	___	407	447	___
Cigar and tobacco factories	80	1	40	16	___	12	11	___
Clothing industries—								
Shirt, collar, and cuff factories	90	6	36	22	___	13	13	___
Suit, coat, cloak, and overall factories	221	3	107	44	___	31	36	___
All other clothing factories	379	26	145	67	___	65	76	___
Food industries—								
Bakeries	46	___	31	5	___	5	5	___
Candy factories	211	2	125	35	___	18	31	___
Slaughter and packing houses	62	1	26	7	___	8	20	___
All other food factories	65	___	35	10	___	9	11	___
Paper box factories	47	___	31	4	___	8	4	___
Printing and publishing	353	3	208	58	___	40	44	___
Shoe factories	277	10	118	60	___	46	43	___
Textile industries—								
Carpet mills	65	1	42	12	___	9	1	___
All other textile mills	51	1	22	7	___	10	11	___
Tinware, enamelware, etc., factories	46	___	17	6	___	8	15	___
All other industries	714	21	333	109	___	125	126	___
Servants	1,848	28	53	26	___	60	162	1,519
Stenographers and typists	3,298	75	1,739	604	___	379	499	2
Tailoresses	56	6	18	8	___	11	13	___
Teachers (school)	1,534	94	463	215	___	153	292	317
Telegraph operators	80	4	39	11	___	11	15	___
Telephone operators	691	13	353	130	___	70	118	7
Trained nurses	568	17	65	30	___	33	90	333
Waitresses	466	7	44	26	___	49	247	93
All other occupations	430	48	158	65	___	52	92	15
MARRIED								
All occupations	3,699	327	273	121	2,310	139	432	97
Agents	8	2	___	___	5	1	___	___
Artists, sculptors, and teachers of art	8	___	1	___	7	___	___	___
Attendants and helpers (professional service)	13	___	1	___	9	___	3	___
Barbers, hairdressers, and manicurists	40	4	3	1	21	3	8	___
Boarding and lodging house keepers	172	32	1	___	137	___	___	2
Bookkeepers, cashiers, and accountants	149	6	15	12	87	10	19	___
Charwomen and cleaners	34	5	___	1	24	1	3	___
Clerks (except clerks in stores)	175	12	30	13	97	6	17	___
Clerks in stores	128	___	13	10	83	4	18	___
College presidents and professors	3	___	___	___	1	___	2	___
Compositors, linotypers, and typesetters	8	3	1	1	3	___	___	___
Dressmakers and seamstresses (not in factory)	159	19	5	___	117	5	12	1
Elevator tenders	16	1	1	___	12	___	2	___
Floorwalkers and forewomen in stores	11	___	___	1	8	2	___	___
Forewomen and overseers (manufacturing)	16	2	___	1	10	1	2	___
Housekeepers and stewardesses	84	11	___	___	36	5	10	22
Janitors and sextons	40	5	___	1	32	1	1	___
Laborers (manufacturing) (n. o. s.[1])	64	6	2	1	50	1	4	___
Food industries	12	1	1	___	10	___	___	___
All other industries	52	5	1	1	40	1	4	___
Laborers, steam and street railroad	42	3	___	1	35	1	2	___
Laundresses (not in laundry)	181	31	1	2	132	5	8	1
Laundry operatives	121	6	12	8	70	7	17	1

[1] Not otherwise specified.

TABLE 170.—FAMILY RELATIONSHIP OF GAINFULLY EMPLOYED WOMEN, BY MARITAL CONDITION AND SPECIFIED OCCUPATION, FOR 11 SELECTED CITIES: 1920—Continued

GAINFULLY EMPLOYED WOMEN 16 YEARS OF AGE AND OVER

OCCUPATION AND MARITAL CONDITION	Total	Heads of families	Living with— Father	Mother	Husband	Other relative	Boarding or lodging	Living with employer

ST. PAUL, MINN.—Continued

MARRIED—continued

OCCUPATION AND MARITAL CONDITION	Total	Heads of families	Father	Mother	Husband	Other relative	Boarding or lodging	Living with employer
Librarians	5		1		3		1	
Manufacturers, officials, and managers	14	1	1		9	1	2	
Messenger, bundle, and office girls	5		3		2			
Midwives and nurses (not trained)	70	6	4		44	6	9	1
Milliners and millinery dealers	51	5	6	3	28	5	4	
Musicians and teachers of music	48	5	3	1	32	2	5	
Packers, wholesale and retail trade	8	1	4	1	2			
Religious, charity, and welfare workers	13	1	2		9			1
Restaurant, café, and lunch room keepers	23	4		1	16		2	
Retail dealers	86	6	7		70		3	
Saleswomen (stores)	334	24	23	11	216	12	48	
Semiskilled operatives (manufacturing) (n. o. s.)[1]	508	30	48	22	324	22	62	
Cigar and tobacco factories	41		3	3	31	1	3	
Clothing industries—								
Shirt, collar, and cuff factories	30	2	5		18	1	4	
Suit, coat, cloak, and overall factories	32	2	2		25		3	
All other clothing factories	94	3	5	4	64	4	14	
Food industries—								
Bakeries	5				5			
Candy factories	29	2	3	2	18	1	3	
Slaughter and packing houses	32	2	5	4	18	1	2	
All other food factories	12	2		1	9			
Paper box factories	2						2	
Printing and publishing	30	1	6	3	13	3	4	
Shoe factories	31	2	5		17		7	
Textile industries—								
Carpet mills	11	1	1	1	7	1		
All other textile mills	20		2		16	1	1	
Tinware, enamelware, etc., factories	7		1		5		1	
All other industries	132	13	10	4	78	9	18	
Servants	367	40	3	4	207	13	46	54
Stenographers and typists	166	7	35	11	78	7	28	
Tailoresses	26	2	1		19	2	2	
Teachers (school)	60	5	5	3	43	1	3	
Telegraph operators	6		1		5			
Telephone operators	62	3	19	7	19	4	10	
Trained nurses	15	1	1		4	1	3	5
Waitresses	189	15	10	2	82	7	64	9
All other occupations	171	23	9	3	121	3	12	
WIDOWED OR DIVORCED								
All occupations	2,941	1,581	185	138		277	516	244
Agents	10	4	2			1	3	
Artists, sculptors, and teachers of art	4	2				2		
Attendants and helpers (professional service)	5	3	1				1	
Barbers, hairdressers, and manicurists	20	9	1	2		2	6	
Boarding and lodging house keepers	194	190		3		1		
Bookkeepers, cashiers, and accountants	75	21	17	8		8	21	
Charwomen and cleaners	43	35	2	1		1	3	1
Clerks (except clerks in stores)	134	54	22	16		15	24	3
Clerks in stores	63	20	10	8		12	13	
College presidents and professors	4	1	1	1			1	
Compositors, linotypers, and typesetters	5	3	1				1	
Dressmakers and seamstresses (not in factory)	202	142	5	8		18	28	1
Elevator tenders	7	3		1		1	2	
Floorwalkers and forewomen in stores	6	4		1			1	
Forewomen and overseers (manufacturing)	11	4	2	2		1	2	
Housekeepers and stewardesses	194	61	6	3		18	30	76
Janitors and sextons	27	19	2			2	3	1

[1] Not otherwise specified

TABLE **170.**—FAMILY RELATIONSHIP OF GAINFULLY EMPLOYED WOMEN, BY MARITAL CONDITION AND SPECIFIED OCCUPATION, FOR 11 SELECTED CITIES: 1920—Continued

OCCUPATION AND MARITAL CONDITION		GAINFULLY EMPLOYED WOMEN 16 YEARS OF AGE AND OVER						
	Total	Heads of families	Living at home				Boarding or lodging	Living with employer
			Living with—					
			Father	Mother	Husband	Other relative		

ST. PAUL, MINN.—Continued

WIDOWED OR DIVORCED—continued								
Laborers (manufacturing) (n. o. s.[1])	32	25	2			2	3	
Food industries	11	10				1		
All other industries	21	15	2			1	3	
Laborers, steam and street railroad	14	9	1			3	1	
Laundresses (not in laundry)	173	147	3	3		9	10	1
Laundry operatives	71	40	7	2		7	13	2
Librarians	4	2				1	1	
Manufacturers, officials, and managers	12	9	1			2		
Messenger, bundle, and office girls	1		1					
Midwives and nurses (not trained)	83	37	4	3		14	18	7
Milliners and millinery dealers	43	17	2	2		5	17	
Musicians and teachers of music	26	15	4	2		3	2	
Packers, wholesale and retail trade	5	4		1				
Religious, charity, and welfare workers	11	7				1	3	
Restaurant, café, and lunch room keepers	19	16					3	
Retail dealers	76	61		3		5	6	1
Saleswomen (stores)	225	104	23.	15		32	51	
Semiskilled operatives (manufacturing) (n. o. s.[1])	309	173	23	22		33	58	
Cigar and tobacco factories	5	4				1		
Clothing industries—								
Shirt, collar, and cuff factories	17	12	1	2		1	1	
Suit, coat, cloak, and overall factories	35	19	1	2		5	8	
All other clothing factories	76	42	5	2		10	17	
Food industries—								
Bakeries	4	3					1	
Candy factories	16	9	1	2		1	3	
Slaughter and packing houses	17	11	2			1	3	
All other food factories	3	2				1		
Paper box factories	1	1						
Printing and publishing	11	2	3	4		1	1	
Shoe factories	16	8	2	1		1	4	
Textile industries—								
Carpet mills	6	3	1	1		1		
All other textile mills	9	6				2	1	
Tinware, enamelware, etc., factories	7	2	2	2			1	
All other industries	86	49	5	6		8	18	
Servants	413	141	7	9		33	86	137
Stenographers and typists	70	24	15	8		6	16	1
Tailoresses	19	8				2	8	1
Teachers (school)	40	16	5	2		9	8	
Telegraph operators	3	1		1			1	
Telephone operators	25	6	6	4		3	6	
Trained nurses	30	8	1			6	5	10
Waitresses	104	46	2	6		10	40	
All other occupations	129	90	6	1		9	21	2

KANSAS CITY, MO.

ALL CLASSES								
All occupations	39,925	5,824	7,704	3,671	6,279	3,766	9,442	3,239
Actresses and showwomen	206	7	21	8	28	6	136	
Agents	120	12	39	18	19	10	20	2
Artists, sculptors, and teachers of art	119	12	34	11	25	14	22	1
Attendants and helpers (professional service)	123	6	42	12	17	17	29	
Barbers, hairdressers, and manicurists	328	70	35	16	84	27	95	1
Boarding and lodging house keepers	1,171	818	3	9	300	10	26	5
Bookkeepers, cashiers, and accountants	2,751	193	846	457	266	300	682	7
Clerks (except clerks in stores)	3,525	199	1,219	484	363	406	844	10
Clerks in stores	1,428	68	431	171	238	169	351	
Compositors, linotypers, and typesetters	72	6	17	9	13	7	20	
Demonstrators	62	7	4	4	19	4	24	

[1] Not otherwise specified.

TABLE 170.—FAMILY RELATIONSHIP OF GAINFULLY EMPLOYED WOMEN, BY MARITAL CONDITION AND SPECIFIED OCCUPATION, FOR 11 SELECTED CITIES: 1920—Continued

OCCUPATION AND MARITAL CONDITION	Total	Heads of families	Living at home—Living with—				Boarding or lodging	Living with employer
			Father	Mother	Husband	Other relative		

KANSAS CITY, MO.—Continued

OCCUPATION AND MARITAL CONDITION	Total	Heads of families	Father	Mother	Husband	Other relative	Boarding or lodging	Living with employer
ALL CLASSES—Continued								
Dressmakers and seamstresses (not in factory)	1,052	363	61	43	236	141	201	7
Elevator tenders	96	14	15	13	22	9	22	1
Forewomen and overseers (manufacturing)	114	20	20	11	28	15	20	
Healers (except osteopaths, physicians, and surgeons)	87	32	3	3	22	8	19	
Hotel keepers and managers	127	81	1	1	27	5	10	2
Housekeepers and stewardesses	869	178	19	13	81	90	135	353
Insurance agents and officials	67	10	17	11	7	8	14	
Janitors and sextons	156	58	3	6	54	14	16	5
Laborers (manufacturing) (n. o. s.¹)	469	89	78	33	113	48	107	1
Building, general, and not specified laborers	115	25	9	4	38	4	34	1
Food industries—								
Slaughter and packing houses	124	32	7	8	28	16	33	
Other food factories	69	12	17	7	11	7	15	
All other industries	161	20	45	14	36	21	25	
Laborers, porters, and helpers in stores	67	6	12	6	23	9	10	1
Laborers, steam railroad	91	40	4	4	28	6	9	
Laundresses (not in laundry)	1,744	641	47	50	599	91	298	18
Laundry operatives	983	210	102	71	270	90	239	1
Librarians	53	6	16	4		10	16	1
Manufacturers, officials, and managers	103	29	21	9	22	7	15	
Messenger, bundle, and office girls	97	5	43	17	7	13	12	
Midwives and nurses (not trained)	586	84	22	18	56	92	194	120
Milliners and millinery dealers	504	60	84	54	92	64	150	
Musicians and teachers of music	506	74	121	53	105	58	90	5
Packers, wholesale and retail trade	87	7	29	7	9	16	19	
Photographers	57	4	19	1	10	5	17	1
Physicians and surgeons	69	23	6	5	13	2	16	4
Real estate agents and officials	84	42	2	4	21	1	14	
Religious, charity, and welfare workers	168	35	16	8	22	13	32	42
Restaurant, café, and lunch room keepers	133	38	6	9	44	12	22	2
Retail dealers	378	95	36	21	136	31	56	3
Saleswomen (stores)	2,132	242	413	190	457	253	574	3
Semiskilled operatives (manufacturing) (n. o. s.¹)	3,013	426	649	277	737	300	621	3
Chemical and allied industries	53	9	21	2	10	2	9	
Clothing industries	755	146	119	49	180	108	152	1
Food industries—								
Bakeries	272	27	96	24	64	13	48	
Candy factories	238	16	69	21	56	20	56	
Slaughter and packing houses	183	33	22	29	52	19	28	
All other food factories	74	7	16	7	26	5	13	
Iron and steel industries	71	10	9	5	27	4	12	
Printing and publishing	426	27	121	50	80	50	97	1
Textile industries—								
Sail, awning, and tent factories	83	14	20	8	24	7	10	
All other textile mills	58	10	9	5	27	1	6	
All other industries	800	127	147	77	191	67	190	1
Servants	4,668	621	144	171	667	267	1,040	1,758
Stenographers and typists	5,126	221	1,770	780	318	550	1,480	7
Tailoresses	202	55	13	12	51	28	42	1
Teachers (school)	1,566	170	405	214	59	169	368	181
Telegraph operators	276	14	88	31	30	33	80	
Telephone operators	1,204	55	431	187	95	138	289	9
Trained nurses	1,040	62	40	11	32	49	235	611
Waitresses	1,062	125	53	48	224	60	493	59
All other occupations	984	191	204	76	190	91	218	14

¹ Not otherwise specified.

TABLE 170.—FAMILY RELATIONSHIP OF GAINFULLY EMPLOYED WOMEN, BY MARITAL CONDITION AND SPECIFIED OCCUPATION, FOR 11 SELECTED CITIES: 1920—Continued

OCCUPATION AND MARITAL CONDITION	GAINFULLY EMPLOYED WOMEN 16 YEARS OF AGE AND OVER							
	Total	Heads of families	Living at home				Boarding or lodging	Living with employer
			Living with—					
			Father	Mother	Husband	Other relative		
KANSAS CITY, MO.—Continued								
SINGLE (INCLUDING UNKNOWN)								
All occupations	21,389	1,267	6,712	3,009	------	2,540	5,666	2,195
Actresses and showwomen	94	4	17	4	------	3	66	------
Agents	77	3	37	15	------	9	11	2
Artists, sculptors, and teachers of art	76	5	32	9	------	12	17	1
Attendants and helpers (professional service)	84	4	35	11	------	12	22	------
Barbers, hairdressers, and manicurists	111	19	24	9	------	14	44	1
Boarding and lodging house keepers	118	107	2	3	------	1	3	2
Bookkeepers, cashiers, and accountants	1,976	85	760	399	------	244	482	6
Clerks (except clerks in stores)	2,527	71	1,090	425	------	328	608	5
Clerks in stores	923	15	388	137	------	131	252	------
Compositors, linotypers, and typesetters	41	2	14	8	------	5	12	------
Demonstrators	11	------	1	2	------	2	6	------
Dressmakers and seamstresses (not in factory)	307	65	41	33	------	72	92	4
Elevator tenders	32	1	6	10	------	6	8	1
Forewomen and overseers (manufacturing)	48	3	16	10	------	11	8	------
Healers (except osteopaths, physicians, and surgeons)	21	10	3	2	------	1	5	------
Hotel keepers and managers	23	14	1	------	------	4	2	2
Housekeepers and stewardesses	224	27	9	4	------	27	28	129
Insurance agents and officials	45	3	16	11	------	6	9	------
Janitors and sextons	17	4	------	2	------	7	4	------
Laborers (manufacturing) (n. o. s.[1])	157	11	60	19	------	25	42	------
Building, general, and not specified laborers	20	2	5	1	------	------	12	------
Food industries—								
Slaughter and packing houses	36	5	6	4	------	7	14	------
Other food factories	30	1	15	4	------	4	6	------
All other industries	71	3	34	10	------	14	10	------
Laborers, porters, and helpers in stores	27	1	10	6	------	6	3	1
Laborers, steam railroad	9	2	1	1	------	2	3	------
Laundresses (not in laundry)	208	61	26	20	------	19	76	6
Laundry operatives	285	28	77	50	------	39	91	------
Librarians	45	2	16	4	------	7	15	1
Manufacturers, officials, and managers	35	4	17	5	------	3	6	------
Messenger, bundle, and office girls	77	1	40	14	------	12	10	------
Midwives and nurses (not trained)	299	22	18	14	------	36	131	78
Milliners and millinery dealers	286	22	71	46	------	51	96	------
Musicians and teachers of music	261	31	100	42	------	39	44	5
Packers, wholesale and retail trade	55	------	28	7	------	11	9	------
Photographers	32	2	15	1	------	3	10	1
Physicians and surgeons	23	7	4	5	------	------	6	1
Real estate agents and officials	16	9	2	2	------	1	2	------
Religious, charity, and welfare workers	101	8	12	7	------	9	23	42
Restaurant, café, and lunch room keepers	28	5	4	7	------	3	9	------
Retail dealers	95	11	29	13	------	13	27	2
Saleswomen (stores)	976	46	327	144	------	162	295	2
Semiskilled operatives (manufacturing) (n. o. s.[1])	1,241	63	519	207	------	166	285	1
Chemical and allied industries	22	3	12	2	------	------	5	------
Clothing industries	277	24	97	36	------	52	68	------
Food industries—								
Bakeries	134	4	79	18	------	8	25	------
Candy factories	117	4	55	17	------	12	29	------
Slaughter and packing houses	70	7	16	24	------	13	10	------
All other food factories	29	------	12	6	------	3	8	------
Iron and steel industries	20	1	7	3	------	6	3	------
Printing and publishing	218	2	97	38	------	37	44	------
Textile industries—								
Sail, awning, and tent factories	25	------	17	6	------	1	1	------
All other textile mills	12	------	7	4	------	------	1	------
All other industries	317	18	120	53	------	34	91	1

[1] Not otherwise specified.

TABLE 170.—FAMILY RELATIONSHIP OF GAINFULLY EMPLOYED WOMEN, BY MARITAL CONDITION AND SPECIFIED OCCUPATION, FOR 11 SELECTED CITIES: 1920—Continued

OCCUPATION AND MARITAL CONDITION	GAINFULLY EMPLOYED WOMEN 16 YEARS OF AGE AND OVER							
	Total	Heads of families	Living at home				Boarding or lodging	Living with employer
			Living with—					
			Father	Mother	Husband	Other relative		

KANSAS CITY, MO.—Continued

SINGLE (INCLUDING UNKNOWN)—continued								
Servants	2,000	109	99	106	------	117	464	1,105
Stenographers and typists	4,191	130	1,646	705	------	487	1,216	7
Tailoresses	55	8	9	6	------	15	17	------
Teachers (school)	1,375	117	390	206	------	160	328	174
Telegraph operators	193	7	74	26	------	29	57	------
Telephone operators	899	26	389	153	------	112	212	7
Trained nurses	859	29	29	10	------	38	193	560
Waitresses	353	22	37	29	------	30	195	40
All other occupations	453	41	171	60	------	50	122	9
MARRIED								
All occupations	10,347	760	556	292	6,279	364	1,723	373
Actresses and showwomen	88	------	2	3	28	2	53	------
Agents	26	4	------	1	19	------	2	------
Artists, sculptors, and teachers of art	32	2	1	1	25	1	2	------
Attendants and helpers (professional service)	28	------	6	1	17	2	2	------
Barbers, hairdressers, and manicurists	127	11	5	2	84	4	21	------
Boarding and lodging house keepers	396	86	------	1	300	2	6	1
Bookkeepers, cashiers, and accountants	481	15	47	32	266	19	102	------
Clerks (except clerks in stores)	624	23	75	28	363	25	108	2
Clerks in stores	374	11	30	19	238	18	58	------
Compositors, linotypers, and typesetters	20	------	1	1	13	2	3	------
Demonstrators	27	1	1	------	19	------	6	------
Dressmakers and seamstresses (not in factory)	328	40	12	4	236	8	28	------
Elevator tenders	34	------	5	1	22	1	5	------
Forewomen and overseers (manufacturing)	41	4	3	------	28	------	6	------
Healers (except osteopaths, physicians, and surgeons)	32	2	------	------	22	1	7	------
Hotel keepers and managers	41	12	------	------	27	------	2	------
Housekeepers and stewardesses	191	20	2	1	81	8	35	44
Insurance agents and officials	17	5	1	------	7	1	3	------
Janitors and sextons	73	9	2	1	54	3	2	2
Laborers (manufacturing) (n. o. s.[1])	192	24	13	5	113	5	32	------
Building, general, and not specified laborers	63	7	3	2	38	------	13	------
Food industries—								
Slaughter and packing houses	52	.12	------	1	28	2	9	------
Other food factories	22	3	1	1	11	1	5	------
All other industries	55	2	9	1	36	2	5	------
Laborers, porters, and helpers in stores	28	------	2	------	23	1	2	------
Laborers, steam railroad	40	7	1	3	28	------	1	------
Laundresses (not in laundry)	838	93	10	14	599	19	96	7
Laundry operatives	433	36	18	10	270	17	81	1
Librarians	2	1	------	------	------	------	1	------
Manufacturers, officials, and managers	32	6	1	------	22	------	3	------
Messenger, bundle, and office girls	12	------	2	------	7	1	2	------
Midwives and nurses (not trained)	98	6	3	1	56	7	13	12
Milliners and millinery dealers	136	8	7	3	92	6	20	------
Musicians and teachers of music	156	6	12	6	105	5	22	------
Packers, wholesale and retail trade	17	------	1	------	9	1	6	------
Photographers	17	------	2	------	10	1	4	------
Physicians and surgeons	22	2	1	------	13	1	3	2
Real estate agents and officials	28	4	------	------	21	------	3	------
Religious, charity, and welfare workers	36	7	2	------	22	2	3	------
Restaurant, café, and lunch room keepers	62	5	2	------	44	4	6	1
Retail dealers	181	15	4	4	136	9	13	------
Saleswomen (stores)	704	32	44	19	457	31	120	1

[1] Not otherwise specified.

TABLE 170.—FAMILY RELATIONSHIP OF GAINFULLY EMPLOYED WOMEN, BY MARITAL CONDITION AND SPECIFIED OCCUPATION, FOR 11 SELECTED CITIES: 1920—Continued

OCCUPATION AND MARITAL CONDITION	Total	GAINFULLY EMPLOYED WOMEN 16 YEARS OF AGE AND OVER						
		Heads of families	Living at home				Boarding or lodging	Living with employer
			Living with—					
			Father	Mother	Husband	Other relative		

KANSAS CITY, MO.—Continued

MARRIED—continued

Semiskilled operatives (manufacturing) (n. o. s.[1])	1,112	69	71	32	737	47	155	1
Chemical and allied industries	20	------	5	------	10	2	3	-----
Clothing industries	261	23	12	2	180	13	31	-----
Food industries—								
Bakeries	95	5	9	3	64	3	11	-----
Candy factories	88	5	7	1	56	5	14	-----
Slaughter and packing houses	72	1	4	2	52	2	11	-----
All other food factories	32	1	2	------	26	------	3	-----
Iron and steel industries	36	2	2	1	27	1	3	-----
Printing and publishing	150	9	12	5	80	6	37	1
Textile industries—								
Sail, awning, and tent factories	35	2	2	2	24	2	3	-----
All other textile mills	31	2	------	1	27	1	------	-----
All other industries	292	19	16	15	191	12	39	-----
Servants	1,399	106	28	24	667	41	259	274
Stenographers and typists	595	16	70	33	318	25	133	-----
Tailoresses	68	6	------	3	51	4	4	-----
Teachers (school)	91	7	7	3	59	2	13	-----
Telegraph operators	58	1	8	2	30	3	14	-----
Telephone operators	187	4	23	15	95	11	38	1
Trained nurses	71	4	4	------	32	1	14	16
Waitresses	446	24	8	9	224	14	161	6
All other occupations	306	26	19	10	190	9	50	2

WIDOWED OR DIVORCED

All occupations	8,189	3,797	436	370	------	862	2,053	671
Actresses and showwomen	24	3	2	1	------	1	17	-----
Agents	17	5	2	2	------	1	7	-----
Artists, sculptors, and teachers of art	11	5	1	1	------	1	3	-----
Attendants and helpers (professional service)	11	2	1	------	------	3	5	-----
Barbers, hairdressers, and manicurists	90	40	6	5	------	9	30	-----
Boarding and lodging house keepers	657	625	1	5	------	7	17	2
Bookkeepers, cashiers, and accountants	294	93	39	26	------	37	98	1
Clerks (except clerks in stores)	374	105	54	31	------	53	128	3
Clerks in stores	131	42	13	15	------	20	41	-----
Compositors, linotypers, and typesetters	11	4	2	------	------	------	5	-----
Demonstrators	24	6	2	2	------	2	12	-----
Dressmakers and seamstresses (not in factory)	417	258	8	6	------	61	81	3
Elevator tenders	30	13	4	2	------	2	9	-----
Forewomen and overseers (manufacturing)	25	13	1	1	------	4	6	-----
Healers (except osteopaths, physicians, and surgeons)	34	20	------	1	------	6	7	-----
Hotel keepers and managers	63	55	------	1	------	1	6	-----
Housekeepers and stewardesses	454	131	8	8	------	55	72	180
Insurance agents and officials	5	2	------	------	------	1	2	-----
Janitors and sextons	66	45	1	3	------	4	10	3
Laborers (manufacturing) (n. o. s.[1])	120	54	5	9	------	18	33	1
Building, general, and not specified laborers	32	16	1	1	------	4	9	1
Food industries—								
Slaughter and packing houses	36	15	1	3	------	7	10	-----
Other food factories	17	8	1	2	------	2	4	-----
All other industries	35	15	2	3	------	5	10	-----
Laborers, porters, and helpers in stores	12	5	------	------	------	2	5	-----
Laborers, steam railroad	42	31	2	------	------	4	5	-----
Laundresses (not in laundry)	698	487	11	16	------	53	126	5
Laundry operatives	265	146	7	11	------	34	67	-----

[1] Not otherwise specified.

TABLE 170.—FAMILY RELATIONSHIP OF GAINFULLY EMPLOYED WOMEN, BY MARITAL CONDITION AND SPECIFIED OCCUPATION, FOR 11 SELECTED CITIES: 1920—Continued

OCCUPATION AND MARITAL CONDITION	GAINFULLY EMPLOYED WOMEN 16 YEARS OF AGE AND OVER							
			Living at home					
				Living with—				
	Total	Heads of families	Father	Mother	Husband	Other relative	Boarding or lodging	Living with employer

KANSAS CITY, MO.—Continued

WIDOWED OR DIVORCED—continued

Librarians	6	3	-----	-----	-----	3	-----	-----
Manufacturers, officials, and managers	36	19	3	4	-----	4	6	-----
Messenger, bundle, and office girls	8	4	1	3	-----	-----	-----	-----
Midwives and nurses (not trained)	189	56	1	3	-----	49	50	30
Milliners and millinery dealers	82	30	6	5	-----	7	34	-----
Musicians and teachers of music	89	37	9	5	-----	14	24	-----
Packers, wholesale and retail trade	15	7	-----	-----	-----	4	4	-----
Photographers	8	2	2	-----	-----	1	3	-----
Physicians and surgeons	24	14	1	-----	-----	1	7	1
Real estate agents and officials	40	29	-----	2	-----	-----	9	-----
Religious, charity, and welfare workers	31	20	2	1	-----	2	6	-----
Restaurant, café, and lunch room keepers	43	28	-----	2	-----	5	7	1
Retail dealers	102	69	3	4	-----	9	16	1
Saleswomen (stores)	452	164	42	27	-----	60	159	-----
Semiskilled operatives (manufacturing) (n. o. s.[1])	660	294	59	38	-----	87	181	1
Chemical and allied industries	11	6	4	-----	-----	-----	1	-----
Clothing industries	217	99	10	11	-----	43	53	1
Food industries—								
Bakeries	43	18	8	3	-----	2	12	-----
Candy factories	33	7	7	3	-----	3	13	-----
Slaughter and packing houses	41	25	2	3	-----	4	7	-----
All other food factories	13	6	2	1	-----	2	2	-----
Iron and steel industries	15	7	-----	1	-----	1	6	-----
Printing and publishing	58	16	12	7	-----	7	16	-----
Textile industries—								
Sail, awning, and tent factories	23	12	1	-----	-----	4	6	-----
All other textile mills	15	8	2	-----	-----	-----	5	-----
All other industries	191	90	11	9	-----	21	60	-----
Servants	1,269	406	17	41	-----	109	317	379
Stenographers and typists	340	75	54	42	-----	38	131	-----
Tailoresses	79	41	4	3	-----	9	21	1
Teachers (school)	100	46	8	5	-----	7	27	7
Telegraph operators	25	6	6	3	-----	1	9	-----
Telephone operators	118	25	19	19	-----	15	39	1
Trained nurses	110	29	7	1	-----	10	28	35
Waitresses	263	79	8	10	-----	16	137	13
All other occupations	225	124	14	6	-----	32	46	3

ATLANTA, GA.

ALL CLASSES

All occupations	31,553	6,677	4,380	3,064	7,130	3,241	5,324	1,737
Barbers, hairdressers, and manicurists	433	90	32	26	200	41	43	1
Boarding and lodging house keepers	414	312	-----	2	97	3	-----	-----
Bookkeepers, cashiers, and accountants	1,252	67	360	209	133	156	321	6
Charwomen and cleaners	137	54	6	10	42	10	13	2
Clerks (except clerks in stores)	1,691	113	502	274	153	231	416	2
Clerks in stores	217	15	62	30	47	21	42	-----
Dressmakers and seamstresses (not in factory)	908	313	49	35	322	93	91	5
Forewomen and overseers (manufacturing)	79	8	13	15	19	11	13	-----
Housekeepers and stewardesses	253	54	3	9	26	17	41	103
Insurance agents and officials	57	15	7	5	19	4	7	-----
Janitors and sextons	142	62	4	9	40	9	15	3
Laborers (manufacturing) (n.o.s.[1])	400	103	68	36	100	40	50	3
Building, general, and not specified laborers	61	23	3	2	21	3	9	-----
Cotton mills	74	20	8	6	27	8	5	-----
Food industries	65	10	16	6	16	9	7	1
All other industries	200	50	41	22	36	20	29	2

[1] Not otherwise specified.

TABLE **170.**—FAMILY RELATIONSHIP OF GAINFULLY EMPLOYED WOMEN, BY MARITAL CONDITION AND SPECIFIED OCCUPATION, FOR 11 SELECTED CITIES: 1920—Continued

OCCUPATION AND MARITAL CONDITION	GAINFULLY EMPLOYED WOMEN 16 YEARS OF AGE AND OVER							
	Total	Heads of families	Living at home				Boarding or lodging	Living with employer
			Living with—					
			Father	Mother	Husband	Other relative		
ATLANTA, GA.—Continued								
ALL CLASSES—Continued								
Laborers, steam railroad	54	24	4	4	11	9	2	----
Laundresses (not in laundry)	5,549	2,163	163	250	2,330	377	245	21
Laundry operatives	949	286	72	97	243	88	161	2
Midwives and nurses (not trained)	719	142	41	48	114	104	147	123
Milliners and millinery dealers	275	35	53	30	33	47	77	----
Musicians and teachers of music	175	27	49	26	33	19	20	1
Religious, charity, and welfare workers	121	14	14	11	20	8	43	11
Restaurant, café, and lunch room keepers	127	55	3	2	51	3	13	----
Retail dealers	173	44	13	3	71	14	28	----
Saleswomen (stores)	1,278	144	282	129	226	163	331	3
Semiskilled operatives (manufacturing) (n. o. s.¹)	2,712	459	544	329	573	347	460	----
Clothing industries—								
Hat factories (felt)	64	11	12	8	15	8	10	----
Suit, coat, cloak, and overall factories	339	75	40	40	68	56	60	----
All other clothing factories	402	94	37	30	80	73	88	----
Food industries—								
Candy factories	376	33	125	47	58	46	67	----
All other food factories	57	9	15	7	13	8	5	----
Printing and publishing	143	20	26	27	29	17	24	----
Textile industries—								
Cotton mills	624	92	132	65	172	45	118	----
All other textile mills	146	27	25	21	34	19	20	----
All other industries	561	98	132	84	104	75	68	----
Servants	6,501	1,479	348	527	1,506	619	879	1,143
Stenographers and typists	2,972	168	930	481	229	347	815	2
Tailoresses	57	14	3	6	16	8	10	----
Teachers (school)	1,028	93	275	168	125	130	205	32
Telegraph operators	187	5	64	28	14	21	55	----
Telephone operators	662	25	191	77	31	75	262	1
Trained nurses	621	49	16	29	37	52	182	256
Waitresses	346	46	34	33	61	36	131	5
All other occupations	1,064	199	175	126	208	138	206	12
SINGLE (INCLUDING UNKNOWN)								
All occupations	12,659	968	3,628	2,193	------	1,920	3,134	816
Barbers, hairdressers, and manicurists	76	15	18	11	------	14	18	----
Boarding and lodging house keepers	34	32	------	1	------	1	------	----
Bookkeepers, cashiers, and accountants	840	20	303	168	------	128	217	4
Charwomen and cleaners	18	5	1	6	------	1	5	----
Clerks (except clerks in stores)	1,236	29	461	230	------	192	323	1
Clerks in stores	125	4	55	23	------	14	30	----
Dressmakers and seamstresses (not in factory)	190	48	35	19	------	48	38	2
Forewomen and overseers (manufacturing)	29	1	9	9	------	4	6	----
Housekeepers and stewardesses	74	10	1	6	------	8	9	40
Insurance agents and officials	15	1	3	5	------	4	2	----
Janitors and sextons	17	1	2	6	------	2	6	----
Laborers (manufacturing) (n. o. s.¹)	126	13	52	22	------	17	19	3
Building, general, and not specified laborers	7	2	1	2	------	1	1	----
Cotton mills	18	2	7	3	------	4	2	----
Food industries	32	2	14	4	------	7	4	1
All other industries	69	7	30	13	------	5	12	2
Laborers, steam railroad	12	2	3	3	------	3	1	----
Laundresses (not in laundry)	526	175	69	114	------	90	68	10
Laundry operatives	265	48	50	57	------	42	68	----
Midwives and nurses (not trained)	256	11	34	30	------	40	86	55
Milliners and millinery dealers	162	8	49	24	------	33	48	----
Musicians and teachers of music	100	14	42	18	------	13	13	----
Religious, charity, and welfare workers	81	5	14	10	------	6	36	10
Restaurant, café, and lunch room keepers	15	6	1	1	------	------	7	----
Retail dealers	29	1	8	3	------	5	12	----
Saleswomen (stores)	656	31	239	94	------	115	175	2

¹ Not otherwise specified

TABLE 170.—FAMILY RELATIONSHIP OF GAINFULLY EMPLOYED WOMEN, BY MARITAL CONDITION AND SPECIFIED OCCUPATION, FOR 11 SELECTED CITIES: 1920—Continued

OCCUPATION AND MARITAL CONDITION	GAINFULLY EMPLOYED WOMEN 16 YEARS OF AGE AND OVER							
	Total	Heads of families	Living at home				Boarding or lodging	Living with employer
			Living with—					
			Father	Mother	Husband	Other relative		

ATLANTA, GA.—Continued

SINGLE (INCLUDING UNKNOWN)—continued								
Semiskilled operatives (manufacturing) (n. o. s.¹)	1,059	56	418	215	-----	196	174	-----
Clothing industries—								
Hat factories (felt)	29	1	8	7	-----	5	8	-----
Suit, coat, cloak, and overall factories	125	14	31	25	-----	31	24	-----
All other clothing factories	134	18	28	19	-----	32	37	-----
Food industries—								
Candy factories	214	2	111	33	-----	36	32	-----
All other food factories	25	1	12	6	-----	5	1	-----
Printing and publishing	62	-----	21	18	-----	12	11	-----
Textile industries—								
Cotton mills	179	6	84	40	-----	25	24	-----
All other textile mills	44	1	17	11	-----	6	9	-----
All other industries	247	13	106	56	-----	44	28	-----
Servants	1,830	213	251	324	-----	287	388	417
Stenographers and typists	2,284	72	845	421	-----	310	634	2
Tailoresses	11	2	1	2	-----	2	4	-----
Teachers (school)	772	55	262	151	-----	111	162	31
Telegraph operators	153	2	59	25	-----	20	47	-----
Telephone operators	524	9	170	61	-----	64	219	1
Trained nurses	463	19	13	21	-----	36	145	229
Waitresses	128	8	22	17	-----	23	54	4
All other occupations	503	53	138	96	-----	91	120	5
MARRIED								
All occupations	11,112	1,084	468	472	7,130	353	1,151	454
Barbers, hairdressers, and manicurists	260	18	6	9	200	9	17	1
Boarding and lodging house keepers	135	38	-----	-----	97	-----	-----	-----
Bookkeepers, cashiers, and accountants	277	14	28	24	133	10	66	2
Charwomen and cleaners	68	14	3	2	42	3	3	1
Clerks (except clerks in stores)	291	12	29	26	153	20	51	-----
Clerks in stores	67	2	7	2	47	2	7	-----
Dressmakers and seamstresses (not in factory)	407	45	7	7	322	5	18	3
Forewomen and overseers (manufacturing)	34	4	4	4	19	-----	3	-----
Housekeepers and stewardesses	66	5	-----	3	26	1	15	16
Insurance agents and officials	27	2	-----	-----	19	-----	3	-----
Janitors and sextons	60	12	1	-----	40	1	3	3
Laborers (manufacturing) (n. o. s.¹)	161	17	12	9	100	4	19	-----
Building, general, and not specified laborers	32	2	2	-----	21	1	6	-----
Cotton mills	35	3	1	2	27	1	1	-----
Food industries	22	2	1	1	16	1	1	-----
All other industries	72	10	8	6	36	1	11	-----
Laborers, steam railroad	27	10	1	1	11	4	-----	-----
Laundresses, (not in laundry)	2,961	339	63	80	2,330	61	78	10
Laundry operatives	404	49	16	24	243	21	50	1
Midwives and nurses (not trained)	209	27	6	6	114	9	28	19
Milliners and millinery dealers	50	5	1	2	33	1	8	-----
Musicians and teachers of music	54	2	5	4	33	4	6	-----
Religious, charity, and welfare workers	23	1	-----	1	20	-----	1	-----
Restaurant, café, and lunch room keepers	65	12	2	-----	51	-----	-----	-----
Retail dealers	88	6	1	-----	71	3	7	-----
Saleswomen (stores)	392	17	28	21	226	16	83	1
Semiskilled operatives (manufacturing) (n. o. s.¹)	997	79	69	71	573	45	160	-----
Clothing industries—								
Hat factories	17	-----	1	-----	15	-----	1	-----
Suit, coat, cloak, and overall factories	116	14	5	8	68	7	14	-----
All other clothing factories	118	9	2	6	80	8	13	-----
Food industries—								
Candy factories	107	12	7	10	58	2	18	-----
All other food factories	20	1	1	1	13	1	3	-----
Printing and publishing	52	2	1	7	29	1	8	-----
Textile industries—								
Cotton mills	334	21	32	17	172	14	78	-----
All other textile mills	58	4	5	6	34	3	6	-----
All other industries	175	15	12	16	104	9	19	-----

¹ Not otherwise specified.

TABLE 170.—FAMILY RELATIONSHIP OF GAINFULLY EMPLOYED WOMEN, BY MARITAL CONDITION AND SPECIFIED OCCUPATION, FOR 11 SELECTED CITIES: 1920—Continued

OCCUPATION AND MARITAL CONDITION	GAINFULLY EMPLOYED WOMEN 16 YEARS OF AGE AND OVER							
	Total	Heads of families	Living at home				Boarding or lodging	Living with employer
			Living with—					
			Father	Mother	Husband	Other relative		
ATLANTA, GA.—Continued								
MARRIED—continued								
Servants	2,687	285	63	105	1,506	85	256	387
Stenographers and typists	455	14	55	29	229	19	109	.....
Tailoresses	25	3	1	1	16	2	2	.....
Teachers (school)	175	4	12	5	125	3	26	.....
Telegraph operators	22	1	3	2	14	.....	2	.....
Telephone operators	89	5	14	10	31	6	23	.....
Trained nurses	66	3	2	3	37	4	9	8
Waitresses	142	9	10	6	61	2	53	1
All other occupations	328	29	17	15	208	13	45	1
WIDOWED OR DIVORCED								
All occupations	7,782	4,625	284	399	.....	968	1,039	467
Barbers, hairdressers, and manicurists	97	57	8	6	.....	18	8	.....
Boarding and lodging house keepers	245	242	.....	1	.....	2	.....	.....
Bookkeepers, cashiers, and accountants	135	33	29	17	.....	18	38	.....
Charwomen and cleaners	51	35	2	2	.....	6	5	1
Clerks (except clerks in stores)	164	72	12	18	.....	19	42	1
Clerks in stores	25	10	.....	5	.....	5	5	.....
Dressmakers and seamstresses (not in factory)	311	220	7	9	.....	40	35	.....
Forewomen and overseers (manufacturing)	16	3	.....	2	.....	7	4	.....
Housekeepers and stewardesses	113	39	2	.....	.....	8	17	47
Insurance agents and officials	15	11	2	.....	.....	.....	2	.....
Janitors and sextons	65	49	1	3	.....	6	6	.....
Laborers (manufacturing) (n. o. s.[1])	113	73	4	5	.....	19	12	.....
Building, general, and not specified laborers	22	19	.....	.....	.....	1	2	.....
Cotton mills	21	15	.....	1	.....	3	2	.....
Food industries	11	6	1	1	.....	1	2	.....
All other industries	59	33	3	3	.....	14	6	.....
Laborers, steam railroad	15	12	.....	.....	.....	2	1	.....
Laundresses (not in laundry)	2,062	1,649	31	56	.....	226	99	1
Laundry operatives	280	189	6	16	.....	25	43	1
Midwives and nurses (not trained)	254	104	1	12	.....	55	33	49
Milliners and millinery dealers	63	22	3	4	.....	13	21	.....
Musicians and teachers of music	21	11	2	4	.....	2	1	1
Religious, charity, and welfare workers	17	8	.....	1	.....	2	6	.....
Restaurant, café, and lunch room keepers	47	37	.....	1	.....	3	6	.....
Retail dealers	56	37	4	.....	.....	6	9	.....
Saleswomen (stores)	230	96	15	14	.....	32	73	.....
Semiskilled operatives (manufacturing) (n. o. s.[1])	656	324	57	43	.....	106	126	.....
Clothing industries—								
Hat factories (felt)	18	10	3	1	.....	3	1	.....
Suit, coat, cloak, and overall factories	98	47	4	7	.....	18	22	.....
All other clothing factories	150	67	7	5	.....	33	38	.....
Food industries—								
Candy factories	55	19	7	4	.....	8	17	.....
All other food factories	12	7	2	.....	.....	2	1	.....
Printing and publishing	29	17	1	2	.....	4	5	.....
Textile industries—								
Cotton mills	111	65	16	8	.....	6	16	.....
All other textile mills	44	22	3	4	.....	10	5	.....
All other industries	139	70	14	12	.....	22	21	.....
Servants	1,934	981	34	98	.....	247	235	339
Stenographers and typists	233	82	30	31	.....	18	72	.....
Tailoresses	21	9	1	3	.....	4	4	.....
Teachers (school)	81	34	1	12	.....	16	17	1
Telegraph operators	12	2	1	2	.....	1	6	.....
Telephone operators	49	11	7	6	.....	5	20	.....
Trained nurses	92	27	1	5	.....	12	28	19
Waitresses	76	29	2	10	.....	11	24	.....
All other occupations	233	117	20	15	.....	34	41	6

[1] Not otherwise specified.

Table 170.—Family Relationship of Gainfully Employed Women, by Marital Condition and Specified Occupation, for 11 Selected Cities: 1920—Continued

OCCUPATION AND MARITAL CONDITION	GAINFULLY EMPLOYED WOMEN 16 YEARS OF AGE AND OVER							
	Total	Heads of families	Living at home				Boarding or lodging	Living with employer
			Living with—					
			Father	Mother	Husband	Other relative		
LOUISVILLE, KY.								
ALL CLASSES								
All occupations	33,655	6,469	7,505	4,185	5,144	3,882	4,118	2,352
Actresses and showwomen	52	4	7	5	6	3	27	-----
Agents	59	12	12	1	6	10	15	3
Attendants and helpers (professional service)	63	6	16	15	8	8	9	1
Barbers, hairdressers, and manicurists	194	32	26	21	76	17	22	-----
Boarding and lodging house keepers	582	426	2	1	141	12	-----	-----
Bookkeepers, cashiers, and accountants	1,550	85	722	332	53	205	149	4
Charwomen and cleaners	135	50	5	7	40	18	10	5
Clerks (except clerks in stores)	1,550	103	697	320	57	184	187	2
Clerks in stores	649	51	264	115	54	91	74	-----
Dressmakers and seamstresses (not in factory)	1,416	420	163	136	233	218	123	123
Forewomen and overseers (manufacturing)	132	16	41	33	9	18	14	1
Housekeepers and stewardesses	575	107	24	19	46	69	63	247
Janitors and sextons	181	86	8	7	45	22	10	3
Laborers (manufacturing) (n. o. s.)	722	180	112	67	155	72	135	1
Cigar and tobacco factories	374	108	35	28	91	24	88	-----
Lumber and furniture industries	55	9	9	10	9	10	7	1
All other industries	293	63	68	29	55	38	40	-----
Laborers, porters, and helpers in stores	54	10	12	8	10	5	8	1
Laborers, steam railroad	59	27	4	4	7	11	6	-----
Laundresses (not in laundry)	3,978	1,566	131	160	1,511	311	275	24
Laundry operatives	563	86	117	78	105	75	51	51
Manufacturers, officials, and managers	58	14	14	8	5	12	5	-----
Messenger, bundle, and office girls	110	3	67	24	-----	9	7	-----
Midwives and nurses (not trained)	458	102	31	27	43	90	95	70
Milliners and millinery dealers	277	36	92	39	20	57	32	1
Musicians and teachers of music	242	37	72	34	38	32	21	8
Religious, charity, and welfare workers	134	21	18	11	13	11	22	38
Restaurant, café, and lunch room keepers	68	29	7	3	22	1	6	-----
Retail dealers	392	182	25	18	116	39	11	1
Saleswomen (stores)	1,614	153	613	284	134	259	169	2
Semiskilled operatives (manufacturing) (n. o. s.)	6,870	1,202	1,724	1,008	1,116	776	1,040	4
Chemical and allied industries	73	10	26	18	8	10	11	8
Cigar and tobacco factories	3,416	764	490	382	801	260	716	3
Clothing industries—								
Suit, coat, cloak, and overall factories	548	100	146	94	69	89	50	-----
All other clothing factories	703	108	194	119	77	122	83	-----
Food industries—								
Candy factories	190	12	92	33	6	27	20	-----
Fruit and vegetable canning, etc	133	17	53	20	22	13	8	-----
All other food factories	127	11	52	27	13	16	8	-----
Iron and steel industries	104	9	46	20	7	14	8	-----
Lumber and furniture industries—								
Furniture factories	77	6	25	26	4	12	4	-----
All other woodworking factories	100	2	47	19	12	13	7	-----
Printing and publishing	237	12	120	50	4	29	21	1
Shoe factories	72	8	26	15	1	14	8	-----
Textile industries—								
Cotton mills	177	19	62	24	14	36	22	-----
Woolen and worsted mills	247	34	95	51	18	34	15	-----
All other textile mills	112	20	38	15	16	15	8	-----
All other industries	554	70	212	105	42	71	54	-----
Servants	4,309	847	281	268	717	429	656	1,111
Stenographers and typists	2,374	59	1,177	534	53	281	269	1
Tailoresses	441	96	84	79	33	110	39	-----
Teachers (school)	1,257	120	311	196	62	168	163	237
Telegraph operators	62	4	32	8	7	3	8	-----
Telephone operators	613	25	274	155	9	76	74	-----
Trained nurses	606	47	37	27	15	42	113	325
Waitresses	326	65	50	25	47	26	93	20
All other occupations	930	160	233	108	132	112	117	68

[1] Not otherwise specified.

6436°—29——23

TABLE **170.**--FAMILY RELATIONSHIP OF GAINFULLY EMPLOYED WOMEN, BY MARITAL CONDITION AND SPECIFIED OCCUPATION, FOR 11 SELECTED CITIES: 1920—Continued

OCCUPATION AND MARITAL CONDITION	GAINFULLY EMPLOYED WOMEN 16 YEARS OF AGE AND OVER							
	Total	Heads of families	Living at home				Boarding or lodging	Living with employer
			Living with—					
			Father	Mother	Husband	Other relative		

LOUISVILLE, KY.—Continued

SINGLE (INCLUDING UNKNOWN)

All occupations	18,429	1,542	6,656	3,483	------	2,609	2,376	1,763
Actresses and showwomen	27	2	6	4	------	2	13	-----
Agents	39	6	10	1	------	9	10	3
Attendants and helpers (professional service)	37	------	15	13	------	4	4	1
Barbers, hairdressers, and manicurists	59	6	20	16	------	10	7	-----
Boarding and lodging house keepers	75	67	1	------	------	7	-----	-----
Bookkeepers, cashiers, and accountants	1,297	25	673	301	------	183	113	2
Charwomen and cleaners	24	7	1	4	------	7	3	2
Clerks (except clerks in stores)	1,286	42	655	287	------	160	140	2
Clerks in stores	499	14	249	102	------	77	57	-----
Dressmakers and seamstresses (not in factory)	703	115	139	114	------	151	66	118
Forewomen and overseers (manufacturing)	85	3	32	27	------	16	6	1
Housekeepers and stewardesses	235	22	16	11	------	26	25	135
Janitors and sextons	30	8	3	4	------	10	4	1
Laborers (manufacturing) (n. o. s.[1])	293	45	90	48	------	43	66	1
Cigar and tobacco factories	126	34	25	16	------	11	40	-----
Lumber and furniture industries	26	2	6	7	------	6	4	1
All other industries	141	9	59	25	------	26	22	-----
Laborers, porters, and helpers in stores	27	1	11	7	------	4	4	-----
Laborers, steam railroad	10	------	1	2	------	5	2	-----
Laundresses (not in laundry)	534	231	62	78	------	55	97	11
Laundry operatives	303	23	104	57	------	45	30	44
Manufacturers, officials, and managers	32	3	8	6	------	11	4	-----
Messenger, bundle, and office girls	103	1	67	24	------	7	4	-----
Midwives and nurses (not trained)	203	25	23	17	------	37	59	42
Milliners and millinery dealers	209	20	86	33	------	47	22	1
Musicians and teachers of music	157	24	61	31	------	26	9	6
Religious, charity, and welfare workers	100	15	17	10	------	7	15	36
Restaurant, café, and lunch room keepers	13	4	4	2	------	-----	3	-----
Retail dealers	100	43	19	14	------	18	5	1
Saleswomen (stores)	1,142	47	542	245	------	206	101	1
Semiskilled operatives (manufacturing) (n. o. s.[1])	3,677	282	1,493	811	------	535	554	2
Chemical and allied industries	44	3	22	6	------	9	4	-----
Cigar and tobacco factories	1,316	176	386	264	------	144	344	2
Clothing industries—								
Suit, coat, cloak, and overall factories	330	19	132	81	------	62	36	-----
All other clothing factories	450	31	167	98	------	95	59	-----
Food industries—								
Candy factories	153	2	87	30	------	20	14	-----
Fruit and vegetable canning, etc	79	2	43	19	------	11	4	-----
All other food factories	87	1	46	24	------	12	4	-----
Iron and steel industries	73	1	40	15	------	11	6	-----
Lumber and furniture industries—								
Furniture factories	58	1	23	22	------	9	3	-----
All other woodworking factories	77	------	44	18	------	11	4	-----
Printing and publishing	204	4	111	49	------	27	13	-----
Shoe factories	53	1.	25	14	------	9	4	-----
Textile industries—								
Cotton mills	116	4	57	22	------	24	9	-----
Woolen and worsted mills	168	9	81	46	------	25	7	-----
All other textile mills	58	2	33	11	------	9	3	-----
All other industries	411	26	196	92	------	57	40	-----
Servants	1,805	194	192	168	------	205	293	753
Stenographers and typists	2,156	39	1,133	507	------	263	213	1
Tailoresses	280	34	76	75	------	73	22	-----
Teachers (school)	1,090	85	293	186	------	151	144	231
Telegraph operators	52	4	29	8	------	3	8	-----
Telephone operators	545	14	256	144	------	72	59	-----
Trained nurses	500	30	33	20	------	33	92	292
Waitresses	148	17	34	15	------	17	54	11
All other occupations	554	44	202	91	------	84	68	65

[1] Not otherwise specified.

TABLE 170.—FAMILY RELATIONSHIP OF GAINFULLY EMPLOYED WOMEN, BY MARITAL CONDITION AND SPECIFIED OCCUPATION, FOR 11 SELECTED CITIES: 1920—Continued

OCCUPATION AND MARITAL CONDITION	GAINFULLY EMPLOYED WOMEN 16 YEARS OF AGE AND OVER							
	Total	Living at home					Boarding or lodging	Living with employer
		Heads of families	Living with—					
			Father	Mother	Husband	Other relative		

LOUISVILLE, KY.—Continued

MARRIED

OCCUPATION AND MARITAL CONDITION	Total	Heads of families	Father	Mother	Husband	Other relative	Boarding or lodging	Living with employer
All occupations	8,078	865	447	306	5,144	342	809	165
Actresses and showwomen	18	1			6	1	10	
Agents	11	1			6		4	
Attendants and helpers (professional service)	13	1	1	1	8		2	
Barbers, hairdressers, and manicurists	92	8	2	2	76		4	
Boarding and lodging house keepers	182	40			141	1		
Bookkeepers, cashiers, and accountants	126	12	26	10	53	8	15	2
Charwomen and cleaners	53	5	3	1	40		3	1
Clerks (except clerks in stores)	124	6	21	14	57	6	20	
Clerks in stores	79	2	10	5	54	3	5	
Dressmakers and seamstresses (not in factory)	311	33	7	7	233	10	17	4
Forewomen and overseers (manufacturing)	20	3	3	1	9	1	3	
Housekeepers and stewardesses	93	8	2	2	46	13	8	14
Janitors and sextons	61	8	3	1	45	1	2	1
Laborers (manufacturing) (n. o. s.[1])	273	37	14	11	155	14	42	
Cigar and tobacco factories	170	25	8	7	91	8	31	
Lumber and furniture industries	15	1	1	2	9	1	1	
All other industries	88	11	5	2	55	5	10	
Laborers, porters, and helpers in stores	17	2	1	1	10	1	1	1
Laborers, steam railroad	16	5	1		7	1	2	
Laundresses (not in laundry)	1,941	217	43	32	1,511	57	75	6
Laundry operatives	155	9	8	9	105	8	9	7
Manufacturers, officials, and managers	11	2	3	1	5			
Messenger, bundle, and office girls	1						1	
Midwives and nurses (not trained)	70	8	2		43	5	10	2
Milliners and millinery dealers	31		3	3	20	2	3	
Musicians and teachers of music	52	1	6		38	1	6	
Religious, charity, and welfare workers	20		1	1	13	2	1	2
Restaurant, café, and lunch room keepers	30	4	2		22	1	1	
Retail dealers	146	19	4	1	116	5	1	
Saleswomen (stores)	237	15	33	11	134	12	31	1
Semiskilled operatives (manufacturing) (n. o. s.[1])	1,964	244	124	107	1,116	81	291	1
Chemical and allied industries	18	3	3		10	1	1	
Cigar and tobacco factories	1,408	190	60	69	801	48	240	
Clothing industries—								
Suit, coat, cloak, and overall factories	95	8	5	4	69	7	2	
All other clothing factories	125	9	13	10	77	5	11	
Food industries—								
Candy factories	16	1	3	1	6	2	3	
Fruit and vegetable canning, etc	32	2	5		22	1	2	
All other food factories	21	1	2	2	13	2	1	
Iron and steel industries	17	2	2	3	7	1	2	
Lumber and furniture industries—								
Furniture factories	10	2	1	1	4	1	1	
All other woodworking factories	17		1	1	12	1	2	
Printing and publishing	18	3	5	1	4	1	3	1
Shoe factories	4			1	1		2	
Textile industries—								
Cotton mills	35	5	2	2	14	4	8	
Woolen and worsted mills	39	3	8	3	18	3	4	
All other textile mills	29	6	2	4	16	1		
All other industries	80	9	12	5	42	3	9	
Servants	1,259	126	48	49	717	72	147	100
Stenographers and typists	135	1	25	14	53	11	31	
Tailoresses	54	6	3		33	7	5	
Teachers (school)	91	3	12	3	62	3	6	2
Telegraph operators	10		3		7			
Telephone operators	24	1	5	1	9		8	
Trained nurses	41	2	3	2	15	3	5	11
Waitresses	105	9	6	7	47	6	22	8
All other occupations	212	26	19	9	132	6	18	2

[1] Not otherwise specified.

TABLE 170.—FAMILY RELATIONSHIP OF GAINFULLY EMPLOYED WOMEN, BY MARITAL CONDITION AND SPECIFIED OCCUPATION, FOR 11 SELECTED CITIES: 1920—Continued

OCCUPATION AND MARITAL CONDITION	GAINFULLY EMPLOYED WOMEN 16 YEARS OF AGE AND OVER							
	Total	Living at home					Boarding or lodging	Living with employer
		Heads of families	Living with—					
			Father	Mother	Husband	Other relative		

LOUISVILLE, KY.—Continued

OCCUPATION AND MARITAL CONDITION	Total	Heads of families	Father	Mother	Husband	Other relative	Boarding or lodging	Living with employer
WIDOWED OR DIVORCED								
All occupations	7,148	4,062	402	396		931	933	424
Actresses and showwomen	7	1	1	1			4	
Agents	9	5	2			1	1	
Attendants and helpers (professional service)	13	5		1		4	3	
Barbers, hairdressers, and manicurists	43	18	4	3		7	11	
Boarding and lodging house keepers	325	319	1	1		4		
Bookkeepers, cashiers, and accountants	127	48	23	21		14	21	
Charwomen and cleaners	58	38	1	2		11	4	2
Clerks (except clerks in stores)	140	55	21	19		18	27	
Clerks in stores	71	35	5	8		11	12	
Dressmakers and seamstresses (not in factory)	402	272	17	15		57	40	1
Forewomen and overseers (manufacturing)	27	10	6	5		1	5	
Housekeepers and stewardesses	247	77	6	6		30	30	98
Janitors and sextons	90	70	2	2		11	4	1
Laborers (manufacturing) (n. o. s.[1])	156	98	8	8		15	27	
Cigar and tobacco factories	78	49	2	5		5	17	
Lumber and furniture industries	14	6	2	1		3	2	
All other industries	64	43	4	2		7	8	
Laborers, porters, and helpers in stores	10	7					3	
Laborers, steam railroad	33	22	2	2		5	2	
Laundresses (not in laundry)	1,503	1,118	26	50		199	103	7
Laundry operatives	105	54	5	12		22	12	
Manufacturers, officials, and managers	15	9	3	1		1	1	
Messenger, bundle, and office girls	6	2				2	2	
Midwives and nurses (not trained)	185	69	6	10		48	26	26
Milliners and millinery dealers	37	16	3	3		8	7	
Musicians and teachers of music	33	12	5	3		5	6	2
Religious, charity, and welfare workers	14	6				2	6	
Restaurant, café, and lunch room keepers	25	21	1	1			2	
Retail dealers	146	120	2	3		16	5	
Saleswomen (stores)	235	91	38	28		41	37	
Semiskilled operatives (manufacturing) (n. o. s.[1])	1,229	676	107	90		160	195	1
Chemical and allied industries	11	4	1	2		1	3	
Cigar and tobacco factories	692	398	44	49		68	132	1
Clothing industries—								
Suit, coat, cloak, and overall factories	123	73	9	9		20	12	
All other clothing factories	128	68	14	11		22	13	
Food industries—								
Candy factories	21	9	2	2		5	3	
Fruit and vegetable canning, etc	22	13	5	1		1	2	
All other food factories	19	9	4	1		2	3	
Iron and steel industries	14	6	4	2		2		
Lumber and furniture industries—								
Furniture factories	9	3	1	3		2		
All other woodworking factories	6	2	2			1	1	
Printing and publishing	15	5	4			1	5	
Shoe factories	15	7	1			5	2	
Textile industries—								
Cotton mills	26	10	3			8	5	
Woolen and worsted mills	40	22	6	2		6	4	
All other textile mills	25	12	3			5	5	
All other industries	63	35	4	8		11	5	
Servants	1,245	527	41	51		152	216	258
Stenographers and typists	83	19	19	13		7	25	
Tailoresses	107	56	5	4		30	12	
Teachers (school)	76	32	6	7		14	13	4
Telephone operators	44	10	13	10		4	7	
Trained nurses	65	15	1	5		6	16	22
Waitresses	73	39	10	3		3	17	1
All other occupations	164	90	12	8		22	31	1

[1] Not otherwise specified.

TABLE 170.—FAMILY RELATIONSHIP OF GAINFULLY EMPLOYED WOMEN, BY MARITAL CONDITION AND SPECIFIED OCCUPATION, FOR 11 SELECTED CITIES: 1920—Continued

	GAINFULLY EMPLOYED WOMEN 16 YEARS OF AGE AND OVER							
			Living at home				Boarding or lodging	Living with employer
OCCUPATION AND MARITAL CONDITION	Total	Heads of families		Living with—				
			Father	Mother	Husband	Other relative		

NEW ORLEANS, LA.

ALL CLASSES								
All occupations	48,358	9,149	9,126	6,028	7,013	7,340	6,426	3,276
Actresses and showwomen	75	3	12	14	10	7	29	----
Agents	58	13	9	5	6	14	11	----
Artists, sculptors, and teachers of art	62	6	14	13	6	13	9	1
Attendants and helpers (professional service)	93	5	40	23	3	12	10	----
Barbers, hairdressers, and manicurists	548	121	63	59	169	68	68	----
Boarding and lodging house keepers	1,011	809	5	7	162	12	13	3
Bookkeepers, cashiers, and accountants	1,121	68	440	256	35	210	105	7
Canvassers	50	13	6	3	9	5	14	----
Charwomen and cleaners	95	33	7	6	25	8	16	----
Clerks (except clerks in stores)	1,995	127	765	464	60	378	195	6
Clerks in stores	871	30	374	166	71	161	68	1
College presidents and professors	70	4	14	3	6	11	11	21
Dressmakers and seamstresses (not in factory)	2,907	854	291	349	486	509	369	49
Elevator tenders	74	8	20	12	8	16	10	----
Farm laborers (working out)	102	14	20	3	47	12	5	1
Forewomen and overseers (manufacturing)	131	17	33	28	7	36	10	----
Housekeepers and stewardesses	758	166	38	28	58	106	99	263
Janitors and sextons	103	46	3	4	25	10	10	5
Laborers (manufacturing) (n. o. s.[1])	1,108	187	245	137	160	178	195	6
Building, general, and not specified laborers	168	39	19	3	39	14	50	4
Cigar and tobacco factories	64	9	21	10	5	14	5	----
Food industries	149	23	33	25	17	28	23	----
Textile industries—								
Cotton mills	171	35	35	11	25	34	30	1
All other textile mills	90	8	27	13	8	14	20	----
Tinware, enamelware, etc., factories	52	3	20	11	3	11	4	----
All other industries	414	70	90	64	63	63	63	1
Laborers, porters, and helpers in stores	116	11	20	14	33	25	12	1
Laborers, steam railroad	82	23	12	10	15	11	11	----
Laundresses (not in laundry)	7,282	2,439	222	263	2,604	745	963	46
Laundry operatives	646	100	115	81	94	130	115	11
Manufacturers, officials, and managers	81	33	8	4	10	14	12	----
Messenger, bundle, and office girls	55	5	21	13	2	12	2	----
Midwives and nurses (not trained)	841	161	45	45	118	123	109	240
Milliners and millinery dealers	224	19	79	46	8	47	25	----
Musicians and teachers of music	332	56	87	49	29	52	54	5
Real estate agents and officials	80	50	3	6	9	5	7	----
Religious, charity, and welfare workers	223	24	12	11	8	9	27	132
Restaurant, café, and lunch room keepers	68	35	1	2	19	8	3	----
Retail dealers	769	330	53	38	256	73	18	1
Saleswoman (stores)	2,269	169	863	447	133	451	205	1
Semiskilled operatives (manufacturing)(n. o. s.[1])	5,152	588	1,594	1,022	318	1,084	540	6
Cigar and tobacco factories	1,153	86	413	277	60	230	86	1
Clothing industries—								
Suit, coat, cloak, and overall factories	349	54	72	66	29	105	23	----
All other clothing factories	535	79	117	107	18	145	69	----
Food industries—								
Bakeries	223	26	74	48	5	43	27	----
Candy factories	253	11	115	56	4	45	22	----
All other food factories	359	49	107	49	42	75	35	2
Lumber and furniture industries	104	10	22	29	6	27	10	----
Printing and publishing	84	6	29	21	5	21	2	----
Shoe factories	75	5	36	9	2	19	4	----
Textile industries—								
Cotton mills	497	84	129	88	36	87	73	----
Knitting mills	223	10	118	49	3	36	7	----
All other textile mills	310	51	61	56	23	70	47	2
Tinware, enamelware, etc., factories	132	14	44	23	7	27	17	----
All other industries	855	103	257	144	78	154	118	1

[1] Not otherwise specified.

TABLE 170.—FAMILY RELATIONSHIP OF GAINFULLY EMPLOYED WOMEN, BY MARITAL CONDITION AND SPECIFIED OCCUPATION, FOR 11 SELECTED CITIES: 1920—Continued

		GAINFULLY EMPLOYED WOMEN 16 YEARS OF AGE AND OVER						
			Living at home				Boarding or lodging	Living with employer
OCCUPATION AND MARITAL CONDITION	Total	Heads of families	Living with—					
			Father	Mother	Husband	Other relative		

NEW ORLEANS, LA.—Continued

ALL CLASSES—Continued

Servants	9,967	1,841	719	681	1,622	1,374	2,008	1,722
Stenographers and typists	3,412	85	1,572	834	50	543	326	2
Tailoresses	115	24	9	25	16	24	16	1
Teachers (school)	2,198	221	579	377	51	387	164	419
Telegraph operators	147	7	62	33	4	20	21	-----
Telephone operators	745	20	315	192	10	141	66	1
Trained nurses	735	73	67	54	44	77	136	284
Waitresses	494	59	56	55	52	58	191	23
All other occupations	1,093	252	213	146	155	161	148	18

SINGLE (INCLUDING UNKNOWN)

All occupations	25,282	1,754	8,168	4,939	-----	4,802	3,307	2,312
Actresses and showwomen	30	1	6	9	-----	3	11	-----
Agents	24	5	5	3	-----	8	3	-----
Artists, sculptors, and teachers of art	43	3	10	12	-----	12	5	1
Attendants and helpers (professional service)	73	1	35	19	-----	9	9	-----
Barbers, hairdressers, and manicurists	173	26	39	37	-----	39	32	-----
Boarding and lodging house keepers	172	158	2	2	-----	6	4	-----
Bookkeepers, cashiers, and accountants	942	27	417	232	-----	181	79	6
Canvassers	11	1	3	1	-----	3	3	-----
Charwomen and cleaners	17	3	5	4	-----	1	4	-----
Clerks (except clerks in stores)	1,631	40	715	413	-----	320	138	5
Clerks in stores	691	8	348	148	-----	141	45	1
College presidents and professors	61	4	12	3	-----	10	11	21
Dressmakers and seamstresses (not in factory)	1,214	169	239	275	-----	324	169	38
Elevator tenders	40	-----	17	8	-----	9	6	-----
Farm laborers (working out)	26	-----	17	3	-----	3	3	-----
Forewomen and overseers (manufacturing)	86	6	29	22	-----	23	6	-----
Housekeepers and stewardesses	314	30	25	21	-----	52	42	144
Janitors and sextons	19	4	3	4	-----	4	3	1
Laborers (manufacturing) (n. o. s.[1])	554	35	219	98	-----	104	97	1
Building, general, and not specified laborers	63	8	19	2	-----	9	25	-----
Cigar and tobacco factories	40	-----	19	7	-----	10	4	-----
Food industries	82	6	26	17	-----	22	11	-----
Textile industries—								
Cotton mills	73	5	29	6	-----	17	15	1
All other textile mills	53	-----	26	11	-----	8	8	-----
Tinware, enamelware, etc., factories	39	-----	17	10	-----	8	4	-----
All other industries	204	16	83	45	-----	30	30	-----
Laborers, porters, and helpers in stores	48	-----	17	9	-----	16	5	1
Laborers, steam railroad	22	2	7	6	-----	3	4	-----
Laundresses (not in laundry)	951	255	103	113	-----	167	289	24
Laundry operatives	323	23	92	62	-----	83	56	7
Manufacturers, officials, and managers	38	12	8	2	-----	9	7	-----
Messenger, bundle, and office girls	45	2	20	11	-----	10	2	-----
Midwives and nurses (not trained)	346	18	33	33	-----	50	62	150
Milliners and millinery dealers	174	6	78	39	-----	38	13	-----
Musicians and teachers of music	210	21	74	35	-----	42	33	5
Real estate agents and officials	24	12	2	5	-----	2	3	-----
Religious, charity, and welfare workers	197	16	12	11	-----	5	21	132
Restaurant, café, and lunch room keepers	9	1	1	1	-----	4	2	-----

[1] Not otherwise specified.

TABLE 170.—FAMILY RELATIONSHIP OF GAINFULLY EMPLOYED WOMEN, BY MARITAL CONDITION AND SPECIFIED OCCUPATION, FOR 11 SELECTED CITIES: 1920—Continued

OCCUPATION AND MARITAL CONDITION	GAINFULLY EMPLOYED WOMEN 16 YEARS OF AGE AND OVER							
		Living at home					Boarding or lodging	Living with employer
	Total	Heads of families	Living with—					
			Father	Mother	Husband	Other relative		

NEW ORLEANS, LA.—Continued

SINGLE (INCLUDING UNKNOWN)—continued								
Retail dealers	140	38	38	25	------	35	3	1
Saleswomen (stores)	1,743	49	804	387	------	373	129	1
Semiskilled operatives (manufacturing) (n. o. s.¹)	3,593	115	1,461	863	------	835	313	6
Cigar and tobacco factories	885	17	380	253	------	181	53	1
Clothing industries—								
Suit, coat, cloak, and overall factories	219	10	67	51	------	80	11	----
All other clothing factories	379	25	109	86	------	113	46	----
Food industries—								
Bakeries	144	1	67	40	------	25	11	----
Candy factories	215	4	105	50	------	39	17	----
All other food factories	215	10	94	37	------	58	14	2
Lumber and furniture industries	73	3	18	27	------	17	8	----
Printing, publishing, and engraving	68	2	26	19	------	20	1	----
Shoe factories	61	1	34	8	------	15	3	----
Textile industries—								
Cotton mills	294	14	116	70	------	62	32	----
Knitting mills	191	------	111	44	------	31	5	----
All other textile mills	178	7	56	42	------	48	23	2
Tinware, enamelware, etc., factories	94	1	39	17	------	25	12	----
All other industries	577	20	239	119	------	121	77	1
Servants	4,011	352	533	443	------	662	958	1,063
Stenographers and typists	3,126	49	1,531	795	------	497	252	2
Tailoresses	55	5	7	19	------	17	6	1
Teachers (school)	1,992	154	566	364	------	359	136	413
Telegraph operators	125	1	60	31	------	17	16	----
Telephone operators	665	8	293	176	------	128	59	1
Trained nurses	549	27	56	46	------	56	105	259
Waitresses	224	9	40	37	------	30	92	16
All other occupations	551	58	186	112	------	112	71	12
MARRIED								
All occupations	12,375	1,504	595	544	7,013	785	1,573	361
Actresses and showwomen	38	1	6	5	10	2	14	----
Agents	14	2	2	1	6	------	3	----
Artists, sculptors, and teachers of art	13	1	2	------	6	------	4	----
Attendants and helpers (professional service)	10	------	4	2	3	------	1	----
Barbers, hairdressers, and manicurists	258	26	21	9	169	11	22	----
Boarding and lodging house keepers	257	86	1	1	162	2	4	1
Bookkeepers, cashiers, and accountants	87	12	10	11	35	6	13	----
Canvassers	17	2	------	------	9	------	6	----
Charwomen and cleaners	43	8	2	------	25	3	5	----
Clerks (except clerks in stores)	168	22	31	17	60	16	22	----
Clerks in stores	106	7	11	5	71	3	9	----
College presidents and professors	8	------	2	------	6	------	------	----
Dressmakers and seamstresses (not in factory)	777	116	26	31	486	49	64	5
Elevator tenders	21	4	2	2	8	2	3	----
Farm laborers (working out)	55	2	3	------	47	1	1	1
Forewomen and overseers (manufacturing)	13	------	1	2	7	1	2	----
Housekeepers and stewardesses	150	22	8	4	58	8	29	21
Janitors and sextons	35	2	------	------	25	2	3	3
Laborers (manufacturing) (n. o. s.¹)	333	47	19	24	160	29	52	2
Building, general, and not specified laborers	75	13	------	1	39	2	19	1
Cigar and tobacco factories	14	3	2	2	5	2	------	----
Food industries	46	5	5	6	17	4	9	----
Textile industries—								
Cotton mills	48	7	4	2	25	4	6	----
All other textile mills	12	------	------	------	8	1	3	----
Tinware, enamelware, etc., factories	8	------	3	1	3	1	------	----
All other industries	130	19	5	12	63	15	15	1

¹ Not otherwise specified.

TABLE 170.—FAMILY RELATIONSHIP OF GAINFULLY EMPLOYED WOMEN, BY MARITAL CONDITION AND SPECIFIED OCCUPATION, FOR 11 SELECTED CITIES: 1920—Continued

OCCUPATION AND MARITAL CONDITION	GAINFULLY EMPLOYED WOMEN 16 YEARS OF AGE AND OVER							
	Total	Heads of families	Living at home				Boarding or lodging	Living with employer
			Living with—					
			Father	Mother	Husband	Other relative		

NEW ORLEANS, LA.—Continued

OCCUPATION AND MARITAL CONDITION	Total	Heads of families	Father	Mother	Husband	Other relative	Boarding or lodging	Living with employer
MARRIED—continued								
Laborers, porters, and helpers in stores	51	5	2	3	33	3	5	----
Laborers, steam railroad	25	2	1	1	15	2	4	----
Laundresses (not in laundry)	3,751	471	81	88	2,604	162	339	6
Laundry operatives	194	24	11	12	94	19	32	2
Manufacturers, officials, and managers	16	4	---	---	10	---	2	---
Messenger, bundle, and office girls	6	1	1	2	2	---	---	---
Midwives and nurses (not trained)	212	13	7	4	118	18	17	35
Milliners and millinery dealers	25	4	1	4	8	3	5	----
Musicians and teachers of music	55	2	10	4	29	---	10	---
Real estate agents and officials	23	9	---	1	9	---	4	---
Religious, charity, and welfare workers	11	1	---	---	8	---	2	---
Restaurant, café, and lunch room keepers	25	6	---	---	19	---	---	---
Retail dealers	329	37	11	7	256	9	9	----
Saleswomen (stores)	245	19	31	14	133	18	30	----
Semiskilled operatives (manufacturing) (n. o. s.¹)	744	100	69	72	318	74	111	----
Cigar and tobacco factories	140	15	17	13	60	19	16	----
Clothing industries—								
Suit, coat, cloak, and overall factories	58	9	1	10	29	3	6	----
All other clothing factories	48	6	2	10	18	4	8	----
Food industries—								
Bakeries	26	4	3	4	5	5	5	----
Candy factories	19	1	6	3	4	3	2	----
All other food factories	88	12	9	4	42	8	13	----
Lumber and furniture industries	15	5	---	---	6	3	1	---
Printing and publishing	11	2	3	1	5	---	---	---
Shoe factories	7	2	1	---	2	1	1	---
Textile industries—								
Cotton mills	90	14	7	5	36	8	20	----
Knitting mills	13	2	4	2	3	1	1	----
All other textile mills	60	7	4	8	23	8	10	----
Tinware, enamelware, etc., factories	16	2	3	1	7	1	2	----
All other industries	153	19	9	11	78	10	26	----
Servants	3,413	368	142	150	1,622	280	582	269
Stenographers and typists	146	3	28	18	50	14	33	----
Tailoresses	30	4	1	4	16	---	5	---
Teachers (school)	87	10	5	6	51	7	7	1
Telegraph operators	12	1	---	2	4	2	3	----
Telephone operators	34	2	7	6	10	5	4	----
Trained nurses	88	8	6	2	44	8	13	7
Waitresses	175	14	12	12	52	12	66	7
All other occupations	275	36	18	18	155	14	33	1
WIDOWED OR DIVORCED								
All occupations	10,701	5,891	363	545	-----	1,753	1,546	603
Actresses and showwomen	7	1	---	---	-----	2	4	---
Agents	20	6	2	1	-----	6	5	---
Artists, sculptors, and teachers of art	6	2	2	1	-----	1	---	---
Attendants and helpers (professional service)	10	4	1	2	-----	3	---	---
Barbers, hairdressers, and manicurists	117	69	3	13	-----	18	14	---
Boarding and lodging house keepers	582	565	2	4	-----	4	5	2
Bookkeepers, cashiers, and accountants	92	29	13	13	-----	23	13	1
Canvassers	22	10	3	2	-----	2	5	---
Charwomen and cleaners	35	22	---	2	-----	4	7	---
Clerks (except clerks in stores)	196	65	19	34	-----	42	35	1
Clerks in stores	74	15	15	13	-----	17	14	---
College presidents and professors	1	---	---	---	-----	1	---	---
Dressmakers and seamstresses (not in factory)	916	569	26	43	-----	136	136	6
Elevator tenders	13	4	1	2	-----	5	1	---
Farm laborers (working out)	21	12	---	---	-----	8	1	---
Forewomen and overseers (manufacturing)	32	11	3	4	-----	12	2	---
Housekeepers and stewardesses	294	114	5	3	-----	46	28	98

¹ Not otherwise specified.

TABLE 170.—FAMILY RELATIONSHIP OF GAINFULLY EMPLOYED WOMEN, BY MARITAL CONDITION AND SPECIFIED OCCUPATION, FOR 11 SELECTED CITIES: 1920—Continued

OCCUPATION AND MARITAL CONDITION	Total	Heads of families	Living at home — Living with— Father	Mother	Husband	Other relative	Boarding or lodging	Living with employer
NEW ORLEANS, LA.—Continued								
WIDOWED OR DIVORCED—continued								
Janitors and sextons	49	40				4	4	1
Laborers (manufacturing) (n. o. s.[1])	221	105	7	15		45	46	3
Building, general, and not specified laborers	30	18				3	6	3
Cigar and tobacco factories	10	6		1		2	1	
Food industries	21	12	2	2		2	3	
Textile industries—								
Cotton mills	50	23	2	3		13	9	
All other textile mills	25	8	1	2		5	9	
Tinware, enamelware, etc., factories	5	3				2		
All other industries	80	35	2	7		18	18	
Laborers, porters, and helpers in stores	17	6	1	2		6	2	
Laborers, steam railroad	35	19	4	3		6	3	
Laundresses (not in laundry)	2,580	1,713	38	62		416	335	16
Laundry operatives	129	53	12	7		28	27	2
Manufacturers, officials, and managers	27	17		2		5	3	
Messenger, bundle, and office girls	4	2				2		
Midwives and nurses (not trained)	283	130	5	8		55	30	55
Milliners and millinery dealers	25	9		3		6	7	
Musicians and teachers of music	67	33	3	10		10	11	
Real estate agents and officials	33	29	1			3		
Religious, charity, and welfare workers	15	7		1		4	4	
Restaurant, café, and lunch room keepers	34	28		1		4	1	
Retail dealers	300	255	4	6		29	6	
Saleswomen (stores)	281	101	28	46		60	46	
Semiskilled operatives (manufacturing) (n. o. s.[1])	815	373	64	87		175	116	
Cigar and tobacco factories	128	54	16	11		30	17	
Clothing industries—								
Suit, coat, cloak, and overall factories	72	35	4	5		22	6	
All other clothing factories	108	48	6	11		28	15	
Food industries—								
Bakeries	53	21	4	4		13	11	
Candy factories	19	6	4	3		3	3	
All other food factories	56	27	4	8		9	8	
Lumber and furniture industries	16	2	4	2		7	1	
Printing and publishing	5	2		1		1	1	
Shoe factories	7	2	1	1		3		
Textile industries—								
Cotton mills	113	56	6	13		17	21	
Knitting mills	19	8	3	3		4	1	
All other textile mills	72	37	1	6		14	14	
Tinware, enamelware, etc., factories	22	11	2	5		1	3	
All other industries	125	64	9	14		23	15	
Servants	2,543	1,121	44	88		432	468	390
Stenographers and typists	140	33	13	21		32	41	
Tailoresses	30	15	1	2		7	5	
Teachers (school)	119	57	8	7		21	21	5
Telegraph operators	10	5	2			1	2	
Telephone operators	46	10	15	10		8	3	
Trained nurses	98	38	5	6		13	18	18
Waitresses	95	36	4	6		16	33	
All other occupations	267	158	9	16		35	44	5

[1] Not otherwise specified.

TABLE **171.**—GAINFULLY OCCUPIED WOMEN LIVING AT HOME, BY RACE, NATIVITY, AND MARITAL CONDITION, CLASSIFIED ACCORDING TO NUMBER OF OTHER EMPLOYED MEMBERS IN THE FAMILY AND WHETHER THERE ARE BOARDERS OR LODGERS, FOR 11 SELECTED CITIES: 1920

		GAINFULLY EMPLOYED WOMEN 16 YEARS OF AGE AND OVER LIVING AT HOME						
RACE, NATIVITY, AND MARITAL CONDITION AND NUMBER OF OTHER GAINFULLY EMPLOYED MEMBERS OF FAMILY	Total number			Living in families having—				
		Boarders or lodgers	No boarders or lodgers	Unemployed members				
				None	1	2	3	4 or more
FALL RIVER, MASS.								
All classes[1]	17,192	1,218	15,974	3,645	5,188	3,412	2,033	2,914
In family having—								
No other employed member	1,476	170	1,306	661	460	214	84	57
1 other	5,789	448	5,341	1,702	1,747	1,047	613	680
2 others	3,992	273	3,719	757	1,321	789	459	666
3 or more others	5,935	327	5,608	525	1,660	1,362	877	1,511
Single (including unknown)	10,696	604	10,092	1,454	3,603	2,229	1,294	2,116
In family having—								
No other employed member	752	79	673	320	299	101	21	11
1 other	2,237	134	2,103	423	863	422	237	292
2 others	2,786	158	2,628	385	1,009	557	322	513
3 or more others	4,921	233	4,688	326	1,432	1,149	714	1,300
Married	5,236	489	4,747	1,659	1,289	982	625	681
In family having—								
No other employed member	246	28	218	93	68	46	20	19
1 other	3,172	286	2,886	1,129	782	572	337	352
2 others	950	87	863	269	241	192	127	121
3 or more others	868	88	780	168	198	172	141	189
Widowed or divorced	1,260	125	1,135	532	296	201	114	117
In family having—								
No other employed member	478	63	415	248	93	67	43	27
1 other	380	28	352	150	102	53	39	36
2 others	256	28	228	103	71	40	10	32
3 or more others	146	6	140	31	30	41	22	22
Native white—Native parentage	1,912	111	1,801	346	672	403	211	280
In family having—								
No other employed member	222	22	200	75	80	41	16	10
1 other	605	29	576	153	202	116	64	70
2 others	485	24	461	74	181	104	53	73
3 or more others	600	36	564	44	209	142	78	127
Native white—Foreign or mixed parentage	8,310	408	7,902	1,327	2,734	1,731	958	1,560
In family having—								
No other employed member	506	47	459	174	188	95	31	18
1 other	2,218	119	2,099	604	772	390	209	243
2 others	1,950	101	1,849	305	693	385	219	348
3 or more others	3,636	141	3,495	244	1,081	861	499	951
Foreign-born white	6,907	692	6,215	1,937	1,772	1,269	857	1,072
In family having—								
No other employed member	729	97	632	400	189	75	36	29
1 other	2,931	297	2,634	930	766	535	335	365
2 others	1,550	148	1,402	372	447	300	186	245
3 or more others	1,697	150	1,547	235	370	359	300	433
Negro	61	7	54	34	10	9	6	2
In family having—								
No other employed member	19	4	15	12	3	3	1	
1 other	34	3	31	14	7	6	5	2
2 others	6		6	6				
3 or more others	2		2	2				

[1] Includes Indians.

TABLE 171.—GAINFULLY OCCUPIED WOMEN LIVING AT HOME, BY RACE, NATIVITY, AND MARITAL CONDITION, CLASSIFIED ACCORDING TO NUMBER OF OTHER EMPLOYED MEMBERS IN THE FAMILY AND WHETHER THERE ARE BOARDERS OR LODGERS, FOR 11 SELECTED CITIES: 1920—Continued

RACE, NATIVITY, AND MARITAL CONDITION AND NUMBER OF OTHER GAINFULLY EMPLOYED MEMBERS OF FAMILY	GAINFULLY EMPLOYED WOMEN 16 YEARS OF AGE AND OVER LIVING AT HOME							
	Total number	Boarders or lodgers	No boarders or lodgers	Living in families having— Unemployed members				
				None	1	2	3	4 or more
PROVIDENCE, R. I.								
All classes [1]	25,339	2,727	22,612	5,448	8,354	5,135	2,768	3,634
In family having—								
No other employed member	3,126	734	2,392	1,445	1,006	414	150	111
1 other	8,443	983	7,460	2,515	2,782	1,503	749	894
2 others	6,365	509	5,856	928	2,246	1,423	744	1,024
3 or more others	7,405	501	6,904	560	2,320	1,795	1,125	1,605
Single (including unknown)	17,771	1,457	16,314	2,243	6,594	3,928	2,122	2,884
In family having—								
No other employed member	1,598	306	1,292	628	662	213	60	35
1 other	4,674	438	4,236	731	1,944	971	455	573
2 others	5,024	341	4,683	523	1,884	1,164	605	848
3 or more others	6,475	372	6,103	361	2,104	1,580	1,002	1,428
Married	4,749	688	4,061	1,890	1,117	754	450	538
In family having—								
No other employed member	373	100	273	136	113	72	32	20
1 other	2,800	374	2,426	1,372	595	361	223	249
2 others	899	120	779	249	248	172	100	130
3 or more others	677	94	583	133	161	149	95	139
Widowed or divorced	2,819	582	2,237	1,315	643	453	196	212
In family having—								
No other employed member	1,155	328	827	681	231	129	58	56
1 other	969	171	798	412	243	171	71	72
2 others	442	48	394	156	114	87	39	46
3 or more others	253	35	218	66	55	66	28	38
Native white—Native parentage	6,468	789	5,679	1,497	2,406	1,364	625	576
In family having—								
No other employed member	1,001	271	730	452	356	128	46	19
1 other	2,423	297	2,126	698	927	464	191	143
2 others	1,545	130	1,415	224	592	390	156	183
3 or more others	1,499	91	1,408	123	531	382	232	231
Native white—Foreign or mixed parentage	12,051	1,004	11,047	1,871	4,193	2,628	1,422	1,937
In family having—								
No other employed member	1,032	183	849	387	386	174	57	28
1 other	3,228	301	2,927	819	1,157	599	279	374
2 others	3,310	238	3,072	402	1,253	736	390	529
3 or more others	4,481	282	4,199	263	1,397	1,119	696	1,006
Foreign-born white	5,989	767	5,222	1,644	1,569	1,051	664	1,061
In family having—								
No other employed member	881	214	667	455	231	94	42	59
1 other	2,442	322	2,120	804	618	408	254	358
2 others	1,371	122	1,249	240	370	274	192	295
3 or more others	1,295	109	1,186	145	350	275	176	349
Negro	828	166	662	434	185	92	57	60
In family having—								
No other employed member	212	66	146	151	33	18	5	5
1 other	348	63	285	192	80	32	25	19
2 others	138	18	120	62	30	23	6	17
3 or more others	130	19	111	29	42	19	21	19

[1] Includes Indians.

TABLE 171.—GAINFULLY OCCUPIED WOMEN LIVING AT HOME, BY RACE, NATIVITY, AND MARITAL CONDITION, CLASSIFIED ACCORDING TO NUMBER OF OTHER EMPLOYED MEMBERS IN THE FAMILY AND WHETHER THERE ARE BOARDERS OR LODGERS, FOR 11 SELECTED CITIES: 1920—Continued

RACE, NATIVITY, AND MARITAL CONDITION AND NUMBER OF OTHER GAINFULLY EMPLOYED MEMBERS OF FAMILY	GAINFULLY EMPLOYED WOMEN 16 YEARS OF AGE AND OVER LIVING AT HOME							
	Total number	Boarders or lodgers	No boarders or lodgers	Living in families having—				
				Unemployed members				
				None	1	2	3	4 or more

ROCHESTER, N. Y. ——

All classes [1]	28,657	4,020	24,637	6,329	9,340	5,681	3,328	3,979
In family having—								
No other employed member	3,235	853	2,382	1,448	1,073	438	168	108
1 other	10,563	1,575	8,988	3,294	3,264	1,823	1,044	1,138
2 others	7,144	867	6,277	1,013	2,511	1,510	953	1,157
3 or more others	7,715	725	6,990	574	2,492	1,910	1,163	1,576
Single (including unknown)	18,992	2,265	16,727	2,357	7,001	4,152	2,433	3,049
In family having—								
No other employed member	1,717	405	1,312	687	691	234	62	43
1 other	5,479	765	4,714	813	2,191	1,098	615	762
2 others	5,312	566	4,746	485	1,994	1,156	751	926
3 or more others	6,484	529	5,955	372	2,125	1,664	1,005	1,318
Married	6,682	1,089	5,593	2,720	1,617	1,052	632	661
In family having—								
No other employed member	432	114	318	153	149	61	40	29
1 other	3,991	618	3,373	2,059	803	538	328	263
2 others	1,329	208	1,121	372	379	263	147	168
3 or more others	930	149	781	136	286	190	117	201
Widowed or divorced	2,983	666	2,317	1,252	722	477	263	269
In family having—								
No other employed member	1,086	334	752	608	233	143	66	36
1 other	1,093	192	901	422	270	187	101	113
2 others	503	93	410	156	138	91	55	63
3 or more others	301	47	254	66	81	56	41	57
Native white—Native parentage	11,000	1,777	9,223	2,630	3,821	2,154	1,204	1,191
In family having—								
No other employed member	1,417	434	983	653	497	185	52	30
1 other	4,210	677	3,533	1,331	1,393	740	398	348
2 others	2,761	370	2,391	415	1,047	582	358	359
3 or more others	2,612	296	2,316	231	884	647	396	454
Native white—Foreign or mixed parentage	11,817	1,351	10,466	2,071	4,150	2,537	1,421	1,638
In family having—								
No other employed member	1,098	242	856	453	388	156	64	37
1 other	3,737	492	3,245	1,021	1,300	672	351	393
2 others	3,049	313	2,736	358	1,144	676	405	466
3 or more others	3,933	304	3,629	239	1,318	1,033	601	742
Foreign-born white	5,622	850	4,772	1,527	1,315	967	686	1,127
In family having—								
No other employed member	691	164	527	323	181	95	51	41
1 other	2,514	391	2,123	884	551	403	287	389
2 others	1,284	174	1,110	226	300	244	186	328
3 or more others	1,133	121	1,012	94	283	225	162	369
Negro	208	41	167	99	50	19	17	23
In family having—								
No other employed member	29	13	16	19	7	2	1	-----
1 other	100	14	86	56	20	8	8	8
2 others	49	10	39	14	19	8	4	4
3 or more others	30	4	26	10	4	1	4	11

[1] Includes Indians.

TABLE 171.—GAINFULLY OCCUPIED WOMEN LIVING AT HOME, BY RACE, NATIVITY, AND MARITAL CONDITION, CLASSIFIED ACCORDING TO NUMBER OF OTHER EMPLOYED MEMBERS IN THE FAMILY AND WHETHER THERE ARE BOARDERS OR LODGERS, FOR 11 SELECTED CITIES: 1920—Continued

RACE, NATIVITY, AND MARITAL CONDITION AND NUMBER OF OTHER GAINFULLY EMPLOYED MEMBERS OF FAMILY	GAINFULLY EMPLOYED WOMEN 16 YEARS OF AGE AND OVER LIVING AT HOME							
	Total number	Boarders or lodgers	No boarders or lodgers	Living in families having—				
				Unemployed members				
				None	1	2	3	4 or more

PATERSON, N. J.

All classes	15,964	1,413	14,551	3,261	5,283	3,375	1,972	2,073
In family having—								
No other employed member	1,473	298	1,175	605	503	232	73	60
1 other	5,734	517	5,217	1,666	1,853	1,097	567	551
2 others	4,039	309	3,730	616	1,442	836	566	579
3 or more others	4,718	289	4,429	374	1,485	1,210	766	883
Single (including unknown)	10,561	753	9,808	1,193	3,864	2,443	1,449	1,612
In family having—								
No other employed member	731	129	602	262	316	114	25	14
1 other	2,745	205	2,540	393	1,106	603	307	336
2 others	3,031	200	2,831	310	1,136	667	447	471
3 or more others	4,054	219	3,835	228	1,306	1,059	670	791
Married	3,946	418	3,528	1,441	1,063	702	394	346
In family having—								
No other employed member	229	49	180	69	74	56	16	14
1 other	2,471	241	2,230	1,049	629	403	218	172
2 others	761	80	681	219	232	125	93	92
3 or more others	485	48	437	104	128	118	67	68
Widowed or divorced	1,457	242	1,215	627	356	230	129	115
In family having—								
No other employed member	513	120	393	274	113	62	32	32
1 other	518	71	447	224	118	91	42	43
2 others	247	29	218	87	74	44	26	16
3 or more others	179	22	157	42	51	33	29	24
Native-white—Native parentage	3,555	382	3,173	766	1,281	730	420	358
In family having—								
No other employed member	424	95	329	159	153	80	20	12
1 other	1,237	116	1,121	370	432	231	110	94
2 others	977	93	884	170	370	196	119	122
3 or more others	917	78	839	67	326	223	171	130
Native white—Foreign or mixed parentage	7,226	516	6,710	1,034	2,548	1,707	923	1,014
In family having—								
No other employed member	472	94	378	172	191	76	20	13
1 other	2,129	163	1,966	515	755	460	200	199
2 others	1,871	116	1,755	178	711	438	272	272
3 or more others	2,754	143	2,611	169	891	733	431	530
Foreign-born white	4,932	471	4,461	1,338	1,401	915	609	669
In family having—								
No other employed member	523	91	432	239	146	74	32	32
1 other	2,250	226	2,024	713	646	392	251	248
2 others	1,150	96	1,054	251	353	199	170	177
3 or more others	1,009	58	951	135	256	250	156	212
Negro	251	44	207	123	53	23	20	32
In family having—								
No other employed member	54	18	36	35	13	2	1	3
1 other	118	12	106	68	20	14	6	10
2 others	41	4	37	17	8	3	5	8
3 or more others	38	10	28	3	12	4	8	11

TABLE **171.**—GAINFULLY OCCUPIED WOMEN LIVING AT HOME, BY RACE, NATIVITY, AND MARITAL CONDITION, CLASSIFIED ACCORDING TO NUMBER OF OTHER EMPLOYED MEMBERS IN THE FAMILY AND WHETHER THERE ARE BOARDERS OR LODGERS, FOR 11 SELECTED CITIES: 1920—Continued

RACE, NATIVITY, AND MARITAL CONDITION AND NUMBER OF OTHER GAINFULLY EMPLOYED MEMBERS OF FAMILY	GAINFULLY EMPLOYED WOMEN 16 YEARS OF AGE AND OVER LIVING AT HOME							
	Total number	Living in families having—						
		Boarders or lodgers	No boarders or lodgers	Unemployed members				
				None	1	2	3	4 or more

CINCINNATI, OHIO

All classes [1]	40,709	3,875	36,834	11,263	13,448	7,931	4,156	3,911
In family having—								
No other employed member	7,685	1,332	6,353	4,002	2,278	888	323	194
1 other	15,191	1,400	13,791	5,179	4,976	2,584	1,269	1,183
2 others	9,504	680	8,824	1,457	3,447	2,222	1,243	1,135
3 or more others	8,329	463	7,866	625	2,747	2,237	1,321	1,399
Single (including unknown)	26,635	1,799	24,836	4,136	10,280	6,000	3,136	3,083
In family having—								
No other employed member	3,552	475	3,077	1,584	1,349	439	117	63
1 other	8,365	562	7,803	1,436	3,527	1,732	835	835
2 others	7,411	421	6,990	715	2,917	1,818	1,020	941
3 or more others	7,307	341	6,966	401	2,487	2,011	1,164	1,244
Married	7,308	996	6,312	3,775	1,606	984	510	433
In family having—								
No other employed member	911	200	711	439	249	124	67	32
1 other	4,668	571	4,097	2,779	928	503	250	208
2 others	1,174	154	1,020	431	290	227	115	111
3 or more others	555	71	484	126	139	130	78	82
Widowed or divorced	6,766	1,080	5,686	3,352	1,562	947	510	395
In family having—								
No other employed member	3,222	657	2,565	1,979	680	325	139	99
1 other	2,158	267	1,891	964	521	349	184	140
2 others	919	105	814	311	240	177	108	83
3 or more others	467	51	416	98	121	96	79	73
Native white—Native parentage	19,224	1,689	17,535	4,104	6,679	4,155	2,182	2,104
In family having—								
No other employed member	3,099	551	2,548	1,411	1,042	405	142	99
1 other	7,058	584	6,474	1,869	2,452	1,416	692	629
2 others	4,896	336	4,560	606	1,796	1,185	684	625
3 or more others	4,171	218	3,953	218	1,389	1,149	664	751
Native white—Foreign or mixed parentage	14,209	907	13,302	3,403	5,231	2,846	1,492	1,237
In family having—								
No other employed member	2,743	293	2,450	1,316	907	346	130	44
1 other	4,712	297	4,415	1,398	1,816	785	382	331
2 others	3,390	177	3,213	440	1,330	815	435	370
3 or more others	3,364	140	3,224	249	1,178	900	545	492
Foreign-born white	2,717	269	2,448	1,134	581	439	264	299
In family having—								
No other employed member	715	94	621	466	140	57	30	22
1 other	1,165	107	1,058	509	239	186	112	119
2 others	477	36	441	113	120	96	62	86
3 or more others	360	32	328	46	82	100	60	72
Negro	4,554	1,008	3,546	2,620	956	489	218	271
In family having—								
No other employed member	1,124	393	731	808	188	78	21	29
1 other	2,255	411	1,844	1,402	469	197	83	104
2 others	741	131	610	298	201	126	62	54
3 or more others	434	73	361	112	98	88	52	84

[1] Includes Indians and Japanese.

TABLE 171.—GAINFULLY OCCUPIED WOMEN LIVING AT HOME, BY RACE, NATIVITY, AND MARITAL CONDITION, CLASSIFIED ACCORDING TO NUMBER OF OTHER EMPLOYED MEMBERS IN THE FAMILY AND WHETHER THERE ARE BOARDERS OR LODGERS, FOR 11 SELECTED CITIES: 1920—Continued

RACE, NATIVITY, AND MARITAL CONDITION AND NUMBER OF OTHER GAINFULLY EMPLOYED MEMBERS OF FAMILY	GAINFULLY EMPLOYED WOMEN 16 YEARS OF AGE AND OVER LIVING AT HOME							
	Total number	Boarders or lodgers	No boarders or lodgers	Living in families having—				
				Unemployed members				
				None	1	2	3	4 or more
INDIANAPOLIS, IND.								
All classes [1]	27,624	4,612	23,012	8,069	8,653	5,290	2,812	2,800
In family having—								
No other employed member	4,528	1,413	3,115	2,358	1,332	564	165	109
1 other	11,589	1,821	9,768	4,028	3,566	2,058	1,050	887
2 others	6,622	844	5,778	1,174	2,306	1,477	846	819
3 or more others	4,885	534	4,351	509	1,449	1,191	751	985
Single (including unknown)	14,525	1,847	12,678	2,086	5,447	3,276	1,790	1,926
In family having—								
No other employed member	1,748	423	1,325	778	660	234	47	29
1 other	5,061	654	4,407	672	2,105	1,134	595	555
2 others	4,195	435	3,760	403	1,582	1,027	599	584
3 or more others	3,521	335	3,186	233	1,100	881	549	758
Married	7,705	1,281	6,424	3,579	1,902	1,118	580	526
In family having—								
No other employed member	587	191	396	239	195	84	36	33
1 other	4,631	720	3,911	2,643	969	550	269	200
2 others	1,561	244	1,317	502	496	274	148	141
3 or more others	926	126	800	195	242	210	127	152
Widowed or divorced	5,394	1,484	3,910	2,404	1,304	896	442	348
In family having—								
No other employed member	2,193	799	1,394	1,341	477	246	82	47
1 other	1,897	447	1,450	713	492	374	186	132
2 others	866	165	701	269	228	176	99	94
3 or more others	438	73	365	81	107	100	75	75
Native white—Native parentage	18,068	2,867	15,201	4,695	5,897	3,699	1,936	1,841
In family having—								
No other employed member	2,815	823	1,992	1,386	885	374	106	64
1 other	7,609	1,133	6,476	2,340	2,453	1,459	746	611
2 others	4,529	565	3,964	685	1,637	1,069	597	541
3 or more others	3,115	346	2,769	284	922	797	487	625
Native white—Foreign or mixed parentage	4,210	475	3,735	916	1,467	897	454	476
In family having—								
No other employed member	601	136	465	269	205	86	24	17
1 other	1,502	183	1,319	423	524	306	130	119
2 others	1,038	95	943	149	389	237	142	121
3 or more others	1,069	61	1,008	75	349	268	158	219
Foreign-born white	770	121	649	239	208	118	91	114
In family having—								
No other employed member	159	38	121	83	43	23	3	7
1 other	325	47	278	116	74	46	42	47
2 others	166	21	145	24	57	21	21	43
3 or more others	120	15	105	16	34	28	25	17
Negro	4,572	1,149	3,423	2,217	1,080	575	331	369
In family having—								
No other employed member	952	416	536	619	199	81	32	21
1 other	2,151	458	1,693	1,148	514	247	132	110
2 others	888	163	725	316	223	149	86	114
3 or more others	581	112	469	134	144	98	81	124

[1] Includes Chinese.

TABLE **171.**—GAINFULLY OCCUPIED WOMEN LIVING AT HOME, BY RACE, NATIVITY, AND MARITAL CONDITION, CLASSIFIED ACCORDING TO NUMBER OF OTHER EMPLOYED MEMBERS IN THE FAMILY AND WHETHER THERE ARE BOARDERS OR LODGERS, FOR 11 SELECTED CITIES: 1920—Continued

RACE, NATIVITY, AND MARITAL CONDITION AND NUMBER OF OTHER GAINFULLY EMPLOYED MEMBERS OF FAMILY	GAINFULLY EMPLOYED WOMEN 16 YEARS OF AGE AND OVER LIVING AT HOME							
	Total number	Living in families having—						
		Boarders or lodgers	No boarders or lodgers	Unemployed members				
				None	1	2	3	4 or more
ST. PAUL, MINN.								
All classes [1]	20,151	2,904	17,247	3,791	6,577	4,415	2,612	2,756
In family having—								
No other employed member	2,430	674	1,756	997	786	392	147	108
1 other	7,045	1,124	5,921	1,808	2,251	1,422	801	763
2 others	5,101	629	4,472	615	1,670	1,263	706	847
3 or more others	5,575	477	5,098	371	1,870	1,338	958	1,038
Single (including unknown)	14,800	1,775	13,025	1,571	5,275	3,531	2,122	2,301
In family having—								
No other employed member	1,287	302	985	482	494	210	68	33
1 other	4,324	605	3,719	498	1,639	1,020	580	587
2 others	4,178	466	3,712	340	1,426	1,084	601	727
3 or more others	5,011	402	4,609	251	1,716	1,217	873	954
Married	3,170	560	2,610	1,370	740	505	276	279
In family having—								
No other employed member	271	80	191	82	79	53	23	34
1 other	1,955	334	1,621	1,042	407	257	135	114
2 others	577	103	474	166	157	112	66	76
3 or more others	367	43	324	80	97	83	52	55
Widowed or divorced	2,181	569	1,612	850	562	379	214	176
In family having—								
No other employed member	872	292	580	433	213	129	56	41
1 other	766	185	581	268	205	145	86	62
2 others	346	60	286	109	87	67	39	44
3 or more others	197	32	165	40	57	38	33	29
Native white—Native parentage	5,649	900	4,749	1,089	1,883	1,246	702	729
In family having—								
No other employed member	707	212	495	291	223	115	49	29
1 other	2,124	354	1,770	536	675	430	246	237
2 others	1,469	203	1,266	175	497	358	191	248
3 or more others	1,349	131	1,218	87	488	343	216	215
Native white—Foreign or mixed parentage	11,367	1,423	9,944	1,680	3,868	2,655	1,564	1,600
In family having—								
No other employed member	1,119	300	819	386	406	207	73	47
1 other	3,631	535	3,096	779	1,247	796	438	371
2 others	2,937	314	2,623	306	979	767	417	468
3 or more others	3,680	274	3,406	209	1,236	885	636	714
Foreign-born white	2,761	472	2,289	834	740	466	320	401
In family having—								
No other employed member	539	130	409	275	141	67	25	31
1 other	1,083	177	906	370	284	173	106	150
2 others	633	102	531	120	174	126	93	120
3 or more others	506	63	443	69	141	100	96	100
Negro	370	108	262	187	86	47	25	25
In family having—								
No other employed member	65	32	33	45	16	3		1
1 other	204	57	147	122	45	22	10	5
2 others	62	10	52	14	20	12	5	11
3 or more others	39	9	30	6	5	10	10	8

[1] Includes Indians and Japanese.

TABLE 171.—GAINFULLY OCCUPIED WOMEN LIVING AT HOME, BY RACE, NATIVITY, AND MARITAL CONDITION, CLASSIFIED ACCORDING TO NUMBER OF OTHER EMPLOYED MEMBERS IN THE FAMILY AND WHETHER THERE ARE BOARDERS OR LODGERS, FOR 11 SELECTED CITIES: 1920—Continued

		GAINFULLY EMPLOYED WOMEN 16 YEARS OF AGE AND OVER LIVING AT HOME						
RACE, NATIVITY, AND MARITAL CONDITION AND NUMBER OF OTHER GAINFULLY EMPLOYED MEMBERS OF FAMILY	Total number	Boarders or lodgers	No boarders or lodgers	Living in families having—				
				Unemployed members				
				None	1	2	3	4 or more
KANSAS CITY, MO.								
All classes [1]	27,244	5,728	21,516	8,976	8,180	5,046	2,600	2,442
In family having—								
No other employed member	4,859	1,836	3,023	2,399	1,462	627	224	147
1 other	12,109	2,382	9,727	4,810	3,427	2,045	1,011	816
2 others	5,994	950	5,044	1,233	1,952	1,375	690	744
3 or more others	4,282	560	3,722	534	1,339	999	675	735
Single (including unknown)	13,528	2,250	11,278	2,199	4,913	3,038	1,677	1,701
In family having—								
No other employed member	1,769	571	1,198	744	682	234	69	40
1 other	4,748	797	3,951	700	1,842	1,092	595	519
2 others	3,842	560	3,282	478	1,376	957	484	547
3 or more others	3,169	322	2,847	277	1,013	755	529	595
Married	8,251	1,723	6,528	4,312	1,885	1,137	524	393
In family having—								
No other employed member	675	261	414	276	205	123	41	30
1 other	5,458	1,087	4,371	3,376	1,073	577	259	173
2 others	1,371	230	1,141	499	370	276	124	102
3 or more others	747	145	602	161	237	161	100	88
Widowed or divorced	5,465	1,755	3,710	2,465	1,382	871	399	348
In family having—								
No other employed member	2,415	1,004	1,411	1,379	575	270	114	77
1 other	1,903	498	1,405	734	512	376	157	124
2 others	781	160	621	256	206	142	82	95
3 or more others	366	93	273	96	89	83	46	52
Native white—Native parentage	16,900	3,485	13,415	5,033	5,347	3,327	1,720	1,473
In family having—								
No other employed member	2,739	990	1,749	1,205	909	399	147	79
1 other	7,657	1,464	6,193	2,780	2,294	1,380	686	517
2 others	3,926	655	3,271	718	1,340	927	481	460
3 or more others	2,578	376	2,202	330	804	621	406	417
Native white—Foreign or mixed parentage	4,975	784	4,191	1,183	1,633	1,050	547	562
In family having—								
No other employed member	750	267	483	338	242	117	29	24
1 other	1,842	300	1,542	587	560	345	194	156
2 others	1,202	128	1,074	170	421	307	131	173
3 or more others	1,181	89	1,092	88	410	281	193	209
Foreign-born white	1,192	203	989	396	271	178	136	211
In family having—								
No other employed member	245	63	182	118	63	29	20	15
1 other	527	102	425	195	126	78	52	76
2 others	238	26	212	62	34	42	37	63
3 or more others	182	12	170	21	48	29	27	57
Negro	4,174	1,255	2,919	2,362	929	490	197	196
In family having—								
No other employed member	1,124	515	609	738	248	81	28	29
1 other	2,081	516	1,565	1,246	447	242	79	67
2 others	628	141	487	283	157	99	41	48
3 or more others	341	83	258	95	77	68	49	52

[1] Includes Indians.

TABLE 171.—GAINFULLY OCCUPIED WOMEN LIVING AT HOME, BY RACE, NATIVITY, AND MARITAL CONDITION, CLASSIFIED ACCORDING TO NUMBER OF OTHER EMPLOYED MEMBERS IN THE FAMILY AND WHETHER THERE ARE BOARDERS OR LODGERS, FOR 11 SELECTED CITIES: 1920—Continued

RACE, NATIVITY, AND MARITAL CONDITION AND NUMBER OF OTHER GAINFULLY EMPLOYED MEMBERS OF FAMILY	GAINFULLY EMPLOYED WOMEN 16 YEARS OF AGE AND OVER LIVING AT HOME							
	Total number	Living in families having—						
		Boarders or lodgers	No boarders or lodgers	Unemployed members				
				None	1	2	3	4 or more
ATLANTA, GA.								
All classes	24,492	4,336	20,156	9,250	6,186	3,984	2,423	2,649
In family having—								
No other employed member	4,531	1,211	3,320	2,439	1,166	541	239	146
1 other	10,703	1,661	9,042	4,767	2,545	1,636	870	885
2 others	5,325	844	4,481	1,431	1,500	962	680	752
3 or more others	3,933	620	3,313	613	975	845	634	866
Single (including unknown)	8,709	1,432	7,277	1,819	2,511	1,745	1,200	1,434
In family having—								
No other employed member	1,068	281	787	565	314	111	50	28
1 other	2,790	458	2,332	599	858	604	339	390
2 others	2,600	351	2,249	425	776	520	408	471
3 or more others	2,251	342	1,909	230	563	510	403	545
Married	9,507	1,475	8,032	4,556	2,157	1,318	700	776
In family having—								
No other employed member	823	201	622	391	233	115	53	31
1 other	5,902	807	5,095	3,316	1,192	712	344	338
2 others	1,644	272	1,372	595	452	264	152	181
3 or more others	1,138	195	943	254	280	227	151	226
Widowed or divorced	6,276	1,429	4,847	2,875	1,518	921	523	439
In family having—								
No other employed member	2,640	729	1,911	1,483	619	315	136	87
1 other	2,011	396	1,615	852	495	320	187	157
2 others	1,081	221	860	411	272	178	120	100
3 or more others	544	83	461	129	132	108	80	95
Native white—Native parentage	10,033	1,956	8,077	2,261	2,744	2,098	1,415	1,515
In family having—								
No other employed member	1,414	419	995	533	449	243	122	67
1 other	4,088	731	3,357	1,226	1,109	816	467	470
2 others	2,556	441	2,115	348	742	578	426	462
3 or more others	1,975	365	1,610	154	444	461	400	516
Native white—Foreign or mixed parentage	618	93	525	127	181	110	81	119
In family having—								
No other employed member	72	22	50	26	27	9	8	2
1 other	230	39	191	67	62	42	26	33
2 others	157	22	135	21	51	29	20	36
3 or more others	159	10	149	13	41	30	27	48
Foreign-born white	243	30	213	49	58	35	36	65
In family having—								
No other employed member	34	7	27	12	9	5	5	3
1 other	103	14	89	29	21	14	8	31
2 others	58	8	50	5	11	8	15	19
3 or more others	48	1	47	3	17	8	8	12
Negro	13,598	2,257	11,341	6,813	3,203	1,741	891	950
In family having—								
No other employed member	3,011	763	2,248	1,868	681	284	104	74
1 other	6,282	877	5,405	3,445	1,353	764	369	351
2 others	2,554	373	2,181	1,057	696	347	219	235
3 or more others	1,751	244	1,507	443	473	346	199	290

TABLE 171.—GAINFULLY OCCUPIED WOMEN LIVING AT HOME, BY RACE, NATIVITY, AND MARITAL CONDITION, CLASSIFIED ACCORDING TO NUMBER OF OTHER EMPLOYED MEMBERS IN THE FAMILY AND WHETHER THERE ARE BOARDERS OR LODGERS, FOR 11 SELECTED CITIES: 1920—Continued

RACE, NATIVITY, AND MARITAL CONDITION AND NUMBER OF OTHER GAINFULLY EMPLOYED MEMBERS OF FAMILY	GAINFULLY EMPLOYED WOMEN 16 YEARS OF AGE AND OVER LIVING AT HOME							
	Total number	Boarders or lodgers	No boarders or lodgers	Living in families having—				
				Unemployed members				
				None	1	2	3	4 or more
LOUISVILLE, KY.								
All classes [1]	27,185	3,587	23,598	8,881	7,543	4,996	2,725	3,040
In family having—								
No other employed member	5,024	1,209	3,815	2,915	1,272	531	187	119
1 other	10,300	1,371	8,929	4,010	2,844	1,646	909	891
2 others	6,300	657	5,643	1,278	1,903	1,415	809	895
3 or more others	5,561	350	5,211	678	1,524	1,404	820	1,135
Single (including unknown)	14,290	1,263	13,027	2,443	4,647	3,257	1,792	2,151
In family having—								
No other employed member	1,883	361	1,522	961	599	230	63	30
1 other	4,156	404	3,752	666	1,541	930	512	507
2 others	4,049	300	3,749	480	1,335	991	575	668
3 or more others	4,202	198	4,004	336	1,172	1,106	642	946
Married	7,104	1,047	6,057	3,631	1,544	909	513	507
In family having—								
No other employed member	708	186	522	391	178	80	32	27
1 other	4,281	587	3,694	2,574	835	408	238	226
2 others	1,295	186	1,109	466	315	244	127	143
3 or more others	820	88	732	200	216	177	116	111
Widowed or divorced	5,791	1,277	4,514	2,807	1,352	830	420	382
In family having—								
No other employed member	2,433	662	1,771	1,563	495	221	92	62
1 other	1,863	380	1,483	770	468	308	159	158
2 others	956	171	785	332	253	180	107	84
3 or more others	539	64	475	142	136	121	62	78
Native white—Native parentage	12,409	1,353	11,056	2,513	3,786	2,756	1,573	1,781
In family having—								
No other employed member	1,814	382	1,432	838	539	269	111	57
1 other	4,415	519	3,896	1,067	1,391	920	535	502
2 others	3,343	289	3,054	383	1,042	842	486	590
3 or more others	2,837	163	2,674	225	814	725	441	632
Native white—Foreign or mixed parentage	5,076	376	4,700	1,047	1,677	1,137	580	635
In family having—								
No other employed member	838	114	724	366	287	123	33	29
1 other	1,583	132	1,451	401	581	307	159	135
2 others	1,190	77	1,113	158	412	300	164	156
3 or more others	1,465	53	1,412	122	397	407	224	315
Foreign-born white	638	53	585	221	149	101	61	106
In family having—								
No other employed member	166	20	146	113	35	12	3	3
1 other	215	20	195	61	44	38	31	41
2 others	145	10	135	29	39	27	19	31
3 or more others	112	3	109	18	31	24	8	31
Negro	9,055	1,803	7,252	5,097	1,931	998	511	518
In family having—								
No other employed member	2,205	693	1,512	1,597	411	127	40	30
1 other	4,085	698	3,387	2,479	828	381	184	213
2 others	1,622	281	1,341	708	410	246	140	118
3 or more others	1,143	131	1,012	313	282	244	147	157

[1] Includes Indians.

TABLE 171.—GAINFULLY OCCUPIED WOMEN LIVING AT HOME, BY RACE, NATIVITY, AND MARITAL CONDITION, CLASSIFIED ACCORDING TO NUMBER OF OTHER EMPLOYED MEMBERS IN THE FAMILY AND WHETHER THERE ARE BOARDERS OR LODGERS, FOR 11 SELECTED CITIES: 1920—Continued

RACE, NATIVITY AND MARITIAL CONDITION AND NUMBER OF OTHER GAINFULLY EMPLOYED MEMBERS OF FAMILY	Total number	GAINFULLY EMPLOYED WOMEN 16 YEARS OF AGE AND OVER LIVING AT HOME						
		Boarders or lodgers	No boarders or lodgers	Living in families having—				
				Unemployed members				
				None	1	2	3	4 or more

NEW ORLEANS, LA.

All classes [1]	38,656	6,313	32,343	10,855	9,753	6,982	4,640	6,426
In family having—								
No other employed member	5,786	1,890	3,896	2,922	1,525	739	340	260
1 other	13,646	2,315	11,331	4,859	3,558	2,270	1,364	1,595
2 others	9,439	1,216	8,223	1,873	2,593	1,949	1,283	1,741
3 or more others	9,785	892	8,893	1,201	2,077	2,024	1,653	2,830
Single (including unknown)	19,663	2,314	17,349	2,993	5,428	4,079	2,887	4,276
In family having—								
No other employed member	1,832	524	1,308	847	625	214	90	56
1 other	5,150	667	4,483	929	1,632	1,070	667	852
2 others	5,631	572	5,059	652	1,647	1,279	848	1,205
3 or more others	7,050	551	6,499	565	1,524	1,516	1,282	2,163
Married	10,441	1,891	8,550	4,441	2,315	1,570	944	1,171
In family having—								
No other employed member	1,055	334	721	462	276	162	85	70
1 other	5,642	1,013	4,629	2,900	1,211	726	387	418
2 others	2,125	350	1,775	700	506	382	234	303
3 or more others	1,619	194	1,425	379	322	300	238	380
Widowed or divorced	8,552	2,108	6,444	3,421	2,010	1,333	809	979
In family having—								
No other employed member	2,899	1,032	1,867	1,613	624	363	165	134
1 other	2,854	635	2,219	1,030	715	474	310	325
2 others	1,683	294	1,389	521	440	288	201	233
3 or more others	1,116	147	969	257	231	208	133	287
Native white—Native parentage	14,950	2,001	12,949	1,999	3,980	3,226	2,408	3,337
In family having—								
No other employed member	1,591	493	1,098	571	523	275	124	98
1 other	4,293	629	3,664	799	1,248	912	616	718
2 others	4,042	444	3,598	358	1,129	958	687	910
3 or more others	5,024	435	4,589	271	1,080	1,081	981	1,611
Native white—Foreign or mixed parentage	5,657	755	4,902	1,179	1,570	1,173	736	999
In family having—								
No other employed member	900	225	675	364	287	145	70	34
1 other	1,817	250	1,567	468	524	366	231	228
2 others	1,416	140	1,276	207	439	308	190	272
3 or more others	1,524	140	1,384	140	320	354	245	465
Foreign-born white	1,139	183	956	339	256	185	127	232
In family having—								
No other employed member	271	80	191	158	58	18	13	24
1 other	398	45	353	117	92	67	39	83
2 others	255	40	215	44	72	42	36	61
3 or more others	215	18	197	20	34	58	39	64
Negro	16,904	3,374	13,530	7,336	3,947	2,398	1,368	1,855
In family having—								
No other employed member	3,023	1,092	1,931	1,829	657	301	132	104
1 other	7,135	1,391	5,744	3,473	1,694	925	478	565
2 others	3,724	592	3,132	1,264	953	641	370	496
3 or more others	3,022	299	2,723	770	643	531	388	690

[1] Includes Indians, Chinese, and other races.

TABLE 172.—WOMEN LIVING AT HOME AND EMPLOYED IN CERTAIN IMPORTANT OCCUPATIONS, CLASSIFIED ACCORDING TO NUMBER OF OTHER EMPLOYED MEMBERS IN THE FAMILY AND WHETHER THERE ARE BOARDERS OR LODGERS, FOR THE 11 SELECTED CITIES COMBINED: 1920

OCCUPATION AND NUMBER OF OTHER EMPLOYED MEMBERS IN THE FAMILY	GAINFULLY EMPLOYED WOMEN 16 YEARS OF AGE AND OVER LIVING AT HOME							
	Total number	Living in families having—						
		Boarders or lodgers	No boarders or lodgers	None	Unemployed members			
					1	2	3	4 or more
BOOKKEEPERS, CASHIERS, AND ACCOUNTANTS	15,735	1,633	14,102	2,036	6,056	3,662	1,973	2,008
In family having—								
No other employed member	1,590	302	1,288	387	739	312	94	58
1 other	5,372	617	4,755	1,049	2,057	1,144	615	507
2 others	4,347	393	3,954	393	1,723	1,072	552	607
3 or more others	4,426	321	4,105	207	1,537	1,134	712	836
CLERKS (except clerks in stores)	20,343	2,165	18,178	2,597	7,294	4,848	2,765	2,839
In family having—								
No other employed member	1,818	324	1,494	454	802	371	123	68
1 other	6,810	801	6,009	1,329	2,498	1,466	801	716
2 others	5,777	597	5,180	486	2,166	1,450	840	835
3 or more others	5,938	443	5,495	328	1,828	1,561	1,001	1,220
CLERKS IN STORES	6,871	693	6,178	1,168	2,110	1,534	961	1,098
In family having—								
No other employed member	509	89	420	143	196	108	34	28
1 other	2,494	267	2,227	642	756	485	317	294
2 others	1,924	176	1,748	234	625	455	268	342
3 or more others	1,944	161	1,783	149	533	486	342	434
DRESSMAKERS AND SEAMSTRESSES (not in factory) [1]	6,814	1,015	5,799	2,742	1,972	1,043	533	524
In family having—								
No other employed member	1,618	370	1,248	914	426	188	62	28
1 other	2,716	392	2,324	1,193	768	372	207	176
2 others	1,399	163	1,236	431	441	250	130	147
3 or more others	1,081	90	991	204	337	233	134	173
LAUNDRESSES (not in laundry) [2]	20,855	3,835	17,020	10,599	4,674	2,646	1,356	1,580
In family having—								
No other employed member	5,057	1,483	3,574	3,244	1,040	431	193	149
1 other	9,794	1,543	8,251	5,212	2,150	1,214	560	658
2 others	3,658	539	3,119	1,478	940	551	316	373
3 or more others	2,346	270	2,076	665	544	450	287	400
SALESWOMEN (stores)	14,523	1,600	12,923	3,017	4,708	3,012	1,818	1,968
In family having—								
No other employed member	1,695	324	1,371	628	627	266	112	62
1 other	5,504	637	4,867	1,606	1,724	1,040	540	594
2 others	3,669	375	3,294	506	1,234	845	526	558
3 or more others	3,655	264	3,391	277	1,123	861	640	754
SEMISKILLED OPERATIVES, CLOTHING INDUSTRIES [1] (n. o. s. [3])	7,283	643	6,640	1,842	2,236	1,460	797	948
In family having—								
No other employed member	1,012	127	885	500	322	132	36	22
1 other	2,813	268	2,545	923	839	497	263	291
2 others	1,737	140	1,597	271	581	365	248	272
3 or more others	1,721	108	1,613	148	494	466	250	363
SERVANTS	22,459	4,156	18,303	11,374	4,957	2,802	1,532	1,794
In family having—								
No other employed member	5,052	1,371	3,681	3,368	1,015	412	151	106
1 other	9,861	1,718	8,143	5,595	2,057	1,088	561	560
2 others	4,364	674	3,690	1,607	1,133	726	415	483
3 or more others	3,182	393	2,789	804	752	576	405	645
STENOGRAPHERS AND TYPISTS	27,009	2,787	24,222	2,834	9,919	6,854	3,831	3,571
In family having—								
No other employed member	2,161	413	1,748	426	1,048	469	146	72
1 other	9,055	1,072	7,983	1,458	3,437	2,116	1,131	913
2 others	7,841	719	7,122	600	2,881	2,090	1,186	1,084
3 or more others	7,952	583	7,369	350	2,553	2,179	1,368	1,502

[1] Includes 5 cities only   [2] Includes 6 cities only.   [3] Not otherwise specified.

TABLE 172.—WOMEN LIVING AT HOME AND EMPLOYED IN CERTAIN IMPORTANT OCCUPATIONS, CLASSIFIED ACCORDING TO NUMBER OF OTHER EMPLOYED MEMBERS IN THE FAMILY AND WHETHER THERE ARE BOARDERS OR LODGERS, FOR THE 11 SELECTED CITIES COMBINED: 1920—Continued

OCCUPATION AND NUMBER OF OTHER EMPLOYED MEMBERS IN THE FAMILY	GAINFULLY EMPLOYED WOMEN 16 YEARS OF AGE AND OVER LIVING AT HOME							
	Total number			Living in families having—				
		Boarders or lodgers	No boarders or lodgers	Unemployed members				
				None	1	2	3	4 or more
TEACHERS (school)	11,384	1,266	10,118	2,275	4,578	2,444	1,166	921
In family having—								
No other employed member	1,958	349	1,609	683	842	296	97	40
1 other	4,124	475	3,649	970	1,651	833	390	280
2 others	2,811	255	2,556	398	1,168	666	322	257
3 or more others	2,491	187	2,304	224	917	649	357	344

TABLE 173.—WOMEN LIVING AT HOME AND EMPLOYED IN CERTAIN IMPORTANT OCCUPATIONS, CLASSIFIED BY MARITAL CONDITION, ACCORDING TO NUMBER OF OTHER EMPLOYED MEMBERS IN THE FAMILY, AND WHETHER THERE ARE BOARDERS OR LODGERS, FOR 11 SELECTED CITIES: 1920

OCCUPATION, MARITAL CONDITION, AND NUMBER OF OTHER GAINFULLY EMPLOYED MEMBERS OF FAMILY	GAINFULLY EMPLOYED WOMEN 16 YEARS OF AGE AND OVER LIVING AT HOME							
	Total number			Living in family having—				
		Boarders or lodgers	No boarders or lodgers	Unemployed members				
				None	1	2	3	4 or more
FALL RIVER, MASS.								
BOOKKEEPERS, CASHIERS, AND ACCOUNTANTS								
All classes	461	22	439	48	174	118	50	71
In family having—								
No other employed member	29	3	26	3	12	10	3	1
1 other	111	7	104	17	49	20	12	13
2 others	142	2	140	18	56	37	11	20
3 or more others	179	10	169	10	57	51	24	37
Single (including unknown)	421	22	399	33	165	110	46	67
In family having—								
No other employed member	25	3	22	2	12	9	1	1
1 other	87	7	80	5	43	16	12	11
2 others	135	2	133	17	54	37	9	18
3 or more others	174	10	164	9	56	48	24	37
Married	30	-------	30	14	8	1	4	3
In family having—								
No other employed member	2	-------	2	-------	-------	-------	2	-----
1 other	18	-------	18	12	5	-------	-------	1
2 others	7	-------	7	1	2	-------	2	2
3 or more others	3	-------	3	1	1	1	-------	-----
Widowed or divorced	10	-------	10	1	1	7	-------	1
In family having—								
No other employed member	2	-------	2	1	-------	1	-------	-----
1 other	6	-------	6	-------	1	4	-------	1
2 others	-------	-------	-------	-------	-------	-------	-------	-----
3 or more others	2	-------	2	-------	-------	2	-------	-----

TABLE **173.**—WOMEN LIVING AT HOME AND EMPLOYED IN CERTAIN IMPORTANT OCCUPATIONS, CLASSIFIED BY MARITAL CONDITION, ACCORDING TO NUMBER OF OTHER EMPLOYED MEMBERS IN THE FAMILY, AND WHETHER THERE ARE BOARDERS OR LODGERS, FOR 11 SELECTED CITIES: 1920—Continued

OCCUPATION, MARITAL CONDITION, AND NUMBER OF OTHER GAINFULLY EMPLOYED MEMBERS OF FAMILY	GAINFULLY EMPLOYED WOMEN 16 YEARS OF AGE AND OVER LIVING AT HOME							
	Total number	Boarders or lodgers	No boarders or lodgers	Living in family having—				
				Unemployed members				
				None	1	2	3	4 or more
FALL RIVER, MASS.—Continued								
CLERKS (EXCEPT CLERKS IN STORES)								
All classes	271	9	262	31	96	73	35	36
In family having—								
No other employed member	20	------	20	5	8	4	3	------
1 other	72	5	67	12	33	18	5	4
2 others	67	2	65	9	28	15	4	11
3 or more others	112	2	110	5	27	36	23	21
Single (including unknown)	244	8	236	22	89	67	33	33
In family having—								
No other employed member	17	------	17	5	8	3	1	------
1 other	55	5	50	4	28	15	5	3
2 others	64	1	63	9	27	13	4	11
3 or more others	108	2	106	4	26	36	23	19
Married	23	1	22	9	6	5	------	3
In family having—								
No other employed member								
1 other	16	------	16	8	4	3	------	1
2 others	3	1	2	------	1	2	------	------
3 or more others	4	------	4	1	1	------	------	2
Widowed or divorced	4	------	4	------	1	1	2	------
In family having—								
No other employed member	3	------	3	------	------	1	2	------
1 other	1	------	1	------	1	------	------	------
2 others	------	------	------	------	------	------	------	------
3 or more others	------	------	------	------	------	------	------	------
CLERKS IN STORES								
All classes	188	11	177	23	67	37	34	27
In family having—								
No other employed member	9	1	8	1	6	1	1	------
1 other	46	2	44	7	19	10	6	4
2 others	62	2	60	11	19	8	13	11
3 or more others	71	6	65	4	23	18	14	12
Single (including unknown)	142	7	135	10	52	28	33	19
In family having—								
No other employed member	5	------	5	------	3	1	1	------
1 other	26	------	26	1	13	6	6	------
2 others	47	2	45	5	17	6	12	7
3 or more others	64	5	59	4	19	15	14	12
Married	41	3	38	12	12	8	1	8
In family having—								
No other employed member	1	------	1	------	1	------	------	------
1 other	19	2	17	6	5	4	------	4
2 others	15	------	15	6	2	2	1	4
3 or more others	6	1	5	------	4	2	------	------
Widowed or divorced	5	1	4	1	3	1	------	------
In family having—								
No other employed member	3	1	2	1	2	------	------	------
1 other	1	------	1	------	1	------	------	------
2 others	------	------	------	------	------	------	------	------
3 or more others	1	------	1	------	------	1	------	------

TABLE **173.**—WOMEN LIVING AT HOME AND EMPLOYED IN CERTAIN IMPORTANT OCCUPATIONS, CLASSIFIED BY MARITAL CONDITION, ACCORDING TO NUMBER OF OTHER EMPLOYED MEMBERS IN THE FAMILY, AND WHETHER THERE ARE BOARDERS OR LODGERS, FOR 11 SELECTED CITIES: 1920—Continued

OCCUPATION, MARITAL CONDITION, AND NUMBER OF OTHER GAINFULLY EMPLOYED MEMBERS OF FAMILY	GAINFULLY EMPLOYED WOMEN 16 YEARS OF AGE AND OVER LIVING AT HOME							
	Total number	Boarders or lodgers	No boarders or lodgers	Living in family having—				
				Unemployed members				
				None	1	2	3	4 or more
FALL RIVER, MASS.—Continued								
SALESWOMEN (STORES)								
All classes	489	29	460	79	192	110	48	60
In family having—								
No other employed member	38	5	33	11	15	5	5	2
1 other	148	2	146	35	50	29	13	21
2 others	120	13	107	20	45	28	15	12
3 or more others	183	9	174	13	82	48	15	25
Single (including unknown)	378	20	358	45	158	89	37	49
In family having—								
No other employed member	21	3	18	8	8	2	2	1
1 other	91	1	90	12	34	21	9	15
2 others	102	10	92	15	38	25	15	9
3 or more others	164	6	158	10	78	41	11	24
Married	88	9	79	30	26	15	8	9
In family having—								
No other employed member	6	2	4	2	3	------	1	------
1 other	52	1	51	21	15	7	3	6
2 others	14	3	11	4	6	2	------	2
3 or more others	16	3	13	3	2	6	4	1
Widowed or divorced	23	------	23	4	8	6	3	2
In family having—								
No other employed member	11	------	11	1	4	3	2	1
1 other	5	------	5	2	1	1	1	------
2 others	4	------	4	1	1	1	------	1
3 or more others	3	------	3	------	2	1	------	------
SEMISKILLED—COTTON MILLS								
All classes	11,890	870	11,020	2,602	3,353	2,293	1,413	2,229
In family having—								
No other employed member	856	85	771	410	250	112	48	36
1 other	4,227	343	3,884	1,308	1,203	747	443	526
2 others	2,628	187	2,441	502	811	536	301	478
3 or more others	4,179	255	3,924	382	1,089	898	621	1,189
Single (including unknown)	6,703	421	6,282	926	2,086	1,321	808	1,562
In family having—								
No other employed member	401	45	356	195	156	39	8	3
1 other	1,274	91	1,183	284	461	212	125	192
2 others	1,684	108	1,576	230	565	341	188	360
3 or more others	3,344	177	3,167	217	904	729	487	1,007
Married	4,372	394	3,978	1,330	1,078	841	537	586
In family having—								
No other employed member	171	20	151	66	47	29	14	15
1 other	2,697	235	2,462	916	673	503	297	308
2 others	775	66	709	207	198	165	108	97
3 or more others	729	73	656	141	160	144	118	166
Widowed or divorced	815	55	760	346	189	131	68	81
In family having—								
No other employed member	284	20	264	149	47	44	26	18
1 other	256	17	239	108	69	32	21	26
2 others	169	13	156	65	48	30	5	21
3 or more others	106	5	101	24	25	25	16	16

TABLE 173.—WOMEN LIVING AT HOME AND EMPLOYED IN CERTAIN IMPORTANT OCCUPATIONS, CLASSIFIED BY MARITAL CONDITION, ACCORDING TO NUMBER OF OTHER EMPLOYED MEMBERS IN THE FAMILY, AND WHETHER THERE ARE BOARDERS OR LODGERS, FOR 11 SELECTED CITIES: 1920—Continued

		GAINFULLY EMPLOYED WOMEN 16 YEARS OF AGE AND OVER LIVING AT HOME						
OCCUPATION, MARITAL CONDITION, AND NUMBER OF OTHER GAINFULLY EMPLOYED MEMBERS OF FAMILY	Total number			Living in family having—				
		Boarders or lodgers	No boarders or lodgers	Unemployed members				
				None	1	2	3	4 or more

FALL RIVER, MASS.—Continued

SEMISKILLED—ALL OTHER TEXTILE MILLS								
All classes	562	27	535	63	189	120	62	128
In family having—								
No other employed member	24	1	23	3	10	7	2	2
1 other	128	8	120	35	41	25	13	14
2 others	160	8	152	23	54	29	15	39
3 or more others	250	10	240	2	84	59	32	73
Single (including unknown)	456	17	439	27	164	99	52	114
In family having—								
No other employed member	11	1	10		6	3	1	1
1 other	82	3	79	13	30	18	9	12
2 others	132	5	127	13	49	23	12	35
3 or more others	231	8	223	1	79	55	30	66
Married	81	7	74	31	18	16	7	9
In family having—								
No other employed member	7		7	3	2	2		
1 other	39	4	35	20	8	7	3	1
2 others	19	1	18	7	3	4	3	2
3 or more others	16	2	14	1	5	3	1	6
Widowed or divorced	25	3	22	5	7	5	3	5
In family having—								
No other employed member	6		6		2	2	1	1
1 other	7	1	6	2	3		1	1
2 others	9	2	7	3	2	2		2
3 or more others	3		3			1	1	1
SERVANTS								
All classes	211	12	199	109	47	18	20	17
In family having—								
No other employed member	65	5	60	39	17	5	3	1
1 other	76	5	71	44	12	8	6	6
2 others	44	2	42	20	13		4	7
3 or more others	26		26	6	5	5	7	3
Single (including unknown)	85	1	84	34	24	10	8	9
In family having—								
No other employed member	20		20	12	7	1		
1 other	27	1	26	13	5	4	2	3
2 others	18		18	7	7		1	3
3 or more others	20		20	2	5	5	5	3
Married	63	5	58	36	7	6	7	7
In family having—								
No other employed member	11	1	10	5		4	1	1
1 other	35	3	32	23	5	2	2	3
2 others	13	1	12	5	2		3	3
3 or more others	4		4	3			1	
Widowed or divorced	63	6	57	39	16	2	5	1
In family having—								
No other employed member	34	4	30	22	10		2	
1 other	14	1	13	8	2	2	2	
2 others	13	1	12	8	4			1
3 or more others	2		2	1			1	

TABLE 173.—WOMEN LIVING AT HOME AND EMPLOYED IN CERTAIN IMPORTANT OCCUPATIONS, CLASSIFIED BY MARITAL CONDITION, ACCORDING TO NUMBER OF OTHER EMPLOYED MEMBERS IN THE FAMILY, AND WHETHER THERE ARE BOARDERS OR LODGERS, FOR 11 SELECTED CITIES: 1920—Continued

OCCUPATION, MARITAL CONDITION, AND NUMBER OF OTHER GAINFULLY EMPLOYED MEMBERS OF FAMILY	GAINFULLY EMPLOYED WOMEN 16 YEARS OF AGE AND OVER LIVING AT HOME							
				Living in family having—				
	Total number	Boarders or lodgers	No boarders or lodgers	Unemployed members				
				None	1	2	3	4 or more
FALL RIVER, MASS.—Continued								
STENOGRAPHERS AND TYPISTS								
All classes	432	15	417	39	160	109	67	57
In family having—								
No other employed member	21	------	21	1	12	7	1	------
1 other	142	6	136	12	59	35	25	11
2 others	117	5	112	16	42	31	10	18
3 or more others	152	4	148	10	47	36	31	28
Single (including unknown)	402	14	388	29	150	103	65	55
In family having—								
No other employed member	17	------	17	1	9	7	------	------
1 other	131	6	125	4	59	32	25	11
2 others	111	4	107	14	40	30	10	17
3 or more others	143	4	139	10	42	34	30	27
Married	24	1	23	9	7	5	1	2
In family having—								
No other employed member								
1 other	10	------	10	8	------	2	------	------
2 others	5	1	4	1	2	1	------	1
3 or more others	9	------	9	------	5	2	1	1
Widowed or divorced	6	------	6	1	3	1	1	------
In family having—								
No other employed member	4	------	4	------	3	------	1	------
1 other	1	------	1	------	------	1	------	------
2 others	1	------	1	1	------	------	------	------
3 or more others								
TEACHERS (SCHOOL)								
All classes	650	19	631	111	275	152	67	45
In family having—								
No other employed member	98	8	90	28	44	22	3	1
1 other	187	5	182	39	81	38	17	12
2 others	174	5	169	24	81	36	24	9
3 or more others	191	1	190	20	69	56	23	23
Single (including unknown)	631	18	613	107	272	146	62	44
In family having—								
No other employed member	91	8	83	28	44	16	2	1
1 other	178	4	174	36	79	38	14	11
2 others	172	5	167	24	80	36	23	9
3 or more others	190	1	189	19	69	56	23	23
Married	12	------	12	3	1	4	3	1
In family having—								
No other employed member	4	------	4	------	------	4	------	------
1 other	6	------	6	2	1	------	2	1
2 others	1	------	1	------	------	------	1	------
3 or more others	1	------	1	1	------	------	------	------
Widowed or divorced	7	1	6	1	2	2	2	------
In family having—								
No other employed member	3	------	3	------	------	2	1	------
1 other	3	1	2	1	1	------	1	------
2 others	1	------	1	------	1	------	------	------
3 or more others								

TABLE **173.**—WOMEN LIVING AT HOME AND EMPLOYED IN CERTAIN IMPORTANT OCCUPATIONS, CLASSIFIED BY MARITAL CONDITION, ACCORDING TO NUMBER OF OTHER EMPLOYED MEMBERS IN THE FAMILY, AND WHETHER THERE ARE BOARDERS OR LODGERS, FOR 11 SELECTED CITIES: 1920—Continued

OCCUPATION, MARITAL CONDITION, AND NUMBER OF OTHER GAINFULLY EMPLOYED MEMBERS OF FAMILY	GAINFULLY EMPLOYED WOMEN 16 YEARS OF AGE AND OVER LIVING AT HOME							
	Total number	Boarders or lodgers	No boarders or lodgers	Living in family having—				
				Unemployed members				
				None	1	2	3	4 or more
PROVIDENCE, R. I.								
BOOKKEEPERS, CASHIERS, AND ACCOUNTANTS								
All classes	1,697	122	1,575	191	727	409	202	168
In family having—								
No other employed member	144	24	120	35	70	27	8	4
1 other	538	42	496	96	232	117	47	46
2 others	467	25	442	32	211	117	58	49
3 or more others	548	31	517	28	214	148	89	69
Single (including unknown)	1,513	103	1,410	131	664	361	192	165
In family having—								
No other employed member	115	17	98	26	59	19	8	3
1 other	442	35	407	51	204	99	43	45
2 others	430	23	407	26	194	105	57	48
3 or more others	526	28	498	28	207	138	84	69
Married	123	11	112	44	36	33	9	1
In family having—								
No other employed member	6	2	4	2	2	2	------	------
1 other	72	5	67	37	17	13	4	1
2 others	29	2	27	5	14	9	1	------
3 or more others	16	2	14	------	3	9	4	------
Widowed or divorced	61	8	53	16	27	15	1	2
In family having—								
No other employed member	23	5	18	7	9	6	------	1
1 other	24	2	22	8	11	5	------	------
2 others	8	------	8	1	3	3	------	1
3 or more others	6	1	5	------	4	1	1	------
CLERKS (EXCEPT CLERKS IN STORES)								
All classes	2,005	169	1,836	251	818	477	221	238
In family having—								
No other employed member	156	25	131	34	82	30	6	4
1 other	620	57	563	130	253	126	63	48
2 others	560	50	510	53	231	157	62	57
3 or more others	669	37	632	34	252	164	90	129
Single (including unknown)	1,770	144	1,626	165	745	424	205	231
In family having—								
No other employed member	123	21	102	24	70	20	5	4
1 other	497	47	450	69	220	108	56	44
2 others	512	43	469	43	211	142	60	56
3 or more others	638	33	605	29	244	154	84	127
Married	163	17	146	71	51	24	13	4
In family having—								
No other employed member	9	2	7	1	4	4	------	------
1 other	91	7	84	57	23	4	5	2
2 others	33	4	29	8	16	7	2	------
3 or more others	30	4	26	5	8	9	6	2
Widowed or divorced	72	8	64	15	22	29	3	3
In family having—								
No other employed member	24	2	22	9	8	6	1	------
1 other	32	3	29	4	10	14	2	2
2 others	15	3	12	2	4	8	------	1
3 or more others	1	------	1	------	------	1	------	------

TABLE **173.**—WOMEN LIVING AT HOME AND EMPLOYED IN CERTAIN IMPORTANT OCCUPATIONS, CLASSIFIED BY MARITAL CONDITION, ACCORDING TO NUMBER OF OTHER EMPLOYED MEMBERS IN THE FAMILY, AND WHETHER THERE ARE BOARDERS OR LODGERS, FOR 11 SELECTED CITIES: 1920—Continued

OCCUPATION, MARITAL CONDITION, AND NUMBER OF OTHER GAINFULLY EMPLOYED MEMBERS OF FAMILY	GAINFULLY EMPLOYED WOMEN 16 YEARS OF AGE AND OVER LIVING AT HOME							
	Total number	Boarders or lodgers	No boarders or lodgers	Living in family having—				
				Unemployed members				
				None	1	2	3	4 or more
PROVIDENCE, R. I.—Continued								
CLERKS IN STORES								
All classes	413	27	386	84	122	87	64	56
In family having—								
No other employed member	27	4	23	11	10	4	1	1
1 other	133	10	123	36	45	21	19	12
2 others	137	6	131	26	43	29	21	18
3 or more others	116	7	109	11	24	33	23	25
Single (including unknown)	314	16	298	41	100	71	52	50
In family having—								
No other employed member	18	3	15	6	9	3	------	------
1 other	84	4	80	11	33	19	12	9
2 others	112	3	109	16	38	22	19	17
3 or more others	100	6	94	8	20	27	21	24
Married	69	6	63	32	18	8	7	4
In family having—								
No other employed member	1	------	1	1	------	------	------	------
1 other	37	4	33	21	9	------	5	2
2 others	17	1	16	8	5	3	------	1
3 or more others	14	1	13	2	4	5	2	1
Widowed or divorced	30	5	25	11	4	8	5	2
In family having—								
No other employed member	8	1	7	4	1	1	1	1
1 other	12	2	10	4	3	2	2	1
2 others	8	2	6	2	------	4	2	------
3 or more others	2	------	2	1	------	1	------	------
SALESWOMEN (STORES)								
All classes	1,143	107	1,036	245	421	218	108	151
In family having—								
No other employed member	123	25	98	51	51	15	2	4
1 other	415	39	376	111	150	69	35	50
2 others	285	20	265	50	96	60	31	48
3 or more others	320	23	297	33	124	74	40	49
Single (including unknown)	753	51	702	96	300	154	82	121
In family having—								
No other employed member	60	10	50	20	34	5	------	1
1 other	209	13	196	28	85	42	23	31
2 others	217	12	205	26	76	45	26	44
3 or more others	267	16	251	22	105	62	33	45
Married	272	34	238	105	84	39	17	27
In family having—								
No other employed member	19	4	15	6	7	3	1	2
1 other	163	17	146	74	47	18	7	17
2 others	51	8	43	16	14	13	4	4
3 or more others	39	5	34	9	16	5	5	4
Widowed or divorced	118	22	96	44	37	25	9	3
In family having—								
No other employed member	44	11	33	25	10	7	1	1
1 other	43	9	34	9	18	9	5	2
2 others	17	------	17	8	6	2	1	------
3 or more others	14	2	12	2	3	7	2	------

TABLE **173.**—WOMEN LIVING AT HOME AND EMPLOYED IN CERTAIN IMPORTANT OCCUPATIONS, CLASSIFIED BY MARITAL CONDITION, ACCORDING TO NUMBER OF OTHER EMPLOYED MEMBERS IN THE FAMILY, AND WHETHER THERE ARE BOARDERS OR LODGERS, FOR 11 SELECTED CITIES: 1920—Continued

OCCUPATION, MARITAL CONDITION, AND NUMBER OF OTHER GAINFULLY EMPLOYED MEMBERS OF FAMILY	GAINFULLY EMPLOYED WOMEN 16 YEARS OF AGE AND OVER LIVING AT HOME							
	Total number	Living in family having—						
		Boarders or lodgers	No boarders or lodgers	Unemployed members				
				None	1	2	3	4 or more

PROVIDENCE, R. I.—Continued

SEMISKILLED—JEWELRY FACTORIES

All classes	1,935	184	1,751	306	612	384	257	376
In family having—								
No other employed member	157	30	127	57	48	23	18	11
1 other	610	65	545	171	215	93	61	70
2 others	506	45	461	53	156	116	77	104
3 or more others	662	44	618	25	193	152	101	191
Single (including unknown)	1,428	116	1,312	116	479	310	204	319
In family having—								
No other employed member	65	10	55	20	25	10	7	3
1 other	356	36	320	42	153	68	37	56
2 others	403	35	368	35	125	94	64	85
3 or more others	604	35	569	19	176	138	96	175
Married	351	43	308	130	89	55	38	39
In family having—								
No other employed member	29	7	22	10	7	5	5	2
1 other	198	19	179	102	44	20	21	11
2 others	76	9	67	13	23	18	8	14
3 or more others	48	8	40	5	15	12	4	12
Widowed or divorced	156	25	131	60	44	19	15	18
In family having—								
No other employed member	63	13	50	27	16	8	6	6
1 other	56	10	46	27	18	5	3	3
2 others	27	1	26	5	8	4	5	5
3 or more others	10	1	9	1	2	2	1	4

SEMISKILLED—WOOLEN AND WORSTED MILLS

All classes	2,972	227	2,745	594	863	587	344	584
In family having—								
No other employed member	249	30	219	90	92	38	14	15
1 other	1,057	85	972	325	303	184	87	158
2 others	739	55	684	112	236	140	95	156
3 or more others	927	57	870	67	232	225	148	255
Single (including unknown)	1,933	131	1,802	235	635	405	240	418
In family having—								
No other employed member	127	17	110	42	62	17	2	4
1 other	475	32	443	92	174	81	44	84
2 others	546	41	505	59	191	112	66	118
3 or more others	785	41	744	42	208	195	128	212
Married	807	74	733	279	174	130	89	135
In family having—								
No other employed member	47	3	44	12	13	12	7	3
1 other	495	46	449	203	111	76	36	69
2 others	151	12	139	41	33	20	27	30
3 or more others	114	13	101	23	17	22	19	33
Widowed or divorced	232	22	210	80	54	52	15	31
In family having—								
No other employed member	75	10	65	36	17	9	5	8
1 other	87	7	80	30	18	27	7	5
2 others	42	2	40	12	12	8	2	8
3 or more others	28	3	25	2	7	8	1	10

TABLE **173.**—WOMEN LIVING AT HOME AND EMPLOYED IN CERTAIN IMPORTANT OCCUPATIONS, CLASSIFIED BY MARITAL CONDITION, ACCORDING TO NUMBER OF OTHER EMPLOYED MEMBERS IN THE FAMILY, AND WHETHER THERE ARE BOARDERS OR LODGERS, FOR 11 SELECTED CITIES: 1920—Continued

OCCUPATION, MARITAL CONDITION, AND NUMBER OF OTHER GAINFULLY EMPLOYED MEMBERS OF FAMILY	GAINFULLY EMPLOYED WOMEN 16 YEARS OF AGE AND OVER LIVING AT HOME							
	Total number	Boarders or lodgers	No boarders or lodgers	Living in family having—				
				Unemployed members				
				None	1	2	3	4 or more

PROVIDENCE, R. I.—Continued

SEMISKILLED—ALL OTHER TEXTILE MILLS								
All classes	2,371	183	2,188	423	604	479	334	531
In family having—								
No other employed member	186	31	155	84	51	28	8	15
1 other	827	69	758	228	210	150	97	142
2 others	597	44	553	75	177	123	75	147
3 or more others	761	39	722	36	166	178	154	227
Single (including unknown)	1,541	97	1,444	148	443	321	238	391
In family having—								
No other employed member	79	10	69	31	29	13	2	4
1 other	364	25	339	50	125	63	48	78
2 others	449	26	423	43	147	89	56	114
3 or more others	649	36	613	24	142	156	132	195
Married	616	57	559	198	109	122	81	106
In family having—								
No other employed member	23	3	20	10	4	7	2	
1 other	392	39	353	158	68	73	43	50
2 others	111	12	99	19	19	26	18	29
3 or more others	90	3	87	11	18	16	18	27
Widowed or divorced	214	29	185	77	52	36	15	34
In family having—								
No other employed member	84	18	66	43	18	8	4	11
1 other	71	5	66	20	17	14	6	14
2 others	37	6	31	13	11	8	1	4
3 or more others	22	---	22	1	6	6	4	5
SERVANTS								
All classes	707	91	616	382	141	80	47	57
In family having—								
No other employed member	212	41	171	146	37	15	7	7
1 other	296	33	263	167	57	27	23	22
2 others	109	9	100	51	24	18	4	12
3 or more others	90	8	82	18	23	20	13	16
Single (including unknown)	215	23	192	108	45	27	15	20
In family having—								
No other employed member	65	9	56	53	6	3	2	1
1 other	56	5	51	27	14	5	5	5
2 others	49	5	44	22	9	10	2	6
3 or more others	45	4	41	6	16	9	6	8
Married	234	37	197	124	44	32	16	18
In family having—								
No other employed member	25	7	18	12	5	5	2	1
1 other	147	24	123	90	25	15	10	7
2 others	36	3	33	16	11	4	1	4
3 or more others	26	3	23	6	3	8	3	6
Widowed or divorced	258	31	227	150	52	21	16	19
In family having—								
No other employed member	122	25	97	81	26	7	3	5
1 other	93	4	89	50	18	7	8	10
2 others	24	1	23	13	4	4	1	2
3 or more others	19	1	18	6	4	3	4	2

TABLE **173.**—WOMEN LIVING AT HOME AND EMPLOYED IN CERTAIN IMPORTANT OCCUPATIONS, CLASSIFIED BY MARITAL CONDITION, ACCORDING TO NUMBER OF OTHER EMPLOYED MEMBERS IN THE FAMILY, AND WHETHER THERE ARE BOARDERS OR LODGERS, FOR 11 SELECTED CITIES: 1920—Continued

OCCUPATION, MARITAL CONDITION, AND NUMBER OF OTHER GAINFULLY EMPLOYED MEMBERS OF FAMILY	GAINFULLY EMPLOYED WOMEN 16 YEARS OF AGE AND OVER LIVING AT HOME							
	Total number	Living in family having—						
		Boarders or lodgers	No boarders or lodgers	Unemployed members				
				None	1	2	3	4 or more
PROVIDENCE, R. I.—Continued								
STENOGRAPHERS AND TYPISTS								
All classes	1,775	136	1,639	147	748	465	217	198
In family having—								
No other employed member	124	17	107	17	61	35	9	2
1 other	538	54	484	59	245	129	62	43
2 others	563	39	524	45	229	154	69	66
3 or more others	550	26	524	26	213	147	77	87
Single (including unknown)	1,673	125	1,548	114	720	438	207	194
In family having—								
No other employed member	110	16	94	13	58	29	8	2
1 other	485	46	439	35	232	122	55	41
2 others	544	39	505	43	222	146	67	66
3 or more others	534	24	510	23	208	141	77	85
Married	78	7	71	27	23	16	8	4
In family having—								
No other employed member	5	-------	5	1	2	2	-------	-------
1 other	44	6	38	21	11	4	6	2
2 others	16	-------	16	2	7	5	2	-------
3 or more others	13	1	12	3	3	5	-------	2
Widowed or divorced	24	4	20	6	5	11	2	-------
In family having—								
No other employed member	9	1	8	3	1	4	1	-------
1 other	9	2	7	3	2	3	1	-------
2 others	3	-------	3	-------	-------	3	-------	-------
3 or more others	3	1	2	-------	2	1	-------	-------
TEACHERS (SCHOOL)								
All classes	1,080	82	998	188	469	252	89	82
In family having—								
No other employed member	170	26	144	61	81	19	7	2
1 other	338	27	311	64	155	73	23	23
2 others	279	15	264	42	115	77	25	20
3 or more others	293	14	279	21	118	83	34	37
Single (including unknown)	1,000	72	928	158	449	230	86	77
In family having—								
No other employed member	151	22	129	54	73	16	6	2
1 other	298	22	276	49	145	62	22	20
2 others	263	15	248	35	114	72	24	18
3 or more others	288	13	275	20	117	80	34	37
Married	44	4	40	19	10	11	1	3
In family having—								
No other employed member	4	-------	4	2	2	-------	-------	-------
1 other	27	3	24	11	6	7	1	2
2 others	8	-------	8	5	1	1	-------	1
3 or more others	5	1	4	1	1	3	-------	-------
Widowed or divorced	36	6	30	11	10	11	2	2
In family having—								
No other employed member	15	4	11	5	6	3	1	-------
1 other	13	2	11	4	4	4	-------	1
2 others	8	-------	8	2	-------	4	1	1
3 or more others	-------	-------	-------	-------	-------	-------	-------	-------

TABLE **173.**—WOMEN LIVING AT HOME AND EMPLOYED IN CERTAIN IMPORTANT OCCUPATIONS, CLASSIFIED BY MARITAL CONDITION, ACCORDING TO NUMBER OF OTHER EMPLOYED MEMBERS IN THE FAMILY, AND WHETHER THERE ARE BOARDERS OR LODGERS, FOR 11 SELECTED CITIES: 1920—Continued

OCCUPATION, MARITAL CONDITION, AND NUMBER OF OTHER GAINFULLY EMPLOYED MEMBERS OF FAMILY	GAINFULLY EMPLOYED WOMEN 16 YEARS OF AGE AND OVER LIVING AT HOME							
	Total number	Boarders or lodgers	Living in family having—					
			No boarders or lodgers	Unemployed members				
				None	1	2	3	4 or more
ROCHESTER, N. Y.								
BOOKKEEPERS, CASHIERS, AND ACCOUNTANTS								
All classes	2,009	228	1,781	272	860	414	223	240
In family having—								
No other employed member	215	36	179	62	100	38	9	6
1 other	632	83	549	123	266	121	60	62
2 others	565	72	493	53	249	119	64	80
3 or more others	597	37	560	34	245	136	90	92
Single (including unknown)	1,756	194	1,562	171	775	373	208	229
In family having—								
No other employed member	167	28	139	42	81	32	8	4
1 other	511	71	440	61	235	106	52	57
2 others	522	64	458	41	233	108	62	78
3 or more others	556	31	525	27	226	127	86	90
Married	188	27	161	80	56	32	11	9
In family having—								
No other employed member	17	4	13	5	6	3	1	2
1 other	102	10	92	58	24	11	6	3
2 others	34	7	27	10	10	10	2	2
3 or more others	35	6	29	7	16	8	2	2
Widowed or divorced	65	7	58	21	29	9	4	2
In family having—								
No other employed member	31	4	27	15	13	3	-----	-----
1 other	19	2	17	4	7	4	2	2
2 others	9	1	8	2	6	1	-----	-----
3 or more others	6	-----	6	-----	3	1	2	-----
CLERKS (EXCEPT CLERKS IN STORES)								
All classes	2,735	334	2,401	334	1,039	604	357	401
In family having—								
No other employed member	189	44	145	57	86	31	8	7
1 other	864	127	737	165	334	174	88	103
2 others	779	88	691	68	324	177	102	108
3 or more others	903	75	828	44	295	222	159	183
Single (including unknown)	2,364	272	2,092	193	929	541	330	371
In family having—								
No other employed member	145	32	113	37	73	23	7	5
1 other	678	100	578	65	291	150	78	94
2 others	702	72	630	50	297	160	96	99
3 or more others	839	68	771	41	268	208	149	173
Married	279	43	236	107	87	44	23	18
In family having—								
No other employed member	16	3	13	5	5	4	1	1
1 other	152	21	131	89	37	13	8	5
2 others	57	13	44	11	24	14	5	3
3 or more others	54	6	48	2	21	13	9	9
Widowed or divorced	92	19	73	34	23	19	4	12
In family having—								
No other employed member	28	9	19	15	8	4	-----	1
1 other	34	6	28	11	6	11	2	4
2 others	20	3	17	7	3	3	1	6
3 or more others	10	1	9	1	6	1	1	1

TABLE **173.**—WOMEN LIVING AT HOME AND EMPLOYED IN CERTAIN IMPORTANT OCCUPATIONS, CLASSIFIED BY MARITAL CONDITION, ACCORDING TO NUMBER OF OTHER EMPLOYED MEMBERS IN THE FAMILY, AND WHETHER THERE ARE BOARDERS OR LODGERS, FOR 11 SELECTED CITIES: 1920—Continued

OCCUPATION, MARITAL CONDITION, AND NUMBER OF OTHER GAINFULLY EMPLOYED MEMBERS OF FAMILY	GAINFULLY EMPLOYED WOMEN 16 YEARS OF AGE AND OVER LIVING AT HOME							
	Total number	Living in family having—						
		Boarders or lodgers	No boarders or lodgers	Unemployed members				
				None	1	2	3	4 or more

ROCHESTER, N. Y.—Continued

CLERKS IN STORES								
All classes	747	96	651	167	231	152	91	106
In family having—								
No other employed member	74	24	50	28	30	12	2	2
1 other	280	40	240	86	80	53	32	29
2 others	191	15	176	33	63	46	22	27
3 or more others	202	17	185	20	58	41	35	48
Single (including unknown)	483	55	428	58	172	101	71	81
In family having—								
No other employed member	42	13	29	9	22	8	1	2
1 other	131	17	114	19	49	29	17	17
2 others	136	11	125	16	48	32	20	20
3 or more others	174	14	160	14	53	32	33	42
Married	201	26	175	86	44	35	15	21
In family having—								
No other employed member	11	4	7	6	4	1	------	------
1 other	126	16	110	62	25	18	11	10
2 others	40	3	37	13	10	9	2	6
3 or more others	24	3	21	5	5	7	2	5
Widowed or divorced	63	15	48	23	15	16	5	4
In family having—								
No other employed member	21	7	14	13	4	3	1	------
1 other	23	7	16	5	6	6	4	2
2 others	15	1	14	4	5	5	------	1
3 or more others	4	------	4	1	------	2	------	1
SALESWOMEN (STORES)								
All classes	1,081	150	931	303	365	204	113	96
In family having—								
No other employed member	127	38	89	53	48	16	8	2
1 other	455	69	386	185	144	70	30	26
2 others	263	22	241	49	93	61	31	29
3 or more others	236	21	215	16	80	57	44	39
Single (including unknown)	588	77	511	79	237	133	72	67
In family having—								
No other employed member	60	20	40	19	28	9	4	------
1 other	182	27	155	32	85	37	11	17
2 others	162	13	149	20	61	38	21	22
3 or more others	184	17	167	8	63	49	36	28
Married	355	45	310	160	94	48	30	23
In family having—								
No other employed member	23	4	19	7	8	4	3	1
1 other	216	29	187	129	44	21	17	5
2 others	79	8	71	20	26	17	9	7
3 or more others	37	4	33	4	16	6	1	10
Widowed or divorced	138	28	110	64	34	23	11	6
In family having—								
No other employed member	44	14	30	27	12	3	1	1
1 other	57	13	44	24	15	12	2	4
2 others	22	1	21	9	6	6	1	------
3 or more others	15	------	15	4	1	2	7	1

TABLE **173.**—WOMEN LIVING AT HOME AND EMPLOYED IN CERTAIN IMPORTANT OCCUPATIONS, CLASSIFIED BY MARITAL CONDITION, ACCORDING TO NUMBER OF OTHER EMPLOYED MEMBERS IN THE FAMILY, AND WHETHER THERE ARE BOARDERS OR LODGERS, FOR 11 SELECTED CITIES: 1920—Continued

OCCUPATION, MARITAL CONDITION, AND NUMBER OF OTHER GAINFULLY EMPLOYED MEMBERS OF FAMILY	GAINFULLY EMPLOYED WOMEN 16 YEARS OF AGE AND OVER LIVING AT HOME							
	Total number	Boarders or lodgers	No boarders or lodgers	Living in family having—				
				Unemployed members				
				None	1	2	3	4 or more

ROCHESTER, N. Y.—Continued

SEMISKILLED—CLOTHING INDUSTRIES								
All classes	1,757	203	1,554	352	471	357	223	354
In family having—								
No other employed member	137	33	104	57	43	23	8	6
1 other	728	84	644	217	166	142	88	115
2 others	424	45	379	44	123	73	66	118
3 or more others	468	41	427	34	139	119	61	115
Single (including unknown)	985	93	892	113	290	210	136	236
In family having—								
No other employed member	60	12	48	29	23	5	2	1
1 other	261	29	232	38	72	57	31	63
2 others	273	24	249	21	79	42	49	82
3 or more others	391	28	363	25	116	106	54	90
Married	603	78	525	191	130	109	74	99
In family having—								
No other employed member	24	5	19	4	8	6	2	4
1 other	397	47	350	162	71	71	51	42
2 others	114	15	99	17	30	22	14	31
3 or more others	68	11	57	8	21	10	7	22
Widowed or divorced	169	32	137	48	51	38	13	19
In family having—								
No other employed member	53	16	37	24	12	12	4	1
1 other	70	8	62	17	23	14	6	10
2 others	37	6	31	6	14	9	3	5
3 or more others	9	2	7	1	2	3		3
SEMISKILLED—SHOE FACTORIES								
All classes	1,760	190	1,570	384	537	349	198	292
In family having—								
No other employed member	148	26	122	55	46	34	7	6
1 other	605	73	532	206	181	86	60	72
2 others	465	45	420	82	132	98	58	95
3 or more others	542	46	496	41	178	131	73	119
Single (including unknown)	1,145	100	1,045	144	381	248	142	230
In family having—								
No other employed member	88	11	77	31	32	19	2	4
1 other	279	33	246	48	100	42	34	55
2 others	333	27	306	35	102	73	44	79
3 or more others	445	29	416	30	147	114	62	92
Married	459	64	395	187	123	68	37	44
In family having—								
No other employed member	14	3	11	3	7	3	1	
1 other	271	35	236	141	68	31	19	12
2 others	103	14	89	36	24	21	10	12
3 or more others	71	12	59	7	24	13	7	20
Widowed or divorced	156	26	130	53	33	33	19	18
In family having—								
No other employed member	46	12	34	21	7	12	4	2
1 other	55	5	50	17	13	13	7	5
2 others	29	4	25	11	6	4	4	4
3 or more others	26	5	21	4	7	4	4	7

TABLE 173.—WOMEN LIVING AT HOME AND EMPLOYED IN CERTAIN IMPORTANT OCCUPATIONS, CLASSIFIED BY MARITAL CONDITION, ACCORDING TO NUMBER OF OTHER EMPLOYED MEMBERS IN THE FAMILY, AND WHETHER THERE ARE BOARDERS OR LODGERS, FOR 11 SELECTED CITIES: 1920—Continued

OCCUPATION, MARITAL CONDITION, AND NUMBER OF OTHER GAINFULLY EMPLOYED MEMBERS OF FAMILY	GAINFULLY EMPLOYED WOMEN 16 YEARS OF AGE AND OVER LIVING AT HOME							
	Total number	Living in family having—						
		Boarders or lodgers	No boarders or lodgers	Unemployed members				
				None	1	2	3	4 or more

ROCHESTER, N. Y.—Continued

SERVANTS								
All classes	619	126	493	301	131	74	57	56
In family having—								
No other employed member	163	49	114	106	33	11	9	4
1 other	254	50	204	137	43	29	23	22
2 others	105	20	85	30	35	16	13	11
3 or more others	97	7	90	28	20	18	12	19
Single (including unknown)	171	31	140	68	37	24	.21	21
In family having—								
No other employed member	38	11	27	33	2	1	1	1
1 other	47	10	37	19	10	5	8	5
2 others	42	8	34	8	17	7	5	5
3 or more others	44	2	42	8	8	11	7	10
Married	246	50	196	129	56	25	20	16
In family having—								
No other employed member	40	11	29	16	18	3	3	-----
1 other	134	30	104	84	17	15	10	8
2 others	40	6	34	15	12	5	6	2
3 or more others	32	3	29	14	9	2	1	6
Widowed or divorced	202	45	157	104	38	25	16	19
In family having—								
No other employed member	85	27	58	57	13	7	5	3
1 other	73	10	63	34	16	9	5	9
2 others	23	6	17	7	6	4	2	4
3 or more others	21	2	19	6	3	5	4	3
STENOGRAPHERS AND TYPISTS								
All classes	2,621	283	2,338	254	1,052	665	343	307
In family having—								
No other employed member	157	29	128	40	73	31	6	7
1 other	822	105	717	119	332	192	100	79
2 others	777	78	699	62	324	181	112	98
3 or more others	865	71	794	33	323	261	125	123
Single (including unknown)	2,426	258	2,168	185	988	630	325	298
In family having—								
No other employed member	133	28	105	29	65	27	5	7
1 other	726	91	635	68	309	177	93	79
2 others	742	73	669	58	306	175	108	95
3 or more others	825	66	759	30	308	251	119	117
Married	157	21	136	57	56	24	13	7
In family having—								
No other employed member	10	-----	10	5	4	1	-----	-----
1 other	84	12	72	48	21	10	5	-----
2 others	30	5	25	3	17	6	3	1
3 or more others	33	4	29	1	14	7	5	6
Widowed or divorced	38	4	34	12	8	11	5	2
In family having—								
No other employed member	14	1	13	6	4	3	1	-----
1 other	12	2	10	3	2	5	2	-----
2 others	5	-----	5	1	1	-----	1	2
3 or more others	7	1	6	2	1	3	1	-----

TABLE 173.—WOMEN LIVING AT HOME AND EMPLOYED IN CERTAIN IMPORTANT OCCUPATIONS, CLASSIFIED BY MARITAL CONDITION, ACCORDING TO NUMBER OF OTHER EMPLOYED MEMBERS IN THE FAMILY, AND WHETHER THERE ARE BOARDERS OR LODGERS, FOR 11 SELECTED CITIES: 1920—Continued

OCCUPATION, MARITAL CONDITION, AND NUMBER OF OTHER GAINFULLY EMPLOYED MEMBERS OF FAMILY	GAINFULLY EMPLOYED WOMEN 16 YEARS OF AGE AND OVER LIVING AT HOME							
				Living in family having—				
	Total number	Boarders or lodgers	No boarders or lodgers	Unemployed members				
				None	1	2	3	4 or more
ROCHESTER, N. Y.—Continued								
TAILORESSES								
All classes	2,395	238	2,157	508	662	490	297	438
In family having—								
No other employed member	202	30	172	59	73	31	25	14
1 other	1,012	102	910	329	267	170	108	138
2 others	534	56	478	80	143	108	77	126
3 or more others	647	50	597	40	179	181	87	160
Single (including unknown)	1,208	106	1,102	117	405	272	156	258
In family having—								
No other employed member	83	9	74	27	34	14	6	2
1 other	316	34	282	39	129	59	34	55
2 others	322	27	295	32	102	59	48	81
3 or more others	487	36	451	19	140	140	68	120
Married	920	100	820	310	187	172	112	139
In family having—								
No other employed member	34	6	28	4	13	5	6	6
1 other	606	61	545	261	116	95	66	68
2 others	157	22	135	33	29	36	24	35
3 or more others	123	11	112	12	29	36	16	30
Widowed or divorced	267	32	235	81	70	46	29	41
In family having—								
No other employed member	85	15	70	28	26	12	13	6
1 other	90	7	83	29	22	16	8	15
2 others	55	7	48	15	12	13	5	10
3 or more others	37	3	34	9	10	5	3	10
TEACHERS (SCHOOL)								
All classes	1,124	144	980	258	467	226	105	68
In family having—								
No other employed member	225	48	177	93	88	32	7	5
1 other	456	54	402	113	188	88	47	20
2 others	242	28	214	32	115	48	31	16
3 or more others	201	14	187	20	76	58	20	27
Single (including unknown)	965	112	853	184	424	203	95	59
In family having—								
No other employed member	196	35	161	76	81	27	7	5
1 other	366	40	326	65	172	75	39	15
2 others	215	24	191	25	99	46	29	16
3 or more others	188	13	175	18	72	55	20	23
Married	110	17	93	57	25	13	8	7
In family having—								
No other employed member	9	3	6	6	2	1	------	------
1 other	73	12	61	43	12	7	7	4
2 others	18	2	16	7	8	2	1	------
3 or more others	10	------	10	1	3	3	------	3
Widowed or divorced	49	15	34	17	18	10	2	2
In family having—								
No other employed member	20	10	10	11	5	4	------	------
1 other	17	2	15	5	4	6	1	1
2 others	9	2	7	------	8	------	------	1
3 or more others	3	1	2	1	1	------	------	1

TABLE 173.—WOMEN LIVING AT HOME AND EMPLOYED IN CERTAIN IMPORTANT OCCUPATIONS, CLASSIFIED BY MARITAL CONDITION, ACCORDING TO NUMBER OF OTHER EMPLOYED MEMBERS IN THE FAMILY, AND WHETHER THERE ARE BOARDERS OR LODGERS, FOR 11 SELECTED CITIES: 1920—Continued

OCCUPATION, MARITAL CONDITION, AND NUMBER OF OTHER GAINFULLY EMPLOYED MEMBERS OF FAMILY	GAINFULLY EMPLOYED WOMEN 16 YEARS OF AGE AND OVER LIVING AT HOME							
	Total number	Boarders or lodgers	No boarders or lodgers	Living in family having—				
				Unemployed members				
				None	1	2	3	4 or more
PATERSON, N. J.								
BOOKKEEPERS, CASHIERS, AND ACCOUNTANTS								
All classes	720	60	660	66	257	178	112	107
In family having—								
No other employed member	44	6	38	6	21	15	1	1
1 other	208	21	187	27	74	50	31	26
2 others	187	9	178	18	70	47	26	26
3 or more others	281	24	257	15	92	66	54	54
Single (including unknown)	668	56	612	50	239	167	107	105
In family having—								
No other employed member	35	4	31	5	16	12	1	1
1 other	184	19	165	15	68	47	29	25
2 others	177	9	168	15	65	45	26	26
3 or more others	272	24	248	15	90	63	51	53
Married	39	1	38	15	12	9	3	-----
In family having—								
No other employed member	4	1	3	-----	2	2	-----	-----
1 other	19	-------	19	12	4	2	1	-----
2 others	9	-------	9	3	4	2	-----	-----
3 or more others	7	-------	7	-----	2	3	2	-----
Widowed or divorced	13	3	10	1	6	2	2	2
In family having—								
No other employed member	5	1	4	1	3	1	-----	-----
1 other	5	2	3	-----	2	1	1	1
2 others	1	-------	1	-----	1	-----	-----	-----
3 or more others	2	-------	2	-----	-----	-----	1	1
CLERKS (EXCEPT CLERKS IN STORES)								
All classes	602	50	552	75	231	156	73	67
In family having—								
No other employed member	35	9	26	8	17	7	1	2
1 other	167	14	153	33	60	45	16	13
2 others	211	14	197	26	94	47	22	22
3 or more others	189	13	176	8	60	57	34	30
Single (including unknown)	553	46	507	55	220	148	68	62
In family having—								
No other employed member	29	8	21	6	15	6	1	1
1 other	143	13	130	18	55	42	16	12
2 others	199	14	185	24	92	45	18	20
3 or more others	182	11	171	7	58	55	33	29
Married	35	2	33	14	10	5	3	3
In family having—								
No other employed member	3	-------	3	-----	1	1	-----	1
1 other	20	1	19	12	5	2	-----	1
2 others	8	-------	8	1	2	1	3	1
3 or more others	4	1	3	1	2	1	-----	-----
Widowed or divorced	14	2	12	6	1	3	2	2
In family having—								
No other employed member	3	1	2	2	1	-----	-----	-----
1 other	4	-------	4	3	-----	1	-----	-----
2 others	4	-------	4	1	-----	1	1	1
3 or more others	3	1	2	-----	1	1	1	1

TABLE **173.**—WOMEN LIVING AT HOME AND EMPLOYED IN CERTAIN IMPORTANT OCCUPATIONS, CLASSIFIED BY MARITAL CONDITION, ACCORDING TO NUMBER OF OTHER EMPLOYED MEMBERS IN THE FAMILY, AND WHETHER THERE ARE BOARDERS OR LODGERS, FOR 11 SELECTED CITIES: 1920—Continued

OCCUPATION, MARITAL CONDITION, AND NUMBER OF OTHER GAINFULLY EMPLOYED MEMBERS OF FAMILY	GAINFULLY EMPLOYED WOMEN 16 YEARS OF AGE AND OVER LIVING AT HOME							
	Total number	Boarders or lodgers	No boarders or lodgers	Living in family having—				
				Unemployed members				
				None	1	2	3	4 or more
PATERSON, N. J.—Continued								
CLERKS IN STORES								
All classes	179	13	166	19	66	41	26	27
In family having—								
No other employed member	14	3	11	2	5	4	------	3
1 other	53	4	49	12	19	11	4	7
2 others	51	3	48	4	19	9	11	8
3 or more others	61	3	58	1	23	17	11	9
Single (including unknown)	134	11	123	6	55	32	21	20
In family having—								
No other employed member	10	3	7	2	4	3	------	1
1 other	29	3	26	3	16	4	3	3
2 others	41	2	39	1	16	8	8	8
3 or more others	54	3	51	------	19	17	10	8
Married	38	2	36	10	9	8	5	6
In family having—								
No other employed member	3	------	3	------	1	1	------	1
1 other	21	1	20	7	3	6	1	4
2 others	8	1	7	2	2	1	3	------
3 or more others	6	------	6	1	3	------	1	1
Widowed or divorced	7	------	7	3	2	1	------	1
In family having—								
No other employed member	1	------	1	------	------	------	------	1
1 other	3	------	3	2	------	1	------	------
2 others	2	------	2	1	1	------	------	------
3 or more others	1	------	1	------	1	------	------	------
SALESWOMEN (STORES)								
All classes	486	39	447	81	179	109	53	64
In family having—								
No other employed member	47	5	42	14	17	14	2	------
1 other	148	13	135	38	53	28	12	17
2 others	130	13	117	17	55	22	16	20
3 or more others	161	8	153	12	54	45	23	27
Single (including unknown)	367	24	343	37	147	82	44	57
In family having—								
No other employed member	27	2	25	7	15	5	------	------
1 other	85	6	79	11	34	20	8	12
2 others	109	10	99	9	48	19	15	18
3 or more others	146	6	140	10	50	38	21	27
Married	83	11	72	27	25	18	8	5
In family having—								
No other employed member	4	1	3	------	------	3	1	------
1 other	53	5	48	21	17	7	4	4
2 others	14	3	11	5	5	2	1	1
3 or more others	12	2	10	1	3	6	2	------
Widowed or divorced	36	4	32	17	7	9	1	2
In family having—								
No other employed member	16	2	14	7	2	6	1	------
1 other	10	2	8	6	2	1	------	1
2 others	7	------	7	3	2	1	------	1
3 or more others	3	------	3	1	1	1	------	------

TABLE 173.—WOMEN LIVING AT HOME AND EMPLOYED IN CERTAIN IMPORTANT OCCUPATIONS, CLASSIFIED BY MARITAL CONDITION, ACCORDING TO NUMBER OF OTHER EMPLOYED MEMBERS IN THE FAMILY, AND WHETHER THERE ARE BOARDERS OR LODGERS, FOR 11 SELECTED CITIES: 1920—Continued

	GAINFULLY EMPLOYED WOMEN 16 YEARS OF AGE AND OVER LIVING AT HOME							
OCCUPATION, MARITAL CONDITION, AND NUMBER OF OTHER GAINFULLY EMPLOYED MEMBERS OF FAMILY	Total number	Living in family having—						
		Boarders or lodgers	No boarders or lodgers	Unemployed members				
				None	1	2	3	4 or more
PATERSON, N. J.—Continued								
SEMISKILLED—CLOTHING INDUSTRIES								
All classes	683	65	618	166	211	154	87	65
In family having—								
No other employed member	81	13	68	30	26	15	7	3
1 other	285	27	258	93	63	47	31	21
2 others	137	10	127	33	39	33	21	11
3 or more others	180	15	165	10	53	59	28	30
Single (including unknown)	414	29	385	64	141	107	57	45
In family having—								
No other employed member	46	6	40	15	19	8	3	1
1 other	119	7	112	26	46	23	13	11
2 others	94	5	89	17	30	24	15	8
3 or more others	155	11	144	6	46	52	26	25
Married	209	26	183	75	58	34	26	16
In family having—								
No other employed member	7	------	7	2	2	2	1	------
1 other	146	19	127	56	43	21	18	8
2 others	35	3	32	14	7	6	5	3
3 or more others	21	4	17	3	6	5	2	5
Widowed or divorced	60	10	50	27	12	13	4	4
In family having—								
No other employed member	28	7	21	13	5	5	3	2
1 other	20	1	19	11	4	3	------	2
2 others	8	2	6	2	2	3	1	------
3 or more others	4	------	4	1	1	2	------	------
SEMISKILLED—SILK MILLS								
All classes	8,212	584	7,628	1,722	2,609	1,665	1,028	1,188
In family having—								
No other employed member	586	93	493	234	218	91	28	15
1 other	3,006	227	2,779	943	947	549	281	286
2 others	2,081	147	1,934	329	691	401	307	353
3 or more others	2,539	117	2,422	216	753	624	412	534
Single (including unknown)	5,195	316	4,879	580	1,775	1,139	748	953
In family having—								
No other employed member	271	40	231	96	128	37	6	4
1 other	1,260	89	1,171	197	491	260	138	174
2 others	1,516	94	1,422	161	504	310	247	294
3 or more others	2,148	93	2,055	126	652	532	357	481
Married	2,365	202	2,163	882	658	414	219	192
In family having—								
No other employed member	103	20	83	29	39	23	9	3
1 other	1,518	119	1,399	654	398	249	124	93
2 others	443	42	401	128	146	72	44	53
3 or more others	301	21	280	71	75	70	42	43
Widowed or divorced	652	66	586	260	176	112	61	43
In family having—								
No other employed member	212	33	179	109	51	31	13	8
1 other	228	19	209	92	58	40	19	19
2 others	122	11	111	40	41	19	16	6
3 or more others	90	3	87	19	26	22	13	10

TABLE 173.—WOMEN LIVING AT HOME AND EMPLOYED IN CERTAIN IMPORTANT OCCUPATIONS, CLASSIFIED BY MARITAL CONDITION, ACCORDING TO NUMBER OF OTHER EMPLOYED MEMBERS IN THE FAMILY, AND WHETHER THERE ARE BOARDERS OR LODGERS, FOR 11 SELECTED CITIES: 1920—Continued

OCCUPATION, MARITAL CONDITION, AND NUMBER OF OTHER GAINFULLY EMPLOYED MEMBERS OF FAMILY	GAINFULLY EMPLOYED WOMEN 16 YEARS OF AGE AND OVER LIVING AT HOME							
	Total number	Boarders or lodgers	No boarders or lodgers	Living in family having—				
				Unemployed members				
				None	1	2	3	4 or more
PATERSON, N. J.—Continued								
SEMISKILLED—ALL OTHER TEXTILE MILLS								
All classes	894	101	793	210	212	181	126	165
In family having—								
No other employed member	84	18	66	43	17	8	9	7
1 other	373	36	337	119	81	72	48	53
2 others	215	22	193	34	61	58	22	40
3 or more others	222	25	197	14	53	43	47	65
Single (including unknown)	452	46	406	55	123	100	67	107
In family having—								
No other employed member	27	6	21	16	8	1	1	1
1 other	124	8	116	21	32	26	22	23
2 others	130	13	117	12	39	43	10	26
3 or more others	171	19	152	6	44	30	34	57
Married	339	38	301	116	75	67	40	41
In family having—								
No other employed member	19	4	15	9	5	2	2	1
1 other	215	24	191	83	44	42	22	24
2 others	67	6	61	17	18	10	10	12
3 or more others	38	4	34	7	8	13	6	4
Widowed or divorced	103	17	86	39	14	14	19	17
In family having—								
No other employed member	38	8	30	18	4	5	6	5
1 other	34	4	30	15	5	4	4	6
2 others	18	3	15	5	4	5	2	2
3 or more others	13	2	11	1	1		7	4
SERVANTS								
All classes	213	36	177	106	41	27	16	23
In family having—								
No other employed member	58	14	44	36	12	4	3	3
1 other	89	13	76	55	14	9	4	7
2 others	37	4	33	10	9	8	4	6
3 or more others	29	5	24	5	6	6	5	7
Single (including unknown)	62	9	53	22	16	9	7	8
In family having—								
No other employed member	20	3	17	11	7		1	1
1 other	14		14	6	2	3	2	1
2 others	12	3	9	2	3	3	1	3
3 or more others	16	3	13	3	4	3	3	3
Married	86	13	73	50	15	7	5	9
In family having—								
No other employed member	10	4	6	7	1	1	1	
1 other	48	8	40	37	8			3
2 others	18		18	5	5	4	2	2
3 or more others	10	1	9	1	1	2	2	4
Widowed or divorced	65	14	51	34	10	11	4	6
In family having—								
No other employed member	28	7	21	18	4	3	1	2
1 other	27	5	22	12	4	6	2	3
2 others	7	1	6	3	1	1	1	1
3 or more others	3	1	2	1	1	1		

TABLE **173.**—WOMEN LIVING AT HOME AND EMPLOYED IN CERTAIN IMPORTANT OCCUPATIONS, CLASSIFIED BY MARITAL CONDITION, ACCORDING TO NUMBER OF OTHER EMPLOYED MEMBERS IN THE FAMILY, AND WHETHER THERE ARE BOARDERS OR LODGERS, FOR 11 SELECTED CITIES: 1920—Continued

OCCUPATION, MARITAL CONDITION, AND NUMBER OF OTHER GAINFULLY EMPLOYED MEMBERS OF FAMILY	Total number	GAINFULLY EMPLOYED WOMEN 16 YEARS OF AGE AND OVER LIVING AT HOME						
				Living in family having—				
		Boarders or lodgers	No boarders or lodgers	Unemployed members				
				None	1	2	3	4 or more
PATERSON, N. J.—Continued								
STENOGRAPHERS AND TYPISTS								
All classes	903	57	846	61	383	255	125	79
In family having—								
No other employed member	43	10	33	4	22	14	3	-----
1 other	262	13	249	23	110	74	27	28
2 others	279	19	260	22	134	59	42	22
3 or more others	319	15	304	12	117	108	53	29
Single (including unknown)	862	53	809	49	370	246	119	78
In family having—								
No other employed member	41	9	32	4	21	13	3	-----
1 other	238	10	228	12	104	69	25	28
2 others	275	19	256	21	132	59	41	22
3 or more others	308	15	293	12	113	105	50	28
Married	30	3	27	9	11	4	5	1
In family having—								
No other employed member	-----	-----	-----	-----	-----	-----	-----	-----
1 other	19	3	16	9	6	3	1	-----
2 others	2	-----	2	-----	1	-----	1	-----
3 or more others	9	-----	9	-----	4	1	3	1
Widowed or divorced	11	1	10	3	2	5	1	-----
In family having—								
No other employed member	2	1	1	-----	1	1	-----	-----
1 other	5	-----	5	2	-----	2	1	-----
2 others	2	-----	2	1	1	-----	-----	-----
3 or more others	2	-----	2	-----	-----	2	-----	-----
TEACHERS (SCHOOL)								
All classes	719	52	667	93	328	164	85	49
In family having—								
No other employed member	93	9	84	27	41	17	5	3
1 other	220	26	194	32	100	51	22	15
2 others	192	6	186	20	94	42	26	10
3 or more others	214	11	203	14	93	54	32	21
Single (including unknown)	691	50	641	85	319	156	83	48
In family having—								
No other employed member	88	9	79	25	41	16	4	2
1 other	209	25	184	29	97	46	22	15
2 others	184	6	178	18	90	40	26	10
3 or more others	210	10	200	13	91	54	31	21
Married	19	1	18	6	7	6	-----	-----
In family having—								
No other employed member	1	-----	1	-----	-----	1	-----	-----
1 other	9	-----	9	3	2	4	-----	-----
2 others	6	-----	6	2	3	1	-----	-----
3 or more others	3	1	2	1	2	-----	-----	-----
Widowed or divorced	9	1	8	2	2	2	2	1
In family having—								
No other employed member	4	-----	4	2	-----	-----	1	1
1 other	2	1	1	-----	1	-----	1	-----
2 others	2	-----	2	-----	1	1	-----	-----
3 or more others	1	-----	1	-----	-----	-----	1	-----

TABLE 173.—WOMEN LIVING AT HOME AND EMPLOYED IN CERTAIN IMPORTANT OCCUPATIONS, CLASSIFIED BY MARITAL CONDITION, ACCORDING TO NUMBER OF OTHER EMPLOYED MEMBERS IN THE FAMILY, AND WHETHER THERE ARE BOARDERS OR LODGERS, FOR 11 SELECTED CITIES: 1920—Continued

OCCUPATION, MARITAL CONDITION, AND NUMBER OF OTHER GAINFULLY EMPLOYED MEMBERS OF FAMILY	GAINFULLY EMPLOYED WOMEN 16 YEARS OF AGE AND OVER LIVING AT HOME							
	Total number	Boarders or lodgers	No boarders or lodgers	Living in family having—				
				Unemployed members				
				None	1	2	3	4 or more
CINCINNATI, OHIO								
BOARDING AND LODGING HOUSE KEEPERS								
All classes	629	547	82	425	118	45	19	22
In family having—								
No other employed member	335	290	45	252	54	15	8	6
1 other	209	184	25	134	39	18	8	10
2 others	63	55	8	32	20	7	2	2
3 or more others	22	18	4	7	5	5	1	4
Single (including unknown)	107	95	12	82	16	5	2	2
In family having—								
No other employed member	80	71	9	65	10	4	1	
1 other	21	20	1	14	3	1	1	2
2 others	5	3	2	2	3			
3 or more others	1	1		1				
Married	229	195	34	151	37	22	10	9
In family having—								
No other employed member	58	48	10	42	9	4	2	1
1 other	129	113	16	89	19	10	6	5
2 others	31	26	5	19	6	4	1	1
3 or more others	11	8	3	1	3	4	1	2
Widowed or divorced	293	257	36	192	65	18	7	11
In family having—								
No other employed member	197	171	26	145	35	7	5	5
1 other	59	51	8	31	17	7	1	3
2 others	27	26	1	11	11	3	1	1
3 or more others	10	9	1	5	2	1		2
BOOKKEEPERS, CASHIERS, AND ACCOUNTANTS								
All classes	2,313	127	2,186	236	966	576	271	264
In family having—								
No other employed member	241	21	220	50	129	47	7	8
1 other	773	41	732	126	334	166	86	61
2 others	690	35	655	40	286	188	89	87
3 or more others	609	30	579	20	217	175	89	108
Single (including unknown)	2,071	113	1,958	152	894	522	254	249
In family having—								
No other employed member	188	17	171	34	106	35	7	6
1 other	645	37	608	64	303	145	80	53
2 others	658	32	626	37	278	178	81	84
3 or more others	580	27	553	17	207	164	86	106
Married	133	7	126	55	36	26	9	7
In family having—								
No other employed member	17	1	16	5	8	3		1
1 other	86	3	83	49	18	11	4	4
2 others	13	2	11		4	4	3	2
3 or more others	17	1	16	1	6	8	2	
Widowed or divorced	109	7	102	29	36	28	8	8
In family having—								
No other employed member	36	3	33	11	15	9		1
1 other	42	1	41	13	13	10	2	4
2 others	19	1	18	3	4	6	5	1
3 or more others	12	2	10	2	4	3	1	2

TABLE **173.**—WOMEN LIVING AT HOME AND EMPLOYED IN CERTAIN IMPORTANT OCCUPATIONS, CLASSIFIED BY MARITAL CONDITION, ACCORDING TO NUMBER OF OTHER EMPLOYED MEMBERS IN THE FAMILY, AND WHETHER THERE ARE BOARDERS OR LODGERS, FOR 11 SELECTED CITIES: 1920—Continued

OCCUPATION, MARITAL CONDITION, AND NUMBER OF OTHER GAINFULLY EMPLOYED MEMBERS OF FAMILY	GAINFULLY EMPLOYED WOMEN 16 YEARS OF AGE AND OVER LIVING AT HOME							
	Total number	Living in family having—						
		Boarders or lodgers	No boarders or lodgers	Unemployed members				
				None	1	2	3	4 or more
CINCINNATI, OHIO—Continued								
CLERKS (EXCEPT CLERKS IN STORES)								
All classes	2,859	174	2,685	323	1,139	700	356	341
In family having—								
No other employed member	318	35	283	84	139	56	23	16
1 other	952	56	896	138	402	208	113	91
2 others	815	45	770	61	343	198	115	98
3 or more others	774	38	736	40	255	238	105	136
Single (including unknown)	2,585	152	2,433	238	1,061	642	327	317
In family having—								
No other employed member	230	21	209	53	107	46	13	11
1 other	832	51	781	91	374	181	102	84
2 others	773	44	729	56	329	186	109	93
3 or more others	750	36	714	38	251	229	103	129
Married	141	8	133	44	43	29	12	13
In family having—								
No other employed member	25	2	23	3	13	4	2	3
1 other	77	4	73	35	19	11	7	5
2 others	24	------	24	4	9	8	1	2
3 or more others	15	2	13	2	2	6	2	3
Widowed or divorced	133	14	119	41	35	29	17	11
In family having—								
No other employed member	63	12	51	28	19	6	8	2
1 other	43	1	42	12	9	16	4	2
2 others	18	1	17	1	5	4	5	3
3 or more others	9	------	9	------	2	3	------	4
CLERKS IN STORES								
All classes	914	61	853	161	317	179	127	130
In family having—								
No other employed member	83	8	75	26	36	12	6	3
1 other	332	16	316	90	106	61	38	37
2 others	264	18	246	27	104	55	31	47
3 or more others	235	19	216	18	71	51	52	43
Single (including unknown)	720	43	677	86	266	150	108	110
In family having—								
No other employed member	52	5	47	13	24	10	4	1
1 other	226	9	217	37	88	43	30	28
2 others	234	13	221	19	90	50	30	45
3 or more others	208	16	192	17	64	47	44	33
Married	115	11	104	47	36	15	9	8
In family having—								
No other employed member	6	------	6	2	4	------	------	------
1 other	73	6	67	40	14	10	3	6
2 others	20	3	17	4	12	2	1	1
3 or more others	16	2	14	1	6	3	5	1
Widowed or divorced	79	7	72	28	15	14	10	12
In family having—								
No other employed member	25	3	22	11	8	2	2	2
1 other	33	1	32	13	4	8	5	3
2 others	10	2	8	4	2	3	------	1
3 or more others	11	1	10	------	1	1	3	6

TABLE **173.**—WOMEN LIVING AT HOME AND EMPLOYED IN CERTAIN IMPORTANT OCCUPATIONS, CLASSIFIED BY MARITAL CONDITION, ACCORDING TO NUMBER OF OTHER EMPLOYED MEMBERS IN THE FAMILY, AND WHETHER THERE ARE BOARDERS OR LODGERS, FOR 11 SELECTED CITIES: 1920—Continued

OCCUPATION, MARITAL CONDITION, AND NUMBER OF OTHER GAINFULLY EMPLOYED MEMBERS OF FAMILY	GAINFULLY EMPLOYED WOMEN 16 YEARS OF AGE AND OVER LIVING AT HOME							
	Total number	Living in family having—						
		Boarders or lodgers	No boarders or lodgers	Unemployed members				
				None	1	2	3	4 or more

CINCINNATI, OHIO—Continued

DRESSMAKERS AND SEAMSTRESSES (NOT IN FACTORY)								
All classes	1,396	133	1,263	571	448	213	91	73
In family having—								
No other employed member	401	58	343	224	112	47	12	6
1 other	532	47	485	233	173	65	35	26
2 others	270	17	253	89	88	45	22	26
3 or more others	193	11	182	25	75	56	22	15
Single (including unknown)	838	51	787	271	325	144	55	43
In family having—								
No other employed member	203	23	180	104	72	22	4	1
1 other	282	14	268	104	113	35	19	11
2 others	189	10	179	49	72	36	14	18
3 or more others	164	4	160	14	68	51	18	13
Married	234	33	201	125	54	30	9	16
In family having—								
No other employed member	32	6	26	18	7	5	1	1
1 other	149	18	131	84	34	17	5	9
2 others	39	4	35	18	8	6	2	5
3 or more others	14	5	9	5	5	2	1	1
Widowed or divorced	324	49	275	175	69	39	27	14
In family having—								
No other employed member	166	29	137	102	33	20	7	4
1 other	101	15	86	45	26	13	11	6
2 others	42	3	39	22	8	3	6	3
3 or more others	15	2	13	6	2	3	3	1
LAUNDRESSES (NOT IN LAUNDRY)								
All classes	2,621	441	2,180	1,535	528	281	138	139
In family having—								
No other employed member	783	202	581	551	126	57	26	23
1 other	1,282	168	1,114	781	256	130	57	58
2 others	363	48	315	142	106	55	32	28
3 or more others	193	23	170	61	40	39	23	30
Single (including unknown)	297	53	244	189	56	22	5	25
In family having—								
No other employed member	135	32	103	116	14	2	1	2
1 other	85	14	71	45	21	9	1	9
2 others	41	4	37	14	16	6	2	3
3 or more others	36	3	33	14	5	5	1	11
Married	1,335	207	1,128	767	270	146	83	69
In family having—								
No other employed member	130	48	82	76	32	12	7	3
1 other	901	116	785	578	158	84	43	38
2 others	215	33	182	86	61	35	18	15
3 or more others	89	10	79	27	19	15	15	13
Widowed or divorced	989	181	808	579	202	113	50	45
In family having—								
No other employed member	518	122	396	359	80	43	18	18
1 other	296	38	258	158	77	37	13	11
2 others	107	11	96	42	29	14	12	10
3 or more others	68	10	58	20	16	19	7	6

TABLE **173.**—WOMEN LIVING AT HOME AND EMPLOYED IN CERTAIN IMPORTANT OCCUPATIONS, CLASSIFIED BY MARITAL CONDITION, ACCORDING TO NUMBER OF OTHER EMPLOYED MEMBERS IN THE FAMILY, AND WHETHER THERE ARE BOARDERS OR LODGERS, FOR 11 SELECTED CITIES: 1920—Continued

OCCUPATION, MARITAL CONDITION, AND NUMBER OF OTHER GAINFULLY EMPLOYED MEMBERS OF FAMILY	GAINFULLY EMPLOYED WOMEN 16 YEARS OF AGE AND OVER LIVING AT HOME							
	Total number			Living in family having—				
		Boarders or lodgers	No boarders or lodgers	Unemployed members				
				None	1	2	3	4 or more
CINCINNATI, OHIO—Continued								
SALESWOMEN (STORES)								
All classes	2,531	173	2,358	464	884	544	346	293
In family having—								
No other employed member	367	41	326	146	128	52	30	11
1 other	921	69	852	221	334	174	100	92
2 others	606	32	574	60	208	148	113	77
3 or more others	637	31	606	37	214	170	103	113
Single (including unknown)	1,955	116	1,839	232	748	441	278	256
In family having—								
No other employed member	211	18	193	74	90	27	14	6
1 other	632	44	588	89	266	130	75	72
2 others	527	25	502	38	193	131	95	70
3 or more others	585	29	556	31	199	153	94	108
Married	269	17	252	114	63	48	31	13
In family having—								
No other employed member	32	5	27	10	11	7	4	
1 other	168	10	158	85	37	22	14	10
2 others	40	1	39	15	6	8	9	2
3 or more others	29	1	28	4	9	11	4	1
Widowed or divorced	307	40	267	118	73	55	37	24
In family having—								
No other employed member	124	18	106	62	27	18	12	5
1 other	121	15	106	47	31	22	11	10
2 others	39	6	33	7	9	9	9	5
3 or more others	23	1	22	2	6	6	5	4
SEMISKILLED—CLOTHING INDUSTRIES								
All classes	2,488	142	2,346	649	859	477	247	256
In family having—								
No other employed member	458	39	419	248	141	50	13	6
1 other	875	51	824	282	306	136	73	78
2 others	587	29	558	76	243	128	75	65
3 or more others	568	23	545	43	169	163	86	107
Single (including unknown)	1,774	80	1,694	300	695	363	205	211
In family having—								
No other employed member	233	12	221	119	88	19	6	1
1 other	539	29	510	101	235	94	49	60
2 others	473	18	455	45	211	99	66	52
3 or more others	529	21	508	35	161	151	84	98
Married	370	26	344	182	82	63	18	25
In family having—								
No other employed member	58	7	51	22	19	14	2	1
1 other	233	12	221	139	42	28	13	11
2 others	60	5	55	18	19	14	2	7
3 or more others	19	2	17	3	2	7	1	6
Widowed or divorced	344	36	308	167	82	51	24	20
In family having—								
No other employed member	167	20	147	107	34	17	5	4
1 other	103	10	93	42	29	14	11	7
2 others	54	6	48	13	13	15	7	6
3 or more others	20		20	5	6	5	1	3

TABLE **173.**—WOMEN LIVING AT HOME AND EMPLOYED IN CERTAIN IMPORTANT OCCUPATIONS, CLASSIFIED BY MARITAL CONDITION, ACCORDING TO NUMBER OF OTHER EMPLOYED MEMBERS IN THE FAMILY, AND WHETHER THERE ARE BOARDERS OR LODGERS, FOR 11 SELECTED CITIES: 1920—Continued

OCCUPATION, MARITAL CONDITION, AND NUMBER OF OTHER GAINFULLY EMPLOYED MEMBERS OF FAMILY	GAINFULLY EMPLOYED WOMEN 16 YEARS OF AGE AND OVER LIVING AT HOME							
	Total number		Living in family having—					
		Boarders or lodgers	No boarders or lodgers	Unemployed members				
				None	1	2	3	4 or more

CINCINNATI, OHIO—Continued

SEMISKILLED—FOOD INDUSTRIES								
All classes	998	65	933	260	297	185	127	129
In family having—								
No other employed member	160	18	142	83	46	16	6	9
1 other	390	29	361	129	109	68	45	39
2 others	254	9	245	36	78	58	39	43
3 or more others	194	9	185	12	64	43	37	38
Single (including unknown)	594	29	565	80	203	128	89	94
In family having—								
No other employed member	45	3	42	25	16	2	------	2
1 other	207	14	193	33	71	41	31	31
2 others	175	5	170	13	61	46	28	27
3 or more others	167	7	160	9	55	39	30	34
Married	235	18	217	104	56	29	23	23
In family having—								
No other employed member	39	2	37	17	9	6	3	4
1 other	134	11	123	71	32	14	10	7
2 others	48	4	44	13	10	7	8	10
3 or more others	14	1	13	3	5	2	2	2
Widowed or divorced	169	18	151	76	38	28	15	12
In family having—								
No other employed member	76	13	63	41	21	8	3	3
1 other	49	4	45	25	6	13	4	1
2 others	31	------	31	10	7	5	3	6
3 or more others	13	1	12	------	4	2	5	2
SEMISKILLED—SHOE FACTORIES								
All classes	1,602	77	1,525	337	607	309	174	175
In family having—								
No other employed member	223	18	205	99	79	28	13	4
1 other	552	24	528	166	206	100	34	46
2 others	402	20	382	49	155	91	52	55
3 or more others	425	15	410	23	167	90	75	70
Single (including unknown)	1,192	51	1,141	152	514	236	145	145
In family having—								
No other employed member	114	8	106	46	56	10	1	1
1 other	358	13	345	63	160	67	30	38
2 others	336	15	321	27	140	76	48	45
3 or more others	384	15	369	16	158	83	66	61
Married	222	13	209	111	48	32	15	16
In family having—								
No other employed member	30	4	26	14	6	2	7	1
1 other	139	5	134	79	32	20	3	5
2 others	36	4	32	15	6	6	2	7
3 or more others	17	------	17	3	4	4	3	3
Widowed or divorced	188	13	175	74	45	41	14	14
In family having—								
No other employed member	79	6	73	39	17	16	5	2
1 other	55	6	49	24	14	13	1	3
2 others	30	1	29	7	9	9	2	3
3 or more others	24	------	24	4	5	3	6	6

TABLE **173.**—WOMEN LIVING AT HOME AND EMPLOYED IN CERTAIN IMPORTANT OCCUPATIONS, CLASSIFIED BY MARITAL CONDITION, ACCORDING TO NUMBER OF OTHER EMPLOYED MEMBERS IN THE FAMILY, AND WHETHER THERE ARE BOARDERS OR LODGERS, FOR 11 SELECTED CITIES: 1920—Continued

	GAINFULLY EMPLOYED WOMEN 16 YEARS OF AGE AND OVER LIVING AT HOME							
OCCUPATION, MARITAL CONDITION, AND NUMBER OF OTHER GAINFULLY EMPLOYED MEMBERS OF FAMILY	Total number			Living in family having—				
		Boarders or lodgers	No boarders or lodgers	Unemployed members				
				None	1	2	3	4 or more
CINCINNATI, OHIO—Continued								
SERVANTS								
All classes	2,816	383	2,433	1,509	596	334	178	199
In family having—								
No other employed member	827	125	702	588	133	61	24	21
1 other	1,205	169	1,036	696	264	116	62	67
2 others	455	50	405	154	116	93	44	48
3 or more others	329	39	290	71	83	64	48	63
Single (including unknown)	914	120	794	361	240	134	76	103
In family having—								
No other employed member	264	44	220	202	42	16	4	
1 other	266	40	226	95	84	31	21	35
2 others	194	20	174	38	61	44	20	31
3 or more others	190	16	174	26	53	43	31	37
Married	1,018	145	873	624	195	103	50	46
In family having—								
No other employed member	126	23	103	77	26	11	6	6
1 other	666	91	575	455	125	49	22	15
2 others	145	16	129	67	26	27	14	11
3 or more others	81	15	66	25	18	16	8	14
Widowed or divorced	884	118	766	524	161	97	52	50
In family having—								
No other employed member	437	58	379	309	65	34	14	15
1 other	273	38	235	146	55	36	19	17
2 others	116	14	102	49	29	22	10	6
3 or more others	58	8	50	20	12	5	9	12
STENOGRAPHERS AND TYPISTS								
All classes	4,004	214	3,790	298	1,585	1,054	553	514
In family having—								
No other employed member	317	27	290	41	181	69	18	8
1 other	1,281	74	1,207	138	544	319	144	136
2 others	1,140	56	1,084	75	436	303	181	145
3 or more others	1,266	57	1,209	44	424	363	210	225
Single (including unknown)	3,832	204	3,628	247	1,530	1,017	537	501
In family having—								
No other employed member	282	23	259	28	166	63	17	8
1 other	1,196	70	1,126	110	518	303	136	129
2 others	1,110	55	1,055	68	430	294	177	141
3 or more others	1,244	56	1,188	41	416	357	207	223
Married	91	6	85	33	27	17	8	6
In family having—								
No other employed member	7	1	6	3	3	1		
1 other	55	4	51	23	16	9	5	2
2 others	17	1	16	5	4	5	1	2
3 or more others	12		12	2	4	2	2	2
Widowed or divorced	81	4	77	18	28	20	8	7
In family having—								
No other employed member	28	3	25	10	12	5	1	
1 other	30		30	5	10	7	3	5
2 others	13		13	2	2	4	3	2
3 or more others	10	1	9	1	4	4	1	

TABLE **173.**—WOMEN LIVING AT HOME AND EMPLOYED IN CERTAIN IMPORTANT OCCUPATIONS, CLASSIFIED BY MARITAL CONDITION, ACCORDING TO NUMBER OF OTHER EMPLOYED MEMBERS IN THE FAMILY, AND WHETHER THERE ARE BOARDERS OR LODGERS, FOR 11 SELECTED CITIES: 1920—Continued

OCCUPATION, MARITAL CONDITION, AND NUMBER OF OTHER GAINFULLY EMPLOYED MEMBERS OF FAMILY	GAINFULLY EMPLOYED WOMEN 16 YEARS OF AGE AND OVER LIVING AT HOME							
				Living in family having—				
	Total number	Boarders or lodgers	No boarders or lodgers	Unemployed members				
				None	1	2	3	4 or more
CINCINNATI, OHIO—Continued								
TAILORESSES								
All classes	1,213	59	1,154	388	380	201	125	119
In family having—								
No other employed member	247	16	231	136	72	20	11	8
1 other	452	28	424	178	142	58	39	35
2 others	265	13	252	52	87	61	26	39
3 or more others	249	2	247	22	79	62	49	37
Single (including unknown)	816	31	785	200	291	148	89	88
In family having—								
No other employed member	139	10	129	85	41	9	3	1
1 other	239	7	232	65	97	35	19	23
2 others	214	12	202	35	76	49	22	32
3 or more others	224	2	222	15	77	55	45	32
Married	206	19	187	101	42	26	23	14
In family having—								
No other employed member	22	1	21	8	8	3	3	
1 other	146	17	129	84	26	14	13	9
2 others	27	1	26	7	6	8	4	2
3 or more others	11		11	2	2	1	3	3
Widowed or divorced	191	9	182	87	47	27	13	17
In family having—								
No other employed member	86	5	81	43	23	8	5	7
1 other	67	4	63	29	19	9	7	3
2 others	24		24	10	5	4		5
3 or more others	14		14	5		6	1	2
TEACHERS (SCHOOL)								
All classes	1,299	106	1,193	259	597	262	123	58
In family having—								
No other employed member	306	35	271	96	144	46	17	3
1 other	540	37	503	121	243	105	44	27
2 others	285	25	260	31	136	67	30	21
3 or more others	168	9	159	11	74	44	32	7
Single (including unknown)	1,128	89	1,039	196	544	233	105	50
In family having—								
No other employed member	273	31	242	86	129	40	15	3
1 other	435	27	408	76	210	92	35	22
2 others	266	24	242	26	133	64	25	18
3 or more others	154	7	147	8	72	37	30	7
Married	117	13	104	46	37	17	12	5
In family having—								
No other employed member	8	1	7	3	5			
1 other	87	10	77	36	29	10	8	4
2 others	13		13	4	2	3	3	1
3 or more others	9	2	7	3	1	4	1	
Widowed or divorced	54	4	50	17	16	12	6	3
In family having—								
No other employed member	25	3	22	7	10	6	2	
1 other	18		18	9	4	3	1	1
2 others	6	1	5	1	1		2	2
3 or more others	5		5		1	3	1	

TABLE **173.**—WOMEN LIVING AT HOME AND EMPLOYED IN CERTAIN IMPORTANT OCCUPATIONS, CLASSIFIED BY MARITAL CONDITION, ACCORDING TO NUMBER OF OTHER EMPLOYED MEMBERS IN THE FAMILY, AND WHETHER THERE ARE BOARDERS OR LODGERS, FOR 11 SELECTED CITIES: 1920—Continued

OCCUPATION, MARITAL CONDITION, AND NUMBER OF OTHER GAINFULLY EMPLOYED MEMBERS OF FAMILY	GAINFULLY EMPLOYED WOMEN 16 YEARS OF AGE AND OVER AT HOME							
	Total number	Boarders or lodgers	No boarders or lodgers	Living in family having—				
				Unemployed members				
				None	1	2	3	4 or more
CINCINNATI, OHIO—Continued								
TELEPHONE OPERATORS								
All classes	1,087	67	1,020	108	413	275	166	125
In family having—								
No other employed member	80	13	67	22	39	9	6	4
1 other	310	23	287	37	126	77	43	27
2 others	322	15	307	34	114	78	56	40
3 or more others	375	16	359	15	134	111	61	54
Single (including unknown)	995	61	934	79	391	257	150	118
In family having—								
No other employed member	56	9	47	11	32	7	2	4
1 other	276	23	253	25	120	68	39	24
2 others	304	14	290	29	111	75	52	37
3 or more others	359	15	344	14	128	107	57	53
Married	40	4	36	17	8	7	4	4
In family having—								
No other employed member	4	3	1	3	1			
1 other	20		20	10	3	4	2	1
2 others	11	1	10	4	2	2	1	2
3 or more others	5		5		2	1	1	1
Widowed or divorced	52	2	50	12	14	11	12	3
In family having—								
No other employed member	20	1	19	8	6	2	4	
1 other	14		14	2	3	5	2	2
2 others	7		7	1	1	1	3	1
3 or more others	11	1	10	1	4	3	3	
INDIANAPOLIS, IND.								
BOOKKEEPERS, CASHIERS, AND ACCOUNTANTS								
All classes	1,692	216	1,476	303	660	377	188	164
In family having—								
No other employed member	208	47	161	75	91	30	5	7
1 other	670	90	580	160	246	145	71	48
2 others	453	43	410	53	166	116	66	52
3 or more others	361	36	325	15	157	86	46	57
Single (including unknown)	1,284	157	1,127	147	547	302	152	136
In family having—								
No other employed member	143	30	113	49	72	15	3	4
1 other	462	60	402	49	202	115	56	40
2 others	365	33	332	35	135	96	56	43
3 or more others	314	34	280	14	138	76	37	49
Married	268	35	233	119	77	34	25	13
In family having—								
No other employed member	13	3	10	3	4	4	1	1
1 other	162	23	139	101	35	13	11	2
2 others	59	8	51	14	24	11	6	4
3 or more others	34	1	33	1	14	6	7	6
Widowed or divorced	140	24	116	37	36	41	11	15
In family having—								
No other employed member	52	14	38	23	15	11	1	2
1 other	46	7	39	10	9	17	4	6
2 others	29	2	27	4	7	9	4	5
3 or more others	13	1	12		5	4	2	2

TABLE **173.**—WOMEN LIVING AT HOME AND EMPLOYED IN CERTAIN IMPORTANT OCCUPATIONS, CLASSIFIED BY MARITAL CONDITION, ACCORDING TO NUMBER OF OTHER EMPLOYED MEMBERS IN THE FAMILY, AND WHETHER THERE ARE BOARDERS OR LODGERS, FOR 11 SELECTED CITIES: 1920—Continued

OCCUPATION, MARITAL CONDITION, AND NUMBER OF OTHER GAINFULLY EMPLOYED MEMBERS OF FAMILY	GAINFULLY EMPLOYED WOMEN 16 YEARS OF AGE AND OVER AT HOME							
	Total number	Living in family having—		Unemployed members				
		Boarders or lodgers	No boarders or lodgers	None	1	2	3	4 or more
INDIANAPOLIS, IND.—Continued								
CLERKS (EXCEPT CLERKS IN STORES)								
All classes	2,149	240	1,909	317	777	540	269	246
In family having—								
No other employed member	214	38	176	62	94	38	13	7
1 other	836	97	739	176	312	200	82	66
2 others	616	67	549	57	220	169	90	80
3 or more others	483	38	445	22	151	133	84	93
Single (including unknown)	1,625	165	1,460	142	631	425	215	212
In family having—								
No other employed member	136	24	112	40	69	21	3	3
1 other	560	58	502	45	251	150	61	53
2 others	517	56	461	42	180	142	81	72
3 or more others	412	27	385	15	131	112	70	84
Married	351	48	303	145	82	68	34	22
In family having—								
No other employed member	26	3	23	9	8	4	3	2
1 other	209	30	179	117	38	32	13	9
2 others	68	7	61	12	25	18	7	6
3 or more others	48	8	40	7	11	14	11	5
Widowed or divorced	173	27	146	30	64	47	20	12
In family having—								
No other employed member	52	11	41	13	17	13	7	2
1 other	67	9	58	14	23	18	8	4
2 others	31	4	27	3	15	9	2	2
3 or more others	23	3	20	------	9	7	3	4
CLERKS IN STORES								
All classes	867	108	759	175	284	190	116	102
In family having—								
No other employed member	79	15	64	21	31	18	4	5
1 other	369	44	325	103	117	63	30	36
2 others	252	30	222	33	93	64	33	29
3 or more others	167	19	148	18	43	45	29	32
Single (including unknown)	511	57	454	44	179	127	79	82
In family having—								
No other employed member	45	7	38	10	20	11	2	2
1 other	178	15	163	16	72	35	29	26
2 others	174	21	153	11	59	52	27	25
3 or more others	114	14	100	7	28	29	21	29
Married	255	36	219	101	81	40	20	13
In family having—								
No other employed member	8	4	4	3	4	1	------	------
1 other	148	21	127	76	36	17	13	6
2 others	57	6	51	13	29	8	3	4
3 or more others	42	5	37	9	12	14	4	3
Widowed or divorced	101	15	86	30	24	23	17	7
In family having—								
No other employed member	26	4	22	8	7	6	2	3
1 other	43	8	35	11	9	11	8	4
2 others	21	3	18	9	5	4	3	------
3 or more others	11	------	11	2	3	2	4	------

TABLE **173.**—WOMEN LIVING AT HOME AND EMPLOYED IN CERTAIN IMPORTANT OCCUPATIONS, CLASSIFIED BY MARITAL CONDITION, ACCORDING TO NUMBER OF OTHER EMPLOYED MEMBERS IN THE FAMILY, AND WHETHER THERE ARE BOARDERS OR LODGERS, FOR 11 SELECTED CITIES: 1920—Continued

OCCUPATION, MARITAL CONDITION, AND NUMBER OF OTHER GAINFULLY EMPLOYED MEMBERS OF FAMILY	GAINFULLY EMPLOYED WOMEN 16 YEARS OF AGE AND OVER AT HOME							
	Total number			Living in family having—				
		Boarders or lodgers	No boarders or lodgers	None	Unemployed members			
					1	2	3	4 or more
INDIANAPOLIS, IND.—Continued								
DRESSMAKERS AND SEAMSTRESSES (NOT IN FACTORY)								
All classes	915	171	744	440	257	116	51	51
In family having—								
No other employed member	245	58	187	165	54	22	3	1
1 other	387	70	317	187	104	49	28	19
2 others	175	29	146	66	61	24	13	11
3 or more others	108	14	94	22	38	21	7	20
Single (including unknown)	278	46	232	98	107	39	13	21
In family having—								
No other employed member	72	17	55	44	21	6	1	-----
1 other	97	18	79	36	34	13	6	8
2 others	59	10	49	11	30	9	4	5
3 or more others	50	1	49	7	22	11	2	8
Married	297	47	250	153	77	37	16	14
In family having—								
No other employed member	21	5	16	12	5	4	-----	-----
1 other	175	25	150	94	42	21	12	6
2 others	66	8	58	36	20	6	2	2
3 or more others	35	9	26	11	10	6	2	6
Widowed or divorced	340	78	262	189	73	40	22	16
In family having—								
No other employed member	152	36	116	109	28	12	2	1
1 other	115	27	88	57	28	15	10	5
2 others	50	11	39	19	11	9	7	4
3 or more others	23	4	19	4	6	4	3	6
LAUNDRESSES (NOT IN LAUNDRY)								
All classes	1,571	380	1,191	807	372	189	103	100
In family having—								
No other employed member	383	156	227	258	81	24	12	8
1 other	766	147	619	402	183	90	50	41
2 others	273	49	224	104	72	45	22	30
3 or more others	149	28	121	43	36	30	19	21
Single (including unknown)	127	38	89	62	36	14	6	9
In family having—								
No other employed member	46	21	25	37	7	2	-----	-----
1 other	35	8	27	15	13	3	2	2
2 others	27	3	24	6	9	7	2	3
3 or more others	19	6	13	4	7	2	2	4
Married	806	136	670	397	203	97	49	60
In family having—								
No other employed member	66	25	41	31	23	4	5	3
1 other	506	70	436	281	116	52	28	29
2 others	149	28	121	59	43	25	7	15
3 or more others	85	13	72	26	21	16	9	13
Widowed or divorced	638	206	432	348	133	78	48	31
In family having—								
No other employed member	271	110	161	190	51	18	7	5
1 other	225	69	156	106	54	35	20	10
2 others	97	18	79	39	20	13	13	12
3 or more others	45	9	36	13	8	12	8	4

TABLE **173.**—WOMEN LIVING AT HOME AND EMPLOYED IN CERTAIN IMPORTANT OCCUPATIONS, CLASSIFIED BY MARITAL CONDITION, ACCORDING TO NUMBER OF OTHER EMPLOYED MEMBERS IN THE FAMILY, AND WHETHER THERE ARE BOARDERS OR LODGERS, FOR 11 SELECTED CITIES: 1920—Continued

OCCUPATION, MARITAL CONDITION, AND NUMBER OF OTHER GAINFULLY EMPLOYED MEMBERS OF FAMILY	GAINFULLY EMPLOYED WOMEN 16 YEARS OF AGE AND OVER AT HOME							
	Total number	Living in family having—						
		Boarders or lodgers	No boarders or lodgers	Unemployed members				
				None	1	2	3	4 or more
INDIANAPOLIS, IND.—Continued								
SALESWOMEN (STORES)								
All classes	1,507	226	1,281	426	528	285	151	117
In family having—								
No other employed member	217	50	167	104	70	30	11	2
1 other	667	97	570	231	208	125	58	45
2 others	374	53	321	66	167	72	40	29
3 or more others	249	26	223	25	83	58	42	41
Single (including unknown)	803	101	702	109	330	192	97	75
In family having—								
No other employed member	93	21	72	39	37	14	3	-----
1 other	276	31	245	29	113	75	35	24
2 others	249	30	219	29	116	56	30	18
3 or more others	185	19	166	12	64	47	29	33
Married	473	66	407	226	132	59	29	27
In family having—								
No other employed member	30	2	28	15	9	4	1	1
1 other	310	43	267	170	73	34	16	17
2 others	86	17	69	28	39	12	3	4
3 or more others	47	4	43	13	11	9	9	5
Widowed or divorced	231	59	172	91	66	34	25	15
In family having—								
No other employed member	94	27	67	50	24	12	7	1
1 other	81	23	58	32	22	16	7	4
2 others	39	6	33	9	12	4	7	7
3 or more others	17	3	14	-----	8	2	4	3
SEMISKILLED—CLOTHING INDUSTRIES								
All classes	1,237	153	1,084	384	389	225	121	118
In family having—								
No other employed member	170	25	145	77	64	23	5	1
1 other	533	76	457	205	168	91	35	34
2 others	306	31	275	66	101	61	43	35
3 or more others	228	21	207	36	56	50	38	48
Single (including unknown)	583	71	512	97	214	122	71	79
In family having—								
No other employed member	61	8	53	23	26	8	4	-----
1 other	194	27	167	34	80	45	14	21
2 others	163	18	145	22	62	37	20	22
3 or more others	165	18	147	18	46	32	33	36
Married	363	45	318	174	86	53	30	20
In family having—								
No other employed member	13	2	11	4	7	2	-----	-----
1 other	223	33	190	130	49	23	15	6
2 others	89	9	80	27	25	17	13	7
3 or more others	38	1	37	13	5	11	2	7
Widowed or divorced	291	37	254	113	89	50	20	19
In family having—								
No other employed member	96	15	81	50	31	13	1	1
1 other	116	16	100	17	39	23	6	7
2 others	54	4	50	17	14	7	10	6
3 or more others	25	2	23	5	5	7	3	5

TABLE **173.**—WOMEN LIVING AT HOME AND EMPLOYED IN CERTAIN IMPORTANT OCCUPATIONS, CLASSIFIED BY MARITAL CONDITION, ACCORDING TO NUMBER OF OTHER EMPLOYED MEMBERS IN THE FAMILY, AND WHETHER THERE ARE BOARDERS OR LODGERS, FOR 11 SELECTED CITIES: 1920—Continued

OCCUPATION, MARITAL CONDITION, AND NUMBER OF OTHER GAINFULLY EMPLOYED MEMBERS OF FAMILY	GAINFULLY EMPLOYED WOMEN 16 YEARS OF AGE AND OVER AT HOME								
	Total number			Living in family having—					
		Boarders or lodgers	No boarders or lodgers	Unemployed members					
				None	1	2	3	4 or more	

INDIANAPOLIS, IND.—Continued

	Total number	Boarders or lodgers	No boarders or lodgers	None	1	2	3	4 or more
SERVANTS								
All classes	2,141	462	1,679	1,012	479	308	144	198
In family having—								
No other employed member	458	156	302	303	90	46	11	8
1 other	975	189	786	511	213	128	64	59
2 others	430	72	358	137	105	89	37	62
3 or more others	278	45	233	61	71	45	32	69
Single (including unknown)	539	104	435	167	137	103	46	86
In family having—								
No other employed member	94	30	64	71	14	7	2	
1 other	187	40	147	48	65	35	19	20
2 others	133	18	115	29	23	41	14	26
3 or more others	125	16	109	19	35	20	11	40
Married	902	160	742	509	188	100	44	61
In family having—								
No other employed member	84	27	57	47	23	8	3	3
1 other	553	92	461	370	95	50	19	19
2 others	174	25	149	68	48	27	11	20
3 or more others	91	16	75	24	22	15	11	19
Widowed or divorced	700	198	502	336	154	105	54	51
In family having—								
No other employed member	280	99	181	185	53	31	6	5
1 other	235	57	178	93	53	43	26	20
2 others	123	29	94	40	34	21	12	16
3 or more others	62	13	49	18	14	10	10	10
STENOGRAPHERS AND TYPISTS								
All classes	3,304	338	2,966	416	1,299	807	418	364
In family having—								
No other employed member	325	61	264	76	163	65	13	8
1 other	1,251	139	1,112	231	499	272	155	94
2 others	971	79	892	77	394	248	142	110
3 or more others	757	59	698	32	243	222	108	152
Single (including unknown)	2,801	266	2,535	221	1,166	703	377	334
In family having—								
No other employed member	253	48	205	59	134	46	10	4
1 other	993	109	884	85	450	233	136	89
2 others	852	56	796	51	354	217	130	100
3 or more others	703	53	650	26	228	207	101	141
Married	366	50	316	164	88	64	27	23
In family having—								
No other employed member	17	2	15	1	7	6		3
1 other	210	25	185	136	33	24	12	5
2 others	93	18	75	21	34	22	10	6
3 or more others	46	5	41	6	14	12	5	9
Widowed or divorced	137	22	115	31	45	40	14	7
In family having—								
No other employed member	55	11	44	16	22	13	3	1
1 other	48	5	43	10	16	15	7	
2 others	26	5	21	5	6	9	2	4
3 or more others	8	1	7		1	3	2	2

TABLE **173.**—WOMEN LIVING AT HOME AND EMPLOYED IN CERTAIN IMPORTANT OCCUPATIONS, CLASSIFIED BY MARITAL CONDITION, ACCORDING TO NUMBER OF OTHER EMPLOYED MEMBERS IN THE FAMILY, AND WHETHER THERE ARE BOARDERS OR LODGERS, FOR 11 SELECTED CITIES: 1920—Continued

OCCUPATION, MARITAL CONDITION, AND NUMBER OF OTHER GAINFULLY EMPLOYED MEMBERS OF FAMILY	Total number	GAINFULLY EMPLOYED WOMEN 16 YEARS OF AGE AND OVER LIVING AT HOME						
				Living in family having—				
		Boarders or lodgers	No boarders or lodgers	Unemployed members				
				None	1	2	3	4 or more
INDIANAPOLIS, IND.—Continued								
TEACHERS (SCHOOL)								
All classes	1,218	153	1,065	314	481	245	101	77
In family having—								
No other employed member	283	50	183	97	85	35	9	7
1 other	572	68	504	164	230	106	37	35
2 others	258	19	239	34	115	61	33	15
3 or more others	155	16	139	19	51	43	22	20
Single (including unknown)	959	114	845	188	406	208	90	67
In family having—								
No other employed member	201	44	157	82	74	32	7	6
1 other	394	41	353	66	185	83	32	28
2 others	228	16	212	26	101	54	32	15
3 or more others	136	13	123	14	46	39	19	18
Married	201	27	174	105	56	27	6	7
In family having—								
No other employed member	7	------	7	4	2	1	------	------
1 other	154	22	132	90	39	16	4	5
2 others	24	3	21	6	11	6	1	------
3 or more others	16	2	14	5	4	4	1	2
Widowed or divorced	58	12	46	21	19	10	5	3
In family having—								
No other employed member	25	6	19	11	9	2	2	1
1 other	24	5	19	8	6	7	1	2
2 others	6	------	6	2	3	1	------	------
3 or more others	3	1	2	------	1	------	2	------
TELEPHONE OPERATORS								
All classes	1,023	130	893	142	356	218	153	154
In family having—								
No other employed member	68	16	52	23	26	13	2	4
1 other	357	59	298	72	126	79	35	45
2 others	320	31	289	34	122	57	56	51
3 or more others	278	24	254	13	82	69	60	54
Single (including unknown)	846	98	748	89	299	185	130	143
In family having—								
No other employed member	43	8	35	13	18	10	1	1
1 other	278	44	234	36	103	66	30	43
2 others	284	27	257	28	108	50	50	48
3 or more others	241	19	222	12	70	59	49	51
Married	125	19	106	42	41	20	16	6
In family having—								
No other employed member	7	2	5	3	2	1	------	1
1 other	61	10	51	33	17	7	3	1
2 others	27	4	23	5	11	4	6	1
3 or more others	30	3	27	1	11	8	7	3
Widowed or divorced	52	13	39	11	16	13	7	5
In family having—								
No other employed member	18	6	12	7	6	2	1	2
1 other	18	5	13	3	6	6	2	1
2 others	9	------	9	1	3	3	------	2
3 or more others	7	2	5	------	1	2	4	------

TABLE **173.**—WOMEN LIVING AT HOME AND EMPLOYED IN CERTAIN IMPORTANT OCCUPATIONS, CLASSIFIED BY MARITAL CONDITION, ACCORDING TO NUMBER OF OTHER EMPLOYED MEMBERS IN THE FAMILY, AND WHETHER THERE ARE BOARDERS OR LODGERS, FOR 11 SELECTED CITIES: 1920—Continued

OCCUPATION, MARITAL CONDITION, AND NUMBER OF OTHER GAINFULLY EMPLOYED MEMBERS OF FAMILY	GAINFULLY EMPLOYED WOMEN 16 YEARS OF AGE AND OVER LIVING AT HOME							
	Total number	Living in family having—						
		Boarders or lodgers	No boarders or lodgers	Unemployed members				
				None	1	2	3	4 or more
ST. PAUL, MINN.								
BOOKKEEPERS, CASHIERS, AND ACCOUNTANTS								
All classes	1,450	168	1,282	176	557	352	186	179
In family having—								
No other employed member	133	32	101	32	51	33	12	5
1 other	463	66	397	90	178	99	51	45
2 others	399	38	361	37	161	94	51	56
3 or more others	455	32	423	17	167	126	72	73
Single (including unknown)	1,266	137	1,129	102	521	311	166	166
In family having—								
No other employed member	104	24	80	26	43	23	9	3
1 other	362	48	314	30	163	82	45	42
2 others	367	34	333	32	151	85	48	51
3 or more others	433	31	402	14	164	121	64	70
Married	130	22	108	65	25	24	9	7
In family having—								
No other employed member	9	3	6	3	3	3	------	------
1 other	86	15	71	56	13	12	4	1
2 others	23	4	19	4	7	6	2	4
3 or more others	12	------	12	2	2	3	3	2
Widowed or divorced	54	9	45	9	11	17	11	6
In family having—								
No other employed member	20	5	15	3	5	7	3	2
1 other	15	3	12	4	2	5	2	2
2 others	9	------	9	1	3	3	1	1
3 or more others	10	1	9	1	1	2	5	1
CLERKS (EXCEPT CLERKS IN STORES)								
All classes	2,623	296	2,327	242	957	650	377	397
In family having—								
No other employed member	202	37	165	57	83	43	12	7
1 other	804	103	701	99	306	192	105	102
2 others	738	94	644	51	274	193	95	125
3 or more others	879	62	817	35	294	222	165	163
Single (including unknown)	2,358	257	2,101	161	876	600	347	374
In family having—								
No other employed member	159	27	132	41	70	37	7	4
1 other	667	85	582	46	264	172	93	92
2 others	691	84	607	41	257	183	89	121
3 or more others	841	61	780	33	285	208	158	157
Married	158	19	139	55	47	31	11	14
In family having—								
No other employed member	9	4	5	2	4	1	1	1
1 other	94	8	86	46	23	16	5	4
2 others	29	6	23	5	14	6	1	3
3 or more others	26	1	25	2	6	8	4	6
Widowed or divorced	107	20	87	26	34	19	19	9
In family having—								
No other employed member	34	6	28	14	9	5	4	2
1 other	43	10	33	7	19	4	7	6
2 others	18	4	14	5	3	4	5	1
3 or more others	12	------	12	------	3	6	3	------

TABLE 173.—WOMEN LIVING AT HOME AND EMPLOYED IN CERTAIN IMPORTANT OCCUPATIONS, CLASSIFIED BY MARITAL CONDITION, ACCORDING TO NUMBER OF OTHER EMPLOYED MEMBERS IN THE FAMILY, AND WHETHER THERE ARE BOARDERS OR LODGERS, FOR 11 SELECTED CITIES: 1920—Continued

OCCUPATION, MARITAL CONDITION, AND NUMBER OF OTHER GAINFULLY EMPLOYED MEMBERS OF FAMILY	GAINFULLY EMPLOYED WOMEN 16 YEARS OF AGE AND OVER LIVING AT HOME							
	Total number	Boarders or lodgers	No boarders or lodgers	Living in family having—				
				Unemployed members				
				None	1	2	3	4 or more
ST. PAUL, MINN.—Continued								
CLERKS IN STORES								
All classes	934	93	841	92	283	250	145	164
In family having—								
No other employed member	51	3	48	10	21	13	5	2
1 other	302	35	267	47	89	83	44	39
2 others	258	28	230	19	79	71	36	53
3 or more others	323	27	296	16	94	83	60	70
Single (including unknown)	774	76	698	44	243	211	127	149
In family having—								
No other employed member	35	3	32	6	15	9	4	1
1 other	219	27	192	13	72	66	35	33
2 others	224	20	204	14	67	61	32	50
3 or more others	296	26	270	11	89	75	56	65
Married	110	13	97	39	23	30	8	10
In family having—								
No other employed member	2	------	2			1	------	1
1 other	65	6	59	33	11	14	3	4
2 others	25	6	19	3	9	9	2	2
3 or more others	18	1	17	3	3	6	3	3
Widowed or divorced	50	4	46	9	17	9	10	5
In family having—								
No other employed member	14	------	14	4	6	3	1	------
1 other	18	2	16	1	6	3	6	2
2 others	9	2	7	2	3	1	2	1
3 or more others	9	------	9	2	2	2	1	2
SALESWOMEN (STORES)								
All classes	1,281	167	1,114	301	385	259	162	174
In family having—								
No other employed member	156	29	127	60	50	28	5	13
1 other	507	71	436	156	146	102	50	53
2 others	302	42	260	51	89	60	46	56
3 or more others	316	25	291	34	100	69	61	52
Single (including unknown)	821	105	716	105	273	182	123	138
In family having—								
No other employed member	69	12	57	27	23	13	2	4
1 other	253	39	214	32	85	58	35	43
2 others	222	29	193	23	72	50	33	44
3 or more others	277	25	252	23	93	61	53	47
Married	286	34	252	140	64	40	22	20
In family having—								
No other employed member	22	3	19	7	8	2	------	5
1 other	190	22	168	111	37	26	10	6
2 others	57	9	48	18	13	9	8	9
3 or more others	17	------	17	4	6	3	4	------
Widowed or divorced	174	28	146	56	48	37	17	16
In family having—								
No other employed member	65	14	51	26	19	13	3	4
1 other	64	10	54	13	24	18	5	4
2 others	23	4	19	10	4	1	5	3
3 or more others	22	------	22	7	1	5	4	5

TABLE **173.**—WOMEN LIVING AT HOME AND EMPLOYED IN CERTAIN IMPORTANT OCCUPATIONS, CLASSIFIED BY MARITAL CONDITION, ACCORDING TO NUMBER OF OTHER EMPLOYED MEMBERS IN THE FAMILY, AND WHETHER THERE ARE BOARDERS OR LODGERS, FOR 11 SELECTED CITIES: 1920—Continued

OCCUPATION, MARITAL CONDITION, AND NUMBER OF OTHER GAINFULLY EMPLOYED MEMBERS OF FAMILY	GAINFULLY EMPLOYED WOMEN 16 YEARS OF AGE AND OVER LIVING AT HOME							
	Total number	Living in family having—						
		Boarders or lodgers	No boarders or lodgers	Unemployed members				
				None	1	2	3	4 or more
ST. PAUL, MINN.—Continued								
SERVANTS								
All classes	624	115	509	265	141	90	57	71
In family having—								
No other employed member	134	32	102	72	32	16	7	7
1 other	302	63	239	140	62	45	25	30
2 others	107	14	93	34	27	15	12	19
3 or more others	81	6	75	19	20	14	13	15
Single (including unknown)	167	26	141	40	39	32	23	33
In family having—								
No other employed member	28	6	22	17	8	3		
1 other	59	12	47	14	11	13	10	11
2 others	38	6	32	5	10	7	5	11
3 or more others	42	2	40	4	10	9	8	11
Married	267	45	222	132	64	33	19	19
In family having—								
No other employed member	30	5	25	8	11	6	2	3
1 other	165	33	132	95	33	18	8	11
2 others	46	6	40	17	13	5	6	5
3 or more others	26	1	25	12	7	4	3	
Widowed or divorced	190	44	146	93	38	25	15	19
In family having—								
No other employed member	76	21	55	47	13	7	5	4
1 other	78	18	60	31	18	14	7	8
2 others	23	2	21	12	4	3	1	3
3 or more others	13	3	10	3	3	1	2	4
STENOGRAPHERS AND TYPISTS								
All classes	2,988	369	2,619	282	1,113	766	458	369
In family having—								
No other employed member	210	62	148	41	98	44	18	9
1 other	959	140	819	154	367	212	124	102
2 others	885	82	803	48	307	275	141	114
3 or more others	934	85	849	39	341	235	175	144
Single (including unknown)	2,797	344	2,453	207	1,062	737	437	354
In family having—								
No other employed member	180	54	126	33	85	39	15	8
1 other	860	128	732	92	352	205	113	98
2 others	853	79	774	44	293	270	136	110
3 or more others	904	83	821	38	332	223	173	138
Married	138	16	122	68	32	17	12	9
In family having—								
No other employed member	11	3	8	4	2	2	2	1
1 other	82	8	74	61	12	3	4	2
2 others	21	3	18	2	10	3	4	2
3 or more others	24	2	22	1	8	9	2	4
Widowed or divorced	53	9	44	7	19	12	9	6
In family having—								
No other employed member	19	5	14	4	11	3	1	
1 other	17	4	13	1	3	4	7	2
2 others	11		11	2	4	2	1	2
3 or more others	6		6		1	3		2

TABLE 173.—WOMEN LIVING AT HOME AND EMPLOYED IN CERTAIN IMPORTANT OCCUPATIONS, CLASSIFIED BY MARITAL CONDITION, ACCORDING TO NUMBER OF OTHER EMPLOYED MEMBERS IN THE FAMILY, AND WHETHER THERE ARE BOARDERS OR LODGERS, FOR 11 SELECTED CITIES: 1920—Continued

OCCUPATION, MARITAL CONDITION, AND NUMBER OF OTHER GAINFULLY EMPLOYED MEMBERS OF FAMILY	GAINFULLY EMPLOYED WOMEN 16 YEARS OF AGE AND OVER LIVING AT HOME							
	Total number	Living in family having—						
		Boarders or lodgers	No boarders or lodgers	Unemployed members				
				None	1	2	3	4 or more
ST. PAUL, MINN.—Continued								
TEACHERS (SCHOOL)								
All classes	1,014	112	902	177	436	208	111	82
In family having—								
No other employed member	159	24	135	61	66	20	9	3
1 other	341	42	299	73	129	74	37	28
2 others	253	29	224	26	104	70	29	24
3 or more others	261	17	244	17	137	44	36	27
Single (including unknown)	925	101	824	146	413	189	103	74
In family having—								
No other employed member	147	21	126	56	63	17	9	2
1 other	279	35	244	51	112	62	32	22
2 others	244	28	216	23	102	67	28	24
3 or more others	255	17	238	16	136	43	34	26
Married	57	5	52	23	14	11	4	5
In family having—								
No other employed members	4	1	3	2	------	1	------	1
1 other	46	3	43	20	13	7	2	4
2 others	4	1	3	1	1	2	------	------
3 or more others	3	------	3	------	------	1	2	------
Widowed or divorced	32	6	26	8	9	8	4	3
In family having—								
No other employed member	8	2	6	3	3	2	------	------
1 other	16	4	12	2	4	5	3	2
2 others	5	------	5	2	1	1	1	------
3 or more others	3	------	3	1	1	------	------	1
KANSAS CITY, MO.								
BOARDING AND LODGING HOUSE KEEPERS								
All classes	1,140	851	289	749	220	100	46	25
In family having—								
No other employed member	586	471	115	435	91	38	14	8
1 other	398	274	124	242	88	42	15	11
2 others	97	64	33	52	25	8	9	3
3 or more others	59	42	17	20	16	12	8	3
Single (including unknown)	113	88	25	94	10	6	2	1
In family having—								
No other employed member	92	73	19	80	6	4	2	------
1 other	16	12	4	11	3	2	------	------
2 others	2	2	------	1	1	------	------	------
3 or more others	3	1	2	2	------	------	------	1
Married	389	268	121	225	87	40	25	12
In family having—								
No other employed member	77	62	15	46	16	10	3	2
1 other	241	162	79	154	51	18	9	9
2 others	46	25	21	18	13	7	7	1
3 or more others	25	19	6	7	7	5	6	------
Widowed or divorced	638	495	143	430	123	54	19	12
In family having—								
No other employed member	417	336	81	309	69	24	9	6
1 other	141	100	41	77	34	22	6	2
2 others	49	37	12	33	11	1	2	2
3 or more others	31	22	9	11	9	7	2	2

TABLE **173.**—WOMEN LIVING AT HOME AND EMPLOYED IN CERTAIN IMPORTANT OCCUPATIONS, CLASSIFIED BY MARITAL CONDITION, ACCORDING TO NUMBER OF OTHER EMPLOYED MEMBERS IN THE FAMILY, AND WHETHER THERE ARE BOARDERS OR LODGERS, FOR 11 SELECTED CITIES: 1920—Continued

OCCUPATION, MARITAL CONDITION, AND NUMBER OF OTHER GAINFULLY EMPLOYED MEMBERS OF FAMILY	GAINFULLY EMPLOYED WOMEN 16 YEARS OF AGE AND OVER LIVING AT HOME							
	Total number			Living in family having—				
		Boarders or lodgers	No boarders or lodgers	Unemployed members				
				None	1 •	2	3	4 or more
KANSAS CITY, MO.—Continued								
BOOKKEEPERS, CASHIERS, AND ACCOUNTANTS								
All classes	2,062	327	1,735	392	784	425	243	218
In family having—								
No other employed member	270	80	190	73	127	42	16	12
1 other	857	132	725	232	296	161	108	60
2 others	532	71	461	68	213	131	53	67
3 or more others	403	44	359	19	148	91	66	79
Single (including unknown)	1,488	233	1,255	142	628	343	197	178
In family having—								
No other employed member	173	50	123	38	100	19	10	6
1 other	538	90	448	52	224	128	86	48
2 others	432	59	373	42	178	114	44	54
3 or more others	345	34	311	10	126	82	57	70
Married	379	52	327	190	103	44	27	15
In family having—								
No other employed member	19	8	11	4	7	4	3	1
1 other	250	30	220	162	50	21	13	4
2 others	71	10	61	19	29	12	5	6
3 or more others	39	4	35	5	17	7	6	4
Widowed or divorced	195	42	153	60	53	38	19	25
In family having—								
No other employed member	78	22	56	31	20	19	3	5
1 other	69	12	57	18	22	12	9	8
2 others	29	2	27	7	6	5	4	7
3 or more others	19	6	13	4	5	2	3	5
CLERKS (EXCEPT CLERKS IN STORES)								
All classes	2,671	401	2,270	507	873	597	360	334
In family having—								
No other employed member	260	62	198	57	118	60	16	9
1 other	1,107	172	935	311	336	216	138	106
2 others	700	104	596	81	247	168	100	104
3 or more others	604	63	541	58	172	153	106	115
Single (including unknown)	1,914	284	1,630	202	690	456	297	269
In family having—								
No other employed member	167	37	130	31	81	41	10	4
1 other	679	115	564	81	249	162	102	85
2 others	553	83	470	50	209	130	85	79
3 or more others	515	49	466	40	151	123	100	101
Married	514	69	445	246	118	79	36	35
In family having—								
No other employed member	27	9	18	6	13	5	1	2
1 other	335	37	298	206	62	31	22	14
2 others	89	14	75	21	25	24	7	12
3 or more others	63	9	54	13	18	19	6	7
Widowed or divorced	243	48	195	59	65	62	27	30
In family having—								
No other employed member	66	16	50	20	24	14	5	3
1 other	93	20	73	24	25	23	14	7
2 others	58	7	51	10	13	14	8	13
3 or more others	26	5	21	5	3	11	-------	7

TABLE 173.—WOMEN LIVING AT HOME AND EMPLOYED IN CERTAIN IMPORTANT OCCUPATIONS, CLASSIFIED BY MARITAL CONDITION, ACCORDING TO NUMBER OF OTHER EMPLOYED MEMBERS IN THE FAMILY, AND WHETHER THERE ARE BOARDERS OR LODGERS, FOR 11 SELECTED CITIES: 1920—Continued

OCCUPATION, MARITAL CONDITION, AND NUMBER OF OTHER GAINFULLY EMPLOYED MEMBERS OF FAMILY	GAINFULLY EMPLOYED WOMEN 16 YEARS OF AGE AND OVER LIVING AT HOME							
	Total number	Living in family having—						
		Boarders or lodgers	No boarders or lodgers	Unemployed members				
				None	1	2	3	4 or more
KANSAS CITY, MO.—Continued								
CLERKS IN STORES								
All classes	1,077	153	924	243	318	243	126	147
In family having—								
No other employed member	68	15	53	14	26	17	7	4
1 other	494	70	424	167	140	81	57	49
2 others	272	37	235	40	79	70	33	50
3 or more others	243	31	212	22	73	75	29	44
Single (including unknown)	671	91	580	81	215	168	87	120
In family having—								
No other employed member	31	11	20	8	13	5	3	2
1 other	228	28	200	32	77	51	32	36
2 others	210	30	180	25	63	53	27	42
3 or more others	202	22	180	16	62	59	25	40
Married	316	50	266	141	71	61	26	17
In family having—								
No other employed member	8	1	7	2	2	3	1	
1 other	227	35	192	124	46	28	19	10
2 others	47	5	42	11	13	17	3	3
3 or more others	34	9	25	4	10	13	3	4
Widowed or divorced	90	12	78	21	32	14	13	10
In family having—								
No other employed member	29	3	26	4	11	9	3	2
1 other	39	7	32	11	17	2	6	3
2 others	15	2	13	4	3		3	5
3 or more others	7		7	2	1	3	1	
DRESSMAKERS AND SEAMSTRESSES (NOT IN FACTORY)								
All classes	844	178	666	411	253	98	50	32
In family having—								
No other employed member	228	71	157	137	61	20	8	2
1 other	381	69	312	195	103	42	24	17
2 others	152	23	129	63	50	21	11	7
3 or more others	83	15	68	16	39	15	7	6
Single (including unknown)	211	38	173	75	87	22	18	9
In family having—								
No other employed member	51	14	37	27	17	5	1	1
1 other	79	13	66	31	33	6	6	3
2 others	46	6	40	10	18	7	8	3
3 or more others	35	5	30	7	19	4	3	2
Married	300	56	244	154	84	39	10	13
In family having—								
No other employed member	28	9	19	12	12	4		
1 other	186	29	157	110	41	22	6	7
2 others	52	10	42	26	17	5	1	3
3 or more others	34	8	26	6	14	8	3	3
Widowed or divorced	333	84	249	182	82	37	22	10
In family having—								
No other employed member	149	48	101	98	32	11	7	1
1 other	116	27	89	54	29	14	12	7
2 others	54	7	47	27	15	9	2	1
3 or more others	14	2	12	3	6	3	1	1

TABLE **173.**—WOMEN LIVING AT HOME AND EMPLOYED IN CERTAIN IMPORTANT OCCUPATIONS, CLASSIFIED BY MARITAL CONDITION, ACCORDING TO NUMBER OF OTHER EMPLOYED MEMBERS IN THE FAMILY, AND WHETHER THERE ARE BOARDERS OR LODGERS, FOR 11 SELECTED CITIES: 1920—Continued

OCCUPATION, MARITAL CONDITION, AND NUMBER OF OTHER GAINFULLY EMPLOYED MEMBERS OF FAMILY	GAINFULLY EMPLOYED WOMEN 16 YEARS OF AGE AND OVER LIVING AT HOME							
	Total number	Boarders or lodgers	No boarders or lodgers	Living in family having—				
				None	Unemployed members			
					1	2	3	4 or more

KANSAS CITY, MO.—Continued

LAUNDRESSES (NOT IN LAUNDRY)								
All classes	1,428	335	1,093	801	306	169	75	77
In family having—								
No other employed member	440	161	279	276	87	49	12	16
1 other	714	131	583	432	146	78	30	28
2 others	194	32	162	75	57	28	14	20
3 or more others	80	11	69	18	16	14	19	13
Single (including unknown)	126	26	100	68	28	14	8	8
In family having—								
No other employed member	52	18	34	40	9	2	1	
1 other	41	5	36	17	10	6	3	5
2 others	19	1	18	8	5	3	1	2
3 or more others	14	2	12	3	4	3	3	1
Married	735	142	593	424	155	83	40	33
In family having—								
No other employed member	83	37	46	38	22	14	6	3
1 other	503	82	421	329	96	46	18	14
2 others	111	19	92	47	32	15	9	8
3 or more others	38	4	34	10	5	8	7	8
Widowed or divorced	567	167	400	309	123	72	27	36
In family having—								
No other employed member	305	106	199	198	56	33	5	13
1 other	170	44	126	86	40	26	9	9
2 others	64	12	52	20	20	10	4	10
3 or more others	28	5	23	5	7	3	9	4
SALESWOMEN (STORES)								
All classes	1,555	255	1,300	465	491	312	162	125
In family having—								
No other employed member	198	50	148	74	78	28	14	4
1 other	759	131	628	299	207	148	65	40
2 others	368	50	318	64	131	96	38	39
3 or more others	230	24	206	28	75	40	45	42
Single (including unknown)	679	89	590	94	249	156	87	93
In family having—								
No other employed member	73	24	49	28	30	12	2	1
1 other	248	28	220	32	95	62	31	28
2 others	215	24	191	21	83	55	25	31
3 or more others	143	13	130	13	41	27	29	33
Married	583	97	486	278	136	100	48	21
In family having—								
No other employed member	28	2	26	6	9	11	2	
1 other	385	72	313	231	64	55	26	9
2 others	106	16	90	30	35	28	8	5
3 or more others	64	7	57	11	28	6	12	7
Widowed or divorced	293	69	224	93	106	56	27	11
In family having—								
No other employed member	97	24	73	40	39	5	10	3
1 other	126	31	95	36	48	31	8	3
2 others	47	10	37	13	13	13	5	3
3 or more others	23	4	19	4	6	7	4	2

TABLE **173.**—WOMEN LIVING AT HOME AND EMPLOYED IN CERTAIN IMPORTANT OCCUPATIONS, CLASSIFIED BY MARITAL CONDITION, ACCORDING TO NUMBER OF OTHER EMPLOYED MEMBERS IN THE FAMILY, AND WHETHER THERE ARE BOARDERS OR LODGERS, FOR 11 SELECTED CITIES: 1920—Continued

OCCUPATION, MARITAL CONDITION, AND NUMBER OF OTHER GAINFULLY EMPLOYED MEMBERS OF FAMILY	GAINFULLY EMPLOYED WOMEN 16 YEARS OF AGE AND OVER LIVING AT HOME							
	Total number	Living in family having—						
		Boarders or lodgers	No boarders or lodgers	Unemployed members				
				None	1	2	3	4 or more
KANSAS CITY, MO.—Continued								
SERVANTS								
All classes	1,870	523	1,347	1,032	417	226	100	95
In family having—								
No other employed member	419	186	233	273	100	29	10	7
1 other	947	224	723	566	200	107	43	31
2 others	311	64	247	143	70	48	26	24
3 or more others	193	49	144	50	47	42	21	33
Single (including unknown)	431	126	305	183	117	60	33	38
In family having—								
No other employed member	100	47	53	79	17	3	1	
1 other	147	37	110	46	48	29	12	12
2 others	91	21	70	37	26	14	10	4
3 or more others	93	21	72	21	26	14	10	22
Married	866	210	656	547	158	90	39	32
In family having—								
No other employed member	80	32	48	44	20	9	3	4
1 other	597	138	459	422	101	45	19	10
2 others	133	27	106	66	28	19	8	12
3 or more others	56	13	43	15	9	17	9	6
Widowed or divorced	573	187	386	302	142	76	28	25
In family having—								
No other employed member	239	107	132	150	63	17	6	3
1 other	203	49	154	98	51	33	12	9
2 others	87	16	71	40	16	15	8	8
3 or more others	44	15	29	14	12	11	2	5
STENOGRAPHERS AND TYPISTS								
All classes	3,639	581	3,058	611	1,345	852	460	371
In family having—								
No other employed member	392	113	279	109	163	83	28	9
1 other	1,426	241	1,185	349	516	281	164	116
2 others	991	144	847	101	372	268	122	128
3 or more others	830	83	747	52	294	220	146	118
Single (including unknown)	2,968	459	2,509	322	1,167	740	395	344
In family having—								
No other employed member	305	83	222	79	138	60	19	9
1 other	1,025	184	841	119	433	231	137	105
2 others	874	125	749	77	330	245	103	119
3 or more others	764	67	697	47	266	204	136	111
Married	462	74	388	252	112	52	34	12
In family having—								
No other employed member	15	6	9	8	3	4		
1 other	315	42	273	218	54	24	15	4
2 others	85	15	70	21	31	16	13	4
3 or more others	47	11	36	5	24	8	6	4
Widowed or divorced	209	48	161	37	66	60	31	15
In family having—								
No other employed member	72	24	48	22	22	19	9	
1 other	86	15	71	12	29	26	12	7
2 others	32	4	28	3	11	7	6	5
3 or more others	19	5	14		4	8	4	3

TABLE **173.**—WOMEN LIVING AT HOME AND EMPLOYED IN CERTAIN IMPORTANT OCCUPATIONS, CLASSIFIED BY MARITAL CONDITION, ACCORDING TO NUMBER OF OTHER EMPLOYED MEMBERS IN THE FAMILY, AND WHETHER THERE ARE BOARDERS OR LODGERS, FOR 11 SELECTED CITIES: 1920—Continued

OCCUPATION, MARITAL CONDITION, AND NUMBER OF OTHER GAINFULLY EMPLOYED MEMBERS OF FAMILY	GAINFULLY EMPLOYED WOMEN 16 YEARS OF AGE AND OVER LIVING AT HOME							
	Total number	Boarders or lodgers	No boarders or lodgers	Living in family having—				
				Unemployed members				
				None	1	2	3	4 or more

KANSAS CITY, MO.—Continued

TEACHERS (SCHOOL)								
All classes	1,017	166	851	225	402	244	91	55
In family having—								
No other employed member	218	47	171	76	89	40	11	2
1 other	396	72	324	89	150	100	32	25
2 others	268	39	229	47	120	62	23	16
3 or more others	135	8	127	13	43	42	25	12
Single (including unknown)	873	146	727	156	372	215	81	49
In family having—								
No other employed member	177	41	136	58	82	29	7	1
1 other	327	62	265	51	135	89	29	23
2 others	243	35	208	38	113	57	20	15
3 or more others	126	8	118	9	42	40	25	10
Married	78	10	68	41	13	14	6	4
In family having—								
No other employed member	11	2	9	4	2	3	2	
1 other	49	5	44	31	8	6	2	2
2 others	15	3	12	5	3	4	2	1
3 or more others	3		3	1		1		1
Widowed or divorced	66	10	56	28	17	15	4	2
In family having—								
No other employed member	30	4	26	14	5	8	2	1
1 other	20	5	15	7	7	5	1	
2 others	10	1	9	4	4	1	1	
3 or more others	6		6	3	1	1		1
TELEPHONE OPERATORS								
All classes	906	130	776	160	270	217	118	141
In family having—								
No other employed member	75	25	50	21	35	10	6	3
1 other	340	43	297	84	98	91	31	36
2 others	264	31	233	36	69	70	45	44
3 or more others	227	31	196	19	68	46	36	58
Single (including unknown)	680	94	586	77	208	164	103	128
In family having—								
No other employed member	46	13	33	13	21	7	3	2
1 other	223	29	194	26	76	66	24	31
2 others	217	25	192	24	52	57	42	42
3 or more others	194	27	167	14	59	34	34	53
Married	148	15	133	72	34	30	6	6
In family having—								
No other employed member	6	1	5	2	4			
1 other	91	8	83	57	16	12	3	3
2 others	27	4	23	9	8	8	1	1
3 or more others	24	2	22	4	6	10	2	2
Widowed or divorced	78	21	57	11	28	23	9	7
In family having—								
No other employed member	23	11	12	6	10	3	3	1
1 other	26	6	20	1	6	13	4	2
2 others	20	2	18	3	9	5	2	1
3 or more others	9	2	7	1	3	2		3

TABLE 173.—WOMEN LIVING AT HOME AND EMPLOYED IN CERTAIN IMPORTANT OCCUPATIONS, CLASSIFIED BY MARITAL CONDITION, ACCORDING TO NUMBER OF OTHER EMPLOYED MEMBERS IN THE FAMILY, AND WHETHER THERE ARE BOARDERS OR LODGERS, FOR 11 SELECTED CITIES: 1920—Continued

OCCUPATION, MARITAL CONDITION, AND NUMBER OF OTHER GAINFULLY EMPLOYED MEMBERS OF FAMILY	GAINFULLY EMPLOYED WOMEN 16 YEARS OF AGE AND OVER LIVING AT HOME							
	Total number	Living in family having—						
		Boarders or lodgers	No boarders or lodgers	Unemployed members				
				None	1	2	3	4 or more
KANSAS CITY, MO.—Continued								
TRAINED NURSES								
All classes	194	47	147	79	37	47	20	11
In family having—								
No other employed member	50	16	34	35	6	6	3	
1 other	88	18	70	28	17	27	10	6
2 others	33	9	24	12	7	10	2	2
3 or more others	23	4	19	4	7	4	5	3
Single (including unknown)	106	28	78	35	21	29	13	8
In family having—								
No other employed member	29	10	19	23	3	3		
1 other	38	10	28	6	5	15	8	4
2 others	19	5	14	4	6	8		1
3 or more others	20	3	17	2	7	3	5	3
Married	41	10	31	22	9	6	3	1
In family having—								
No other employed member	4	2	2	2	1		1	
1 other	31	4	27	16	8	5	1	1
2 others	5	3	2	3		1	1	
3 or more others	1	1		1				
Widowed or divorced	47	9	38	22	7	12	4	2
In family having—								
No other employed member	17	4	13	10	2	3	2	
1 other	19	4	15	6	4	7	1	1
2 others	9	1	8	5	1	1	1	1
3 or more others	2		2	1		1		
WAITRESSES								
All classes	510	137	373	273	116	70	26	25
In family having—								
No other employed member	104	47	57	54	28	13	5	4
1 other	272	68	204	164	56	32	7	13
2 others	88	12	76	42	20	14	7	5
3 or more others	46	10	36	13	12	11	7	3
Single (including unknown)	118	27	91	43	35	20	8	12
In family having—								
No other employed member	28	12	16	18	8	1	1	
1 other	30	7	23	4	12	7	1	6
2 others	38	2	36	16	10	6	3	3
3 or more others	22	6	16	5	5	6	3	3
Married	279	60	219	180	53	30	11	5
In family having—								
No other employed member	21	7	14	9	6	2	3	1
1 other	205	48	157	144	37	19	2	3
2 others	36	3	33	22	5	5	3	1
3 or more others	17	2	15	5	5	4	3	
Widowed or divorced	113	50	63	50	28	20	7	8
In family having—								
No other employed member	55	28	27	27	14	10	1	3
1 other	37	13	24	16	7	6	4	4
2 others	14	7	7	4	5	3	1	1
3 or more others	7	2	5	3	2	1	1	

TABLE **173.**—WOMEN LIVING AT HOME AND EMPLOYED IN CERTAIN IMPORTANT OCCUPATIONS, CLASSIFIED BY MARITAL CONDITION, ACCORDING TO NUMBER OF OTHER EMPLOYED MEMBERS IN THE FAMILY, AND WHETHER THERE ARE BOARDERS OR LODGERS, FOR 11 SELECTED CITIES: 1920—Continued

OCCUPATION, MARITAL CONDITION, AND NUMBER OF OTHER GAINFULLY EMPLOYED MEMBERS OF FAMILY	GAINFULLY EMPLOYED WOMEN 16 YEARS OF AGE AND OVER LIVING AT HOME							
				Living in family having—				
	Total number	Boarders or lodgers	No boarders or lodgers	Unemployed members				
				None	1	2	3	4 or more
ATLANTA, GA.								
BOOKKEEPERS, CASHIERS, AND ACCOUNTANTS								
All classes	925	150	775	143	273	209	148	152
In family having—								
No other employed member	91	27	64	17	35	20	13	6
1 other	378	58	320	88	115	82	52	41
2 others	240	35	205	16	77	58	39	50
3 or more others	216	30	186	22	46	49	44	55
Single (including unknown)	619	92	527	50	200	150	97	122
In family having—								
No other employed member	49	15	34	8	24	9	4	4
1 other	208	33	175	16	77	59	27	29
2 others	187	26	161	11	58	44	30	44
3 or more others	175	18	157	15	41	38	36	45
Married	209	36	173	77	52	35	29	16
In family having—								
No other employed member	12	2	10	2	5	2	3	------
1 other	132	15	117	64	27	18	16	7
2 others	35	8	27	5	16	7	6	1
3 or more others	30	11	19	6	4	8	4	8
Widowed or divorced	97	22	75	16	21	24	22	14
In family having—								
No other employed member	30	10	20	7	6	9	6	2
1 other	38	10	28	8	11	5	9	5
2 others	18	1	17	------	3	7	3	5
3 or more others	11	1	10	1	1	3	4	2
CLERKS (EXCEPT CLERKS IN STORES)								
All classes	1,273	212	1,061	211	397	260	208	197
In family having—								
No other employed member	129	31	98	25	55	30	15	4
1 other	499	77	422	138	157	83	60	61
2 others	352	56	296	34	116	65	72	65
3 or more others	293	48	245	14	69	82	61	67
Single (including unknown)	912	142	770	83	296	194	175	164
In family having—								
No other employed member	66	15	51	10	33	12	8	3
1 other	294	42	252	35	108	61	46	44
2 others	291	47	244	25	93	51	65	57
3 or more others	261	38	223	13	62	70	56	60
Married	240	41	199	103	68	34	18	17
In family having—								
No other employed member	16	4	12	2	8	4	2	------
1 other	159	23	136	93	33	16	9	8
2 others	42	5	37	7	20	5	4	6
3 or more others	23	9	14	1	7	9	3	3
Widowed or divorced	121	29	92	25	33	32	15	16
In family having—								
No other employed member	47	12	35	13	14	14	5	1
1 other	46	12	34	10	16	6	5	9
2 others	19	4	15	2	3	9	3	2
3 or more others	9	1	8	------	------	3	2	4

TABLE **173.**—WOMEN LIVING AT HOME AND EMPLOYED IN CERTAIN IMPORTANT OCCUPATIONS, CLASSIFIED BY MARITAL CONDITION, ACCORDING TO NUMBER OF OTHER EMPLOYED MEMBERS IN THE FAMILY, AND WHETHER THERE ARE BOARDERS OR LODGERS, FOR 11 SELECTED CITIES: 1920—Continued

OCCUPATION, MARITAL CONDITION, AND NUMBER OF OTHER GAINFULLY EMPLOYED MEMBERS OF FAMILY	Total number	Boarders or lodgers	No boarders or lodgers	None	1	2	3	4 or more

ATLANTA, GA.—Continued

CLERKS IN STORES

All classes	175	20	155	39	46	38	28	24
In family having—								
No other employed member	13	3	10	3	2	4	2	2
1 other	79	9	70	29	18	14	10	8
2 others	43	5	38	4	13	10	8	8
3 or more others	40	3	37	3	13	10	8	6
Single (including unknown)	95	12	83	11	30	15	20	19
In family having—								
No other employed member	6	1	5	1	2	1	1	1
1 other	27	5	22	5	8	3	7	4
2 others	33	3	30	3	9	5	8	8
3 or more others	29	3	26	2	11	6	4	6
Married	60	5	55	24	15	12	5	4
In family having—								
No other employed member	1	------	1	------	------	1	------	------
1 other	43	4	39	22	9	7	1	4
2 others	7	1	6	1	4	2	------	------
3 or more others	9	------	9	1	2	2	4	------
Widowed or divorced	20	3	17	4	1	11	3	1
In family having—								
No other employed member	6	2	4	2	------	2	1	1
1 other	9	------	9	2	1	4	2	------
2 others	3	1	2	------	------	3	------	------
3 or more others	2	------	2	------	------	2	------	------

LAUNDRESSES (NOT IN LAUNDRY)

All classes	5,283	778	4,505	2,546	1,260	726	343	408
In family having—								
No other employed member	1,238	287	951	742	291	118	58	29
1 other	2,489	307	2,182	1,237	555	361	154	182
2 others	933	120	813	393	251	122	72	95
3 or more others	623	64	559	174	163	125	59	102
Single (including unknown)	448	72	376	230	103	62	19	34
In family having—								
No other employed member	136	28	108	105	20	9	1	1
1 other	114	25	89	57	23	23	5	6
2 others	109	10	99	47	32	10	6	14
3 or more others	89	9	80	21	28	20	7	13
Married	2,873	345	2,528	1,307	675	431	190	270
In family having—								
No other employed member	233	50	183	118	67	27	17	4
1 other	1,793	204	1,589	896	396	255	103	143
2 others	492	52	440	196	127	74	33	62
3 or more others	355	39	316	97	85	75	37	61
Widowed or divorced	1,962	361	1,601	1,009	482	233	134	104
In family having—								
No other employed member	869	209	660	519	204	82	40	24
1 other	582	78	504	284	136	83	46	33
2 others	332	58	274	150	92	38	33	19
3 or more others	179	16	163	56	50	30	15	28

TABLE **173.**—WOMEN LIVING AT HOME AND EMPLOYED IN CERTAIN IMPORTANT OCCUPATIONS, CLASSIFIED BY MARITAL CONDITION, ACCORDING TO NUMBER OF OTHER EMPLOYED MEMBERS IN THE FAMILY, AND WHETHER THERE ARE BOARDERS OR LODGERS, FOR 11 SELECTED CITIES: 1920—Continued

OCCUPATION, MARITAL CONDITION, AND NUMBER OF OTHER GAINFULLY EMPLOYED MEMBERS OF FAMILY	GAINFULLY EMPLOYED WOMEN 16 YEARS OF AGE AND OVER LIVING AT HOME							
				Living in family having—				
	Total number	Boarders or lodgers	No boarders or lodgers	Unemployed members				
				None	1	2	3	4 or more

ATLANTA, GA.—Continued

SALESWOMEN (STORES)								
All classes	944	147	797	218	247	189	134	156
In family having—								
No other employed member	111	30	81	26	43	26	9	7
1 other	424	51	373	144	95	75	48	62
2 others	230	43	187	33	65	54	36	42
3 or more others	179	23	156	15	44	34	41	45
Single (including unknown)	479	68	411	52	138	92	93	104
In family having—								
No other employed member	44	12	32	9	22	7	4	2
1 other	158	14	144	22	40	33	28	35
2 others	149	24	125	14	45	29	28	33
3 or more others	128	18	110	7	31	23	33	34
Married	308	41	267	128	61	57	28	34
In family having—								
No other employed member	14	3	11	2	5	2	2	3
1 other	196	18	178	107	32	25	14	18
2 others	53	15	38	11	14	19	5	4
3 or more others	45	5	40	8	10	11	7	9
Widowed or divorced	157	38	119	38	48	40	13	18
In family having—								
No other employed member	53	15	38	15	16	17	3	2
1 other	70	19	51	15	23	17	6	9
2 others	28	4	24	8	6	6	3	5
3 or more others	6	------	6	------	3	------	1	2
SERVANTS								
All classes	4,479	757	3,722	2,455	992	502	262	268
In family having—								
No other employed member	991	240	751	658	202	89	28	14
1 other	2,071	311	1,760	1,293	403	205	93	77
2 others	868	132	736	361	240	113	76	78
3 or more others	549	74	475	143	147	95	65	99
Single (including unknown)	1,075	163	912	463	272	158	83	99
In family having—								
No other employed member	192	49	143	149	29	8	4	2
1 other	326	46	280	140	91	52	26	17
2 others	295	29	266	111	85	42	27	30
3 or more others	262	39	223	63	67	56	26	50
Married	2,044	305	1,739	1,256	415	184	88	101
In family having—								
No other employed member	212	43	169	137	46	24	2	3
1 other	1,305	186	1,119	914	219	96	38	38
2 others	334	54	280	148	95	39	27	25
3 or more others	193	22	171	57	55	25	21	35
Widowed or divorced	1,360	289	1,071	736	305	160	91	68
In family having—								
No other employed member	587	148	439	372	127	57	22	9
1 other	440	79	361	239	93	57	29	22
2 others	239	49	190	102	60	32	22	23
3 or more others	94	13	81	23	25	14	18	14

TABLE **173.**—WOMEN LIVING AT HOME AND EMPLOYED IN CERTAIN IMPORTANT OCCUPATIONS, CLASSIFIED BY MARITAL CONDITION, ACCORDING TO NUMBER OF OTHER EMPLOYED MEMBERS IN THE FAMILY, AND WHETHER THERE ARE BOARDERS OR LODGERS, FOR 11 SELECTED CITIES: 1920—Continued

OCCUPATION, MARITAL CONDITION, AND NUMBER OF OTHER GAINFULLY EMPLOYED MEMBERS OF FAMILY	GAINFULLY EMPLOYED WOMEN 16 YEARS OF AGE AND OVER LIVING AT HOME							
		Living in family having—						
	Total number	Boarders or lodgers	No boarders or lodgers	Unemployed members				
				None	1	2	3	4 or more
ATLANTA, GA.—Continued								
STENOGRAPHERS AND TYPISTS								
All classes	2,155	342	1,813	382	625	512	288	348
In family having—								
No other employed member	209	40	169	55	85	40	17	12
1 other	831	149	682	218	241	187	89	96
2 others	622	96	526	85	183	157	96	101
3 or more others	493	57	436	24	116	128	86	139
Single (including unknown)	1,648	246	1,402	180	502	415	243	308
In family having—								
No other employed member	130	28	102	32	55	25	10	8
1 other	551	96	455	72	184	140	69	86
2 others	533	75	458	57	161	136	88	91
3 or more others	434	47	387	19	102	114	76	123
Married	346	59	287	164	73	59	28	22
In family having—								
No other employed member	14	1	13	5	6	2	1	------
1 other	222	35	187	132	39	35	12	4
2 others	63	15	48	22	17	11	6	7
3 or more others	47	8	39	5	11	11	9	11
Widowed or divorced	161	37	124	38	50	38	17	18
In family having—								
No other employed member	65	11	54	18	24	13	6	4
1 other	58	18	40	14	18	12	8	6
2 others	26	6	20	6	5	10	2	3
3 or more others	12	2	10	------	3	3	1	5
TEACHERS (SCHOOL)								
All classes	791	168	623	190	267	149	105	80
In family having—								
No other employed member	96	31	65	33	39	13	8	3
1 other	316	62	254	99	95	58	35	29
2 others	179	27	152	32	66	30	28	23
3 or more others	200	48	152	26	67	48	34	25
Single (including unknown)	579	121	458	102	208	120	82	67
In family having—								
No other employed member	70	24	46	22	32	9	5	2
1 other	194	40	154	40	64	44	25	21
2 others	148	20	128	22	56	27	23	20
3 or more others	167	37	130	18	56	40	29	24
Married	149	27	122	63	41	17	19	9
In family having—								
No other employed member	5	------	5	------	2	1	2	------
1 other	99	15	84	52	23	8	9	7
2 others	19	4	15	5	7	2	4	1
3 or more others	26	8	18	6	9	6	4	1
Widowed or divorced	63	20	43	25	18	12	4	4
In family having—								
No other employed member	21	7	14	11	5	3	1	1
1 other	23	7	16	7	8	6	1	1
2 others	12	3	9	5	3	1	1	2
8 or more others	7	3	4	2	2	2	1	------

TABLE 173.—WOMEN LIVING AT HOME AND EMPLOYED IN CERTAIN IMPORTANT
OCCUPATIONS, CLASSIFIED BY MARITAL CONDITION, ACCORDING TO NUMBER
OF OTHER EMPLOYED MEMBERS IN THE FAMILY, AND WHETHER THERE ARE
BOARDERS OR LODGERS, FOR 11 SELECTED CITIES: 1920—Continued

	GAINFULLY EMPLOYED WOMEN 16 YEARS OF AGE AND OVER LIVING AT HOME							
OCCUPATION, MARITAL CONDITION, AND NUMBER OF OTHER GAINFULLY EMPLOYED MEMBERS OF FAMILY	Total number			Living in family having—				
		Boarders or lodgers	No boarders or lodgers	Unemployed members				
				None	1	2	3	4 or more

LOUISVILLE, KY.

BOOKKEEPERS, CASHIERS, AND ACCOUNTANTS								
All classes	1,397	96	1,301	120	521	356	186	214
In family having—								
No other employed member	142	17	125	21	72	33	13	3
1 other	441	41	400	55	171	111	51	53
2 others	391	23	368	31	152	93	59	56
3 or more others	423	15	408	13	126	119	63	102
Single (including unknown)	1,182	66	1,116	65	467	304	155	191
In family having—								
No other employed member	100	11	89	7	59	26	7	1
1 other	348	28	320	22	151	87	41	47
2 others	342	17	325	24	140	77	49	52
3 or more others	392	10	382	12	117	114	58	91
Married	109	13	96	32	26	22	17	12
In family having—								
No other employed member	7	1	6	1	3	1	1	1
1 other	56	7	49	25	11	11	6	3
2 others	27	3	24	5	8	6	6	2
3 or more others	19	2	17	1	4	4	4	6
Widowed or divorced	106	17	89	23	28	30	14	11
In family having—								
No other employed member	35	5	30	13	10	6	5	1
1 other	37	6	31	8	9	13	4	3
2 others	22	3	19	2	4	10	4	2
3 or more others	12	3	9	------	5	1	1	5
CLERKS (EXCEPT CLERKS IN STORES)								
All classes	1,361	98	1,263	151	452	360	213	185
In family having—								
No other employed member	143	19	124	36	62	32	8	5
1 other	440	44	396	67	168	98	60	47
2 others	397	21	376	22	114	124	77	60
3 or more others	381	14	367	26	108	106	68	73
Single (including unknown)	1,144	80	1,064	87	389	314	186	168
In family having—								
No other employed member	96	13	83	19	44	23	5	5
1 other	330	34	296	27	140	76	50	37
2 others	364	19	345	18	106	115	68	57
3 or more others	354	14	340	23	99	100	63	69
Married	104	5	99	33	31	15	14	11
In family having—								
No other employed member	11	1	10	3	4	2	2	------
1 other	61	4	57	29	16	5	4	7
2 others	17	------	17	------	5	5	5	2
3 or more others	15	------	15	1	6	3	3	2
Widowed and divorced	113	13	100	31	32	31	13	6
In family having—								
No other employed member	36	5	31	14	14	7	1	------
1 other	49	6	43	11	12	17	6	3
2 others	16	2	14	4	3	4	4	1
3 or more others	12	------	12	2	3	3	2	2

TABLE **173.**—WOMEN LIVING AT HOME AND EMPLOYED IN CERTAIN IMPORTANT OCCUPATIONS, CLASSIFIED BY MARITAL CONDITION, ACCORDING TO NUMBER OF OTHER EMPLOYED MEMBERS IN THE FAMILY, AND WHETHER THERE ARE BOARDERS OR LODGERS, FOR 11 SELECTED CITIES: 1920—Continued

OCCUPATION, MARITAL CONDITION, AND NUMBER OF OTHER GAINFULLY EMPLOYED MEMBERS OF FAMILY	GAINFULLY EMPLOYED WOMEN 16 YEARS OF AGE AND OVER LIVING AT HOME							
	Total number	Living in family having—						
		Boarders or lodgers	No boarders or lodgers	Unemployed members				
				None	1	2	3	4 or more
LOUISVILLE, KY.—Continued								
CLERKS IN STORES								
All classes	575	37	538	89	170	129	84	103
In family having—								
No other employed member	54	6	48	21	18	13	2	-----
1 other	179	14	165	35	56	33	27	28
2 others	169	14	155	18	50	40	28	33
3 or more others	173	3	170	15	46	43	27	42
Single (including unknown)	442	27	415	43	133	102	69	95
In family having—								
No other employed member	26	4	22	9	11	5	1	-----
1 other	126	10	116	12	44	25	20	25
2 others	137	11	126	12	39	34	22	30
3 or more others	153	2	151	10	39	38	26	40
Married	74	5	69	26	19	14	10	5
In family having—								
No other employed member	3	------	3	1	1	1	-----	-----
1 other	36	3	33	17	7	4	6	2
2 others	20	1	19	4	6	5	3	2
3 or more others	15	1	14	4	5	4	1	1
Widowed or divorced	59	5	54	20	18	13	5	3
In family having—								
No other employed member	25	2	23	11	6	7	1	-----
1 other	17	1	16	6	5	4	1	1
2 others	12	2	10	2	5	1	3	1
3 or more others	5	------	5	1	2	1	------	1
DRESSMAKERS AND SEAMSTRESSES (NOT IN FACTORY)								
All classes	1,170	138	1,032	466	330	210	97	67
In family having—								
No other employed member	294	48	246	160	74	38	13	9
1 other	438	52	386	191	123	68	33	23
2 others	238	23	215	65	78	56	23	16
3 or more others	200	15	185	50	55	48	28	19
Single (including unknown)	519	37	482	157	167	114	49	32
In family having—								
No other employed member	98	10	88	50	30	14	4	-----
1 other	160	8	152	52	53	37	12	6
2 others	129	8	121	29	50	28	11	11
3 or more others	132	11	121	26	34	35	22	15
Married	290	33	257	130	76	45	20	19
In family having—								
No other employed member	33	5	28	15	13	3	-----	2
1 other	161	22	139	85	36	19	9	12
2 others	54	6	48	17	10	18	5	4
3 or more others	42	------	42	13	17	5	6	1
Widowed or divorced	361	68	293	179	87	51	28	16
In family having—								
No other employed member	163	33	130	95	31	21	9	7
1 other	117	22	95	54	34	12	12	5
2 others	55	9	46	19	18	10	7	1
3 or more others	26	4	22	11	4	8	------	3

TABLE **173.**—WOMEN LIVING AT HOME AND EMPLOYED IN CERTAIN IMPORTANT OCCUPATIONS, CLASSIFIED BY MARITAL CONDITION, ACCORDING TO NUMBER OF OTHER EMPLOYED MEMBERS IN THE FAMILY, AND WHETHER THERE ARE BOARDERS OR LODGERS, FOR 11 SELECTED CITIES: 1920—Continued

OCCUPATION, MARITAL CONDITION, AND NUMBER OF OTHER GAINFULLY EMPLOYED MEMBERS OF FAMILY	GAINFULLY EMPLOYED WOMEN 16 YEARS OF AGE AND OVER LIVING AT HOME							
	Total number	Living in family having—						
		Boarders or lodgers	No boarders or lodgers	Unemployed members				
				None	1	2	3	4 or more
LOUISVILLE, KY.—Continued								
LAUNDRESSES (NOT IN LAUNDRY)								
All classes	3,679	690	2,989	1,987	784	410	234	264
In family having—								
No other employed member	923	280	643	638	179	64	20	22
1 other	1,667	266	1,401	941	341	168	91	126
2 others	658	96	562	280	165	91	60	62
3 or more others	431	48	383	128	99	87	63	54
Single (including unknown)	426	86	340	255	87	32	27	25
In family having—								
No other employed member	193	52	141	159	27	5	1	1
1 other	95	20	75	49	29	6	7	4
2 others	57	7	50	27	16	4	6	4
3 or more others	81	7	74	20	15	17	13	16
Married	1,860	253	1,607	935	404	219	143	159
In family having—								
No other employed member	143	50	93	69	43	18	8	5
1 other	1,144	144	1,000	665	223	106	66	84
2 others	348	37	311	138	83	50	33	44
3 or more others	225	22	203	63	55	45	36	26
Widowed or divorced	1,393	351	1,042	797	293	159	64	80
In family having—								
No other employed member	587	178	409	410	109	41	11	16
1 other	428	102	326	227	89	56	18	38
2 others	253	52	201	115	66	37	21	14
3 or more others	125	19	106	45	29	25	14	12
SALESWOMEN (STORES)								
All classes	1,443	108	1,335	232	490	333	172	216
In family having—								
No other employed member	166	19	147	52	80	23	6	5
1 other	494	40	454	108	171	102	57	56
2 others	394	29	365	40	124	103	51	76
3 or more others	389	20	369	32	115	105	58	79
Single (including unknown)	1,040	71	969	105	373	260	130	172
In family having—								
No other employed member	96	10	86	26	49	14	4	3
1 other	309	23	286	28	127	72	40	42
2 others	312	22	290	30	100	86	38	58
3 or more others	323	16	307	21	97	88	48	69
Married	205	14	191	73	59	35	16	22
In family having—								
No other employed member	19	4	15	3	13	1	1	1
1 other	110	6	104	58	24	17	7	4
2 others	37	1	36	4	9	9	5	10
3 or more others	39	3	36	8	13	8	3	7
Widowed or divorced	198	23	175	54	58	38	26	22
In family having—								
No other employed members	51	5	46	23	18	8	1	1
1 other	75	11	64	22	20	13	10	10
2 others	45	6	39	6	15	8	8	8
3 or more others	27	1	26	3	5	9	7	3

TABLE **173.**—WOMEN LIVING AT HOME AND EMPLOYED IN CERTAIN IMPORTANT OCCUPATIONS, CLASSIFIED BY MARITAL CONDITION, ACCORDING TO NUMBER OF OTHER EMPLOYED MEMBERS IN THE FAMILY, AND WHETHER THERE ARE BOARDERS OR LODGERS, FOR 11 SELECTED CITIES: 1920—Continued

OCCUPATION, MARITAL CONDITION, AND NUMBER OF OTHER GAINFULLY EMPLOYED MEMBERS OF FAMILY	Total number	GAINFULLY EMPLOYED WOMEN 16 YEARS OF AGE AND OVER LIVING AT HOME						
		Living in family having—						
		Boarders or lodgers	No boarders or lodgers	Unemployed members				
				None	1	2	3	4 or more
LOUISVILLE, KY.—Continued								
SEMISKILLED—CIGAR AND TOBACCO FACTORIES								
All classes	2,697	439	2,258	1,270	577	343	205	302
In family having—								
No other employed member	592	159	433	441	84	35	25	7
1 other	1,122	163	959	618	231	121	77	75
2 others	535	69	466	158	139	94	47	97
3 or more others	448	48	400	53	123	93	56	123
Single (including unknown)	970	122	848	264	238	162	100	206
In family having—								
No other employed member	165	43	122	132	23	7	3	
1 other	242	29	213	58	63	48	31	42
2 others	270	27	243	54	72	46	27	71
3 or more others	293	23	270	20	80	61	39	93
Married	1,168	190	978	713	220	116	59	60
In family having—								
No other employed member	162	47	115	122	15	17	5	3
1 other	723	96	627	493	130	48	30	22
2 others	181	25	156	73	44	32	15	17
3 or more others	102	22	80	25	31	19	9	18
Widowed or divorced	559	127	432	293	119	65	46	36
In family having—								
No other employed member	265	69	196	187	46	11	17	4
1 other	157	38	119	67	38	25	16	11
2 others	84	17	67	31	23	16	5	9
3 or more others	53	3	50	8	12	13	8	12
SEMISKILLED—CLOTHING INDUSTRIES								
All classes	1,118	80	1,038	291	306	247	119	155
In family having—								
No other employed member	166	17	149	88	48	21	3	6
1 other	392	30	362	126	106	81	36	43
2 others	283	25	258	52	75	70	43	43
3 or more others	277	8	269	25	77	75	37	63
Single (including unknown)	685	36	649	90	215	175	86	119
In family having—								
No other employed member	70	7	63	29	26	10	1	4
1 other	197	11	186	31	63	53	20	30
2 others	188	12	176	20	57	49	34	28
3 or more others	230	6	224	10	69	63	31	57
Married	207	19	188	107	33	30	17	20
In family having—								
No other employed member	17	1	16	10	1	4	1	1
1 other	111	10	101	68	18	10	9	6
2 others	55	8	47	20	9	12	4	10
3 or more others	24		24	9	5	4	3	3
Widowed or divorced	226	25	201	94	58	42	16	16
In family having—								
No other employed member	79	9	70	49	21	7	1	1
1 other	84	9	75	27	25	18	7	7
2 others	40	5	35	12	9	9	5	5
3 or more others	23	2	21	6	3	8	8	3

TABLE **173.**—WOMEN LIVING AT HOME AND EMPLOYED IN CERTAIN IMPORTANT OCCUPATIONS, CLASSIFIED BY MARITAL CONDITION, ACCORDING TO NUMBER OF OTHER EMPLOYED MEMBERS IN THE FAMILY, AND WHETHER THERE ARE BOARDERS OR LODGERS, FOR 11 SELECTED CITIES: 1920—Continued

OCCUPATION, MARITAL CONDITION, AND NUMBER OF OTHER GAINFULLY EMPLOYED MEMBERS OF FAMILY	GAINFULLY EMPLOYED WOMEN 16 YEARS OF AGE AND OVER LIVING AT HOME							
	Total number	Boarders or lodgers	No boarders or lodgers	Living in family having—				
				Unemployed members				
				None	1	2	3	4 or more

LOUISVILLE, KY.—Continued

SERVANTS								
All classes	2,542	425	2,117	1,413	560	282	146	141
In family having—								
No other employed member	625	137	488	456	129	26	9	5
1 other	1,095	183	912	670	225	101	43	56
2 others	477	73	404	199	118	81	46	33
3 or more others	345	32	313	88	88	74	48	47
Single (including unknown)	759	124	635	338	180	110	63	68
In family having—								
No other employed member	178	37	141	141	30	5	2	
1 other	209	43	166	87	57	30	15	20
2 others	191	28	163	73	49	37	17	15
3 or more others	181	16	165	37	44	38	29	33
Married	1,012	143	869	633	198	92	44	45
In family having—								
No other employed member	103	20	83	60	31	7	2	3
1 other	640	87	553	465	96	41	16	22
2 others	176	28	148	82	45	23	15	11
3 or more others	93	8	85	26	26	21	11	9
Widowed or divorced	771	158	613	442	182	80	39	28
In family having—								
No other employed member	344	80	264	255	68	14	5	2
1 other	246	53	193	118	72	30	12	14
2 others	110	17	93	44	24	21	14	7
3 or more others	71	8	63	25	18	15	8	5
STENOGRAPHERS AND TYPISTS								
All classes	2,104	126	1,978	173	747	565	320	299
In family having—								
No other employed member	160	21	139	25	80	39	12	4
1 other	695	51	644	87	256	180	94	78
2 others	625	37	588	28	233	162	102	100
3 or more others	624	17	607	33	178	184	112	117
Single (including unknown)	1,942	111	1,831	124	707	530	299	282
In family having—								
No other employed member	138	15	123	21	72	35	9	1
1 other	614	46	568	48	240	167	87	72
2 others	594	34	560	25	224	150	97	98
3 or more others	596	16	580	30	171	178	106	111
Married	104	9	95	38	25	20	12	9
In family having—								
No other employed member	5	1	4		2	1	1	1
1 other	59	4	55	33	13	7	3	3
2 others	22	3	19	3	7	7	3	2
3 or more others	18	1	17	2	3	5	5	3
Widowed or divorced	58	6	52	11	15	15	9	8
In family having—								
No other employed member	17	5	12	4	6	3	2	2
1 other	22	1	21	6	3	6	4	3
2 others	9		9		2	5	2	
3 or more others	10		10	1	4	1	1	3

TABLE **173.**—WOMEN LIVING AT HOME AND EMPLOYED IN CERTAIN IMPORTANT OCCUPATIONS, CLASSIFIED BY MARITAL CONDITION, ACCORDING TO NUMBER OF OTHER EMPLOYED MEMBERS IN THE FAMILY, AND WHETHER THERE ARE BOARDERS OR LODGERS, FOR 11 SELECTED CITIES: 1920—Continued

OCCUPATION, MARITAL CONDITION, AND NUMBER OF OTHER GAINFULLY EMPLOYED MEMBERS OF FAMILY	GAINFULLY EMPLOYED WOMEN 16 YEARS OF AGE AND OVER LIVING AT HOME							
	Total number	Boarders or lodgers	No boarders or lodgers	Living in family having—				
				Unemployed members				
				None	1	2	3	4 or more
LOUISVILLE, KY.—Continued								
TEACHERS (SCHOOL)								
All classes	857	75	782	180	332	201	75	69
In family having—								
No other employed member	160	22	138	48	76	23	9	4
1 other	298	26	272	73	117	55	28	25
2 others	209	17	192	38	80	58	20	13
3 or more others	190	10	180	21	59	65	18	27
Single (including unknown)	715	58	657	128	293	176	58	60
In family having—								
No other employed member	133	18	115	39	69	16	8	1
1 other	226	19	207	41	97	44	21	23
2 others	187	11	176	31	72	56	17	11
3 or more others	169	10	159	17	55	60	12	25
Married	83	12	71	29	28	13	9	4
In family having—								
No other employed member	5	1	4		3	1		1
1 other	51	5	46	23	17	8	2	1
2 others	14	6	8	5	5		3	1
3 or more others	13		13	1	3	4	4	1
Widowed or divorced	59	5	54	23	11	12	8	5
In family having—								
No other employed member	22	3	19	9	4	6	1	2
1 other	21	2	19	9	3	3	5	1
2 others	8		8	2	3	2		1
3 or more others	8		8	3	1	1	2	1
NEW ORLEANS, LA.								
BOARDING AND LODGING HOUSE KEEPERS								
All classes	995	785	210	577	214	109	43	52
In family having—								
No other employed member	509	410	99	332	95	57	10	15
1 other	314	250	64	171	77	35	17	14
2 others	113	83	30	52	34	10	11	6
3 or more others	59	42	17	22	8	7	5	17
Single (including unknown)	168	135	33	119	30	9	6	4
In family having—								
No other employed member	111	88	23	84	19	5	2	1
1 other	43	39	4	30	7	3	1	2
2 others	11	6	5	3	4	1	3	
3 or more others	3	2	1	2				1
Married	252	201	51	138	62	24	13	15
In family having—								
No other employed member	62	52	10	39	14	3	2	4
1 other	134	105	29	75	33	15	8	3
2 others	33	27	6	17	12	3	1	
3 or more others	23	17	6	7	3	3	2	8
Widowed or divorced	575	449	126	320	122	76	24	33
In family having—								
No other employed member	336	270	66	209	62	49	6	10
1 other	137	106	31	66	37	17	8	9
2 others	69	50	19	32	18	6	7	6
3 or more others	33	23	10	13	5	4	3	8

TABLE **173.**—WOMEN LIVING AT HOME AND EMPLOYED IN CERTAIN IMPORTANT OCCUPATIONS, CLASSIFIED BY MARITAL CONDITION, ACCORDING TO NUMBER OF OTHER EMPLOYED MEMBERS IN THE FAMILY, AND WHETHER THERE ARE BOARDERS OR LODGERS, FOR 11 SELECTED CITIES: 1920—Continued

OCCUPATION, MARITAL CONDITION, AND NUMBER OF OTHER GAINFULLY EMPLOYED MEMBERS OF FAMILY	GAINFULLY EMPLOYED WOMEN 16 YEARS OF AGE AND OVER LIVING AT HOME							
	Total number	Boarders or lodgers	No boarders or lodgers	Living in family having—				
				None	Unemployed members			
					1	2	3	4 or more
NEW ORLEANS, LA.—Continued								
BOOKKEEPERS, CASHIERS, AND ACCOUNTANTS								
All classes	1,009	117	892	89	277	248	164	231
In family having—								
No other employed member	73	9	64	13	31	17	7	5
1 other	301	36	265	35	96	72	46	52
2 others	281	40	241	27	82	72	36	64
3 or more others	354	32	322	14	68	87	75	110
Single (including unknown)	857	92	765	63	239	208	144	203
In family having—								
No other employed member	48	4	44	8	24	9	4	3
1 other	223	22	201	20	77	52	38	36
2 others	258	37	221	23	73	68	34	60
3 or more others	328	29	299	12	65	79	68	104
Married	74	12	62	17	18	20	11	8
In family having—								
No other employed member	9	1	8	3	2	3	1	-----
1 other	38	5	33	11	10	10	3	4
2 others	12	3	9	2	5	2	2	1
3 or more others	15	3	12	1	1	5	5	3
Widowed or divorced	78	13	65	9	20	20	9	20
In family having—								
No other employed member	16	4	12	2	5	5	2	2
1 other	40	9	31	4	9	10	5	12
2 others	11	-----	11	2	4	2	-----	3
3 or more others	11	-----	11	1	2	3	2	3
CLERKS (EXCEPT CLERKS IN STORES)								
All classes	1,794	182	1,612	155	515	431	296	397
In family having—								
No other employed member	152	24	128	29	58	40	18	7
1 other	449	49	400	60	137	106	71	75
2 others	542	56	486	24	175	137	101	105
3 or more others	651	53	598	42	145	148	106	210
Single (including unknown)	1,488	145	1,343	96	441	369	244	338
In family having—								
No other employed member	97	15	82	16	43	23	10	5
1 other	339	36	303	28	110	91	51	59
2 others	457	47	410	15	151	119	85	87
3 or more others	595	47	548	37	137	136	98	187
Married	146	16	130	27	34	31	24	30
In family having—								
No other employed member	26	4	22	4	7	8	5	2
1 other	48	5	43	19	11	6	7	5
2 others	42	3	39	2	12	10	8	10
3 or more others	30	4	26	2	4	7	4	13
Widowed or divorced	160	21	139	32	40	31	28	29
In family having—								
No other employed member	29	5	24	9	8	9	3	-----
1 other	62	8	54	13	16	9	13	11
2 others	43	6	37	7	12	8	8	8
3 or more others	26	2	24	3	4	5	4	10

TABLE **173.**—WOMEN LIVING AT HOME AND EMPLOYED IN CERTAIN IMPORTANT OCCUPATIONS, CLASSIFIED BY MARITAL CONDITION, ACCORDING TO NUMBER OF OTHER EMPLOYED MEMBERS IN THE FAMILY, AND WHETHER THERE ARE BOARDERS OR LODGERS, FOR 11 SELECTED CITIES: 1920—Continued

OCCUPATION, MARITAL CONDITION, AND NUMBER OF OTHER GAINFULLY EMPLOYED MEMBERS OF FAMILY	GAINFULLY EMPLOYED WOMEN 16 YEARS OF AGE AND OVER LIVING AT HOME							
	Total number	Boarders or lodgers	No boarders or lodgers	Living in family having—				
				Unemployed members				
				None	1	2	3	4 or more
NEW ORLEANS, LA.—Continued								
CLERKS IN STORES								
All classes	802	74	728	76	206	188	120	212
In family having—								
No other employed member	37	7	30	6	11	10	4	6
1 other	227	23	204	30	67	55	30	45
2 others	225	18	207	19	63	53	32	58
3 or more others	313	26	287	21	65	70	54	103
Single (including unknown)	645	53	592	45	172	152	101	175
In family having—								
No other employed member	21	3	18	4	8	4	2	3
1 other	156	14	142	10	52	41	19	34
2 others	195	15	180	15	54	45	30	51
3 or more others	273	21	252	16	58	62	50	87
Married	97	10	87	26	20	19	11	21
In family having—								
No other employed member	5	2	3	2	-------	1	1	1
1 other	51	6	45	18	12	8	7	6
2 others	11	1	10	2	3	4	-------	2
3 or more others	30	1	29	4	5	6	3	12
Widowed or divorced	60	11	49	5	14	17	8	16
In family having—								
No other employed member	11	2	9	-------	3	5	1	2
1 other	20	3	17	2	3	6	4	5
2 others	19	2	17	2	6	4	2	5
3 or more others	10	4	6	1	2	2	1	4
DRESSMAKERS AND SEAMSTRESSES (NOT IN FACTORY)								
All classes	2,489	395	2,094	854	684	406	244	301
In family having—								
No other employed member	450	135	315	228	125	61	26	10
1 other	978	154	824	387	265	148	87	91
2 others	564	71	493	148	164	104	61	87
3 or more others	497	35	462	91	130	93	70	113
Single (including unknown)	1,007	109	898	265	320	182	91	149
In family having—								
No other employed member	128	39	89	61	47	15	3	2
1 other	333	34	299	121	99	51	28	34
2 others	264	24	240	43	89	59	23	50
3 or more others	282	12	270	40	85	57	37	63
Married	708	107	601	286	168	109	69	76
In family having—								
No other employed member	61	20	41	24	17	13	6	1
1 other	382	58	324	179	91	54	30	28
2 others	159	19	140	59	40	23	14	23
3 or more others	106	10	96	24	20	19	19	24
Widowed or divorced	774	179	595	303	196	115	84	76
In family having—								
No other employed member	261	76	185	143	61	33	17	7
1 other	263	62	201	87	75	43	29	29
2 others	141	28	113	46	35	22	24	14
3 or more others	109	13	96	27	25	17	14	26

TABLE **173.**—WOMEN LIVING AT HOME AND EMPLOYED IN CERTAIN IMPORTANT OCCUPATIONS, CLASSIFIED BY MARITAL CONDITION, ACCORDING TO NUMBER OF OTHER EMPLOYED MEMBERS IN THE FAMILY, AND WHETHER THERE ARE BOARDERS OR LODGERS, FOR 11 SELECTED CITIES: 1920—Continued

OCCUPATION, MARITAL CONDITION, AND NUMBER OF OTHER GAINFULLY EMPLOYED MEMBERS OF FAMILY	GAINFULLY EMPLOYED WOMEN 16 YEARS OF AGE AND OVER LIVING AT HOME							
	Total number	Boarders or lodgers	No boarders or lodgers	Living in family having—				
				Unemployed members				
				None	1	2	3	4 or more
NEW ORLEANS, LA.—Continued								
LAUNDRESSES (NOT IN LAUNDRY)								
All classes	6,273	1,211	5,062	2,923	1,424	871	463	592
In family having—								
No other employed member	1,290	397	893	779	276	119	65	51
1 other	2,876	524	2,352	1,419	669	387	178	223
2 others	1,237	194	1,043	484	289	210	116	138
3 or more others	870	96	774	241	190	155	104	180
Single (including unknown)	638	143	495	322	134	78	39	65
In family having—								
No other employed member	202	65	137	158	31	10	3	----
1 other	182	38	144	83	49	18	10	22
2 others	135	25	110	48	31	29	13	14
3 or more others	119	15	104	33	23	21	13	29
Married	3,406	545	2,861	1,540	749	502	264	351
In family having—								
No other employed member	286	82	204	138	70	38	19	21
1 other	1,930	308	1,622	999	421	258	105	147
2 others	686	96	590	272	149	113	78	74
3 or more others	504	59	445	131	109	93	62	109
Widowed or divorced	2,229	523	1,706	1,061	541	291	160	176
In family having—								
No other employed member	802	250	552	483	175	71	43	30
1 other	764	178	586	337	199	111	63	54
2 others	416	73	343	164	109	68	25	50
3 or more others	247	22	225	77	58	41	29	42
SALESWOMEN (STORES)								
All classes	2,063	199	1,864	203	526	449	369	516
In family having—								
No other employed member	145	32	113	37	47	29	20	12
1 other	566	55	511	78	166	118	72	132
2 others	597	58	539	56	161	141	109	130
3 or more others	755	54	701	32	152	161	168	242
Single (including unknown)	1,613	153	1,460	108	435	358	294	418
In family having—								
No other employed member	78	17	61	14	33	16	10	5
1 other	386	46	340	33	129	83	46	95
2 others	486	44	442	37	134	117	89	109
3 or more others	663	46	617	24	139	142	149	209
Married	215	13	202	46	43	43	36	47
In family having—								
No other employed member	12	3	9	4	2	3	2	1
1 other	111	4	107	32	24	21	13	21
2 others	45	3	42	5	10	10	9	11
3 or more others	47	3	44	5	7	9	12	14
Widowed or divorced	235	33	202	49	48	48	39	51
In family having—								
No other employed member	55	12	43	19	12	10	8	6
1 other	69	5	64	13	13	14	13	16
2 others	66	11	55	14	17	14	11	10
3 or more others	45	5	40	3	6	10	7	19

TABLE **173.**—WOMEN LIVING AT HOME AND EMPLOYED IN CERTAIN IMPORTANT OCCUPATIONS, CLASSIFIED BY MARITAL CONDITION, ACCORDING TO NUMBER OF OTHER EMPLOYED MEMBERS IN THE FAMILY, AND WHETHER THERE ARE BOARDERS OR LODGERS, FOR 11 SELECTED CITIES: 1920—Continued

OCCUPATION, MARITAL CONDITION, AND NUMBER OF OTHER GAINFULLY EMPLOYED MEMBERS OF FAMILY	GAINFULLY EMPLOYED WOMEN 16 YEARS OF AGE AND OVER LIVING AT HOME							
	Total number	Living in family having—						
		Boarders or lodgers	No boarders or lodgers	Unemployed members				
				None	1	2	3	4 or more

NEW ORLEANS, LA.—Continued

SEMISKILLED—CIGAR AND TOBACCO FACTORIES								
All classes	1,066	106	960	111	253	207	183	312
In family having—								
No other employed member	66	12	54	28	23	5	5	5
1 other	282	29	253	49	81	52	38	62
2 others	303	26	277	17	89	68	50	79
3 or more others	415	39	376	17	60	82	90	166
Single (including unknown)	831	73	758	44	201	170	156	260
In family having—								
No other employed member	29	5	24	8	16	1	4	----
1 other	185	13	172	13	57	39	29	47
2 others	249	19	230	11	74	57	40	67
3 or more others	368	36	332	12	54	73	83	146
Married	124	16	108	40	30	22	13	19
In family having—								
No other employed member	10	2	8	7	3	------	------	-----
1 other	65	8	57	28	18	7	6	6
2 others	27	5	22	3	6	7	4	7
3 or more others	22	1	21	2	3	8	3	6
Widowed or divorced	111	17	94	27	22	15	14	33
In family having—								
No other employed member	27	5	22	13	4	4	1	5
1 other	32	8	24	8	6	6	3	9
2 others	27	2	25	3	9	4	6	5
3 or more others	25	2	23	3	3	1	4	14
SEMISKILLED—TEXTILE MILLS								
All classes	901	86	815	138	194	194	149	226
In family having—								
No other employed member	87	22	65	41	16	19	8	3
1 other	268	29	239	51	78	46	43	50
2 others	248	19	229	28	56	52	52	60
3 or more others	298	16	282	18	44	77	46	113
Single (including unknown)	601	42	559	50	125	135	108	183
In family having—								
No other employed member	26	5	21	12	7	4	2	1
1 other	155	10	145	14	47	30	28	36
2 others	180	14	166	14	38	41	36	51
3 or more others	240	13	227	10	33	60	42	95
Married	132	15	117	39	35	21	15	22
In family having—								
No other employed member	16	3	13	4	5	5	1	1
1 other	62	8	54	24	17	5	6	10
2 others	30	3	27	6	7	5	7	5
3 or more others	24	1	23	5	6	6	1	6
Widowed or divorced	168	29	139	49	34	38	26	21
In family having—								
No other employed member	45	14	31	25	4	10	5	1
1 other	51	11	40	13	14	11	9	4
2 others	38	2	36	8	11	6	9	4
3 or more others	34	2	32	3	5	11	3	12

TABLE 173.—WOMEN LIVING AT HOME AND EMPLOYED IN CERTAIN IMPORTANT OCCUPATIONS, CLASSIFIED BY MARITAL CONDITION, ACCORDING TO NUMBER OF OTHER EMPLOYED MEMBERS IN THE FAMILY, AND WHETHER THERE ARE BOARDERS OR LODGERS, FOR 11 SELECTED CITIES: 1920—Continued

		GAINFULLY EMPLOYED WOMEN 16 YEARS OF AGE AND OVER LIVING AT HOME							
OCCUPATION, MARITAL CONDITION, AND NUMBER OF OTHER GAINFULLY EMPLOYED MEMBERS OF FAMILY	Total number			Living in family having—					
		Boarders or lodgers	No boarders or lodgers	Unemployed members					
				None	1	2	3	4 or more	

NEW ORLEANS, LA.—Continued

SERVANTS

	Total number	Boarders or lodgers	No boarders or lodgers	None	1	2	3	4 or more
All classes	6,237	1,226	5,011	2,790	1,412	861	505	669
In family having—								
No other employed member	1,100	386	714	691	230	110	40	29
1 other	2,551	478	2,073	1,316	564	313	175	183
2 others	1,421	234	1,187	468	376	245	149	183
3 or more others	1,165	128	1,037	315	242	193	141	274
Single (including unknown)	1,990	329	1,661	723	490	277	189	311
In family having—								
No other employed member	278	105	173	206	50	14	4	4
1 other	555	91	464	210	158	75	51	61
2 others	548	75	473	155	155	86	66	86
3 or more others	609	58	551	152	127	102	68	160
Married	2,562	517	2,045	1,304	539	334	181	204
In family having—								
No other employed member	265	93	172	137	68	39	9	12
1 other	1,413	273	1,140	873	269	139	75	57
2 others	503	102	401	185	127	96	41	54
3 or more others	381	49	332	109	75	60	56	81
Widowed or divorced	1,685	380	1,305	763	383	250	135	154
In family having—								
No other employed member	557	188	369	348	112	57	27	13
1 other	583	114	469	233	137	99	49	65
2 others	370	57	313	128	94	63	42	43
3 or more others	175	21	154	54	40	31	17	33

STENOGRAPHERS AND TYPISTS

	Total number	Boarders or lodgers	No boarders or lodgers	None	1	2	3	4 or more
All classes	3,084	326	2,758	171	862	804	582	665
In family having—								
No other employed member	203	33	170	17	110	42	21	13
1 other	848	100	748	68	268	235	147	130
2 others	871	84	787	41	227	252	169	182
3 or more others	1,162	109	1,053	45	257	275	245	340
Single (including unknown)	2,872	287	2,585	135	801	753	544	639
In family having—								
No other employed member	172	26	146	10	98	35	17	12
1 other	758	88	670	49	241	212	132	124
2 others	817	71	746	35	215	239	156	172
3 or more others	1,125	102	1,023	41	247	267	239	331
Married	113	24	89	23	34	25	17	14
In family having—								
No other employed member	7	3	4	------	3	1	3	------
1 other	58	8	50	15	21	13	6	3
2 others	24	8	16	5	4	4	4	7
3 or more others	24	5	19	3	6	7	4	4
Widowed or divorced	99	15	84	13	27	26	21	12
In family having—								
No other employed member	24	4	20	7	9	6	1	1
1 other	32	4	28	4	6	10	9	3
2 others	30	5	25	1	8	9	9	3
3 or more others	13	2	11	1	4	1	2	5

TABLE **173.**—WOMEN LIVING AT HOME AND EMPLOYED IN CERTAIN IMPORTANT OCCUPATIONS, CLASSIFIED BY MARITAL CONDITION, ACCORDING TO NUMBER OF OTHER EMPLOYED MEMBERS IN THE FAMILY, AND WHETHER THERE ARE BOARDERS OR LODGERS, FOR 11 SELECTED CITIES: 1920—Continued

OCCUPATION, MARITAL CONDITION, AND NUMBER OF OTHER GAINFULLY EMPLOYED MEMBERS OF FAMILY	GAINFULLY EMPLOYED WOMEN 16 YEARS OF AGE AND OVER LIVING AT HOME							
	Total number	Living in family having—						
		Boarders or lodgers	No boarders or lodgers	Unemployed members				
				None	1	2	3	4 or more

NEW ORLEANS, LA.—Continued

TEACHERS (SCHOOL)								
All classes	1,615	189	1,426	280	524	341	214	256
In family having—								
No other employed member	200	49	151	63	89	29	12	7
1 other	460	56	404	103	163	85	68	41
2 others	472	45	427	72	142	115	53	90
3 or more others	483	39	444	42	130	112	81	118
Single (including unknown)	1,443	153	1,290	230	471	304	198	240
In family having—								
No other employed member	162	32	130	51	73	24	9	5
1 other	395	46	349	81	144	71	61	38
2 others	428	40	388	60	131	104	48	85
3 or more others	458	35	423	38	123	105	80	112
Married	79	14	65	23	21	20	6	9
In family having—								
No other employed member	10	2	8	1	5	2	1	1
1 other	32	8	24	13	7	10	2	------
2 others	25	4	21	6	7	6	2	4
3 or more others	12	------	12	3	2	2	1	4
Widowed or divorced	93	22	71	27	32	17	10	7
In family having—								
No other employed member	28	15	13	11	11	3	2	1
1 other	33	2	31	9	12	4	5	3
2 others	19	1	18	6	4	5	3	1
3 or more others	13	4	9	1	5	5	------	2